Abstracts of

York County Pennsylvania

WILLS

1749-1819

F. Edward Wright

HERITAGE BOOKS
2009

HERITAGE BOOKS
AN IMPRINT OF HERITAGE BOOKS, INC.

Books, CDs, and more—Worldwide

For our listing of thousands of titles see our website
at
www.HeritageBooks.com

Published 2009 by
HERITAGE BOOKS, INC.
Publishing Division
100 Railroad Ave. #104
Westminster, Maryland 21157

Copyright © 1998 F. Edward Wright

All rights reserved. No part of this book may be reproduced or transmitted in any form or by any means, electronic or mechanical, including photocopying, recording or by any information storage and retrieval system without written permission from the author, except for the inclusion of brief quotations in a review.

International Standard Book Numbers
Paperbound: 978-1-58549-387-6
Clothbound: 978-0-7884-8133-8

INTRODUCTION

These wills were abstracted under the auspices of the Historical Society of Pennsylvania in the early 1900s. Copies were made available to various libraries in Pennsylvania and microfilm copies made by the Genealogical Society of Utah (LDS). Originally the abstracts were arranged in alphabetical order. In this version we have re-arranged the entries in chronological order.

Index To The Probate Inventories Of York County, Pennsylvania 1749-1850, compiled by David A. and Brenda L. Paup, was published in 1992 by Family Line Publications. These are listings of file name (decedent), date, township or borough, occupations, husband or wife, and other comments.

York County was established in 1749 from Lancaster County and in 1800 Adams County was founded from York County. One must consider these dates when looking for the records.

We extend our appreciation to the staffs of the Historical Society of Pennsylvania (1300 Locust Street, Philadelphia, PA 19107) and encourage use and support of its facilities and to the Genealogical Society of Pennsylvania whose collections are housed in the Historical Society Library. We also encourage membership in the Genealogical Society of Pennsylvania (address same as HSP).

The Historical Society of York County (250 East Market St., York, PA 17403) houses an excellent collection of genealogy and historical information. Their modern and pleasant facilities and operation amply fill the needs of the researcher.

> F. Edward Wright
> Westminster, Maryland
> 1995

--- --, ---   --- --, 1776
Dorman, John. Executor: Omitted. (Will on file, but not copied.)

Jul 15, 1780   --- --, ----
Bollinger, Anna Mary. Executor: Jacob Hagy. Manheim Township. Widow of Jacob Bollinger. Children: Abraham, Jacob, Christian, Michael, Catharine and Eva.

--- --, ----   --- --, ----
Eyster, Daniel. Executor: Elizabeth Eyster. (This will was not filed or copied, and was removed by certiorari.)

May 31, 1777   --- --, ----
Bollinger, Jacob. (German will.)

--- --, ----   --- --, ----
Eichelberger, Frederick. (Will was not copied, but said to be in the files.)
Apr 1, 1770   --- --, 1770
Bollinger, Isaac. Executors: Peter Vongend and Jacob Krouse. Codorus Township. Wife: Catharine Bollinger. Child: Frederick.

--- --, ----   --- --, 1776
Gantzer, Andrew. Executor: Omitted. (This will is on file, but not copied on the records.)

--- --, ----   --- --, 1776
Hoh, Martin. Executor: Omitted. (Will not copied on records.)

--- --, ----   --- --, 1776
Ohard, Patrick. This will has not been copied on the records, but is on file.

--- --, ----   --- --, 1776
Cross, Thomas. (This will not copied, but on file.)

--- --, ----   --- --, 1776
Ducket, Thomas. Executor: Omitted. (Will on file, but not copied.)

--- --, ----   --- --, 1776
Elliott, John. Executor: Omitted. (This will is said to be in the file, but not copied in the records.)

--- --, ----   --- --, 1776
Clay, Nicholas. (This will not copied, but on file.)

--- --, ----   --- --, 1777
Quickel, Peter. Township: Omitted. Will not on the records, see files.

--- --, ----   --- --, 1777
Brown, George. Will filed but not copied on records.

--- --, ----   --- --, 1777
Bix, Christian. Will filed but not copied.

Dec 27, 1784   --- 14, 1785
Holtzinger, Jacob. Executors: Thomas Hartley and Edward Crawford. York County. Wife: Omitted. Legatees: Brothers-in-law Thomas Hartley and Edward Crawford.

--- --, ----   May 21, ----
Dubs, Salome. Executor: Daniel Dubs. (German will.)

Jan 11, 1749   Jan 21, 1749
Henderson, John. Executor: James Henderson. Dover Township. Children: John, Francis, William, and James.

Oct 10, 1749   Jan 29, 1749
Simenton, Ann. Executor: William Boyd and William McGanghy. Marsh Creek Township. Legatees: Margaret Boyd (sister), Mary and Margaret Boyd (nieces) and a nephew (Boyd - first name not given), (children of Margaret.)

Jan 7, 1749   Jan 31, 1749
Stevinson, James. Executors: George and James Stevinson. Straban Township. Wife: Margaret Stevinson. Children: James, William, Elizabeth and George.

Jan 11, 1749   Jan 31, 1749
McFerson, ---. Executor: Robert McFerson. Township: Omitted. Children: Hugh, Jane, and John.

Sep 10, 1749   Oct 24, 1749
Johnston, Daniel. Executor: Thomas Johnston. Chanceford Township. Children: Thomas, Mary, Robert, and Catharine.

Oct 20, 1749   Oct 28, 1749
Person, John. Executors: Adam Lenn and Andrew Leviston. Lancaster County (called in will "Rock Creek Co."). Wife: Jenn Person. Children: William, Benjamin, (and two other sons whose names were not given.)

Dec 23, 1748   Nov 1, 1749
Wilson, Patrick. Executors: William Wilson and James Jameson. Reading Township. Wife: Janet Wilson. Children: Yeancy wife of McCarry, Samuel, McCartha, Garret and Marmaduke.

Aug 31, 1749   Nov 26, 1749
Alexander, Jeddiah. Executors: Anne Alexander and Eleas Alexander. York County. Wife: Anne Alexander. Brothers: Isaac, Francis, William, Eleas. Sister: Esther.

Aug 4, 1750   Jan 4, 1750
Taylor, John. Executor: George Taylor. Fawn Township. Children: John, George, Robert and Thomas.

Feb 11, 1746   Feb 6, 1750
Shamberger, Baltzer. Executor: Margaret Shamberger. Lancaster County. Wife: Margaret Shamberger.

Feb 7, 1750   Feb 15, 1750
Loyd, William. Executor: Daniel Kenly. Township: Omitted. Father's name: Walter Loyd. Legatees: Mary Beon and Mary Artiss, friends living in Philadelphia, PA.

Nov 3, 1750   Feb 17, 1750 (?)
Anderson, William. Executor and wife omitted. York County. Children: James and Rachel.

Sep 28, 1850   Feb 20, 1750
Sharp, Kezia. Executors: Thomas Alexander and Thomas Sharp. York County. Child: Kezia.

Jan 5, 1749   Apr 24, 1750
McGaughy, William. Executors: Margaret and John McGaughy. Hamiltonsban Township. Wife: Margaret McGaughy. Children: John, James, William, and Alexander.

Feb 17, 1750   Apr 25, 1750
Black, John. Executors: Samuel Murry and William Black. Cumberland

Township. Children: Mary, William, John, James and Mathew.

Apr 17, 1750   May 24, 1750
Gison, John. Executors: Mary Gibson and Andrew Thompson. York County. Wife and Children: (Names and number of children not given.)

Nov 8, 1748   Jun 7, 1750
Robinson, James. Executor: Mary Robinson. Lancaster County. Wife: Mary Robinson. Child: Abraham.

Jul 20, 1749   Jun 11, 1750
Carson, William. Executors: Mary Carson and John Mickle. Minallen Township. Wife: Mary Carson. Children: William, Rachel, and Ann.

Sep 4, 1750   Sep 24, 1750
Torance, David. Executor: Archibald Torance. Omitted Township. Wife: (Name not given.) Children: John and Sarah.

Oct 10, 1750   Oct 27, 1750
Dill, Matthew. Executors: Mary and James Dill. York County. Wife: Mary Dill. Children: James, Thomas, Matthew, Mary, John, Nancy, and Sarah.

Jul 21, 1750   Nov 20, 1750
McGennis, Dennis. Executors: Aaron Torrens and Samuel Mitchell. Virginia Township. Children: James, John, and William.

Aug 4, 1750   Dec 12, 1750
Shoolsbank, Joseph. Executor: Mary Shoolsbank. Hellam Township. Wife: Mary Shoolsbank. Children: Michael, William and Philip.

Feb 24, 1750   Apr 15, 1751
Miner, Thomas. Executors: Thomas Miner and John Reed. Cumberland Township. Wife: Mary Miner. Child: Thomas, and two sons-in-law - John Reed and William Baxter (wives' names not given). Grandson: Samuel Miner.

Mar 18, 1751   May 2, 1751
Osburn, Thomas. Executor: Omitted. Mt. Pleasant Township. Legatees: Francis Osburn (mother), Noble Osburn (brother), and Margaret Osburn (sister).

Mar 14, 1751   May 2, 1751
Robinson, Thomas. Executors: Patricia Wattson and Martha Galt. Mt. Joy Township. Children: John, Elizabeth, Mary and Margaret

Jul 9, 1751   Jul 29, 1751
Mappen, Moses. Executors: Thomas Cox and Henry Clark. Warrington Township. Wife: Mary Mappen.

Aug 5, 1751   Sep 30, 1751
Cessna, John. Executors: Priscella Cessna and Peter Stout. Newberry Township. Wife: Priscella Cessna. Children: (Names and number not recorded.)

Nov 22, 1751   Nov 22, 1751
Gilkey, John. Executors: Walter Gilkey and William Hodge. Tyrone Township. Child: Mary.

Nov 4, 1751   Jan 15, 1752
Stall, Jacob. Executor: Anna Maria Stall. Township: Omitted. Wife: Mary Stall.

Dec 20, 1751   Feb 5, 1752
Whittlesay, Eli. Executor: Omitted. Legatee: Mr. Balm (who lives in New England).

Oct 27, 1757   Mar 14, 1752
Far, George. Executors: John Bradly and Hannah Far. Township omitted. Wife: Hannah Far.

Oct 16, 1751   Mar 26, 1752
Early, Edward. Executor: Omitted. Newberry Township. Child: Daniel. Grandchildren: John, Sarah, Catharine, Daniel, and Patrick.

May 10, 1752   Jun 9, 1752
Taylor, Benjamin. Executors: Moses Grodden and Joseph Coulson. Hellam Township. Children: John, Benj., Ann, Grace and Rebecca.

Feb 16, 1751   Jun 11, 1752
Honing, Nicholas. Executors: Conrad Low and Joseph Wagoner. York County Wife: Elizabeth Honing. Child: John.

Jul 11, 1752   Aug 1, 1752
Cambel, Thomas. Executor: Samuel Boyd. York County. Wife:

Elizabeth Cambel. Children: John, Janet, and Marthon.

Sep 19, 1752   Oct 16, 1752
Cohoon, John. Executors: Rachel and Thomas Cohoon. Manchester Township. Wife: Rachel Cohoon. Child: Thomas.

Mar 7, 1752   Nov 3, 1752
Betty, Walter. Executors: William Betty, Samuel Betty and William Lindsey. Reign Township. Children: Samuel, William, Esther wife of ---- McCoy, and Mary wife of ---- Lindsey.

Jun 22, 1752   Dec 19, 1752
Park, William. Executors: Francis Beaty and Samuel McFarran. Manallen Township. Legatees: Jennet Dean (mother) wife of Hans Dean, and Ann Smith and Mary Park (sisters).

Mar 10, 1750   Dec 28, 1752
Frazier, James. Executors: John Garretson and Rebecca Frazier. Newberry Township. Wife: Rebecca Frazier. Child: James.

Oct 14, 1753   Nov 30, 1753
Dickson, William. Executors: James Eger and William Shaw. Chanceford Township. Wife: Sarah Dickson. Children: John and Margaret.

Jan 13, 1754   Feb 22, 1754
Towle, Ambrose. Executors: William Smart and Hugh Whiteford. Omitted Township. Wife: Sarah Towle. Children: Jean, Henry and Lettis.

Jan 3, 1754   Mar 15, 1754
Benner, Henry. Executor: (omitted). Manheim Township. Wife: Anna Mary Benner. Children: Adam, Philip, Henry, Elizabeth, Mary, Anna, Eve and Barbara.

Jan 26, 1754   Mar 16, 1754
Spangler, George. Executors: Bernhart Lowman, George Kuntz and Rosanna Spangler. Manchester Township. Wife: Rosanna Spangler. Child: George.

Aug 21, 1754   Jul 27, 1754
Shrom, Anna Maria. Executors: Philip and Henry Kreeber. Manchester Township. Children: George, Nicolas, David and John.

Jul 22, 1754   Aug 19, 1754
Widebach, Henry. Executor: Anna Wideback. Huntington Township.
Wife: Anna Marcant Wideback. Children: John, Abraham. There was a
son-in-law Michael Miller - wife's name not given.

Mar 14, 1754   Aug 19, 1754
Saylor, Benjamin. Executors: Catharine Saylor. Township: Omitted.
Wife: (Name not given.) There were children mentioned in will, but
(Names and number not given.)

Sep 10, 1754   Nov 16, 1754
Hill, John. Executor: Rachel Hill. York County. Wife: Rachel Hill.
Children: Jane, Mary, Elizabeth, Samuel, Edward, John, Robert, James,
and Margaret.

Apr 9, 1754   Jan 24, 1755
McCall, John. Executors: Alexander McCall and Samuel McCall. Tyrone
Township. Children: John, Elizabeth, Margaret, Martha, James, Jennet,
Samuel, and Thomas.

Dec 25, 1754   Feb 20, 1755
Dods, William, Executors: James and William Dods. Warrington
Township. Wife: Janet Dods. Children: John, Joseph, William, Francis,
Margaret, Jean, Mary, Agness, Rosena, and Sarah.

Feb 1, 1755   Apr 2, 1755
Love, John. Executors: William Love and Michael Drumgold. Township:
Omitted. Wife: Elizabeth Love. Children: Jane, Margaret, Eleanor and
William.

Mar 31, 1755   Apr 16, 1755
Deell, Adam. Executors: Maria Deell and Jacob Bilmyer. York County.
Wife: Mary Catharine Deell. Children: Nicholas, George, Daniel, Corll,
Evagreda, Peter, Adam, Maria, and Englis.

Apr 21, 1755   May 2, 1755
McClellan, William. Executors: William McClellan. Cumberland
Township. Children: William, Elizabeth, John, Jacob, David, and Mary.

Feb 8, 1754   May 26, 1755
McClean, John. Executor: John McClean. York County. Children:
John, James, Catharine, William. Son-in-law: Henry Blick (wife's name
not given).

Apr 4, 1755   Aug 19, 1755
Maul, Bartholomew. Executors: John Getting and James Rudesiltz. York
County. Wife: Mary Elizabeth Maul. Children: George, Catharine,
Peter, Mary, and Tullinar.

Jun 30, 1755   Aug 22, 1755
Welty, Peter. Executors: Michael Danner and John Welty. Manheim
Township. Wife: Catharine Welty. Children: John and Abraham.

May 29, 1755   Aug 25, 1755
Hill, Alexander. Executor: Eleanor Hill. York County. Wife: Eleanor
Hill. Children: Alexander, Samuel, John, and Elizabeth.

Apr 6, 1754   Nov 7, 1755
Dinkle, Daniel. Executor: Anshilla Dinkle. York Town. Wife: Mary
Dinkle. Children: Daniel, Peter, Margaret, Anna, Mary, and Dorothea.

Apr 12, 1755   Jan 26, 1756
Wallace, William. Executors: Anna and Moses Wallace. Chanceford
Township. Wife: Anna Wallace. Children: Joseph and Mary.

Nov 16, 1755   Jan 27, 1756
Wallace, Daniel. Executor: Moses Wallace. Fawn Township. Wife: Jean
Wallace. Legatees: (Bros.) MOses, John and Ludwick.

Jan 17, 1756   Feb 4, 1756
Bard, Martin. Executors: Francis Bard and Jacob Foutz. Germany
Township. Wife Savilla Bard. Children: Philip, Steom, Catharine,
Francis, Susanna and Fornica.

Apr 5, 1755   Feb 16, 1756
Turner, David. Executor: William Ross. ---- Township. Wife: Ann
Turner. Children: Ann, Sarah, Robert, Lydia, David and John.

Jan 8, 1756   Feb 18, 1756
Miller, Sarah. Executor: William Ross. Cumberland Township. Children:
Nathaniel and John.

Feb 2, 1756   Feb 23, 1756
Marker, Mathias. Executors: John Strior and Jacob Strior. Germany
Township. Wife: Catharine Marker. Children: Six (four boys and two
girls, names not given).

May 20, 1756   Jul 28, 1756
Freetz, Philip. Executors: John and Henry Shultz. Hellam Township.
Wife: Anna Catharine Freetz. Children: Philip, Adam, Elizabeth, Anna,
and Julianna.

Aug 5, 1756   Oct 13, 1756
Moore, Samuel. Executors: Quinton Armstrong and Charles McMullen.
Cumberland Township. Wife: Jean Moore. Children: Thomas, David and
Samuel.

Nov 6, 1756   Jan 26, 1757
Mather, Jean. Executor: Henry Pickart. York County. Children: Sarah,
Richard, Jean and son-in-law Henry Pickart (wife's name not given).

Jun 27, 1756   Mar 16, 1757
Lambard, Mathias. Executors: Jacob and Casper Lambard. Manchester
Township. Wife: Omitted. Children: Jacob, Casper, George, Ann, and
Catharine.

Apr 27, 1756   May 12, 1757
Miller, Matthew. Executor: William Ross. Township: Omitted.
Children: James, Anna, and Susanna. Grandson: James Ross (parents'
names not given).

Apr 23, 1755   May 28, 1757
Ramsey, James. Executor: Mary Ramsey. York County. Wife: Mary
Ramsey. Children: James and Mary.

May 17, 1757   Jun 10, 1757
Leyty, Christian. Executors: Catharine and John Leyty. Reading
Township. Wife: Catharine Leyty. Children: John and Jonas.

Nov 23, 1753   Jul 11, 1757
Dorrough, John. Executors: Joseph Wilson and Thomas Gray. Reading
Township. Wife: Mary Dorrough. Children: Margaret, William, and
Joseph.

Sep 16, 1757   Sep 28, 1757
Schall, Fent. Executors: Susanna Schall and Henry Schultz. York Town
Township. Wife: Susanna Schall. Child: John.

--- --, ---   Oct 20, 1757
Degrosch, John. Executor: Marilis Degrosch. (German will.)

May 3, 1756   Nov 2, 1757
Myer, John. Executor: Hy. Myer. York Township. Children: John, Christian, Barbara wife of Jacob Coffman, Cary wife of Peter Brillhart, Catharine, and Henry.

Nov 1, 1777   Nov 23, 1757
Ross, James. Executors: William Garretson and William Griffeth. Warrington Township. Wife: Rebecca Ross. Children: John, Elizabeth, George, Richard, Ann, Sarah, James, Mary, Eleanor, Rebecca and Susanna.

Nov 18, 1757   Dec 13, 1757
Retow, Abraham. Executors: Metzel and J. Crouster. Reading Township. Wife: Mary Retow. Child: Francis. N.B. This is spelled Lerue in the indexes and on the records.

Nov 18, 1757   Dec 13, 1757
Lerue, Abraham. (The name on the will signed Retow.) Executors: U. Metzel and Y. Crouster. Reading Township. Wife: Mary Lerue (or Retow). Child: Francis.

Sep 14, 1751   Jan 3, 1758
Lehman, Peter. Executors: Barbara Lehman and Peter Freed. York County. Wife: Barbara Lehman. Children: Peter and Barbara. Son-in-law: Abraham Blasser (wife's name not given).

Jun 9, 1755   Feb 2, 1758
Coons, Catharine. Executors: Philip Sawer and George Umkatone. Heidelburg Township. Child: John. Grandchildren: Juliana, Fronica, and Catharine (children of John).

Mar 3, 1758   Mar 22, 1758
Beightely, Samuel. Executors: Samuel Beightely and Jacob Danner. Manheim Township. Wife: Martha Beightely. Children: Christian, Martin and Samuel.

Mar 28, 1755   Apr 26, 1758
Houseman, Philip. Executors: Christian Fingery and Anthony Kirkhan. York County. Wife: Omitted. Children: (Names and number not given.)

Mar 14, 1758   May 2, 1758
Reynolds, Samuel. Executors: Martha Reynolds, Samuel Perry and David

McGrew (Magaw). Cumberland Township. Wife: Martha Reynolds. Child: Mary.

May 10, 1750   May 8, 1758
McDonaugh, Henry. Executor: Margaret McDonaugh. Cumberland Township. Wife: Margaret McDonaugh. Children: John, Elizabeth, Mary, Joseph, Henry, Ann, and Jean.

Apr 13, 1758   May 11, 1758
McCorrison, William. Executor: William McCorrison. Chanceford Township. Wife: Margery McCorrison. Children: William, John, and Cary.

May 11, 1758   May 15, 1758
Bay, Hugh. Executors: Andrew Bay and James Smith. York Township. Brother: Andrew Bay.

Oct 8, 1757   May 23, 1758
Davis, Walter.. Executors: James Agnew and John Davis. Hamiltonsban Township. Wife: Mary Davis. Children: Mary and James.

Oct 8, 1757   May 23, 1758
Dunbar, William. Executors: James McKee and Isaac McKinly. (The wife's name was not given. The entire estate was left to her.)

May 3, 1758   May 30, 1758
Hood, Elizabeth. Executor: James Caldwell. York County. Brother-in-law: James Caldwell.

Aug 25, 1757   May 31, 1758
Campbell, William. Executors: Elizabeth Campbell and Thomas Minshall. York County. Wife: Elizabeth Campbell. Children: Jane, Mary, Elizabeth, John, Ann, William, Thomas, and Martha.

Dec 2, 1757   Jun 17, 1758
Scott, John. Executors: Richard Brown and Janet Scott. Straban Township. Wife: Janet Scott. Children: John, David and Richard.

Mar 19, 1758   Jun 22, 1758
Hoghan, Nicholas. Executor: Catharine Hoghan. Heidelberg Township. Wife: Chatronary Hoghan. Children: Ann, and (three other children whose names are not given.)

Jul 14, 1750   Jun 28, 1758
Lilley, Samuel. Executor: Thomas Lelley. Conewago Township. Wife: Omitted. Child: Thomas.

--- --, ----   Jul 24, 1758
Evans, Joseph. Executor and Township omitted. (This will was not in the records, and there is no mention of its being in the files.)

Jul 19, 1758   Aug 13, 1758
Updegraef, Harman. Executor: Joseph Updegraef. Omitted Township. Wife: Anna Ursula Updegraef. Children: Derick, John, William and Herman.

Apr 22, 1758   Aug 18, 1758
Darby, John. Executor: James Darby. York County. Wife: Barbara Darby. Children: John, Margaret, Elizabeth, and Mary.

--- --, ----   Aug 22, 1758
Croll, Christian. Executors: Elizabeth Croll, Philip Croll, and Martin Eykelberger. Township omitted. Wife: Elizabeth Croll. Children: Michael, Philip, John, Henry, and Mary.

Sep 28, 1757   Oct 4, 1758
Bard, Savilla. Executor: Peter Bard. Township omitted. Children: Peter, Francis, Martin, Barne, Paul and Philip.

--- --, ----   Oct 17, 1758
Fletzer, Jacob. Executor: omitted. (Will not copied on records.)

Dec 16, 1754   Nov 17, 1758
Stentz, Henry. Executor: Omitted. Hellam Township. Wife: Maria Dorothea Stentz. Children of the second Wife: Leonard, Maria, Jacob and John. Children of the first wife: Anna, Catharine and Dorothea.

Nov 7, 1758   Dec 14, 1758
Moore, Robert. Executors: Thomas Stockton and Samuel McFarran. Manallen Township. Wife: Jean Moore. Children: William, Robert, and James.

Jan 29, 1759   Feb 3, 1759
Wigle, Martin. Executors: Deiter Ulher and Martin Eichelberger. York County. Wife: Dorothea Wigle. Children: Bastian, Martin, Jacob, Leonard, Peter, Henry, Julianna and Elizabeth.

Aug 21, 1757   Mar 13, 1759
McCan, Timothy. Executor: Omitted. Maryland. Child: Daniel. Grandchildren: Patrick and Ann McCan.

Jan 23, 1759   Mar 19, 1759
Kerr, John. Executors: Martha and George Kerr. Hamiltonsban Township. Wife: Martha Kerr. Children: George, William, John, Samuel, James, Thomas, and Andrew.

Feb 8, 1759   Mar 20, 1759
Armstrong, Thomas. Executor: John Armstrong. Cumberland Township. Children: William, John, Elenor, Margaret. Son-in-law: James Orr (wife's name not given).

May 19, 1756   Mar 26, 1759
Murphy, Alexander. Executors: James Murphy and James McWilliam. Straban Township. Children: James and Archibald.

Dec 14, 1758   Jun 6, 1759
Read, James. Executors: John Ralston of Carrolls Delight, Maryland. Cumberland Township. Children: John and William. Grandchildren: James Read (son of John) and Margaret, John, James and Robert (children of William).

Aug 29, 1754   Jun 26, 1759
Jones, Charles. Executor: Elizabeth Jones. Yorktown Township. Wife: Elizabeth Jones. Children: Robert, and (others whose names were not given.)

--- --, ----   Jun 27, 1759
McNeil, John. Executor: Omitted. Cumberland Township. Brothers: Robert and Ephriam.

Jul 4, 1759   Aug 14, 1759
Copland, William. Executors: Thomas Copland and Robert Miller. Newberry Township. Wife: Elizabeth Copland. Children: Thomas, (and three other sons whose names are not given.)

Sep 2, 1759   Oct 20, 1759
Owings, Robert. Executors: Hannah and Robert Owings. Baltimore County. Wife: Hannah Owings. Children: Robert, Thomas, Joshua, William, Charles, John, Mary, Rachael, Hannah, and Susanna.

Dec 3, 1753   Oct 29, 1759
Wright, John Executors: Eleanor and James Wright. Hellam Township.
Wife: Eleanor Wright. Children: Robert, John, (and two daughters - names not given).

Apr 27, 1759   Apr 28, 1760
Spangler, Casper. Executors: Michael Bard, Barnet and Judith Spangler. Township: Omitted. Wife: Judith Spangler. Children: Judith wife of Henry Baker, Philip and Barnet.

Sep 28, 1759   Apr 28, 1760
Carson, Samuel. Executors: Janeat and David Carson. Mount Pleasant Township. Wife: Janeat Carson. Children: Elizabeth, John, George, David, William, and Samuel.

Aug 6, 1759   Apr 28, 1760
Clark, Timothy. Executor: Mary Clark. Reading Township. Wife: Margaret Clark. Children: Hannah, Eleanor, Elizabeth, and Margaret wife of Daniel Coyle.

May 21, 1760   Jun 9, 1760
Day, John. Executors: John Garritson, Rebecca and Joseph Day. Newberry Township. Wife: Omitted. Children: Joseph, Stephen, Rebecca, Silvina, Thomas, Samuel, and Solomon. Grandchild: Rebecca Garritson (daughter of John Garritson, mother's name not recorded).

Oct 1, 1760   Oct 7, 1760
Cron, Henrich. Executors: Michael Swope and Barbara Cron. York Town Township. Wife: Barbara Cron. Children: Henry and Elizabeth.

Sep 3, 1760   Oct 13, 1760
Bealley, Joseph. Executor: Alexander McCarter. Township omitted. Wife: Elizabeth Hannah Bealley. Child: Elizabeth.

Aug 12, 1754   Nov 20, 1760
Morthland, Hugh. Executors: Rebecca Morthland. Warrington Township. Wife: Rebecca Morthland. Children: William, Charles, Samuel, Agness, Rebecca, Margaret, and Hugh.

Jan 19, 1760   Nov 22, 1760
Heslet, James. Executor: Mary Heslet. Yorktown Township. Children: John, Sarah, William, James, and Robert.

Jan 2, 1761   Jan 8, 1761
Sohn, George. Executors: John Sohn and George Keintz. York Town
Township. Children: Jacob, Margaret and Elizabeth.

Dec 8, 1760   Jan 26, 1761
Lautshaw, Jacob. Executors: Mary and Isaac Lautshaw. Reading
Township. Wife: Mary Lautshaw. Children: Joseph, Isaac, Peter, Mary,
John, and Elizabeth.

Mar 9, 1761   Mar 16, 1761
McMullen, James. Executors: Jean McMullen and John Curran.
Strasburg Township. Wife: Jean McMullen. Children: Mary and Robert.

Dec 14, 1759   Mar 20, 1761
Paxton, Nathaniel. Executors: John and Joseph Paxton. Township:
Omitted. Wife: Hannah Paxton. Children: Nathaniel and others,
(Names and number not given.)

Mar 14, 1759   Apr 14, 1761
Thompson, Andrew. Executors: Eleanor and John Thompson. Mt.
Pleasant Township. Wife: Eleanor Thompson. children: Ephriam, John,
Andrew, William, Margaret, Isaac and George.

Feb 24, 1761   Apr 15, 1761
Ocher, John. Executors: John Nesbit and Henry Flick. Warrington
Township. Children: Hannickel, Christiana, Margaret, and Susanna.

Aug 12, 1761   Aug 20, 1761
Hale, Thomas. Executor: Hannah Hale. Warrington Township. Wife:
Hannah Hale. Children: John, Sarah, and Joseph.

Jul 3, 1761   Aug 27, 1761
Morrison, Margery. Executor: Francis Houlton. Township: Omitted.
Children: Francis, Ann, Elizabeth, Mary, and Margery.

Feb 19, 1761   Oct 8, 1761
McAdams, John. Executors: Joseph Ross and Sarah McAdams. York
County. Wife: Sarah McAdams. Child: Samuel.

Feb 21, 1761   Oct 30, 1761
Jones, Engel. Executors: Jacob Bealer and Daniel Dole. Manheim
Township. Wife: Mary E. Jones. Children: Elizabeth, Michael, and
Mary.

Feb 20, 1762   Mar 3, 1762
Shaw, John. Executors: Jean Shaw and Joseph Mason. Chanceford Township. Wife: Margaret Shaw. Children: Robert, Jean and William.

Oct 12, 1761   Mar 12, 1762
Martin, Edward. Executor: Mary Martin. Newberry Township. Wife: Mary Martin. Child: Mary.

Feb 18, 1762   Mar 13, 1762
Mearns, William. Executor: John Barns. Windsor Township. Children: Agness, Martha, and Elizabeth.

Jan 7, 1762   Apr 24, 1762
Low, Joshua. Executors: Mary and Caleb Low. Manchester Township. Wife: Mary Low. Child: Joshua.

Mar 30, 1762   Apr 27, 1762
Herback, Yost. Executors: John Herback and Jacob Welshover. Hellam Township. Wife: Mary Eliza Herback. Children: George, John, Leonard, Mary, Catharine, Jacob, and Margaret.

Apr 2, 1756   Jul 26 1762
Young, David. Executor: Margaret Young. Cumberland Township. Wife: Margaret Young. Children: Margaret, David, Eleanor, James and Nancy.

Sep 4, 1761   Oct 2, 1762
Shannon, Andrew. Executors: George Leviston and William Biggors. Straban Township. Wife: Mary Shannon. Children: William, Mary, Sarah, Margaret, Richard, Samuel and Rebecca.

Mar 16, 1761   Oct 18, 1762
Rogers, John. Executors: Adam and Eleanor Rogers. Township: Omitted. Wife: Eleanor Rogers. Children: William and John.

Aug 30, 1762   Nov 1, 1762
Houck, Bernard. Executors: Eve and Jacob Houck. Manheim Township. Children: Jacob, Philip, George, Eva, and Elizabeth.

Jul 18, 1762   Nov 9, 1762
Saltzgeber, Detrick. Executors: Margaret Saltzgeber and Abraham Gehler. Paradise Township. Wife: Margaret Saltzgeber. Children: Jacob, Casper, Margaret, Elizabeth and Mary. There was a son-in-law, Abraham Gehler (his wifes' name not given).

Nov 2, 1762   Nov 12, 1762
Honsicker, Jacob. Executors: Catharine Honsicker and Michael Danner. Manheim Township. Wife: Catharine Hunsicker.

Oct 20, 1762   Dec 10, 1762
Taylor, Robert. Executors: John Taylor and Hugh Whiteford. York County. Wife: Jean Taylor. Children: Eleanor, John and Hugh.

Jan 23, 1763   Jan 27, 1763
Davis, Thomas. Executor: William Davis. York County. Wife: Anna Davis. Children: (Names and number not given.)

Feb 7, 1763   Feb 28, 1763
Welshance, Jacob. Executors: Jacob Welshance and Henry Gerlack. York County. Wife: Elizabeth Welshance. Children: Jacob, David, Conrad, Magdalena and Eve.

Dec 18, 1762   Mar 19, 1763
Houser, John. Executors: George Werly and Hansly Mayer. Cordorus Township. Wife: Mary Houser. Children: John, Peter, Henry, Jacob, George, Elizabeth, and Yuleyane.

Feb 2, 1763   Mar 22, 1763
Liggit, John. Executors: Margaret and Alexander Liggit. Windsor Township. Wife: Margaret Liggit. Children: Alexander, Francis, George, John, and Elizabeth.

Apr 13, 1763   Jun 2, 1763
Ellison, John. Executor: Matthew Ellison. York County. Children: Matthew, Mary, and Ellen. Grandchild: Mary (child of Matthew).

May 26, 1763   Jun 15, 1763
Laird, Samuel. Executor: James Laird. Fawn Township. Wife: Jennet Laird. Children: Martha, Sarah, Margaret, Mary, and Anna.

Sep 2, 1763   Oct 13, 1763
Spangler, Rudolph. Executors: George Keentz and Adam Lightner. York County. Wife: Catharine Spangler. Children: Elizabeth and Henry.

Sep 20, 1763   Oct 18, 1763
Mirs, John Jr. Executor: Henry Strickler, Christian Stoner, and Christian Shanke. Windsor Township. Wife: Elizabeth Mirs. Child: Elizabeth.

Oct 2, 1763   Nov 29, 1763
Lora, Henrich. Executors: Anthony Amen and George Feavour. Windsor Township. Wife: Omitted. Children: (Names and number not given.)

Oct 24, 1763   Jan 23, 1764
White, Archibald. Executor: Archibald White. Fawn Township. Legatees: (Bros.) James (and others - names not stated).

--- ---, ----   Feb 29, 1764
Unkafare, George. Executors: Michael Carle and Leonard Geisel. Omitted Township. (German will.)

May 3, 1764   Mar 27, 1764
Hamel, James. Executor: William Dunlap. Tyrone Township. Children: Mary, Rachel Rodgers (stepdaughter), and William Carson (stepson).

--- ---, ----   Mar 27, 1764
Finley, James. Executor: John Withrow. Hamiltonsban Township. Wife: Jean Finley. Child: Margaret.

--- ---, ----   Apr 5, 1764
Harman, Honickle. Executor: Esther Harman. Township: Omitted. German will.

Dec 19, 1763   Jun 5, 1764
Buchannan, William. Executor: Ebenezer Newtin. Fawn Township. Wife: Jane Buchannan. Children: James, William, Thomas, Elizabeth and Margaret.

--- ---, ----   Oct 12, 1764
Wirt, Henry. Executor: Omitted. Manheim Township. Will not copied on records - see files.

--- ---, ----   Nov 23, 1764
Wampfler, Christian. Executor: Abraham Weldie and Johannes Hunsecher. Omitted Township. (German will.)

Apr 17, 1759   Nov 29, 1764
Stagner, Nicholas. Executors: Samuel Moser and Adam Haindly. Windsor Township. Wife: Catharine Stagner. Children: Isaac, Mary wife of John Brandon and Richard.

Nov 1, 1764   Jan 5, 1765
Noblit, Abraham. Executor: Anna Noblit. Newberry Township. Wife: Anna Noblit. Children: Thomas, John, and William.

Dec 25, 1764   Jan 15, 1765
Uhler, Dietrich. Executors: M. Eichelberger and George Myer. Manchester Township. Wife: Margaret Uhler. Children: Adam, Erasmus, Valentine, Andrew, Rosanna, Barbara, Eve, Elizabeth, Savenah and Catherine.

Nov 6, 1764   Feb 28, 1765
Asper, John. Executors: George Asper and Ursella Asper. Reading County. Children: George, Elizabeth and Frederick.

Aug 13, 1764   Mar 26, 1765
Willis, Henry. Executor: William Willis. Newberry Township. Wife: Rachel Willis. Children: William, Joshua, Richard, Mary and Catharine.

Aug 3, 1763   Mar 27, 1765
Bixler, John. Executor: John Miller. Manheim Township. Wife: Matalina Bixler. Children: Jacob, John, Samuel, Mary wife of John Miller and Elizabeth.

Feb 7, 1764   May 31, 1765
Weyerman, William. Executors: Henry Weyerman and Archibald McGrew. Huntington Township. Children: Henry, William, John, Nicholas, Hannah and Gertrude.

Jan 13, 1766   Jun 24, 1765 (?)
Albright, George. Executors: Adam Taylor and Conrad Brubaker. Windsor Township. Children: Peter and Philip.

Jul 31, 1765   Sep 19, 1765
Wilson, William. Executors: Samuel and Walter Beaty. Reading Township. Wife: Susanna Wilson. Children: William, Elizabeth, Jean and (son-in-law) Robert Laughlin (wife's name not given). Grandchildren: Jean and Samuel Laughlin.

Jan 8, 1766   May 13, 1766
Ledder, Jacob. Executor: Margaret Ledder. Yorktown Township. Wife: Omitted. Children: (Names and number not given.)

Mar 9, 1766   May 16, 1766
McClentor, James. Executor: Jean McGee. Chanceford Township.
Children: Jenny and Jean.

Feb 15, 1766   Jun 9, 1766
Cooper, Peter. Executors: Margaret Cooper and George Kautz.
Shrewsbury Township. Wife: Margaret Cooper. Children: Adam, Peter,
Eve, and Elizabeth.

Oct 19, 1763   Jun 9, 1766
Criglo, John. Executors: Margaret Cooper and George Kautz. Mt. Joy
Township. Wife: Elizabeth Criglo. Children: (Names and number not
recorded.)

Oct 27, 1765   Jun 10, 1766
Noel, John. Executors: Margaret and Nicholas Bettinger. Paradise
Township. Wife: Margaret Noel. Children: Andrew, John, Peter, Jacob,
Nicholas, Casper, and Philip.

May 2, 1766   Jun 10, 1766
Leard, John. Executors: William and Martha Leard. Cumberland
Township. Wife: Martha Leard. Children: John, William, Mary, and
Martha.

Feb 28, 1766   Jun 13, 1766
King, Abraham. Executor: George King. York County. Wife: Omitted.
Children: George, Eve wife of Thomas Fisher, and Abraham.
Grandchildren: Mrs. Stephen Wible and Mrs. Reinhart Reaploge (children
of George).

May 20, 1766   Jul 29, 1766
Elliker, Casper. Executors: Nicholas Miller and Henry Elliker. York
County. Wife: Susanna Elliker. Child: Henry.

Mar 26, 1764   Jul 31, 1766
Shonard, John. Executors: Eleanor Shonard and William Fulton.
Shrewsbury Township. Wife: Eleanor Shonard. Children: Jonathan,
Abraham, John, Thomas, William, Mary, Susan, Margaret, Eleanor and
Elizabeth.

Aug 6, 1765   Aug 21, 1766
Griffe, Stephen. Executors: Peter and Mary Mundorff. Yorktown
Township. Children: Eve, Sarah, and Magdalena.

Apr 26, 1766   Aug 26, 1766
Dobs, Oswald. Executors: Adam Kreber and John S. Muller. Manheim Township. Wife: Salome Dobs. Children: Daniel, Oswald, (and six others whose names were not given.)

Jul 29, 1766   Aug 29, 1766
McCandles, Alexander. Executor: James McCandles. Fawn Township. Wife: Sarah McCandles. Children: Jean, Martha, William, Alexander, Margaret, Sarah, and James.

Oct 26, 1765   Sep 2, 1766
Dods, William. Executors: Susanna and Joseph Dods. York County. Wife: Susanna Dods. Children: Janet, Mary and Joseph.

Oct 19, 1765   Sep 24, 1766
Montgomery, Hugh. Executor: John and James Montgomery. Shrewsbury Township. Wife: Margaret Montgomery. Children: William, Jean, John, James, Hugh, Martha, and Elizabeth.

Feb 3, 1766   Sep 26, 1766
Ham, Valleendin. Executors: Lewis and Jacob May. Dover Township. Wife: Louisa Ham. Children: Baltzer, Christian, and Mary.

Aug 11, 1766   Oct 1, 1766
Geinling, Barnhard. Executor: Christiana Geinling. Township: Omitted. Wife: Christiana Geinling. Child: Barhard.

Aug 9, 1766   Oct 20, 1766
How, Abraham. Executors: Elizabeth and Samuel How. York County. Wife: Elizabeth How. Children: Abraham and Mary.

--- --, ----   Oct 27, 1766
Nelson, William. Executor: Omitted. Warrington Township. This will has not been copied on the records, but is on file.

Nov 6, 1766   Nov 26, 1766
Tull, Ulrich. Executor: Elizabeth Tull. Paradise Township. Wife: Elizabeth Tull.

Apr 12, 1766   Nov 27, 1766
Thompson, Alexander. Executors: Thomas and John Praxton. Cumberland Township. Wife: Esther Thompson. Sons-in-law: Thomas Morton and George Williams (names of wives not given). Grandchild:

Jane Williams.

Apr 9, 1762   Dec 9, 1766
Schaum, John. Executors: Mary Ann and Isaac Schaum. Germany Township. Children: Isaac, Elizabeth, Leonard and Nicholas.

Oct 31, 1766   Dec 22, 1766
Hosselberger, George. Executors: Maria Hosselberger and George Stake. Yorktown Township. Wife: Maria Hosselberger. Children: George, Philip, Michael, and Catharine.

Dec 13, 1766   Dec 22, 1766
Long, George. Executor: Elizabeth Long. Dover Township. Wife: Elizabeth Long. Children: (Names and number not given.)

Oct 29, 1765   Feb 11, 1767
McCarrll, John. Executor: James McCarrll. Straban Township. Wife: Omitted. Children: James, Elizabeth, Ann, Mary, and Esther. Grandchild: John McCarrll (son of James).

Feb 23, 1767   Mar 24, 1767
Young, Margaret. Executors: John Linn and David Young. Cumberland Township. Children: James, Margaret, Agness and John Davison and David.

Jun 13, 1766   Mar 26, 1767
Turner, William. Executors: Rebecca Turner and Alexander Mc Carter. Straban Township. Wife: Rebecca Turner. There were six children - names not given.

Sep 2, 1766   Mar 26, 1767
McGrew, Finley. Executors: William Delap and Archibald McGrew. Tyrone Township. Wife: Elizabeth McGrew. Children: James, Peter, Nathan, William, and Finley.

May 19, 1758   Mar 30, 1767
Upp, Jacob. Executor: Peter Pence. Dover Township. Wife: Catharine Upp. Children: Nicholas, Elizabeth and Peter Pence, Jacob, Catharine, Louisa and (son-in-law) Christopher Knertzer (wife's name not given). Grandchildren: Nicholas, Andrew, Baltzer, Anna, Margaret and Catharine Knertzer

Aug 23, 1764   Apr 3, 1767
Swevans, Ann. Executor: George Swope. Paradise Township. Children: George and six daughters (names not given).

Mar 14, 1767   Apr 8, 1767
Shall, George. Executors: George Keentz and Gotlieb Zeigler. Township: Omitted. Wife: Vliana Shall. Children: Barbara, Mary, Catharine and George.

--- --, ----   Apr 8, 1767
Hiestand, Jacob. Executor: Jacob Updegraff. Township: Omitted. (German will.)

Nov 16, 1765   Apr 13, 1767
Dickson, Samuel. Executor: James Dickson. Straban Township. Wife: Jane Dickson. Children: Mary, Margaret (?) wife of ---- Buchanan, Isabella, Jane, Elizabeth, Samuel, and James. Granddaughter: Margaret (child of Margaret (?)).

Mar 6, 1767   Apr 15, 1767
Spengler, Rosina. Executor: George Spengler. Manchester Township. Children: George and Henry.

Jan 13, 1767   Apr 15, 1767
Summers, Robert. Executors: Joseph Watson and Joseph Bogle. Chanceford Township. Wife: Agness Summers. Children: John and Elizabeth.

Feb 13, 1767   May 13, 1767
Hesslet, Joseph. Executors: Esther Heslet and William Shekley. Cumberland Township. Wife: Esther Hesslet. Children: Mary and Agness.

Oct 28, 1765   May 26, 1767
Wallace, Alexander. Executors: James Wallace and John Orr. Shrewberry Township. Wife: Agness Wallace. Children: Elizabeth, William, Margaret, Jean, Sarah, Christiana and James. N.B. There was a bequest to Alexander, James, Joseph and Agness Tompson.

Feb 12, 1767   May 26, 1767
Long, Henry. Executor: Margaret Long. Windsor Township. Wife: Margaret Long. Children: Matthew, Elizabeth, Margaret, Mary, Jennet, and Henry.

Dec 31, 1766   Jul 27, 1767
Hodge, William. Executors: Margaret and William Hodge. Reading
Township. Wife: Margaret Hodge. Children: Samuel, William, John,
Mary wife of Richard Say, Margaret wife of George Hodge, and Sarah.
Grandchild: William (son of Margaret).

Dec 2, 1766   Aug 14, 1767
Drungold, Michael. Executors: William Love and James Dixon. Straban
Township. Wife: Margaret Drungold. Children: John, Alexander, and
James.

Jun 30, 1767   Sep 24, 1767
Ness, Mathias. Executors: Jacob Ness and Peter Low. Manchester
Township. Children: Jacob, Henry, Catharine, Susan, and Mary.
Grandchild: Peter Ness (parents' names not given).

Sep 10, 1767   Oct 1, 1767
Parker, Rebecca. Executors: Andrew Mays and Moses Ginkin.
Cumberland Township. Children: James, George, Margaret, Mary, and
Rebecca.

Sep 8, 1767   Oct 1, 1767
Boyd, William. Executors: Margaret Boyd and Moses Boyd. Cumberland
Township. Wife: Margaret Boyd. Children: James, Moses, William,
Samuel, Robert, Isabella and Margaret.

Oct 6, 1767   Oct 29, 1767
Reed, John. Executors: Thomas and John Reed. Straban Township.
Wife: Fanny Reed. Children: Jane, Fanny, Hannah, Rebecca, Matthew,
William, Samuel, Thomas and John.

Jan 17, 1767   Nov 16, 1767
Straley, Andrew. Executors: Peter Wertz, Philip Fainman and Andrew
Fraimer. Reading Township. Wife: Name not given. There were
children, but (Names and number not given.) Mentioned in will as "My
wife and children".

Mar 13, 1764   Nov 27, 1767
Morgan, Thomas. Executor: Nathaniel Morgan. Chanceford Township.
Children: Nathaniel, William, Elizabeth, John, and Mary wife of John
Dakin. Grandchildren: George and Dorothea Dakin.

May 28, 1767   Nov 30, 1767
Underwood, Alexander. Executors: William Underwood. Warrington Township. Children: Samuel, Thomas, Joseph, William, Mary, Benjamin, Frazier, Jane, Ruth, Elicher and John.

Nov 20, 1767   Dec 10, 1767
Rorahbah, Jacob. Executor: Margaret Rorahbah. Mt. Joy Township. Wife: Margaret Rorahbah. Brothers: Lairriah and John. Sister: Barbara Rorahbah.

Nov 20, 1767   Jan 16, 1768
Neff, Peter. Executor: Anna Neff. Newberry Township. Wife: Anna Neff. Children: John and Elizabeth.

Jan 12, 1768   Feb 17, 1768
Dickson, James. Executor: John Morrison. Chanceford Township. Children: Margaret, Hannah, and Ann.

Jan 1, 1768   Mar 24, 1768
Vance, Ezekiel. Executors: Elenaor Vance and Alexander Brown. Omitted Township. Wife: Eleanor Vance. Child: William.

Mar 18, 1762   Apr 11, 1768
Jost, Conrad. Executors: George Trone and George Mather. Manheim Township. Wife: Christiana Jost. Children: Herman, and (four others whose names were not given.)

Mar 30, 1768   Apr 11, 1768
Michael, Paul. Executor: Christiana Michael. Windsor Township. Wife: Christiana Michael. Children: Henry, William, Margaret, Catharine wife of Adam Polasei. (There was a younger daughter whose name was not given. She was the wife of Lorance Polasei.)

Apr 9, 1768   Apr 26, 1768
Collings, John. Executor: John Collings. Reading Township. Children: Joseph, John, Mary, and Rose.

Apr 3, 1768   Apr 28, 1768
Becker, George. Executors: Henry Bondabush and John Becker. Berwick Township. Wife: Elizabeth Becker. Children: John, George, Daniel, Elizabeth wife of Henry Brissel, Susanna and Catharine.

--- --, ----   Apr 30, 1768
Lohra, Michael. Executors: Henry Krober, Regena Lohra, and Henry Schneck. (German will.)

Apr 7, 1769   May 8, 1768
McGrew, Nathan. Executors: Rachel and Finley McGrew. Township: Omitted. Wife: Rachel McGrew. Child: Rebecca.

May 3, 1768   Jun 10, 1768
Watson, Hugh. Executors: Elizabeth and Patrick Watson. Straban Township. Wife: Elizabeth Watson. Children: Sarah, John, Daniel, William, Katharine, Hugh and George.

Jun 17, 1768   Aug 20, 1768
Worley, Francis. Executors: Daniel Worley and John Updegraff. Manchester Township. Children: Daniel, Jacob, Martha, Henry, Samuel, James, Francis, Thomas, Mary wife of Peter Shugart and Lydia wife of George Eickelberger
P.S. About that will of Francis Worley of York Co. - dated 17 June 1768; probated 23 Aug 1768. Although the abstract at HSP does not mention his wife Charity, my certified copy <u>does</u> mention her to such an extent that there is no doubt she was living when he wrote the will. So I think this is all the proof that is necessary to indicate the abstract is wrong. Perhaps a notation could be inserted in the page saying the complete will should be consulted as the abstract is inaccurate? (It also mentions a daughter Martha, whose name does <u>not</u> appear in the will.)
Note from Miss Elizabeth Lery regarding original will of Francis Worley on file in the Register of Wills office, Youk County, Penna.
Photostat of Will: Francis Worley, York Co., PA 1768
<u>Eight</u> sons are named: Daniel, Jacob, Samuel, James, Francis, Nathan, Henry and Thomas. Daughters: Mary Shugart and Lydia Eikelberger (Martha in abstract was probably mis-reading of Nathan).

Mar 3, 1766   Sep 5, 1768
Evin, John. Executor: John Thompson. Mt. Pleasant Township. Children: Alexander, Martha, Isaac, Robert and Samuel.

Sep 22, 1766   Sep 17, 1768
Bosler, Frederick. Executor: Fornica Bosler. York Township. Wife: Fornica Bosler. Brother: Ulerick Bosler.

Aug 24, 1761   Oct 1, 1768
McPherson, James. Executors: Robert McPherson and James Ferguson.

York County. Children: Francis wife of ---- Davies, and Robert.
Grandchildren: Janet, Hugh and Agness Davies (Robert's child), Jannet
McPherson, and Janet and Mary Boyd ((parents' names not given).

Aug 26, 1768   Nov 7, 1768
Bardt, George. Executors: Abraham Hule and Michael Clapsadle.
Berwick Township. Wife: Barbara Bardt. Children: George, Paul,
Barbara, Susanna, Anna, Catharine, Mandilena and Mariles.

Apr 12, 1768   Nov 9, 1768
Bahn, Henry. Executors: George Kuntz and Jacob Shickley. Hellam
Township. Wife: Eva Bahn. Children: John, Johannes, Jacob, Elizabeth,
Catharine, Eva, Juliana and Anna.

Nov 11, 1768   Nov 19, 1768
Kirkpatrick, David. Executors: Susanna Kirkpatrick, James Lefer, and
John McKinley. Chanceford Township. Wife: Susanna Kirkpatrick.
Children: Hugh, James, David, Mary, Hannah, and Elizabeth.

--- --, ----   Nov 30, 1768
McCaskey, Neall. Executor: William McCaskey. Fawn Township.
(German will.)

Oct 31, 1768   Dec 16, 1768
Hendrix, William. Executor: Elizabeth Worley. Hanover Township.
Brother: James. Cousin: Elizabeth Worley.

Jan 11, 1765   Jan 3, 1769
Homan, Michael. Executors: Michael Kinefelter and Elizabeth Homan.
Shrewsbury Township. Wife: Elizabeth Homan. Children: Godleap, and
(others whose names are not given.)

Dec 5, 1768   Feb 3, 1769
Alexander, John. Executor: Hugh Scott. York County. Children:
Samuel, John, Pedons, Lindsey, and Rebecca wife of Porter. John and
Jane (children of Rebecca).

Jan 17, 1769   Feb 18, 1769
Shelly, Peter. Executors: Daniel Shelly and John Plow. Newberry
Township. Wife: Catharine Shelly. Children: Mary, Ann and Peter.

Mar 14, 1769   Apr 7, 1769
Butler, Thomas. Executor: Thomas Lilly. Heidleberg Township. Wife:

Sarah Butler. Children: Thomas, Margaret and Mary.

Jan 5, 1769   Apr 11, 1769
Price, Joseph. Executors: Ephriam Johnson and Hugh Eagon. Fawn Township. Legatee: Phebe Price (sister).

Jan 13, 1763   May 8, 1769
Hagenberger, Reinhart. Executor: Omitted. Manchester Township. Wife: Rosina Hagenberger. Children: John, and Mary wife of Andrew Miller.

May 8, 1769   May 30, 1769
Hughes, Jonathan. Executor: Omitted. Manheim Township. Child: John. Grandchildren: Eleanor (daughter of John) wife of Blackburn. Great Grandchildren: Joseph, Abigal, Thomas, and Anthony (children of Eleanor).

Jan 7, 1761   Aug 31, 1769
Mains, Culbert. Executors: Robert Mains and Thomas Baldwin. Tyrone Township. Children: Robert and Elizabeth. Grandchildren: Robert, Culbert, and Isaac Mains.

--- ---, ----   Sep 1, 1769
Cowgell, Henry. Executors: Alice and Henry Cowgell, and George Payne. Fawn Township. Wife: Alice Cowgell. Children: Henry, John, Sarah, Rachel, Lydia, Allen, and Alice.

Aug 15, 1767   Sep 18, 1769
Knertzer, Baltzer. Executors: Baltzer Knertzer and George Kuntz. Yorktown Township. Wife: Catharine Knertzer. Children: George, Baltzer, Catharine, and Dorothea wife of Andrew Miller. Stepson: Andrew Grass. Grandchildren: Nicholas, Andrew, Baltzer, Margaret, and Catharine (children of George).

Dec 30, 1768   Oct 30, 1769
Montfort, Peter. Executors: Abraham Banta, John and Abraham Montfort. York County. Wife: Johannah Montfort. Children: Peter, Anamary, John, Margaret, Sarah, and Catharine.

Sep 12, 1769   Oct 30, 1769
Galbreaith, John. Executors: Catharine and John Galbreaith. Mt. Pleasant Township. Wife: Catharine Galbreaith. Children: John, Agness, Elizabeth, Rebecca, Cathren, Robert and John.

Oct 3, 1769   Oct 30, 1769
Miller, Joseph. Executors: Nicholas Wireman and Margaret Miller. York County. Wife: Margaret Miller. Children: Levi, Eli, and Phebe.

Sep 23, 1769   Nov 18, 1769
Mitchel, John George. Executor: Peter Strecher. Township: Omitted. Wife: Catharine Mitchel. Children: John (and four others whose names were not given.)

Jun 14, 1768   Dec 6, 1769
Komfort, Mary Veronica. Executor: Andreas Komfort. Township: Omitted. Wife of Leonard Komfort. Children: Ann, Andrew, and John.

Sep 10, 1769   Dec 28, 1769
Wilkinson, John. Executors: Robert Wilkinson and Ellis Lewis. Newburry Township. Wife: Diriah Wilkinson. Children: William, John, Robert and Ann wife of Cornelius Ryan.

Dec 29, 1769   Jan 9, 1770
Sheffer, David. Executors: Philip Sheffer and Baltzer Cobar. Shrewsbury Township: Catharine Sheffer. Children: Philip, Natalina, Elizabeth, Anna, Maria, Charles, David, McArillis wife of Baltzer Cobar, Margaret and Katharine wife of George Yearman.

--- --, ----   Jan 29, 1770
Hessey, John. Executors: Reed Hershey and William Matthew. Newberry Township. (German will.)

Jan 12, 1770   Feb 12, 1770
Bentzel, Johannes. Executor: Sophia Bentzel. Township omitted. Wife: Sophia Bentzel.

Jan 4, 1770   Mar 8, 1770
Rowan, Andrew. Executor: Andrew Rowan. Fawn Township. Wife: Agnes Rowan. Children: William, Jean, Susanna, Andrew, Agnes, Margaret and Mary.

--- --, ----   Mar 12, 1770
Drorbach, Adam. Executors: Wilhelm and Nicholas Drorbach. German will.

Oct 15, 1769   Mar 13, 1770
Newland, William. Executors: Hannah and William Newland. Menallen

Township. Wife: Hannah Newland. Children: William, James, Anna, Elijah, David, John, Deborah, and Benjamin.

Feb 3, 1770 Mar 21, 1770
Lowman, Barnet. Executors: Christopher Lowman and Jacob Bott. York Township. Wife: Anna Margaret Lowman. Children: Christopher, Gotleep, Magdalena, and Ann.

Jun 7, 1769 Mar 26, 1770
Mummert, Dietrich. Executors: Philip Heneman and B. Hockinbough. Reading Township. Children: William, Margaret wife of David Erhart, Mary wife of Samuel Webster, Susanna wife of Philip Jacobs, Elizabeth wife of Abraham How, and Catharine.

Apr 20, 1770 May 7, 1770
Johnston, Benjamin. Executors: Ephriam and Jacob Johnston. Wife: Mary Johnston. Children: Caleb, Ephriam, Jacob, Robert, Ann, and Able.

Apr 26, 1770 May 14, 1770
Beitler, Jacob. Executors: Barbara Beitler and Daniel Beitler. Hellam Township. Wife: Barbara Beitler. Children: Jacob, Ann and John.

Oct 10, 1776 Jun 7, 1770
Leman, Rude. Executors: Frena and Christian Leman. Hellam Township. Wife: Frena Leman. Children: John, Maney, David, and Barbara.

Dec 1, 1769 Jun 9, 1770
Cannon, John. Executor: Thomas Cannon. Newberry Township. Wife: Elizabeth Cannon. Children: Agness, William, Samuel, Hannah, Mary, Robert, Elizabeth, Jane, and Thomas.

Apr 5, 1770 Jun 19, 1770
Hara, Charles. Executor: Mary Hara. Chanceford Township. Wife: Mary Hara. Children: Daniel and Patraick.

Mar 21, 1770 Jul 21, 1770
Herrington, Jacob. Executors: Mary Herrington and George Lefever. York County. Wife: Omitted. Children: (Names and number not given.)

Jun 30, 1770 Jul 31, 1770
Dombar, John. Executor: Archibald McGrew. York County. Children: James, Margaret wife of William McCreary, Janet wife of James Reead,

Mary wife of Andrew Miller, and John.

Apr 7, 1768   Aug 3, 1770
McClery, John. Executor: Daniel Griffith. Hopewell Township. Wife: Martha McClery. Children: Andrew, John, Sarah, and Mary.

Sep 6, 1770   Sep 20, 1770
Shultz, Samuel. Executors: George Keentz and Margaret Shultz. York Town Township. Wife: Margaret Shultz.

Jun 1, 1770   Sep 20, 1770
Didrich, William. Executors: Modelena Featory and Adam Winterode. York County. Wife: Modelena Didrich. Children: (Names and number not given.)

Sep 10, 1770   Sep 27, 1770
Ament, George. Executors: Adam Gartner and Catharine Ament. Hellam Township. Wife: Catharine Ament. Children: George, Jacob, Marilla wife of Adam Gartner, Catharine wife of Conrad Hoak. Barbara (child of George). Jacob and Catharine Shultz (two grandchildren, Mother's name not given).

Aug 11, 1770   Oct 20, 1770
Stuck, Conrad. Executors: Michael Newman, Peter and Martin Stuck. Cordorus Township. Wife: Margaret Stuck. Children: Peter, Martin, Jacob, Hannah, Susanna and Eve wife of Andrew Shettler.

Sep 24, 1770   Oct 31, 1770
Agnew, James. Executors: John Agnew and David Agnew. Hamiltonsban Township. Wife: Rebecca Agnew. Children: John, James, David, Samuel, Jean wife of Scott, Martha wife of Patterson.

Jul 23, 1770   Nov 27, 1770
Wilson, Jasper. Executors: John Wilson and Leonard Hattan. Tyrone Township. Wife: (name not given). Child: Louise and William Ford.

Oct 9, 1770   Dec 3, 1770
Spangler, Baltzer. Executors: Baltzer Spangler and Michael Swope. York County. Wife: Magdalena Spangler. Children: George, Baltzer, Michael, John, Rudolph, Daniel, Juliana wife of ---- Bickle and Elizabeth wife of Francis Koombs. Grandchildren: Frederick, Hannah, Magdalena and Elizabeth Bickle.

Aug 6, 1770   Dec 6, 1770
Bisking, Casper. Executors: Philip Haniman and Christian Close.
Reading Township. Wife: Mary Bisking. Children: John, Jacob, Henry,
Catharine and Mary.

Dec 24, 1770   Jan 28, 1771
Petit, James. Executor: Leonhard Leas. Berwick Township. Wife:
Priscilla Petit. Children: Hannah, Thomas, James, Keziah wife of Daniel
Clark, Priscilla, Abigail, and Eve. Grandchildren: William Stephenson and
Stephen Petit (parents' names not given), and Evis Baup (daughter of
Jacob Baup).

Dec 15, 1770   Jan 28, 1771
Bear, Henry. Executor and Township omitted. Wife: Elizabeth Bear.
Children: Henry, Samuel, John, Abraham, Barbara, Hannah, Elizabeth,
Salome, Mary, Sarah, Nancy and Michael (a child by his former wife).

May 3, 1770   Jan 28, 1771
Cronemiller, Martin. Executors: Philip King and Martin Starbock.
Manchester Township. Wife: Anna Elizabeth. Children: Martin,
Thomas, Dorothea, George, Philip, Jacob, and John.

Jan 21, 1771   Feb 4, 1771
McKnight, James. Executors: William Walker and George Duffield.
Minallen Township. Children: Mary wife of Joseph Brouster.
Grandchild: Mary Brouster.

Jun 30, 1766   Mar 20, 1771
Hartzough, George. Executors: Ann Maria Hartzough and John
Heckenthon. Yorktown Township. Wife: Ann Maria Hartzough.
Children: Magdalena, Catharine, Dorothea, Anna, Maria, and Andrew.

Feb 15, 1771   Mar 21, 1771
Hoover, Christian. Executor: Mary Hoover. Heidleberg Township. Wife:
Mary Hoover.

Mar 15, 1771   Mar 27, 1771
Sutor, William. Executor: John Sutor. Township: Omitted. Wife:
Sarah Sutor.

Oct 26, 1769   Apr 20, 1771
Grever, Anthony. Executors: Philip Poards and Adam Bottenfield.
Manheim Township. Wife: Margaret Grever. Children: Adam, Mary

wife of Christian Lipe, Anna Maria wife of Christian Greenwalt, Margaret wife of Tobias Suer, Catharine wife of David Kiser, and Elizabeth.

Mar 13, 1771   May 6, 1771
Evans, Henry. Executors: Elizabeth Evans and Joseph Moore. Windsor Township. Wife: Elizabeth Evans. Child: Mary.

May 7, 1771   May 15, 1771
Fackler, Adam. Executors: Gottlieb Zeigler and Frederick Yence. Yorktown Township. Wife: Maria F. Fackler. Children: Gottleib, Jacob, George, Magdalena, Eva, Catharine, and Elizabeth.

May 1, 1771   May 16, 1771
Keiffer, Peter. Executor: Dorothea Keiffer. Yorktown Township. Wife: Dorothea Keiffer. Children: Peter, Ann, Catharine, Margaret, Dorothea, and John.

Apr 4, 1771   May 21, 1771
Thomas, John. Executors: Rebecca and John Thomas. Warrington Township. Wife: Rebecca Thomas. Children: John, Eleanor, Rebecca, Sarah, Dinah and Jonah.

Dec 27, 1770   Jun 28, 1771
Davison, James. Executor: Nicholas Wereman. York County. Wife: Olivia Davison. Children: William, John, Sarah, Eleanor, and Olivia.

May 10, 1771   Jul 1, 1771
Hoke, Frederick. Executors: John and Andrew Hoke. Manchester Township. Brothers: Conrad, Casper, Henry, and Andrew.

Jun 1, 1771   Jul 30, 1771
Gyer, Paul. Executor: John Hay. Yorktown Township. Wife: Anna Catharine Gyer.

Jun 3, 1771   Aug 12, 1771
Tormin, Benedict. Executors: Michael Berkey and Michael Breassel. Cordorus Township. Wife: Anna Mary Tormin. Children: Samuel, John (and others, their names not given).

Feb 13, 1769   Sep 16, 1771
Schartz, Michael. Executor: Omitted. Newberry Township. Wife: Mary Schartz. Children: Andrew, Philip, George, Michael and Margelton. N.B. He was called Michael Black.

Jun 25, 1771   Sep 20, 1771
Smith, Henry. Executors: Margaret Smith and Michael Trease. Hellam Township. Wife: Maggie Smith. Children: George, Rosanna wife of Lorentz Crone, Catharine wife of Anthony Oler, Elizabeth wife of Frantz Bishop, Barbara wife of Jacob Harbaugh and Magdalena wife of George Deats.

Aug 20, 1771   Oct 1, 1771
Hutton, Joseph. Executors: William Penrose and William Matthews. Newberry Township. Wife: Betty Hutton. Children: Joseph, Joshua, Rachel, Betty, and Simeon.

Apr 19, 1766   Oct 17, 1771
McKesson, Alexander. Executors: John, James, Alexander, and William McKesson. Hamiltonsban Township. Wife: Mary McKesson. Children: John, Margaret wife of Andrew Cochran, James, Mary, Alexander, William, and Ebenezer.

Oct 19, 1771   Oct 29, 1771
Nagle, John. Executors: Mathias Bowser and William Mummer. Paradise Township. Wife: Catharine Nagle. Children: John, Jacob, Margaret wife of William Hart, and Catharine and Christian Dick.

Oct 19, 1771   Oct 29, 1771
Noell, Peter. Executors: John Heidler and Peter Noell. Paradise Township. Wife: Margaret Noell. Children: John, Peter, Daniel, Barbara wife of Peter Straspach, Magdalena, Margaret, Mary wife of Anthony Sell.

Aug 8, 1770   Oct 31, 1771
Boyd, John. Executors: John Edmunds and William McMillen. Warrington Township. Children: William, Samuel, George, Sarah wife of ---- Leech, Ann wife of ---- Bready, Elizabeth wife of Stedham, and Jane. Granddaughter Jane Marsh (parents' names not recorded).

Feb 5, 1769   Nov 1, 1771
McCoullath, William. Executors: Isaac Sadler and John Pope. Tyrone Township. Children: Anna wife of Robert Wilson, Esther, William, Elizabeth, Samuel. Children of first wife (viz): Mary wife of Andrew Park, Margaret wife of George Phillipse, Isabella wife of Robert Irwin, and Jane wife of William Bruse.

Aug 26, 1771   Nov 30, 1771
Petterson, Nathan. Executors: Sarah and Andrew Petterson. Straban

Township. Wife: Sarah Petterson. Children: Andrew, John, James, Eleanor, Sarah, Nathan, Mary, and Iabella.

May 17, 1771   Jan 6, 1772
Leibenstein, George. Executors: Catharine and Jacob Lienbenstein. Manchester Township. Wife: Catharine Leibenstein. Children: John, Adam, Maria, Elizabeth, George, Ann, Christian, Jacob, Catharine, Eve, and Michael. *(Not correct.)*

Oct 29, 1771   Jan 9, 1772
Crawford, John. Executors: Jane Dunwoodie and William McClain. Hamiltonsban Township. Child: Jane wife of ---- Dunwoodie. Brother: James Crawford. Grandchild: John Dunwoodie.

Oct 28, 1771   Jan 18, 1772
Sheteron, Henry. Executor: Anna Maria Sheteron. Shrewsburry Township. Wife: Anna Maria Sheteron. Children: Leonard, Casper, Jacob, Catharine, Anna, Trowne and Margaret.

May 16, 1771   Feb 11, 1772
Erwin, Joseph. Executor: John Erwin. Reading Township. Wife: Mary Erwin. Children: John, James, and Sarah.

Oct 14, 1771   Feb 17, 1772
Bierer, Conrad. Executors: Barbara Bierer and Rienhart Butt. York Township. Wife: Barbara Bierer (Names and number of children not given).

Apr 18, 1772   Feb 19, 1772 (?)
Ammon, Conrad. Executor: Jacob Ammon. Paradise Township. Child: Jacob. Stepdaughters: Elizabeth wife of Henry Luchenbach, Scharlot wife of John Wolf, Margaret wife of George Inglefritz, Anna wife of Tobias Helljet.

Feb 14, 1772   Mar 4, 1772
Dogoma, Eve. Executor: Abraham Lovine. Berwick Township.

Feb 1, 1772   Mar 4, 1772
Degoma, Adam. Executor: Abraham Lovine. Berwick Township. Wife: Eve Degoma.

Aug 6, 1771   Mar 4, 1772
Noll, Francis. Executors: Michael Danner and Michael Carl. Hanover

Township. Wife: Anna Margaret Noll. Children: Henry, Anthony, Anna, and Elizabeth.

Jan 27, 1772   Mar 11, 1772
Hamilton, Hance. Executors: John Hamilton, Robert McPerson, and Edie. Manallen Township. Children: Thomas, Sarah wife of Alexander McKeen, Hance, Guain, Mary wife of Hugh McKeen, George, William, and James.

Nov 27, 1771   Mar 19, 1772
Christ, Leonard. Executor: Maria Christ. York Town Township. Wife: Maria Magdalena Christ. Children: (Five children whose names are not given.)

Aug 14, 1770   Mar 23, 1772
Wallace, Agness. Executors: Gavin Allison and William Gemmill. Hopewell Township. Children: Margaret, Geen, Sarah, Christianna, William Ebram, Peter and James.

Mar 8, 1772   Mar 26, 1772
Styer, Tobias. Executor: Jacob Eversolt. Manheim Township. Children: Tobias and Magdalena wife of Jacob Eversolt.

Apr 12, 1769   Apr 2, 1772
Malawn, Mathias. Executors: Mathias and John Malawn. Reading Township. Children: Mathias, John, Rebecca, Hannah, Catharine wife of William Mummert, Mary wife of John Lighty, and Anna wife of Jacob Holl.

Nov 2, 1771   Apr 10, 1772
Robinson, Henry. Executors: John and Mary Robinson. Township: Omitted. Wife: (Name not given.) Children: Sarah, Robert, William, Henry and John. Grandson: James Robinson (parents' names not given).

Mar 3, 1772   Apr 11, 1772
Flowers, John. Executor: Mary Flowers. Shrewsbury Township. Wife: Mary Flowers. Children: Elizabeth, John, Thomas, Ann, Sarah, David, James, Mary, and Alice.

Jan 16, 1772   Apr 11, 1772
Spinckel, William. Executors: John Bushong, Henry and William Spinckel. York County. Wife: Catharine Spinckel. Children: William, Henry, Peter, Jacob, Daniel, Margaret wife of Tobias Hendricks, Elizabeth wife of John Bushong, Catharine wife of George Long, Charlotte wife of

Nicholas Tin, Anna, Eve wife of Abraham Immel and Mary wife of Martin Shroder.

Jan 11, 1770   May 13, 1772
Lan, Christman. Executors: John Emich and Peter Lan. Manchester Township.. Wife: Anna Oleva Lan. Children: Philip, Peter, Michael, Anna wife of Elias Eister, and Maria wife of Casper Kerber.

Mar 6, 1772   May 15, 1772
Wampler, Ludwick. Executors: George Keentz and Catharine Wampler. York Town Township. Wife: Catharine Wampler. Children: Ludwick and Joseph.

Apr 12, 1769   May 29, 1772
Vonseyoc, Aaron. Executors: Rebecca Vonseyoc and Archibald McGrew. Berwick Township. Wife: Rebecca Vonseyoc. Children: Cornelius, Isabella wife of Henry Freeman, Tobitha wife of Edward Williams, Aaron, Moses and Enoch.

Mar --, 1 772   Jun 1, 1772
Kromein, Thomas. Executor: Dorothea Kromein. Yorktown Township. Wife: Dorothea Kromein. Child: Sabina wife of Ludwig Hetig.

Apr 9, 1771   Jun 22, 1772
Vanaersdalen, Joannes. Executors: Henry Banta, Cornelius and Elam Vanaersdalen. Berwick Township. Wife: Nettie Vanaersdalen. Children: Antie, Jannek, David, Johanna and Isaac.

Mar 22, 1769   Jun 23, 1772
Fulton, James. Executors: James and Andrew Fulton. Hopewell Township. Wife: Jean Fulton. Children: John, James, William, Jennet, Andrew, Hugh, and David.

May 26, 1772   Jun 24, 1772
Fox, Henry. Executors: Jesaus King and George Brown. Reading Township. Wife: Catharine Fox. Children: Justina and Henry.

Oct 9, 1764   Jul 28, 1772
Bott, Herman. Executor: Jacob Bott. Manchester Township. Wife: (not recorded). Children: Reinhard, Jacob, Cookas wife of John Cookas, and Adelia wife of John Hagener.

May 27, 1772   Jul 31, 1772
Galbraith, James. Executor: Robert Galbraith. Straban Township. Wife: Omitted. Children: Isabella, Robert, William, James, and Nancy.

May 24, 1772   Aug 3, 1772
Peter, Philip. Executors: Gottfried Frey and Gottfried Frey, Jr. York Town Township. Children: Magdalena wife of Philip Entler, Catharine wife of Peter Krieger, and Barbara.

Jul 16, 1769   Sep 23, 1772
Vanderbilt William. Executors: Jacob Vanderbilt and Cornelius Cozine. --- Township. Wife: Lea Vanderbilt. Children: David, Ida, Nelly, Maria and Catharine. N.B The father of the writer of this will was Jacob Vanderbilt of Summerset Co., in "The Jersey."

Sep 9, 1772   Oct 14, 1772
Marlen, William. Executor: William McMillan. Chanceford Township. Wife: Mary Marlen. Children: Mary, Jean, John, and Rachel.

Oct 3, 1772   Nov 10, 1772
Shram, George. Executors: Joseph Welchans and Jacob Shram. Manchester Township. Wife: Elizabeth Shram. There were nine children, names not given.

Apr 4, 1772   Nov 16, 1772
Johnson, Elizabeth. Executors: Samuel McMillin and Andrew McDowell. Warrington Township. Child: Susanna.

Oct 26, 1769   Nov 21, 1772
Imswiller, Peter. Executor: Peter Imswiller. Windsor Township. Wife: Mary Eva Imswiller. Children: (Names and number not given.)

Nov 17, 1772   Dec 1, 1772
Opp, Peter. Executors: Jacob Opp and Daniel Messerly. Dover Township. Children: Catharine wife of Conrad Becker, Sophia wife of Andrew Blechhard, Dorothea wife of Adam Metzgar, Margaret wife of Martin Wenkel, Elizabeth, Peter, Jacob, Barbara, Magdalena, Andrew, and Maria.

Nov 25, 1772   Dec 3, 1772
Gantzer, Matthias. Executors: Casper Lambert and Jacob Shrettrone. Dover Township. Wife: Catharine Gantzer. Children: Catharine and Elizabeth.

Feb 8, 1770   Dec 11, 1772
Cully, Thomas. Executor: William Cully. Martic Township (Lancaster County). Children: John, Thomas, Mary wife of James Parks, and William.

Nov 7, 1772   Jan 2, 1773
Miller, Andrew. Executors: George Miller and Daniel Noll. Cordorus Township. Wife: Barbara Miller. Children: Jacob, (and others whose names were not given.)

Mar 2, 1773   Mar 25, 1773
Buchanan, John. Executors: Samuel McConoughy and James McCarra. Cumberland Township. Children: Samuel, James, McCarrel and Simpson.

Feb 13, 1773   Mar 31, 1773
Leinbacher, Henry. Executors: Conrad Leinbacher and Gerhard Greff. Dover Township. Wife: Catharine Leinbacher. Children: Conrad, Felix, Anna wife of Mathias Schmeiser, and Catharine wife of Gerhard Greff.

May 15, 1773   Apr 26, 1773
Ruble, Peter. Executors: Christian Ruble and Hans Kerr. Cordorus Township. Wife: Anna Ruble. Children: Matthew, Christian, Abraham and Peter.

Mar 8, 1773   Apr 26, 1773
Long, James. Executor: Mary Long. Windsor Township. Wife: Mary Long. Child: Henry.

--- --, ----   May 4, 1773
Lephart, Henry. Executors: Henry and George Lephart. Hellam Township. Wife: Catharine Lephart. Children: John, Jacob, Henry, George, Valentine, and Mary.

Apr 6, 1773   Jun 1, 1773
McCulloch, Samuel. Executors: John Agnew and Michael Kinhead. Hamiltonsban Township. Wife: Margaret McCulloch. Children: Mary and Samuel.

Apr 13, 1773   Jun 1, 1773
Michael, Stophel. Executor: George Mortar. Manheim Township. Wife: Ann Michael. Children: William, Jean, and Anna.

May 3, 1773   Jun 7, 1773
Baltzly, Jacob. Executors: Joseph Baltzly and Nicholas Feyerston. Paradise Township. Children: Joseph, Henry, Elizabeth, Barbara, Anna and Mary.

Jun 1, 173   June 19, 1773
Wolf, Johannes. Executor: Henry Wolf. Manchester Township. Children: Jacob, Elizabeth wife of Nicholas Shaffer, John, Peter, Anna, Margaret wife of George Shuck, Barbara Thomas, Johannes, George, Tobias, Catharine and Sabina.

Jan 22, 1772   Jul 13, 1773
Lehman, Peter. Executor: Mary Lehman. York County. Wife: Maria Lehman. Children: Jacob, Mary, and eight others whose names were not given.

Jul 9, 1773   Jul 16, 1773
Nicol, William. Executors: Mary Nicol and Samuel Nelson. Chanceford Township. Wife: Mary Nicol. Children: James, William, Samuel, and Sarah.

Jul 13, 1773   Jul 26, 1773
Staab, Adam. Executors: George, John, Jacob, Henry and Philip Staab. Mt. Pleasant Township. Wife: Anna Staab. Children: George, John, Henry, Jacob, Philip, Catharine and Anna.

Jan 23, 1773   Jul 26, 1773
Dentzler, Frederick. Executor: Charles Barnitz. York Town. Wife: Gertrude Dentzler.

Jan 21, 1773   Aug 2, 1773
Wicker, Baltzer. Executor: Margaret Wicker. York Town Township. Wife: Margaret Wicker. Children: Margaret and Maria.

Dec 3, 1767   Aug 16, 1773
Young, Dewalt. Executors: Andrew Schriber and Peter Young. Heidelberg Township. Children: Andrew, Barbara wife of John Burns, Ann wife of Jacob Lehman, Hannah wife of Leonard Ketzmiller and Margaretta wife of George Sponseller. Grandchild: Ann Sponseller.

Mar 23, 1763   Aug 18, 1773
Vance, Charles. Executors: Hugh and Thomas Vance. Cumberland Township. Wife: (Name not given). Children: Hugh, Thomas, Robert,

Sarah, Hannah and Mary.

Jan 9, 1773   Aug 20, 1773
Vance, John. Executor: William Griffin York County. Legatees (Bro. and Sisters) Jean, Elizabeth, Agness and Samuel Vance.

Jan 16, 1773   Aug 20, 1773
Johnston, James. Executor: Sarah Johnston. York County. Wife: Sarah Johnston. Children: Agness, Elizabeth, Eleanor, Jean, Mary, Sarah, and Margaret.

May 8, 1773   Aug 25, 1773
Welsh, Jacob. Executor: Elizabeth and John Welsh. York Town Township. Wife: Elizabeth Welsh. Children: (the names and number not given).

Oct 3, 1772   Oct 13, 1773
Rockenbaugh, Mathias. Executor: Catharine Rockenbaugh. York Town Township. Wife: Catharine Rockenbaugh. Child: Jacob.

Jul 14, 1773   Oct 15, 1773
Larimer, William. Executor: James Larimer. Hanover Township. Wife: Jane Larimer. Children: Victor and Mary.

Jun 7, 1776   Oct 25, 1773
McBride, Hugh. Executor: Daniel McBride. Mt. Joy Township. Wife: Margaret McBride. Children: Neal and Daniel. Grandchildren: William Cearson, Duncan McDonald, and George Darby (parents' names not given).

Jun 22, 1773   Nov 1, 1773
Smith, Jacob. Executor: Jacob Smith. Dover Township. Children: Jacob, John, Adam, Peter and Margaret wife of Frederick Myer.

Aug 5, 1773   Nov 9, 1773
Karwer, Henry. Executor: Michael Beller. Manheim Township. Wife: Mary Elizabeth Karwer. Children: (Names and number not given.)

May 30, 1766   Nov 16, 1773
Gohn, Adam. Executors: Catharine and Henry Gohn. Windsor Township. Wife: Omitted. Children: Henry, Sophia, Catharine, John, Elizabeth, Mary, Magdalena, Peter, Margaret, and Philip.

Mar 19, 1772   Dec 3, 1773
McConnell, Ebenezer. Executors: James and William McKesson.
Hamiltonsban Township. Sister: Margaret McConnell.

Nov 17, 1773   Dec 4, 1773
Scheibley, Christian. Executors: Esther Scheibley and Christian West.
York County. Wife: Esther Scheibley. Children: John, Christian, Esther,
Barbara wife of David Smith, Susanna and Elizabeth.

Dec 15, 1773   Jan 6, 1774
Young, Andrew. Executor: Agness Young. Chanceford Township. Wife:
Agness Young. Children: Andrew, William, Robert, Agness, Margaret,
Jean, Isabel and Griziel.

--- --, ----   Feb 7, 1774
Cronebaugh, Peter. Executors: Jacob Cronebaugh, George and Philip
Zeigler. Dover Township. Wife: Elizabeth Cronebaugh. Children:
George, Elizabeth, Eve, Henry, Jacob, and Philip.

Feb 7, 1774   Mar 25, 1774
Pott, William. Executors: George Hicker and Herman Wireman.
Huntington Township. Wife: Margaret Pott. Children: William, Jacob,
John, Degenbart, Benjamin, and Catharine.

Nov 21, 1773   Mar 25, 1774
Davy, John. Executor: Henry Werman. Huntington Township. Wife:
Mary Davy. Children: Samuel, Ann, Jonathan, George, Rachel, and Mary.

Oct 17, 1771   Mar 25, 1774
Neal, Letiss. Executors: Letiss Henderson and Caleb Baile. Monaghan
Township. Children: Hugh, David, Matthew, Mary, and Letiss.
Grandchildren: John, Susanna, and David Neal (children of Hugh).

Feb 5, 1774   Mar 26, 1774
Hassler, Michael. Executor: Margaret Hassler. Cordorus Township.
Wife: Margaret Hassler. Children: Joseph, Michael, Christian,
Magdalena, George, and Abraham.

Mar 8, 1774   Apr 7, 1774
Shull, Frederick. Executors: L. Zimmerman and C. Newcomer.
Warrington Township. Wife: Solomena Shull. Children: Mary, Jacob,
Sally, Barbara, John, Peter, Joseph and Samuel.

Mar --, 1774   Apr 8, 1774
Leonhart, Peter. Executors: William Leonhart and Daniel Nesserly. Dover Township. Wife: Margaret Leonhart. Children: Philip, Jacob, George, Christopher, Henry, Peter, Frederick, Godrey, and William.

Mar 31, 1774   Apr 11, 1774
Edger, James. Executors: Patrick Scott and James Edger. Fawn Township. Wife: Margaret Edger. Children: James, Samuel, Hugh, and William.

Mar 12, 1774   Apr 11, 1774
Steel, Thomas. Executors: Rachel and Thomas Steel. Fawn Township. Wife: Rachel Steel. Children: Thomas, Rachel, Martha, John, David, Margaret and William.

Dec 17, 1773   Apr 15, 1774
Kerckhart, Anthony. Executor: John Herbach and Jacob Rieman. York County. Wife: Veronica Kerckhart. Children: (Names and number not given.)

Oct 19, 1773   Apr 25, 1774
Buntin, Thomas. Executors: Mary Buntin and Buntin. Warrington Township. Wife: Mary Buntin. Children: John, Thomas, Mary and Rachel.

Apr 23, 1774   May 16, 1774
Horst, Jacob. Executors: Barbara Horst and Christian Furrey. Newberry Township. Wife: Barbara Horst. Children: Jacob, John, Daniel, Barbara, Ann, and Amanuel.

Feb 16, 1774   Jun 25, 1774
McAnulty, John. Executors: John and Mary McAnulty. Chanceford Township. Wife: Mary McAnulty. Children: James, William, John, Michael, and Jeseph.

May 12, 1772   June 24, 1774
Wallace, Margaret. Executor: Thomas Douglas. Cumberlnad Township. Legatee: (Bro.) Samuel Shannon.

Jul 1, 1774   Sep 6, 1774
McNutt, John. Executors: James Russell, Susanna, and Francis McNutt. Manallen Township. Wife: Susanna McNutt. Child: Francis. Brothers: Samuel and Francis McNutt.

Aug 26, 1774   Sep 7, 1774
McCracken, Anthony. Executors: Alexander Adams and William McElwain. Hamiltonsban Township. Wife: Mary McCracken. Children: James, Mary wife of Alexander Adams, Rebecca wife of Archibald Fletcher, and Elizabeth wife of William McElwain.

Jul 5, 1774   Sep 30, 1774
Cooper, John. Executors: Thomas Wheeler, Nicholas and Thomas Cooper. Fawn Township. Wife: Hannah Cooper. Children: John, Priscilla, Sarah, and Hannah.

Apr 2, 1773   Oct 1, 1774
Welsh, John. Executor: James Rankin. Newberry Township. Legatee: (Bro.) James Welsh.

--- --, ----   Oct 1, 1774
Livingston, George. Executors: Andrew and Adam Livingston. York County. Will not copied on records.

Aug 4, 1774   Oct 1, 1774
Mier, Jacob. Executors: Christian Lepe and Samuel Miller. Newberry Township. Wife: Katharine Mier. Children: Martin, Jacob, Emanuel, and Daniel.

Sep 17, 1774   Oct 20, 1774
Brandon, John. Executors: James and Walter Brandon. Huntington Township. Wife: Mary Brandon. Children: Thomas, John, Joseph, William, Alexander, James, Walter and Richard. Grandchild: John (son of Thomas).

Apr 26, 1770   Oct 27, 1774
Neely, Margaret. Executors: Thomas Neely and William Walker. Tyrone Township. Wife: Jean Neely. Children: Samuel, Jackson, James, Jonathan, William, Margaret, Mary, Jean, Agness wife of James Carithers, Elizabeth, John, and Sarah wife of Alexander McCurdy.

Aug 23, 1774   Nov 8, 1774
Brouster, John. Executors: Ann Brouster and John Linn. Cumberland Township. Wife: Ann Brouster. Children: William, Mary and Margaret.

Oct 13, 1774   Nov 9, 1774
Ginter, Dewalt. Executor: Christiana Ginter. Dover Township. Wife: Christiana Ginter. Child: Anna.

Nov 26, 1774   Dec 9, 1774
Morrison, Janet. Executors: Joseph Morrison and William Buchanan. Cumberland Township. Legatees: Catharine Boyd (cousin) and others.

Nov 16, 1774   Dec 9, 1774
Erwin, William. Executor: John Stosach. Cumberland Township. Wife: Rachel Erwin. Children: Arthur, Archibald, and Mary.

Jun 12, 1771   Jan 2, 1775
Keentz, George. Executors: Maria E. Keentz and Adam Lightner. Yorktown Township. Wife: Maria Elizabeth Keentz.

Oct 15, 1774   Jan 6, 1775
Wintermeyer, Philip. Executor: Philip Wintermeyer. Manchester Township. Wife: Anna Gertrude Wintermeyer. Children: Anthony, Dorothea wife of Peter Keifer and Julianna wife of Philip Gentzler.

Feb 21, 1774   Jan 31, 1775
McAlister, Charles. Executor: James McAlister. Hamiltonsban Township. Wife: Rosanna McAlister. Children: James, Alexander, Mary wife of James Holliday, Margaret wife of Samuel Gingles, and John. Grandson: Charles Holliday.

Dec 21, 1774   Feb 1, 1775
Sumberland, John. Executors: Henry Slagle and William Sumberland. Berwick Township. Wife: Elizabeth Sumberland. Children: William, John, James and Jean.

--- --, ----   Feb 2, 1775
Hoober, George. Executors: John Hoober and Thomas Fisher. Mt. Pleasant Township. Wife: Barbara Hoober. Children: John, and Barbara wife of Conrad Staley.

Nov 12, 1774   Feb 3, 1775
Roseborough, Robert. Executors: William Garretson and Samuel Morthland. Cumberland Township. Wife: Mary Roseborough. Children: Eleanor and John

Mar 26, 1772   Feb 3, 1775
Roseborough, John. Executors: William Garretson and Samuel Morthland. Monaghan Township. Legatees: Robert (brother) and Eleanor (sisters - another mentioned in will, but name not given).

Nov 25, 1773   Mar 2, 1775
Graybill, John. Executor: Anna Graybill. Lancaster County. Wife: Anna Graybill. Children: Christian, Barbara, Anna, Johannes, and Eve.

Feb 24, 1775   Mar 28, 1775
Erhart, David. Executors: Philip and Margaret Erhart. Reading Township. Wife: Margaret Erhart. Children: Philip, Catharine, Susanna, Esther, David, John, Margaret, Anthony, Barbara, Ann and Elizabeth.

Oct 19, 1773   Mar 29, 1775
Eshleman, Peter. Executors: Chrisle Like and John Eshleman. Newberry Township. Wife: Margaret Eshleman. Children: John, Jacob, Ann, and Elizabeth.

Oct 21, 1772   Apr 6, 1775
Hall, Edward. Executors: William and Edward Hall. Cumberland Township. Wife: Else Hall. Children: Elizabeth wife of James Entrikin, Mary wife of John Williams, William, Esther, Jean, Edward, and John.

Apr 2, 1775   Apr 25, 1775
Morrison, John. Executor: Joseph Morrison. Chanceford Township. Children: William, Samuel, Hannah, Mary, Joseph, and John.

--- --, ----   Apr 27, 1775
King, Victor. Executors: A. McGrew and H. Kinly *(King?)*. York County. Letters granted. (Note: "There was no will." However, see the following.) Will of Victor King, of Tyrone Township of York County, Pennsylvania (one of three brothers who was among the early settlers in Adams County, then York County, near the present site of Gettysburg) made and executed October 25, 1774. His "trusty friend" Archibald McGrew, Esq., and his son Hugh King, were appointed executors. Signed, sealed, pronounced and acknowledged in prescence of William Ross, James Dickson, and William King.

Apr 14, 1775   May 1, 1775
Mansperger, Martin. Executor: George Mansperger. Newberry Township. Children: John, George, and Margaret.

Mar 22, 1775   May 6, 1775
Heneman, Philip. Executors: Mary and Philip Heneman. Reading Township. Wife: Mary Heneman. Children: John, Philip, Mary, Catharine, and Margaret wife of Peter Fox.

Apr 4, 1774   May 30, 1775
Bruckhard, Michael. Executors: Barbara Bruckhard and Jacob Bruckhard. Kellam Township. Wife: Barbara Bruckhard. Children: Jacob, John, Michael, Philip and Magdalena.

May 10, 1775   Jun 21, 1775
Knipple, Anna Maria. Executor: Peter Lind. Manchester Township. Wife of Christopher Knipple. Child: Baltzer.

Jan 25, 1773   Jul 7, 1775
Hussey, Nathan. Executor: Joseph Updegraff. Yorktown Township. Children: Mary Webb wife of Joseph Updegraff, Hannah, and Susanna wife of ---- Updegraff. Grandchildren: Ambrose, Nathan and Edith (children of Susanna).

Jun 20, 1770   Jul 27, 1775
Warner, Adam. Executor: Jacob Warner. Germany Township. Wife: Catharina Warner. Children: Jacob, George, Christopher, Francy wife of Henry Bruther, John and Catharine wife of Jacob Fouts.

May 5, 1775   Jul 28, 1775
Buchanan, James. Executor: James Edge. Fawn Township. Wife: Margaret Buchanan.

Jun 17, 1775   Aug 14, 1775
Kendworthy, David. Executors: Charles Coulson and Rebecca Kendworth. Huntington Township. Wife: Rebecca Kendworthy.

--- --, ----   Aug 25, 1775
Neischwanger, Peter. Executor: Joseph Neischwanger. York County. (German will.)

Jan 3, 1775   Sep 2, 1775
Melhorn, Simon. Executors: Michael Melhorn and Conrad Becker. Manchester Township. Wife: Barbara Melhorn. Children: Michael, George, John, Andrew, Mary wife of ---- Kromlick, and Magdalena. Grandchildren: Henry and Anna Kromlick.

--- --, ----   Sep 4, 1775
Elsroth, Valentine. Executor: Susanna Elsroth. York County. German will.

Aug 16, 1775   Sep 13, 1775
Burger, Mathias. Executors: Michael Danner and David Newman. Hanover Township. Wife: Margaret Burger. Children: George, and Elizabeth wife of Charles Breederline.

Jul 4, 1775   Sep 15, 1775
Zong, Henry. Executor: Margaret Zong. Germany Township. Wife: Margaret Zong. Children: Philibina wife of --- Sharron, John and Eva. Grandchildren: Eva and Margaret Sharron.

Feb 25, 1774   Sep 18, 1775
Campbell, John. Executors: Adam and John Campbell. Windsor Township. Wife: Anna Campbell. Children: William, John, James, Charles, and Ann.

--- ---, ----   Oct 9, 1775
Fackler, Jacob. Executors: Gotleib Zeigler and Frederick Jans. Yorktown Township. Wife: Magdalena Fackler. Children: (Names not given.) Sons-in-law: Gotlieb Zeigler and Frederick Jans.

Aug 11, 1775   Oct 21, 1775
Phillips, Edmond. Executor: Nathan Phillips. Warrington Township. Wife: Elizabeth Phillips. Children: Phebe, Mary, Jane, Patience, Elizabeth, and John.

Oct 15, 1775   Nov 13, 1775
Walter, Joseph. Executor: John Hay. York County. Wife: Anna Maria Walter. Children: Marilis wife of Jacob Newman and Anna.

Nov 4, 1775   Nov 20, 1775
Dalman, John. Executor: John Bushangin. York County. Wife: Ann Dalman. Children: Henry, John, Rejena, and Ann.

Nov 7, 1775   Nov 27, 1775
Jacobs, Samuel. Executors: Philip Jacobs and Peter Deardorff. Berwick Township. Wife: Magdalena Jacobs. Children: Daniel, Samuel (and five others whose names were not given.)

May 9, 1769   Nov 27, 1775
Jamison, Samuel. Executors: Philip Jacobs and Peter Deardorff. York County. Wife: Sarah Jamison. Children: Susanna, Samuel, and Robert.

Jul 6, 1775   Dec 6, 1775
McGrew, John. Executors: Archibald and William McGrew. Huntington Township. Wife: Elizabeth McGrew. Children: Archibald, Catharine wife of William Boyd, and William. Grandchildren: John and Archibald McGrew (sons of Archibald), and James, Robert, and John Maxwell (parents' names not given).

--- ---, ----   Jan 2, 1776
Gouff, Philip. Executors: Daniel Messerly and Frederick Sham. Dover Township. German will.

--- ---, ----   Jan 29, 1776
Stephans, Peter. Executors: Leonard Jenewein and Henry Martin. Township: Omitted. (German will.)

Nov 24, 1775   Jan 29, 1776
Glasick, John. Executors: Jacob Bear and Barnet Zeigler. Cordorus Township. Wife: Omitted. Children: Rachel, Mary, and Samuel.

Dec 4, 1775   Feb 7, 1776
Deardorff, John. Executors: Christian Cloas and Abraham Stouffer. Reading Township. Children: Anthony, Christiana wife of Michael Boserman, Margaret wife of ---- Thomey, Barbara wife of William Thomas, Hannah wife of Nicholas Myers, Catharine wife of Adam Cunkeland, Abraham, Susanna, John, and Daniel.

May 20, 1773   Feb 13, 1776
Porter, David. Executors: Agness and Alexander Porter. Cumberland Township. Children: Alexander, Andrew, David, Samuel, and Agness. Niece: Mary Porter, daughter of brother Matthew Porter.

Feb 28, 1776   Mar 12, 1776
Chamberlin, Jeremiah. Executors: John and James Chamberlin. Reading Township. Wife: Margaret Chamberlin. Children: James, John, Nemen, and Martha.

Dec 8, 1775   Mar 25, 1776
Cavin, James. Executors: Jean and Alexander Cavin. Cumberland Township. Wife: Jean Cavin. Children: Alexander, Fergus, James, John, and Elizabeth.

Mar 21, 1770   Mar 27, 1776
Goodbred, Ludwick. Executor: Turless Goodbred. Yorktown Township.

Wife: Turless Goodbred. Child: Philip.

Mar 9, 1776   Mar 29, 1776
King, Nicholas. Executor: Ann E. Cronemiller. Yorktown Township. Wife: Susanna King. Children: Godfrey, Ann wife of ---- Cronemiller, Philip, and Barbara wife of Adam Willhelm.

Oct 11, 1773   Apr 1, 1776
Lauson, Moses. Executor: Mary Lauson. Cordorus Township. Wife: Omitted. Children: Benj., Joseph, Francis, Richard, and Edward.

--- ---, ----   May 1, 1776
Wilson, James. Executor: Omitted. Hamiltonsban Township. (Will not recorded - see files.)

--- ---, ----   May 1, 1776
McElhenny, Elizabeth, Executor: Omitted. Mt. Joy Township. (Will not on records, but on file.)

--- ---, ----   May 6, 1776
Seegrist, Hans Urick. Executors: Casper Lichtenberger and Baltzer Zumwalt. Township: Omitted. Will not on records, but on file.

--- ---, ----   Jul 9, 1776
Spangler, Henry. Executors: John Bushong, Stophel Lowman and John G. Spangler. York County. Will not on records, but on file.

--- ---, ----   Jul 17, 1776
Jolly, John. Executor: John Jolly. Will not recorded.

--- ---, ----   Aug 6, 1776
Shaffer, Nicholas. Executors: Jacob and Michael Shaffer. York Town Township. Will not on records, but on file.

--- ---, ----   Aug 14, 1776
Ruby, Casper. Executors: Christian Stoner and Henry Lephard. Windsor Township. (Note on the records - see files).

--- ---, ----   Aug 31, 1776
Redett, Andrew. Executors: Christopher Houk and John Reditt. York County. (Will not copied - see files.)

51

--- --, ----   Sep 16, 1776
Lighty, Jonas. Executor: Omitted. Reading Township. (Will on file, but not on records.)

--- --, ----   Oct 18, 1776
Meem, John. Executor: Omitted: York Town Township. (Will not copied, but on file.)

--- --, ----   Dec 14, 1776
Kantz, Elizabeth. Executor: Valentine Kantz. Yorktown Township. (Will not copied, but on file.)

--- --, ----   Dec 25, 1776
Murphy, James. Executor: Omitted. Cumberland Township. (Will not copied, see file.)

Feb 17, 1777   Jan 18, 1777
Schwartz, Andreas. Executors: Elizabeth Schwartz. York Town Township. Wife: Elizabeth Schwartz. The names and number of children not given.

Apr 3, 1776   Jan 24, 1777
Bob, Thomas. Executor: John Linn. Cumberland Township. Wife: Jannet Bob. Children: James, John, Robert, Elizabeth and Jenette.

--- --, ----   Feb 22, 1777
Cinagan, Charles. Executor: Omitted. Legatee: Samuel Harkins, (a friend.)

--- --, ----   Mar 4, 1777
Wilson, Thomas. Executor: Joseph Jefferies. York County. (Will not on records - see files.)

--- --, ----   Mar 11, 1777
Strickler, John. Executors: Samuel Landis and Jacob Strickler. Township: Omitted. Will not on records, see files.

--- --, ----   Mar 24, 1777
Stuckslager, Albertus. Executors: Christian Beechley and Nicholas Bovhar. Cumberland Township. Will not copied, see files.

Jan 5, 1777   Apr 11, 1777
Holtzenger, Elizabeth. Executors: Thomas Hartley and Joseph

Donaldson. Yorktown Township. Children: Catharine, Joseph, Barnet, Elizabeth, and Jacob.

Feb 11, 1777   Apr 23, 1777
McCurry, William. Executor: Matthew Kilgore. Chanceford Township. Brothers: James, John, George, and Joseph.

Dec 9, 1776   Apr 26, 1777
Denwody, Hugh. Executors: Michael Finly, Jean and David Denwody. Wife: Jean Denwody. Hamiltonsban Township. Children: Ronana, James, John, David, Hugh, and Robert.

Feb 23, 1777   Apr 29, 1777
Ramsay, William. Executors: Martha Ramsay and Samuel Gattlip. Hamiltousban Township. Wife: Martha Ramsay. Child: Raymond. Grandchildren: Reynold Ramsay and Mary Clark (Parents names not given).

Mar 12, 1777   Apr 29, 1777
Johnston, Alexander. Executors: Samuel Edie and John Thompson. Cumberland Township. Nephews: Thomas Johnston (son of Brother Jacob), and John Johnston. Bequests to Thomas Latta and wife Debora of Cumberland Township.

Feb 12, 1777   May 7, 1777
Leard, Robert. Executors: John Blair and William Leard. Cumberland Township. Wife: Omitted. Children: John, William, and Joseph.

Mar 5, 1777   May 9, 1777
Haller, Christopher. Executors: John Steckendom and John Rothrock. Yorktown Township. Wife: Anne Maria Haller. Children: Susanna wife of Abraham Etter.

Feb 10, 1777   May 10, 1777
Ross, William. Executors: Alexander Ross, John Nesbit and William Porter. Warrington Township. Wife: Jean Ross. Children: Martha, Jean, Alexander, Mary, William, James, Elizabeth and Ann.

Apr 25, 1777   May 13, 1777
Anderson, Jean. Executor: John Scott. Straban Township. Children: Robert, Jean and Susanna. Sons-in-law: Andrew McKee and Benjamin Micawee (wives' names not recorded).

--- --, ----   May 22, 1777
Venus, Philip. Executors: Elizabeth Venus and Conrad Schwartz. (This was an administration account, there was no will.)

Mar 31, 1777   May 30, 1777
Morrison, Jane. Executor: Adam Black. Cumberland Township. Legatees: Mary Morrison (mother), Joseph and Mary Morrison (brother and sister).

Apr 20, 1777   Jun 4, 1777
Byer, John. Executors: Margaret Byer and Jacob Byer. Windsor Township. Wife: Margaret Byer. Children: Jacob, Philip, Henry, John, George, Peter, Elizabeth, Treat and Mary.

--- --, ----   Jun 6, 1777
Gauff, Philip. Executors: Frederick Shahr and George Kann. Dover Township. German will.

Apr 15, 1777   Jun 9, 1777
McGown, Andrew. Executor: Mary McGown. York County. Wife: Mary McGown. Children: Robert, William, Samuel, Andrew, John, and James.

--- --, ----   Jun 21, 1777
Myer, George. Executors: Valentine Shultz and Balthus Rudiselly. York County. (German will.)

Mar 8, 1777   Jun 26, 1777
Monfort, John. Executors: Peter Francis, John and Larence Monfort. York County. Wife: Cneartie Monfort. Children: Peter, Francis, John, Larence, and Mary.

--- --, ----   Jul 11, 1777
Keentz, Mary Elizabeth. Executor: ---- Nichlas. (Letters granted. No will.)

Feb 18, 1777   Jul 15, 1777
McGahey, John. Hamiltonsban Township. Wife: Mary McGahey. Children: Martha, Mary, Thomas, Jann, and Alexander.

Feb 25, 1777   Jul 26, 1777
King, Henry. Executors: Frederick Yonce and Andrew Hertzog. Yorktown Township. Children: Henry, Maria, and Catharine.

Mar 15, 1777   Aug 6, 1777
Parks, John. Executors: Robert and Andrew Parks. Warrington Township. Wife: Mary Parks. Children: Robert, Margaret wife of James, Hoge, John, Jane wife of William Morrow, Mary, and Martha wife of John Gibson.

--- ---, ----   Sep 15, 1777
McCosh, Nathaniel. Executors: Mary McCosh and John Semple. Strabant Township. Wife: Mary McCosh. Children: John, Sarah, Samuel, and James.

Jul 20, 1777   Sep 15, 1777
Black, Jane. Executors: John Blackburn and David Jardin. Manallen Township. Brothers: Robert and Jordon. Children of Robert: John, David and Sarah. Children of Jordon: Jane, Spiner and Elizabeth.

Jun 8, 1777   Sep 28, 1777
Kurtz, Christopher. Executors: Martin Kurtz and Adam Vonderau. Fawn Township. Wife: Philipina Kurtz. Children: Michael, John, Thomas, Catharine wife of George Keentz, Christiana wife of Philip Sneider, Elizabeth, Peter, and Martin. Stepson: Adam Vonderau.

Sep 13, 1776   Oct 7, 1777
Bingham, Hugh. Executor: Omitted. Hamiltonsban Township. Children: Samuel, William, Robert, Hugh, Elizabeth, and Mary wife of ---- McKinley. Grandchildren: Mary, John and Hugh (children of Mary).

Jul 17, 1777   Oct 18, 1777
Fulton, Jane. Executors: Andrew Fulton. Hopewell Township. Widow of James Fulton. Children: David, Andrew, and Hugh.

Aug 27, 1776   Oct 24, 1777
Campbell, George. Executors: Isabella Campbell and John Reed. Chanceford Township. Wife: Isabella Campbell. Children: Janet, Marrion, George, Isabella, and Margaret.

--- ---, ----   Nov 3, 1777
Feeser, Jacob. Executors: Anna and Nicholas Feeser. York County. German will.

Sep 27, 1777   Nov 8, 1777
McCullough, Hugh. Executors: Michael McAnulty and Thomas Lager. Reading Township. Wife: Mary McCullough. Children: Hugh, and Mary

wife of ---- McAnulty. Grandchildren: Agness Eager (parents' names not given), Robert, John, Mary, and Agness McAnulty.

Feb 8, 1777   Nov 13, 1777
Livingston, William. Executors: William McCreary and Thomas Duglas. Hamilton Township. Wife: Omitted. Children: John, Margaret, and William.

Apr 21, 1777   Nov 15, 1777
Cox, John. Executor: Jacob Bear. Newberry Township. Wife: Elizabeth Cox. Children: Elizabeth and Conrad.

Sep 22, 1777   Nov 19, 1777
Hunter, Thomas. Executor: William Hunter. Newberry Township. Wife: Mary Hunter. Children: Nancy, James, Ephriam, Jane, Mary, Margaret, Alice, Joseph, and William. Grandchildren: Allen Hay, Thomas and William Aston (parents' names not given).

Mar 16, 1773   apr 11, 1778
Gentzler, Conrad. Executor: Adam Leitner. Yorktown Township. Wife: Gertrude Gentzler. Children: Magdalena, Philip, George, and Conrad.

Dec 29, 1777   Jan 10, 1778
Boyd, Moses. Executors: William McClean and James Black. Cumberland Township. Wife: Catharine Boyd. Children: Margaret, Sarah and Jane.

Jan 6, 1778   Feb 12, 1778
Farra, James. Executors: Samuel Farra. Dover Township. Children: William, Rebecca wife of Isaac Norton, Mary, Sarah, Katharine, and Samuel. Grandchildren: James, Thomas, Martha, and John (children of William), and Joseph (son of Rebecca).

Feb 25, 1777   Feb 25, 1778
Hayns, Philip. Executors: Philip Rothrock and William Lanaus. Manchester Township. Wife: Christiana Hayns. Children: Catharine, Susanna, Jacob, Barbara, Philip, Elizabeth, Christiana, and Eve.

--- --, ----   Feb 26, 1778
Lauman, Gottleib. Executors: Christopher Lauman and Jacob Bott. Yorktown Township. Wife: Anna Maria Lauman. Children: Catharine and Mary.

Mar 12, 1775   Mar 18, 1778
Long, Michael. Executors: Daniel Peterman and John Schreiber. Manchester Township. Wife: Regina Magdalena Long. Children: Michael, Andrew, and Peter.

Mar 10, 1778   Mar 24, 1778
Craig, Elizabeth. Executor: Abraham Scott. York County. Bequests to sister Margaret Craig, (niece) Mary Scott, and nephew Abraham Scott.

Nov 12, 1777   Mar 26, 1778
White, Elizabeth. Executors: Elizabeth White. York County. Children: Joseph, James, Mary, Sarah wife of Joseph Jackson, Andrew and Elizabeth.

Mar 22, 1778   Apr 4, 1778
Kuhn, Frederick. Executors: Catharine Kuhn and Jacob Small. Berwick Township. Wife: Catharine Kuhn. Children: Mary, Jacob, Susanna, George, Barbara wife of Jacob Small, and Catharine wife of John Keawey. Note: A son, Henry Kuhn, is named in the original will.

Mar 2, 1773   Apr 7, 1778
Immel, Leonard. Executors: Michael Ebert, John and Michael Immel. York County Wife: Maria Immel. Children: John, Michael, Barbara wife of Henry Bentzel, Christiana wife of Martin Hambrecht, Sevilla wife of Michael Schriver, Margaret wife of George Lefler, Magdalena, and Eva.

Aug 11, 1777   Apr 8, 1778
Leatherman, Michael. Executors: Margaret and Conrad Leatherman. Yorktown Township. Wife: Margaret Leatherman. Child: Conrad.

Jan 29, 1778   Apr 10, 1778
Shelter, Christian. Executors: Mary and Andrew Shelter. Township: Omitted. Wife: Mary Shelter. Children: Jacob, Christian, Frederick, Michael, Henry and John.

Dec 4, 1777   Apr 10, 1778
Eliot, John J. Executors: Robert Willey and James Eliot. Tyrone Township. Wife: Anne Eliot. Child: James.

Feb 8, 1778   Apr 23, 1778
Fishel, Philip. Executors: Henry Fishel and Frantz J. Raymer. Paradise Township. Wife: Barbara Fishel. Children: John, Elizabeth, Peter, and Margaret.

Jun 20, 1775   Apr 28, 1778
Lanius, Jacob. Executors: Jacob, Henry, and William Lanius. Yorktown Township. Children: Jacob, Harvey, William, John, Mary wife of Christopher Weider, Catharine wife of Frederick Rohmer, Juliana wife of Michael Fisher, and Magdalena wife of Ephriam Colver.

May 20, 1777   Apr 29, 1778
Clingan, George. Executor: Thomas Clingan. Hamiltonsban Township. Wife: Margaret Clingan. Children: Thomas, Mary wife of ---- Wilson, Margaret, Hannah, Elizabeth, Catharine, and David. Grandson: Samuel Wilson (son of Mary).

Sep 2, 1777   Apr 29, 1778
Parker, Samuel. Executor: James Parker. Chanceford Township. Children: James, Anna wife of William Morrison, and John.

Nov 13, 1776   Apr 30, 1778
Carson, John. Executors: Jacob Gibson and James Edge. Township and wife: Omitted. Child: Janet wife of John Mason. Sister's sons Matthew and William Guilliland, and cousin Robert Carson, living in Comchanvale, Ireland, were the parties named in the will.

Apr 7, 1778   May 1, 1778
Schmeiser, Mathias. Executors: Michael and Jacob Schmeiser. Manchester Township. Children: Dorothea wife of Peter Hoke, Rosanna wife of George Moul, Sabina wife of Jacob Swope, Elizabeth wife of Leonard Euhilberger, Anna wife of Martin Ebert and Susanna.

Mar 28, 1778   May 7, 1778
Horn, Jacob. Executor: Lewis Williams. Monaghan Township. Legatee: Mary Steele (daughter of George Steele).

Nov 22, 1777   May 23, 1778
Spahr, Michael. Executors: Daniel Messerly and Frederick Spahr. Dover Township. Wife: Barbara Spahr. Children: Michael, Elizabeth, Eve, Catharine, Peter and Frederick.

Apr 16, 1778   Jun 4, 1778
Wallace, James. Executors: Andrew Proudfoot and Agness Wallace. Hopewell Tonwship. Wife: Agness Wallace. Children: Agness wife of John Gammel and Margaret wife of James Harper. Grandchildren: Margaret, William and James Gammel.

May 5, 1778   Jun 5, 1778
Neilson, Hugh. Executor: William Gemmill. Hopewell Township.
Children: John, Agness, and Robert.

May 15, 1775   Jun 8, 1778
Galbreaith, Thomas. Executor: Robert Galbreaith. Mt. Pleasant Township. Wife: Catharine Galbreaith.

--- ---, ----   Jun 13, 1778
Frederick, Andrew., Jr. Executors: Nicholas Dundinger, Daniel and Anna Dundinger. Paradise Township. Wife: Ann Elizabeth Frederick. Children: Michael, Andrew, Catharine wife of Anthony Snyder, Magdalena wife of Peter Thorn, Elizabeth, Susanna, and Juliana.

Mar 5, 1775   Aug 17, 1778
Frut, Peter. Executors: Juliana Frut. York County. Wife: Juliana Frut. Children: Jacob, John, Christian, Peter, and Ann.

Jul 6, 1778   Aug 19, 1778
Benodt, Francis. Executors: George Gump and Francis Miller. York Town Township. Children: John, Jacob, Henry, Mary, Marials and Catharine.

May 29, 1778   Sep 8, 1778
Hunter, James Jr.. Executors: Samuel and Joseph Hunter. Mt. Joy Township. Wife: Isabella Hunter. Children: Joseph, Samuel, Elizabeth, Mary, James, and Isabella.

May 14, 1777   Sep 21, 1778
Hughs, Tamer. Executor: Thomas Lilly. Berwick Township. Children: Thomas, Francis, John, Ann, Charles, Daniel, Henry, Joseph, Patrick, and Christian.

May 9, 1777   Sep 21, 1778
Hughs, Patrick. Executor: Thomas Hughs. Berwick Township. Wife: Tamer Hughs. Children: Francis, Thomas, John, Ann, James, Charles, Daniel, Joseph, Mary, Hannah, Patrick, and Catharine.

Nov 15, 1778   Sep 30, 1778
Hear, Michael. Executors: Elizabeth Hear and John Eiler. Manheim Township. Wife: Elizabeth Hear. Children: John and Elizabeth.

Sep 18, 1778   Oct 8, 1778
Roberts, Patrick. Executor: Rachel Roberts. Hopewell Township. Wife: Rachel Roberts. Children: John, Zachariah, Jacob, Moses, Benjamin, Mary, Ann and Peter.

Sep 5, 1778   Oct 19, 1778
Crowell, Michael. Executors: Anna Maria and Michael Crowell. Straban Township. Wife: Anna Maria Crowell. Children: William, Conrad, George, Henry, Peter, Michael, Catharine wife of Vernor M., Elizabeth wife of Michael Live, Sarah wife of Peter Vichely, Elizabeth wife of John Sharp, and Anna.

Sep 11, 1778   Oct 29, 1778
Bracken, James. Executors: Lewis Lewis and John McGrue. Menallen Township. Wife: Mary Bracken. Children: James, Caleb and Thomas.

Apr 8, 1775   Aug 19, 17788
Read, Hugh. Executor: John Read. York County. Wife: Mary Read. Children: John, James, Mary wife of John Abrinethey, Jean wife of Joseph Litch, Margaret, Agness, Elizabeth wife of James Litch and Hugh.

Mar 10, 1777   Jan 7, 1779
Knues, Daniel. Executors: Francis Knues and Henry Wireman. Menallen Township. Wife: Elizabeth Knues. Children: Eve, Henry, Mary, Elizabeth, and Daniel.

Jun 4, 1777   Jan 29, 1779
Mills, Robert. Executors: James and John Mills. Newberry Township. Children: Mary, Susanna, Elizabeth, and John.

Dec 11, 1778   Feb 5, 1779
Wilson, Thomas. Executors: Hugh and Thomas Wilson. Cumberland Township. Wife: Isabella Wilson. Children: Hugh, Thomas, John, Samuel, Sarah, James (and two sons-in-law - William and John Mitchel - their wives' names not given).

--- --, ----   Feb 8, 1779
Crombach, George. Executor: Barbara Crombach. Township: Omitted. (German will.)

Apr 4, 1778   Feb 18, 1779
McKinley, John. Executors: John Finley and Margaret McKinley. Chanceford Township. Wife: Margaret McKinley. Child: David.

Apr 25, 1777   Feb 23, 1779
Scriner, George. Executor: Mary E. Scriner. Tyrone Township. Wife: Elizabeth Scriner. Children: Mary, Catharine and Margaret.

Feb 27, 1775   Feb 27, 1779
Stickler, Jacob. Executors: Magdalena and George Stickler. Warrington Township. Wife: Magdalena Stickler. Children: George, Peter, Christopher and Ann. Grandson: John Stickler (son of Christopher).

May 13, 1778   Mar 1, 1779
Houlton, Francis. Executor: William Houlton. York County. Wife: Mary Houlton. Children: John, William, Margery, Mary, Joseph, Samuel, Ann, Benjamin, and Elizabeth.

Jan 12, 1779   Mar 1, 1779
Ziegel, Gottleib. Executors: Frederick Zeigel and Frederick Zonce. York Town Township. Wife: Mary Barbara Ziegel. Children: Mary, Magdalena wife of George Fry, Gottleib and Thomas.

Jan 8, 1779   Mar 1, 1779
Bittle, George. Executors: Michael Bael and Thomas Bittle. Germany Township. Wife: (Name not given.) Children: Salome, Margaret and Eve.

Jan 1, 1779   Mar 1, 1779
Hughs, Rowland. Executors: Elizabeth and William Hughs. York County. Wife: Elizabeth Hughs. Children: John, William, Elizabeth, Robert, James, Samuel, Isabella, and Symly.

Oct 16, 1772   Mar 1, 1779
Caldwell, William. Executors: Jean and Robert Caldwell. Fawn Township. Wife: Jean Caldwell. Children: Janet, Jean, Martha, Elizabeth, Catharine, Mary, and Isabell.

Jna 11, 1779   Mar 17, 1779
Wetzel, Jacob. Executors: James Paxton and James McIlhenney. Mt. Joy Township. Wife: Mary Wetzel. Children: Jacob (there were others - but names and number not given).

Mar 15, 1779   Mar 29, 1779
Sheely, George. Executors: Stophel Sheely and Abraham Mosser. York County. Wife: Catharine Sheely. Children: George, Henry, Godfrey, Stophel, Abraham, John and Elizabeth. Grandchild: Mary Lamberger (parents names not given).

Oct 17, 177   Mar 31, 1779
McDowel, John. Executors: Jeseph Read and William McDowel. Chanceford Township. Children: Margaret wife of Isaac Williams, Elizabeth, William, John, and Agness. Grandchild: Mary Williams.

Sep 8, 1777   Apr 1, 1779
Hobson, Francis. Executors: Joseph Hobson and William Hatton. Manheim Township. Wife: Omitted. Children: Joseph, and (others whose names were not given.)

Mar 9, 1779   Apr 2, 1779
Young, William. Executor: John Schooler. Chanceford Township. Children: John, James, Andrew, William, Elizabeth, Margaret and Mary.

Feb 1, 1778   Apr 3, 1779
Schuler, Andrew. Executors: Christian and Christly Schuler. Newberry Township. Wife: Christiana Schuler. Children: John, George and Mary.

--- --, ----   Apr 12, 1779
Beek, Burk. Executor: Magdelina Beek. (German will.)

Mar 17, 1779   Apr 28, 1779
Edger, Margaret. Executor: Abraham Scott. Fawn Township. Stepson: James Edger. Sister's Children: Christian and Abraham Scott.

Sep 3, 1769   Apr 28, 1779
Myer, Johannes. Executor: Omitted. Dover Township. Wife: Maria Catharine Myer.

Mar 26, 1776   Apr 30, 1779
Kinkcaid, Samuel. Executor: Michael Kinkcaid. York County. Brother: John Kinkcaid. Sister: Mary Kinkcaid.

Jan 9, 1779   May 8, 1779
Roland, Robert. Executor: Margaret Roland. Fawn Township. Wife: Margaret Roland. Children: Margaret, James, John, Matthew, Mary, Ann, Agness and Isabella.

Apr 8, 1777   May 18, 1779
Frankelberger, John. Executors: John and William Frankelberger. Paradise Township. Wife: Barbara Frankelberger. Children: John, Henry, Elizabeth, Philip, William, Margaret, Jacob, Conrad, Barbara, George, Caty, and Molly.

Aug 19, 1778   May 20, 1779
Geyer, Adam. Executors: Sabina M. Geyer, Peter and Paul Geyer.
Windsor Township. Wife: Sabina Margaret Geyer. Children: George,
Paul, Conrad, Peter, Anna, Catharine, and Maria.

May 3, 1779   Jun 2, 1779
Crawford, Hugh. Executor: James Crawford. Berwick Township. Wife:
Mary Crawford. Children: Hannah, James, William, and Margaret.

Apr 20, 1779   Jun 4, 1779
Hering, Henry. Executor: Nicholas Biedmyer. Paradise Township.
Children: Philip, Mary wife of Adam Fauster, Elizabeth wife of George
Miller, Dorothea wife of George Madok, Catharine wife of Nicholas
Michael, Henry, and Christiana wife of Adam Fauster. Grandchildren:
Henry and George Miller (children of Elizabeth), and Margaret and
Dorothea Kap, and Mary Emler (parents' names not given).

May 1, 1779   Jun 21, 1779
Ziegel, Frederick. Executors: John Herbach and Maria M. Zeigel. York
Township. Wife: Maria Zeigel. Children: Barbara, Ann, Maria,
Christianna, Elizabeth and Jacob.

Jun 7, 1779   Jul 2, 1779
Hagen, Edward. Executors: Thomas Fisher and Patrick McSherry. Mt.
Pleasant Township. Wife: Elizabeth Hagen. Children: Henry, John,
Patrick, Edward, James, David, and Andrew. Grandson: Peter McClain
(parents' names not given).

Jul 12, 1774   Jul 15, 1779
Wilson, Henry. Executor: Andrew Wilson. Monaghan Township.
Children: Jannet wife of James Sharp and Andrew. Grandchildren:
James and Agness Dill and Mary Williams (the names of their parents not
given). Legatees: (Sisters) Jannet and Mary Wilson - living in Ireland.

Mar 20, 1777   Jul 19, 1779
Maier, Christian. Executors: John and Christian Maier. York County.
Wife: Elizabeth Maier. Children: Francis, Andrew, Christian, and
Hannah.

--- ---, ----   Aug 14, 1779
Zell, Bartholomew. Executors: B. Zell and Peter Kaub. York County.
(German will.)

Jun 8, 1779   Aug 19, 1779
Spencer, William. Executors: John Blackburn and John Jordan.
Manallen Township. Wife: Jean Spencer. Children: William, John,
Mary, Isaac, Robert and Thomas.

Oct 28, 1776   Aug 30, 1779
Mohr, Philip Henry. Executors: Catharine Mohr and Peter Rheil. Dover
Township. Wife: Catharine Mohr. Children: George, Mary, and Sophia
wife of ---- Valentine. Grandchildren: Philip and Daniel Valentine.

--- --, ----   Sep 4, 1779
Hershner, Lawrence. Executors: John Cron and Henry Libhart. York
County. German will.

Aug 16, 1779   Sep 15, 1779
Wilson, James. Executors: Esther Wilson and John Thompson.
Hamiltonsban Township. Wife: Esther Wilson. Children: Jean and
James.

Jun 28, 1779   Oct 26, 1779
Nebinger, Andress. Executors: Anna Maria and George Nebinger. York
Town Township. Wife: Anna Maria Nebinger. Children: George and
Catharine wife of George Weller.

Jan 29, 1779   Oct 26, 1779
Cossine, Peter. Executors: Williampe Cossine and Lemon Vanarsdalen.
York County. Wife: Williampe Cossine. Children: Cornelius, Martinus,
Elizabeth, and Peter.

Sep 8, 1779   Nov 5, 1779
Nailer, James. Executors: James McCurdy and William Nailer.
Newberry Township. Wife: Elizabeth Nailer. Children: William, Ralph,
James, John, Thomas, Ewing, and Mary.

Dec 1, 1778   Nov 12, 1779
Slagel, Mary. Executors: Daniel and Jacob Slagel. Barwick Township.
Children: Daniel, Jacob, Catharine, Christopher, Magdalena, Susanna and
Henry.

Mar 14, 1779   Nov 15, 1779
Urey, Antone. Executors: Casper Lambert and Michael Urey.
Warrington Township. Wife: Barbara Urey. Children: John and
Elizabeth.

Jul 5, 1777   Nov 18, 1779
Hatton, Edward. Executors: Adam Semonds and Archibald McGrew.
Hungtinton Township. Children: John, James, Ann wife of Roland
McRandles, Robert, and Mary wife of Adam Seymonds. Grandchildren:
Joseph McRandles (son of Ann), and Edward, James, Leonard, Jane and
Rachel Hatton (children of Robert).

Nov 5, 1777   Dec 2, 1779
McNagten, Neal. Executors: Thomas and John McNagten. Tyrone
Township. Wife: Elizabeth McNagten. Children: Elizabeth wife of
George Duffield, Sarah wife of Alexander Blackburn, Margery wife of
William Robinson, Margaret, Thomas, and John.

Nov 7, 1779   Dec 15, 1779
Emmitt, Josiah. Executors: William and Sarah Porter. York County.
Wife: Sarah Emmitt. Children: Mary, Sarah, and Susanna.
Grandchildren: Josiah, Mary and Sarah (children of Mary Emmitt,
husband's name not given).

May 5, 1775   Jan 17, 1780
Weller, George. Executors: Henry Lanius and William Lanius. York
County. Wife: Anna Eve Weller. Children: Martin, George, Elizabeth
and Philip Rathrock and Savena.

Jan 11, 1780   Jan 31, 1780
Scholl, John Jacob. Executors: John Ottman and Henry Kessler.
Cordorus Township. Wife: Catharine Scholl. Children: John, Dorothea,
Mary and Catharine.

Nov 25, 1777   Feb 2, 1780
Schlothauer, Nicholas. Executor: A.E. Schlothauer. Manheim Township.
Wife: Anna Schlothauer. Child: Anthony.

--- --, ----   Mar 6, 1780
Cramer, Daniel. Executors: Jacob Shares and Haefer Cramer. (German
will.)

--- --, ----   Mar 7, 1780
Kramer, Daniel. Executors: Jacob Shaves and Halfor Kramer. (German
will.)

Mar 25, 1779   Mar 21, 1780
Ross, Hugh. Executor: William Ross. Chanceford Township. Wife:

Elizabeth Ross. Children: William, Joseph, Elizabeth wife of Alexander McCandless, Mary wife of Joseph Reed. Grandchild: Hugh Reed.

Jan 9, 1780   Mar 28, 1780
Cabell, Philip. Executor: Michael Miller. Warrington Township. Wife: Mary Cabell. Children: Abraham, Barbara, Benjamin, Jacob and Salome.

Mar 27, 1789   Apr 8, 1780
Meyer, Magdalena. Executor: Ignatus Leitner. Cordorus Township. Child: John. Granddaughter: Magdalena Meyer.

Jan 8, 1780   May 11, 1780
Ramsay, Thomas. Executors: Mary and Alexander Ramsay. Dover Township. Wife: Mary Ramsay. Children: Alexander, Oliver and Mary. Grandchildren: William, Mary, Sarah (children of Oliver).

Oct 5, 1778   May 26, 1780
Gartner, Adam. Executors: Philip Gartner and George Maul. Yorktown Township. Wife: Elizabeth Gartner. Children: Jacob and Elizabeth.

May 13, 1780   Jun 14, 1780
Bosler, Veronica. Executors: Joseph Wilsham and Killean Small. York Town Township. Legatees: The Elders of the German Reformed Church of York Town.

Mar 19, 1780   Jul 25, 1780
Owings, John. Executors: Mary Ann and Joseph Owings. York County. Wife: Mary Ann Owings.

Sep 9, 1779   Aug 8, 1780
Machlan, John. Executor: Jacob Vore. Warrington Township. Wife: Rebecca Machlan. Children: Mary, George, Lydia, John, William, Elizabeth, Margaret, James, and Sarah.

Jun 20, 1780   Aug 10, 1780
Karl, Michael. Executor: George Karl. Berwick Township. Wife: Anna Maria Karl. Children: Martin, George, and Anna wife of Casper Kinacre.

Jun 23, 1780   Aug 17, 1780
Frey, Martin. Executors: Anna Mary Frey and Killian Small. Yorktown Township. Wife: Anna Mary Frey. Children: Martin, Anna, Margaret, and Elizabeth.

Aug 17, 1779   Aug 31, 1780
Wilson, Charles. Executors: Robert and Charles Wilson. Mt. Joy
Township. Wife: Mary Wilson. Children: John, James, Elizabeth, Mary,
Anne, Robert, Charles and Thomas.

Dec 23, 1779   Sep 8, 1780
Jack, James. Executors: John Jack and Benjamin Reed. Hamiltonsban
Township. Wife: Agness Jack. Children: Lidia, John, James, Elizabeth,
Jean wife of ---- Wilkey, Agness wife of ---- Kernahan, Sarah, Andrew, and
Esther. Grandchildren: James Wilkey and James Kernahan.

Oct 2, 1780   Oct 7, 1780
Sweeney, Isaac. Executor: James Sweeney. Cumberland Township.
Legatees: Miles Sweeney (father), Thomas, John, Mary and Ann Sweeney
(brothers and sisters).

Jul 18, 1780   Oct 9, 1780
Johnson, Ephriam. Executors: John, Ephriam, and John Johnson.
Carrols Tract Township. Wife: Agness Johnson. Children: Elizabeth
wife of Samuel Agnew, James, Ephriam, and John. Grandchild: Ephriam
(son of Ephriam).

Aug 17, 1780   Oct 23, 1780
Grove, Henry. Executor: Jacob Grove. Manchester Township. Wife:
Anna Mary Grove. Children: Jacob, Elizabeth, Catharine, George, and
Henry.

Oct 10, 1780   Oct 31, 1780
Reed, John. Executors: Robert McCortel and Thomas McFarland.
Cumberland Township. Legatees: Margaret McCortel (mother), Daniel
and William Reed (brothers), Mary McCormick wife of James McCormick
and Margaret Colwell (sisters).

May 18, 1780   Nov 2, 1780
Sharp, James. Executors: Jean Sharp, Samuel Wallace and William
Hunter. Newberry Township. Wife: Jean Sharp. Children: Robert,
James, Jannet, Hannah, Ann and Dorcas.

Jun 12, 1780   Nov 7, 1780
Sipe, George. Executors: George and Henry Sipe. Cumberland
Township. Wife: Elizabeth Sipe. Children: George, Henry, Elizabeth,
Mary, Jean, Charles and Sarah.

Apr 6, 1779   Nov 14, 1780
Bracken, Thomas. Executors: Archibald McGrew and William Bracken. Monaghan Township. Wife: Martha Bracken. Children: William, John, Thomas, James, Hannah wife of Nicholas Bishop, Mary wife of James Guttory, Margaret wife of Archibald McGrew, and Jean wife of Mathew Dill.

Nov 10, 1780   Nov 21, 1780
Sennard, Eleanor. Executors: Thomas Grove and William Gemmell. Hopewell Township. Children: Jonathan, Sarah, Mary, Susanna, Abraham, John, Thomas, William, Margaret, Eleanor and Elizabeth.

Jul 5, 1779   Dec 2, 1780
McNagten, Elizabeth. Executors: Thomas and John McNagten. Tyrone Township. Children: Elizabeth wife of George Duffield, Sarah wife of Alexander Blackburn, Margery wife of William Robinson, Margaret, Thomas and John. Grandson: John McNagten (son of Thomas).

Nov 9, 1780   Dec 11, 1780
Auman, Jacob. Executors: Henry Werby and Christopher Bricker. Wife: Mary Elizabeth Auman. Manheim Township. Children: Margaret, George, John, Michael (?), (stepdaughter) Mary wife of William Struck, (stepson) Michael Jones. George and Jacob (?) (children of George).

Sep 19, 1777   Dec 21, 1780
Spangler, Susanna. Executor: Christian Lawman. York Township. Wife of Henry Spangler. Children: Susanna. (There were others, but names and number not given.)

Feb 3, 1777   Jun 27, 1780.
Klunk, Peter. Executors: Martin and Peter Klunk. Berwick Township. Wife: Mary Klunk. Children: Martin, Elizabeth, Peter, Margaret, Ann, and Magdalena.

Aug 26, 1780   Jan 9, 1781
Bentz, Philip. Executors: Michael Stahn, Henry Yessler and Henry Bentz. York Town Township. Wife: Mary Elizabeth Bentz. Children: Henry, Peter, Christian, Philip, Elizabeth wife of Michael Hahn, Margaret wife of Henry Yessler, and Rosina wife of John Hahn.

--- --, ----   Jan 11, 1781
Morgenstern, John. Executors: Valentine Fisher and C. Morningstar. York County. (German will.)

Nov 9, 1780   Jan 13, 1781
Miller, Peter. Executors: Charles Diehl and Barnet Zeigler. Cordorus Township. Wife: Ann Elizabeth Miller. Children: Susanna, Barbara, Jacob, Johannes, and Philip.

Jun 21, 1781   Feb 15, 1781
Kueny, Henry. Executors: Samuel Flickinger and Henry Hohff. Germany Township. Wife: Anna Kueny. Children: John, (and others whose names were not given).

--- --, ----   Feb 17, 1781
Walter, Henry. Executors: John Smith and Valentine Wilt. Cordorus Township. (German will.)

--- --, ----   Feb 27, 1781
Erhart, William. Executors: Thomas and Jacob Erhart. York County. German will.

Jan 13, 1769   Feb 29, 1781
Diggs, Edward. Executor: Omitted. St. Mary's County, Maryland. Children: Elizabeth, Eleanor, Mary, John, Edward, and Ann.

May 20, 1777   Mar 1, 1781
Furman, Stephen. Executors: Catharine and Michael Furman. Manheim Township. Wife: Catharine Furman. Children: Catharine, Valentine, and Eva.

Feb 5, 1781   Mar 12, 1781
Loboob, Michael. Executors: Dorothea Loboob and John Heidler. Berwick Township. Wife: Dorothea Loboob. Children: Michael, Maria, Elizabeth, and Christiana.

Feb 20, 1781   Mar 14, 1781
Kuntz, William. Executor: John Keiffer. York County. Wife: Elizabeth Kuntz. Children: Elizabeth and Catharine.

Jan 10, 178   Mar 15, 1781
McCall, Matthew. Executors: Susanna McCall and Samuel Nelson. Chanceford Township. Wife: Susanna McCall. Children: Robert (and three daughters whose names were not given.))

Feb 15, 1781   Mar 17, 1781
Palm, Jacob. Executor: Sebastian Obolt. Mt. Pleasant Township. Wife:

Ann Palm. Son-in-law: Jacob Rider (wife's name not given).

May 21, 1777   Mar 19, 1781
Probst, Jacob. Executors: Frederick Vonce, and George Wehr. York Town Township. Wife: Anna Elizabeth Probst. Children: John, Anna wife of George Spangler, and Marilis wife of Jacob Funk.

Nov 15, 1780   Mar 26, 1781
Miller, John. Executors: James Taggert and Edward Abbot. Berwick Township. Wife: Alice Miller. Children: Deborah, Ebenezer, and Joshua.

Jan 18, 1781   Mar 28, 1781
Griffith, David. Executors: William Smith and David Griffith. Hopewell Township. Wife: Hannah Griffith. Children: Even, Susanna wife of John Forsyth, David, Sarah, Esther, and Hannah.

Dec 4, 1778   Apr 6, 1781
Hobias, Frederick. Executors: Barnet Zeigler and Christian Rohrbaugh. Cordorus Township. Wife: Margaret Hobias. Children: (Names and number not given.)

Feb 8, 1781   Apr 28, 1781
Eichelberger, Martin. Executors: Adam, Jacob, and Martin Eichelberger. Manchester Township. Wife: Anna Maria Eichelberger. Children: George, Frederick, Jacob, Barnet, Martin, Susanna, and Mary.

Aug 5, 1778   May 15, 1781
Apple, Elias. Executor: Eliza Apple. Wife: Eliza Apple. Dover Township. Children: James and Christian.

Dec 6, 1774   May 22, 1781
Harper, Samuel. Executor: Samuel Harper. Hopewell Township. Wife: Jennet Harper. Children: Jean, Agness, Samuel, and James.

--- ---, ----   May 24, 1781
Billinger, Jacob. Executors: Michael Billinger and Andrew Billinger. York Town Township. German will.

May 9, 1781   May 31, 1781
Feisser, John. Executors: Peter Feisser and John Heuisen. Dover Township. Wife: Elizabeth Feisser. Child: Peter.

Mar 30, 1781   Jun 15, 1781
McCurdy, Robert. Executors: John McCurdy and James McFarland. Berwick Township. Wife: Omitted. Children: John, Margaret, Sarah, Mary, Agness, and Jeseph. Grandchildren: Margaret (daughter of Joseph).

Aug 9, 1780   Jun 15, 1781
Houts, John. Executors: Christopher Houts, William Geary and Rudolph Spangler. York County. Wife: Ida Houts. Children: Christopher, Jacob, John, Margaret, Elizabeth, Christiana, and Catharine wife of William Geary.

Feb 9, 1781   Jun 15, 1781
Mayes, John. Executors: Dorcas and Charles Mayer. Paradise Township. Wife: Dorcas Mayes. Child: William.

Nov 23, 1788   Jun 23, 1781
Snellbecker, Jacob. Executor: John Budisell. York County. Wife: Catharine Snellbecker. Children: George and Barbara wife of Mathias Eicholtz.

May 5, 1781   Jun 30, 1781
Mixell, Conrad. Executors: John Mixell. Newberry Township. Wife: Barbara Mixell. Children: John, George, Adam, Mary, Catharine, Margaret, Elizabeth, and Jacob.

--- ---, ----   Jul 30, 1781
Wolff, George. Executors: Anne E. Wolff and Jacob Schmeiser. York County. (German will.)

May 20, 1781   Jul 30, 1781
Low, Philip. Executors: Jacob Schmutzer and Peter Minger. Manchester Township. Children: Gertrude wife of Frederick Miller, Henry, Elizabeth, Andrew, Michael, and Magdalena.

Jul 16, 1781   Aug 2, 1781
Eichelberger, Barnett. Executors: James Werley and Daniel Barterett. York County. Bequests were left to the following: Daniel Barnett, son of sister Susanna Barnett, and Mary Eichelberger, daughter of brother George Eichelberger.

Apr 7, 1781   Aug 3, 1781
Hupard, Adam. Executors: Catharine and Adam Hupard. Manheim

Township. Wife: Catharine Hupard. Children: Adam, Catharine wife of Peter Welch, Eve, and Anamary.

Apr 9, 1781   Aug 16, 1781
Neal, Thomas. Executor: John Neal. Fawn Township. Children: Thomas, John, Margaret, and Agness.

Dec 22, 1774   Aug 20, 1781
Hentz, Philip. Executor: Peter Wolff. Manchester Township. Wife: Barbara Hentz. Children: Nicholas, Mark, Philip, Mary, Elizabeth, Catharine, Henry, Anna, Maria, John, Peter, and Martin.

Jan 22, 1781   Aug 21, 1781
Cochran, Andrew. Executors: Margaret Cochran, James McKesson, and William McKesson. Cawelsbury, Hanover Township. Wife: Margaret Cochran. Nieces and Nephew: Mary Cochran (daughter of brother James), Mary Cochran (daughter of brother John), and Andrew Cochran (son of brother John).

Jul 25, 1781   Aug 22, 1781
Frederick, Anna Elizabeth. Executors: Daniel Ammer and Daniel Ammer, Jr. Paradise Township. Widow of Andrew Frederick. Children: John, Susanna, and Elizabeth.

Sep 7, 1781   Sep 17, 1781
Ottinger, Jacob. Executors: Conrad Eisenhardt and Jacob Ottinger. Manchester Township. Wife: Hannah Ottinger. Children: Jacob, Henry, Peter, Clara, Elizabeth wife of George Eisenhardt, Henry, Hannah wife of Michael Frederick, Peter, and Dorothea wife of John Dettemer.

Jun 16, 1789   Oct 13, 1781
Headrich, Jacob. Executors: Elizabeth Headrich and John Ruhl. Cordorus Township. Wife: Elizabeth Haedrich. Children: Christian, Elizabeth wife of Nicholas Wolfgang, Catharine, Christely, John, Appolonia, and Abraham.

Sep 12, 1781   Oct 15, 1781
Riehl, William. Executor: John Heckendorn. York Town Township. Wife: Gertrude Riehl. Children: Catharine wife of Harman Hookas and Margaret wife of Daniel Dinkel. Grandchildren: (Five children of Margaret - names not given).

Sep 12, 1781   Nov 6, 1781
Marlin, William. Executor: James Logue. Chanceford Township. Wife: Elizabeth Marlin. Children: Agness, Jean, Susanna, Rachel, and Mary. Grandchildren: William Speer and William Martin (parents' names not given).

Oct 27, 1781   Nov 14, 1781
Hoke, John. Executors: Andrew Hoke and George Rudy. Manchester Township. Wife: Sabina Hoke. Children: Frederick, Sabina, Daniel, John, and George.

Mar 4, 1777   Nov 24, 1781
Stewart, John. Executors: Elizabeth and John Stewart. York Township. Wife: Elizabeth Stewart. Children: John, Mathias, Jacob, Abraham, David, Freny, Elizabeth, Mary and Barbara.

Sep 13, 1781   Nov 27, 1781
Bush, John. Executors: Henry Lenus and Jacob Lenus. York Township. Wife: Anna Bush. Children: John, Jacob, Elizabeth, Christiana, Anna wife of Christopher Kline, Catharine, Jieleana, Rosina, Barbara, and stepdaughter Anna wife of Frantz J. Milen.

Dec 5, 1780   Nov 29, 1781
Steel, John. Executor: James Ferguson. Hamiltonsban Township. Wife: Elizabeth Steel. Sons-in-law: William Brown, James Ferguson and William Fenley. (Their wives' names not given.)

Nov 1, 1781   Dec 7, 1781
Fulton, William. Executors: Thomas Allen, and Mary and John Fulton. York County. Wife: Mary Fulton. Children: John, Alexander, James, Elijah, and Mary.

Dec 2, 1778   Dec 16, 1781
Wertz, John. Executors: Philip Senft and Yost Runk. Cordorus Township. Children: Catharine wife of John Ottman, Jacob, Elizabeth wife of George Steighletter, Daniel, Peter and Rosinna.

May 12, 1781   Jan 2, 1782
Swing, Michael. Executors: Killian Small and Jacob Welshantz. York Town Township. Children: George, Michael and Margaret wife of Lawrence Ettare.

Sep 5, 1781   Jan 8, 1782
Craff, Barbara. Executors: Michael Dondel and Charles Barnitz. York Town. Children: Margaret, George, Juliana, Barbara, Mary, Ludwig, and Jacob.

Jan 31, 1777   Jan 11, 1782
Cowan, William. Executor: Robert Cowan. York County. (Sister:) Sarah Carson.

Feb 16, 1777   Jan 11, 1782
Cowan, Alexander. Executors: William Eahen and William Whiteford. Harford Township. Brothers and Sisters: Robert, Henry, Jenny, Gun, and Samuel. (Living in Ireland).

Dec 28, 1781   Jan 11, 1782
Hershaw, Christian. Executors: John Weltz and Christian Bear. Manheim Township. Child: Mary wife of Adam Frank.

Dec 25, 1781   Jan 26, 1782
Eisenhard, Conrad. Executors: Philip Zeigler and Emanuel Herman. Manchester Township. Wife: Catharine Eisenhard. Children: Conrad, Ann, and George.

Aug 8, 1779   Jan 29, 1782
Bower, Frederick. Executors: Ludwig Rosemiller and George Male. Huntington Township. Wife: (Not recorded.) Children: George and Frederick.

--- --, ----   Feb 16, 1782
Bardt, Stephen. Executors: Catharine Bardt and Christopher Smith. German will.

Feb 5, 1782   Feb 22, 1782
Landes, Christian. Executors: Samuel and Henry Landes. Windsor Township. Wife: Maria Landes. Children: Barbara wife of Stephen Landes, Magdalena wife of Henry Strickler, John, Christian, Samuel, Jacob, Henry, Abraham, Benjamin, Elizabeth, Daniel, and David.

Feb 14, 1782   Feb 23, 1782
Sower, Adam. Executors: M. Forry, A. Berd and Christian Leib. Berwick Township. Wife: (Name not given.) Children: Catharine, Elizabeth, David, Adam, Daniel, Jacob, Mary, Susan and Juliana wife of (name not given). Grandchildren: Jacob, John, George, Martin, Catharine and Eve

(children of Juliana).

Feb 3, 1782   Mar 1, 1782
Baldwin, Nathaniel. Executors: John Gritt and Charles Wintersmith. Hanover Township. Legatee: Brother-in-law Daniel Fagot "who is an officer at New Orleans".

Dec 18, 1781   Mar 4, 1782
Cronester, John. Executors: Barbara Cronester and Henry Wesseler. Huntington Township. Wife: Barbara Cronester. Children: John, Susanna, Elizabeth, Conrad, and Mary.

Feb 27, 1780   Mar 9, 1782
Duncan, James. Executor: John Duncan. Chanceford Township. Children: John, Sarah, Rudsand, Jean, and Elizabeth.

Feb 10, 1782   Mar 12, 1782
Baumgarner, John. Executor: George Mansperger. Township Omitted. Wife: Mary Baumgarner.

May 15, 1777   Mar 20, 1782
Brackon, John. Executor: Elizabeth Bracken. Huntington Township. Wife: Elizabeth Bracken. Children: Thomas, John, Martha, Christian, Elizabeth, Margaret and Mary.

--- --, ----   Apr 2, 1782
Gillerees, Robert. Executors: Agness Gillerees and Thomas Aller. Fawn Township. Wife: Agness Gillerees. Children: John, Margaret, Robert, James, and William.

Aug 14, 1781   Apr 6, 1782
Becker, Frederick. Executors: John Adam Becker and Killean Lichtenberger. Manchester Township. Wife: Anna Becker. Children: John, Adam, Mary wife of Christopher Greenewald, and Anna wife of Jacob Shoemaker (of Bucks County).

Feb 7, 1782   Apr 23, 1782
Richter, George. Executors: Barbara Richter and Martin Reisinger. Dover Township. Wife: Barbara Richter. The names and number of children not given.

Jun 17, 1780   May 1, 1782
McChance, David. Executors: George and John McChance. Straban

Township. Wife: Margaret McChance. Children: Andrew, David, and George.

Feb 14, 1777   May 1, 1782
McClure, Thomas. Executors: John Parks and John McClure. Mt. Pleasant Township. Wife: Margaret McClure. Children: Mary and Elizabeth.

Mar 25, 1776   May 2, 1782
White, James. Executor: James White. Reading Township. Wife: Elizabeth White. Children: James, Peter, Andrew, Henry, Elizabeth and Charity.

Jan 12, 1782   May 9, 1782
Reid, Joseph. Executors: James and Samuel Reid. York County. Testees: Francis Harbison, William and Thomas Reid. Signers of Will: James R. Reid, Samuel Reid and Joseph Reid. N.B. This will was drawn making each Brother the legatee of the others in case, as stated in will, of "accident or sickness incurred, while engaged in Public Services during these Critical Times".

--- --, ----   May 13, 1782
Meyer, Michael. Executor: Peter Brillhart. York County. (German will.)

Mar 23, 1782   May 15, 1782
Fickes, Valentine. Executors: Elizabeth and Jacob Fickes. Huntington Township. Wife: Elizabeth Fickes. Children: Jacob, Rebecca, Elizabeth, Margaret, Abraham, John, Isaac, and Valentine.

Mar 11, 1780   May 27, 1782
Swope, George. Executors: Anna Maria Swope and Joseph Wilson. Paradise Township. Wife: Anna Maria Swope. Children: (One son and one daughter, names not given.)

May 11, 1781   May 28, 1782
Trine, Jacob. Executors: Omitted. Heidleberg Township. Wife: Rose Trine. Children: Peter, Jacob, Christian, Elizabeth and Margaret.

Apr 1, 1774   Jun 7, 1782
Withrow, John. Executor: William McLean. Hamiltonsban Township. Children: William, Jean wife of William McLean and Margaret wife of John Agnew. There were nine grandchildren - chlidren of William and four children of Jean (names not given).

Apr 3, 1781   Jun 8, 1782
McDonald, Martha. Executors: Robert McPherson. Cumberland Township. Children: Mary and Samuel.

--- --, ----   Jun 8, 1782
Weisz, Casper. Executors: John Baker and Casper White. York County. (German will.)

May 7, 1782   Jun 11, 1782
Curry, Ann. Executor: William Hamilton. Manallen Township. Children: Elinor wife of William McBride, Mary wife of Thomas White, and Francis wife of William Hamilton. Grandchildren: Ann, Mary, James, and William (children of Francis).

Apr 12, 1782   Jun 14, 1782
Lieninger, George. Executors: Philip Long and Martin Minter. Manheim Township. Wife: Catharine Lieninger. Children: (Names not given.)

--- --, ----   Jun 14, 1782
Frey, Gottfried. Executors: John Hay and John Welsh. York County. German will.

May 8, 1781   Jun 25, 1782
Baker, Mathias. Executors: Mathias Baker and Christian Hemler. Heidelberg Township. Children: Mathias, Mary, and Ann wife of ---- Hemler.

May 1, 1781   Jul 30, 1782
McClellan, William. Executors: Mary McClellan and William Mitchell. Warrington Township. Wife: Mary McClellan. Children: John, Margaret, William, Mary, Elizabeth, and Jane.

Feb 13, 1782   Aug 20, 1782
Percel, Richard Sr. Executors: Richard Percel and Henry Slagle. Berwick Township. Children: Isaac, Richard, Peter, Rulit, John, Hilgath, Mary, Sarah, Catharine, Hannah, and Elizabeth.

Jun 4, 1782   Aug 29, 1782
Johnston, Ephriam. Executors: Margaret and James Johnston. Manallen Township. Wife: Margaret Johnston. Children: Ephriam, Nathan, Sarah, Agness, Margaret, and Elizabeth.

Jul 24, 1782   Sep 12, 1782
McAlister, James. Executors: Mary McAlister and James Marshall.
Hamiltonsban Township. Wife: Mary McAlister. Children: Charles,
Hugh, Sarah, and James.

Feb 2, 1777   Sep 23, 1782
Atherton, Thomas. Executor: Richard Atherton. Wife: Abigael
Atherton. Warrington Township. Children: Richard, Henry and
Elizabeth.

Jun 11, 1781   Sep 27, 1782
Schneider, Adam. Executors: Henry Wireman and William Delap.
Manallen Township. Children: Adam, Abraham, John, Sarah wife of John
Kegy, Marlina wife of Jacob Letshaw and Eve wife of George Brown.
Grandson: Samuel Grabill (parents name not given).

Aug 1, 1779   Oct 1, 1782
Smith, John. Executors: Andrew Porter. Cumberland Township.
Children: William, Agness wife of William McGaughey, Mary wife of
Andrew Porter, Robert, Sarah wife of William Parks, David and Elizabeth.

Mar 7, 1782   Oct 5, 1782
Owings, Joshua. Executor: Hannah Owings. Hanover Township.
Legatees: Hannah and Susanna Owings (sisters).

Feb 15, 1782   Oct 7, 1782
Hunter, Joseph. Executor: Alexander Hunter. Mt. Joy Township.
Children: Joseph, Alexander, Agness wife of ---- Denwoody, Francis wife
of ---- Denwoody, and Sarah wife of ---- Tompson. Grandchildren: Sarah
Tompson (daughter of Sarah), Joseph Hunter (son of Alexander), Sarah
Denwoody (daughter of Agness), and Joseph and Sarah Denwoody
(children of Francis).

Mar 6, 1777   Oct 14, 1782
Stahl, Henry. Executors: Jacob Forman and Ludwick Rudsilly. Manheim
Township. Wife: Matalena Stahl. Children: Jacob, Henry and four
daughters (names not given).

Mar 31, 1777   Oct 16, 1782
Allison, Gavin. Executors: James Allison and James Maffit. Wife: Jean
Allison. Hopewell Township. Children: Alexander, Margaret, John,
Agness, Joseph, Jean, James and William.

May 25, 1782   Oct 16, 1782
Brillhart, Peter. Executor: Peter Brillhart. Codorus Township.
Children: Peter, John, Jacob, Christian, Elizabeth wife of Samuel Pixler, Mary wife of Joseph Grabell, Eve wife of Samuel Flickinger, Anna and Barbara.

May 28, 1776   Nov 11, 1782
Geip, Nicholas. Executor: Omitted. Hellam Township. Wife: Charlotte Geip. Children: Nicholas, Ann wife of Michael King, Mary wife of Peter Ditty, Elizabeth wife of Peter Kline, Peter, and Henry.

Aug 7, 1782   Dec 5, 1782
Reid, Joseph. Executors: John M. Creary and William Ross. Chanceford Township. Wife: Jennet Reid. Children: John, Jean, James, Joseph, Elizabeth, George and William.

Nov 7, 1782   Dec 9, 1782
Leas, Leonard. Executors: Mathias Maloan and Michael Kimmel. Reading Township. Children: William, Mary wife of George Neas, Ursilla wife of John Cough, Eleanor wife of ---- Fahnstick, Abraham, John, Benjamin, Catharine, Jacob, Sarah, and Daniel. Granddaughter: Mary Jones (parents' names not given).

Feb 18, 1782   Dec 11, 1782
Amerman, Henry. Executors: Cornelius Vanarsdalen, James Brinkelhof and John Muntfort. Wife: Jean Amerman. Mount Pleasant Township. Children: James, Simon, Anne, Mary, Henry, Milly and Gerret.

Nov 21, 1782   Dec 25, 1782
Henry, George. Executors: William Henry and James Long. Chanceford Township. Wife: Elizabeth Henry. Children: William, Elizabeth, and George.

Mar 29, 1777   Jan 2, 1783
Weaver, Melcher. Executors: B. Anghingbourgh and Peter Deardorf. Reading Township. Children: David, Barbara, John, Melcher and Elizabeth.

Nov 24, 1782   Jan 3, 1783
Chesney, William. Executors: Elizabeth Chesney and William Chalmers. Newberry Township. Wife: Elizabeth Chesney. (Niece and Nephews:) Jane wife of Moses Wallace, Isabella wife of Hugh Wilson, Grizal wife of Alexander Wilson, Joseph Fulton, and Richard Fulton.

Dec 28, 1782   Jan 9, 1783
Gibson, John. Executors: Jennet and James Gibson. Hopewell Township. Wife: Jennet Gibson. Children: (Names and number not given.)

Nov 6, 1782   Feb 5, 1783
Martin, Thomas. Executors: Sarah Martin and James McGanghy. Cumberland Township. Wife: Sarah Martin. Children: Thomas, James, Sarah, and Jennet.

Oct 18, 1782   Feb 27, 1783
Hunt, John. Executors: Rodger Hunt and Robert Johnson. Huntington Township. Wife: Jane Hunt. Children: Elizabeth, John, Mary, Rodger, Samuel, Edward, William, and Margaret wife of William Bowman.

Apr 9, 1782   Feb 28, 1783
Edmundson, John. Executors: Sarah and Joseph Edmundson. Warrington Township. Wife: Sarah Edmundson. Children: Joseph, Esther, Thomas, Sarah, John, Rachel, and Caleb.

--- --, ----   Mar 3, 1783
McFerran, John. Executor: Samuel McFerran. Cumberland Township. Wife: Martha McFerran. Children: Samuel, Andrew, William, Elizabeth, Mary, Jane, Agness, Susanna, Martha, and Anne. Grandchild: John McFerran (son of William).

Oct 4, 1782   Mar 5, 1783
Brown, Joseph. Executors: William Orr and Robert Cester. Straban Township. Children: Sarah, Rebecca, Martha and Mary.

Sep 26, 1782   Mar 18, 1783
Harman, Adam. Executor: George Harman. Huntington Township. Wife: Elizabeth Harman. Children: George, Frederick, John, and Elizabeth wife of ---- Prose.

Oct 15, 1802   Mar 18, 1783
Hart, David. Executor: Andrew Hart. Hamiltonsban Township. Wife: Omitted. Children: John, Margaret, Mary, Andrew, Isabella, Jean, and Elijah. Grandchildren: David (son of John), and David (son of Andrew).

Feb 3, 1783   Mar 25, 1783
Forney, Philip. Executors: Adam Forney and Andrew Shriner. Heidelburg Township. Wife: Elizabeth Forney. Children: Adam, Samuel,

David, Peter, Jacob, Mary wife of Ludwick Shriver, Louise wife of Leonhard Lease, Elizabeth wife of Daniel Saunnot, Hannah, Susanna, and Salome.

Oct 19, 1782   Mar 26, 1783
Grimes, Nathan. Executor: George Lewis Leffer. York County. Wife: Mary Grimes. Children: (Names and number not given.)

Aug 13, 1774   Apr 10, 1783
Bear, Abraham. Executors: Fornica Bear and John Bear. Manchester Township. Wife: Fornica Bear. Children: Jacob, John Henry, Samuel, Mary wife of John Fetter, and Barbara wife of Isaac Sittler.

Apr 18, 1782   Apr 11, 1783
Bentz, Whyrich. Executors: Henry Wolf and John Hay. York Town Township. Wife: Anna Maria Bentz. Children: Whyrich, Jacob, Peter, Catharine wife of Jacob Heller, Anna wife of George Rudy, Susanna wife of Abraham Frostle, Elizabeth wife of Peter Deckart, Lizzie wife of Jacob Sidler, and Ursula wife of Henry King.

Jun 2, 1778   Apr 12, 1783
Shields, John. Executors: George Watt and Alexander Porter. Cumberland Township. Children: Margaret wife of Benjamin Sterret, Eleanor wife of --- McIlherson, Jennet wife of John Murdock, John and Robert. Son-in-law: George Watt (wifes' name not given). Grandchildren: John, Jennet, Martha and Mary Watt.

Mar 20, 1783   Apr 15, 1783
Gelwicks, Frederick. Executors: Nicholas Gelwicks and Philip Myers. Hanover Township. Wife: Mary Dorothea Gelwicks. Children: Peter, Daniel, Charles, Eve wife of Philip Myers, George, and Nicholas.

--- --, ----   Apr 16, 1783
Brenner, Adam. Executor: Anna Maria Brenner. German will.

--- --, ----   Apr 30, 1783
Hildebrand, John. Executors: Felix Hildebrand and Jacob Swartz. York County.

Apr 18, 1782   May 3, 1783
Hendricks, Samuel. Executors: Alice and Nathan Hendricks. Manallen Township. Wife: Alice Hendricks. Children: Nathan, Stephen, Samuel, Ann, Martha, Mary, Patience, Lydia, Elizabeth, and Hannah.

Mar 3, 1783   May 13, 1783
Butler, Sarah. Executor: Boston Obalt. Heidleberg Township. Child: Mary.

Feb 5, 1777   May 13, 1783
McDowell, James. Executor: Omitted. Manheim Township. Wife: Agness McDowell.

Apr 15, 1783   May 13, 1783
Emery, Samuel. Executor: William Leth. Township omitted. Bequests were made to the following: Capt. Le Brown Debelleowe, Charles Martin R. M. Legion, and to Sgt. William Bawcutt.

May 2, 1783   May 15, 1783
William, Peter. Executors: Henry Markle and Frederick William. Cordorus Township. Children: Peter, Elizabeth and Frederick.

--- --, ----   May 20, 1783
Meyer, Henry. Executors: Magdalena and John Meyer. York County. (German will.)

Apr 15, 1775   May 26, 1783
Lehn, Jonathan. Executors: Samuel Arnold. Paradise Township. Wife: Margaret Lehn. Children: Peter, John, Catharine, Elizabeth, Hannah, and Mary.

Jul 11, 1776   May 29, 1783
Huggins, Jacob. Executor: Ann Huggins. Manchester Township. Wife: Ann Huggins. Children: George, Margaret, and Isabella.

--- --, ----   Jun 10, 1783
Koch, Johannes. Executors: Mary Koch and Frederick Rider. York County. (German will.)

May 10, 1783   Jun 20, 1783
Maurer, Herman. Executors: Daniel Messerly and John Retrof. Dover Township. Wife: Anna Maria Maurer. Children: John, Catharine, Juliana, Elizabeth, George, and Adam.

--- --, ----   Jul 12, 1783
McWilliams, James. Executors: Alexander Brown and John McWilliam. York County. (Will not on record, but on file.)

Jun 2, 1783   Jul 14, 1783
Croll, John. Executors: Peter Shultz and George Lewis Lefler.
Manchester Township. Wife: Clara Croll. Children: John, Daniel,
Magdalena wife of Frederick, Hubly, and Susanna.

Mar 12, 1782   Aug 16, 1783
McFarlan, William. Executors: James McFarlan and J. Chamberlin.
Reading Township. Wife: Sarah McFarlan. Children: James, Mary wife
of John Johnston, Alice wife of Robert Fleming, and Thomas.

--- --, ----   Sep 12, 1783
Moore, Elizabeth. Executors: E. Langworthy and Michael Dondell. York
Town Township. (German will.)

Aug 8, 1783   Sep 20, 1783
Hohf, Henry. Executors: Stephen Patery, Henry Danner, and Daniel
Uttz. Manheim Township. Wife: Mary Hohf. Children: Anna, Barbara,
and Nicholas.

Aug 4, 1782   Oct 1, 1783
Flemming, John. Executors: William McPherson and James Getty.
Cumberland Township. Wife: Elizabeth Flemming. Children: (Five
children, names not given.)

Oct 18, 1772   Oct 3, 1783
Furrer, Christian. Executors: Benjamin Brackbill, Elizabeth and Henry
Furrer. Newberry Township. Wife: Elizabeth Furrer. Children: Henry,
Daniel, Christian, and Samuel.

Sep 28, 1780   Oct 16, 1783
Derstein, Michael. Executors: John Frichler and Henry Strickler.
Hellam Township. Wife: Barbara Derstein. Children: Michael,
Magdalena, Christly, Barbara, Mary, and Elizabeth.

Jun 23, 1783   Oct 17, 1783
Cuthbertson, William. Executor: David Denwoody. Cumberland
Township. Wife: Rosanna Cuthbertson. Child: William. Grandchildren:
Lettis, Allen, Nancy, and Rosanna.

Jul 22, 1783   Oct 22, 1783
Miller, Harman. Executors: Conrad Brubaker and Michael Miller.
Windsor Township. Children: Michael, Lovice, Frederick, Herman,
Simeon, Christian, Henry, and Conrad.

Jul 28, 1783   Oct 31, 1783
White, John. Executors: James Johnson and Moses McLean. Cumberland Township. Wife: Dorcas White. Children: Henry, John, Isaah, Ann wife of James McLean, Robert, William and Stephen.

Feb --, 1783   Nov 10, 1783
Little, Casper. Executors: Adam Winterote and Andrew Little. Mt. Joy Township. Wife: Susanna Little. Children: John, Joseph, Adam, Jacob, David, Peter, Susanna, Catharine, Hannah, Andrew, Trony, Henry, Samuel, and George.

Oct 21, 1783   Nov 10, 1783
Bonine, James. Executors: Daniel and Thomas Bonine. Township omitted. Children: Elizabeth wife of Thomas Prier, Daniel, Thomas and James.

Mar 16, 1778   Nov 12, 1783
Wertz, Wilhelmus. Executor: Peter Dierdorf. Reading Township. Legatees: (Bro. and Sister) Peter and Margaret wife of Detrich Fanstick.

Apr 23, 1777   Nov 13, 1783
Hatton, Robert. Executors: Leonard Hatton and James Maxwell. Huntington Township. Wife: Elizabeth Hatton. Children: Edward, James, Jane, Rachel, and Leonard.

Oct 3, 1783   Nov 15, 1783
Baughman, John. Executor: Jacob Baughman. Warrington Township. Children: Jacob, John, Anna, Mary and Franey.

Oct 21, 1783   Nov 29, 1783
Eaby, John J. Executors: Henry Tyson and Stephen Landrs. Windsor Township. Wife: Magdalena Eaby. Children: John, Christian, Magdalena, Henry, Jacob, Elizabeth, Barbara, and Ann.

Nov 17, 1783   Nov 29, 1783
Love, William. Executors: John Love and Elisha Kirk. Yorktown Township. Wife: Mary Love. Children: Thomas and James.

Nov 19, 1783   Dec --, 1783
Bauer, Martin. Executors: Henry Wolf and Michael Welsh. Manchester Township. Wife: Rosina Bauer. There were five children, their names were not recorded.

Oct 10, 1774   Dec 15, 1783
Buchanan, John. Executor: Omitted. Warrington Township. Children: John, Jacob, Anna, Barbara, Mary and Fornica.

Oct 18, 1783   Feb 20, 1784
Monfort, Peter. Executors: G. Vanarsdael and Lawrence Monfort. York County. Wife: Charity Monfort.

--- --, ----   Feb 22, 1784
Quickel, George. Executors: John Hameisse and Frederick Eicholtz. York County. (German will.)

Mar 12, 1783   Feb 23, 1784
Pather, Philip. Executors: Bernhart Allewelt and Henry Slagle. Berwick Township. Wife: Anna Barbara Pather. Children: Elizabeth wife of Bernhart Allewelt, Margaret wife of Herman Roat, Catharine wife of Andrew Maurer, and Susanna wife of Wendle Rockey.

Apr 10, 1780   Feb 26, 1784
Pecher, Simon. Executor: John Beeker. Reading Township. Children: John, Mary wife of ---- Bodenhimer, Eve wife of ---- Myers, and Elizabeth wife of Michael Coal. Grandchildren: Simeon and Henry (sons of John).

Jul 20, 1781   Feb 26, 1784
Sullivan, Timothy. Executor: Samuel Moore. York County. Legatees: Samuel Moore of Carrols Delight, Maryland.

Apr 10, 1780   Feb 26, 1784
Becker, Simon. Executor: John Becker. Reading Township. Children: John, Mary, Eve, and Elizabeth wife of Michael Coal. Grandchild: Henry (son of John).

Aug 25, 1781   Mar 2, 1784
Miller, Casper. Executors: Catharine Miller and Daniel Musser. York Town Township. Wife: Catharine Miller.

Jun 17, 1783   Mar 8, 1784
Simpson, James Executors: James Speer and James McMordie. Cumberland Township. Wife: Agness Simpson. Children: Agness, Alexander and Jonathan.

Oct 2, 1782   Mar 19, 1784
Kehler, Martin. Executors: Peter Dihl and Philip Shickard. York

Township. Children: (Six whose names were not given.)

Jul 6, 1783   Mar 23, 1784
Miller, Nicholas. Executors: L. Snearinger and G. Ketsmiller. Germany Township. Wife: Catharine Miller. Children: Jacob and Nicholas.

Sep 22, 1783   Mar 23, 1784
Cochran, John. Executors: William Cochran and William Porter. Hamiltonsban Township. Wife: Sarah Cochran. Children: William, Andrew, and (four others whose names are not given.) *(? - James, John, Oliver, and Mary wife of James ----.)*

Feb 5, 1784   Mar 25, 1784
Rautenbush, Henry. Executors: Samuel Arnold and Peter Deardorff. Berwick Township. Wife: Anna Rautenbush. Children: John, Soloman, Daniel, Michael, Elizabeth wife of John Baker, Jacob, Esther, Henry, and Caty wife of Christian Grove.

Mar 11, 1784   Mar 31, 1784
Thompson, James. Executor: Alexander Thompson. Hopewell Township. Legatees: (Bros. and Sister) Alexander, Joseph, Allen and Agness Tompson.

Jul --, 1776   Apr 5, 1784
Hussey, Riccord. Executor: Marian Hussey. Warrington Township. Wife: Marian Hussey. Children: Amos, (names and number of others not given.)

Apr 8, 1783   Apr 6, 1784
Krebs, Ludwig. Executors: George Krebs and Barnet Zeigler. Cordorus Township. Wife: Margaret Krebs. Children: Margaret, Jeremiah, Peter, George, Elizabeth, and Katharina.

Feb 13, 1781   Apr 6, 1784
Murray, John. Executor: Thomas Johnson. Hamiltonsban Township. Wife: Elizabeth Murray. Child: Mary.

Jan 17, 1777   Apr 7, 1784
Cook, Peter. Executors: Samuel and Jesse Cook. Warrington Township. Wife: Sarah Cook. Children: Jesse, Joseph, Samuel, Hannah, Ann, Sarah, and Peter.

Dec 12, 1783   Apr 7, 1784
Cook, Ann. Executor: Benjamin Walker. Warrington Township.
Brothers: Samuel and Peter. Sister: Hannah. Nieces: Rebecca and
Sarah (children of Samuel).

Dec 30, 1782   Apr 15, 1784
Raymer, Frederick. Executors: John Raymer and Jacob Lanius.
Manchester Township. Wife: Catharine Raymer. Children: John and
Adam.

Nov 27, 1783   Apr 22, 1784
Smith, Joseph. Executor: Barbara Smith. York Town Township. Wife:
Barbara Smith.

Dec 23, 1783   May 11, 1784
Kerr, Josiah. Executors: William Kerr and James McIlhenny. Mt.
Pleasant Township. Wife: Mary Kerr. Children: Josiah, Alexander,
Susanna wife of John Coulter, and William. Grandchildren: Josiah and
John (children of Alexander), Jannet, Mary, Susanna, Martha, and John
Coulter.

Apr 20, 1784   May 18, 1784
Shaffer, Paul. Executors: Anna E. Shaffer and Henry Tyson. Windsor
Township. Wife: Anna E. Shaffer. Children: Abigal wife of Henry
Albright, Barbara wife of John Dellinger, Christiana wife of Jacob
Denbinger and Catharine wife of --- Imsrviller.

Feb 14, 1784   May 20, 1784
Owings, Susanna. Executor: Hannah Owings. Hanover Township.
Legatees: Hannah Owings (mother) and Hannah Owings (sister).

Aug 17, 1782   May 26, 1784
Benedict, Melchoir. Executors: John Hay and Grace Lewis Lifler. Dover
Township. Wife: Catharine Benedict.

Apr 16, 1804   Jun 17, 1784
Paxton, John. Executors: Mary and Isaac Paxton. Mt. Joy Township.
Wife: Mary Paxton. Children: John, Isaac, Sarah wife of Thomas Fergus,
and Elizabeth.

--- --, ----   Jul 8, 1784
Sharer, Jacob. Executors: Philip Grenn and John D. Sharer. York
County. (German will.)

Dec 28, 1781   Jul 16, 1784
Sultzberger, Jacob. Executor: Anna B. Sultzberger. York Town Township. Wife: Anna B. Sultzberger. Children: Andrew and Maria.

May 6, 1784   Jul 27, 1784
Scott, William. Executors: William Porter and William Cochran. Hamiltonsban Township. Wife: Jean Scott. Children: Anne, Margaret, William, Leivinia, Martha and Mary.

--- --, ----   Aug 1, 1784
Geentil, Adam. Executor and Wife: Anna Margaret Geentil. York County. German will.

May 29, 1782   Aug 2, 1784
Shupp, Jacob. Executors: Martin Shupp and Conrad Swope. Mt. Pleasant Township. Wife: Barbara Shupp. Children: Martin, Peter, Jacob and Louis.

Jun 6, 1784   Aug 6, 1784
Fleming, Robert. Executors: Dorothea and Samuel Fleming. Hamiltonsban Township. Wife: Dorothea Fleming.

Oct 14, 1783   Aug 7, 1784
Walter, Jacob. Executor: George Walter and John Leveston. Cordorus Township. Wife: Margaret Walter. Children: George, Anna wife of George Raus, Catharine wife of Henry Bower, Barbara wife of John Leveston and Margaret. Grandchild: Catharine Raus.

Sep 5, 1782   Aug 25, 1784
Pope, John. Executors: Archibald McGrew and William Delap. Tyrone Township. Legatees: Samuel Pope (brother), and Elizabeth (sister) wife of Daniel Hammond.

Jul 7, 1784   Sep 9, 1784
Peterman, Michael. Executors: John Herbach and Henry Tyson. Windsor Township. Wife: Anna Mary Peterman. Children: Margaret, Catharine wife of Jacob Lefever, Elizabeth wife of John Bollinger, Annamary wife of John Mealhoof, Richard, George, Andrew, Jacob, and John.

Jun 23, 1784   Sep 16, 1784
Geiselman, Michael. Executors: Michael Geiselman and Barnet Zeigler. Shrewsbury Township. Wife: Margaret Geiselman. Children: George,

Michael, Frederick, John, Jacob, Elizabeth wife of Frederick Rumel, Magdalena wife of John Kunkle, Catharine wife of George Walter, Eve wife of Samuel Moser, and Christiana wife of Jacob Correl.

Sep 19, 1784   Sep 29, 1784
Wysong, Ludwig. Executor: Philip Slentz. Heidelberg Township. Wife: Mary Wysong. Child: Ludwig.

Mar 26, 1784   Oct 6, 1784
Lackey, George Executors: Alexander Lackey and Daniel Menteith. Mt. Pleasant Township. Wife: Sarah Lackey. Children: Sarah, Alexander, Catharine, Mary, and Margaret.

Feb 7, 1788   Oct 11, 1784
Meloan, Hannah. Executors: Mathias Meloan and William Mummer. Reading Township. Legatees: Mathias and John (brothers).

--- --, ----   Oct 13, 1784
Kissinger, Conrad. Executors: Elizabeth Kissinger and Peter Diehl. York County. (German will.)

Sep 3, 1784   Oct 13, 1784
Road, Jacob. Executors: Abraham Road and Jacob Brubaker. Paradise Township. Wife: Anna Maria Road. Children: Elizabeth, Christian, Catharine, Joseph, Anna, Ferona, Jacob, Maria and Magdalena.

Oct 3, 1784   Oct 13, 1784
Stump, Mathias. Executors: John Stump and Daniel Ammer. Paradise Township. Wife: Margaret Stump. Children: John, Margaret, Barbara, Elizabeth, Catharine and Mathias.

Sep 15, 1784   Oct 27, 1784
Pofelberger, John. Executors: George Pofelberger and Nicholas Langel. Mt. Pleasant Township. Wife: Margaret Pofelberger. Children: George, John, Peter, Barbara, Margaret, and Katharine.

Sep 14, 1784   Oct 29, 1784
Miller, Michael Executors: John Montorff, Henry Miller, and Hugh Morthland. Huntington Township. Children: Henry, John, Catharine, Margaret, Elizabeth wife of John Fickies, and Susanna.

--- --, ----   Nov 8, 1784
Walter, John. Executor: Mary E. Walter. York County. (German will.)

May 26, 1783   Nov 9, 1784
Spangler, Mary. Executor: John Spangler. York County. Children: George, Balser, Michael, Rudy, Daniel, Juliana wife of Francis Bikel, Elizabeth wife of Francis Huntz and John. Grandchildren: Magdalena, Hannah, John and Elizabeth Bikel.

Jan 5, 1784   Nov 12, 1784
Painter, Valentine. Executor: Jacob Sponseller. Mt. Joy Township. Wife: Magdalena Painter. Children: Andrew, Jacob, George, John, and Christiana.

Jun 2, 1776   Dec 16, 1784
Schneider, Theobald. Executor: Simon Clear. Manheim Township. Wife: Susanna Schneider. Children: Theobald, Mary wife of Jacob Roth, Margaret wife of ---- Schitz and Henry.

Feb 3, 1783   Dec 24, 1784
Hull, Isaac. Executor: Samuel Hull. Warrington Township. Children: Mary, Samuel, Elizabeth, Magdalena, and Ann.

Dec 24, 1784   Jan 4, 1785
Faller, John. Executor: Adam Faller. Mt. Pleasant Township. Wife: (Name not given.) Children: Adam, Maria, Dorothea, and Elizabeth wife of ---- Miller. Grandchildren: John and Magdalena (chldren of Elizabeth).

Dec 29, 1784   Jan 13, 1785
Mayrs, Henry. Executors: Adam Wenteroth and Robert McIlhenny. Mt. Joy Township. Wife: Barbara Mayrs. Children: Barbara, Catharine, Jacob, Henry, John, and George.

--- --, ----   Jan 22, 1785
Kline, Adam. Executors: Christian Lehman and John Reisinger. York County. (German will.)

Apr 29, 1771   Jan 26, 1785
Noll, Philip. Executor: George Noll. Barwick Township. Wife: Elizabeth Noll. Children: John, Susanna wife of Frederick Galvix, George, Christiana wife of ---- Graseas, and Mary.

Dec 29, 1784   Feb 8, 1785
Rhode, Anthony, township of Manchster, York Co., yeoman. Executors: John Rhodes and Christian Lepe. Manchester Township. Wife: Magdalena Rhode. Children: Henry, John, Frainey wife of ---- Strickler,

Christian, Anthony, Frederick, Magdalena wife of ---- Culp and Elizabeth. Part of the will is quoted herein: That my plantation with all the buildings and what thereunto belongs to be praised and put to public sale and my wife to have no part thereof, and said Plantation to be publicly advertised three months before the sale thereof and whoever byeth said Plantation to pay three hundred pounds down at the time of said sale, which sum is to be equally divided between by four eldest children, their heirs or assigns, to wit; Henry Rhodes, John Rhodes, and Frainy Prinimen, formerly Rhodes, and Ann Strickler, formerly Rhodes, at the time of said vandoe, and the remainder part of the price of said plantation to be paid in sale as follows; that is to say, seventy-five pounds in one year after the vandoe, and the same sum of seventy-five pounds yearly every year until the whole be paid, which I give and bequeath in the following manner; that is to say, the first seventy-five pounds to be equally divided between Christian Rhode and Anthony Rhode, Jr., the second payment of seventy-five pounds to be divided equally between Madlene Coulp, formerly Rhode, and Frederick Rhode, and Elizabeth Rhode, and the third payment of seventy-five pounds to be paid unto my two forementioned sons Christian and Anthony, and the fourth payment of seventy-five pounds to be paid unto my forementioned daughter Madlene's son Frederick and daughter ----, the fifth payment of seventy-five pounds and all ---- to more, is to be equally divided among my above named children at the time of payment of each sums or to their heirs and executors, administrators or assigns by my executors hereafter named and likewise every other sum herein mentioned as above described.
To my son Anthony five pounds besides what is already mentioned.

May 12, 1784   Feb 12, 1785
Ziegler, Jacob. Executor: George Zeigler. Huntington Township. Wife: Anna Mary Zeigler. Children: George, Margaret and Jacob.

Jan 8, 1785   Feb 25, 1785
Shoe, Henry. Executors: Susanna Shoe and Frederick Woeff. Berwick Township. Wife: Susanna Shoe. Children: Elizabeth, Susanna, John, Henry and Frederick.

Sep 18, 1784   Mar 3, 1785
Loop, Christian. Executors: John Holk and Frederick Long. Newberry Township. Wife: Christiana Loop.

Nov 25, 1784   Mar 9, 1785
Armor, Thomas. Executor: Robert Bigham. York Township. Child: Thomas. Cousins: Robert Bigham and Thomas Bigham.

Jul 2, 1778   Mar 12, 1785
McAlester, Grabriel. Executor: James McAlester. Mt. Joy Township. Children: John, Elen wife of Hugh Cumins, and James.

Nov 29, 1784   Mar 22, 1785
Campbel, Archibald. Executor: Thomas Campbel. Monaghan Township. Sister: Sarah wife of Joseph McDowell. Brother: John Campbel.

Feb 2, 1785   Mar 25, 1785
Holl, George. Executor: Mary Horf. Manheim Township. Wife: Barbara Holl.

Nov 27, 1784   Mar 27, 1785
Rockey, Henry. Executors: John Adam Yagy and Peter Meyer. Dover Township. Wife: Susanna Rockey. Children: Christopher, Hans, Margaret, Barbara wife of Nicholas Welsh.

Feb 20, 1785   Apr 5, 1785
Rieger, John. Executors: George Kuntz and John Rieger. York County. Wife: Anna Lees Rieger. Child: Jacob. Son-in-law: George Kuntz (wifes' name not given).

Mar 26, 1785   Apr 9, 1785
Spies, Peter. Executors: Killian and George P. Zeigler. Dover Township. Wife: Susanna Spies. Children: Jacob, Peter, Katharine and George.

Dec 12, 1784   Apr 12, 1785
Roose, Frederick. Executors: Andrew Roose and Elinure Underwood. Warrington Township. Wife: Christiana Roose. Children: Andrew, Barbara, Frederick and Rosanna.

Jan 7, 1785   Apr 12, 1785
Pence, Joseph. Executors: Elihn Underwood, Catharine and John Pence. Warrington Township. Wife: Catharine Pence. Children: Michael, Henry, Catharine, John, Joseph, Mary, Philip, and Elizabeth.

Apr 18, 1780   Apr 20, 1785
Murray, Duncan. Executors: Michael Kincaid and David McClellan. Hamiltonsban Township. Wife: Eleanor Murray. Child: John.

Jul 9, 1777   Apr 21, 1785
Crow, Leonard. Executor: Michael Crow. Hellam Township. Wife: Susanna Crow. Children: Susanna, Michael, Alexander, Elizabeth wife of

Paul Kemberly, Catharine wife of Nicholas Esminger, Anna wife of George Strow, and Susanna wife of George Gartner.

Mar 19, 1784   Apr 21, 1785
Smith, John. Executor: James Smith. Huntington Township. Wife: Margaret Smith. Children: George, John, Eleanor wife of Robert Crawford, Elizabeth wife of James Smith and Hugh.

Sep 2, 1784   Apr 22, 1785
Newcomer, Christian. Executors: George and Christian Newcomer. Warrington Township. Wife: Anna Newcomer. Children: George, Christian, and Sally wife of Isaac Deardorff.

Nov 24, 1774   May 4, 1785
Beekar, William. Executors: John Heckman and Christiana Beekar. York Town Township. Wife: Christiana Beekar. Children: Peter, Adolph, Christopher, George and Coleman. Grandchildren: Catharine and Anna (children of Adolph).

Apr 5, 1783   May 6, 1785
Williams, Benjamin. Executors: Martha Williams and James Cadwalader. Warrington Township. Wife: Martha Williams. Child: Sara. Grandchildren: Hannah Smith and Sarah and Jane Ratcakin (parents' names not given).

Nov 24, 1774   May 17, 1785
Fisher, Nicholas. Executor: Valentine Fisher. Manheim Township. Wife: Christiana Fisher. Children: Peter, Adolph, Christopher, George, and Coleman. Grandchildren: Ann and Maria (children of Adolph).

Aug 18, 1785   May 19, 1785
Young, William. Executor: Samuel Young. Manallen Township. Children: Samuel, Agness, Amelia wife of Andrew Mitchel, Mary and Ann.

--- --, ----   May 23, 1785
Shaffer, Anna Margaret. Executor: Peter Feiser. York County. (German will.)

Aug 29, 1783   May 26, 1785
Mays, Charles. Executors: Samuel Mays. Menallen Township. Wife: Dorcas Mays. Children: Charles, Elizabeth, John, William, and Samuel. Grandchildren: Charles and Elizabeth Mays (children of Charles).

93

Apr 27, 1782   Jun 1, 1785
Blair, Brise. Executors: John Blair and Brise Blair. Warrington Township. Wife: (Name not given.) Children: John, Brise, James, Mary wife of William Anderson, Anna, Susanna, Jane, Eleanor, and Barbara wife of James Anderson.

May 5, 1785   Jun 1, 1785
Bricker, Christopher. Executor: John Brise Blair, Jr. Manheim Township. Wife: Margaret Bricker. Children: Jacob, Juliana and Ann.

Sep 29, 1784   Jun 3, 1785
Ebert, Michael. Executors: Michael, Philip and Martin Ebert. Manchester Township. Wife: Eve Ebert. Children: Michael, Martin, Philip, Elizabeth, Helena, John, and Adam.

May 9, 1783   Jun 9, 1785
Hess, Valentine. Executors: Jacob Kinser and Isaac Hess. Huntington Township. Wife: Rachel Hess. Children: Isaac, Valentine, Henry, and Elizabeth wife of ---- Wafe. Grandchild: Martin (son of Elizabeth).

Mar 10, 1785   Jun 14, 1785
Yost, Nicholas, Jr. Executor: Robert Yost. Shrewsbury Township. Wife: Rachel Yost. Children: (the names and number not given).

May 12 1785   Jul 2, 1785
Underwood, William. Executors: Benj. and Elihu Underwood. Warrington Township. Wife: Ruth Underwood. Children: William, Lydia, Jane, Ruth, Hannah, Jesse, Rachel, Anna, Obed, Eliher and Zephina. Grandchild: Hannah Underwood (parents' names not given).

Jun 15, 1785   Jul 4, 1785
Kreber, Philip. Executor: Adam Kreber. Yorktown Township. Wife: Christiana Kreber. Brothers: Adam and Martin Kreber.

Apr 24, 1782   Jul 15, 1785
Haeffner, Mattheis. Executor: Christian Schroth. Manheim Township. Wife: Margaret Haeffner. Children: Ann wife of Conrad Ludwig, Apolon, and Mary. Grandchildren: Jacob, Conrad, George, and Abraham (sons of Ann).
Will of Mattheis Haeffner of Manheim Township, York County, Pennsylvania. Dated 24 April 1782. Wife Markret, oldest daughter Anna Mary, daughter Apolon. Four sons of my oldest daughter Anna Mary, that is to say Jacob Loudwick and Conrad Loudwick and George Michael

Loudwick and Abraham Loudwick. The above named Jacob Loudwick (oldest son of my oldest daughter). The above named four sons of Christopher Loudwick, deceased. I make and nominate my trusty nephu, Christopher Schroth, to be my whole and sole executor. Witnesses: Nicholas Wofgang, George Hellman, Jacob Brunkhard, Mattheisz Haeffner.

Jul 4, 1785   Jul 20, 1785
Myer, Martin. Executor: Conrad Shindler. Township: Omitted. Children: Jacob, Martin, and Catharine.

Mar 28, 1785   Jul 27, 1785
Dehoff, Henry. Executor: Nicholas Weyant. Manchester Township. Children: Anna M. Nicholas Weyant, George, and Nicholas.

Jul 4, 1785   Aug 9, 1785
Bonine, Thomas. Executors: Daniel Bonine and Samuel Kroan. Newberry Township. Wife: Mary Bonine. Brother: Daniel Bonine.

Feb 9, 1784   Aug 24, 1785
Chambers, Robert. Executors: William Walker and William Delap. Manallen Township. Children: Henry, James, Arthur, Agness wife of Thomas Stewart, John, and Roland.

Feb 24, 1785   Aug 24, 1785
Finley, Michael. Executors: Joseph and Ebeneer Finley. York County. Wife: Ann Finley. Children: Joseph and Ebenezer.

Sep 14, 1781   Sep 1, 1785
Frank, David. Executor: Michael Carle. Manheim Township. Wife: Anna Mary Frank.

Aug 16, 1785   Sep 16, 1785
Penrose, William. Executor: Thomas and John Penrose. Huntington Township. Wife: Ann Penrose. Children: William, Mary, Jane, Phebe, Ann, Susanna, Thomas, and John.

May 5, 1785   Oct 5, 1785
Stauffer, Abraham. Executors: Isaac Deardorff and Christiana Stauffer. Monaghan Township. Wife: Christiana Stauffer. Children: John, Henry, Anna, Rebecca. Sons-in-law: Jacob Lerue and Henry Smith (wives' names not given).

Dec 5, 1774   Oct 14, 1785
Heckendorn, John. Executor: William Lanius. Yorktown Township. Wife: Barbara Heckendorn. Children: John, Barbara, Catharine, Elizabeth, Ann, Maria, and Christian. William Lanius was a son-in-law, wife's name not given.

Aug --, 1784   Oct 19, 1785
Hayney, Patrick. Executor: Jonathan Pain. York County. Children: Patrick, Mary, Ann, Catharine, Sarah, and Edward. Grandson: Edward (son of Edward).

Jul 29, 1782   Oct 26, 1785
Scannal, Lorentz. Executors: Nicholas and Catharine Marshall. Germany Township. Wife: Catharine Scannal. Children: (Names and number not given.)

Jan 20, 1785   Oct 26, 1785
Wilson, George, Executors: Benj. Wilson and Jonathan Wright. Manallen Township. Children: Benj., Lydia wife of John Griff, Sarah wife of William Rusk and (son-in-law James Hammond - wife's name not given). Grandchild: George Hammond.

Oct 7, 1785   Oct 31, 1785
Climmer, Valentine. Executors: Elizabeth Clemer and Adam Winteroth. Petersburg Township, York County. Wife: Margaret Climmer. Children: John, George, Elemer, and Susanna.

Sep 29, 1785   Nov 2, 1785
Rankin, John. Executors: Elizabeth Rankin. York Town Township. Wife: Elizabeth Rankin. Children: John, Moses, Hanna and Rebecca.

Oct 3, 1785   Nov 21, 1785
Ammer, Daniel Executors: Daniel Ammer and Samuel Arnold. Wife: Barbara Ammer. Paradise Township. Children: Daniel, Anna wife of John Jeigler, Barbara wife of Valentine Fickies, and Catharine wife of Michael Winebright.

Aug 13, 1785   Dec 2, 1785
Boyd, William. Executors: Catharine Boyd, Archibald Boyd and James Marwell. Cumberland Township. Wife: Catharine Boyd. Children: William, Robert, Archibald, John, Benjamin, Mary wife of John Caven, Janet and Elizabeth.

Oct 17, 1785   Dec 5, 1785
Klein, Gerlack. Executor: William Moneyer. Berwick Township.
Children: Catharine wife of Jacob Heitzel, Ann wife of Mathias Smock,
Eve wife of William Moneyer, John, and Christian.

Dec 2, 1785   Dec 22, 1785
Beacor, Philip. Executors: Elizabeth Beacor and Casper Snar. Manallan
Township. Wife: Elizabeth Beacor. Children: Frederick, John, Julian,
Mary, Studebacker, Christiana, Ann, Eve, Margaret, Rosen, Elizabeth,
Barbara and Susanna.

May 5, 1776   Dec 24, 1785
Hoff, Adam. Executors: Juleana and Francis Hoff. Cordorus Township.
Children: Francis, (names and number of others not given.)

Sep 23, 1782   Jan 19, 1786
Kelly, Thomas. Executor: John Kelly. Chanceford Township. Wife:
Mary Kelly. Children: James, John, Egemyah wife of Robert Mickey, and
Rebecca.

Oct 30, 1783   Jan 21, 1786
Reiter, Lawrence. Executors: John Mate and John Meyer. Windsor
Township. Wife: Gertrude Reiter. Children: Christopher, Lawrence,
John and Catharine.

Nov 22, 1785   Jan 28, 1786
Hawmmel, Philip. Executors: Anna Mary Hawmmel and Andrew Poully.
Paradise Township. Wife: Anna Mary Hawmmel. Children: Elizabeth,
Jacob, Anna, Eve, Daniel, and Conrad.

Jan 1, 1786   Feb 1, 1786
Jonce, John. Executors: Samuel Landis and Frederick Fetz. Windsor
Township. Wife: Elizabeth Jonce. Children: Magdalena, Catharine, and
Barbara.

Feb 10, 1786   Feb 22, 1786
Sheritz, Arnold. Executor: David Nickey. Manheim Township. Wife:
Catharine Sheritz. Children: Jacob, Conrad and Ludwick.

Aug 6, 1781   Feb 24, 1786
Miller, Henry. Executor: Abraham Miller. Newberry Township. Wife:
Margaret Miller. Children: Henry, John, Adam, Fanny, Barbara, and
Margaret.

Jan 11, 1786   Feb 25, 1786
Appleman, John. Executors: Anne Appleton and Christian Weist. Wife: Anna Margaret Appleman. Paradise Township. Children: Philip, John, Henry, Jacob, Lena, Margaret, Elizabeth, Christiana, Katharine wife of Eppleman, and Conrad.

Jan 11, 1786   Feb 25, 1786
Eppleman, John. Executors: Margaret Eppleman and Christian Weist. Paradise Township. Wife: Anna Margaret Eppleman. Children: Philip, John, Henry, Conrad, Jacob, Lena, Elizabeth, Christiana, and Katharine.

Feb 5, 1786   Mar 1, 1786
Shetter, John. Executors: John Herman, Dorothea and Martin Shetter. Newberry Township. Wife: Dorothea Shetter. Children: John, Andrew, Barbara, Elizabeth, Merea, Margaret, Mady, Samuel, Eve, David and Susanna.

Jan 27, 1786   Mar 8, 1786
Abbot, John. Executors: Archibald McGrew and John McGrew. Wife: Alice Abott. Berwick Township. Children: Edward, Margaret wife of John Green, Thomas, Eleanor wife of James Mackey, Alice wife of Donaldson, Catharine and Elizabeth.

Feb 6, 1776   Mar 10, 1786
Fishell, John. Executor: Michael Fishell. Yorktown Township. Wife: Anna Maria Fishell. Children: Adam, Michael, Rosina wife of George Geyer, John, Anna wife of Andrew Borheck, and Margaret wife of Hey Lenius.

Sep 1, 1784   Mar 14, 1786
Wildt, Nicholas. Executors: Valentine Wildt and Jonas Rudisilly. Manchester Township. Children: Valentine, John, Adam, Samuel, George, Mary, Elizabeth and Ann.

Jan 29, 1786   Mar 27, 1786
Neely, Joseph. Executor: Christian Wart. Tyrone Township. Children: Joseph, Peter, Henry, Mary, William, and Catharine.

Mar 5, 1786   Mar 29, 1786
McIlheny, Robert. Executors: William and Robert McIlheny. Straban Township. Wife: Agness McIlheny. Children: William, Violet wife of John McClure, Margaret wife of Samuel Moody, Anna wife of William King. Granddaughter: Agness Elliott (parents' names not given).

Dec 20, 1785   Mar 29, 1786
Monges, Charles. Executors: Michael Miller and F. Lichenknecht. Windsor Township. Wife: Mary Elizabeth Monges. Children: Michael, Mary, Elizabeth, Peter, Ann, John, Adam, and Jacob.

May 12, 1786   Apr 27, 1786
Ewing, James. Executors: William Ewing, Alexander Porter and Moses McClain. Franklin Township. Wife: Eleanor Ewing. Children: William, Elizabeth, Margaret, Martha, Ann, Eleanor, and Thomas.

Jun 12, 1785   May 6, 1786
Heibley, Jacob. Executors: Sophia and Paul Heibley. Shrewsbury Township. Wife: Sophia Heibley. Children: Magdalena, Christopher, Michael, Sophia, Anna, Paul, Christian, John, Juliano, Jacob.

Oct 17, 1777   May 17, 1786
Adams, John. Executor: Samuel Adams. Hamiltonsban Township. Children: Samuel, Mary wife of Robert Patton, Samuel (son of Samuel).

Oct 25, 1785   May 18, 1786
McClean, Archibald. Executors: Moses McClean and Jacob Barnetz. York Town Township. Children: Alexander, Elizabeth wife of Thomas Clingan, Mary wife of Jacob Barnitz, Ann wife of Samuel Leech, Rebecca wife of Samuel Erwin, and Esther. Grandson: Archibald McClean (parents' names not given).

Apr 6, 1786   Jun 10, 1786
Greesemer, Henry. Executors: Elizabeth and Adam Greesemer. Heidelberg Township. Wife: Elizabeth Greesemer. Children: Catharine and Adam.

Jun 9, 1786   Jun 23, 1786
Felker, Frederick. Executor: Dorothea Felker. Manchester Township. Wife: Dorothea Felker. Children: Yost, Frederick, and Christiana.

--- --, ----   Jun 24, 1786
Wagoner, Yost. Executors: Adam Eichelberger and John Kerr. Manheim Township. (German will.)

--- --, 1785   Jul 5, 1786
Deshner, John. Executors: George Dice and Daniel Cayler. Windsor Township. Wife: Anna Deshner. Children: George, Barbara wife of Henry Renbarger, Mary wife of George Dice, and Elizabeth wife of Daniel

Cayler.

--- --, ----　　　Jul 7, 1786
Keffer, Frederick. Executor: George Kuntz. Township: Omitted. (German will.)

Jun 19, 1786　　Jul 22, 1786
Stover, Christian. Executors: Christian Stover, Henry Strickler and Henry Leiphard. Hellam Township. Wife: Anna Maria Stover. Children: Christian, Henry, Catharine and Elizabeth. Grandchild: Peter Sansany (parents' name not given).

Mar 8, 1786　　Jul 26, 1786
Sell, Abraham. Executors: James and Adam Sell. Germany Township. Wife: Hannah Sell. Children: Jacob, Adam, Catharine wife of Henry Mayr and Eve wife of Nicholas Dill.

Jul 8, 1786　　Jul 27, 1786
Bender, Jacob. Executors: Conrad Bender and Catharine Bender. Manallen Wife: Catharine Bender. Children: Henry, Jacob, John, Michael, Elizabeth wife of Jacob Males, and Mary wife of Hy Snider.

Aug 5, 1786　　Aug 30, 1786
Cosine, Cornelius. Executors: Francis Cassat, George Williams, and David Beaty. Straban Township. Wife: Mary Cosine. Children: John, Garard, Anaty wife of Simon Vanasdale, Leine wife of John Bodine, Ann wife of Barnet Smock, Jane wife of Abraham Broca, Elizabeth wife of Peter Banta, and Cornelius.

Aug 3, 1786　　Sep 12, 1786
Housman, Jacob. Executors: Charles and Michael Housman. Windsor Township. Wife: Barbara Housman. Children: Michael, Christian, Christiana wife of Jacob Hance, Catharine wife of John Gohn, and Charles.

Oct 10, 1783　　Sep 28, 1786
Dotterer, Michael. Executor: Omitted. Children: Michael, Sophia, Anny, Margaret, Mary, and Conrad.

Jul 26, 1786　　Oct 3, 1786
Hellman, Jacob. Executors: Andrew Billmeyer and Jacob Welshantz. Yorktown Township. Wife: Magdalena Hellman. Children: (Two children whose names were not given.)

--- --, ----   Oct 3, 1786
Strohmenger, Jacob. Executors: George Adich and George Weinhold.
Windsor Township. (German will.)

Aug 12, 1785   Oct 4, 1786
Klein, John Ludwig or John Ludwig Little. (The signature on the will is
John Ludwig Little, but on the records "Klein".) Executor: Frederick
Kline (or Little). Germany Township. Wife: Mary Eva Kline (or Little)
Children: Peter, Frederick, and Margaret wife of ---- Franciscus.

Aug 12, 1785   Oct 4, 1786
Little, John Ludwig. Executor: Frederick Little. Germany Township.
Wife: Mary Eva Little. Children: Peter, Frederick, and Margaret.

Mar 15, 1785   Oct 14, 1786
Sinn, George Christian. Executors: Christopher Lawman and Christian
Sinn. York Town Township. Children: Christian, Mary, Barbara,
Catharine and Mary wife of ---- Lawman. Grandchildren: Catharine,
Mary, Susanna and Christian Lawman.

Jan 10, 1786   Oct 18, 1786
West, Samuel. Executors: G. West and J. Jonest. Fawn Township.
Wife; Priscilla West. Children: Jonathan, George, Rachel, Phebe and
Priscilla.

Aug 3, 1786   Oct 25, 1786
Penry, Robert. Executors: James Robinson. Township: Omitted. Wife:
Eleanor Penry. Children: Elizabeth, Alle, and James (Elizabeth and Alle
reside in Ireland).

Apr 28, 1786   Nov 1, 1786
Hoover, John George. Executors: Adam and George Hoover. Dover
Township. Wife: Mary Hoover. Children: Adam and George.

May 14, 1776   Nov 11, 1786
Bodine, John. Executor: Simon Vanarsdalen. York County. Wife: Lume
Bodine. Children: Abraham, (there were other children, but names and
number were not recorded).

Sep 28, 1786   Nov 14, 1786
Adich, John. Executors: John Adich and Jacob Hart. Township omitted.
Wife: Maria Magdalena Adich (maiden name was Haas). Children:
Henry, Peter, George, John, Maria and Elizabeth.

Feb 4, 1776   Nov 16, 1786
McBride, Jean. Executor: Robert Orr. Mt. Pleasant Township.
Children: James, Andrew, Susanna, and Margaret.

Dec 12, 1780   Nov 23, 1786
King, Charles. Executor: Barbara King. York County. Wife: Barbara King. Child: Jacob.

Jul 5, 1784   Dec 6, 1786
McIntyre, Alexander. Executors: Andrew McIlvain and David Adams. Berwick Township. Children: John, Jane wife of Hugh Caldwell, Sarah wife of John Kerr, and Martha wife of David Adams. Grandchildren: William Hall Caldwell and two other children of Jane, and four children of John (names not given).

Mar 2, 1786   Dec 18, 1786
Hunt, Roger. Executor: Edward Hunt. Huntington Township. Mother: Jane Hunt. Sister: Elizabeth Hunt. Brother: Edward Hunt.

Nov 7, 1786   Jan 3, 1787
Helman, John. Executors: Barnet Zeigler and John Kroll. Cordorus Township. Wife: Anamary Helman. Children: Philip, Michael, and Catharine wife of Peter Kuntz. (The oldest daughter, name not given, was married to Godfrey Klindiens.)

Nov 10, 1785   Jan 10, 1787
Rudisere, Jacob. Executor: Jacob Herback. Manchester Township. Children: Jacob, Jonas, Philip, Baltzer, John, Henry, Catharine wife of John Rever, Elizabeth wife of Michael Ebech, Barbara wife of Godfrey Leib, Susanna wife of Andrew Smith, Dorothea wife of George Meyer and Mary wife of Andrew Ritter.

Dec 26, 1786   Jan 11, 1787
Kohler, Andrew. Executor: Andrew Kohler. Manchester Township. Wife: Maria Kohler. Children: Joseph, Andrew, (and seven others whose names were not given.)

Jan 13, 1787   Jan 26, 1787
Grey, Thomas. Executor: William Grey. Berwick Township. Wife: Elizabeth Gray. Children: John, Isabella wife of John Weilley, William, Elizabeth wife of John Ewing, Joseph, and Thomas.

Sep 25, 1786   Jan 31, 1787
Clapsadle, Michael. Executor: Adam Casper. Mount Pleasant Township.
Wife: Catharine Clapsadle. Children: Francis, George, Paul, Michael,
Daniel, Catharine, Mary, and Barbara wife of Adam Crasser.

Apr 9, 1777   Feb 23, 1787
Gribble, John. Executors: Elias Pierson and Alexander Sanderson.
Huntington Township. Wife: Jane Gribble. Children: John, Vevi,
Elizabeth, Mary, Vincent, Archibald, and Jane.

Jan 17, 1787   Feb 24, 1787
Milliron, John. Executors: Regena Milliron and David Mickey. Hanover
Township. Wife: Regena Milliron. Child: Jacob.

--- --, ----   Mar 21, 1787
Flory, Magdalena. Executor: Henry Strickler. York County. German
will.

Dec 4, 1786   Mar 21, 1787
Hantz, Andrew. Executors: Catharine and John Hantz. Dover Township.
Wife: Catharine Hantz. Children: John, Andrew, Jacob, Barbara, and
Catharine.

--- --, ----   Mar 27, 1787
Staab, Catharine. Executors: Sebastian Obolt. Heidelberg Township.
(German will.)

Mar 9, 1784   Mar 30, 1787
Christ, Philip. Executor: Peter Wolf. Paradise Township. Children:
Adam and John.

Jan 22, 1787   Mar 31, 1787
Ressler, Mathias. Executors: Joseph Bear and George Meller. Newberry
Township. Wife: Catharine Ressler. Children: Michael, Catharine,
Henry, Dena and Elizabeth.

Oct 19, 1786   Apr 17, 1787
Good, David. Executors: Henry Tyson and Charles Guth. Windsor
Township. Wife: Anna Mary Good. Children: David and Anna.
Grandchildren: John Mouch, John, Ann and Mary Mosey. (parents' names
not given).

May 3, 1778   Apr 24, 1787
Montgomery, Patrick. Executor: John Montgomery. Manallen Township.
Child: James.

Nov. 10, 1786   May 12, 1787
Wagoner, Margaretta. Executor: David Nickey. Manheim Townsihp.
Widow of Joseph Wagoner. Child: Catharine wife of (name not given).
Grandchildren: Ann and Margaret (daughters of Catharine).

Jan 24, 1787   May 22, 1787
Meyer, Nicholas. Executors: John and William Meyer. Huntington
Township. Children: John, Ludwig, William, Philip, Peter, David,
Nicholas, Mary, Margaret, Susanna, Albert, Jacob, and Elizabeth.

Jun 21, 1786   May 24, 1787
Whiteford, Hugh. Executor: Omitted. Harford County, MD. Wife: Ann
Whiteford. Children: John, Anna, Mary and Hugh.

Sep 19, 1787   May 29, 1787
Updegraff, Jacob. Executors: Joseph and Jacob Updegraff. York Town
Township. Wife: Barbara Updegraff. Children: Joseph, Jacob and Peter.

Dec 10, 1783   Jun 5, 1787
Morgan, William. Executor: Benjamin Tyson. Windsor Township.
Children: John, Elizabeth wife of John Ament, Nathaniel, Mary wife of
Benj. Tyson, David, Margaret, and William. Grandchild: Catharine
Morgan (child of John).

--- --, ----   Jun 15, 1787
Shailey, Jacob. Executors: John and Andrews Shailey. Mt. Joy Township.
(German will.)

Mar 8, 1787   Jun 20, 1787
Yost, Nicholas. Executors: George Strake and Conrad Lamb. York
County. Wife: Catharine Yost. Children: Abraham, Mary wife of Conrad
Lamb, Ann wife of Francis Streithoff and Catharine wife of Jacob
Burnhart.

Apr 23, 1787   Jun 22, 1787
Hammond, John. Executors: Nathan Hammond and William Griffith.
Manallen Township. Wife: Deobrah Hammond. Children: Nathan, Sarah
wife of William Griffith, Elizabeth wife of John Wright, Mary wife of

Aaron Garrison, and Tamer wife of John Garrison.

May 18, 1781   Jul 11, 1787
Sneidman, Bastian. Executor: Stephen Reep. Hellam Township. Wife: Loreena Sneidman. Child: Daniel.

Sep 29, 1785   Jul 28, 1787
Troup, Paul. Executors: Benj. Fahnestick and Henry Tramb. Reading Township. Wife: Mary Troup. Children: Henry, Peter, John, Paul, Robert, Philip, Mary and Margaret.

Nov 13, 1779   Aug 2, 1787
Lilly, Anna. Executor: Thomas Lilly. Berwick Township. Child: Thomas.

Jan 1, 1787   Aug 3, 1787
Ritchey, Matthew. Executors: Andrew Tompson and William Walker. Tyrone Township. Wife: Rachel Ritchey. Children: David, John, Robert, Mary wife of Matthew Mitchel, Agness wife of Benj. Brown, Jean wife of Ebenezer Mitchel, Isabella wife of James Rickel, Rebecca, Matthew, James, Anna wife of Adam Ritchey, Margaret, William and George. Grandchild: Matthew Mitchel (son of Jean).

Sep 30, 1784   Aug 15, 1787
Braneman, William. Executors: Mary Braneman and Joseph Brillhardt. Cordorus Township. Wife: Mary Braneman. Children: Christian, Johanna, William, David, Richard, Sarah and Anna.

--- --, ----   Aug 18, 1787
Nenkoment, Ulrich. Executor: Magdalena Nenkoment. Hellam Township. (German will.)

Apr 16, 1787   Aug 28, 1787
Vanarsdalen, Cornelius. Executors: Simon and William Vanarsdalen. Straban Township. Wife: Jenne Vanarsdalen. Children: Simon, Luck, William, John, Ida, Anna and Margaret.

Nov 16, 1782   Aug 28, 1787
Vanarsdalen, Garret. Executors: Simon and William Vanarsdalen. York County. Wife: Tracey Vanarsdalen. Children: Garret, Jack, Joseph, Alleda, Janetec, Charity and Sarah. Grandchildren: Ida and Creasy Vanarsdalen (parents' names not given).

Sep 7, 1787   Sep 21, 1787
Wolf, Jonas. Executors: Henry Hull and Garret Dorland. Berwick Township. Wife: Appolonia Wolf. Children: Jacob, John, Appolonia, Catharine, Adam, Christianna, Frederick, Elizabeth and Andrew.

Aug 10, 1787   Sep 21, 1787
Briegner, Barbara. Executors: Andrew Young and Jacob Noel. Berwick Township. Sister: Catharine wife of Andrew Young.

Jun 17, 1782   Sep 26, 1787
Sarback, Jacob. Executor: Christian Sarback. Berwick Township. Wife: Catharine Sarback. Children: Christiana, Elizabeth, Jacob, David, Susanna, Michael and Catharina wife of Christian Rafinsberger.

--- --, ----   Oct 15, 1787
Young, John Nicholas. Executors: Christian Young and George Adick. Windsor Township. (German will.)

Oct 30, 1785   Oct 29, 1787
Leech, Thomas Sr. Executor: Thomas Leech. Warrington Township. Wife: Sarah Leech. Children: Rachel, Jane, Sarah, and Thomas.

Mar 2, 1787   Nov 16, 1787
McPike, Daniel. Executors: David Moore and James Sweeney. Cumberland Township. Children: William, Anna, James, and John. Grandchildren: Margaret and William (children of William).

Nov 4, 1785   Dec 10, 1787
Wein, Jacob. Executor: Henry Wein. Heidelberg Township. Wife: Elizabeth Wein. Children: Adam and Henry.

Jan 15, 1782   Dec 15, 1787
Pressel, David. Executors: Catharine and Valentine Pressel. Berwick Township. Wife: Catharine Pressel. Children: Daniel, Catharine, David, Mary, and Elizabeth.

--- --, ----   Dec 15, 1787
Bressel, David. Executors: Catharine Russel and Valentine Russel. Berwick Township. There was no will, letters testamentary were granted to the parties stated.

May 26, 1781   Dec 31, 1787
Arthur, Thomas. Executor: Thomas Wherry. Newberry Township.

Wife: Mary Arthur. Child: Issah.

Dec 10, 1787   Jan 10, 1788
Cook, Joseph. Executor: Elizabeth Cook. Warrington Township. Wife: Elizabeth Cook. Child: John. Stepdaughter: Mary Holland (widow of Thomas Holland).

Dec 21, 1787   Jan 14, 1788
McKinley, William. Executors: Nathaniel Paxton and Elizabeth McKinley. Hamiltonsban Township. Wife: Elizabeth McKinley. Children: Phebe wife of ---- Cochran, William, Sarah, Elizabeth, Margaret, Ann, and James. Grandchildren: Isabella, William, and Phebe Cochran, and Elizabeth McKinley (daughter of James).

--- ---, ----   Jan 14, 1788
Bingel, Leonard. Executors: Barbara Bingel and Jacob Pritt. York County. German will.

Jul 30, 1787   Jan 31, 1788
Walker, Joseph, Executors: James Dixon and Samuel Walker. York County. Wife: Margaret Walker. Children: James, Samuel, Grace wife of Hugh McCurdy, Mary wife of Joseph Walker and Sarah wife of Thomas Porter. Grandchildren: Mary McCurdy and Letitia Walker (child of Mary).

Dec 10, 1787   Jan 31, 1788
Miller, John. Executor: William King. Straban Township. Child: Rebecca wife of Thomas Anderson.

Jan 4, 1788   Jan 31, 1788
McKinley, Isaac. Executors: James Weakley and William Gilliland. Menallen Township. Wife: Elizabeth McKinley. Children: Martha, Elizabeth wife of David Lusk, and Rebecca wife of James Weakley. Grandchild: Rebecca Long (child of William Long, mother's name not given). Stepson John Stockton.

Nov 25, 1787   Feb 1, 1788
Eichelberger, Adam. Executors: Frederick and Magdalena Eichelberger. Wife: Magdalena Eichelberger. Manheim Township. Children: Frederick, Michael, Samuel, Adam, Joseph, Susanna, and Salome.

May 11, 1782   Feb 8, 1788
Seifert, Adam. Executors: Michael and Anna Maria Seifert. Dover Township. Wife: Anna Maria Seifert. Child: Michael.

Mar 18, 1785   Feb 19, 1788
Miller, Jacob. Executor: Tobias Leib. York County. Wife: Sebilla Catharine Miller. Children: (Names and number not given.)

Jan 29, 1788   Mar 5, 1788
Lambert, Jacob Jr. Executors: Jacob and John Lambert. Dover Township. Wife: Mary Lambert. Children: Jacob, Ann, Elizabeth, George, John, Mary, Catharine wife of John Yoner, and Matalina.

Mar 7, 1787   Mar 7, 1788
Teeterich, Joseph. Executor: Joseph Teeterich. Mt. Pleasant Township. Wife: Mary Teeterich. Children: Joseph, Catharine and Joseph McCain (a son-in-law wife's name not given). Grandchlid: Joseph McCain.

May 17, 1785   Mar 13, 1788
Schryock, John. Executors: John Schyock and Michael Fackler. Manchester Township. Wife: Anna M. Schryock. Children: Christian, Leonard, Michael, Helena, Jacob and John. Son-in-law: Michael Fackler (wifes' name not given.) Anna Magdalena.

Feb 20, 1788   Mar 15, 1788
Correl, Jacob. Executors: Magdalena Correl and Jacob Correl. York Town. Wife: Magdalena Correl. Children: Jacob, (and others whose names were not given.)

Aug 21, 1787   Mar 18, 1788
Fullerton, John. Executors: Samuel Fullerton and John Sutor. Chanceford Township. Wife: Jean Fullerton. Children: Mary wife of ---- Mathers. Grandchildren: Jean and John (children of Mary).

Feb 29, 1788   Mar 21, 1788
Yother, John. Executors: Edward Hunt and Jacob Kinzer. Reading Township. Wife: Esther Yother. Children: Elizabeth and Jacob.

Feb 14, 1787   Mar 24, 1788
Poe, Alexander. Executor: Nicholas Findly. Franklin Township. Wife: Margaret Poe. Children: John, Sarah wife of James Marlin, Margaret wife of Thomas Ormond. Grandchildren: Alexander Poe Ormond, Alexander Marlin, and Mary Pedan (parents' names not given.)

Jul --, 1787   Mar 25, 1788
Yoner, Nicholas. Executor: Daniel May. Dover Township. Wife: Elizabeth Yoner.

Dec 26, 1785   Mar 28, 1788
Frankeberger, John. Executor: Omitted. Paradise Township. Wife: Margaret Frankeberger.

Mar 22, 1788   Apr 3, 1788
Kennedy, David. Executor: Mary Kennedy. Hopewell Township. Wife: Mary Kennedy. Children: (Names and number not given.)

Mar 20, 1788   Apr 21, 1788
Lanius, Jacob. Executors: Henry and William Lanius. Hellam Township. Wife: Barbara Lanius. Children: Catharine, Jacob, John, William, and Barbara (a stepdaughter).

Feb 29, 1788   Apr 24, 1788
McCullough, James. Executor: Jacob McCullough. Fawn Township. Children: John, Sarah, Rebecca, Mary, Margaret, Jacob, and William. Grandson: Andrew Stewart (parents' names not given).

Apr 12, 1783   May 1, 1788
Kerr, John. Executors: Thomas Douglas and John Morron. Hamiltonsban Township. Wife: Agness Kerr. Children: James, Mary, Eliza, Margaret, Nancy, Robert, William, John, and Joseph.

Sep 6, 1783   May 2, 1788
Holdsworth, Samuel. Executors: William Walker and John Semple. Straban Township. Wife: Jane Holdsworth. Children: John, Joseph, Margaret wife of James Deepson, and Catharine wife of James Eatten. Grandchildren: Samuel and John Eatten (sons of Catharine), and four children of Margaret whose names were not given.

Dec 3, 1786   May 26, 1788
Smith, John. Executors: Joseph and William Smith. Hopewell Township. Children: James, Rebecca, Mary, John, Martha wife of John Griffith, David, Francis, Samuel, Joseph and Ann wife of Robert Whitton.

Apr 10, 1786   May 27, 1788
Kitzmiller, Martin. Executor: George Kitzmiller. Manheim Township. Wife: Juliana Kitzmiller. Children: Jacob, John, Catharine wife of Adam Stam, and Mary wife of Henry Kline. Grandchildren: Mary Kline, John,

Leonard, Juliana, Elizabeth, and Ann Stam.

--- --, ----   May 31, 1788
Ort, Milzer. Executor: Ludwig Ort. Windsor Township. This will not copied on the records.

Jan 20, 1788   Jun 9, 1788
Hose, Philip. Executor: Magdalena Hose. York County. Wife: Magdalena Hose. Children: Jacob, Elizabeth wife of George Fink, Eve wife of Philip Barker, Peter, Philip, and Dietrich.

May 15, 1788   Jun 11, 1788
McClure, James. Executors: Samuel and John Edie. Cumberland Township. Wife: Agness McClure. Children: Sarah, Jane, Elizabeth, Ann, Agness, Mary, and Margaret. (This is spelled in will "McLure").

Jun 3, 1788   Jul 4, 1788
Shaefer, Christofel. Executors: Christiana Shaefer and George Overdorph. Windsor Township. Wife: Christiana Shaefer. Children: Elizabeth wife of George Overdorph, Christiana and Anna.

Aug 25, 1788   Sep 22, 1788
Sheffer, Henry. Executors: Elizabeth and Henry Sheffer. Windsor Township. Wife: Elizabeth Sheffer. Children: Henry, Elizabeth, John and Christiana.

Jul 10, 1785   Jul 29, 1788
Quickel, Michael. Executors: Henry Mathias and John Kochenour. Dover Township. Wife: Barbara Quickel. Children: John, Michael, Barbara wife of ---- Krider, Elizabeth wife of Michael Kreider, Maria wife of Conrad Ensminger, Catharine wife of Jacob Barr, Anna, and Baltzer. Stepson and daughter: Henry Bohmer, and Mary wife of Philip Miller.

May 16, 1788   Aug 8, 1788
Immel, John. Executors: Reinhart Bott and Jacob Schmeiser. York County. Wife: Dorothea Immel. Children: Daniel and George.

--- --, ----   Aug 12, 1788
Marcks, John. Executor: Sybilla Marcks. York County. (German will.)

Jun 14, 1788   Aug 12, 1788
Rowes, Lucas. Executors: Johanna, Sophia and John Rowes. York Town Township. Wife: Johanna Rowes. Children: John, Becky (and two

others names not given).

Mar 31, 1788   Aug 16, 1788
Hoover, Martin. Executors: John Herr and Joseph Shick. Hellam Township. Wife: Catharine Hoover. Children: Martin, Joseph, Isaac, David, Christian, Mary, and Catharine. Grandchild: Jacob Martin, Jr. (a son of Jacob Martin, who was a son-in-law of Martin Hoover, wife's name not given).

Aug 4, 1788   Aug 27, 1788
Craig, John. Executors: Thomas Lalta and Robert Craig. Cumberland Township. Wife: Ann Craig. Brother: Bobet Craig. Niece: Jean Craig (child of Robert).

Sep 21, 1787   Sep 8, 1788
Dewis, Henry. Executors: Paul Rider and Daniel May. Dover Township. Wife: Mary Barbara Dewis. Children: Henry, John, Catharine wife of George Harbold, Christiana wife of Paul Rider, Elizabeth wife of John Sturt, Mary, Dorothea wife of William Harbolt, and Margaret wife of William Bear.

Mar 7, 1783   Oct 13, 1788
Miller, Ludwig. Executors: Anna, Nicholas and Ludwig Miller. Germany Township. Wife: Anna Barbara Miller. Children: Ann, Nicholas, Ludwig, and Barbara wife of Henry Moyer.

Sep 2, 1786   Oct 16, 1788
McCune, Thomas. Executor: Thomas McCune. Mt. Joy Township. Children: Samuel, Martha, Sarah, and Thomas. Grandchildren: Samuel McCune, Jr., Sarah Alexander (child of Samuel Alexander), and Peter, Thomas, Sarah, and Bleam Davison (children of son-in-law James Davison) (none of the mothers' names were given).

Jun 25, 1786   Oct 17, 1788
Blackburn, John. Executors: James and Alexander Blackburn. Tyrone Township. Wife: Agnes Blackburn. Children: James, William, John, Mary wife of William McGrew, Hannah and Sarah.

Sep 15, 1788   Oct 23, 1788
McCandless, James. Executors: R. and Alexander McCandless. Fawn Township. Wife: Ruthia McCandless. Children: Sarah, Esther, Alexander, James, and William.

Jan 2, 1787   Oct 31, 1788
Henly, John. Executor: Robert J. Chester. York County. Sole Legatee: Robert Johnson Chester.

Aug 5, 1788   Nov 3, 1788
Weller, Martin. Executors: John Spangler and Martin Ebert. York County. Wife: Catharine Weller. Children: Eve and Catharine.

Aug 16, 1788   Nov 25, 1788
McGee, Patrick. Executors: James McGee and John Kelly. Chanceford Township. Wife: Jean McKee. Children: James, John, Robert, Patrick and Polly. (Two sons-in-law Richard McAnulty and William Duglas wives' names not given).

Jul 12, 1784   Nov 27, 1788
Holl, Abraham. Executors: Philip Myers and Peter Wine Bremmer. Berwick Township. Children: Henry, John, Philip, Mary, Abraham, Andrew, Peter, George, Catharine, Jacob, and Nicholas.

Sep 22, 1788   Nov 29, 1788
Morrison, Hans. Executors: John Semple, Hugh and James Morrison. Straban Township. Wife: Elizabeth Morrison. Children: Ann, Hugh, James, Ebenezer, and John. Grandchild: Richard Morrison (parents' names not given).

--- --, ----   Nov. 17, 1788
Wolf, George. Executors: Dorothea Wolf and Isaac Gordman. York Town Township. (German will.)

Feb 7, 1786   Dec 18, 1788
Buchanan, Walter. Executors: David McClellean, Robert Buchanan, and Walter Buchanan. Franklin Township. Wife: Mary Buchanan. Children: James, William, Robert, Walter, Elizabeth, Jennet, Mary, Margaret and Ann.

Feb 26, 1787   Dec 20, 1788
Felger, Henry. Executors: Anna Mary Felger, John Kroh and Peter Grundy. Manheim Township. Wife: Anna Mary Felger. Children: Jacob, Henry, Eve, Barbara, and Ann.

Sep 15, 1788   Dec 31, 1788
Shollas, Theobald. Executors: James Patterson, Daniel Galwax and John Range. Mt. Pleasant Township. Wife: Magdalena Shollas. Children:

Susanna wife of James Patterson, Katharine wife of Daniel Galwax, Magdalena wife of John Range and Martha wife of Jacob Grosgras. Grandchildren: Tobias and Andrew Galwax, Samuel Patterson, John and Sholas Range.

Dec 14, 1788   Jan 18, 1789
Dill, Armstrong. Executor: Omitted. York County. Wife: Omitted. Brother: John.

Mar 21, 1788   Jan 24, 1789
Slough, Jacob. Executors: James Esccks and George Hertsel. Straban Township. Children: Susanna, Elizabeth, Mary, Catharine and Rosanna.

Nov 28, 1788   Jan 30, 1789
Jenkins, Moses. Executors: Moses Jenkins and William McPerson. Franklin Township. Wife: Francis Jenkins. Children: Walter and Moses.

Nov 10, 1787   Feb 14, 1789
Kagey, Jacob. Executors: Christian Becktel and Detrick Brubaker. Heidelberg Township. Wife: Barbara Kagey. Children: John, Jacob, Abraham, and Ann wife of Jacob Four.

Feb 7, 1789   Feb 17, 1789
Sippix, Grease. Executor: Cuff Sippix. Warrington Township. Children: Cuff and James. Grandchildren: Sarah, Betsy, Jacob and John Sippix (children of Cuff).

Mar 13, 1789   Mar 16, 1789
Springer, Ann. Executors: William and John Welch. York Boro. Legatees: Mary Kinkaid, Jane Nicolas, Mary and Sarah Welch.

Dec 18, 1788   Mar 16, 1789
Read, Mary. Executor: Daniel Dunwoody. Straban Township. Children: David, William and Minor.

Mar 10, 1789   Mar 25, 1789
Gemmill, J. Jannet. Executors: Andrew Finley and Robert Gemmill. Hopewell Township. Children: John, David, Ann wife of David Weylie, James, and Robert. Grandchildren: Jane (child of Ann), Margaret and William (children of John).

Feb 3, 1789   Mar 25, 1789
Allison, Agness. Executor: Alexander Thompson. Hopewell Township.
Sisters: Margaret, Jean, Elizabeth. Brother: Alexander.

Feb 15, 1789   Mar 31, 1789
Shetley, Frederick. Executors: Elizabeth Shetley and Jacob Young. York Boro. Wife: Elizabeth Shetley. There were two children, names not given.

Feb 2, 1789   Apr 3, 1789
Morningstar, Philip. Executors: Michael Carl and George Morningstar. Manheim Township. Children: George, Henry, Catharine wife of Peter Shultz, Juliana wife of Frederick Sower, Ann wife of Nicholas Hull, Elizabeth wife of John Felty, Salome wife of Philip Morningstar, John, and Adam.

Apr 28, 1788   Apr 4, 1789
Marsh, Peter. Executors: Hugh Moklin and John Brunter. Warrington Township. Children: Mary, Deborah, Jane, Lydia, Rachel, Rebecca, Esther, Jonathan, and John.

Feb 7, 1787   Apr 4, 1789
Herman, Henry. Executors: George Herman and Frederick Wolff. Berwick Township. Children: George, Anna wife of Jacob Hartman, and Maria wife of Henry Decker. Grandchild: George (son of George).

Mar 17, 1789   Apr 8, 1789
McMullen, Jennet. Executor: Agness Brown. Chanceford Township. Children: Mary and Agness.

Mar 3, 1789   Apr 14, 1789
Melhorn, Simon. Executors: Sabastian Obolt and Philip Slentz. York County. Wife: Anna Barbara Melhorn. Children: David, Casper, Andrew, Elizabeth, Mary, Frederick, John, and Barbara.

Jan 18, 1785   Apr 29, 1789
Deardorf, Peter. Executors: Peter Deardorf and Charles Himes. Paradise Township. Wife: Mary Deardorf. Children: Mary wife of Charles Himes, Caty wife of Ludwick Sell, John, and Anthony.

Apr 9, 1789   Apr 30, 1789
West, Charles. Executors: Joseph Glancy and John Albert. Newberry Township. Wife: (name not given). Children: John, Charles, Hannah

(and five others names not given).

Apr 17, 1789   May 3, 1789
Broadenheimer, William. Executors: Henry Holl and Joseph Heine. Reading Township. Wife: Mary Broadenheimer. Children: William, Jacob, Handiel, John, Mary, Ann wife of John Ramgier, Alse wife of Andrew Wolf, Christiana wife of John Speer, and Eve.

Jan 21, 1789   May 9, 1789
Buchanan, Frederick. Executors: Eva Buchanan and David Buchanan. Germany Township. Wife: Eva Mary Buchanan. Children: Frederick, David, Anna wife of George Reinhard, and Ann wife of Henry Zouck.

Jan 7, 1789   May 9, 1789
Thron, John. Executors: John Kehr and Samuel Flickinger. Manheim Township. Wife: Magdalena Thron. Children: Barbara, Samuel, John, Magdalena, Mary, Elizabeth, George and Michael.

Mar 1, 1784   May 9, 1789
Flickinger, Andrew. Executors: Daniel Utz and John Kour. Manheim Township. Children: Hans, Samuel, Peter, Jacob, Barbara wife of Michael Bear, Anna wife of John Keeny, Elizabeth wife of Daniel Utz, Magdalena wife of John Trone, and Andrew.

Mar 23, 1789   May 18, 1789
Helman, Jacob. Executors: Martin and Christian Helman. Hanover Borough. Wife: Barbara Helman. Children: Jacob, Martin, Eve, Margaret, and Michael. Grandchildren: Jacob, Barbara, and William (children of Jacob).

May 7, 1789   May 18, 1789
White, George. Executors: Hannah White and John Forsythe. Paradise Township. Wife: Hannah White. Children: Thomas, William, George, Ann wife of Emas Powell and John. Grandchildren: Thomas and George White (sons of Thomas), Tempest, Joseph and George White (children of William), Sarah and Hannah White (daughters of George) and George, Emas, David, Elizabeth, Hannah and Mary Powell.

Apr 9, 1789   May 18, 1789
McGrew, Robert. Executor: William McGrew. Straban Township. Child: William.

Aug 8, 1786   May 22, 1789
Menteith, John. Executor: Daniel Menteith. Berwick Township. Wife: Janet Menteith. Children: John and Daniel.

May 3, 1789   May 23, 1789
Wanshoung, Conrad, Executor: John Doll. Paradise Township. Wife: Mary Elizabeth Wanshoung. Children: Conrad, Ann wife of Jacob Smith and Margaretta wife of George Metzler. Grandchild: Elizabeth Metzler.

Feb 7, 1784   May 25, 1789
Kirk, Timothy. Executor: Timothy Kirk. Wife: Sarah Kirk. Children: Ezekiel, Rachel wife of Joshua Hutton, Thomas, William, and Jonathon.

--- --, ----   Jun 9, 1789
Schwartz, Andrew. Executors: Conrad Schwartz and Felix Glatfelder. Shrewsbury Township. (German will.)

Apr 9, 1789   Jun 22, 1789
Schmok, Jacob. Executors: Henry Tyson and Barnet Frey. Windsor Township. Wife: Catharine Schmok. Children: John and Jacob.

Oct 7, 1773   Jun 30, 1789
Reed, James. Executors: William and Jane Reed. Fawn Township. Wife: (Name not given.) Children: Jean, Mary, William and James.

Jun 17, 1789   Oct 27, 1789
Riddle, James. Executors: James and David Riddle. York County. Children: John, Robert, James, David, William, Joseph, Joshua, Samuel and George.

Nov 15, 1786   Jul 2, 1789
Willson, Joseph. Executors: Catharine and Joseph Willson. Franklin Township. Wife: Catharine Willson. Children: John, Robert, Thomas, Mary, Elizabeth, Martha, Catharine, Margaret, Joseph and William. Grandchild: Joseph McKee (parents' names not given).

May 25, 1789   Jul 28, 1789
Sultzberger, Anna. Executors: Andrew Sultzberger. York Boro. Children: Andrew and Dorothea. Grandchildren: Elizabeth Houser and Dorothea Henninger (names of the parents not given).

Jun 13, 1787   Jul 29, 1789
Swartz, George. Executors: Peter Brillhart, Simon Munich and Henry

Danner. Shrewsbury Township. Wife: Barbara Swartz.

Aug 3, 1789   Aug 3, 1789
Dapper, Christian. Executor: Andrew Dapper. Manchester Township. Wife: Maria Dapper. Children: Andrew, John, Magdalena, and Elizabeth.

Sep 10, 1788   Aug 12, 1789
Sonday, Jacob. Executors: John Sonday and Michael Frederick. Paradise Township. Wife: Christiana Sonday. Children: Mathias, Joseph, Christiana and Margaret wife of Jacob Rumel.

Jul 22, 1789   Aug 24, 1789
Deitch, Philip. Executors: Christian Lauman and Adam Kreber. York Borough. Children: Hartman, Eve, Margaret wife of Matthew Goodwin.

May 21, 1789   Aug 25, 1789
McCandless, Ruthia. Executors: William Read and Sarah McCandless. Fawn Township. Children: Alexander, James, Sarah, William, and Esther.

Jun 7, 1789   Aug 29, 1789
Frey, Philip. Executors: John Frey and George Obertwiff. York County. Wife: Mary Frey. Child: George.

May 19, 1789   Sep 16, 1789
McDonald, Richard. Executors: Mary McDonald, John Kelly and Joseph Manifold. Hopewell Township. Wife: Mary McDonald. Children: Margaret, Jane, Aquilla, Persilla, Elizabeth, Richard, Mary, Robert, and Agness.

Sep 11, 1789   Sep 18, 1789
Lang, John. Executor: Christian Wolf. York County. Wife: Mary Lang. Children: John, Frederick, and Elizabeth.

Nov 5, 1784   Oct 9, 1789
Gilleland, John. Executors: Samuel and William Gilleland. Menallen Township. Wife: Jane Gilleland. Children: James, Samuel, and William.

Aug 17, 1789   Nov 9, 1789
Stake, George. Executors: Catharine Stake, John Hay and Henry Miller. York Boro. Wife: Catharine Stake. Children: Mary wife of ---- Shugart, Michael, George, Christian, Jacob, Peggy, Lehna and Elizabeth. Grandchild: Catharine Shugart.

Nov 3, 1789   Nov 9, 1789
Gartman, Isaac. Executors: George Shuck and Patrick Sullivan. York Borough. Wife: Elizabeth Gartman. Children: Isaac, Mary wife of Jacob Rudy, and Magdalena.

May 7, 1788   Nov 12, 1789
Mate, John. Executors: Henry and Peter Geipe. Hellam Township. Children: John, Casper, Philip, Anna wife of John Lephart, Magdalena wife of George Mentel, and Appolonia wife of Valentine Lephard.

Jan 17, 1769   Nov 14, 1789
McMullen, Robert. Executors: Robert Matthew, Samuel McMullen, and Samuel Nelson. Warrington Township. Wife: Omitted. Son-in-law: John Johnston (the name of his wife and the other children were not given).

Nov 5, 1789   Nov 16, 1789
Schonk, Joseph. Executors: Martin Ebbert and George Schouk. York Boro. Wife: Elizabeth Schonk. Children: George, John, and Barbara.

Sep 14, 1789   Nov 16, 1789
Welsh, Michael. Executors: David Cremer and John Welsh. York Borough. Wife: Barbara Welsh. Children: Elizabeth, John, Henry, Catharine wife of David Cremer, Barbara, Jacob and Michael.

Aug 13, 1782   Nov 17, 1789
Caruthers, James. Executor: James Caruthers. Monaghan Township. Wife: Jean Caruthers. Children: John, James, Thomas, and Andrew.

Oct 25, 1789   Dec 2, 1789
Beidle, Barbara. Executor: Henry Strickler. Hellam Township. Children: Ann wife of Daniel Flurey, and Freney.

Jun 7, 1784   Dec 2, 1789
Grofe, Michael. Executor: William Mummert. Paradise Township. Children: Valentine, John, Margaret wife of Peter Devolt, and Magdalena wife of Andrew Habersock.

Jun 9, 1787   Dec 3, 1789
Mickle, John. Executors: Owen McRail and Finley McGrew. Manallen Township. Wife: Jane Mickle. Children: Sarah wife of John Mickle, Elijah, Mary wife of John Sheperd, Hannah wife of William Royl, and Jane wife of Thomas Royl.

Nov 11, 1789   Dec 3, 1789
Reider, Gertraut. Executor: John M. Fissei. York Boro. Legatees: John Michael Fissei.

Mar 4, 1784   Dec 7, 1789
Toland, James. Executor: Elizabeth Toland. Newberry Township. Wife: Elizabeth Toland. Children: Elizabeth, James, Thomas, Mary, William, Margaret, Susanna and Anne wife of Robert Murdough.

Nov 24, 1786   Dec 9, 1789
Rhorback, Christian. Executors: Christian Rhorback and Barney Zeigler. Township: Omitted. Wife: Susanna Rhorback. Children: Christian, Lawrence, Henry and John.

Nov 9, 1789   Dec 18, 1789
Comfort, Andrew. Executors: Mary E. Comfort and Christian Close. Berwick Township. Wife: Mary E. Comfort. Children: Andrew, Henry, John, Jacob, and Mary.

Nov 16, 1789   Dec 19, 1789
Myer, Jacob. Executors: Peter Myer and Martin Cronmiller. York Borough. Wife: Anna Barbara Myer. Children: Frederick, Catharine wife of John Koch, Peter, John, Barbara wife of Martin Cronmiller, Margaret wife of George Fink, George, Henry, and Jacob.

Aug 9, 1789   Dec 23, 1789
Winebremmer. Executors: Jacob Beltz and Henry Hoke. Hanover Township. Wife: Barbara Winebremmer. Child: Justina wife of Daniel Glabsatle.

Aug 25, 1789   Jan 1, 1790
Brown, Thomas. Executor: Jacob Gibson. York County. Wife: Mary Brown. Children: James, William, John, Elizabeth, Susanna and Mary.

Jan 16, 1790   Jan 4, 1790
Kuny, John. Executors: Henry Danner and John Kuny. Germany Township. Wife: Anna Kuny. Children: Anna wife of Adam Gisler. Grandchildren: Magdalena and John Gisler.

Oct 13, 1788   Jan 28, 1790
Emmit, Sarah. Executor: Joseph Emmit. York County. Children: Susanna, Mary and Sarah. Grandchildren: Hannah and John Adair (parents' names not given).

Jan 7, 1788   Jan 28, 1790
Elder, James. Executors: Benj. Elder and William Porter. Hamiltonsban Township. Children: Mary, Andrew, Joseph, Benjamin, Rosana, and James.

Jan 5, 1781   Jan 29, 1790
Ensminger, Henry. Executor: George Ensminger. Newberry Township. Wife: Christiana Ensminger. Children: George, Conrad, Catharine wife of Samuel Grove, and Magdalena wife of Philip Wallick.

Dec 19, 1789   Jan 29, 1790
Houck, Lorentz. Executor: John Thomas. Hanover Township. Wife: Anna Mary Houck. Children: Jacob and Peter.

Dec 22, 1787   Jan 30, 1790
Nehrbas, Frances. Executors: Catharine Nehrbas and Jacob Weigel. Dover Township. Wife: Catharine Nehrbas.

Mar 18, 1784   Feb 1, 1790
Shoup, Andrew. Executors: William How and Mathias Hallerpeter. York County. Children: Dorothea, Peter, Mathias and Christian. Son-in-law: William How (wifes' name not given). N.B. This wills land in Penn Township, North Cumberland County, Pennsylvania.

Jan 17, 1785   Feb 4, 1790
Fissel, Gillian. Executor: Jost Runk. Cordorus Township. Wife: Barbara Fissel. Children: Henry, Elizabeth, Catharine, Adam, and Margaret.

Aug 17, 1789   Feb 11, 1790
Chester, Robert Johnston. Executors: Elizabeth Chester and James Chester. Berlin Township. Wife: Elizabeth Chester. Children: William, Richard, John and Mary.

Jan 9, 1790   Feb 24, 1790
Leamer, Conrad. Executors: Elizabeth Leamer and Thomas McCreary. Warrington Township. Wife: Elizabeth Leamer.

Jan 4, 1785   Feb 27, 1790
Kepner, Catharine. Executors: Tobias Kepner and Peter Ickis. Berwick Township. Children: Andrew, Tobias, William, Elizabeth wife of John Betz, Dorothea wife of Peter Ickis, Henry, Tobias, and Mary wife of Samuel Knisel.

Mar 11, 1788   Mar 22, 1790
Sellix, Thomas. Executors: Tobias Sellix and William Gelland. Menallen Township. Children: Agness wife of John Cord, Margaret wife of Thomas McIuown, Mary wife of Thomas Feelly and Thomas. Grandchild: Hamilton Sellix (son of Thomas).

Jul 13, 1789   Mar 22, 1790
McQuown, Laurence. Executors: John McQuown and William Gilliland. Menallen Township. Wife: Jean McQuown. Children: Thomas, John, James, William, Catharine wife of Isaac Leany, Elizabeth wife of Able Hasty, Mary wife of George McCreary, Jean wife of David Pantan, Rebecca wife of Benj. Stewart, Margaret, Eleanor, David, and Laurence.

--- --, ----   Mar 23, 1790
Robenstein, Albrak. Executor: Omitted. Township: Omitted. Wife: Christiana Robenstein. Children: David and Leonard.

Jan 9, 1790   Mar 25, 1790
Houck, Jacob. Executors: Catharine Houck and Christian Mieheimer. Hanover Township. Wife: Christiana Houck. Children: Hannah, Elizabeth, and Susanna.

Feb 23, 1789   Apr 1, 1790
Gottwalt, Jacob. Executors: Mary C. and Andrew Gottwalt. Manchester Township. Wife: Maria Catharine Gottwalt. Children: Jacob, Elizabeth wife of ---- Coppinhoffer, Andrew, Catharine, and George. Grandchild: Elizabeth Coppinhoffer (child of Elizabeth).

Dec 7, 1775   Apr 3, 1790
Hoopard, George. Executors: Catharine Hoopard and Jacob Rudisell. Mt. Pleasant Township. Wife: Catharine Hoopard. Children: Catharine, John, Daniel, Eve, Mary, George, Christiana, and Elizabeth.

Jan 15, 1789   Apr 7, 1790
Berger, Andrew. Executor: Valentine Berger. Manheim Township. Wife: Catharine Berger. Children: Catharine, and Barbara wife of Andrew Beaty.

Mar 28, 1789   Apr 7, 1790
Harbold, George. Executors: Philip, Jacob, Julius, and Casper Bensyl. Dover Township. Wife: Catharine Harbold. Children: William, Leonard, Henry, Michael, and Elizabeth wife of Casper Bensyl.

Jan 13, 1790   Apr 8, 1790
Eberhard, John. Executors: Catharine Eberhard and Francis Groff. Cordorus Township. Wife: Catharine Eberhard. Children: Abraham, Eve, and a young son.

Nov 7, 1789   Apr 9, 1790
Lauer, Mathias. Executors: Catharine Lauer and George Mather. Manheim Township. Wife: Catharine Lauer. Children: Conrad, John, Mathias, Henry, Abraham, Jacob, Ludwick, Anamary, Margaret, Elizabeth, Catharine, and Christiana.

Feb 18, 1790   Apr 10, 1790
Lechner, George. Executor: Anthony Hinkle. Manheim Township. Children: George, Micheal, John, Catharine wife of Adam Lomer, Lena wife of John Fissel, Salome wife of Anthony Hinkle, Elizabeth wife of Elias Wood, Christiana wife of John Kline, and Juliana wife of Andrew Senff. Grandchildren: George and Michael Lechner (sons of George), and Mary and John Lechner (children of John).

Oct 22, 1789   Apr 10, 1790
Slagle, Jacob. Executors: Jacob Rudisell and Henry Slagle. Berwick Township. Wife: Barbara Slagle. Children: Christopher, Louise wife of Mathias Smisser, Susanna, Jacob, Helena wife of Conrad Sherman, Magdalena wife of George Eyster, George, Catharine wife of Godlip Smith, Salomy, David, Christiana, John, Mary, Gloria, Joshua, Elizabeth and Eve.

Mar 2, 1790   Apr 21, 1790
Oiler, Valentine. Executors: Jacob Eyler and Francis Knouse. Manallen Township. Wife: Susanna Oiler. Children: Jacob, John, Magdalena, Frederick, Valentine, Katharine wife of Peter Arndt, Mary wife of Peter Kackler, Christiana wife of Peter Hind, and Susanna.

Mar 7, 1790   Apr 24, 1790
Kirk, Elisha. Executor: William Welsch. York Borough. Wife: Ruth Kirk. Children: Aquila and Priscilla.

Nov 13, 1786   Apr 27, 1790
Schnerr, Casper. Executor: Simon Essick. Manallen Township. Wife: Madlen Schnerr. Children: Catharine wife of John Bender, Mary, Ule wife of Simon Essick and Elizabeth.

Apr 17, 1790   Apr 29, 1790
Kniselley, Samuel. Executors: Tobias Kepner, Mary and John Kniselley.

Dover Township. Wife: Mary Kniselley. Children: John, Abraham, and Mary wife of Tobias Kepner.

Jun 17, 1789   Apr 29, 1790
McClelland, David. Executors: Jacob and William McClelland. Hamiltonsban Township. Wife: Jannet McClelland. Children: Walter, David, John, Robert, William, David, Elizabeth, Jannet, and Mary.

Nov 17, 1789   Apr 30, 1790
Eichelberger, Magdalena. Executor: Jacob Eichelberger. Hanover Township. Children: Ludwick, Jacob and Leonard. Grandchildren: Gloria, Barbara, and Elizabeth Hoke (children of Andrew Hoke, mother's name not given); Catharine Smyser (daughter of Jacob Smyser, mother's name not given); Frederick and Magdalena Eichelberger (children of Ludwick).

Apr 23, 1790   May 1, 1790
Fischel, Wendel. Executors: Christian Wist and Barned Spangler. Paradise Township. Wife: Margaret Fischel. Children: Barbara, John, Henry, Margaret wife of John Hans, Mary wife of Peter Marx, Ann wife of Theobald Scheyerman, and Philip.

Apr 1, 1790   May 10, 1790
Hoffman, Matthias. Executor: Michael Hoffman. Manheim Township. Wife: Anna Elizabeth Hoffman.

--- --, ----   May 17, 1790
Harnist, John. Executors: Barbara Harnist and Peter Raab. York County. German will.

May 3, 1790   May 21, 1790
Diel, Nicholas. Executors: Peter and Nicholas Diel. York Township. Wife: Catharine Diel. (Legacies to nephews and nieces, children of brothers Daniel and Adam Diel.)

Mar 4, 1790   May 22, 1790
Miller, Martin. Executors: Jacob Colar and Andrew Smith. Shrewsbury Township. Children: Henry, Catharine, Eve, Barbara, Mary, Margaret, Martin and Elizabeth.

Jun 21, 1789   May 24, 1790
Berlin, Jacob. Executors: Nicholas Berlin and Frederick Berlin. Berwick Township. Wife: Anna Margaretta Berlin. Children: Nicolas, Frederick,

Christiana wife of Martin Weigel, and Catharine wife of Michael Finch.

May 12, 1790   May 29, 1790
Peterman, Dorothea. Executor: Isaac Gartman. York Town Township.
Child: Barbara wife of John Stop.

May 10, 1790   Jun 4, 1790
Hall, Michael. Executors: Henry Danner and George Petry. Cordorus Township. Wife: Christiana Hall. Children: Christiana and Isaac.

May 22, 1790   Jun 4, 1790
Apfel, George. Executors: Daniel Dubs and Samuel Wildisin. Manheim Township. Wife: Anna Apfel. Sister: Margaret wife of Samuel Wildisin. Brother: Wendle.

--- ---, ----   Jun 7, 1790
Wideman, Sebastian. Executors: Frederick Mummer and Dietrich Brubaker. Cordorus Township. (German will.)

May 28, 1790   Jun 7, 1790
Grier, David. Executors: Jennet Grier, James Riddle and Henry Miller. Yorktown Township. Wife: Jennet Grier. Children: Agness, Mary, Jennet, and Margaret.

Sep 2, 1789   Jun 7, 1790
Byer, Samuel. Executors: John Byer and Christopher Hollinger. Hamiltonsban Township. Wife: Mary Byer. Children: David, Jonas, Samuel, Barbara wife of John Stockslagle, Esther wife of Abraham Beam, and Mary.

Feb 2, 1790   Jun 9, 1790
Landis, Samuel. Executors: Henry Strickler and Henry Kendrich. Windsor Township. Wife: Barbara Landis. Children: Magdalena, Anna wife of Christian Neighcomer, Barbara wife of Frederick Fitz and Elizabeth.

May 22, 1790   Jun 29, 1790
Thompson, William. Executors: Robert Thompson and Francis Allen. Cumberland Township. Wife: Eleanor Thompson. Children: Robert, Mary, Phebe, Ruth, Sarah, Martha, Elizabeth, Susanna, and Eleanor. Son-in-law Francis Allison (wife's name not given). Grandchildren: John Thompson, Sarah, John and Mary McDermond (their parents' names not

given).

Apr 19, 1790   Jul 5, 1790
Bott, Reinhardt. Executor: Adam Kreber. Manchester Township. Wife: Mary Elizabeth Bott. Children: George and Barbara. (Granddaughter:) Catharine Wendler (parents' names not recorded).

Nov 21, 1789   Aug 2, 1790
Shefer, John. Executors: Christiana Shefer and Michael Dondel. York Boro. Wife: Christiana Shefer.

Sep 8, 1789   Aug 5, 1790
Bixler, John. Executors: Susanna Bixler and Jacob Bixler. Windsor Township. Wife: Susanna Bixler. Children: Christley, Jose, and (son-in-law) John Bay (wife's not given).

Jan 3, 1790   Aug 21, 1790
Sahler, Isaac. Executor: Eleanor Sahler. Manchester Township. Wife: Eleanor Sahler.

Mar 12, 1789   Aug 25, 1790
Pettit, Thomas. Executors: Rebecca and Thomas Pettit. Dover Township. Wife: Rebecca Pettit. Children: Priscilla, Thomas, Lucia wife of Patrick Donalson, Hannah wife of John Hooper, and Rebecca wife of Gabriel Gill.

Jun 16, 1790   Aug 25, 1790
Webb, Eleanor. Executor: Benj. Tompkins. Fawn Township. (Bro. and Sister) Elizabeth Bolen and Evan Evans.

--- --, ----   Aug 26, 1790
Derris, John. Executors: Elizabeth Derris and George Kann. York County. German will.

--- --, ----   Aug 26, 1790
Hess, Ulrich. Executors: Ursula and Henry Hess. Shrewsbury Township. German will.

Nov 13, 1789   Aug 30, 1790
Reinecker, Casper. Executors: Conrad Reinecker and Jacob Rudisell. Hanover Township. Children: Conrad, Maney, Gloria, George, Anna wife of Jacob Eyechelberger, Catharine wife of George Kuhn, Elizabeth wife of George Sherman and Nancy.

Jul 13, 1790   Aug 31, 1790
Shnyder, Jacob. Executor: George Shnyder. York Boro. Children: George, Jacob, Susanna wife of Peter Vogt and Elizabeth.

Nov 29, 1784   Sep 13, 1790
Jones, Robert. Executor: Jacob Worley. Manchester Township. Wife: Margery Jones. Children: Margaret, Robert, Henry, Elizabeth wife of Henry Cunningham, Mary wife of Arthur Cunningham, Hannah wife of Thomas Oldham, and Rachel wife of Francis Worley.

Dec 2, 1789   Sep 20, 1790
Peter, Peter. Executor: John Ensminger. York County. Wife: Mary Margaret Peter. Children: Magdalena, Anna, and Henry.

Jan 7, 1790   Oct 2, 1790
Girbin, Mary. Executor: Alexander Dobbin. Cumberland Township. Child: Elizabeth wife of James Breden. Grandchild: Walter Breden.

May 7, 1790   Oct 4, 1790
Trimmer, Peter. Executor: Andrew Trimmer. Reading Township. Legatees: (Bros. and Sisters) Christiana, Mary, Sophia, Ann, Nelly, Salome, Andrew, John, David, Mathias, and William Trimmer.

Jun 1, 1790   Oct 5, 1790
Nevis, Martin. Executors: George Williamson and John Montfort. Mt. Pleasant Township. Wife: Ida Nevis. Children: John, Christopher, and one daughter whose name was not given.

Dec 28, 1786   Oct 11, 1790
Ringer, George. Executors: Peter Mundorf and Samuel Gross. Manchester Township. Wife: Catharine Ringer. Children: Michael, John, George, Catharine and Christiana.

Aug 12, 1790   Oct 19, 1790
Bower, George. Executors: Nicholas Miller and David Flock. Huntington Township. Child: Michael.

Sep 9, 1790   Oct 29, 1790
Harrison, John. Executor: Ann Harrison. Monaghan Township. Wife: Ann Harrison. Children: Thomas and Hannah.

Oct 5, 1790   Nov 9, 1790
Kunkel, John. Executor: Catharine Kunkle. Dover Township. Wife: Catharine Kunkel. Children: Jacob and Eve.

Jun 16, 1790   Dec 16, 1790
Kennedy, William. Executors: William Scott, James Short, and John Strawbradge. Yorktown Township. Brothers: Alexander and George Kennedy. (This will is for property on Front Street, Philadelphia, extending along the Delawar River.)

Dec 19, 1790   Jan 5, 1791
Zollinger, Peter. Executor: Jacob Wiest. Paradise Township. Wife: Elizabeth Zollinger. Children: Catharine wife of Adam Pieper, Veronica wife of Daniel Ammer, Elizabth wife of Bernard Spangler, Ulrich, John, Henry and Peter. (Step-daughter:) Elizabeth Yoe.

Dec 1, 1789   Jan 28, 1791
Poe, Margaret. Executor: William Gillilans. Cumberland Township. Children: John, Mary, Margaret wife of ---- Orman, and Sarah wife of ---- Marlin. Grandchildren: Alexander Finley, David and Mary Paden (parents' names not given), Margaret Orman (child of Margaret), and David Marlin (son of Sarah).

Jan 18, 1791   Feb 14, 1791
Spengler, Henry. Executors: Andrew and Adam Hope. Paradise Township. Wife: Clara Spengler. Children: Lydia, Adam and John.

Sep 28, 1789   Feb 26, 1791
Pflieger, Frederick. Executors: Martin Ebert and Peter Feiser. York County. Wife: Maria Margaret Pflieger. Children: Jacob, George, John, Abraham, Michael, Henry, and Christiana wife of Michael Hess.

--- --, ----   Feb. 16, 1791
Degan, John. Executors: Elizabeth Degan and Peter Brillhart. German will.

Jul 21, 1787   Mar 8, 1791
Donnalson, John. Executor and Township omitted. Wife: Elizabeth Donnalson. Child: William.

Apr 11, 1786   Mar 15, 1791
Shearer, Jacob. Executors: Barnet Zeigler and John Ruhl. Cordorus Township. Wife: Maria Shearer. Children: John, George, Henry, Jacob and Daniel.

Mar 1, 1791   Mar 18, 1791
Fisher, Frederick. Executors: John Casper Fisher and Peter Sprinckel.

York Township. Wife: Elizabeth Fisher. Children: John, Margaret wife of ---- Sprinckel, Casper, Catharine wife of Adam Beecher, Anna wife of John Epple, and Christopher.

Apr 23, 1787   Mar 23, 1791
Fedroe, Philip. Executor: Joseph Fedroe. Newberry Township. Wife: Mary Fedroe. Children: Philip, Michael, Joseph, John, and Andrew.

Jan 18, 1791   Mar 24, 1791
Ewing, Robert. Executors: Samuel and John Ewing. Mt. Pleasant Township. Brothers: Isaac and Samuel Ewing. Sister: Martha wife of Noble Osburn. Nephew: Robert Ewing (son of Samuel).

Nov 2, 1790   Apr 5, 1791
Jordan, Joshia. Executor: Lydia Jordan. York Borough. Wife: Lydia Jordan. Child: Elisha.

Feb 26, 1791   Apr 6, 1791
Marlin, John. Executors: James Logue and John Reed. Chanceford Township. Child: James. Grandchildren: Hannah Sinclaire, John and William Marlin (parents' names not given), Rachel Marlin wife of John Marlin.

Feb 19, 1784   Apr 7, 1791
Kuntz, John. Executors: Abraham Kuntz and Barnet Zeigler. Cordorus Township. Wife: Catharine Kuntz. Children: Abraham, Anna wife of Adam Michael, and Peter.

Feb 27, 1784   Apr 21, 1791
Miller, Peter. Executors: Anna Mary and Nicholas Miller. Tyrone Township. Wife: Anna Mary Miller. Children: Mary, Margaret, Ann, and Nicholas. Grandson: John Martin (parents' names not given).

Apr 12, 1791   Apr 27, 1791
McKee, Joseph. Executors: Thoms McKee and John Riddle. York County. Children: Thomas, William, Betsy, John, and Sally. Grandchildren: Joseph, Thomas and John (children of John McKee), and Robert, Joseph and James Parks (children of James Parks, wife's name not given).

Jun 29, 1790   Apr 28, 1791
Reed, William. Executors: Mary Reed and Samuel Morrison. York County. Wife: Mary Reed. Children: Thomas, Mary, Jane, James,

Samuel and Margaret.

--- --, ----   May 9, 1791
Winebremmer, Catharine. Executor: Jacob Beltz. Heidelberg Township. (German will.)

Jun 27, 1789   May 21, 1791
Welch, George Executors: William Welch and Mary Brown. Manchester Township. Children: Sarah, Margaret wife of Isaac Springer, Jane wife of John Nicholas and Mary wife of --- Brown. Grandchildren: George, John, Phebe and Sarah Brown.

--- --, ----   May 21, 1791
Leininger, George. Executors: Magdalena Leininger and George Schaedel. Dover Township. (German will.)

May 1, 1791   May 23, 1791
Pike, John. Executors: George Harris and Robert Miller. Newberry Township. Wife: Elizabeth Pike. Children: Pheby wife of John Richman, Ruth, Mosey, John, and Rebecca wife of Abraham Vernon.

Jun 16, 1779   May 23, 1791
Stagner, Catharine. Executor: Christopher Wohlfaurt. Windsor Township. Children: Charlotte wife of Peter Gangeree, Mary wife of Stofel Wohlfaurt and Peter. Grandchild: Catharine Wohlfaurt.

Feb 2, 1785   May 25, 1791
Bailey, Daniel. Executors: Sarah Bailey and William Mitchel. Monagan Township. Wife: Sarah Bailey. Children: Andrew, John, Rachel, Jane, Elizabeth and Nancy.

Apr 5, 1788   May 26, 1791
Campbell, John. Executor: James Johnston. Franklin Township. Children: Agness wife of ---- Mullin and wife of Harkam (married twice), and Jennet wife of Mark Millikin. Grandchildren: Henry and John (children of Agness).

Apr 6, 1791   May 31, 1791
Stewart, James. Executor: Andrew Stewart. Hamiltonsban Township. Wife: Mary Stewart. Children: Hugh, William, Andrew, Mary wife of ---- Walker and Elizabeth. Grandchildren: John, Stewart and Sarah Richards (parents' name not given).

May 24, 1791   May 31, 1791
Stewart, Hugh. Executors: Andrew and William Stewart. Hamiltousban Township. Child: Sarah. Legatees: Andrew, Stewart, Mary Walker and Elizabeth Stewart (brothers and sisters).

--- ---, ----   Jun 8, 1791
Fittler, Philip. Executors: Peter Fittler and Conrad Bender. Tyrone Township. German will.

Feb 12, 1791   Jun 21, 1791
Townsley, John. Executors: William Townsley and James Barr. Mt. Joy Township. Wife: Jean Townsley. Children: George, James, Robert, Margaret, and William. Grandchildren: Margaret Townsley (daughter of George) and John Townsley (son of Robert).

Apr 19, 1791   Jun 25, 1791
Sprochell, Joanna. Executor: Baltzer Rudisell. York Boro. Children: Elizabeth and Susanna wife of Michael Berth.

Jun 3, 1791   Jul 25, 1791
Ziegler, Nicholas. Executors: Michael and Nicholas Zeigler. Cordorus Township. Wife: Catharine Ziegler. Children: Elizabeth wife of Adam Fessel, Catharine wife of John Henick, Jacob, Michael and Nicholas.

Dec 30, 1788   Jul 25, 1791
Bager, John. Executors: John, George, William and Christina Bager. Berwick Township. Wife: Elizabeth Bager. Children: George, Samuel, John, William, and Catharine wife of Martin Slaup.

--- ---, ----   Jul 27, 1791
Keller, Jacob. Executors: Christian Keller and Andrew Meyer. Shrewsbury Township. (German will.)

Jan 25, 1789   Jul 27, 1791
Moll, Henry. Executor: Ludwig Moll. Warrington Township. Children: Ludwig, Margaret, Mary, Catharine, John, and Henry.

Dec 13, 1788   Jul 28, 1791
Shollas, Magdalena. Executor: Daniel Beatty. Mt. Pleasant Township. Children: Susanna wife of James Patterson, Christiana wife of Daniel Galwax and Magdalena wife of John Range. Grandchildren: Theobald and Elizabeth Range and Magdalena Galwax.

Dec 9, 1790   Jul 29, 1791
Zinlaub, George. Executor: Christiana Zinlaub. Germany Township.
Children: Christiana, Catharine and Henry Heisman, Ann and Margaret.

Apr 15, 1790   Aug 20, 1791
Coulson, Charles. Executors: William and Francis Coulson. Monaghan Township. Children: William, David, Francis, John, Jane wife of Niblock. Grandchildren: Rebecca (daughter of William), Charles and William (children of David), and Mary (child of Niblock).

Jul 24, 1791   Aug 22, 1791
Shank, John. Executors: Samuel Flickinger and Jacob Shank. Franklin Township. Wife: Mary Shank. Children: Myri, Jacob, Michael, Christian, Adam, Elizabeth and Franey. Son-in-law: Henry Hoober (wifes' name not given).

Aug 19, 1791   Sep 12, 1791
Nunnamacher, Abraham. Executor: Henry Lochner. York Borough. Wife: Christiana Nunnamacher. Children: Anna wife of Henry Lochner, and Nicholas.

Jan 7, 1785   Sep 23, 1791
Whinery, Robert. Executor: William Whinery. Newberry Township. Children: Thomas, Catharine, William and Hannah wife of --- McCreary. Grandchild: Sarah McCreary.

Jan 26, 1789   Sep 27, 1791
McKean, Robert. Executors: Thomas and Alexander McKean. Cumberland Township. Children: John, Mary wife of ---- Trimble, Hugh, Thomas, James, Alexander, and Martin. Grandchildren: Agness and John Trimble.

Sep 11, 1791   Oct 24, 1791
McMillan, John. Executors: Thomas and John McMillan. Warrington Township. Children: Abigail, Thomas, John, and James.

Jan 7, 1790   Oct 29, 1791
Weinand, John. Executors: Philip Weinand and Andrew Bally. Paradise Township. Children: Margaret wife of Jacob Dietrich, Philip and Jacob.

Oct 17, ----   Nov 7, 1791
Kohl, Jacob. Executor: Omitted. Chester County. Wife: Mary Kohl. Brother: John Kohl. (This is spelled "Cohl" in the Indexes and Records,

but the will has it "Kohl".)

Oct 17, 1791   Nov 7, 1791
Coal, Jacob. Executor: Jacob Rose. Chester County. Wife: Mary Coal.
Brother: John Coal.

Apr 18, 1787   Nov 18, 1791
March, George. Executors: Jacob March and Daniel May. Dover
Township. Wife: Mary Catharine March. Children: John, Jacob,
Catharine, Nancy, Polly, Susanna, Gertrude, and Andony.

Sep 20, 1791   Nov 28, 1791
Wilson, William. Executor: Tempest Tucker. Paradise Township.
Legatee: (Sister) Mary wife of Tempest Tucker.

Nov 5, 1787   Dec 31, 1791
Bigler, Jacob. Executor: Jacob May. Dover Township. Wife: Suvia
Bigler. Children: Jacob, Joseph, Barbara and Matalina.

Dec 8, 1791   Jan 7, 1792
Sherritz, Ludwig. Executors: Conrad Sherritz and Philip W. Werking.
Manheim Township. Wife: Margaret Sherritz. Children: Margaret,
Elizabeth, Frederick, Catharine and Mary.

Nov 13, 1791   Jan 28, 1792
Meyer, John. Executors: Henry Myer and Barnard Spangler. Paradise
Township. Wife: Margaret Meyer. Children: Henry, David, Michael,
Catharine, John, and Anna.

Jan 9, 1792   Feb 18, 1792
Arthur, Isaas. Executor: Thomas Whinriy. Brother: Thomas Arthur.

Nov 9, 1791   Feb 23, 1792
King, Philip. Executors: Peter Diehl, Philip and Jacob King. Manchester
Township. Wife: Catharine King. Children: Philip, Jacob, Henry,
Elizabeth, Peter, Barbara, George, Adam, Catharine, and Anna.

Jan 9, 1792   Feb 25, 1792
Burkholder, Henry. Executor: George Robinet. Huntington Township.
Children: John, Henry, Jacob, Mary wife of ---- Stum, Barbara wife of
James Saunderson, Sarah, Elizabeth, Rachel and Hannah.

Feb 23, 1792   Mar 26, 1792
Keller, George. Executors: Christiana Rohrebach and Veronica Keller. Cordorus Township. Wife: Veronica Keller. Children: George, Christian, Henry, Christiana, and Elizabeth.

Jan 2, 1792   Mar 27, 1792
Wilson, Mary. Executor: John McGrew. Tyrone Township. Child: John. Grandchildren: Catharine and John Wilson.

Mar 3, 1792   Mar 27, 1792
Plunket, Thomas. Executor: Francis Plunket. Tyrone Township. Legatees: Eleanor and Francis Plunket. N.B. - The relationship is not stated in the will.

Jan 16, 1782   Mar 28, 1792
Paxton, Andrew. Executor: Jennet Paxton. Chanceford Township. Wife: Jennet Paxton. Children of second wife: Jean, Ann, and Margaret. Children of first wife: James and Andrew. N.B. - The Rev. James Clarkson and Alex. Downing were appointed by the will to be the guardians of these children.

Feb 4, 1792   Mar 29, 1792
Hoopert, George. Executor: Catharine Hoopert. Mt. Pleasant Township. Sisters: Catharine, and (three others whose names were not given.)

Mar 24, 1787   Mar 30, 1792
Randels, William. Executor: Samuel Garretson. Children: Hannah, Martha, William, Hugh and Jannett.

Jan 14, 1789   Mar 30, 1792
Orin, Benjamin. Executor: Thomas Campbell. Monaghan Township. Wife: Elizabeth Orin. Children: Rebecca wife of William Kearns, John, Rachel wife of Samuel Stitt, Mary wife of Enis Jaimeson, Benjamin, Thomas, Elizabeth, and William.

Sep 8, 1788   Apr 11, 1792
Walter, Henry. Executors: Christopher Lowman and Michael Gunacker. York Borough. Wife: Elizabeth Walter. Children: Catharine wife of Michael Eberly and Barbara wife of Michael Gunacker (of Lancaster).

Apr 5, 1792   Apr 21, 1792
Smelser, Philip. Executors: Philip and Michael Smelser. Windsor Township. Children: Philip and Michael. (The names of the wife and

other children not given.)

Oct 7, 1771   Apr 30, 1792
Jacobs, Philip. Executors: Samuel Arnold and Philip Altland. Paradise Township. Wife: Barbara Jacobs. Children: Philip, Abraham, Mally wife of Philip Altland, Catharine wife of Henry Vance, Samuel, Susanna, John, Nancy, Daniel, Henry, Elizabeth, Salome, William, and Peter.

Dec 19, 1789   Apr 30, 1792
Johnston, William. Executors: William Weakley and James Chamberlin. Reading Township. Wife: Jennet Johnston. Children: William, and Mary wife of James Ellot. Grandchildren: William, James, Mary, Margaret, Jennet, John, and Samuel Ellot.

Oct 18, 1785   May 1, 1792
Goody, George. Executors: Anne Elizabeth Goody and Leonard Jenewin. Manheim Township. Wife: Anna Elizabeth Goody. Children: (Names and number not given.)

Jul 15, 1789   May 4, 1792
Wilson, Ann. Executors: James Maxwell and Robert Delap. Tyrone Township. Legatees: (Sisters) Mary Wilson and Elizabeth Lawrence.

Feb 16, 1791   May 7, 1792
Kemerly, Jacob. Executor: Michael Miller. Windsor Township. Children: Jacob and Margaret wife of ---- Towbenberger. Grandchild: Margaret (daughter of Margaret) wife of Peter Shoenberger.

May 27, 1777   May 11, 1792
Krebs, Christiana. Executor: Peter Krebs. Germany Township. Children: Peter, Anna, Christian, John, Henry, George, and Mary. (This name is spelled "Crebs" on the will.)

Aug 16, 1790   May 19, 1792
Livingston, John. Executors: James and John Livingston. York County. Wife: Sarah Livingston. Children: Mary, Sarah, Agness, Eals, Jean, William, James, and John.

Dec 20, 1790   May 21, 1792
Matthew, William. Executor: Hannah Matthew. York Borough. Wife: Hannah Matthew.

Jul 25, 1785   May 22, 1792
Maxwell, John. Executors: James Maxwell and Alexander McGrew.
Tyrone Township. Wife: Isabella Maxwell. Children: James, Robert, and
John. Granddaughter: Isabella Maxwell (parents' names not given).

--- ---, ----   May 29, 1792
Koch, George. Executors: John Koch and Peter Meyer. York Borough.
(German will.)

Apr 4, 1790   Jun 4, 1792
Neff, Henry. Executors: Christian Eby and Andrew Mayer. Cordorus
Township. Wife: Catharine Neff. Children: Henry, Mary, Anna,
Magdalena, and Elizabeth.

May 18, 1792   Jun 20, 1792
Larimer, John. Executors: William Larimer and Samuel Hunter. Mt. Joy
Township. Wife: Esther Larimer. Brothers: Robert, Thomas, and
William Larimer.

Apr 20, 1792   Jun 25, 1792
Lauman, Catharine. Executor: Christian Sinn. York Borough. Legatees:
Mother, Ann Piles; brother, Christian; sisters, Mary and Susanna Lauman;
and uncle, Christian Sinn.

Apr 12, 1792   Jul 18, 1792
Seitz, Benjamin. Executors: Adam Forney and Jacob Eiselberger.
Heidelberg Township. Wife: Anna Seitz. Children: Aaron, Jacob and
John Hagy (wifes' name not given).

Jun 19, 1792   Sep 5, 1792
Horney, Benedict. Executors: Elizabeth Horney and John Eckert.
Germany Township. Wife: Elizabeth Horney. Children: Henry, (son-in-
law John Eckert wife's name not given.)

Apr 4, 1792   Sep 17, 1792
Gump, George. Executors: John Rothrack and George Goodyear. York
Borough. Wife: Salome Gump. Children: Hannah, Barbara, Rosana,
Catharine, Dorothea, John, Margaret wife of Leonard Hehl, and Elizabeth
wife of Frederick Stein.

May 18, 1779   Oct 3, 1792
Swartzback, Adam. Executor: John Swartzback. Becks Co. Pa. Wife:
Magdalena Swartzback. Children: Anna wife of --- Ottilia, John (and a

son-in-law Ludwig Reigle - wife's name not given) K.B. There was a bequest in will of thirty shillings for the Community at Ephrata for "Pivus causes."

Mar 19, 1792   Oct 5, 1792
Spangler, Peter. Executor: Peter Spangler. Tyrone Township. Wife: (Name not given.) Children: Peter and Sons-in-law - John Snyuder, Henry Stover and Jacob Swartz (the names of their wives not given).

Oct 12, 1792   Oct 30, 1792
Gross, Jacob. Executor: Omitted. Dover Township. Wife: Omitted. Children: Esther and Samuel.

Sep 7, 1788   Nov 13, 1792
Hossack, Thomas. Executor: Henry Hossack. Franklin Township. Wife: Mary Hossack. Children: John, David, Mary wife of Robert Black, and Jean wife of James Cowen.

Oct 5, 1792   Nov 16, 1792
Bateman, Andrew. Executor: Omitted. Township. Wife: Elizabeth Bateman. Children: William, Andrew, Isaac, Reuben and Rachel.

Sep 29, 1792   Nov 24, 1792
Guse, John. Executors: Davolt Snyder and Jacob Keller. Cordorus Township. Wife: Omitted. Children: (Names and number not given.)

Oct 8, 1792   Nov 28, 1792
Heltzel, Tobias. Executors: John Beyer and John Joseph. Paradise Township. Wife: Anna Heltzel. Children: Scharlot wife of Martin Schultz, Henry, Philip, Eve wife of John Boss, Sophia wife of William Haines, Catharine wife of Jacob Geiger, Margaret, John, and Tobias.

Oct 28, 1792   Nov 29, 1792
Strickler, Henry. Executors: Christian Steiner and Henrich Strickler. Hellam Township. Wife: Ann Strickler. Children: Jacob, Henrich and Anna.

Nov 8, 1792   Dec 10, 1792
Wolf, Henry. Executors: George Overdurff and Adam Paulos. Windsor Township. Wife: Mary Wolf. Children: Henry (there were others - but names are not given).

Nov 19, 1792   Dec 21, 1792
Douglas, Thomas. Executors: Thomas McClellan and Robert
Cunningham. Cumberland Township. Wife: Margaret Douglas.
Children: Robert, William, Archibald, and Timothy.

Dec 2, 1792   Dec 22, 1792
McAlister, Abigail. Executor: Richard McAlister. Hanover Township.
Legatee: Richard McAlister (father).

Feb 18, 1779   Dec 27, 1792
Moore, Alexander. Executors: Thomas and Griziel Mickle. Hopewell
Township. Legatee: Griziel Mickle (sister).

Dec 5, 1777   Jan 3, 1793
Herold, Peter. Executor: William Baxter. Newberry Township. Wife:
Rebecca Herold. Children: Peter and Mary.

Mar 16, 1791   Jan 4, 1793
Hummel, Barbara. Executors: George and Jacob Meyer. York County.
Children: Frederick, Catharine, George, and Jacob.

Nov 10, 1792   Jan 9, 1793
Kennard, Anthony. Executors: John Balderston and John Cox. Fawn
Township. Wife: Elizabeth Kennard. Children: Hannah, Elizabeth,
Phebe, Eby, Anthony, Mary, Joseph, Tacy, and Levi.

Jan 12, 1788   Jan 29, 1793
Petery, Stephen. Executors: Henry Danner and George Petery.
Cordorus Township. Wife: Anna Petery. Children: Michael, George,
Stephen, Jacob, Magdalena, Henry, and Anna.

Oct 25, 1792   Feb 2, 1793
Garretson, William. Executors: Elisha Underwood and Aaron Garretson.
Warrington Township. Children: William, John, Aaron, Anna wife of
Elisha Underwood, Sarah wife of James Wickersham, Marion wife of
Thomas McCrery, Naomi wife of James Thomas, and Elizabeth wife of
Joseph Blackford.

Jul 14, 1792   Feb 4, 1793
Yost, Catharine. Executors: Abraham Yost and Conrad Lamb. York
Borough. Children: Nicholas, Abraham, Elizabeth and Catharine.

Dec 18, 1792   Feb 15, 1793
Stouck, Godfrey. Executor: Charlotte Stouck. Dover Township. Wife: Charlotte Stouck. Children: John, George, Elizabeth and Mary.

Nov 29, 179   Mar 4, 1793
McMullin, Hugh. Executors: John Thompson and Edward Ohaall. Monaghan Township. Wife: Omitted. Children: Mary wife of James O. Nail, Ealse wife of Jesse Fulton, Jane, Elizabeth, Hugh, and George.

Oct 19, 1788   Mar 5, 1793
Slenker, Andrew. Executors: Elizabeth and Martin Slenker. Windsor Township. Wife: Elizabeth Slenker. Children: Martin, Andrew, John and Jacob.

Dec 22, 1792   Mar 6, 1793
Bolt, Jonas. Executors: George and Philip Zeigler. Manchester Township. Wife: Catharine Bolt. Children: Peter, Christiana, Elizabeth and Susan.

Jan 14, 1789   Mar 7, 1793
Wilson, Andrew. Executor: Andrew Wilson. Monaghan Township. Children: Daniel, John, Francis, Margaret, Janet, Rebecca and Andrew.

Jul 22, 1791   Mar 8, 1793
Paxton, Samuel. Executor: Nathaniel Paxton. Cumberland Township. Wife: Rachel Paxton. Children: John, Samuel, Thomas, Jane, Isabella, Nathaniel, Hugh, George, Benj., Robert, Jonathan, Moses, David, Joseph, Grisle, Sarah, Margery, and Mary.

Feb 2, 1793   Mar 9, 1793
Grimes, Margaret. Executors: Joseph Homer and James Edger. Chanceford Township. Children: David, John, Conrad and Henry.

Dec 9, 1792   Mar 26, 1793
Magold, George. Executor: Omitted. Berwick Township. Wife: Elizabeth Magold. Children: Barbara wife of Peter Zollinger and Catharine wife of Henry Sumofon.

--- --, ----   Mar 28, 1793
Todd, Joseph. Executors: James Todd and John Love. Newberry Township. Children: Owen and Hannah.

--- --, ----   Apr 8, 1793
Seitz, John. Executors: Henry Koeller, Catharine Seitz and Joseph Seitz.
Strasburg Township. (German will.)

Mar 5, 1793   Apr 16, 1793
Reed, Margaret. Executor: Arthur Orr. Township: Omitted. Children:
Jane, Hugh, Arthur and John.

May 11, 1793   May 15, 1793
Bengham, Hugh. Executor: William Bengham. Hamiltonsban Township.
Wife: (Name not given.) Children: John, Hugh, Thomas and Zearr.

Nov 14, 1792   May 20, 1793
Witterecht, Michael. Executors: Philip Windemere and John Jacoby.
Manchester Township. Children: George, Peter, Jacob, Michael and
Philip. Grandchild: Michael Meow (parents' names not given).

Apr 5, 1773   May 21, 1793
Snodgrass, James. Executors: Joseph Snodgrass and Nathaniel Paxton.
Franklin Township. Legatees: (Mother:) Agnes Snodgrass (Brothers and
Sisters) Robert, Sarah, William, Mary, John and Joseph.

May 24, 1793   Jun 1, 1793
Young, Frederick. Executor: Anna Maria Young. Mt. Pleasant Township.
Wife: Anna Maria Young. Children: Baltzer (there were others - but
names not given).

Jul 1, 1792   Jun 5, 1793
McIlvain, Alexer. Executors: Rebecca and John McIlvain. Mt. Pleasant
Township. Wife: Rebecca McIlvain. Children: Andrew, John, Moses, and
William.

--- --, ----   Jun 10, 1793
Burchart, Julius. Executors: Peter Shultz and Samuel Gross. Township
omitted. German will.

Dec 21, 1789   Jun 27, 1793
Rathfou, Frederick. Executor: Christian Rathfou. Windsor Township.
Wife: Elizabeth Rathfou. Children: George, Christian, Catharine wife of
Mathias Wrestler, Margaret wife of Frederick Zorger, Frederick, Leonard,
Jacob and Elizabeth wife of Andrew Church.

Jun 1, 1793   Jun 28, 1793
Lindy, John. Executor: Henry Shotter. York Borough. Children: Jacob, John, George, Catharine wife of John Mosser, Rosand wife of John Folke, Eve wife of Andrew Shelly, Christiana wife of Yost Mohr, Elizabeth wife of Philip Schwartzwelder, and Dorothea.

Aug 7, 1792   Jun 30, 1793
King, Thomas. Executors: Salome King and Samuel Mosser. York County. Wife: Salome King. Children: John and Elizabeth.

Nov 4, 1785   Jul 16, 1793
Leech, James. Executor: John McGrew. Tyrone Township. Wife: Barbara Leech. Children: Ann, Jenet, Robert, Samuel, Jean, Henry, James, and Mary.

--- --, ----   Aug 6, 1793
Brunner, Henry. Executors: Christian Brunner and John Haller. Manchester Township. (Letters granted and will not recorded.)

May 28, 1792   Aug 13, 1793
Fries, Michael. Executor: George Deats. Windsor Township. Children: George, Martin, Jacob, David, Ann wife of Adam Hinkle, Simon, Ericona wife of John Fake. Grandchildren: Elizabeth, Christian, Catharine, and David (David's children).

May 3, 1790   Aug 30, 1793
Spangler, Michael. Executor: Rudolph Spangler. York Co. Legatees: (Bros.) George, Baltzer and Rudolph Spangler.

Jun 25, 1792   Aug 30, 1793
McPheson, Robert. Executors: William and John McPherson. Cumberland Township. Legatees: Agness McPherson (mother), and William McPherson (brother), and others.

Dec 19, 1790   Aug 31, 1793
McGrew, James. Executors: James and Alexander McGrew. Menallen Township. Children: James, Simeon, Finley, Deborah wife of Joseph Blackburn, Ann and Mary. Grandchildren: Jean McGrew (daughter of James), Mary Brandon, and Rebecca Hatton (daughters of John Hatton mother's name not given).

Aug 30, 1793   Sep 4, 1793
Helfrich, George. Executors: Matthias Spitter and Baltzer Young. Wife:

Christiana Helfrich. Mt. Pleasant Township. Children: Mary and
Christian.

Jun 16, 1785   Sep 5, 1793
Gardner, Peter. Executors: Jacob Gardner and Henry Leibhart.
Yorktown Township. Children: Michael, George, Martin, Philip, Jacob,
Eve wife of Philip Rester, Elizabeth wife of Christian Kurtz, Margaret wife
of Abraham Lersh, Peter, Henry, Adam, and Catharine wife of ---- Swope.
Grandchild: Elizabeth (daughter of Catharine).

Jul 3, 1793   Sep 5, 1793
Thompson, John. Executors: Esther Thompson, Samuel Cobean and
David Agnew. Hamiltonsban Township. Wife: Esther Thompson.
Children: Anne, Mary, John, Elizabeth and Andrew.

Aug 2, 1793   Sep 6, 1793
Keas, John. Executors: William Hamilton and William Gilland. Straban
Township. Wife: Elizabeth Keas. Children: Margaret, Mary, Catharine
wife of William Hamilton, and Jane.

Aug 6, 1793   Sep 17, 1793
Hammond, James. Executors: George and Thomas Hammond. Tyrone
Township. Wife: Mary Hammond. Children: George, Thomas, James,
John, Mary, and Margaret.

Mar 13, 1790   Oct 6, 1793
Fisher, Thomas. Executors: Robert McIlhenney, Thomas and Catharine
Fisher. Yorktown Township. Wife: Catharine Fisher. Children: George,
Elizabeth, Eve, Catharine, Mary, Thomas, James, and Henry.

Apr 22, 1779   Oct 9, 1793
Brandon, George. Executors: James, George and Thomas Brandon. York
County. Children: John, Thomas, Elizabeth wife of John Brown, and
Jane wife of James Henderson. (Grandchildren:) George (son of John),
and George (son of Elizabeth).

Jan 9, 1788   Oct 12, 1793
Detter, Nicholas. Executor: Lorentz Detter. Reading Township.
Children: Lorentz and Mathias.

Sep 28, 1793   Oct 21, 1793
Dorgis, Henry. Executors: Michael Dorgis and John Rothrock.
Manchester Township. Wife: Dorothea Dorgis. Children: Michael,

Frederick, Henry, Barbara, and Rosinah.

May 31, 1793   Oct 30, 1793
Melaun, John. Executors: Jacob Jones, Mathias and Susanna Melaun. Reading Township. Wife: Susanna Melaun. Children: Rebecca, Hannah, Benj., John, Sarah, Mary, and Susanna.

--- --, ----   Nov 2, 1793
Ehresman, Jacob. Executors: Peter and Andrew Shultz. Manchester Township. (There is no will, letters of administration were granted to the parties named.)

Sep 10, 1793   Nov 2, 1793
Graff, Mathias. Executors: Gertrude Graff and Abraham Frostle. Paradise Township. Wife: Anna Graff. Children: Catharine wife of Peter Heilman, Christian, and Henry.

Jul 18, 1791   Nov 8, 1793
Rorrsich, Michael. Executors: Michael Doudle, Jacob Smyser and John Haller. Manchester Township. Children: George, Dorothea wife of Philip Healman, Christiana wife of John Wilhelm, Eve wife of William Trousheld, Susanna wife of Jacob Mutchler, Mary wife of Jacob Bentz and Catharine wife of George Gauff.

Sep 3, 1793   Nov 9, 1793
Bager, John. Executors: Nicholas Bager and David Nicky. Berwick Township. Wife: Betey Bager. Child: John.

Nov 25, 1792   Nov 14, 1793
Linn, John. Executor: Hugh Linn. Cumberland Township. Children: William, John, Samuel, Margaret, Andrew, David, Jennet, Margaret, and Hugh.

Jul 10, 1793   Dec 2, 1793
Wilson, David. Executor: Joseph Wilson. Mt. Pleasant Township. Wife: Catharine Wilson. Children: John, Mary, Margaret, Joseph, Catharine and William.

Aug 20, 1793   Dec 2, 1793
Degroff, Michael. Executors: Samuel Polly and H. Brinkernot. Mt. Pleasant Township. Wife: Margaret Degroff. Children: Abraham, Hannah, Elizabeth, Esther, Catharine, William, Moses, Richard, James, Samuel, Rachel, Nelly, Ann, and Margaret.

Dec 6, 1792   Dec 10, 1793
Holsable, Erasmus. Executors: Erasmus Holsable and Gotleib Fackler.
Manchester Township. Children: Adam, Henry, Jacob, Erasmus,
Elizabeth wife of Henry Shock, Catharine wife of Jacob Clingman, Barbara
wife of Jacob Fockler, Christiana wife of David Stein, and Margaret wife
of Frederick Hoober.

Dec 9, 1793   Dec 24, 1793
Grimm, Philip. Executors: Barbara and Philip Grimm. York County.
Wife: Barbara Grimm. Children: Peter, Christiana, Michael, Dorothea
wife of Conrad Miller, Daniel and John.

May 27, 1790   Dec 30, 1793
Stewart, Robert. Executor: Stephen McKinley. Chanceford Township.
Children: John, Martha, Robert and Rachel.

Sep 18, 1790   Dec 31, 1793
Strickler, Conrad. Executor: Christian Strickler. Hellam Township.
Wife: Christiana Strickler.

Dec 19, 1793   Dec 31, 1793
Bott, Barbara. Executor: John Heller. Manchester Township. Brother:
George Bott. Sister: Mary Bott.

Aug 1, 1792   Apr 1, 1793.
Bope, Mathias. Executors: John and Ludwick Bope. Cordorus Township.
Children: John, Adam and Burkhardt.

Dec 19, 1793   Jan 14, 1794
Ob, Jacob. Executors: Philip Zeigler and Philip Ob. Dover Township.
Legatees: Peter Ob (nephew) and Christiana Hentz (niece).

Sep 20, 1789   Jan 27, 1794
Simon, Casper. Executors: John Klein and Andrew Senff. Cordorus
Township. Wife: Margaret Simon. Child: John.

May 11, 1791   Feb 11, 1794
Herleman, Sebastian. Executor: Barnet Zeigler. Cordorus Township.
Children: Conrad, and (sons-in-law John and George Houser wives' names
not given).

Jan 4, 1794   Feb 17, 1794
Smyser, Jacob. Executors: Elizabeth, Henry and Jacob Smyser.

Manchester Township. Wife: Elizabeth Smyser. Children: Henry, Jacob (and others - but (Names and number not given.))

Oct 20, 1787   Feb 17, 1794
Pressel, Sarah. Executors: Michael and Valentine Pressel. Berwick Township. Children: Michael, Valentine, Henry, and David. Grandchild: Henry Pressel (son of Henry).

May 30, 1793   Feb 28, 1794
Herman, Eve. Executor: Emanuel Herman. Manchester Township. Children: Emanuel, and Mary wife of Jacob Guth. Grandchildren: Mary (daughter of Emanuel), and David Shettron (parents' names not given).

Feb 1, 1791   Mar 6, 1794
Meyer, Adolph. Executors: Mary Ann and John Meyer. Germany Township. Wife: Mary Ann Meyer. Children: John, Nicholas, Elizabeth, Mary, Ann, Joseph, Michael, and Peter.

Oct 17, 1792   Mar 8, 1794
Apmeyer, Melcher. Executors: Anna Apmeyer and Dietrich Apmeyer. Codorus Township. Wife: Anna Apmeyer. Children: Michael and Christiana.

Nov 20, 1793   Mar 8, 1794
Kehr, John. Executor: Henry Danner. Manheim Township. Wife: Mary Kehr. Children: Christian, Samuel, Mary wife of Samuel Throne, and Elizabeth wife of Michael Bucher.

Feb 27, 1794   Mar 17, 1794
Smith, Jacob. Executors: Margaret and Adam Smith. Dover Township. Wife: Margaret Smith. Children: Elizabeth, Margaret, Barbara and Catharine.

Nov 27, 1793   Mar 25, 1794
Tate, Archibald. Executors: James and William Tate. Cumberland Township. Children: Mary wife of John McLaughlin, Jean wife of John McTeeth, Sarah, William and James.

Sep 25, 1785   Mar 31, 1794
Duncan, Seth. Executors: James Duncan and William Scott. Berwick Township. Wife: Christiana Duncan. Children: James, Hannah wife of John Nickleson, Seth, Matthew, Joseph, William, Martha, John, and Abner. Grandchild: William (son of William).

Jan 17, 1794   Apr 7, 1794
Cox, William. Executor: Naomi Cox. Warrington Township. Wife: Naomi Cox. Children: William, Jesse, Joshua, Susanna wife of John Griest, and Emmy wife of John Morton.

Aug 27, 1787   Apr 8, 1794
Miller, John. Executor: William Miller. Hamiltonsban Township. Wife: Isabella Miller. Children: William, Agness wife of William Reed, and James.

Mar 9, 1794   Apr 14, 1794
Kennard, Hannah. Executor: Jacob Balderston. York County. Child: Jesse.

Mar 4, 1794   May 2, 1794
Ashton, William. Executors: Thomas Ashton and William Ashton. Township omitted. Wife: Margaret Huse Ashton. Children: Richard, Thomas and William.

Mar 29, 1794   May 3, 1794
Basserman, Christiana. Executors: M. Bausman and David Brown. Reading Township. Children: Abraham, Philip, Peter, Daniel, Susanna wife of Daniel Brown, Margaret wife of Peter Kock, Christiana wife of Jacob Deel, Catharine wife of Jacob Sherfig, and Mary.

Apr 9, 1794   May 7, 1794
McMillan, Joanna. Executors: William and Joseph Griffith. Warrington Township. Children: Esther wife of John McMillan, Mary (step-children), Mary, Abraham, Jacob, David, Joseph, Debora, William, and Benj. Griffith. Grandchildren: Ruth and James McMillan.

Sep 1, 1789   May 16, 1794
Kurtz, Nicholas. Executors: George, Peter, and Jacob Kurtz. York Borough. Children: Frederick, George, Christian, John, Elizabeth, Benjamin, Jacob, Daniel, and Mary. Son-in-law: Jacob Goering (wife's name not given).

Nov 30, 1792   May 27, 1794
Marsden, Edward. Executors: Matthew and James Marsden. Mt. Pleasant Township. Wife: Jean Marsden. Children: Matthew, James, Jean, and Elizabeth wife of John White. Grandson: Edward White (son of Elizabeth).

Oct 9, 1789   Jun 9, 1794
Slagle, David. Executors: Braltzer Fitz and George Deitz. Berwick Township. Children: Daniel, Elizabeth wife of Daniel Demerce, Catharine wife of Henry Schlar, Margaret wife of Peter Eyster and Mary wife of John Ablenis.

Jan 10, 1794   Jun 9, 1794
Brehm, Jacob. Executors: Samuel Henry and Jacob Brehm. Warrington Township. Children: Samuel, Henry, Jacob, Breshen and Catharine.

Apr 15, 1794   June 9, 1794
Shultz, Jacob. Executors: Braltzer Fitz and George Dietz. Hellam Township. Wife: Eve Shultz. Children: Jacob, George, Henry, Adam, John, Catharine, Eve, Gertrude, Elizabeth and Susanna.

Aug 28, 1793   Jul 21, 1794
Straeher, Peter. Executors: Adam Huber and Jacob Weigel. Dover Township. Wife: Juliana Straeher. Children: Jacob, Peter, John, Mary Magdalena wife of Jacob Wigle, Andrew, Susanna, Elizabeth, Eve and Catharine wife of Lawrence Bitzel.

Jul 16, 1794   Aug 2, 1794
Sheffer, Jacob. Executor: Jacob Sheffer. Dover Township. Wife: Mary Catharine Sheffer. Children: Jacob, John, Ann wife of Peter Boss, Elizabeth and Margaret.

--- --, ----   Aug 4, 1794
Schuller, John Adam. Executors: Anna Schuller and George Maisk. Newburry Township. (German Will)

Apr 4, 1794   Aug 11, 1794
Rohrbaugh, Zacarias. Executors: Adam Rohrbaugh and Samuel Hunter. Mt. Joy Township. Children: John, Christiana, Barbara, Rachel and Adam.

Sep 21, 1793   Aug 16, 1794
Weltz, Joh. Executors: Jacob Weltz and Christian Rubel. Manheim Township. Wife: Eve Weltz. Children: Catharine wife of Ludwig Geeding, Peter, Barbara wife of Christian Rubel, Mary wife of Peter Eleberger, Ann wife of Abraham Myer, Ferena wife of Joseph Bixler, Eve wife of --- Golding, Elizabeth, Magdalena, Jacob, John, Abraham and Joseph. Grandchild: Nancy Golding.

Jan 7, 1793   Sep 2, 1794
Brokaw, George. Executors: Margaret, Peter and George Brokaw and John Bereau. Mount Pleasant Township. Wife: Margaret Brokaw. Children: George, John, Peter, Abraham, Ann wife of William Hockdelin, Mary wife of Jacob Foutz, Lena wife of Cornelius Lott, and Margaret.

Aug 10, 1786   Sep 5, 1794
Beitzel, John. Executors: John Beitzel and Daniel Rauhauser. Dover Township. Wife: Anna Eliza Beitzel. Children: Jonathan, John, Lorence, Elizabeth, Barbara, Magdalena, Margaret, Christian and Louisa.

Jul 25, 1794   Sep 6, 1794
Lane, Abraham. Executor: Samuel Fahenstock. Berwick Township. Legatees: (Father,) Peter Lane; (Brothers) and (Sisters,) Mary, Catharine, John, Samuel and Thomas Lane.

Mar 4, 1786   Sep 22, 1794
Raser, Adam. Executors: Laurence Raser and Adam Raser. Shrewsbury Township. Wife: Catharine Raser. Children: John, Lawrence, Philip (and six others, names not given).

Sep 10, 1793   Sep 24, 1794
Finley, Aaron. Executors: Michael Finley and David Blythe. York County. Wife: Margaret Finley. Children: Maria and William.

Jun 14, 1794   Oct 4, 1794
Farra, William. Executors: John Farra and Frederick Rose. Warrington Township. Wife: Sarah Farra. Children: Samuel and John.

Jul 3, 1793   Oct 11, 1794
Leshy, Susanna. Executor: Henry Elicker. Warrington Township. Legatees: Stepson, Henry Elicker; son of stepdaughter (name not given), Casper Coxen.

Apr 14, 1791   Oct 24, 1794
Runkle, Jacob. Executors: Jacob Runkle and Jacob Behler. Manheim Township. Wife: Anna Mary Runkle. Children: Ludwick, John, Jacob and Catharine wife of Jacob Behler.

May 13, 1794   Nov 1, 1794
Walter, Elizabeth. Executor: Andrew Gottwalt. York Borough. Widow of Henry Walter. Legatees: (Sister) Catharine Gottwalt, (Niece and Nephews) Catharine, Andrew and George Gottwalt (children of

Catharine).

Jan 6, 1784   Nov 1, 1794
Blackburn, Thomas. Executors: Alice Blackburn and Thomas Blackburn. Manallan Township. Wife: Alice Blackburn. Children: Thomas and John.

Sep 7, 1793   Nov 4, 1794
Dicks, Peter. Executors: Tempest Fricker and Christian Hershey. Paradise Township. Wife: Ruth Dicks. Children: Peter, Job, Martha, Mary, John, Deborah wife of William Alexander, and Sarah wife of Thomas Alexander.

Sep 30, 1793   Nov 21, 1794
Griffith, John. Executors: Martha and James Griffith. Hopewell Township. Wife: Martha Griffith. Children: John, Ann, Sarah, Elizabeth wife of James Allen, Rebecca, Rachel, James, David, and Martha wife of George McCann.

Aug 12, 1794   Dec 2, 1794
Phillips, Priscilla. Executor: Hannah Matthews. Legatee: Hannah Matthews (sister).

Jan 6, 1787   Dec 3, 1794
Buchanan, Andrew. Executor: Elizabeth Buchanan. Monaghan Township. Wife: Elizabeth Buchanan. Child: Elizabeth.

May 26, 1792   Dec 5, 1794
King, William. Executors: Hugh and Victor King. Tyrone Township. Nephews: Hugh and John King (sons of brother Victor).

Jan 10, 1794   Dec 16, 1794
Hutchinson, James. Executor: Robert Hutchinson. Mt. Joy Township. Children: James, John, Ann, Martha, Jennet wife of ---- Leech, Esther, Samuel, and Robert. Grandchild: Samuel (son of Jennet.).

Sep 22, 1794   Dec 31, 1794
Smith, James. Executor: Thomas Smith. York. Co. Children: William, Rebecca and Thomas.

Aug 24, 1794   Jan 23, 1795
Gemmel, David. Executors: Robert and James Gemmel. Hopewell Township. Wife: Jean Gemmel. Children: William, George, Jannet,

John, Margaret, Mary, Thomas, and Ann.

Jan 21, 1795   Jan 27, 1795
Coppenhoeffer, Elizabeth. Executor: Godfrey Lenhart. York Borough.
Children: Elizabeth wife of Godfrey Lenhart, Catharine wife of John
Brenneissy, and Valentine.

Dec 19, 1794   Jan 27, 1795
Becker, Conrad Executors: Mathias Becker and George Eichler.
Manchester Township. Wife: Catharine Becker. Children: Mathias,
Peter, Samuel, Philip, Conrad, Jacob, John, Eve wife of Jacob Hoffman,
Magdalina wife of Valentine Kohler, Barbara wife of Charles Mittmar,
Catharine wife of Christian Mohr, Elizabeth wife of George Eicholtz, Ann,
Margaret, and Mary.

Jul 29, 1794   Feb 5, 1795
Wiley, Joseph. Executors: Elizabeth and Mary Wiley. Fawn Township.
Wife: Elizabeth Wiley. Children: Mary (and two daughers - names not
given).

Dec 28, 1794   Feb 16, 1795
Lewis, Ellis. Executor: Eli Lewis. Newberry Township. Wife: Ruth
Lewis. Children: Eli and Ellis. Grandchildren: Ellis, Ruth, Jacob, and
Mary (children of Ellis).

Feb 5, 1795   Feb 22, 1795
Lehmer, John. Executors: Abraham Bower and George Harman.
Warrington Township. Wife: Elizabeth Lehmer. Children: Eve, William,
Mary wife of Philip Erhart, Henry, John, Eve, Catharine wife of Adam
Schwartz, Philip, Elizabeth, Abraham, Sarah, Jacob, Susanna, and David.

Feb 4, 1792   Mar 2, 1795
McCreary, William. Executors: James Reed and Robert Campbell.
Strabant Township. Wife: Margaret McCreary. Children: John, James,
Jannet, Margaret, and William.

Feb 1, 1793   Mar 6, 1795
Arnold, Peter. Executors: Andrew Ruse and Elihue Winderwood.
Warrington Township. Wife: Margaret Arnold. Children: John, Peter,
Catharine, Margaret, Nicholas, Elizabeth, George, Detter and Christiana.

Nov 1, 1793   Mar 6, 1795
Armstrong, Quintin. Executors: Quintin Armstrong and Isaac Armstrong.

Cumberland Township. Wife: Jennet Armstrong. Children: James, Quintin, John and Isaac.

Jan 7, 1792   Mar 12, 1795
Welshans, Elizabeth. Executor: Conrad Welshans. York Borough. Children: Jacob, Magdalena wife of Henry Meas, David and Eve wife of Christian Miller.

Feb 22, 1795   Mar 16, 1795
Wentz, Philip. Executors: Henry Wentz and Barnet Holtzrapple. Dover Township. Wife: Anna Mary Wentz. Children: John, Henry, Philip, Christiana wife of Adam Rupard, Michael, Jacob, Ann, Margaret and Elizabeth.

Nov 11, 1795   Mar 23, 1795
Lehn, Peter. Executor: Samuel Fahnestock. Berwick Township. Wife: Omitted. Children: Hannah, Thomas, and Abraham.

Aug 13, 1790   Mar 25, 1795
Schantz, Jacob. Executor: Conrad Doll. Berwick Township. Wife: Susanna Schantz. Children: Henry, Peter, Jacob, Juliana and Elizabeth.

Oct 22, 1788   Mar 25, 1795
Grihams, William. Executors: Thomas and Robert Grihams. Menallen Township. Wife: Martha Grihams. Children: Thomas, Ann, Margaret, Robert, and William.

Aug 13, 1790   Mar 25, 1795
Johntz, Jacob. Executor: Conrad Doll. Berwick Township. Wife: Susanna Johntz. Children: Henry, Peter, Jacob, Juliana, and Elizabeth.

Oct 11, 1794   Mar 25, 1795
McFarlan, John. Executors: William Hamilton and William Bogle.

Feb. 12, 1795 Apr 3, 1795
Schwartz, Christian. Paradise Township. Legatees: (Bros. & Sisters) George, Magdalena, Catharine and Sally Schwartz.

Nov 28, 1794   Apr 3, 1795
Ham, Daniel. Executor: Peter Ham. Cordorus Township. Children: John, Jacob, Daniel, and Peter.

Apr 13 1795   Apr 8, 1795
Stemmers, John. Executors: James Thompson and Samuel McCullough. Hamiltonsban Township. Wife: Margaret Stemmers. Children: John and Alexander.

Mar 19, 1795   Apr 9, 1795
Wonder, Stephen. Executor: Sebastian Wonder. Huntington Township. Children: Sebastian, Stephen, Henry, Margaret wife of Godfrey Sidle and Elizabeth wife of Frederick Wailer.

Apr 1, 1790   Apr 13, 1795
Fass, Christian. Executors: George Warner and Richard Auman. Manheim Township. Wife: Elizabeth Fass.

Aug 1, 1788   Apr 21, 1795
Bringman, Frederick. Executor: Omitted. York Borough. Wife: Catharine Bringman. Children: John, (others whose names are not recorded.)

Feb 12, 1791   May 16, 1795
Baer, Christian. Executors: Christian Hershey and Elizabeth Baer. Heidelberg Township. Wife: Elizabeth Baer. Children: Michael, Anne wife of Nicholas Bweher, and (three other daughters whose names are not given.)

Jan 3, 1794   May 25, 1795
Long, Henry. Executors: Philip Christ and J. G. Odeman. Paradise Township. Children: Jacob, Elizabeth wife of Philip Christ, Anna wife of Adam Klinepeter, Catharine wife of Adam Utz, Enis, Susanna, William, Conrad, Henry, and Jacob.

Jan 4, 1795   Jun 3, 1795
Stauffer, Peter. Executors: John Goghenaur, John Hurst and Margaret Stauffer. Newberry Township. Wife: Margaret Stauffer. Children: Jacob, Christian, and a son-in-law Jacob Hurst - who was married to the oldest daughter - name not given.

Jan 1, 1795   Jun 15, 1795
Lan, Michael. Executors: Peter, Michael and Andrew Lan. Manchester Township. Wife: Anna Mary Lan. Children: Michael, Peter (and two daughters whose names were not given.)

May 1, 1790   Jun 16, 1795
Shrieber, Peter. Executor: Jacob Shrieber. Manchester Township. Wife: Margaret Shreiber. Children: Peter, Jacob, John, Michel, Ann wife of George Snellbecker, Maria wife of Henry Rudy, Catharine wife of John Wilot and Eva wife of Henry Borhaf.

May 13, 1795   Jun 24, 1795
Dugles, William. Executors: Daniel Mouteeth and David Demore. Straban Township. Wife: Eunics Dugles. Children: Jean wife of Joseph Taylor, Mary wife of James Steedt, and Margaret wife of James Shield.

May 26, 1795   Jul 1, 1795
Test, George. Executors: George Wogan and William Welch. York Borough. Wife: Margaret Test. Children: George, Anna, Jacob, Isabella and John.

Jul 6, 1795   Aug 7, 1795
McMillan, George. Executors: Joseph Garretson, George and Ann McMillan. Warrington Township. Wife: Ann McMillan. Children: George, Thomas, Jacob, Joseph, Rebecca, Ann, Deborah, and Mary.

Jul 23, 1795   Aug 8, 1795
McQueen, Josiah. Executors: Armstrong Carethers and William Gilliland. Franklin Township. Wife: Isabella McQueen. Children: Susanna, and Elizabeth wife of Armstrong Carethers.

Oct 21, 1787   Aug 12, 1795
Bard, Dorothy. Executor: John Spangler. York Town. Children: George, Barbara wife of Jabob Eichelberger, and Margaret wife of John Spangler.

Feb 2, 1795   Aug 24, 1795
Meyer, Peter. Executor: Mathias Meyer. Cordorus Township. Wife: Elizabeth Meyer. Children: Conrad, Regina, David, Christiana wife of John Hering, Peter, Elizabeth, Adam, Henry, Mathias, and Frederick.

May 28, 1793   Aug 26, 1795
McSherry, Patrick. Executors: Robert McElhenny and James McSherry. Germany Township. Wife: Catherine McSherry. Children: Mary wife of William Owings, John, Barnabus, Catharine, Hugh, Sarah, Patrick, and James. Grandchild: Catharine McSherry (daughter of Patrick).

Aug 31, 1794   Sep 7, 1795
Maxwell, Isabel. Executor: Finley McGrew. Tyrone Township. Legatees: Margaret Mitchel and Mary Dode (sisters), and others.

Aug 1, 1794   Sep 19, 1795
Dickson, James. Executor: John Dickson. Straban Township. Wife: Susanna Dickson. Children: Sarah, Margaret, John, and Samuel.

Sep 14, 1795   Sep 21, 1795
Sarback, Catharine. Executors: Henry Lehmer. Berwick Township. Children: Susanna wife of John Richwine, Jacob, David, Michael, Christiana wife of Jacob Bauin and Elizabeth wife of John Brown. Grandchild: Catharine Brauin.

Nov 11, 1794   Sep 29, 1795
Johnston, James. Executors: William McLean and Thomas Meredith. Franklin Township. Wife: Elizabeth Johnston. Children: Ephriam, William, Jean, and Agness.

Sep 26, 1795   Oct 1, 1795
McCalister, Richard. Executors: Jacob Rudisill, Archibald and Jessee McCalister. Hanover Township. Children: Jean, Archibald, Matthew, Richard, Nancy wife of Patrick Hays, Elizabeth wife of John McCalister, Sally wife of John Anne, and Jessee (to whom he wills his sword and pistols).

Jan 16, 1769   Oct 8, 1795
Vanduyn, David. Executors: David Cassart and George Williamson. York County. Wife: Ida Vandeyne. Children: David, Sarah wife of David Cassart, Cassar wife of George Williamson and Mary wife of (husband's name omitted). Grandchildren: David, Nelly, Ida and Maria (children of Mary - their last name not recorded).

Sep 16, 1795   Oct 21, 1795
Keplinger, Pete. Executors: Daniel and Peter Keplinger. Manheim Township. Wife: Hannah Keplinger. Children: Catharine wife of George Newman, Elizabeth, Daniel, Peter, Anamary wife of John Myer, and Samuel.

Sep 29, 1795   Oct 26, 1795
Mair, Daniel. Executors: Hugh and Thomas Fergus. Bedford Township. Legatees: Hugh Fergus (not a relative), and John and Samuel Fergus, and Agness McClelland (children of Hugh Fergus).

Aug 14, 1793   Oct 29, 1795
Trimmer, Andrew. Executors: Anthony Deardorff and David Trimmer. Reading Township. Children: David, Matthew, William, Mary wife of Anthony Deardorff, Sophia wife of Jacob Brugh, Anna, Christiana wife of Jacob Picking, Eleanor, John, Andrew and Sally wife of ---- Aughinbough. Grandchild: William Aughinbough.

Nov 5, 1791   Oct 30, 1795
Cleaver, Peter. Executors: Peter and John Cleaver. Warrington Township. Wife: Marian Cleaver. Children: Elizabeth, Peter, John, Sarah, and William.

--- --, ----   Oct 31, 1795
Keffer, Mathias. Executors: John Kuhn and Mary Elizabeth Keffer. Berwick Township. Wife: Mary Elizabeth Keffer. Children: Elizabeth, Eve, John, Catharine, Joseph, and Jacob (children of second wife); Ludwig, Mary and Barbara (children of first wife Eve Keffer).

Oct 4, 1795   Nov 5, 1795
Bixler, Christian. Executors: Magdalena Bixler and John Hoover. Manchester Township. Wife: Magdalena Bixler. Children: Christian, Jacob, Joseph, Michael, John, Conrad, Magdalena wife of Peter Waltz, Elizabeth wife of John Hoover, Catharine, and Eve.

Jan 2, 1794   Nov 24, 1795
Stoner, Frederick. Executors: Jacob Stoner and Peter Buss. Paradise Township. Children: Michael, Adam, George and Christiana.

Aug 31, 1789   Nov 30, 1795
Eply, John. Executor: Francis Himes. Manheim Township. Wife: Rosina Eply. Children: Matthias and Hanspeter.

Feb 24, 1794   Dec 5, 1795
Kerr, William. Executors: Alexander McNair and Alexander Russell. Hamiltonsban Township. Wife: Jane Kerr. Children: John, Eleanor, William, James, and David.

Feb 2, 1794   Dec 31, 1795
Peacher, John. Executors: Simon Peacher and Peter Miers. Berwick Township. Children: Simon, Elizabeth, Catharine, Henry, Christiana, and John.

Apr 6, 1795   Jan 1, 1796
Bety, Samuel. Executors: Benjamin Bety and John Polk. Reading Township. Wife: Mary Bety. Children: Benjamin, William, Samuel, John, Jane, Elizabeth wife of George Smith, Susanna wife of Marmyduke Wilson, Esther wife of John Polk, Rachel wife of David Polk, Lilly wife of Ludwick Franks, Margaret wife of Thomas McFarland, and Sarah wife of William Laughlin.

Nov 13, 1795   Jan 9, 1796
Hoffman, Mary. Executors: John Sharp and Frederick Hoffman. Dover Township. Children: Charles, Henry, Daniel, Adam, Frederick, Elizabeth wife of George Miller, Barbara wife of ---- Crombauch, Christiana, and Hannah wife of Jacob Zenk.

Nov 17, 1795   Jan 19, 1796
Brown, Agness. Executors: James Robinson and Samuel Robinson. Chanceford Township. Sister: Mary Lueney.

Dec 18, 1795   Jan 23, 1796
Trump, John. Executors: Mary Trump and Richad Mummard. Paradise Township. Wife: Mary Trump. Children: John and Mary.

Apr --, 1794   Jan 26, 1796
Hancock, James. Executors: John, Benjamin, and Joel Hancock. Newberry Township. Wife: Elizabeth Hancock. Children: James, Elizabeth, Sarah, John, Benjamin, and Joel.

Jan 4, 1796   Feb 11, 1796
Slentz, Philip. Executors: Ludwick Griver and John McCreary. Heidleberg Township. Wife: Marilis Slentz. Children: Jacob and Nicholas.

Dec 13, 1795   Feb 18, 1796
Sox, Nicholas. Executors: Sarah Sox and Benjamin Bower. Huntington Township. Wife: Sarah Sox.

Jan 15, 1796   Feb 26, 1796
Strup, Martin. Executor: Catharine M. Strup. Mt. Pleasant Township. Wife: Catharine Margaret Strup. Children: Daniel, Ann, Mary, Elizabeth, Barbara, Susanna, Rachel, Rebecca, John and Martin.

Jul 29, 1789   Feb 28, 1796
Cooper, William. Executors: William and James Cooper. York County.

Wife: (Name not given.) Children: John, William, Jannet, Finwell, Christiana Elizabeth, Nieely, Mary, Rachel and Robert.

Feb 13, 1796   Mar 3, 1796
Miller, George. Executors: George Petery and Philip Miller. Manheim Township. Wife: Mary Miller. Children: (Names and number not given.)

Mar 11, 1795   Mar 8, 1796
Robinson, Isaac. Executors: Jacob and John Robinson. Hamiltonsban Township. Wife: Jane Robinson. Children: Catharine wife of William Smith, Sarah wife of George White, Mary wife of William Hart, Samuel, Isaac and John.

Feb 18, 1796   Mar 8, 1796
Sheffer, Catharine. Executor: Anthony Slothour. Dover Township. Children: Catharine wife of Anthony Slothour, Elizabeth wife of Conrad Stouchenberger, Barbara wife of Charles Cuin, Margaret wife of Frederick Bakers, Christiana wife of Joseph Seip, Malcher and Philip.

Jan 22, 1793   Mar 11, 1796
Wolff, Peter. Executors: George Bard and Andrew Wolff. Manchester Township. Wife: Catharine Wolff. Children: Dorothea wife of Michael Ege, Elizabeth wife of George Bard, Ann wife of Peter Becker, Adam, Henry, Babara wife of Peter Schmeiser, Catharine and Margaret wife of Christian Eyster. Grandchildren: Peter and Margaret Eyster.

Jan 22, 1796   Mar 12, 1796
Hyre, Frederick. Executor: Jacob Hyre. Newberry Township. Children: Charles, Jacob, Elizabeth, and Magdalena.

--- --, ----   Mar 15, 1796
Miller, Tobias. Executors: Catharine and Michael Miller. Strasburg Township. (German will.)

Nov 25, 1793   Mar 19, 1796
Leib, Christian. Executors: Abraham Leib and Joseph Updegraf. Manchester Township. Children: Abraham, Ann wife of Joseph Updegraf, Catharine wife of John Roth, Elizabeth wife of Christian Miller, Juliana wife of Michael Miller, and Magdalena.

Mar 1, 1796   Mar 21, 1796
Buss, Peter. Executors: Jacob Buss and Baker Jung. Paradise Township. Wife: Elizabeth Buss. Children: John, Jacob, Mary wife of

Baltzer Jung, and Elizabeth.

Mar 24, 196   Apr 2, 1796
Miller, Paul. Executor: Paul Miller. Heidleberg Township. Children: Paul, Elizabeth wife of Michael Zemmerman. Grandchildren: Catharine wife of Martin Hoffman, Elizabeth wife of Andrew Schwrtzman, and Joseph Schwrtzman (parents' names not given).

--- --, ----   Apr 6, 1796
Ellenberger, Peter. Executors: Henry Strickler and Abraham Leib. Manchester Township. German will.

Apr 5, 1793   Apr 21, 1796
Bigham, Patrick. Executor: Samuel Bigham. Mt. Joy Township. Wife: Mary Bigham. Children: Samuel, Hugh, Byran, Eleanor and Agness.

Mar 9, 1796   Apr 23, 1796
McCandless, John. Executor: Mary McCandless. Chanceford Township. Children: James, Katharine wife of James Bradley, George, and Mary.

Dec 18, 1787   May 3, 1796
Logan, John. Executor: Henry Logan. Monaghan Township. Wife: Agness Logan. Child: Henry. Grandchildren: John, Jenny, and Nancy Logan, and John and Agness McGill (parents' names not given).

Feb 2, 1795   May 21, 1796
May, Jacob. Executors: Barbara and Daniel May. Dover Township. Wife: Barbara May. Children: Jones, Jacob, Samuel, Sarah (children of the first wife) (viz.), Daniel May and a daughter the wife of Jacob Rahauser.

May 1, 1780   May 21, 1796
McCall, John. Executor: Omitted. York County. Brothers: Matthew and Robert McCall.

Jan 8, 1787   May 24, 1796
Bentz, Anna Mary. Executor: Abraham Frostel. York Town. Children: Christian, Whyrick, Peter, Anna, Susanna, Elizabeth, Salome, and Ursula.

May 17, 1796   May 30, 1796
Henry, Peter. Executors: Daniel Henry and John Gossweiler. Monaghan Township. Wife: Anna Henry. Children: Peter, Joel, Joseph, Daniel, and Samuel. Grandson: John Henry (parents' names not given).

Feb 23, 1796   Jun 2, 1796
Moser, Samuel. Executors: Henry Tyson and John Herbach. York County. Wife: Solome Moser. Children: Samuel, (and others whose names were not given.)

Feb 21, 1787   Jun 9, 1796
Shriver, Ludwick. Executors: Ludwick and John Shriver. Heidleberg Township. Children: Ludwick, John, Peter, Elizabeth wife of Nicholas Shearly, Catharine wife of Peter Foreman, Susanna wife of Henry Forney, Margaret wife of Henry Hartman and Solome wife of George Clapsaddle.

Dec 7, 1795   Jun 15, 1796
Fox, Peter. Executors: Margaret and John Fox. Reading Township. Wife: Margaret Fox. Children: Catharine, Salome, and Peter.

Apr 7, 1785   Jun 27, 1796
Noblit, Ann. Executor: Robert Hamersby. Newberry Township. Widow of Abraham Noblit. Children: James, John, William, and Mary wife of Robert Hamersly. Grandchildren: Abraham, Rhodes, Ann and Rebecca.

Mar 21, 1791   Aug 6, 1796
Mesemer, Yodorus. Executor: Henry Mesemer. Manheim Township. Wife: Anna Mary Meseman. Children: John, Elizabeth wife of William Knash, Jacob, Henry, and Mary.

Feb 26, 1796   Sep 9, 1796
Ralston, John. Executor: William Anderson. Fawn Township. Wife: Mary Ralston. Legatees: James (brother) and Rebecca Graham (sister).

May 24, 17956   Sep 9, 1796
Slentz, John. Executors: George Heagy and Jacob Stentz. Mt. Joy Township. Wife: Catharine Slentz. (There were three children names not given.)

Oct 5, 1793   Sep 9, 1796
Fegely, Paul. Executors: Conrad Doll and George Belk. Paradise Township. Wife: Elizabeth Fegely. Children: Elizabeth wife of Conrad Doll, Anna wife of George Beck, and Barbara wife of Ludwig Hiner.

Jan 13, 1767   Sep 29, 1796
McKinley, John. Executor: Omitted. Maryland. Wife: Catharine McKinley. Children: Benjamin and Andrew.

--- --, ----   Oct 4, 1796
Mohr, Nicholas. Executors: Philip and Peter Mohr. Manchester Township. (German will.)

Oct 25, 1793   Oct 11, 1796
Miller, Michael. Executor: Jacob Strickler. Hellam Township. Wife: Elizabeth Miller. Children: Elizabeth wife of Conrad Doll, Anna wife of George Beck, and Barbara wife of ---- Ludwig.

Sep 17, 1796   Oct 22, 1796
Boyd, George. Executors: Thomas Leech and John McMillan. Warrington Township. Wife: Catharine Boyd. Children: James, Ann, Jane, and Rachel.

Sep 29, 1796   Oct 25, 1796
McClellan, William. Executors: David Moore, Daniel Edie, and William McClellan. Cumberland Township. Children: Margaret wife of Robert McCracken, Martha, Samuel, William, David, and James.

Apr 24, 1794   Nov 4, 1796
Hamersly, William. Executor: Robert Hamersly. Newberry Township. Sister: Mary Saddler. Brother-in-law: John McDonald. Nephew: Daniel McDonald (son of John).

Aug 4, 1795   Nov 9, 1796
Becthel, George. Executor: Philip Lory. Germany Township. Wife: Mary Ann Becthel. Child: Tobias.

Oct 13, 1796   Nov 14, 1796
Brown, Mary. Executors: John Nicholas and William Welsh. Manchester Township. Children: John, Phebe, and Sarah.

Sep 6, 1796   Nov 17, 1796
Spangler, John. Executors: George Bard and Jacob and Margaret Spangler. York Co. Wife: Margaret Spangler. Children: Sarah, Zacharia, John, William, Rebecca, Mary and Juliana.

Nov 22, 1792   Nov 19, 1796
Messerly, Daniel. Executors: Peter Messerly and John Hoover. Dover Township. Children: Abraham, Peter, Susanna wife of John Hoover, and Anna wife of Jacob Hoover.

Nov 1, 1796   Nov 21, 1796
Long, John. Executors: Conrad Long and James Bolton. Manheim Township. Wife: Anna Maria Long. Children: Conrad, John, Juliana, Christiana, Anna wife of George Erehard, and Elizabeth wife of Jacob Larch.

Nov 19, 1796   Dec 3, 1796
Rupp, Baltzer. Executors: Christian Rupp and Gotlieb Rupp. Hellam Township. Wife: Elizabeth Rupp. Child: Jacob.

Jul 5, 1795   Dec 6, 1796
Marter, George. Executors: Jacob and Henry Marter. Manheim Township. Children: Jacob, George, Catharine wife of Frederick Baucher, Anna wife of Frederick Eyechilberger, and Valentine. Grandson: Ludwig Marter (son of Valentine).

May 11, 1790   Dec 19, 1796
Weems, Thomas. Executors: Henry Black and Jonathan Neely. Mt. Joy Township. Children: John, Elizabeth wife of Jesse McAllister, Mary wife of Henry Black and Sarah wife of Jonathan Nely. Grandchildren: Anna, Sarah, and Elizabeth Black. Anna, Mary and Jennet Neely.

Nov 23, 1796   Dec 25, 1796
Hammer, Conrad. Executors: Paul Miller and John Kuhn. Heidleburg Township. Wife: Catharine Hammer. Children: (Names and number not given.)

Nov 7, 1796   Dec 27, 1796
Miclheim, George. Executors: George McMihlheim and Martin Miller. Manheim Township. Wife: Eve Miclheim. Second wife: Catharine Miclheim. Children of the first wife: Eve wife of Philip Dewalt, and Margaret wife of Philip Danner. Children of the second wife: Catharine, Christian, and George.

Dec 5, 1796   Jan 4, 1797
McGinley, John. Executors: Moses McClean, Joseph and Edward McGinley. Hamiltonsban Township. Wife: Jane McGinley. Children: Mary wife of James Rankin, Margaret wife of Isaac Moore, Abigail wife of William Rankin, Alexander, John, Joseph, and Ebenezer.

Feb 8, 1796   Jan 16, 1797
Byermister, Frederick. Executor: Christopher Byermister. Heidleberg Township. Wife: Anna Byermister. Children: Christopher, Anna wife of

Michael Kline, Elizabeth wife of Frederick Smith, and Christiana wife of Peter Short.

Jan 8, 1797   Jan 28, 1797
Cronbaek, Jacob. Executors: George Philip Zeigler and George Julius. Dover Township. Wife: Christiana Cronbaek. Children: John, Philip, Henry, Elizabeth, and George.

Oct 12, 1796   Feb 4, 1797
Barnitz, Charles. Executors: Jacob Barnitz and Rudolph Spangler. York Borough. Wife: Anna Barbara Barnitz. Children: Charles, George, John, Daniel, Jacob, Michael, Susan, and Rebecca.

--- ---, ----   Feb 17, 1797
Hoffman, Christian. Executors: John Leas and Andrew Spangler. Manheim Township. German will.

--- ---, ----   Mar 2, 1797
Fisher, John. Executors: John Richard and Ludwig Bob. Shrewsbury Township. German will.

--- ---, ----   Mar 6, 1797
Bender, Martin. Executors: Gabriel Smith and Peter Bender. Warrington Township. (Will not copied.)

Nov 6, 1789   Mar 8, 1797
Brown, Richard. Executor: Richard Brown. Straban Township. Wife: Susanna Brown. Children: John, Richard, William, James, and Susanna.

Aug 25, 1795   Mar 9, 1797
Clapsadle, Catin. Executor: Omitted. Child: Michael.

Jan 24, 1797   Mar 19, 1797
Stauseberg, Conrad. Executor: George Lewis Lefler. York Borough. Wife: Elizabeth Stauseberg. Children: John, George, Henry, Andrew, Daniel, Catharine and Joseph.

Dec 9, 1798   Mar 26, 1797
Edgar, William. Executors: Joseph and William Edgar. Hopewell Township. Wife: Libbie Edgar. Children: Joseph, William, David, Ellener wife of William Legget, Jr., Ann, Jennet, and Thomas.

Sep 24, 1791   Mar 27, 1797
Shellbecker, Catharine. Executors: Anna B. Eicholtz and G. Mathias
Eicholtz. Dover Township. Children: Anna and Mathias Eicholtz.

Apr 1, 1797   Jun 6, 1797
Simpson, James. Executors: Joseph Morrison and Marmaduke Wilson.
Franklin Township. Legatees: (Brothers and Sister) Elizabeth, John and
Robert Simpson.

Mar 15, 1791   Apr 3, 1797
Eicholtz, Frederick. Executors: Frederick Eicholtz and John Henisen.
Dover Township. Wife: Catharine Eicholtz. Children: Frederick,
Mathias, and George.

Mar 15, 1797   Apr 6, 1797
Gret, John, Executors: Michael Gret and Peter Storm. Hanover
Township. Wife: Ann Elizabeth Gret. Children: Nicholas, Elizabeth,
Christiana, Eve, Jacob, Michael, Joseph, and Apolonia.

Jan 25, 1797   Apr 11, 1797
Barr, James. Executor: James Barr. Mount Joy Township. Children:
James, Agnes, Sarah and Catharine.

Mar 24, 1794   Apr 11, 1797
Lehman, Christian. Executors: Christian Lehman and Stephen Keeb.
Hellam Township. Wife: Catharine Lehman. Children: Christian,
Abraham, Susanna, John, and Henry.

Mar 11, 1797   Apr 26, 1797
Kauter, Bernhard. Executor: Catharine Kauter. Manchester Township.
Wife: Catharine Kauter. Child: Philip.

Aug 23, 1796   May 6, 1797
Mohr, Peter. Executor: John Wolf. Paradise Township. Children:
Jacob, John, Eve, Catharine, Elizabeth, Barbara, Magdalena, Gertrude,
and Margaret.

Sep 13, 1796   May 11, 1797
Moore, Anthony. Executors: Job and John Moore. Newberry Township.
Children: Job, John, Annamaria, Mordica, and Anna.

Jul 5, 1793   May 19, 1797
Beck, Jacob. Executors: Jacob Beck and Ludwig Bote. Shrewsbury
Township. Children: Jacob, Catharine wife of John Fleitz, Ann wife of

Peter Smith, Mary wife of Paul Brwee, and Elizabeth.

Apr 27, 1794   Jun 5, 1797
Cramer, Helfrig. Executors: Henry and Philip Cramer. Manheim Township. Wife: Eve Elizabeth Cramer. Children: Henry, Philip, John, Anna, and Margaret.

Sep 2, 1793   Jun 5, 1797
Rickey, David. Executors: George Robinett and Andrew Thompson. Huntington Township. Children: Thomas, Andrew, John, David, Esther wife of William Meely, Sarah wife of Alexander Trindle and Hannah wife of John Lamb.

Oct --, 1792   Jun 9, 1797
Albert, Lawrence. Executors: Andrew Albert and Jacob Albert. Huntington Township. Children: Margaret wife of Lawrance Hyas, Andrew, Jacob, Applonia wife of George Herman and John. (Child of Margaret:) Lawrance Hyas.

Jan 20, 1794   Jun 9, 1797
Ross, William. Executor: David Ross. Straban Township. Children: John, David, William, Agness, Susanna wife of George Master and James. Grandchildren: William Ross (son of John), Eleanor, William, Isabella and Jean (children of David).

Aug 7, 1795   Jun 9, 1797
Zeigler, Barnet. Executors: Philip and John Zeigler. Cordorus Township. Wife: Rosina Zeigler. Children: Philip, Barbara Adam, John, Christiana, Sabina and Rosina.

Jan 21, 1795   Jun 10, 1797
Douglas, William. Executor: David Douglas. Chanceford Township. Wife: Elizabeth Douglas. Children: David, James, William, and John.

Dec 28, 1795   Jun 17, 1797
Spence, George. Executor: John Spence. Newberry Township. Children: John.

--- --, ----   Jun 19, 1797
Shannon, Thomas. Executor: Joseph Shannon. Hamiltonsban Township. Wife: Mary Shannon. Children: Joseph and Mary and Henry Cowley. Grandson: Thomas Cowley.

Apr 7, 1786   Jul 17, 1797
Spengler, John George. Executor: John Wolf. York Co. Legatees: (Sisters) Susanna Spengler and Christiana wife of George Diehl and to children of (Bro.) Rudolph Spengler.

May 23, 1795   Aug 14, 1797
Thompson, William. Executors: George Hays and William Thompson. Strabn Township. Children: Sarah wife of George Hays. Grandchildren: William, Charity, George, Adam, Sarah, John, Lessy and Alexander Hays.

May 27, 1797   Sep 2, 1797
Wilson, James. Executor: Richard Wilson. Monaghan Township. Children: Alexander and Richard.

--- --, ----   Sep 12, 1797
Kohlman, Valentine. Executors: Jost Kerbach and Frederick Grunwald. Manheim Township. (German will.)

Aug 20, 1797   Sep 16, 1797
Shotter, Henry. Executors: Dorothea and Henry Shotter. York Borough. Wife: Dorothea Shotter. Children: Anna, Catharine, Elizabeth, Frederick and Margaret.

Mar 23, 1795   Oct 3, 1797
Garretson, John. Executors: Samuel and Joseph Garretson. Newberry Township. Children: Willliam, Joseph, John, Ann, Samuel, Sarah, and Cornelius. Grandchildren: Jacob Garretson (son of William), Elizabeth and Mathias Kirk (parents' names not given), Edward, Jane, Hannah, and Phebe Jones (parents' names not given).

Jul 5, 1797   Oct 12, 1797
Dullinger, George. Executors: Henry Deardorff and Jacob Lerew. Monaghan Township. Wife: Catharine Dullinger. Child: John.

Sep 30, 1795   Oct 28, 1797
Miller, Robert. Executors: Samuel and Thomas Miller. Newberry Township. Wife: Sarah Miller. Children: Thomas, Margaret wife of ----, Samuel, Robert, Mary, and Hannah. Grandchildren: Joseph Miller, Sarah Bonine, and Ruth (last name not given) (parents' names not given).

Sep 16, 1797   Nov 8, 1797
Laumaster, Wendle. Executor: Peter Reisinger. York Borough. Child: Frederick. Grandchild: Elizabeth Laumaster (child of Frederick).

Nov 6, 1797   Nov 21, 1797
Screiber, Jacob. Executors: John Emig and Michael Schreiber. York Borough. Wife: Eliza Screiber. Children: Michael, Maria, Elizabeth, Susanna and Margaret.

Jan 19, 1797   Dec 4, 1797
Packer, Moses. Executors: Philip and George Packer. Warrington Township. Children: Philip, Lydia, George, Hannah wife of Abraham Underwood, John, Moses, James, and Aaron.

--- --, ----   Dec 6, 1797
Minch, Simon. Executors: Simon and Michael Minch. Strasburg Township. (German will.)

Apr 20, 1797   Dec 9, 1797
Gohn, Margaret. Executor: Michael Kawfelt. Windsor Township. Sisters: Anna Gohn and Catharine Albright.

Sep 20, 1797   Dec 15, 1797
Short, James. Executors: John Edie, Conrad Laub and William Davison. York Borough. Wife: Jane Short.

Jan 7, 1795   Jan 18, 1798
Schmith, Barbara. Executors: Peter Diehl, Jacob Barmitz and Frederick Yuce. York Borough. Bequests to Luthern Church York Pa.

Apr 18, 1792   Jan 20, 1798
Fogelson, Philip. Executor: Frederick Klepfer. Warrington Township. Wife: Barbara Fogelson. Children: Nicholas, Catharine, Christiana, Christopher, and Philip.

Dec 20, 1797   Feb 5, 1798
Smith, Barnet. Executor: Henry Eppley. Manchester Township. Wife: Margaret Smith. (There were eight children - names not given.)

Jan 22, 1798   Feb 10, 1798
Herschy, Joseph. Executors: Henry Baer and Nicholas Grove. Paradise Township. Children: Barbara, Anna wife of Christian Miller, Andrew, Christian, Magdalena wife of Emanuel Newschwange, and Elizabeth wife of Henry Strickhouser.

Dec 21, 1795   Mar 5, 1798
Gemmill, John. Executors: Elizabeth Gemmill and John Kelly. Hopewell

Township. Wife: Elizabeth Gemmill. Children: Margaret, William, James, Jannet, Ann, Elizabeth, Mary, Jean, Robert, Sarah, Agness, David, and John.

Dec 5, 1797   Mar 7, 1798
Young, James. Executors: Robert L. Arman and Joseph Walker. York County. Wife: Mary Young. Children: Peggy and --- Moore and (son-in-law) Samuel Johnston (wife's name not given). Grandchildren: James Johnston and James and Matley Moore.

Jan 20, 1790   Mar 9, 1798
Shanck, Elizabeth. Executor: George Schanck. York Borough. Widow of Joseph Shanck. Child: George.

Jan 17, 1798   Mar 17, 1798
Melann, Mathias. Executors: John Melann and Bovins Fahnestock. Reading Township. Wife: Catharine Melann. Children: John, Elizabeth wife of ---- Kilmore, Sarah, Rebecca, Rachel, and Anna.

Feb 12, 1798   Mar 27, 1798
Evans, David. Executors: Thomas Evans and Martin Raffensberger. Warrington Township. Wife: Eve Evans. Children: Sarah, Peter, David, Betsy, and Catharine.

Jan 9, 1798   Mar 27, 1798
Deardorff, Jacob. Executors: Isaac Deardorff and George Robinet. Huntington Township. Wife: Elizabeth Deardorff. Children: Samuel, Daniel, Henry, Jacob, John, Peter, Abraham, Benjamin, Elizabeth, Mary, Hannah, Sarah, and Rebecca.

Mar 1, 1798   Apr 12, 1798
Sely, Henry. Executor: Boris Fahnstock. Berlin Township. Wife: Mary Sely.

Mar 1, 1790   Apr 12, 1798
John, Joshua. Executor: Cornelius Garretson. Newberry Township. Wife: Rachel John. Children: Sarah, Elizabeth, Griffith, Rachel, Isaah, Hannah, Ann, and Isabella wife of ---- Cooper.

Dec 9, 1791   Apr 13, 1798
Kaller, George. Executors: Ulerick Huber and Michael Miller. Manheim Township. Wife: Christiana Kaller. Children: Jacob, Abraham, Elizabeth wife of Jacob Kaller, Catharine wife of Mathias Brobeck, Barbara wife of

Christian Leil, Eve wife of Abraham Miller, Anna wife of Michael Miller, and Christiana.

Jun 4, 1796   Apr 24, 1798
Kaun, Henry. Executors: George and Adam Berd. Hellam Township. Children: Michael, John, Philip, Henry, Daniel, John, Susanna wife of Michael Dersteen, Catharine wife of Frederick Ruhl, Barbara wife of ---- Heyer, (and now married to Jacob Stohly), Mary wife of Philip Decker, and Magdalena wife of John Kauffman. Grandchildren: John and Barbara Heyer, (and four children of Catharine Ruhl whose names were not given.)

Nov 9, 1796   May 5, 1798
Wintermeyer, Anthony. Executors: Valentine and George Wintermeyer. Dover Township. Children: Valentine, George, Elizabeth wife of George Slegers, Julie wife of Patrick Ervin, Anna wife of Casper Youker, Philip, Susanna and Catharine.

Apr 18, 1798   May 5, 1798
Heltzel, Anna Maria. Executor: Frederick Brenner. Paradise Township. Children: Bernard, John, Jacob, Frederick, Catharine wife of Peter Bob, and Christiana wife of Tobias Heltzel.

Apr 18, 1798   May 17, 1798
Baugher, William. Executors: Martin Conrad and James Miller. Berwick Township. Wife: Catharine Baugher. Children: William, Catharine wife of Soloman Hahn, Elizabeth wife of Jacob Regal, Barbara wife of James Dustin, Susan wife of Jacob Overlander, Mary, Christiana, and Hannah.

Mar 1, 1798   May 21, 1798
Dodds, Joseph. Executors: Andrew Tompson and John McGrew. Huntington Township. Wife: Elizabeth Dodds. Children: William, Joseph, Catharine wife of Robert Delap, and Isabella wife of John Meely. Grandchild: Joseph (son of Isabella).

--- --, ----   May 31, 1798
Michenfel, Casper. Executors: Barbara Michenfel and Jacob Adams. Conewago Township. (German will.)

May 11, 1797   Jun 2, 1798
Heible, Christopher. Executors: George and Michael Heible. Hellam Township. Wife: Louisa Catharine Heible. Children: Jacob, George, and Michael.

Aug 21, 1792   Jun 5, 1798
Murphy, John. Executor: Daniel Murphy. Cumberland Township. Wife: Martha Murphy. Children: Samuel, John, Hugh, and Daniel.

Apr 25, 1798   Jun 6, 1798
Clogston, Joseph. Executor: William Bigham. York County. Wife: Jane Clogston. Children: Elizabeth, Mary, Robert, Margaret, John, and William.

Apr 14, 1798   Jun 7, 1798
John, Rachel. Executor: Cornelius Garretson. Newberry Township. Widow of Joshua John. Children: Sarah, Griffith, Rachel, Isaah, Anna, and Hannah.

Apr 29, 1798   Jun 9, 1798
Smith, Valentine. Executors: Sarah Smith and John Bull. Dover Township. Wife: Sarah Smith. Children: John, William and Thomas ?????.

Apr 3, 1795   Jun 12, 1798
Updegraff, Samuel. Executor: Caleb Kirk. York Borough. Wife: Mary Updegraff. Child   Lydia wife of Caleb Kirk.

Jun 11, 1798   Jun 14, 1798
McClean, William. Executors: George Spangler and John Kuntz. York Borough. Wife: Anna Maria McClean.

Jun 16, 1798   Jun 24, 1798
Ehrman, Joseph. Executors: Jacob Kuhn and Appolonia Ehrman. Heidleberg Township. Wife: Catharine Ehrman. Children: Appolonia, Mary wife of Peter Kurk, and Catharine wife of Anthony Trexel. Grandchildren: Furgerson and Mary Kurk (children of Mary), and Joseph, Peter and John Trexel (children of Catharine).

Feb 3, 1798   Jun 30, 1798
Klinedienzt, David. Executors: David and Andrew Klinedienzt. Cordorus Township. Wife: Magdalena Klinedienzt. Children: Godfrey, Daniel, Christian, Andrew, Michael, Eve, and Barbara.

Jun 13, 1795   June 20, 1798
Senft, John Philip. Executors: Andrew and Peter Senft. Cordoruse Township. Wife: Anna Mary Senft. Child: Andrew.

Mar 14, 1798   Jul 25, 1798
Schosp, Adam. Executors: Elizabeth and Stephen Schosp. Manheim Township. Wife: Elizabeth Schosp. Children: Adam, John, Jacob, Peter, Stephen, and Andrew.

Feb 16, 1797   Aug 9, 1798
McDonald, Mary. Executor: John Manifold. Hopewell Township. Children: Richard, Robert, Aquilla, Anna, Elizabeth, Persilla, Jane, and Margaret. Grandchildren: Robert, Grazel, Aquila and Mary (children of Richard).

Jun 9, 1798   Aug 25, 1798
Burkholder, Abraham. Executor: Catharine Burkholder. Chanceford Township. Wife: Catharine Burkholder. Children: Abraham, Elizabeth, and Catharine.

Aug 16, 1798   Sep 5, 1798
Kleindinzt, David, Jr. Executors: Mathias Neas and James Bolton. Hanover Township. Wife: Elizabeth Kleindint. Children: Elizabeth, David, John, Andrew, Polly, and Sabina.

Sep 7, 1798   Oct 1, 1798
Yoder, Martin. Executors: Abraham Lichtenwalter and Jacob Diehl. Mt. Joy Township. Wife: Susanna Yoder. Children: John (there were six others - names not given).

Jun 7, 1798   Oct 1, 1798
Miller, Ludwig. Executors: John and Ludwig Miller. Germany Township. Wife: Margaret Miller. Children: John, Ludwig, Andrew, Simon, and Abraham.

Aug 13, 1798   Oct 8, 1798
Cooper, Thomas. Executor: Stephen Cooper. York County. Wife: Mary Cooper. Children: Stephen, Eccy, and Armfield.

--- --, ----   Oct 9, 1798
Martzen, Catharina. Executor: Jacob March. Paradise Township. (German will.)

Jun 1, 1798   Oct 23, 1798
Klein, John. Executor: Jacob Klein. Manheim Township. Wife: Omitted. Children: Henry, Sally, John, and Elizabeth.

Apr 23, 1798   Oct 26, 1798
Neely, Jackson. Executors: Thomas Neely and Abraham Fickes. Tyrone Township. Wife: Susanna Neely. Children: Samuel, "the second son not yet named, but call him Jackson for the present" (extract from will).

Aug 16, 1790   Nov 9, 1798
Strickler, Christiana. Executor: John Strickler. Hellam Township. Widow of Conrad Strickler. Legatees: (Bros. and Sister) John and Joseph Bixler and Barbara Strickler.

Feb 9, 1798   Nov 16, 1798
McGaughy, James. Executors: William and James McGaughy. Hamiltonsban Township. Wife: Agness McGaughy. Children: Agness, William, Ann, James, Hugh, and Alexander.

Dec 16, 1794   Nov 21, 1798
Herschy, John. Executors: John Herschy and Michael Grove. Manheim Township. Children: Christian, Elizabeth wife of Christian Hershey, Barbara wife of Samuel Bechtel, and Anna wife of Adam Bucher.

Jul 9, 1790   Nov 22, 1798
Fox, Elizabeth. Executors: Jacob Kramer and Jacob Updegroff. York Borough. Children: Abraham, Jacob, Eve and Samuel.

Jul 19, 1790   Dec 5, 1798
Bigham, Robert. Executors: William Bigham, James Agnew and Barbara McSherry. Hamilton Township. Children: Samuel, Abraham, and Eve.

Oct 21, 1798   Dec 16, 1798
Hirdt, Martin. Executor: David Hirdt. Shrewsbury Township. Wife: Christiana Hirdt. Children: Daniel, Eve wife of Jacob Hershner, and Barbara wife of Jacob Heindal.

--- --, ----   Dec 18, 1798
Kintig, Anna. Executors: Peter Guth and Jost Herback. Manchester Township. (German will.)

--- --, ----   Jan 2, 1799
Grasser, Adam. Executor: Jacob Grasser. Berwick Township. Children: Adam, Catharine, Leonhart, Anna, Henry, and Jacob.

Dec 14, 1798   Jan 2, 1799
Campbell, Hugh. Executor: Alexander Campbell. Straban Township.

Wife: Rebecca Campbell. Children: Alexander, Armstrong, Mary, Robert, and Margaret.

Nov 23, 1797   Jan 3, 1799
Hiller, Martin. Executor: John Wampler. Manheim Township. Sons-in-law: John Wampler and John Gossler (wives' names not given). Grandchildren: Mary and Elizabeth Wampler (children of John Wampler, John Adam Tissell, (four other children whose names were not given,) and Mary Eve wife of John Miller (parents' names not given).

Feb 8, 1798   Jan 4, 1799
Wilson, James. Executors: David Wilson and John Agnew. Hamiltonsban Township. Children: Hugh, Martha wife of Edward Hall, James and David. Grandchildren: Jane Wilson (child of Hugh) and James Wilson (son of James).

Dec 12, 1798   Feb 8, 1799
Agnew, James. Executors: John Agnew, James Agnew and James McCreary. Hamilton Township. Wife: Martha Agnew. Children: David and Jane, Margaret (daughter of Jane). Grandchildren whose parents' names are not recorded: James Hunter, James Agnew McCreary, John Agnew McCreary and Andrew Agnew McCreary.

Jan 15, 1790   Feb 9, 1799
Byers, John. Executor: William Byers. Cumberland Township. Wife: Elizabeth Byers. Children: Andrew, William, James, John, Samuel, Margaret, Esther, Martha, Rachel, and Elizabeth.

Sep 26, 1795   Feb 11, 1799
Wogan, Anne. Executor: George Wogan. Manchester Township. Children: George, Margaret and --- Test, Anne and Isabella and Samuel Day. Grandchild: Anne Test.

Jan 8, 1799   Feb 15, 1799
Coleman, Conrad. Executors: Margaret Coleman and John Bull. Dover Township. Wife: Margaret Coleman. Child: Joseph.

May 14, 1791   Feb 16, 1799
Kapp, Martin. Executors: Peter Menges and Jacob Slagle. Manchester Township. Wife: Eve Maria Kapp. Stepchildren: Christian and William Miller, Maria wife of Peter Menges, and Magdalena wife of George Diffenbach.

Jan 30, 1798   Feb 26, 1799
Wilson, James. Executors: Thomas and Robert Wilson. Straban Township. Legatees: (Bros. and Sisters) William, Thomas, Robert, Sarah Long, Elizabeth and Agness Wilson.

Dec 14, 1798   Mar 5, 1799
Kister, Ludwig. Executors: Elizabeth and George Kister. Newberry Township. Wife: Elizabeth Kister. Children: George, (and others whose names were not given.)

Feb 9, 1799   Mar 5, 1799
Cooper, Nicholas. Executor: Stephen Cooper. York County. Wife: Elizabeth Cooper. Children: Mary wife of William Chapman, Nicholas, Alice wife of Ezekiel Jones, Sarah wife of William Barkcley, Stephen, Joshua, Nelly, Priscilla, and Hannah.

Apr 5, 1795   Mar 23, 1799
McCreery, Margaret. Executor: Robert Campbell. Straban Township. Children: Jane and Margaret.

Jun 5, 1794   Mar 23, 1799
Waldenberger, Daniel. Executor: Elizabeth Waldenberger. Cumberland Township. Wife: Elizabeth Waldenberger.

--- --, ----   Mar 26, 1799
Hayd, Anna Mary. Executor: Omitted. York County. German will.

Mar 12, 1799   Mar 26, 1799
Schweisgute, Laurence. Executors: Michael Spangler and John G. Oderman. Paradise Township. Wife: Elizabeth Schweisgute. Children: Adam, Philip, Sophia wife of Henry Clementz, Margaret wife of Godfried Ratz, Catharine wife of Michael Spangler, Elizabeth wife of Peter Actland, Anna wife of Jacob Wagner and John.

Feb 8, 1797   Mar 26, 1799
Slemous, James. Executors: Robert Slemous and John Slemous. Hamiltonsban Township. Legatees: (Bros. and Sisters) Sarah, William, Robert and John Slemous and Margaret wife of John Jack.

Mar 1, 1799   Mar 30, 1799
Werking, Philipina. Executors: Philip Werking and Philip W. Werking. Manchester Township. Children: Philip, Dorothea and Henry. Grandchild: Margaret Werking (daughter of Philip).

Dec 31, 1798   Mar 30, 1799
Stump, Margaret. Executors: Conrad Steiman and Michael Bear. Heidleberg Township. Wife of George Stump. Children: Baltzer, Joseph, Margaret and Henry.

Aug 6, 1794   Apr --, 1799
Hobbach, Peter. Executors: Benjamin Walker and Philip Hobbach. Warrington Township. Children: George, Philip, Conrad, Elizabeth, Mary, Catharine, Christiana, John, and Margaret. Grandson: Jacob Obedier (parents' names not given).

Dec 28, 1798   Apr 6, 1799
Leas, Stephen. Executors: John Leas and Samuel Leas. Monaghan Township. Legatees: (Father,) John Leas; and Brothers and Sisters,) John Jr., Hannah, Samuel, Leonard, Mary, Susanna, Asper, and Philip.

--- --, ----   Apr 15, 1799
Garner, Marks. Executor: Anna Mary Garner. Windsor Township. Wife: Anna Mary Garner. Child: Marks.

Apr 9, 1799   Apr 27, 1799
Eurig, Margaret. Executors: James and Grace Eurig. Paradise Township. Children: John, George, Elizabeth wife of Michael Walsch, and Margaret wife of Casper Hoke.

Jan 2, 1788   Apr 30, 1799
Myer, Michael. Executors: Joseph Meyer. Mt. Pleasant Township. Wife: Catharine Myer. Children: Joseph, Elizabeth, Mary, and Frances.

Mar 16, 1797   May 3, 1799
Long, John. Executors: Rachel and Thomas Long. Newberry Township. Wife: Rachel Long. Children: Isabella, Rachel, Hannah, Jane, Mary, Thomas, and Margaret wife of Joseph Long.

Mar 2, 1799   May 3, 1799
McGinney, Robert. Executors: William and Joseph McGimsey. Hamiltonsban Township. Wife: Mary McGimsey. Children: Joseph, Robert, William, and Anna.

Apr 16, 1799   May 8, 1799
Wehler, Henry. Executors: Henry and Frederick Wehler. Paradise Township. Wife: Catharine Wehler. Children: Catharine wife of John Hereh, Daniel, Henry, John and Frederick. Grandchildren: Henry,

Catharine and George Trimmer (parents' names not given).

May 6, 1799   May 21, 1799
Hoffman, Philip. Executor: John Haller. Manchester Township. Wife: Catharine Hoffman. Children: Six (names not given).

May 10, 1798   May 21, 1799
McIlhenny, Esther. Executor: Samuel McIlhenny. Mt. Joy Township. Widow of Ezekiel McIlhenny. Children: James, Robert, Samuel and Esther Logan (a Legatee who does not appear to be a relative). Grandchildren: Esther (daughter of James), Sophia (daughter of Robert), and Ezekiel (son of Samuel).

Oct 11, 1796   May 25, 1799
Sweeney, Miles. Executors: John and Thomas Sweeney. Cumberland Township. Children: Thomas, Polly, James, John (Son-in-law), James Watson (wife's name not given). Grandchild: Nelly Wilson (Parents name not given).

Jan 25, 1799   May 27, 1799
Kern, Jacob. Executors: Joseph and Jacob Kern. York Borough. Wife: Catharine Kern. Children: John, Jacob, and Joseph. Grandchildren: Elizabeth (child of John), and Catharine (child of Jacob).

Apr 5, 1799   Jun 4, 1799
Ziegler, John. Executors: Henry and George Zeigler. Omitted Township. Wife: Mary Ziegler. Children: Catharine wife of George Wilson, Eve wife of Isaac Deardorff, Philip, Elizabeth, Sarah, Susanna, Daniel, Henry and Volly.

May 20, 1799   Jun 6, 1799
Baker, Peter. Executor: Philip Shriener. Newberry Township. Children: John, David, Joseph, and Mary.

Mar 9, 1792   Jun 8, 1799
Hollopeter, Matthias. Executor: Frederick Hollopeter. Warrington Township. Wife: Barbara Hollopeter. Children: Mary, Susanna, Christiana, Barbara, John, Matthias, Frederick, Andrew, and Abraham.

--- --, ----   Jun 17, 1799
Knaur, David. Executors: Christiana Knaur and Peter Schlosser. Township: Omitted. (German will.)

May 10, 1799   Jun 27, 1799
Black, Robert. Executors: Henry and James Black. Mt. Joy Township.
Wife: Ann Black. Children: Sarah wife of Aaron Deveney, Rachel wife of Samuel Linn, James, and Henry.

--- --, ----   Aug 17, 1799
Bowman, John. Executor: Hy Bowman. German will.
Translation, Will of John (Johann) Bauman, York County.
In the name of God. Amen!
I, John Bauman, living in Codorus Township, York County, Province and State of Pennsylvania, have thought to make my Testament and Last Will while still possessed of good understanding. First I commit my soul into the hands of my God and my body to the earth from which it came. After my death, my body is to be buried according to Christian rites. Also, it is my will that after my death all my debts are to be paid. Also, it is my will that my son, Jacob Bauman, may have the place where I live, after my death, for 400 pounds, and I leave him all my rights therein, that he may possess it after my death and that of my wife. Also, it is my will that in addition to the place he shall have four horses, the necessary harness, a wagon, the plow, the ---, and the windmill, also a cow and a steer; this he is to have with the place for 400 pounds. Also, my son Jacob Bauman is to have his share of the 400 pounds, and after my death and that of his mother, he shall pay yearly 20 pounds to each of his brothers and sisters, in good money, silver or gold, and it is my will that he begin with my eldest son, John Bauman, who is to have five pounds in advance and then 20 pounds out of the place. (Here several words are illegible in the fold of the paper.) My children are to inherit the one the same as the other, and as above stated the beginning is to be made with the oldest son, and then my daughter Elizabeth, who is married to Henry Hess, she receiving 20 pounds in silver or gold, and thereafter my daughter Anna Maria, who is married to Abraham Schwartz, is also to receive 20 pounds in silver or gold. Thereafter my son Henry Bauman, and then my son Philip Bauman and then my daughter Eva Bauman, and when they all have received 20 pounds then he is to begin again with the oldest son and again pay 20 pounds to each in the order stated above. And it is my will that my daughter Eva Bauman shall have on the place a cow, a bed, bedstead and what belongs thereto. Also, it is my will that my son Henry Bauman shall have the loom and the weaving equipment for four pounds. Also, it is my last will that my son Jacob Bauman shall pay nothing from the place to his brothers and sisters until after my death and that of my wife. Also, it is my last will that my son Jacob Bauman from now on shall yearly and every year deliver to me twenty bushels of wheat, ten bushels of corn, eight bushels of maize, half the products of the garden, one-third of the

potatoes, six bushels of turnips and a third of the fruit. Also, three cows are to be kept after the manner of nature, by pasturing in the fields, but in winter they are to be fed in the stable. Also, four sheep are to be pastured in the fields. Also, three hogs. Also, my son Jacob Bauman is to provide as much firewood for the house in summer and winter as the father needs, and must cut it small. (Blotted word.) The father agrees to keep -- horses, but when he does not need the horses, the son Jacob may use them. Also, the father agrees to supply 20 pounds of hemp or flax. Also, it is my last will that my wife Barbara Bauman shall have half the before mentioned products of the place after my death, and she is also to have two cows as long as the youngest daughter remains unmarried. Then she is to have one of the cows. It also is my will that my wife shall have a widow-seat in the house where we live so long as she remains my widow. Also, my son Jacob Bauman shall give her yearly half of the forementioned articles (?) and shall give her yearly one pair of shoes, one bushel of salt. Also, it is my will that my wife shall have one hundredweight pork well cured, also firewood for the house in summer and winter as much as she needs, also one-third of the garden products, also space in the cellar or springhouse. Also, my son Jacob Bauman is to maintain a steer for my wife as long as she lives. Also, my wife shall have one-third part of ??? (one line of typing not properly copied). ...is to have the right to her kitchen utensils, as much as she wishes, also her spinningwheel. Also, it is my last will that the remainder of my house furnishings after my death be divided among my children share and share alike. Also, my son Henrich Bauman is to have the bed on which he lies. Also, it is my last will that my son Henrich Bauman and my son-in-law Henrich Hess shall be my executors. Also, I acknowledge before witnesses that this is my last will and I recall all others ever made ... I acknowledge before witnesses with my hand and seal the 30th July, in the year 1794. (George Waller, Philip Ziegler)

Apr 14, 1799   Jun 27, 1799
Blasser, Nicholas. Executors: Henry and James Black. York Township. Wife: Susanna Blasser. Children: Mathias, Peter, Nicholas, Magdalena wife of Michael Bixler, Susanna wife of Peter Neff, Barbara wife of George Kepp, Catharine wife of Sigmond Austein, Ann, and Philip.

--- --, ----   Jul 19, 1799
Gerner, George. Executors: John Geo. Gerner and Jacob Biehl. Township omitted. German will.

Jun 15, 1799   Jul 27, 1799
Treighler, John. Executors: Jacob Strickler and Andrew Ferree. York

County. Wife: Dorothea Treighler. Children: Barbara, Martin, Anna, Elizabeth, Maria, Magdalena, Catharine, Daniel and Salome.

Sep 6, 1798   Aug 5, 1799
Will, Peter. Executors: John Kuhn and Henry Fink. York County. Children: Nicholas, Henry, Catharine and Peter.

Oct 6, 1792   Aug 9, 1799
Poake, James. Executors: John and Martha Poake. Reading Township. Wife: Anne Poake. Children: David, Martha, Mary, Rachel, Robert, Elizabeth wife of John Neely, and John. Grandchild: James Neely.

May 16, 1799   Aug 17, 1799
Tate, Jeremiah. Executors: Hannah Tate and John Felker. Newberry Township. Wife: Hannah Tate. Children: Abigail, George, Martha and Mary.

Sep 1, 1795   Aug 20, 1799
Vale, Robert. Executors: William and Joshua Vale. Warrington Township. Wife: Sarah Vale. Children: Robert, John, Ann, William and Joshua. Grandchild: Robert Vale (son of John).

Jul 29, 1799   Sep 5, 1799
Swoope, Conrad. Executors: George Charles and John Swoope. Hanover Township. Wife: Gloria Swoope. Children: John, Henry, George and Adam.

Aug 24, 1799   Sep 5, 1799
Patterson, Thomas. Executors: John and Hugh Patterson. Hamiltonsban Township. Wife: Anna Patterson. Children: John, Hugh, Betty wife of William Hunter, Anna wife of William Shields, Mary, and Jenny. Grandchildren: Betty and Anne Shields.

Aug 28, 1798   Oct 1, 1799
Koch, Mary. Executor: John Deardorff. Monaghan Township. Children: John, George, Peter, Elizabeth wife of Peter Updegraff, Jacob, Mary wife of Joseph Bradley, and Salome wife of John Dougherty.

Mar 29, 1799   Oct 7, 1799
Barnitz, Charles. Executors: George and John Barnitz. York Borough. Mother: Ann Barbara Barnitz. Brothers: John, Michael, George, Daniel, and Jacob. Sisters: Susanna and Barbara.

Apr 9, 1799   Oct 8, 1799
Vernon, Aaron. Executors: John Hart and Samuel Miller. Newberry Township. Wife: Mary Vernon. Children: Margaret wife of Daniel Bailey. Sarah wife of John Hart and Tracy. Grandchild: Aaron Bailey.

Sep 21, 1793   Oct 16, 1799
Herschy, Andrew. Executors: Elizabeth Herschy and Deitrich Brubaker. Paradise Township. Children: Anna, Jacob, Christian, Peter and Jospeph.

Oct 7, 1799   Oct 25, 1799
Tate, Isaac. Executors: John Harmon, Jr., and Thomas Luck. Straban Township. Wife: Elizabeth Tate. Children: Izreal, Solomon, (four daughters and one son - their names are not recorded).

Oct 9, 1794   Oct. 28, 1799
Small, John. Executor: John Engle Small. Heldleberg Township. Wife: Mary Small. Children: (The names and number not stated.)

Nov 7, 1796   Nov 15, 1799
Shenberger, John.. Executors: Adam Shenberger and John Ruby. Windsor Township. Children: Adam, Margaret wife of Martin Rape, Mary Susanna, Elizabeth wife of Conrad Piler, Magdalene wife of George Albright, John, Rachel, Michael and Joseph. Grandchildren: Margaret and Emanuel Rape.

Jan 2, 1797   Nov 20, 1799
Myrise, George. Executors: George and Margaret Spanseller. Germany Township. Children: John, Adam, and Margaret wife of George Spanseller. Grandchildren: Christiana Grey (mother's name not given), Elizabeth, George, Catharine and Rachel Spanseller.

--- --, ----   Dec 2, 1799
Schwartz, Henry. Executors: Theobold Schneider and Henry Schwartz. Strasburg Township. (German Will)

May 14, 1799   Dec 17, 1799
Sell, Isaac. Executor: Jacob Sell. Germany Township. Wife: Margaret Sell. Children: Jacob (others but names and number not given.)

Jan 23, 1799   Jan 2, 1800
Huber, John. Executors: Henry Slagle, John, George, David, and Henry Huber. Germany Township. Children: John, George, Andrew, Jacob, Henry, Catharine wife of John Winrote, Michael, and David.

Dec 1, 1799   Jan 5, 1800
Epply, Sophia. Executors: John Epply and John Derr. Newburry Township. Child: John.

Dec 6, 1799   Jan 8, 1800
Hickes, George. Executor: Laurence Hickes. Huntington Township. Wife: Catharinea Hickes. Children: Laurence, Jacob, Mary wife of Philip Myers, Barbara, Catharine, Christiana, John, George, Frederick, and Henry.

Dec 19, 1797   Jan 15, 1800
Hausman, Christian. Executor: Philip Gossler. York Borough. Child: Conrad. Granddaughter: Rebecca Grafins (parents' names not given).

Oct 9, 1794   Jan 16, 1800
Bowen, Thomas. Executor: Benjamin Wilson. Manallin Township. Wife: Jane Bowen. Children: William, Jonathan, Thomas, John, Lydia wife of Thomas Mather, Rachel wife of Patrick Russel, and Sarah wife of Benj. Wilson. Grandchildren: Thomas and David (sons of William).

Dec 26, 1799   Jan 21, 1800
Chambers, John. Executors: Catharine and Henry Chambers. Mt. Pleasant Township. Wife: Catharine Chambers. Children: Jacob, Solomon, John, Henry, Catharine, Rachel, and Rosana.

Aug 16, 1796   Jan 22, 1800
Genter, Nicholas. Executors: John and George Genter. Manchester Township. Wife: Christiana Genter. Children: Conrad, John, and George.

May 29, 1795   Jan 22, 1800
Wierman, Nicholas. Executors: William Wireman and Thomas Thomburg. Hunting Township. Wife: Sarah Weirman. Children: William, Benj., Phebe, Nicholas and (son-in-law) Thomas Thomburg (wife's name not given).

Jun 2, 1798   Feb 8, 1800
Cremer, Adam. Executors: Martin Gartner and Adam Bahn. York Borough. Wife: Ann Elizabeth Cremer. Children: Elizabeth, Adam, Jacob, Catharine, Eve, Abraham, and Peter.

May 7, 1798   Feb 12, 1800
Bogle, Malcolm. Executors: Alexander and William Bogle. Straban

Township. Wife: Elizabeth Bogle. Children: Alexander and William.

Aug 11, 1797   Feb 17, 1800
Mummert, William. Executors: Mathias Mummert and Samuel Fahnestock. Paradise Township. Children: Richard, Mathias, John, William, Jacob, Peggy wife of Christian Swobenland, Anna wife of Ludwig Swobenland, Susanna wife of Jacob Nagel, and Catharine wife of Mathias Myer.

Jan 21, 1800   Mar 10, 1800
Fritzlun, George. Executors: Anna Mary Fritzlun and Jacob Adams. Germany Township. Wife: Anna Mary Fritzlun. Children: (Five children, names not given.)

Jul 7, 1794   Mar 27, 1800
Siegle, Jacob. Executor: Elizabeth Siegle. Hopewell Township. Wife: Elizabeth Siegle. Children: Jacob, George, Anna, Rosanna and Christiana.

Mar 5, 1800   Apr 15, 1800
Stambach, Philip. Executors: Barbara and Jacob Stambach. Cordorus Township. Wife: Barbara Stambach. Children: Jacob, Henry and John.

Jun 7, 1788   May 2, 1800
Fisher, Alice. Executors: William and Elizabeth Randel. Monaghan Township. Children: Jane wife of Caphas Atkinson, James, Isaac, Marian wife of John McAdams, and Elizabeth wife of William Randel. Grandchildren: Mary and Hannah (children of Elizabeth).

--- --, ----   May 12, 1800
Kobell, Jost. Executor and Township: Omitted. (German will.)

Apr 3, 1800   May 13, 1800
Sheely, Christopher. Executors: George Sheely and Frederick Youse. York Borough. Wife: Catharine Sheely. Children: Catharine, Mary, George, and Susanna wife of Peter Schmuck.

Apr 29, 1800   May 21, 1800
Raeber, John. Executors: Ludwick and John Rudiselly. Cordorus Township. Wife: Catharine Raeber. Children: Jonas, Christiana, Henry and Elizabeth.

May 25, 1795   Jun 5, 1800
Lehmer, William. Executors: Thomas McCreary and John Lehmer. Monaghan Township. Wife: Susanna Lehmer. Children: Jacob, William, Henry, John, Susanna, Elizabeth, and Catharine.

May 14, 1800   Jun 14, 1800
Blair, Jane. Executors: John and Brice Blair. Warrington Township. Children: John, Brice and James.

--- ---, ----   Jun 30, 1800
Wehr, George. Executor: Ludwick Shive. York Borough. Wife: Eve Wehr. Children: Elizabeth (five others - names not given).

Jun 4, 1800   June 28, 1800
Shaefer, Frederick. Executors: George Julius and Adam Dick. Dover Township. Wife: Susanna Shaefer. Children: Samuel, John, George, Jacob, Margaret, Catharine, Molly and Sally.

Jun 25, 1800   Aug 4, 1800
Short, Anthony. Executors: John Short and Paul Miller. Heidleberg Township. Wife: Mary Short. Children: John, Anthony, Mary, Joseph, Jacob and Francis.

Jun 6, 1800   Aug 9, 1800
Brehm, Samuel. Executors: Valentine Hughs and Frederick Wealer. Warrington Township. Children: Magdalena wife of Valentine Highgas, and Esther.

Jun 6, 1800   Aug 9, 1800
Preme, Samuel. Executors: Valentine Hegas and Frederick Wealer. Warrington Township. Children: Magdalena wife of Valentine Hegas, and Esther.

Aug 1, 1800   Aug 16, 1800
Cook, Samuel. Executors: Elisha and William Cook. Warrington Township. Children: Hannah wife of Thomas James, Rebecca wife of Joseph Griffith, Sarah wife of William Griffith, Ruth, Elisha, Isreal, and Samuel.

Jan 1, 1800   Aug 23, 1800
Griffith, David. Executors: William Griffith and Thomas Petit. Paradise Township. Wife: Anna Griffith. Children: William, Caleb, and David.

Dec 14, 1798   Aug 27, 1800
Hubley, Frederick. Executors: Magdalena Hubley and Daniel Spangler. Manchester Township. Wife: Magdalena Hubley. Child: Frederick.

Apr 16, 1796   Aug 27, 1800
Wilt, Valentine. Executors: Elizabeth Wilt and John Michel. York Borough. Wife: Elizabeth Wilt. Children: Nicholas, Peter, Velantine, Magdalena, Catharine wife of John Pflieged, Elizabeth, Barbara, Susanna and Anne.

Aug 18, 1800   Oct 14, 1800
Schmuck, Elizabeth. Executors: George Schmuck and Peter Munderff. York Borough. Legatees: (Mother)Catharine Schmuck, (Bros.) John and George Schmuck.

Aug 17, 1796   Nov 3, 1800
Wagner, Barbara. Executor: John Morris. York Borough. Children: John, Mary, Rebecca, Elizabeth wife of Peter Knaub, Catharine wife of Valentine Estel and Barbara wife of David Krahmer.

Jan 18, 1800   Nov 8, 1800
Deardorff, Anthony. Executors: Andrew and Anthony Deardorff. Dover Township. Wife: Ann Mary Deardorff. Children: Peter, Anthony, Paul, Andrew, Catharine wife of Isaac Latshaw, and Christiana wife of Herman Brough.

Oct 31, 1800   Nov 10, 1800
Stine, Abraham. Executor: Frederick Stine. Newberry Township. Legatees: (Father) Frederick Stine, (Bros & Sisters) Catherine, Christiana, Mary, John and Frederick.

--- --, ----   Dec 2, 1800
Mickel, Christian. Executor: George Mickel. Cordorus Township. Wife: Catharine Mickel. Children: John, George, Barbara, Jacob, Henry, Catharine, Elizabeth, Michael, Anna, and Margaret.

Mar 29, 1794   Dec 11, 1800
Dellown, Nicholas. Executor: Adam Faller. Paradise Township. Wife: Hannah Dellown. Children: Barbara wife of Anthony Bereenour, Maria wife of Adam Taller, Catharine wife of Dietrich Velti, Elizabeth wife of Joseph Hilt, and Margaretta.

Mar 15, 1794   Dec 15, 1800

Harrison, Ann. Executor: Thomas Harrison. Monaghan Township. Children: Thomas and Hannah.

Aug 26, 1800   Dec 24, 1800
Hartley, Thomas. Executors: Dr. James Hall and John Forsythe. Yorktown Township. Child: Charles.

Jun 6, 1797   Dec 27, 1800
Renill, Daniel. Executors: Christian and Henry Runkle. Cordorus Township. Wife: Mary Renill. Children: Christian, Peter, Darrell, Jacob, Mary wife of Lelia Cratselder, Barbara wife of Peter Law, , Susanna wife of Adam Erunst and Margaret wife of Conrad Myers.

Dec 4, 1800   Jan 3, 1801
Hyre, Jacob. Executor: Frederick Zorger. Newberry Township. Brother: Charles Hyre. Sister: Elizabeth wife of Jacob Foderman.

May 27, 1799   Jan 10, 1801
Miller, Bernard. Executors: Thomas Pettit and Valentine Miller. Dover Township. Wife: Ursula Miller. Children: George, Magdalena wife of Herman Hellman, Salome wife of George Miller, Catharine wife of Philip Uppach, and Elizabeth wife of George Styvenson.

May 17, 1798   Jan 15, 1801
Rudsill, John. Executor: George Shettler. Dover Township. Wife: Catharine Rudsill. Children: Werrick, John, Barbara wife of George Spihr, Elizabeth wife of Jacob Schreiber, Margaret wife of John Ehrmig, Susanna wife of Henry Herth and Anna wife of John Emig. Grandchildren: John and Michael Emig.

Oct 27, 1800   Jan 17, 1801
Brown, John. Executors: Andrew Warwick and Jane Aron. Hopewell Township. Children: Andrew, Margaret, Ann, Sarah, Robert, John, Martha, and Catharine.

Aug 14, 1796   Feb 14, 1801
Martin, Andrew. Executors: Thomas and John Martin. Newberry Township. Wife: Margaret Martin. Children: Thomas, John, Jean, and Elizabeth.

Feb 16, 1800   Feb 20, 1801
Olligner, Peter. Executors: John Graw and John Olligner. Shrewsbury Township. Wife: Barbara Olligner. Children: Barbara, John, Adam,

Jacob. Children by the first wife: John, Elizabeth wife of Andrew Stein, and Catharine wife of Christian Fisher.

Oct 6, 1800   Feb 21, 1801
Jennings, Esther. Executor: Thomas Jennings. Newberry Township. Sister: Anna Wickersham. Brother: Thomas Jennings.

Dec 12, 1794   Feb 26, 1801
Reinhart, George. Executor: Elias Reinhart. Manheim Township. Children: Anna, Magdalena, Mary, Susanna, George, Simon, Elias, Jacob, Charles, Henry, David, Peter, Catharine, John and Abraham.

Feb 11, 1794   Mar 10, 1801
Spittles, John. Executors: Catharine Spittle and George Smith. Hanover Township. Wife: Catharine Spittle. Child: Mary wife of Smith. Grandchildren: John and Mary Smith.

Mar 19, 1799   Mar 28, 1801
Knisely, Anthony. Executor: Thomas Black. Warrington Township. Wife: Omitted. Children: Anna wife of Jacob Shull, John, Anthony, Eve wife of Andrew Lobach, Abraham, Michael, Jacob, Mary wife of Jacob Hantz, Samuel, George, and Soloman.

Feb 5, 1801   Apr 6, 1801
Throne, Abraham, Jr. Executors: Samuel and John Throne. Manheim Township. Wife: Mary Throne. Legatees: (Bro. and Sisters) Anna, Magdalena, Mary and John Throne.

Apr 8, 1801   Apr 16, 1801
Bush, Herman. Executors: Emanuel Bare and John Miller. Newberry Township. Wife: Barbara Bush. Children: John, Elizabeth, George, Henry, Mary, Catharine, Peter, Susanna, and Mathias.

Jan 12, 1796   Apr 18, 1801
Brothbeck, John. Executors: George Werner and Margaret Brothbeck. Manheim Township. Wife: Margaret Brothbeck. Children: Zacharius, John, Christian, Magdalena, Catharine, Margaret, Elizabeth, Barbara and Ann.

Apr 15, 1801   Apr 27, 1801
Ringer, John. Executors: John Billinger and Frederick Kern. Manchester Township. Wife: Eva Ringer. Children: George and Elizabeth.

Aug 17, 1786   Apr 30, 1801
Hunter, Mary. Executors: Anna Holl and Abraham Lehman. Newberry Township. Children: William, Ephriam, Jacob, Margaret, Jean, Elias, Mary, Allen, and Joseph.

Sep 27, 1800   Apr 30, 1801
Holl, John. Executors: Ann Holl and Abraham Lehman. Hellam Township. Wife: Anna Holl. Children: Martin and Henry.

Aug 31, 1798   May 5, 1801
Cadwalader, James. Executor: David Cadwalader. Warrington Township. Wife: Mary Cadwalader. Children: Mary, Margaret, David, Sarah Evans, and Ruth Stewart.

Mar 27, 1800   May 21, 1801
Wilson, John. Executors: Alexander and William Wilson. Hopewell Township. Wife: Margaret Wilson. Children: William, James, John, David, Margaret and Alexander.

Dec 29, 1800   Jun 8, 1801
Krober, Adam. Executor: John Krober. Manheim Township. Children: John, Catharine wife of Joseph Durnbach, Gertrude, and Elizabeth wife of ---- Unwe.

--- --, ----   Jun 20, 1801
Kutter, Peter. Executors: Samuel Bechtil and Daniel Bar. Township: Omitted. (German will.)

Oct 13, 1798   Jul 18, 1801
Haring, Henry. Executors: Daniel Dubs and Anthony Henkell. Manheim Township. Wife: Juliana Haring. Children: Lewis, Philipena, John, Mary, Jacob, Christiana, Henry, and George.

Jul 3, 1801   Aug 3, 1801
Graybell, Hannah. Executors: John Grier and John Jones. York Borough. Bequests to Uncle Jacob Graybell, and cousins Polly Graybell, Sarah and John Jones.

Feb 3, 1801   Aug 4, 1801
Candler, David. Executors: Catharine Candler and George Barnitz. York Borough. Wife: Catharine Candler.

Apr 15, 1801   Aug 17, 1801
Ralston, Mary. Executor: William Anderson. Fawn Township. Legatees: James Ralston (nephew) and Rebecca Graham (niece).

Jul 1, 1800   Aug 20, 1801
Witterechd, George. Executors: Peter Witterechd and Peter Wittterechd, Jr. Manchester Township. Wife: (name not given). Children: Jacob, Peter, Christiana, Filbina, Catharine, Elizabeth, Annamary, Sarah and Susanna wife of Philip Fackler.

Jul 9, 1794   Sep 14, 1801
Kurtz, Michael. Executors: Michael and Anna Mary Kurtz. York Borough. Wife: Anna Mary Kurtz. Children: Eve wife of Henry Keefer, Margaret wife of John Lessel, Anna wife of George Stelevish, Maria wife of William Jones, Elizabeth wife of John Tuitz, Susanna wife of Philip Tuitz, Nicholas, Michael, and Christiana.

Aug 18, 1801   Sep 18, 1801
Manifold, Joseph. Executors: John and Benj. Manifold. Hopewell Township. Wife: Eleanor Manifold. Children: Joseph, Benjamin, Henry, William, Mary, Lydia, Eleanor, and Anibale. Granddaughter: Rachel Vogan (parents' names not given).

--- --, ----   Oct 6, 1801
Rudy, Michael. Executor: Philip Schreiner. Hellam Township. (German will).

Jul 30, 1800   Oct 7, 1801
Willis, William. Executors: Samuel Willis and John Love. Manchester Township. Children: John, Susannah wife of Samuel Fisher, Hannah wife of Samuel Wilson, Joel, Lydia wife of William Tarquhar, Mary, Betty and Samuel. Grandson: Samuel Speakman (parents' names not given).

Sep 21, 1801   Oct 13, 1801
Ludwick, Laurence. Executors: Godfrey Sumwald and John Ludwick. Shrewsbury Township. Wife: Mary Ludwick. Children: John, George, Philip, Elizabeth, Mary, and Lawrence.

May 24, 1798   Oct 23, 1801
Reisinger, Peter. Executors: John Landis and Samuel Keller. Windsor Township. Wife: Eve Reisinger. Children: John (and seven others whose names are not given.)

Apr 26, 1801   Nov 9, 1801
McDaniel, John. Executor: Jane McDaniel. York County. Wife: Jane McDaniel. Child: James.

Oct 30, 1801   Nov 20, 1801
Underwood, Elihu. Executor: Alexander Underwood. Warrington Township. Wife: Margaret Underwood. Child: Alexander.

Aug 1, 1794   Dec 4, 1801
Updegraff, Joseph. Executor: Mary Updegraff. York Borough. Wife: Mary Updegraff. Children: Josiah, Susanna, Sarah, Israel, Mary, Hannah, Ambrose, Nathan and Edith wife of Eli Kirk.

Sep 16, 1801   Dec 4, 1801
Creighton, Esther. Executor: Robert Gemmill. Hopewell Township. Children: James, Agness wife of William White, Esther wife of Thomas Dickson, and Patty wife of B. L. Purdy. Grandchildren: Esther and Jennet (children of Patty).

Nov 16, 1801   Jan 30, 1802
Nesbit, John. Executors: Alexander Ross and John Nesbit. Warrington Township. Wife: Jane Nesbit. Children: Alexander, Rebecca wife of Samuel Miller, John, William, Jenny wife of John Sanders, Hannah wife of Samuel Metier, Martha wife of George Petre, Mary wife of James Montgomery, and Nancy wife of Thomas Nelson. Grandchildren: George Petre and Mary Nelson.

Jan 6, 1802   Feb 1, 1802
Keller, John. Executors: Mary Keller and John Rubey. Hellam Township. Wife: Mary Keller. Children: John, Christian, Samuel, and Margaret.

Dec 24, 1796   Feb 15, 1802
Smith, Baltzer. Executor: James Smith. Warrington Township. Wife: Magdalene Smith. Children: Elizabeth wife of Machael Harnish, Eve wife of Andrew Hartman, Sarah wife of Michael Leidig, Mary, Salome, John and William.

Dec 28, 1801   Mar 2, 1802
Spangler, Joseph. Executors: Frederick Hike and Jacob Gartner. Dover Township. Wife: Elizabeth Spangler. Children: Jonas, Mary, Peter, Joseph, John, Jacob, Daniel and Elizabeth.

Jul 4, 1801   Mar 8, 1802
Hengst, Michael. Executor: Michael Hengst. York County. Children: Jacob, Michael, Catharine wife of Vandermullen, Margaret wife of Godfrey Kleindrenst, Eve wife of George Philips, and Elizabeth wife of George Wolf.

Mar 5, 1802   Mar 10, 1802
Grove, Thomas. Executors: David Williso and Francis Grove. Chanceford Township. Wife: Margaret Grove. Children: Jacob, Allner, Elizabeth, Cambel, and Thomas.

--- --, ----   Mar 15, 1802
Menges, Michael. Executors: John Brillinger and Peter Mohr. Manchester Township. (German will.)

Mar 15, 1802   Mar 19, 1802
McNary, John. Executors: Joseph Reed and John McNary. Chanceford Township. Children: Elizabeth, Mary, Esther, Margaret, Agness, Jean, Jannet, James, John, and Alexander.

Mar 9, 1802   Mar 25, 1802
Graif, Elizabeth. Executor: Conrad Doll. Paradise Township. Bequests to Adam Fishall and others.

Mar 13, 1802   Apr 12, 1802
Orson, George. Executor: John Orson. Chanceford Township. Children: William, Mary, Anna wife of William Gray, Sarah wife of Charles Gray, George, and Joseph. Grandchildren: Rebecca, Joseph, and Mary (children of George).

Jul 1, 1800   Apr 12, 1802
Disse, Michael. Executor: Andrew Disse. York County. Children: Andrew and John.

Jan 20, 1799   Apr 14, 1802
Kaufman, Soloman. Executors: John Kaufman and George Heckert. York Borough. Children: Catharine, Soloman, John, Henry, Peter, Elizabeth wife of Gotlieb Rupp, Feronica wife of Nicholas Koch, Barbara wife of John Leh, and Susanna wife of George Heckert.

Mar 29, 1802   Apr 16, 1802
Holder, John. Executors: Barbara Holder and Michael Beeker. Windsor Township. Wife: Barbara Holder.

Mar 31, 1802   Apr 30, 1802
Detter, Matthias. Executors: John Detter, Jacob Messoncopp, and Jacob Schaffer. Botts Town (Manchester Township). Wife: Magdalena Detter. Children: John, Nicholas, Catharine wife of Jacob Messoncopp, Magdalena wife of Jacob Schaffer, Elizabeth wife of Frederick Wehn, and Susanna wife of Jacob Erisman. (Magdalena was married twice having eight children by her first husband, Henry Shultz. The names of the children were not given.)

Apr 25, 1802   May 11, 1802
Derres, Benjamin. Executor: John Derres. Township omitted. German will.

May 22, 1802   May 29, 1802
Proudfoot, Robert. Executors: Francis Holler and John Brillinger. Hopewell Township. Wife: Mary Proudfoot. Legatees: Daniel and Rudolph Proudfoot (brothers).

Apr 7, 1800   May 29, 1802
Hoffman, Philip Executors: Francis Holler and John Brillinger. Manchester Township. Children: Sarah wife of Francis Holler, and Jacob. Grandchild: Catharine (daughter of Sarah).

Mar 14, 1802   Jun 15, 1802
Fishel, Henry. Executor: Henry Mather. Manheim Township. Wife: Barbara Fishel. Children: Margaretta, Barbara, John, Michael, Henry, Matalena, Jacob, and Elizabeth.

Jul 14, 1801   Jun 26, 1802
Henry, Michael. Executors: Leonard Esenhower and George Oberdorff. Windsor Township. Children: John, Catharine wife of Ludwig Gich, Elizabeth wife of Leonard Cessenhower, Michael, Magdalena wife of Jacob Graul, Anna wife of John Ohmet, and Christian.

Aug 5, 1795   Jun 29, 1802
Quickel, Barbara. Executor: John Quickel. Dover Township. Children: Anna wife of Conrad Fry, Henry, Barbara wife of Philip Miller, John, and Balthasser. Grandchildren: John and Ann (children of John), and Barbara Miller (child of Barbara).

May 7, 1799   Jul 24, 1802
Lantz, Philip. Executors: Baltzer Colar and Henry Gipe. Windsor Township. Children: Philip, Elizabeth wife of George Sebastian,

Christiana wife of Baltzer Colar, Marelise wife of Michael Sebastian, Catharine wife of Henry Gipe, and Henry.

Jun 11, 1802   Aug 4, 1802
Neil, John. Executors: John Cobb and David Cook. Hellam Township. Wife: Jennet Neil. Children: Hugh, John, James, and William.

Oct 5, 1798   Aug 16, 1802
Nunemacher, Jacob. Executor: Philip Wolfert. Manheim Township. Wife: Margaretta Nunemacher. Children: Jacob, Barbara wife of Peter Baum, Gotleib, Christiana wife of Michael Steffe, Philip, Catharine, Eve, Magdalena wife of George Bear, George, and Jacob.

May 15, 1802   Aug 21, 1802
Wise, Sebastine. Executors: Adam Faller and Michael Dellone. Paradise Township. Wife: Catharine Wise. Children: Joseph, Christianna, Sebastian and Philipina wife of John Noel.

Mar 19, 1798   Aug 28, 1802
Coppenhaffer, Simon. Executors: Michael and Martin Coppenhaffer. Newberry Township. Children: Martin, Simon, Michael, John, Benjamin, Catharine wife of Abraham Rankin, Barbara wife of George McDavit, and Elizabeth wife of John Sands.

Sep 7, 1802   Sep 18, 1802
Wanbaugh, Michael. Executors: Michael Strominger and Henry Hurst. Newburry Township. Wife: Barbara Wanbaugh. Children: Jacob, Michael, Mary, Catharine, John and (two sons-in-law) Michael Sangry and Philip Reignberger (wives' names not given).

Sep 10, 1802   Sep 25, 1802
Jacob, George. Executors: Samuel Heller and John Landis. Windsor Township. Wife: Elizabeth Jacob.

Jul 6, 1802   Oct 6, 1802
Marshel, James. Executor: William Marshel. Shrewsbury Township. Wife: Susanna Marshel. Legatees: Jane McDonald, Susanna Owens, James Wilson, Jane Owens, Elizabeth and William Marshel (no mention of what relation they were to James Marshel).

Dec 1, 1801   Nov 4, 1802
Strickler, Jacob. Executors: Jacob and John Strickler. Hellam Township. Wife: Elizabeth Strickler. Children: John (the names of the others not

given.)

Sep 11, 1802   Nov 16, 1802
Neilson, Samuel. Executors: William Neilson and John Bailey. Monaghan Township. Wife: Mary Neilson. Children: Susanna wife of James McCuer, Margaret, William, Roberts, Elizabeth, Mary wife of John Bailey, Rebecca and Jenny.

Sep 25, 1802   Dec 6, 1802
Spangler, Barnhart. Executor: John Spangler. Paradise Township. Wife: Eve Spangler. Children: John, Jacob Jonas, Elizabeth wife of George Kaetricter and Daniel.

Mar 28, 1802   Dec 9, 1802
Least, Philip. Executor: John Least. Reading Township. Legatees: Brother, John; and others.

Mar 6, 1799   Dec 23, 1802
Kuhl, Peter. Executors: Yost Ruhl and John Weiser. York Township. Wife: Margaret Kuhl. Children: Yost, Margaret, John, and Elizabeth wife of Philip Mate.

Sep 26, 1800   Jan 24, 1803
Reibolt, Andrew. Executors: George Gantz and John Ruhl. Cordorus Township. Children: Barbara wife of John Doll, Martha and Henry.

Dec 24, 1802   Feb 1, 1803
Sanderson, John. Executors: James Sanderson and Alexander Ross. Warrington Township. Wife: Jean Sanderson.

Oct 20, 1802   Feb 4, 1803
Dollman, John. Executor: Dr. John Rouse. York Borough. Wife: Anna Mary Dollman. Children: Mary wife of Michael Schmuck, Catharine wife of Mathew Gibbons, and Elizabeth wife of Jacob Ilgenfritz.

Nov 26, 1802   Feb 6, 1803
Herbach, John. Executors: George Herbach and Michael Hengst. York County. Wife: Magdalena Herbach. Children: Margaret wife of Peter Zeigler, Elizabeth wife of Adam Balm, John, Juliana wife of Michael Hengst, and Polly wife of William Johnston.

May --, 1802   Feb 8, 1803
Crosby, James. Executors: Semon Ainstin and Frederick Hartman.

Windsor Township. Wife: Sarah Crosby. Children: William, John, Rachel, Mary, and David.

Sep 19, 1795   Feb 15, 1803
Elliot, Benjamin. Executors: John Elliot and Enoch Vanscoyoe. Monoghan Township. Children: John, Mary and Lydia.

Jan 9, 1801   Mar 9, 1803
Doudle, Michael. Executors: John Stewart, George Bard, and Michael Dunn. York Borough. Wife: Margaret Doudle. Child: Margaret wife of Robert Dunn.

Jun 17, 1802   Mar 17, 1803
Day, Samuel. Executor: Isabella Day. Manchester Township. Wife: Isabella Day. Children: George, John, Rebecca, and Ann.

Jul 30, 1802   Mar 22, 1803
Miller, Frederick. Executors: George Stabler and Walter Shnyder. Shrewsbury Township. Wife: Catharine Miller. Children: Magdalena, Elizabeth, Christian, Frederick, Anna wife of Jacob Munnamacher, and Catharine wife of Sal Bosert.

Mar 7, 1803   Mar 23, 1803
Cunningham, Benjamin. Executor: William Morrison. Fawn Township. Wife: Jean Cunningham. Children: Ambrose, Benjamin, Hugh, Samuel, Joseph, Mary, Sarah wife of Rev. Parker, Lates wife of Hugh Gibson, Jean wife of James McKuitt, Elizabeth wife of John Crozly, and Ann wife of Samuel Parker.

Feb 28, 1798   Mar 31, 1803
Rothrock, Philip. Executors: John Rothrock and Abraham Grafius. York (Boro). Wife: Eleanor Rothrock. Children: Catharine wife of ---- Bents and Anna wife of ---- Meissenkop. Grandchildren: Jacob, John, Philip, Peter, George, Valentine, Benj., Joseph and Frederick. These are the children of Ann and Catharine. The will does not designate which are their Parents.

Mar 24, 1803   Apr 13, 1803
Miller, Valentine. Executors: Michael Miller and Jacob Mertz. Dover Township. Wife: Omitted. Children: George, (and others whose names were not given.)

Apr 2, 1803   Apr 13, 1803
Fritz, Baltzer. Executors: Abraham Hiestand and Andrew Gerber. Hellam Township. Wife: Elizabeth Fritz. Children: Barbara wife of ---- Dreichler, Elizabeth wife of John Streipler, Magdalena wife of David Newcomer, Anna wife of Abraham Hiestand, Mary wife of Herman Long, Susanna, Christiana wife of ---- Long, Jacob, and John.

Feb 8, 1803   Apr 20, 1803
Ross, Elizabeth. Executor: Omitted. Warrington Township. Legatees: Sarah Linton (sister) and Elizabeth and Sarah Linton (nieces).

Oct 5, 1800   Apr 23, 1803
Shaller, George. Executor: George Shaller. Donnegall Lancaster Co. Children: Eve and George. (N.B. There was a bequest to the Dutch Moravian Church at York Township.)

Apr 13, 1803   Apr 23, 1803
Miller, Jacob. Executors: C. and A. Lichdeberger. Newberry Township. Wife: Susanna Miller. Children: (Names and number not given.)

Sep 11, 1786   May 12, 1803
Kern, Michael. Executors: Henry Keizer and Peter Meyer. Newberry Township. Wife: Judith Kern. Children: Michael, Margaret, Barbara, Catharine, and Eve; and Susanna and Mary (children by second wife).

May 9, 1801   May 14, 1803
Deardorff, Ann. Executor: Joseph March. Dover Township. Children: (Names and number not given in will.)

--- --, ----   Jun 3, 1803
Rudisill, Catharine. Executor: James Emig. Fawn Township. (German will.)

Apr 5, 1798   Jun 24, 1803
Stein, Jacob. Executors: Conrad Swartz and Theobold Snyder. Shrewsbury Township. Wife: Anna Maria Stein. Children: Jacob, Mathias, Andrew, Frederick, Magdalena, Julianna, Catherine, Elizabeth and Anna. Son-in-law Theobold Snyder (wife's name not given).

Jul 7, 1803   Jul 30, 1803
Bixler, John. Executors: Samuel Fleckinger and Daniel Bear. Manheim Township. Wife: Mary Bixler. Children: Abraham, (names and number of other children not recorded.)

--- --, ----   Aug 12, 1803
Stegmer, Jacob. Executor: Joseph Maish. York County. (German will.)

Jun 30, 1803   Aug 16, 1803
Kend, Christian. Executor: Adam Labo. Manheim Township. Wife: Anna Mary Kend. Children: Nicholas, Malin, Susanna, Abraham, and Anna.

Apr 13, 1803   Aug 23, 1803
Bricker, Nicholas. Executor: Jacob Bricker. Manheim Township. Wife: Anna Mary Bricker. Child: Jacob.

Aug 11, 1803   Sep 9, 1803
Starr, John. Executors: Moses Starr and John Cross. Fairview Township. Wife: (name not given). Children: Moses (the number and names of the others not given).

Jul 18, 1803   Sep 12, 1803
Stough, George. Executor: Andrew Stough. Dover Township. Wife: Barbara Stough. Children: Andrew, Jacob, George, John, Frederick, Peter, Lanhart, Henry, Jaccobin and Catharine.

Feb 9, 1803   Sep 24, 1803
Wickersham, Jesse. Executors: Jesse and John Wickersham. Newburry Township. Wife: Ann Wickersham. Children: Ruth, Jesse, John, Hannah, Mary, Lydia and Anna.

May 16, 1802   Sep 24, 1803
Schmuck, Catharine. Executors: George and Michael Schmuck. Windsor Township. Widow of John Schmuck. Children: George, Michael, Catharine wife of Jacob Kennerly, John, Anna wife of John Katz.

Aug 23, 1800   Oct 5, 1803
Gordon, James. Executors: Matthew Gordon. Fawn Township. Children: Isabella, Mary, Catharine, Elizabeth, Martha, Robert, Matthew, and James.

May 6, 1803   Oct 12, 1803
Milheim, Christian. Executors: Henry Shultz and George Milheim. Hanover Township. Children: Elizabeth wife of John File, and Christiana wife of John Eyler.

Mar 14, 1801   Nov 4, 1803
Sample, Cunningham. Executor: Patrick Scott. Township omitted. Wife: Agness Sample. Children: John, Nathaniel, Elizabeth, Catharine, Agness wife of --- Boyd, Mildridge, Ann, Sarah, and (Son-in-law) Hugh Whiteford (wife's name not given). Grandchildren: Cunning and Ann Whiteford. Sons-in-law James R. Kamsey and James Boyd (wife's name not given).

Nov 3, 1803   Nov 8, 1803
Coudry, Leah. Executor: George Mansberger. Newberry Township. Widow of John Condry. Brothers: Garred and Abijah Peters. Sister: Martha Kepler.

Apr 10, 1790   Nov 11, 1803
Schneider, Casper. Executor: Jacob Schneider. Paradise Township. Children: Anthony and Jacob.

Feb 5, 1799   Nov 26, 1803
Bower, John. Executors: Michael and Isaac Bower. Huntington Township. Wife: Elizabeth Bower. Children: Michael, Isaac, John, Susanna, Samuel, Daniel, Elizabeth wife of Christian Herman, Henry, Mary, and Sarah wife of John Melaun.

--- ---, ----   Nov 26, 1803
Wilt, Paul. Executors: George Shettle and John Wilt. Dover Township. (German will.)

Apr 3, 1801   Nov 28, 1803
Shriner, Philip. Executors: Margaret and Martin Shriner. Newberry Township. Wife: Margaret Shriner.

Jun 18, 1803   Dec 6, 1803
Schmith, John. Executor: William Schmith. Cordorus Township. Legatees: (nephews) John, Daniel and David Schmith.

Feb 6, 1803   Dec 10, 1803
Motz, Jacob. Executor: John Stermer. Hopewell Township. Children: Catharine wife of Joseph Brandage, Catharine, and Barbara wife of John Stermer. Grandchild: George Scheaffer (parents' names not given).

Dec 3, 1803   Dec 13, 1803
Underwood, Benjamin. Executors: Joseph and William Griest. Warrington Township. Wife: Susanna Underwood. Children: Nehemiah, William, Michael, Benj. and Mary. Grandchildren: Mary Underwood

(daughter of Nehemiah), Sarah, Martha, Isaac and Mary Underwood (children of William).

Dec 30, 1802   Dec 20, 1803
Liggit, William. Executors: William and Alexander Liggit. Hopewell Township. Children: William, Alexander, Margaret wife of William Smith, and Eleanor wife of Robert Creighton.

Nov 27, 1803   Dec 27, 1803
Emmerick, Mary. Executor: John Emmerick. Newburry Township. Children: Jacob, Catharine, Elizabeth, Barbara, and John.

Apr 19, 1793   Dec 29, 1803
Erion, Jacob. Executor: John Haller. York Borough. Wife: Catharine Erion. Children: George and Jacob.

Oct 7, 1783   Dec 30, 1803
Andrew, Robert. Executors: Lennet Andrew, Martin Armstrong and Anthony Nichol. Chanceford Township. Wife: Jannet Andrew. Children: Elizabeth, Margaret, Robert and James.

Mar 5, 1803   Jan 6, 1804
Wise, George. Executors: Frederick Sawmiller and Isaac Williams. Chanceford Township. Wife: Christianna Wise. Children: Nancy wife of --- Tarnock. Grandchild: Jacob Tarnock.

Nov 8, 1799   Jan 26, 1804
Martin, Samuel. Executor: James Martin. Hopewell Township. Wife: Jean Martin. Children: Andrew, Peter, James, and Elizabeth. Grandchildren: Samuel and Isabel (parents' names not given).

Jan 15, 1804   Feb 11, 1804
Eister, Peter. Executors: John Kinsely, Henry Wolf, and Catharine Eister. Paradise Township. Wife: Catharine Eister. Children: George and Elizabeth.

Oct 16, 1802   Feb 14, 1804
Fry, George. Executor: Conrad Fry. Manchester Township. Wife: Elizabeth Fry. Child: Conrad.

Sep 21, 1796   Feb 14, 1804
Decker, Philip. Executors: Elizabeth Decker and George Dietz, Jr. York Borough. Wife: Elizabeth Decker.

Feb 25, 1797   Feb 20, 1804
Kessler, Michael. Executors: George Fackenroth. Cordorus Township.
Wife: Magdalena Kessler. Children: Michael and Christiana.

Apr 30, 1800   Feb 20, 1804
Forney, Marks. Executor: Adam Forney. Manheim Township. Children:
Christian, Marks, Adam, Eve wife of Christian Werts, Catharine wife of
Nicholas Kiefbraler, and Daniel.

May 7, 1799   Feb 21, 1804
McClarie, Andrew. Executor: John McClarie. Chanceford Township.
Children: Andrew, Margaret wife of McGlauglen, and John.
Grandchildren: James and Margaret McGlauglen.

Mar 4, 1776   Feb 23, 1804
Filey, John. Executor: Jacob Filey. Managhan Township. Wife: Susan
Filey. Children: Mary wife of William Martin, John, Catharine wife of
Jacob Swanger, and Sophia wife of Jacob Wiser.

Feb 16, 1804   Mar 6, 1804
Gohn, John. Executors: Frederick Luder and Jacob Klinefelter.
Chanceford Township. Wife: Catharine Gohn. Children: George, John,
and Rebecca.

Jul 22, 1803   Mar 14, 1804
Filkern, Dorothea. Executors: Adam and Conrad Lichtinberger. York
County. Children: William, George, Frederick, Jacob, and Elizabeth.

Mar 11, 1804   Mar 19, 1804
Miller, John. Executors: Daniel Brewa and Frederick George. Newberry
Township. Children: John, Milley wife of Adam Thomas, Suvley wife of
Henry Kulp, Catharine wife of Daniel Brewa, Elizabeth, and Sarah wife of
Peter Shriner.

Mar 12, 1804   Mar 26, 1804
Strong, James. Executor: Jacob Strong. Windsor Township. Wife:
Mary Strong. Children: Jacob, (there were daughters mentioned but
names or number not given).

--- --, ----   Mar 29, 1804
Spangler, Barnet. Executors: Margaret Spangler and Peter Diehl. York
County. (German will.)

Mar 25, 1804   Mar 31, 1804
Sailor, Casper. Executor: Adam Diehl. Windsor Township. Children: Peter, Susanna, John, (and six others, names not given).

Apr 30, 1802   Apr 2, 1804
Marsh, John. Executors: Jonathan and John Marsh. Warrington Township. Wife: Margaret Marsh. Children: Jonathan, Elizabeth, Margaret, Mary, John, William, Lidia, Hugh, Hannah, Susanna, and Rebecca.

Mar 25, 1804   Apr 3, 1804
Hower, Anthony. Executors: Peter Hower and John Arnold. Chanceford Township. Wife: Barbara Hower. Children: Peter, and sons-in-law John Ackerware and John Arnold (wives' names not given).

Mar 8, 1804   Apr 9, 1804
Major, John. Executors: Thomas and Andrew Major. Fawn Township. Wife: Agness Major. Children: Thomas, John, Anne, Archibald, and Alexander.

Apr 9, 1804   Apr 17, 1804
Wilson, Mary. Executors: James Buchnaan and James Logue. Chanceford Township. Legatees: (Bro.) William Buchanan and nephews-Buchanan.

Mar 27, 1804   Apr 17, 1804
Newman, David. Executor: Andrew Forney. Hanover Township. Children: Michael, David, Magdalena wife of Jacob Metzgar, and William. Grandchild: William Metzgar.

Mar 15, 1802   Apr 19, 1804
Schneider, Peter. Executor: John Brillinger. Manchester Township. Wife: Elizabeth Schneider. Children: Mary, Jacob, Catharine, Philip, Nicholas, Rebecca, Magdalena, Peter, Christiana and Elizabeth.

Dec 25, 1801   Apr 23, 1804
Brillhart, Peter. Executors: Jacob Brillhart and Martin Feigely. Shrewsbury Township. German will.

Mar 28, 1804   May 5, 1804
Myer, Simon. Executors: Elizabeth and Peter Myer. Windsor Township. Wife: Elizabeth Myer. Children: Catharine, Peter, Elizabeth, Sarah, Maria, and Henry.

Apr 8, 1800   May 5, 1804
Schwartz, Charles. Executor: Anna M. Schwartz. Hanover Township. Wife: Anna M. Schwartz. Brother: Christopher.

Nov 7, 1802   May 15, 1804
Sunday, John. Executors: Andrew Sunday and Richard Wummard. Paradise Township. Children: Charles, Andrew, Catharine wife of Casper Salegever and Elizabeth wife of Casper Cox. Grandchild: Catharine Cox.

Apr 9, 1800   May 17, 1804
Purdy, Archibald. Executors: Samuel Harper and Joseph Tompson. Hopewell Township. Children: Jane wife of Samuel Harper, and Mary wife of Joseph Tompson. Grandchildren: Agness, John, Archibald, and Samuel Richman (parents' names not given).

Mar 3, 1804   May 28, 1804
Wilson, Andrew. Executors: Francis Wilson and Alexander McCurdy. Monaghan Township. Legatees: (Bros. and Sisters) Jane, Alexander, Dorcas wife of James Ross, Margaret McCurdy, Jannet Hope, Francis, Daniel, John and Barbara Gillispie.

Mar 5, 1804   Jun 25, 1804
Sinn, Christian. Executor: George Crone and Samuel Ilgenfritz. York Borough. Wife: Margaret Sinn. Children: Rebecca, Anna, John, Jacob and Christian.

Apr 2, 1804   Jun 25, 1804
Crone, John Philip. Executor: Samuel Ilgenfritz. Dover Township. Wife: Mary Elizabeth Crone. Children: George, David, Daniel, Susanna, Christian, Katharine, and Mary.

Apr 18, 1803   Jun 29, 1804
Hurst, John. Executors: Ann Hurst and Adam Brand. Monaghan Township. Wife: Ann Hurst.

Feb 20, 1804   Jul 28, 1804
Forsh, Adam. Executors: John Betzel, John and Barbara Forsh. Dover Township. Wife: Barbara Forsh.

Jun 3, 1804   Aug 1, 1804
Altland, Philip. Executors: Andrew and John Altland. Paradise Township. Children: Philip, Jacob, Peter, George, Andrew, John Catharine wife of Christian Jellers, and Elizabeth wife of John Peck.

Mar 19, 1804   Aug 8, 1804
Smith, Alexander. Executor: Robert Gimmill. Chanceford Township.
Legatee: Catharine Gimmill (Daughter of Robert Gimmill).

Nov 9, 1800   Aug 10, 1804
Trump, Peter. Executor: John Trump. Paradise Township. Wife:
Barbara Trump. Children: Margaret and Michael, Herman and John.

Apr 16, 1801   Aug 13, 1804
Highgas, George. Executor: John Stauffer. Monaghan Township. Wife:
Margaret Highgas. Children: John, Catharine wife of Peter Folke,
Hannah wife of Adam Fry, Sareina, Magdalena wife of Philip Kolp, Mary
wife of Samuel Shirts, Jacob, Elizabeth, Abraham, Henry, and William.

Mar 8, 1804   Aug 13, 1804
Kuntz, Francis. Executor: Elizabeth Kuntz. York Borough. Wife:
Elizabeth Kuntz.

Jul 11, 1804   Aug 20, 1804
Lantzel, George. Executors: Catharine Lantzel. Heidelberg Township.
Wife: Catharine Lantzel. Children: Anna wife of Peter Gladus, and
Catharine.

Aug 4, 1804   Aug 21, 1804
Morningstar, George. Executors: Henry Shultz and Henry Morningstar.
Manheim Township. Children: Henry, Elizabeth, George, Catharine, and
John.

Sep 9, 1803   Aug 28, 1804
Koch, Margaret. Executors: Mary and Richard Koch. York Borough.
Children: Barbara and Mary Koch.

Aug 16, 1804   Aug 30, 1804
Schreiber, Michael. Executor: Peter Kern. Manchester Township. Wife:
Isabella Schreiber. Children: Henry, John, George, Jacob, Elizabeth wife
of John Kleber, Andrew and Peter.

Jan 12, 1803   Sep 1, 1804
Wildasin, Samuel. Executors: Anthony Henkle and Henry Morter.
Manheim Township. Wife: Margaret Wildasin. Children: Peter, George,
Mary wife of Andrew Rudisily, Catharine wife of John Meyer, Eve wife of
Michael Renecker, John, Jacob, Ann wife of Daniel Loeb, Margaret wife of
Henry Hering and Philip.

Jul 30, 1803   Sep 1, 1804
Flore, Valentine. Executors: John Sharp and John Crone. Dover Township. Wife: Elizabeth Flore. Children: Conrad, Susanna wife of Peter Yeger, Anna wife of Adam Yeger, Elizabeth wife of Jacob Banters, Valentine, and Anna.

--- --, ----   Sep 4, 1804
Shindel, Frederick. Executors: Frederick Shindel and Peter Kern. Manchester Township. (German will.)

Aug 17, 1804   Sep 7, 1804
Ziegler, George. Executors: Peter Monges, Martin and Peter Zeigler. West Manchester Township. Children: Martin, Eve, Daniel, Jacob and Peter. (There was a son-in-law, name not given).

May 19, 1801   Sep 13, 1804
Diehl, George. Executors: Daniel and Adam Diehl. Cordorus Township. Wife: Eve Diehl. Children: Daniel, Catharine, Adam, George, Esther, Jacob, Christiana, Ann, John, Charles, and David.

Sep 9, 1804   Sep 25, 1804
Gise, Peter. Executors: Jacob Gise and Tobias Kepner. Children: Susanna and George.

Feb 2, 1794   Sep 27, 1804
Kauffman, Christian. Executor: Philip Kissinger. York Township. Children: Christian, Elizabeth wife of George Meyer, Anna wife of Philip Kissinger, Christiana, and Barbara.

--- --, ----   Sep 29, 1804
Straddler, Jacob. Executors: Christian Hamacher and Jacob Welshans. Hellam Township. (German will.)

Oct 5, 1797   Oct 4, 1804
Ross, George. Executors: Charles Morris and Sarah Ross. Monaghan Township. Wife: Sarah Ross. Children: George, Elizabeth, Richard, Sarah and John. Grandchildren: Elizabeth and Sarah Ginton (Parents names not given).

Apr 10, 1804   Oct 5, 1804
Bohn, Nicholas. Executors: Adam Lichtenberger and Peter Mohr. Manchester Township. Wife: Anna Bohn. Children: Jacob, Ludwig, Elizabeth wife of George Lichtenberger, Catharine wife of Jacob Knab,

Margaret wife of Casper Knob, and Barbara wife of George Ringer.

Jan 1, 1784   Oct 9, 1804
Gould, Thomas. Executors: Catharine Gould and Henry Miller. Newberry Township. Wife: Catharine Gould. Children: Thomas, Mary wife of Moses Pike, Catharine, Jane wife of John Herman, Susanna wife of Freeman Baldy, and Elizabeth.

Sep 11, 1804   Oct 13, 1804
Rudy, Henry. Executors: George Rudy and Philip Heneissen. Dover Township. Wife: Barbara Rudy. Children: Henry and George.

Aug 4, 1804   Oct 20, 1804
Bence, George. Executors: John and Jacob Bence. Washington Township. Wife: Philibbina Bence. Children: Mary, John, George, Elizabeth, Henry, Jacob, Susanna, Caty, and David.

Aug 4, 1804   Oct 20, 1804
Pentz, John. Executors: John and Jacob Pentz. Washington Township. Wife: Philibina Pentz. Children: Mary, John, George, Elizabeth, Henry, Jacob, Susan, Caty, and David. Grandchild: Betsy Beisher (parents' names not given).

Sep 4, 1804   Oct 24, 1804
Spahr, Hans. Executor: John Spahr. Washington Township. Legatee: John Spahr.

Sep 7, 1804   Oct 29, 1804
Miller, Robert. Executors: Joseph Glancy and William Miller. Fairview Township. Wife: Elizabeth Miller. Children: William, Thomas, Elizabeth wife of Haggie Cooper, and Margaret wife of Thomas Warren. Grandson: John Miller (parents' names not given).

--- --, ----   Oct 29, 1804
Raukauser, Daniel. Executors: John Raukauser and Casper Leentenberger. Township: Omitted. (German will.)

Sep 15, 1804   Nov 4, 1804
Asper, George. Executors: Abraham Asper and Philip Asper. Washington Township. Children: Isaas, John, George, Jacob, Philip, Abraham, Frederick, Susanna wife of Henry Bushey, Mary wife of Charles Hoffman, Margaret wife of Andrew Gayer, and Elizabeth wife of Casper Elieker.

Sep 2, 1804   Nov 6, 1804
Weyer, Andrew. Executors: John Weyer and John Lay. West
Manchester Township. Children: Anthony, Michael, John, Benard,
Elizabeth, Susanna, Mary, Margaret, Jacob, Daniel and Lydia.

Nov 1, 1804   Nov 12, 1804
Desenberg, Anthony. Executor: Adam Lichtenberger. Manchester
Township. Wife: Margaret Desenberg. Children: Peter, (and a younger
son whose name was not given.)

Aug 6, 1804   Nov 14, 1804
Sneider, Elizabeth. Executors: Abraham Feed and John School. York
County. Child: David. (This was a deed of gift.)

Aug 12, 1804   Nov 19, 1804
Aulenbaugh, Nicholas. Executors: John and Peter Aulenbaugh. Manheim
Township. Wife: Elizabeth Aulenbaugh. Children: John and Peter.
Granddaughter: Elizabeth wife of Joseph Etzler (parents' names not
recorded).

Sep 30, 1800   Nov 22, 1804
Seffrentz, George. Executors: Catharine Seffrentz and Michael Kurtz.
York Borough. Children: Catharine and Michael Kurtz (and one son -
name not given).

Nov 11, 1804   Nov 27, 1804
Cross, George. Executors: Catharine Cross and John Hooper.
Chanceford Township. Wife: Catharine Cross. (Bequests to heirs of John
Hooper: Mary, Elizabeth and Jannet Hooper.)

Oct 5, 1804   Dec 3, 1804
Read, Joseph. Executors: Janet and Joseph Read. Chanceford Township.
Wife: Janet Read. Children: James, Nicholas, Joseph, James, Margaret
wife of James McNary, William, Esther and Ann. Grandchild: Margaret
Fulton (Parents names not given).

Nov 26, 1804   Dec 8, 1804
Brubacher, Dietrich. Executors: John Brubacher and Samuel Stone.
West Manchester Township. Children: John, Veronica wife of Samuel
Grabill, Mary wife of Samuel Stone, and Ann wife of Christian Lehman.

Feb 21, 1804   Dec 19, 1804
Swartz, Jacob. Executors: Casper Hittabrand and Falicks Glashfatter.

Strasburg Township. Wife: Dorothea Swartz. Children: Jacob, John, Andrew, Felix and Tobias.

Apr 28, 1800   Jan 3, 1805
Hentzel, Casper. Executors: John Summer and Baltzer Hiepert. Manheim Township. Wife: Mary Hentzel. Children: George and Catharine.

Dec 12, 1804   Jan 5, 1805
Hoke, Peter. Executors: Frederick Eichelberger, Jacob and Peter Hoke. West Manchester Township. Wife: Dorothea Hoke. Children: Michael, Peter, Jacob, George, Gloria, Catharine, Sabina wife of John Pentz, and Mary wife of Andrew Schreiber.

Oct 23, 1804   Jan 12, 1805
Gerber, John. Executors: Samuel Harnisch and Samuel Baechtell. Manheim Township. Wife: Catharine Gerber. Children: Christian, Nicholas, and Elizabeth.

May 11, 1803   Jan 17, 1805
Brickner, Peter. Executors: Elizabeth and Kaleb Brickner. Paradise Township. Wife: Elizabeth Brickner. Children: Elizabeth, Peter, Mary, Catharine, John, Emanuel, and Joseph.

Nov 30, 1804   Feb 4, 1805
Crone, John. Executors: Christiana Crone and Philip Hidey. Dover Township. Wife: Christiana Crone. Children: (There were seven children whose names were not given.)

Dec 17, 1804   Feb 11, 1805
Schneider, George. Executors: Elizabeth Schneider and Martin Ebert. York Borough. Wife: Elizabeth Schneider. Children: Daniel, Salome, Margaret, Ann and George.

--- --, ----   Feb 11, 1805
Jacob, John. Executors: George Miller and Ludwick Were. Newberry Township. Wife: Anna Jacob. Children: Elizabeth wife of Jacob Keller, John, Daniel, David, Catharine, Elias, and Mary. Grandchildren: Susanna and John Sharp (parents' names not given).

Jan 15, 1805   Feb 12, 1805
Schlott, Michael. Executors: Mary C. and Adam Schlott. Windsor Township. Wife: Mary Catharine Schlott. Children: John, Susan,

Catharine, Elizabeth, Margaret, Magdalena, Sophia, Michael and Philip.

Oct 2, 1804　　Feb 19, 1805
Fulton, Margaret. Executor: Hugh Fulton. Chanceford Township. Child: Mary.

Dec 27, 1804　　Feb 21, 1805
Wildasin, Samuel. Executors: Jacob Wildasin and Henry Matter. Manheim Township. Wife: Anna Mary Wildasin. Children: (one daughter - name not given).

Apr 3, 1802　　Mar 2, 1805
Brown, Sebastian. Executor: Simon Friss. Hellam Township. Wife: Anna Mary Brown. Children: David, Mathias, Catharine wife of Jacob Leidy, and Magdalena wife of Hey Beam.

--- --, ----　　Mar 6, 1805
Maish, John George. Executor: Joseph Maish. Fairview Township. (German will.)

Jan 30, 1800　　Mar 20, 1805
Billmyer, Helena. Executors: Elizabeth Billmyer and Peter Diehl. York Borough. Children: Michael, Andrew, Rosina wife of Leonard Weigle, Ann wife of Henry Shaffer, and Elizabeth.

Aug 9, 1804　　Mar 21, 1805
Stambach, Jacob. Executors: John and Peter Stambach. Manheim Township. Children: John, Philip and Peter.

Jun 22, 1802　　Apr 30, 1805
Jameson, William. Executors: Mary Jameson and Hugh Anderson. Hopewell Township. Wife: Mary Jameson. Child: William. Sons-in-law: Hugh Anderson and John Dun (wives' names not given).

Feb 5, 1802　　May 1, 1805
Nesbit, Jean. Executor: Alexander Ross. Warrington Township. Legatees: Children of Alexander Ross and Samuel Mateers (names not given).

May 11, 1805　　May 18, 1805
Day, Isabella. Executor: George Wogan. Manchester Township. Children: George, John, Rebecca, and Ann.

Apr 13, 1805   May 20, 1805
Edwards, Edward. Executor: James Patterson. Hopewell Township.
Bequests to Mother, Unity Edwards, and Brother John Edwards.

Oct 11, 1798   May 20, 1805
Bruskhart, Margaret. Executors: Peter Shultz and Samuel Gross.
Manchester Township. German will.

Mar 9, 1805   Jun 20, 1805
Harris, John. Executor: Elizabeth Harris. York Borough. Wife:
Elizabeth Harris.

Jul 7, 1799   Jun 25, 1805
Dressler, George. Executors: John G. Oderman and Christian Wiest.
Paradise Township. Wife: Catharine Dressler. Children: Frederick and
Anna.

Jun 20, 1805   Jul 4, 1805
Sprenckel, George. Executors: Michael Sprenckel and Peter Manges.
West Manchester Township. Wife: Barbara Sprenckel. Children: Anna,
George, Michael, Elizabeth, John, Barbara, Magdalena, Frederick and
Daniel.

Dec 12, 1794   Jul 5, 1805
Bott, Mary Elizabeth. Executor: John Haller. Manchester Township.
Child: Barbara. Granddaughter: Catharine Warner (parents' names not
given).

Dec 7, 1798   Jul 23, 1805
McCoy, John. Executors: John and James McCoy. Windsor Township.
Wife: Elizabeth McCoy. Children: John, James, William, Jenny, Lydia,
and Agness.

Feb 15, 1800   Jul 30, 1805
Senfert, Anna Maria. Executor: John Sharp. Dover Township. Child:
Michael. Grandchildren: (children of Michael) Adam, John, Philip,
George, Catharine wife of Joseph Bower, Barbara, Elizabeth, Mary and
Susanna.

Oct 18, ----   Aug 1, 1805
Gerbrick. Peter. Executors: Jacob Kleinfelter and John Gerber.
Cordorus Township. Children: John, Frederick, George, Michael, Jacob,
Joseph, Margaret wife of George Baley, Maria, Elizabeth, Susan, Eve,

Catharine, and Barbara. Grandchild: Eve Elizabeth Baley (daughter of Margaret).

Jul 20, 1805   Aug 16, 1805
Werner, John Executors: Peter Rigel and George Wehrly. Cordorus Township. Wife: Judith Werner. Children: Anna, Elizabeth, Daniel and Jacob.

Mar 11, 1805   Aug 19, 1805
Lehman, Abraham. Executors: Weirick Bentz and John Lee. York Borough. Wife: Mary Lehman.

Jul 23, 1805   Aug 20, 1805
Miller, John. Executors: Nicholas Gelwecks and Michael Helman. Hanover Borough. Wife: Anna Miller. Children: George, Henry, Solome, Dolly, Joseph, John, Jonathan, Adam, Jacob, and Esther wife of John Sweney. Grandchildren: Jacob, John, George, Elizabeth, and Mary (children of John), Polly Sweney (child of Esther).

May 24, 1803   Sep 4, 1805
Burkholder, Catharine. Executors: Chrisly Sangry and Catharine Sangry. Chanceford Township. Child: Cabien wife of Chrisly Sangry.

Jul 18, 1803   Sep 20, 1805
Thoman, Jacob. Executors: Henry Thoman and Oswald Dupes. Manheim Township. Wife: Suanna Thoman. Children: Magdalena, Elizabeth, John, Henry, Abraham and Rudolph.

Apr 7, 1805   Oct 9, 1805
Welsh, Michael. Executor: Abraham Graffin. York Borough. Wife: Elizabeth Welsh. Children: Elizabeth wife of George Worley, Jacob, Michael, John and Margaret.

May 7, 1805   Oct 11, 1805
Etter, Lawrence. Executors: Mary Etter and Ludwig Bott. Wife: Mary Etter. Shrewsburry Township. Children: Jacob, John, Michael, George, Laurence, Catharine, and Elizabeth.

Jul 1, 1799   Oct 11, 1805
Bobb, Bernard. Executors: Adam Schaffer and Ludwig Bobb. Shrewsbury Township. Wife: Gertrude Bobb. Children: Michael, Barbara wife of Christian Heterick, Margaret wife of Henry Baumgartner, Eve wife of Michael Geip, Ludwig, Henry, and John.

--- --, ----   Oct 25, 1805
Bottenfeld, Philip. Executor: Omitted. German will.

Jan 22, 1797   Oct 26, 1805
Kreber, Philip. Executors: John and Jacob Kreber. Manchester Township. Children: John, Jacob, Margaret wife of Adam Holtzaffel, Susanna wife of George Wetterrecht, Catharine wife of Balthasser Hamm, and Elizabeth wife of Mathias Kline. Granddaughter: Catharine Holtzaffel.

May 21, 1803   Oct 28, 1805
Patterson, Mary. Executors: James Patterson. Chanceford Township. Children: James, Martha wife of Nathan Morris, and Hugh.

Oct 5, 1805   Nov 8, 1805
Grienewalt, Christopher. Executors: Adam Lichtenberger and Peter Mohr. Manchester Township. Wife: Maria Grienewalt. Children: Abraham, John, Frederick, Jacob, Anna, and Catharine wife of John Heistand.

May 27, 1804   Nov 12, 1805
More, Catharine. Executor: David Miesenhelter. Dover Township. Legatee: Valentine Artel.

Mar 21, 1801   Nov 18, 1805
Schenck, Henry. Executors: Deitrick Brubaker and John Schenck. Cordorus Township. Children: Michael, John, Mary Magdalena, Margaret, Henry, Freney wife of John Meyer, Barbara wife of John Hershey, Ann and Elizabeth.

Feb 8, 1805   Nov 20, 1805
McMullen, Samuel. Executors: Alexander Ross and William McMullen. Monaghan Township. Wife: Omitted. Children: William and James.

Nov 12, 1805   Nov 21, 1805
Kepler, Jacob. Executor: Jacob Kepler. Newberry Township. Wife: Catharine Kepler. Children: Jacob, George, Abijah, Nancy, Elizabeth, Mary, Rachel wife of Thomas Farre, and Leah wife of ---- Day. Grandchildren: Rachel and Leah Day.

Jul 6, 1805   Nov 27, 1805
Aushelman, John. Executors: Eve Aushelman and Joseph Sneersy. Hanover Township. Wife: Eve Aushelman. Brother: Christian. Sister:

Catharine Aushelman.

Aug 20, 1802   Nov 28, 1805
Hoffman, John. Executor: Catharine Hoffman. Newberry Township.
Wife: Catharine Hoffman. Children: Eve, Susanna, Magdalena, and Daniel.

Oct 19, 1805   Dec 3, 1805
King, Godfrey. Executor: Philip Jacob King. West Manchester Township.
Wife: Catharine King. Children: George, Philip, Barbara wife of Adam Rutter, Elizabeth wife of Frederick Rockey, and Christiana wife of Jacob Fischel. Grandchild: Charles Fischel.

Sep 29, 1805   Dec 10, 1805
Bentz, George. Executors: Anna Bentz, Jacob Spangler and Samuel Rutter. York Borough. Wife: Anna Maria Bentz. Children: John, William, Polly wife of Samuel Long, Barnet, Elizabeth wife of Nicholas Dell, and Jacob. Grandchildren: Daniel and Elizabeth (children of Barnet).

Dec 19, 1805   Jan 14, 1806
Meyer, John. Executors: John Landis and Henry Tyson. Windsor Township. Wife: Christiana Meyer. Children: (Ten, names not given.)

Aug 27, 1802   Jan 25, 1806
Jacob, George. Executor: George Jacob. Paradise Township. Children: Henry, George, Elizabeth wife of John Trump, and Mary wife of Jacob More.

May 19, 1802   Jan 28, 1806
Shanks, Thomas. Executors: Sarah Shanks and Alexander Ross. Warrington Township. Children: William, David James, Sarah, Elizabeth and Mary.

Jan 29, 1806   Feb 3, 1806
Gartman, Catharine. Executors: Michael Klinefelter and Abraham Danner. York Borough. Children: Catharine, and Elizabeth wife of Thomas Boumgartner.

Sep 10, 1801   Feb 5, 1806
Wittmeyer, Simon. Executors: Simon Wittmeyer and Andrew Hack. Manchester Township. Wife: Mary Wittmeyer. Children: Simon, Magdalena wife of Peter Weigle and Mary wife of Andrew Hack.

Jan 15, 1806   Feb 12, 1806
Schwartz, Abraham. Executors: Anna Maria Schwartz and Jacob Henry. Shrewsbury Township. Wife: Anna Maria Schwartz.

Jan 5, 1805   Feb 18, 1806
Wiley, Joseph. Executors: James Wiley and Samuel Morrison. Fawn Township. Wife: Mary Wiley. Children: James, Sarah wife of James Gammill, Jenny and Mary wife of Samuel Morrison.

--- --, 1803   Feb 19, 1806
Kurtz, Anna Mary. Executor: John Laucks. York Borough. Wife of Michael Kurtz. Children: Christiana, (and two other daughters whose names were not given.)

Oct 11, 1805   Feb 19, 1806
Houck, David. Executors: Maria Houck and John Trone. Hanover Township. Wife: Maria Houck.

Dec 8, 1804   Feb 24, 1806
Erwin, Arthur. Executors: Joseph Person and Margaret Erwin. Fairview Township. Children: Arthur and Margaret. Grandchild: Joseph (son of Arthur). Son-in-law: Joseph Person (wife dead, her name not stated). Three children whose names were not given.

Sep 10, 1805   Mar 5, 1806
Hicks, Laurence. Executors: George Herman and Jacob Retter. Monaghan Township. Wife: Susanna Hicks. Children: Lawrence, Mary, Catharine, Rebecca, and Jacob.

Sep 4, 1801   Mar 14, 1806
Lan, Peter. Executors: George P. Zeigler, John Emig, and Andrew Lan. Cordorus Township. Children: Andrew, George, Magdalena wife of George Gentzer, Anna wife of Daniel Reynold, Catharine wife of Valentine Alt, Susanna wife of Valentine Bergheimer, and Eve wife of Peter Reynold.

Feb 4, 1806   Mar 15, 1806
Smith, George. Executors: Henry Willer and George Smith. Cordorus Township. Wife: Catharine Smith. Children: George, Sophia, Catharine, Susanna, Margaret, John, Magdalena, Elizabeth, Anthony and Juliana.

May 13, 1805   Mar 25, 1806
Ewing, James. Executors: William Barber. Hellam Township. Grandson:

James Ewing Mifflin (mother's name not given).

Mar 7, 1806   Mar 30, 1806
McClellan, David. Executor: John Kelly. Chanceford Township. Wife: Ann McClellan. Child: Margaret.

Jan 20, 1806   Apr 1, 1806
Messing, John. Executor: Sophia C. Messing. Hanover Township. Wife: Sophia Messing. Children: Frederick, Anne and Sophia Nagle (stepdaughter).

Mar 8, 1806   Apr 12, 1806
Reiff, Joseph. Executors: John Mumaugh, John Selly and Abraham Rike. York County. Wife: Catharine Reiff.

Apr 10, 1806   Apr 25, 1806
Deardorff, Anthony. Executors: John and Anthony Deardorff. Washington Township. Wife: Mary Deardorff. Children: John, Samuel, Daniel, David, Anthony, Joseph, Elizabeth, Molly wife of Henry Eckenroad, and Susanna wife of Daniel Brown.

Apr 9, 1806   Apr 26, 1806
Bailey, Hannah. Executor: Manuell McDowell. York County. Children: Margaret, Hannah, Ruth, and Jane.

Feb 15, 1806   May 3, 1806
Nevitt, Hannah. Executor: Elizabeth Cook. Washington Township. Legatees: Jesse and Samuel Cook (brothers).

Aug 5, 1801   May 16, 1806
Harris, George Executors: John Spence and Robert Hamersley. Newberry Township. Wife: Bulah Harris. Children: George, John, Elisha, Richard, James, Elizabeth wife of Joseph Fletcher, Lydia wife of Frederick Darr, Mary wife of Joseph Webb, and Hannah wife of Hugh Reed.

May 2, 1800   May 22, 1806
Hahn, David. Executors: John Thomas and Jacob Hostetter. Hanover Township. Wife: Philipina Hahn. Child: Barbara.

Apr 25, 1806   May 23, 1806
Herr, John. Executors: Martin Huber and Christian Stoner. Hellam Township. Children: Rudy, John, Anna wife of John Stewart, Mary wife

of Christian Stoner, Elizabeth wife of Christian Bucker, Caty wife of Abraham Flury, and Susanna wife of Jacob Fetz.

Aug 26, 1805   May 28, 1806
Guckes, John. Executor: George Slater. York Borough. Children: Julianna, Dorothea, Adam, and Catharine.

Mar 10, 1801   Jun 3, 1806
Updegraff, Herman. Executor: Thomas Evans. Monaghan Township. Wife: Nancy Updegraf. Children: Samuel, Jacob, Peter, Henry, Elizabeth, Herman and Hannah.

--- --, ----   Jun 7, 1806
Fleishaman, Martin. Executor: The Widow. Shrewsbury Township. German will.

--- --, ----   Jun 7, 1806
Manges, Peter. Executors: John Manges and Martin Zeigler. West Manchester Township. Wife: Catharine Manges. Children: John, Peter, Jacob, Margaret wife of John Shaffer, Elizabeth wife of John Fickes, Eve wife of Jacob Eip, and Catharine wife of Martin Zeigler.

Aug 14, 1798   Jun 30, 1806
Feiser, Peter. Executor: Peter Feiser. York Borough. Children: Peter, Christiana wife of Daniel Smith, Elizabeth wife of Tobias Beckel, and Anamary wife of Jacob Strobich.

Apr 5, 1806   Jul 17, 1806
Smith, James. Executors: James Smith, Jr., William Barber and James Johnson. York Borough. Wife: Eleanor Smith. Child: James Smith.

Oct 15, 1804   Aug 1, 1806
Park, William. Executor: Elihu Park. Township: Omitted. Children: Mary, Francis, Elizabeth, Elihu, and Joseph.

Jun 27, 1806   Aug 4, 1806
Zacharias, George. Executors: John Philip Strack and John Young. Manheim Township. Legatees: (Sisters-in-law) Margaret wife of Jacob Casset and Barbara Young.

Jul 19, 1806   Aug 11, 1806
Miller, John. Executors: John and Henry Deardorff. Monaghan Township. Wife: Christiana Miller. Children: George, (and others names

and number not given.)

Jul 10, 1806   Aug 11, 1806
McCleary, John. Executors: Isabella McCleary and William Anderson. Chanceford Township. Wife: Isabella McCleary. Children: Margaret, Agness, John, Nathan, and Jean.

May 13, 1806   Aug 21, 1806
Fiester, Jacob. Executors: Jacob Stoble and Michael Segrist. Windsor Township. Wife: Catharine Fiester. Children: Susanna, and (five other daughters whose names were not given.)

Mar 7, 1801   Aug 22, 1806
Milliken, James. Executor: James Milliken. York County. Wife: Elizabeth Milliken. Children: James, Jean, Thomas, Elizabeth, and Martha. Grandsons: James Taylor and William Colver (parents' names not given).

Jul 2, 1805   Aug 22, 1806
Leas, Valentine. Executor: Henry Wolf. Paradise Township. Wife: Barbara Leas. Children: Daniel, Susanna, Sarah, William, Jacob, Elizabeth, and Margaret.

--- ---, ----   Aug 30, 1806
Bickeler, Magdalena. Executor and Township omitted. German will.

Feb 27, 1801   Aug 30, 1806
Stover, George. Executors: Michael and Jacob Stover. Paradise Township. Legatee: (Bro.) Michael Stover.

--- ---, ----   Oct 14, 1806
Godwald, Andrew. Executors: John Quickel and Andrew Smith. Manchester Township. Wife: Omitted. Children: Jacob, Andrew, John, Catharine, Daniel, Magdalena, Henry, Elizabeth, and George.

--- ---, ----   Oct 20, 1806
Heidler, John. Executors: Judith Heidler and Tobias Kepner. Paradise Township. Wife: Judith Heidler. Children: Catharine, Margaret, Magdalena, Mary, Elizabeth, and John.

Mar 6, 1802   Oct 24, 1806
Lewig, Philip. Executors: Anna Lewig and Adam Brandt. Reading Township. Wife: Anna Lewig.

213

Dec 8, 1805   Nov 19, 1806
Miller, Elizabeth. Executors: William and Thomas Miller. Fairview Township. Widow of Robert Miller. Children: William, Thomas, Margaret wife of Thomas Warren, and Elizabeth wife of Haggie Cooper.

Feb 14, 1806   Dec 8, 1806
Keller, John. Executors: Jacob Keller and Jacob Bossert. Manheim Township. "An old single man." Legatees: Michael Hohf and others.

Jun 14, 1806   Dec 9, 1806
Matthias, Henry. Executors: John and Peter Matthias. Newberry Township. Children: Catharine wife of Peter Zeller, Sophia wife of Jacob Copwalt, Mary wife of John Preneman, Henry, John, Peter, and Elizabeth wife of Henry Bush.

Mar 19, 1804   Dec 9, 1806
Wambach, Peter. Executors: Peter Wambach and David Gear. Windsor Township. Children: Peter and Anna wife of David Pear.

Oct 16, 1806   Dec 30, 1806
Marsh, John. Executors: John Everit and Hugh Marsh. Washington Township. Wife: Catharine Marsh.

Oct 5, 1806   Jan 1, 1807
Meckle, Catharine. Executors: Christian and Michael Meckle. Cordorus Township. Wife: Catharine Meckle. Children: John, Christian, Jacob, Henry, George, Michael, Barbara, Catharine wife of John Binder, Elizabeth wife of John Rudisel, and Anna wife of Jacob Stambach.

Oct 30, 1805   Feb 10, 1807
Liebhart, Valentine. Executors: Jacob Deitz and Henry Liebhart. Township: Omitted. Wife: Appolonia Liebhart. Children: Henry, Catharine, Susanna, John, Jacob, Barbara wife of Mathias Brown, Elizabeth, and Philip.

Sep 13, 1806   Feb 19, 1807
Baer, Jeremiah. Executors: Nicholas Lichty and Harry Wentz. Dover Township. Children: William, Ludwick, Michael, Peter, Margaret wife of Samuel Wilt, Catharine wife of Adam Bitner, Barbara wife of Nicholas Lichty, and Eve wife of Philip Hering.

Feb 5, 1799   Feb 26, 1807
Mamber, Michael. Executor: Michael Mamber. Monaghan Township.

Children: Christiana wife of Frederick Long, and Michael.

Sep 6, 1805   Mar 12, 1807
Grame, Conrad. Executor: T. Grame. Fairview Township. Children: Frederick, Peter, Gertrude wife of Jacob Possiler, Susanna, and Agness wife of John Grubb.

Feb 7, 1806   Mar 19, 1807
Worley, James. Executors: Philip Frederick and Weerick Bentz. West Manchester Township. Wife: Abigail Worley. Children: Nathan and Lydia wife of John Eichelberger. Grandson: James Worley (son of Nathan).

Mar 11, 1807   Mar 25, 1807
Lighty, John. Executor: Abraham Lighty. Washington Township. Legatee: Philip Herman and his heirs.

Mar 11, 1807   Mar 30, 1807
Shettler, Andrew. Executors: Jacob Stuck and Martin Ebert. Cordorus Township. Wife: Eve Shettler. Children: Jacob, Lydia and Barbara. Grandchild: Catharine Beyer (daughter of John Beyer - mother's name not given).

Aug 17, 1804   Apr 9, 1807
Proudfoot, Andrew. Executor: Alexander Tompson. Hopewell Township. Wife: Sarah Proudfoot. Children: James, Alexander, David, and Robert. Grandchildren: Alexander Proudfoot (son of James), and Andrew Proudfoot (son of David).

Apr 13, 1805   Apr 12, 1807
Cummins, John. Executors: William Cummins and Robert Gordan. Township omitted. Wife: Rebecca Cummins. Children: Samuel, William and Jane.

Mar 25, 1795   Apr 18, 1807
Yager, Henry. Executor: Jacob Wert. Manheim Township. Legatee: (Step-Bro.) Jacob Wert.

Feb 3, 1803   Apr 20, 1807
Bauser, Daniel. Executor: Christian Bauser. Manheim Township. Wife: Elizabeth Bauser. Children: Magdalena wife of Nicholas Miller, Elizabeth wife of Conrad Koppenheffer, Benjamin, Esther, Joseph, Mary, Isaac, Jonas, Andrew, Solomon, and Adam.

Sep 22, 1804   Apr 20, 1807
Rudisilly, Jacob. Executor: John Rudisilly. Cordorus Township. Children: John, Ludwig and Elizabeth wife of Abraham Roth. Grandchild: Jacob Rudisilly (son of John).

Apr 13, 1807   Apr 23, 1807
Henry, William. Executor: George Henry. Chanceford Township. Wife: Margery Henry. Children: Jane wife of James Speer, and George.

Dec 7, 1806   May 1, 1807
Hines, James. Executors: Susanna and Anthony Hines. Windsor Township. Children: Sarah, Rosanna, Ruth, Mary, and Susanna.

--- --, ----   May 2, 1807
Finley, Andrew. Executors: Robert Gemmel and Andrew Warwick. Hopewell Township. Nieces and Nephew: Ellener, Baxter, Mary, and Andrew Laird.

Feb --, 1807   May 5, 1807
Sefference, Nancy. Executor: Michael Graham. York Borough. Sister: Martha Sefference.

Apr 28, 1807   May 13, 1807
Hamelton, Margaret. Executor: Robert Cathcart. York County. Legatees: Rev. Robert Cathcart and Sarah Geddes, the daughter of Capt. Henry Geddes.

Aug 8, 1803   May 19, 1807
Smith, Maria Dorothea. Executor: Frederick Youse. York Borough. Children: Peter, Andrew, and Anna wife of Christian Kreitler.

May 2, 1807   May 26, 1807
Bower, George Adam. Executors: Henry Bower and George Meller. Newburry Township. Children: Christopher, Henry, John, Jacob, Eve wife of ---- Hoffman, Christiana wife of ---- Emick, and Martin.

Mar 2, 1805   Jun 15, 1807
Hower, Michael. Executor: Henry Malter. Manheim Township. Wife: Eve Hower. Children: Henry, George, and Elizabeth wife of Isaac Schuh.

Jan 19, 1807   Jun 29, 1807
Leib, Henry. Executors: Henry Leib and Philip Laner. Dover Township. Wife: Magdalena Leib. Children: Henry, John, Nancy, and Magdalena.

May 6, 1807   Jul 18, 1807
Smyser, Martin. Executors: Sarah and Jacob Smyser. York Borough.
Wife: Barbara Smyser.

Apr 1, 1806   Jul 25, 1807
Lorich, Jacob. Executors: Barbara Grenblad and Adam Rossar. Cordorus Township. Children: Barbara wife of Philip Grunblad, Effa wife of William Rachser, and Michael. Granddaughter: Elizabeth Rachser.

Jul 1, 1807   Aug 15, 1807
Laird, Hugh. Executors: William and James Laird. Dover Township. Wife: Mary Laird. Children: William, James, and Jane.

Jul 7, 1807   Aug 26, 1807
Bopp, Peter. Executor: Peter Bott, Jr. Monaghan Township. Wife: Catharine Bott. Children: Catharine, Peter, Mary, and Elizabeth.

Apr 27, 1807   Sep 18, 1807
Stauffer, John. Executors: Jacob Stauffer and Henry Wolf. Paradise Township. Wife: Anna Stauffer. Children: Anna wife of John Brubaker, Barbara wife of Jacob Davis, John, Henry, Elizabeth wife of John Herr and Polly.

Dec 31, 1804   Sep 18, 1807
Weigel, Sebastian. Executors: Peter Weigel and John Haller. West Manchester Township. Children: Peter, Henry, Sebina, Julianna, Elizabeth, Catharine, Susanna, Margaret and Anna.

Jan 15, 1804   Sep 18, 1807
Wilson, William. Executors: Martin Armstrong and Thomas McKinley. Chanceford Township. Legatees: (Bro. and Sister) Jane and Thomas Wilson.

Feb 2, 1803   Sep 23, 1807
Anderson, Jennet. Executors: Robert Anderson and James Anderson. Hopewell Township. Children: Robert, James, John, Andrew and Rachel; Jennet (daughter of James), Esther (daughter of John). Granddaughter: Rachael Wilson (parents' names not recorded).

Jul 2, 1798   Oct 5, 1807
Weber, Philip. Executors: Daniel Weber and Isaac Gartman. York Borough. Wife: Catharine Weber. Children: Abraham, Daniel, Catharine wife of Isaac Garman and Anna wife of John Rothbaust.

Sep 2, 1807   Oct 13, 1807
Pressel, Valentine. Executors: Adam Brand and Abraham Bisel. Washington Township. Wife: Margaret Pressel. Children: Catharine, Margaret, Elizabeth wife of Samuel Tonneras, and Valentine.

Aug 28, 1807   Oct 20, 1807
Losh, Henry. Executors: George Leininger and Henry Sprinkle. Manheim Township. Wife: Catharine Losh. Children: Zacharius, Henry, Elizabeth wife of George Leininger, and Catharine wife of Henry Sprinkle.

Sep 5, 1807   Dec 28, 1807
Finley, Martha. Executors: Martin Gartner and George Bard. Chanceford Township. Grandchildren: Polly Laird and John Finley (parents' names not given). Nieces and Nephews: James Wells, Polly Doman, and Mary Chambers (parents' names not given).

Feb 17, 1797   Dec 28, 1807
Fritz, Philip. Executors: John Gartner and George Bard. Hellam Township. Children: Philip, Fretz, Barbara wife of Michael Cloninger, Catharine wife of Philip Rupp, John, Juleana, Jacob, Henry, and Adam.

Feb 13, 1808   Jan 2, 1808
Burkholder, Christian. Executors: Frederick Burkholder and William Neel, Jr. Chanceford Township. Wife: (Omitted.) Children: Frederick, Christian and William.

--- --, ----   Jan 30, 1808
Dewes, John. Executor and Township omitted. German will.

Dec 9, 1800   Feb 2, 1808
Burn, Joseph. Executors: Robert Ramsey and Martin Clack. Fawn Township. Sisters: Francis and Betsy Burn.

Jan 6, 1808   Feb 6, 1808
Becker, Jacob. Executors: George Gans and Henry Rahl. Shrewsbury Township. Wife: Eva Becker. Children: Polly, Rosana, Leadia, Jacob, and Henry.

Dec 12, 1804   Feb 24, 1808
Becker, Matthias. Executors: William Metzger and John Quickel. Newberry Township. Wife: Elizabeth Becker. Children: (Names and number not recorded.)

Nov 16, 1807   Mar 2, 1808
Irwin, Gerrerd. Executors: William and George Irwin. Fairview Township. Children: William, George, and John.

Sep 11, 1807   Mar 18, 1808
Georing, Jacob. Executors: Jacob Hay and Adam Lichtenberger. York Borough. Wife: Elizabeth Georing. Children: Maria, Sarah, Barbara, Lydia, Elizabeth, Margaret, and John.

Apr 20, 1807   Mar 19, 1808
Hussey, Miriam. Executors: Joseph Griest and Thomas McMillen. Warrington Township. Children: Amos, Miriam, Edith wife of James Marsh, Lydia wife of Jacob Griffith, Rebecca wife of Joseph Griest, Hannah wife of John Marsh, Ruth wife of Mordica Matthews, and Mary wife of Elisha Hunt.

Nov 25, 1796   Mar 28, 1808
Danner, Martin. Executor: Abraham Danner. York Borough. Children: Elizabeth wife of Abraham Wilt, Catharine wife of John Welsh, and Abraham.

Feb 15, 1808   Apr 5, 1808
Huzzy, Nathan. Executors: William Vale and Judia Huzzy. Warringtont Wife: Hannah Huzzy.

Feb 7, 1804   Apr 6, 1808
Noll, Francis. Executors: Nicholas Gewicks and Elizabeth Noll. Hanover Township. Wife: Elizabeth Noll. Children: Jacob, John, George, Susanna, Elizabeth, Mary, and Sarah.

May 7, 1806   Apr 9, 1808
Smith, Michael. Executor: Peter Smith. Dover Township. Wife: Elizabeth Smith. Children: (the names and number not given).

Jun 5, 1808   Jun 7, 1808
Eyen, Catharine. Executors: Henry Mourer and John White. Baltimore, Maryland. Children: Catharine wife of John White, and Charlotte wife of Henry Mourer.

Apr 20, 1808   Jul 4, 1808
Braneman, Samuel. Executors: John Zeigler and Joseph Braneman. Cordorus Township. Children: Samuel, Benjamin, Wilhelm, and Joseph.

Jun 9, 1808   Jul 5, 1808
Ramsay, James. Executors: James and William Ramsay. Fawn Township. Wife: Catharine Ramsay. Children: Sarah, Catharine, James and William. Grandchildren: James, John and Eliza Glasgo and James, John and Samuel Keiper (Parents names not given).

May 7, 1808   Jul 21, 1808
Zerm, Mary. Executor: Jacob Zerm. Dover Township. Child: Margaret.

Oct 29, 1807   Jul 23, 1808
Bergheimer, Valentine. Executors: Daniel Dicke and Henry Bergheimer. Cordorus Township. Wife: Susanna Bergheimer. Children: (Names and number not recorded.)

--- --, ----   Jul 23, 1808
Kerman, Mathias. Executor: John Sheffer. Hellam Township. (German will.)

--- --, ----   Aug 1, 1808
McDonnald, Mary. Executor: Thomas Kilgore. Fawn Township. Legatees: Soloman Kilgore and others who are not relatives.

Jul 22, 1808   Aug 17, 1808
Neill, Thomas. Executors: Rev. Robert Cathcart, Alexander, and Lewis Neill. York County. Child: Lewis. Grandson: Lewis (child of Lewis).

Jul 4, 1808   Sep 10, 1808
Davis, John. Executors: Benjamin Walker and Robert Davis. Warrington Township. Wife: Hannah Davis. Children: Daniel, Robert, Anne, and Elizabeth wife of David Cadwaleder.

Aug 19, 1808   Sep 21, 1808
Young, Tobias. Executors: Elizabeth Young and Christian Brilhart. Cordorus Township. Wife: Elizabeth Young.

Jun 11, 1808   Sep 26, 1808
Kinstler, Rebecca. Executors: John Blasser and Jacob Beck. Shrewsbury Township. (A widow.) Nephew: Frederick Reagan (sister's son).

--- --, ----   Oct 1, 1808
Lanius, Henry. Executor: Christian Lanius. York Borough. (German will.)

Nov 26, 1804   Oct 13, 1808
Kintzlein, Elizabeth. Executor: Henry Lanius. Mt. Joy Township. Widow of Jacob Kintzlein. Children: Susanna, Elizabeth wife of Henry Lanius, Catharine, Magdalena, John, Jacob, and Christian.

Sep 14, 1808   Oct 20, 1808
Miller, Richard. Executors: James Anderson and Jean Miller. Fairview Township. Wife: Jean Miller. Children: Samuel, and Mary.

Oct 1, 1808   Nov 7, 1808
Low, Joshua. Executors: Caleb Low and Jesse Low. Shrewsbury Township. Children: Caleb, Ann, Jesse, and Mary.

--- --, ----   Nov 21, 1808
Shriver, John. Executor: Omitted. Township omitted. (German will.)

Jul 30, 1807   Dec 5, 1808
Morris, Dr. John. Executors: Jacob Hay, Andrew Cramer, and Thomas Eichelberger. York Borough. Wife: Barbara Morris. Children: Charles, and others (Names and number not given.)

Jul 8, 1808   Dec 8, 1808
Smith, Christian. Executor: Adam Smith. Windsor Township. Wife: Mary Anna Smith. Children: Adam, Mary, Barbara wife of Infarth Bower, Christiana, Polly, Margaret wife of John Erhart.

Jul 8, 1808   Dec 10, 1808
Fahs, Henry. Executors: Abraham Fahs and George Siess. Maryland Township. Wife: Anna Maria Fahs. Children: Henry, John, Jacob, Zachariah, and Susanna.

Jun 8, 1807   Dec 20, 1808
Fox, George. Executors: Conrad Fox and George Oberdorph. Windsor Township. Wife: Eve Fox. Children: Conrad, Elizabeth wife of Jacob McClain, Joseph, John, and Eve wife of Robert McCanley.

Jul 3, 1807   Jan 10, 1809
Fisher, John J. Executors: Barbara and John Fisher. York Borough. Wife: Barbara Fisher. Children: George, John, and Charles.

Sep 16, 1808   Jan 12, 1809
Mills, Robert. Executors: Thomas Mills and David Warren. Newberry Township. Legatees: Ann (mother) wife of James Wickersham, Thomas

Mills (brother), and sisters Mary wife of John Wall, Rachel wife of William Wickersham, and Esther Mills.

Feb 10, 1803   Jan 13, 1809
Wolf, Henry. Executors: Peter Dickle and Yost Herbach. York Borough. Children: Henry, Catharine, Peter, George and Elizabeth wife of Peter Dickle.

Oct 7, 1808   Feb 11, 1809
Boyer, John. Executors: Benjamin and Christian Boyer. Manheim Township. Wife: Elizabeth Boyer. Children: Magdalena, Henry, Elizabeth, Daniel, Christian, Susanna wife of Jacob Schnebz, and Benjamin.

Jan 17, 1809   Feb 25, 1809
Sangry, Peter. Executor: George Barringer. Chanceford Township. Wife: Charlotte Sangry. Children: Michael, Christian, Catharine, Elizabeth wife of George Barsinger, Christiana wife of James Hay, Jacob and John.

Mar 9, 1809   Mar 18, 1809
Householder, Henry. Executors: Jacob and John Householder. Hopewell Township. Wife: Mary Householder. Children: Nancy, Elizabeth, Mary, Abraham, Jacob, Henry, and John.

Mar 19, 1809   Mar 27, 1809
Bensel, Casper. Executor: James Julius. Paradise Township. Wife: Elizabeth Bensel. Children: Jacob, John, and Susanna wife of Jacob Wist.

May 22, 1800   Apr 3, 1809
Reiger, Ludwick. Executors: Peter Reiger and Anthony Willet. Cordorus Township. Wife: Gertrude Reiger. Children: Peter, Elizabeth wife of Anthony Willet and Margaret.

Mar 18, 1809   Apr 4, 1809
Young, Henry. Executors: William Young and Michael Helman. Hanover Township. Children: William, Jacob and Elizabeth.

Jan 20, 1806   Apr 5, 1809
Kinsler, Michael. Executor: Rebecca Kinsler. Shrewsbury Township. Wife: Rebecca Kinsler.

Feb 24, 1809   Apr 6, 1809
McCally, John. Executor: John Smith. Chanceford Township. Legatee: William McCally (father).

Dec 22, 1808   Apr 12, 1809
Campbell, John. Executors: Henry Kelly and Elizabeth Campbell. Chanceford Township. Wife: Elizabeth Campbell. Children: Esther, Daniel, John, Rebecca, Sally, Donnal, Elizabeth, Mary, and James.

Jul 25, 1808   Apr 14, 1809
Korbman, Henry. Executors: George Metzgar and Andrew Cramer. York Borough. Wife: Catharine Korbman. Children: John, George, Michael, Catharine wife of Nicholas Welt, Christiana, Eve wife of George Metzgar, and Rosina wife of John Geiselman.

Sep 15, 1808   Apr 25, 1809
Pugh, David. Executors: James Jacobs and John Moore. Township: Omitted. Children: Joseph, Mordica, Lydia wife of James Jacobs, and Sarah wife of John Moore. Grandson: David Pugh (son of Joseph).

Apr 6, 1809   May 15, 1809
Zinn, Philip Jacob. Executors: John Butler and Nicholas Zinn. Dover Township. Wife: Ann Kunta Zinn. Children: John, Jacob, Elizabeth, Margaret, Catharine, Nicholas, Mary, Barbara, Magdalena, Christiana and Adam.

Mar 9, 1801   Jun 3, 1809
Heiges, George. Executor: Jacob Heiges. Monaghan Township. Wife: Elizabeth Heiges. Children: Jacob, Christian, Elizabeth, John, and Mary.

Apr 14, 1809   Jun 16, 1809
Klinepeter, Rudolph. Executors: Jacob Stover and Jacob Boose. Paradise Township. Children: Mary, Adam, Elizabeth wife of Frederick Knetzinger, Henry, Casper, John, Frederick, Margaret wife of John Stump, and Catharine.

Dec 13, 1808   Jun 23, 1809
Gibson, Jacob. Executors: Anna and Jacob Gibson. Fawn Township. Wife: Anna Gibson. Children: Lydia wife of Ambrose Cunningham, Andrew, Joseph, Hugh, Margaret wife of Robert Colvin, George, Mary wife of John Gibson, Anna, Jane, Jacob, and Thomas. Grandchildren: Jacob, John and Ann (children of Hugh).

Mar 9, 1809   Jul 1, 1809
Wamback, George. Executors: Michael Wamback and John Gayley.
Windsor Township. Wife: Anna Mary Wamback. Children: Elizabeth,
Magdalena, Michael, Catharine, George and John.

Dec 20, 1794   Jul 26, 1809
Heibly, Sophia. Executor: Jacob Heibly. York Borough. Children:
Sophia wife of Henry Miller, Jacob, Juliana wife of David Jameson,
Michael, Anna, and John.

Jul 3, 1808   Aug 4, 1809
Edinger, Adam. Executors: Anna Mary Edinger and Adam Edinger.
Dover Township. Wife: Anna Mary Edinger. Children: John, Adam,
Jacob, Jonas, Joseph, Benjamin, Leah, Daniel, Mary, and Elizabeth.

Apr 6, 1809   Aug 5, 1809
Pike, Elizabeth. Executors: Daniel and Moses Pike. Township: Omitted.
Children: David, Moses, John, Phebe wife of John Richmond, Sarah wife
of Isaac Shepherd, Rebecca wife of Abraham Vernon, and Ruth.

Apr 6, 1808   Aug 28, 1809
Nelson, Samuel. Executors: Samuel Nelson and John Kilgore.
Chanceford Township. Wife: Omitted. Children: John, Robert, Rebecca,
Elizabeth, and Samuel. Son-in-law: John Kilgore wife's name not given).

Aug 24, 1809   Sep 2, 1809
Grove, Francis. Executors: Philip Wohlfort and Frederick Grove.
Manheim Township. Wife: Margaret Grove. Children: George,
Catharine, Susanna, John, Elizabeth, and Salley.

Nov 10, 1804   Sep 5, 1809
Torbet, Robert. Executors: Andrew and Robert Torbet. Fawn Township.
Children: Jean, Janet wife of --- Gordan, Agness, Isabella wife of --- Shaw,
Andrew and Robert. Grandchildren: Agness Torbet (child of Andrew)
James Gordan, Nancy and William Shaw.

Aug 9, 1800   Oct 6, 1809
Long, Michael. Executors: Mary C. Long and Jacob Sterbick. York
County. Wife: Mary C. Long. Children: John, and Barbara wife of
Martin Fenter. Grandchildren: Elizabeth Sprenkle (daughter of John),
John and Frederick (sons of John), and John and Susanna Fenter.
Stepson: John Walter.

Jun 6, 1809   Nov 9, 1809
Wilson, James. Executors: David and John Wilson. Hopewell Township.
Wife: Rachel Wilson. Children: Jannett, James, David, Rachel, John,
William and Robert.

Sep 27, 1807   Nov 10, 1809
Dinsmore, John. Executors: Robert Colvin, Martha and Andrew
Dinsmore. Fawn Township. Wife: (Name not given.) Children: George,
Nancy, Martha, Jane, and Polly.

May 27, 1808   Dec 1, 1809
Spangler, Susanna. Executors: Peter Streber and Abraham Grafus.
York County. Legatees: Henry and Elizabeth Spangler. Children of
brother: Robert Spangler.

Aug 6, 1809   Dec 15, 1809
Himan, Gottleib. Executors: John Boyer and Magdalena Himan.
Shrewsbury Township. Wife: Magdalena Himan. Children: John,
Hannah and Jacob.

Jun 13, 1809   Dec 20, 1809
Lawson, Mary. Executor: Edward Lawson. York County. Children:
Benj., Moses, Fanny, Joseph, Richard, Moses, and Edward.

--- --, ----   Dec 30, 1809
Martin, Christian. Executor: Omitted. Hellam Township. (German will.)

Sep 4, 1804   Jan 2, 1810
Lutes, John. Executors: David Maich, John and Margaret Lutes.
Fairview Township. Wife: Margaret Lutes. Children: Elizabeth, Sarah,
Magdalena wife of David Cline, Adam, John, Henry, and Leah wife of
Philip Conrad.

Jan 15, 1810   Jan 27, 1810
Reitinger, Anna. Executor: Michael Reitinger. West Manchester
Township. Child: Michael Reitinger.

Jan 19, 1809   Jan 29, 1810
Edmundson, Thomas. Executors: William and Thomas Edmundson.
Warrington Township. Children: William, Hannah, Abigial, Mary, and
Thomas.

Oct 1, 1805   Jan 30, 1810
Shroll, John. Executors: John Shroll and Adam Lichtenberger. Heillam Township. Children: Catharine, Eve, John, Christian and Anna wife of Valentine Coleman.

Sep 2, 1803   Feb 5, 1810
Buchanan, John. Executors: James and Thomas Buchanan. Chaceford Township. Wife: Jane Buchanan. Children: William, Margaret, Ebeneser, John, Andrew, James, Thomas, Martha, Nancy, Jane, and George.

Nov 20, 1809   Feb 7, 1810
Billet, Magdalena. Executor: Jacob Billet. Hellam Township. Children: Jacob and Eve.

Dec 8, 1806   Feb 16, 1810
Brubaker, Conrad. Executors: James Cross and Francis Werner. Windsor Township. Children: Catharine wife of Francis Wenney, and Henry Myers (a son-in-law, wife's name not recorded).

Feb 3, 1810   Feb 20, 1810
Lauer, Philip. Executor: John Lauer. Dover Township. Wife: Anna Lauer. Children: Anna, Nancy, John, Elizabeth, Molly, Abraham, Susanna, and Philip.

Dec 30, 1809   Feb 23, 1810
Ridar, Frederick. Executors: Benjamin Alexander, John and Frederick Ridar. Washington Township. Children: Epfriam, Frederick, John, Rosanna, Sophia, Catharine, Hannah and Barbara.

--- --, ----   Feb 26, 1810
Derringer, Kilian. Executor: Susanna Derringer. Township omitted. German will.

Feb 7, 1810   Mar 10, 1810
Lauer, Jacob. Executors: John and Philip Lauer. Dover Township. Wife: Magdalena Lauer. Children: John, Elizabeth, Catharine, Magdalena, Barbara, Christiana, Anna, Mary, and Philip.

Jun 22, 1807   Mar 12, 1810
Keller, John. Executors: John Keller, Jacob Bossert and Jacob Buver. Cordorus Township. Wife: Esther Keller. Children: Jacob, John, Esther, Catharine, Elizabeth, and Maria.

Feb 20, 1810   Mar 14, 1810
Enders, Nicholas. Executor: George Enders. Paradise Township. Wife: Susanna Enders. Children: Jacob, Mary, Elizabeth, Esther, Frederick, John, Nicholas, Catharine wife of John Schwartz, Susanna wife of Peter Gierr, and George.

Feb 19, 1807   Mar 16, 1810
Blasser, Peter. Executor: Harman Blasser. York County. Brother: Harman Blasser.

October 7, 1804   Mar 17, 1810
Leckrone, Leonard. Executors: George, Peter, and Leonard Leckrone. West Manchester Township. Children: George, Peter, and Gerard.

Nov 1, 1809   Mar 31, 1810
Morris, John. Executor: Barbara Morris. York Borough. Wife: Barbara Morris. (The wife was the sole Legatee.)

Jan 14, 1810   Apr 3, 1810
Galahar, Abraham. Executors: John Galahar and James Cross. Windsor Township. Wife: Isabella Galahar. Children: Mary, Isabella, and John.

Mar 10, 1809   Apr 10, 1810
Gerlin, Valentine. Executor: Catharine Gerlin. Hellam Township. German will.

Mar 16, 1810   Apr 16, 1810
Barns, William. Executor: David Barns. York County. Child: David.

Mar 28, 1810   Apr 16, 1810
Wamback, Mary. Executor: John L. Miller. Windsor Township. Widow of George Wamback. Children: Michael, Catharine, George and John.

Aug 20, 1803   May 1, 1810
Dehuff, George. Executors: George, Philip and Christian Dehuff. Cordorus Township. Wife: Elizabeth Dehuff. Children: Catherine wife of Samuel Glarrick, Susanna, Barbara wife of Elias Reinhart, Christiana wife of Jacob Shawer, George, John, Christian, Jacob, and Elizabeth wife of Abraham Painder.

Sep 14, 1809   May 10, 1810
Fichel, Michael. Executors: Michael Fischel and John Menges. Paradise Township. Children: Elizabeth wife of Andrew Bentz, Barbara wife of

Henry Fichel, Philip, Conrad, Kratchan wife of Lenhart Reiber, Michael, John, Frederick, and Catharine wife of Abraham Roth. Grandchildren: Elizabeth, Salome, and Henry (children of Catharine).

Aug 5, 1806   May 23, 1810
Heneise, John. Executors: Philip Heneise and Leonard Westheffer. Dover Township. Wife: Margaret Heneise. Children: John, Mary wife of Barnet Feisser, Catharine wife of Leonard Westheffer, and George. Grandchild: Elizabeth Heneise (child of John).

May 12, 1810   May 29, 1810
Stover, Nicholas. Executor: Jacob Stover. Dover Township. Legatee: Jacob Stover (brother).

May 12, 1810   Jun 6, 1810
Conrad, Jacob. Executor: John Conrad. York County. Wife: Agness Conrad. Child: John Conrad.

Apr 25, 1810   Jun 9, 1810
McPherson, William. Executors: William and John McPherson. York Borough. Legatees: William McPherson (father) and John McPherson (brother).

Jun 15, 1806   Jun 9, 1810
Ziegler, Jacob. Executors: Michael and Nicholas Ziegler. Cordorus Township. Wife: Catharine Zeigler. Children: Michael, Peter, Christiana and Catharine.

Feb 11, 1810   Jun 13, 1810
Strickler, John. Executors: John Strickler and Francis Grover. Hilliam Township. Wife: Elizabeth Strickler. Children: Samuel and William.

Feb 18, 1809   June 7, 1810
Tschudy, Nicholas. Executor: Barbara Tschudy. Hanover Township. Wife: Barbara Tschudy. Legatees: (Nephew) Jacob Mermer and four children - Ezra, Maria, Ruth and Jacob Mohler.

Aug 12, 1801   Jul 2, 1810
Trenhler, Dorothea. Executor: Peter Gut. York County. Children: Susanna wife of Jacob Bixler, Eve wife of Mathias Stewart, Elizabeth wife of Joseph Strickler, Catharine wife of Henry Groul, Salome wife of John Strickler and Mary and John Miller.

Jul 5, 1810   Jul 24, 1810
Schmyser, Michael. Executors: John and Peter Schmyser. West Manchester Township. Wife: Anna Maria Schmyser. Children: Peter, Jacob, Michael, Polly, Elizabeth wife of John Ebert, Sarah wife of Daniel Forney, Anna, Susanna wife of John Hay.

Jun 10, 1810   Jul 27, 1810
Allison, Joseph. Executor: William Allison. Chanceford Township. Children: John, James, Garvin and Margaret; Elizabeth (child of Gavin).

Mar 2, 1809   Aug 7, 1810
Gochenouer, Joseph. Executors: Jacob and Michael Gochenouer. Dover Township. Wife: Mary Gochenouer. Children: Christian, Samuel, John, Michael, Abraham, Martin, Joseph, Barbara, Anna, Mary, and Jacob.

Aug 5, 1797   Aug 10, 1810
Thaker, John. Executors: John and William C. Thaker. Chanceford Township. Wife: Jean Thaker. Children: William, John, Samuel and Sarah. Grandchild: John Coin (Parents' names not stated).

Aug 11, 1810   Aug 18, 1810
Nunemacher, Soloman. Executors: John Nunemacher and Henry Ruman. Township: Omitted. Wife: Anna Mary Nunemacher. Children: Barbara wife of David Shaffer, George, Jacob, Daniel, Solomon, Ann, Mary, and Catharine. Grandchild: Hannah Shaffer.

Sep 1, 1794   Aug 21, 1810
Seitz, Joseph. Executors: John and Adam Seitz. Shrewsbury Township. Wife: Anna Elizabeth Seitz. Children: John, Christiana and Adam.

Apr 7, 1810   Sep 29, 1810
Newman, George. Executor: George Newman. Dover Township. Wife: Mary Elizabeth Newman. Children: George, Andrew, Susanna wife of Daniel Jacoby, Anna, Margaret, Elizabeth wife of George Benedict, and Catharine wife of John Jacoby.

--- --, 1810   Sept 1, 1810
Schattel, George. Executor: Henry Stover. Dover Township. Wife: Margaret Schattel. Children: Michael, George, Susanna, Catharine wife of Frederick Stoner and John.

Sep 17, 1805   Oct 6, 1810
Spangler, George. Executors: George and Anna Maria Spangler. York

County. Children: John, Anna, George and Magdalena.

Aug 5, 1808   Oct 20, 1810
Hinego, Michael. Executor: Frederick Fitz. York County. Wife: Elizabeth Hinego.

Aug 15, 1804   Oct 27, 1810
Smith, William. Executors: Katharine Smith and Robert Gemmill. Hopewell Township. Wife: Catharine Smith. Children: Ann wife of John Kelly, Margaret, Samuel, Katharine wife of Samuel Fulton and Sarah wife of Robert Gemmill. Grandchild: Catharine Kelly.

Apr 11, 1810   Nov 6, 1810
McCay, John. Executor: William Anderson, John Livingston, and Robert Gordon. Fawn Township. Niece: Mary Bane.

Sep 8, 1810   Nov 7, 1810
Kincaid, Samuel. Executors: Nancy and Joshua Kincaid. Fawn Township. Wife: Nancy Kincaid. Children: Joseph, Thomas, and Nancy.

Jun 4, 1810   Nov 7, 1810
Newman, Michael. Executors: Michael Helman and John Stark. Manheim Township. Legatees: David Newman (nephew, son of brother David), and Magdalena Diffenbach (sister).

Oct 20, 1810   Nov 15, 1810
Bear, Henry. Executors: Daniel Bear and Peter Hershey. Manchester Township. Wife: Abbe Bear. Children: Wetzy wife of Peter Hershey, Elizabeth wife of Tobias Young, Henry, Anna, Benjamin, Jacob, and Katharine.

Aug 20, 1810   Nov 21, 1810
Hetrick, John. Executor: Christian Hetrick. Manheim Township. Brother and Sisters: Christian, Ann, and Elizabeth Hetrick.

Nov 17, 1809   Nov 28, 1810
Goering, Elizabeth. Executor: Elizabeth Goering. York Borough. Sister: Lydia Zemmerman.

Jun 11, 1805   Dec 2, 1810
Clarkson, James. Executors: Susanna and Andrew Clarkson. York County. Wife: Susanna Clarkson. Children: Elizabeth, Andrew, James, Thomas, Ephriam, Agness, and John.

Jun 10, 1805   Dec 3, 1810
Fucks, George. Executors: John Fucks and John Bowerrax. Manheim Township. Children: John, Catharine wife of George Gabel, Molly wife of John Trifagel, and Margaret wife of John Bowerrax.

Aug 28, 1808   Dec 13, 1810
Rudisell, Jacob. Executors: Henry Feltz and Henry Welsh. Hanover Township. Legatees: Elizabeth (Sister) wife of William Bear and Charlotte Rudisell (Sister).

May 10, 1810   Dec 18, 1810
Busel, Thomas. Executors: John Buss and George Davon. Dover Township. Children: Thomas, Elizabeth wife of John Buss, Magdalena wife of Henry Barmone, and Margaret wife of George Davon.

Feb 30, 1808   Dec 18, 1810
Wallace, William. Executor: Thomas Wallace. Fawn Township. Children: Mary, Jenny, Margaret, Eleanor, Nancy, John and Thomas.

Nov 5, 1810   Dec 25, 1810
Hershey, Christian. Executors: Christian Miller and Henry Strickouser. Paradise Township. Wife: Katharine Hershey. Children: Joseph, (and others whose names were not given.)

Sep 29, 1810   Dec 26, 1810
Siechrist, Jacob. Executors: John Kaufman and Anna McKinney. York Borough. Children: Maria wife of John Kaufman, Ann and Elizabeth.

Sep 29, 1810   Dec 27, 1810
Heckert, Magdalena. Executors: Joseph and George Heckert. York County. Children: Philip, Jacob, George, and Catharine wife of Peter Reisinger.

Dec 20, 1810   Jan 9, 1811
Himes, Francis. Executors: Henry Shultz and Jacob Barnetz. Hanover Township. Wife: Catharine Himes. Children: Catharine, Solome, William, John, George, Elizabeth wife of Richard Chester, and Samuel.

May 7, 1809   Jan 12, 1811
Froesher, Frederick. Executors: Catharine and Peter Froesher. Cordorus Township. Wife: Catharine Froesher. Children: Margaret wife of John Erman, Lutwig, John, Peter, Catharine, Barbara, Charlotte, Rosina, Christiana, Elizabeth, Eve, and Magdalena.

Feb 8, 1810   Jan 15, 1811
Hoff, Francis. Executors: Abraham Heisland and Yost Ranck. Cordorus Township. Wife: Eve Hoff. Child: Adam.

Jun 5, 1798   Jan 21, 1811
Bohly, Daniel. Executors: Rosina Bohly and Henry Ruhl. Shrewsbury Township. Wife: Rosina Bohly.

Jul 19, 1810   Feb 9, 1811
Williams, Mordica. Executors: Benjamin Walker and Jonathan Jessop. Warrington Township. Legatees: (Sisters) Hannah and Sarah Williams.

Jan 16, 1811   Mar 4, 1811
Hersh, Mary. Executor: Benjamin Hersh. Child: John.

Feb 28, 1811   Mar 28, 1811
Frey, Conrad. Executors: William Metzger and Henry Ensminger. Manchester Township. Wife: Barbara Frey. Children: (Names and number not given.)

Jul 20, 1810   Apr 1, 1811
Metzgar, George. Executors: William Metzgar and Philip Baker. Manchester Township. Children: Margaret, William, (and five others whose names were not given.)

Jul 3, 1806   Apr 22, 1811
Gohn, Philip. Executors: John Gohn and Henry Leibhart. Windsor Township. Wife: Elizabeth Gohn. Children: Henry, Jacob, Sophia, George, Elizabeth wife of Henry Leibhart, and Henry.

Jul 12, 1808   May 11, 1811
Wagoner, Daniel. Executor: Anna M. Wagoner. Maryland. Wife: Anna Maria Wagoner. Children: George, Anna, Maria, Elizabeth, Catharine, Samuel and William.

Feb 7, 1811   May 16, 1811
Brillhart, Jacob. Executors: Peter and Samuel Brillhart. Shrewsbury Township. Wife: Margaret Brillhart. Children: Peter, David, Elizabeth, and Samuel.

Apr 18, 1810   May 27, 1811
Garretson, James. Executors: Joseph Garretson and Isaac Kirk. Newberry Township. Wife: Anna Garretson.

Feb 8, 1810   Jun 15, 1811
Updegraff, Herman. Executors: Samuel Willis and Jonathan Jessup.
York Borough. Wife: Susanna Updegraff. Children: Anna wife of John
Love, Mary wife of John Cope and Rhoda wife of Alexander Underwood.

Jan 13, 1810   Jul 20, 1811
Elgar, Joseph. Executors: Margaret and John Elgar. York Borough.
Wife: Margaret Elgar.

Jan 1, 1808   Jul 29, 1811
Oberlin, Christopher. Executor: George Oberlin. Paradise Township.
Wife: Catharine Oberlin. Children: Jacob, Elizabeth wife of Jacob
Hacken, Polly, Hannah, Catharine wife of Jacob Sugar, Christiana wife of
John Shaeffer, and Susanna wife of Michael Waef.

May 6, 1811   July 24, 1811
Galaher, Jennet. Executor: James Cross. Windsor Township. Wife:
Martha Isabella Galaher. Sister: Isabella Galaher. Brother: John
Galaher.

Nov 27, 1810   Aug 2, 1811
Doll, Barbara. Executor: George Goutz. Cordorus Township. Legatee:
Henry Reinbolt.

Jun 9, 1800   Aug 14, 1811
Foust, Martin. Executor: John Foust. Warrington Township. Wife:
Barbara Foust. Children: John, Frederick, Jacob, and Elizabeth wife of
David Deerdorf.

Nov 19, 1810   Aug 15, 1811
Daron, Adam. Executors: David Forringer and Barnet Smith. Hellam
Township. Wife: Barbara Daron. Children: Henry, Adam, Michael,
Philip, John, George, and Jacob.

Feb 3, 1809   Aug 17, 1811
Lenhart, Catharine. Executor: Andrew Cremer. York Borough. Child:
Elizabeth wife of Andrew Cremer.

Jun 1, 1800   Aug 26, 1811
Spangler, Rudolph. Executor: Dorothea Spangler. York Borough. Wife:
Dorothea Spangler. Children: Jacob, Jesse, Daniel, Peter, Catharine wife
of George Barnitz, Elizabeth wife of William Mess, Mary wife of Peter
Small, Margaret wife of Joseph Slagle and Magdalena wife of Charles

Fisher.

Jun 5, 1809 Sep 12, 1811
Stambach, Philip. Executors: Jacob Remack and Adam Hoferman. Corodurs Township. Wife: Anna Maria Stambach. Children: Henry, Elizabeth wife of Christian Kaufman and Michael.

Feb 24, 1811 Sep 26, 1811
Hake, John. Executors: Martin Armstrong and Samuel Hake. Chanceford Township. Wife: Catharine Hake. Children: Samuel, John, William, Frederick, Conrad, Benjamin, Elizabeth, and Jacob.

Aug 6, 1811 Nov 4, 1811
Schenck, Magdalena. Executor: Henry Strickhouser. Cordorus Township. Legatees: (Bro. and Sisters) Maria, Margaret and John.

Dec 19, 1810 Nov 25, 1811
Lewis, Susanna. Executors: John Laferty and Stephen Harry. York Borough. Children: Hannah wife of ---- Krouse. Grandchildren: Elizabeth, Susanna, and Mary Krouse.

Nov 16, 1810 Dec 21, 1811
Small, John. Executors: John and Jacob Small. York Borough. Wife: Philibina Small. Children: Joseph, Catharine wife of Jacob Maleris, Elizabeth, Anna, Enos and William.

May 8, 1810 Dec 23, 1811
McCleary, John. Executor: John McCleary. Hopewell Township. Wife: Jane McCleary. Children: Elizabeth wife of John Allison, John, Martha wife of Alexander Proudfits, Andrew, Sarah, and William.

Dec 18, 1811 Jan 2, 1812
Keiffer, Dorothea. Executor: Ignatus Leitner. York Borough. (Widow of Peter Keiffer.) Children: Ann, Dorothea, John, Peter, Maria, and Catharine wife of Jacob Brenemin.

Dec 19, 1807 Jan 2, 1812
Becker, Philip. Executors: Peter Opp and Peter Eicholtz. West Manchester Township. Wife: Elizabeth Becker. Children: Elizabeth and Catharine.

Dec 30, 1811 Feb 6, 1812
Lottman, George. Executors: John and George Lottman. York

Township. Wife: Barbara Lottman. Children: John, George, Jacob, Mary, Sarah, Elizabeth wife of Thomas Euhilberger, and Catharine.

May 5, 1809   Feb 7, 1812
Morthland, Hugh. Executors: Hugh and Michael Morthland. Washington Township. Wife: Catharine Morthland. Children: Michael, Rebecca wife of Elcock, Hugh, and Catharine wife of John Parker.

Jul 8, 1811   Feb 10, 1812
Deardorff, Henry. Executors: Jonas Deardorff and Adam Enst. Franklin Township. Wife: Mary Deardorff. Children: Jonas, Ira, Joseph, Rebecca wife of Peter Touampf, Ann wife of James Baker, and Jacob.

Oct 6, 1809   Feb 26, 1812
Smith, James. Executors: John Stronan and John Armor. York Borough. Legatee: (Cousins) John and Anne Armor and James Armor. N.B. He bequeaths to the parties named, his sword and pistols and Case of Bottles. The two former to be used in the defense of this country and the latter, he says, "not to be filled too often - unless with water." Recorded in Will Book M. p. 397.

Feb 15, 1811   Feb 28, 1812
Grove, Francis. Executor: Nicholas Strayer. York Borough. Wife: Catharine Grove. Children: George, Frederick, John, Michael, Francis, and Margaret wife of George Shaney.

Aug 16, 1811   Feb 29, 1812
Michael, Wendle. Executor: John Michael. York Borough. Children: Lewis, John, Wendle, Christiana wife of Rudolph Spangler, Margaret wife of Peter Cremer, and Henry. Grandchildren: John and Mary Michael (children of Henry).

Feb 11, 1807   Mar 2, 1812
Hooppert, Catharine. Executors: Henry Felty. Manheim Township. Children: Catharine wife of Peter Welsh, Christiana wife of Henry Welsh, and Polly wife of Henry Felty.

Feb 17, 1812   Mar 18, 1812
Erhard, Michael. Executor: Anthony Willed. Manheim Township. Wife: Margaret Erhard. Children: Michael, Nicholas, Peter, Catharine, Philip, Margaret, and Eve.

Mar 2, 1805   Apr 1, 1812

Irwin, George. Executors: John and Henry Irwin. York Borough. Wife: Martha Irwin. Children: John and Henry.

Mar 10, 1807   Apr 1, 1812
Campbell, Ann. Executor: Joseph Reed. York County. Child: Joseph.

Jul 30, 1805   Apr 3, 1812
Smith, Peter. Executors: Abraham and Peter Smith. Washington Township. Children: Henry, Samuel, Mary wife of William Putt, Peter, Hannah wife of Jacob Myers, Catharine wife of Stoman Brown, Elizabeth wife of Jacob Smith and Abraham.

Oct 1, 1806   Apr 6, 1812
Wilson, Elizabeth, Executors: Robert and Andrew Wilson. Monaghan Township. Children: George, Mary, Margaret, Andrew and Robert. Granddaughter: Margaret Taylor (parents' names not given).

Dec 20, 1809   Apr 9, 1812
Shol, Gacharius. Executors: John Shol and Peter Ryder. Cordorus Township. Wife: Anna Elizabeth Shol. Children: John, Gacharius, Henry, Anna, Peter, Jacob and Isaac.

Nov 12, 1811   Apr 13, 1812
Godfrey, William. Executors: Francis Coulson and James Robinette. Frankum Township. Wife: Hannah Godfrey. Children: Jane wife of Stephen Foulk, John, Mary wife of David George, Thomas, Charles, and Hannah wife of ---- Aliress.

Nov 24, 1810   Apr 14, 1812
Fullerton, William. Executor: James Logue. Lower Chanceford Township. Children: John, Isabella, Margaret, Ann, William, Robert, Adam, Samuel, and Mary.

Apr 2, 1799   Apr 18, 1812
Bergheimer, Valentine. Executor: John Leib. Paradise Township. Wife: Caroline Bergheimer. Child: Henry.

May 16, 1803   Apr 25, 1812
Hershner, Anna. Executor: Henry Hershner. Township: Omitted. Children: Andrew, and Barbara wife of Christian Heureman.

Apr 10, 1812   May 2, 1812
Ernst, Adam. Executors: John Byers, John Higas, and John Ernst.

Franklin Township. Wife: Susanna Ernst. Children: John, Adam, and Samuel.

Oct 13, 1806   May 11, 1812
Smith, Andrew. Executors: Andrew Smith and Michael Coppenheffler. Manchester Township. Children: Andrew, John, George, Henry, Eve, Catharine, Barbara and Magdalena.

Sep 14, 1809   May 12, 1812
Wilson, William, Jr. Executors: Alexander Wallace and Joseph Edgar. Hopewell Township. Children: Margaret wife of Robert Anderson, Jane wife of John McCleary, Agness wife of Joseph Ailkin and David.

Aug 29, 1810   May 25, 1812
Spitzer, Conrad. Executors: John Spitzer and Jacob Hart. Fairview Township. Wife: Barbara Spitzer. Children: John, Susanna wife of Christian Nafe and Ann. Grandchild: Susanna Nafe.

Sep 9, 1805   Jun 11, 1812
Keiler, John. Executors: Henry and Barbara Keiler. Paradise Township. Wife: Barbara Keiler. Child: Henry.

--- --, ----   Jun 12, 1812
Graham, James. Executor: Omitted. Fawn Township. (This will in on the files, but not on the records.)

Jan 13, 1809   Jun 16, 1812
Stewart, Elizabeth. Executors: John Stewart and John Morris. York Borough. Children: Barbara wife of John Morris, John and Abraham.

Jan 13, 1810   Jun 17, 1812
Fishel, Henry. Executors: Henry King and Michael Fishel. Paradise Township. Wife: Anna Maria Fishel. Children: Frederick, Michael, Jacob, Elizabeth, George, and Henry.

May 27, 1812   Jul 4, 1812
Detter, Lawrence. Executors: Peter and Mathias Detter. Washington Township. Wife: Catharine Detter. Children: Catharine wife of Joseph Faerenbach, Peter, Mathias, Nicholas, Margaret wife of William Firestone, Elizabeth wife of Jacob Hartman, Esther, Susanna, Magdalena, and John.

Apr 11, 1812   Jul 8, 1812
Olp, John. Executors: Laurentz Hentil and Adaman Sherer. Shrewsbury

Township. Wife: Catharine Olp. Children: John, Peter, Jacob, Catharine wife of Larentz Hentil, and Dorothea wife of Adam Sherer.

Mar 6, 1812   Aug 12, 1812
Upland, Michael. Executor: Michael Helman. Cordorus Township. Wife: Dorothea Upland. Children: John and Elizabeth and Adam Nace.

Jan 29, 1804   Aug 12, 1812
Hoffman, Catharine. Executor: Thomas W. Bradlee. Monaghan Township. Children: Mary and Leach.

May 22, 1809   Aug 17, 1812
Bely, Jacob. Executors: John Bely and Henry Ruhl. Shrewsbury Township. Wife: Eva Bely. Children: George, Jacob, John, Margaret, Susanna, Rosina, and Elizabeth Folk (stepdaughter).

--- --, ----   Aug 19, 1812
Boyer, Henry. Executors: Henry and John Boyer. Manheim Township. Wife: Barbara Boyer. Children: John, Henry, Magdalena, Christian, and Daniel.

Apr 1, 1784   Sep 3, 1812
Michael, Nicholas. Executor: Anna Maria Michael. Dover Township. Wife: Anna Maria Michael. Child: Adam. Granddaughter: Anna Maria Michael.

Jul 17, 1812   Sep 8, 1812
Kunckel, Baltzer. Executors: Christian Kunckel and Christian Gengrich. Hellam Township. Wife: Anna Maria Kunckel. Children: Catharine wife of Jacob Kohlman, Jacob, Eve wife of Christian Gengrich, Maria wife of John Bixler, and Elizabeth.

Jul 17, 1812   Sep 8, 1812
Gunkle, Balzer. Executors: Charles Gunkle and Christian Gingrich. Hellam Township. Wife: Anna Maria Gunkle. Children: Maria, Catharine wife of Jacob Kohlman, Eve wife of Christian Gingrich, and Anna wife of John Bixler.

Sep 29, 1812   Oct 13, 1812
Stevens, Henry. Executors: Adam Stevens and John Philips. Windsor Township. Wife: Anna Mary Stevens. Children: Adam, Mary and Philip.

--- --, ----   Oct 21, 1812
Leiss, Peter. Executors: Elizabeth Leiss and F. Geiselman. Shrewsbury Township. (German will.)

Apr 8, 1812   Nov 4, 1812
Miller, Martin. Executor: Jacob Miller. Fairview Township. Children: Elizabeth, George, Jacob, Sophia wife of James Patton, Catharine wife of John Bear, and Mary wife of John Backler.

Dec 6, 1804   Nov 19, 1812
Mateer, Mary. Executors: Thomas Warren and Michael Hart. Fairview Township. Legatees: Thomas Warren and James Anderson (not relatives).

Oct 29, 1812   Nov 20, 1812
Ilgenfretz, Martin. Executor: John May, Catharine and Jacob Ilgenfretz. Manchester Township. Wife: Catharine Ilgenfretz. Children: Daniel, Joseph, Martin, Anna wife of Daniel Shribers, Catharine wife of ---- Crose, Juliana wife of John Benedick, Margaret wife of Frederick Dalph, Elizabeth, Sarah, and Hannah.

Mar 12, 1804   Nov 23, 1812
Miller, George. Executors: Anna M. and George Miller. Manchester Township. Wife: Anna Margaret Miller. Children: George, Peter, Barbara, Magdalena, Margaret, Catharine, Elizabeth, and Maria.

Jan 12, 1812   Nov 26, 1812
Adams, Mathew. Executor: Sara Adams. Chanceford Township. Wife: Sara Adams. Child: Mathew.

Apr 2, 1811   Nov 27, 1812
Barnitz, Anna Barbara. Executor: Jacob Barnitz. York Borough. Children: Jacob, Michael, Barbara, and Susanna.

Oct 30, 1811   Dec 8, 1812
Heckert, Philip. Executor: George Heckert and Godleib Zeigal. York Borough. Wife: Dorothea Heckert. Children: Sarah, Mary wife of Joseph Spangler, Daniel, Philip, and Charles.

Apr 15, 1812   Dec 28, 1812
Wilson, Josiah. Executors: Anna Wilson, James Logue, Jr. and James Murphy. Chanceford Township. Wife: Anna Wilson. There were children - but names and number not given.

Jan 6, 1801   Jan 4, 1813
Diehl, Peter. Executors: Nicholas and Daniel Diehl. York County. Children: Nicholas, Jacob, Daniel, Catharine wife of John Brillinger, and Elizabeth wife of Hey King.

Nov 29, 1812   Jan 23, 1813
McCandless, Alexander. Executors: Hannah McCandless and Robert Gorden. Fawn Township. Wife: Hannah McCandless. Children: Agness, Ruthia, James, and John.

Jul 12, 1811   Jan 27, 1813
Witman, Michael. Executors: Jacob Witman and Catharine Witman. Chanceford Township. Wife: Catharine Witman. Children: Jacob and Daniel. Grandchildren: Rebecca, Elizabeth, Mary, William, Christian and Catharine Witman (children of Daniel).

Apr 7, 1812   Feb 23, 1813
Lehman, Frederick. Executors: Jacob Lehman and Jacob Tyson. Windsor Township. Wife: Anna Lehman. Children: Elizabeth wife of Jacob Tyson, and Mary wife of John Kauffelt.

Sep 3, 1812   Mar 10, 1813
Myers, George. Executors: Emanuel Bare and George Zorger. Newberry Township. Wife: Thurley Myers. Children: Mirecles, Eve wife of John Zorger, Mary wife of Peter Zeller, and George.

Mar 19, 1811   Mar 10, 1813
Fahs, Jacob. Executors: John Fahs and Tobias Myer. York Borough. Wife: Catharine Fahs. Children: John, Joseph, Jacob, Philip, Abraham, Tovias, Elizabeth, and Henry.

Feb 17, 1813   Mar 15, 1813
Becker, Grabill. Executor: Frederick Becker. Chanceford Township. Wife: Catharine Becker. Children: Frederick, Henry, and Elizabeth wife of Jacob Mosser.

Feb 5, 1813   Mar 20, 1813
Yienger, Jacob. Executor: "His Father." Newberry Township. Legatees: His father and mother (names not given).

Jan 25, 1812   Mar 23, 1813
McDonald, John. Executors: Jacob James and Elizabeth McDonald. York Borough. Children: John, Susanna, and Elizabeth.

--- --, ----   Mar 27, 1813
Flury, Jacob. Executor: Omitted. Hellam Township. German will.

Mar 4, 1813   Apr 12, 1813
Laird, John. Executors: Janet Laird and Robert Gibson. Fawn Township. Wife: Janet Laird. Children: James, Hugh, Robert, and Rebecca.

Jan 9, 1813   Apr 14, 1813
Tomkins, John. Executors: James Walter and Sarah and Joseph Tomkins. Fawn Township. Wife: Sarah Tomkins. Children: Joseph, Benjamin, John, Jacob and Deborah.

Apr 14, 1813   Apr 27, 1813
Lott, Cyrus. Executor: Nathan Worley. West Manchester Township. Wife: Ruth Lott. Children: James, Hannah, David, John, Mary, Cyrus, Elizabeth, Susanna, and Ruth.

--- --, 1800   Apr 27, 1813
Lefler, George Lewis. Executors: Elizabeth and Mary Lefler. York Borough. Children: Elizabeth and Mary.

Apr 16, 1813   May 15, 1813
Herman, Samuel. Executor: Henry Miller. Newberry Township. Wife: Ann Herman. Children: Mary, Samuel, Abraham, David, Lydia, Joseph, and Susanna.

Aug 19, 1812   Jul 8, 1813
Spangler, Margaret. Executor: George Barnitz. York County. The widow of Casper Spangler. Child: Elizabeth wife of John Herbach. Grandchild: Salome Herbach.

Jul 7, 1813   Aug 2, 1813
Mayer, Frederick. Executors: Jacob Elecker and George Hoober. Warrington Township. Wife: Anna Mayer. Children: Peter, Frederick, Mary, Elizabeth, and Margaret.

May 13, 1808   Aug 3, 1813
Overdeer, John. Executors: John Sharp and David Overdeer. Dover Township. Wife: Freney Overdeer. Children: David, Benj., Catharine, Christian, Peter, John, Jacob, and Hyster wife of John Shetters.

Dec 2, 1803   Aug 10, 1813
Collins, Grace. Executor: Andrew Wallace. Hopewell Township.
Children: Samuel, William, John, Isabell, Ann wife of Andrew Wallace,
and Elizabeth. Grandchildren: William (son of Samuel), and William (son
of Ann). (The following are mentioned in the will, but parents' names
were not given:) Polly, Isabella, William, and Grace McPherson.

Mar 9, 1812   Aug 16, 1813
Simpson, Michael. Executors: Michael Simpson and Jacob M. Haldeman.
Farview Township. Wife: Susanna Simpson. (Nephews and Niece)
Michael Simpson, Joseph and Rebecca Kelso.

Jul 4, 1813   Aug 26, 1813
Mundorff, Peter. Executors: John Stroman and William Macmon. York
Borough. Wife: Mary Magdalena Mundorff.

Jan 15, 1813   Aug 27, 1813
Griffith, James. Executors: John and Jenny Griffith. Hopewell
Township. Wife: Jenny Griffith. Children: John, Martha, Elizabeth,
Jane, William, Robert, and Joseph.

Nov 1, 1811   Aug 30, 1813
Welsh, Jacob. Executors: Anna M., Charles and Henry Welsh.
Washington Township. Wife: Anna Maria Welsh. Children: Jacob,
Charles, Susanna wife of Jesse Updegraff, Elizbeth wife of Martin
Eichelberger, Mary wife of --- Myers and Catharine. Grandchild: Harriet
Nelson (parents' names not given).

May 5, 1813   Sep 24, 1813
Grier, Jennet. Executors: Rev. Robert Cathcart and Charles A. Barnetz.
Yorktown Township. Children: Anna, Jane, and Margaret.

Sept 15, 1808   Oct 16, 1813
Thomas, James. Executor: Benjamin Walker. Warrington Township.
Children: James and Deborah wife of --- Vale. Grandchildren: James,
Robert, Eli, Lydia, Bulah, Ann and Phebe Vale; and Thomas Peadol
(parents' names not given).

Feb 9, 1808   Oct 18, 1813
Haar, Jacob. Executors: Elizabeth and George Haar. Paradise Township.
Wife: Elizabeth Haar.

Oct 25, 1813   Nov 6, 1813
Gesler, Henry. Executors: Henry Slagle and Jacob Smyser. Paradise Township. Wife: Margaret Gesler. Children: Michael, John, Daniel, and Peggy wife of Jacob Smyser.

Mar 1, 1812   Nov 10, 1813
Pedan, Benjamin. Executors: John and Benjamin Pedan. Lower Chanceford Township. Wife: Susanna Pedan. Children: John, Benjamin, Martha, Jannet, Isabella, Susanna, James, David, and Eleanor.

Oct 14, 1813   Nov 11, 1813
Bricker, Jacob. Executors: John Bricker and William Line. Monaghan Township. Wife: Agness Bricker. Children: Jacob, Joseph, and Mary Brandt (stepdaughter).

--- --, ----   Nov 17, 1813
Ortt, Henry. Executor: Omitted. York County. (German will.)

Feb 8, 1813   Nov 22, 1813
Etzler, George. Executors: Michael Etzler and Jacob Barnitz. Heidleberg Township. Wife: Fransina Etzler. Children: George, Andrew, Michael, Catharine wife of William Yound, Mary wife of Jacob Barnitz, and Elizabeth wife of Rev. Henry Heinen.

Oct 8, 1813   Nov 30, 1813
Gemmill, Robert. Executor: Elizabeth Gemmill. Hopewell Township. Sisters: Mary, Jane, and Sarah Gemmill.

Sep 9, 1813   Dec 1, 1813
Sprenkle, Peter. Executors: William and Frederick Sprenkle. York County. Wife: Anna Maria Sprenkle. Children: Peter, William, Frederick, Daniel, John, Anna wife of Lawrence Boerstler, Elizabeth wife of Philip Day, ?? wife of Martin Conawar and Sarah wife of Barnet Phileger. Grandchildren: Daniel, Charles and Polly Phileger.

Dec 9, 1813   Jan 3, 1814
McCauley, William. Executor: James Patterson. Chanceford Township. Wife: Susanna McCauley. Child: Jennet.

Jan 8, 1814   Jan 14, 1814
Shaul, John. Executor: John Shaul. Lower Chanceford Township. Wife: Catharine Shaul. Children: George, John, Mary wife of Henry Weize, Jacob, Joseph, Henry and Catharine wife of David Ellis.

Mar 27, 1803   Jan 31, 1814
Free, Conrad. Executors: Jacob Becker and Henry Ruhl. Shrewsbury Township. Wife: Maria Free. Children: John, Peter, Michael, Elizabeth, Magdalena, Catharine, Maria, and Susanna.

Jun 7, 1802   Feb 2, 1814
Leverknight, Catharine. Executor: Omitted. Windsor Township. Widow of Frederick Leverknight. Children: John and Frederick.

Jul 8, 1810   Feb 12, 1814
Winter, George. Executors: Henry Strickhouser and John Zeigler. Cordorus Township. Wife: Margaret Winter. Children: George, Katharine and George Folkimmer and Kreta wife of Adam Haase. Grandson: John Haase.

Sep 10, 1812   Feb 12, 1814
Au, George. Executor: Henry Strickhouser. Codorus Township. Child: Hannah wife of ---- Miller. Children of Hannah: Henry and Catharine.

Dec 23, 1813   Feb 12, 1814
Michael, John. Executors: Catharine Michael and John Michael. Hanover Township. Wife: Catharine Michael. Children: Elizabeth wife of Samuel Hostetter, John, Catharine, Margaret, Jacob, Anna, William, Henrietta, and Charles.

Jan 24, 1814   Feb 18, 1814
Regan, Daniel. Executors: Joseph and Francis Worley. York Boro. Wife: Ruth Regan. Step-sons: Joseph and Francis Worley.

Sep 23, 1813   Feb 22, 1814
Streber, Peter. Executors: Elizabeth Streber and George Hay. York County. Wife: Elizabeth Streber. Children: Jacob, William, Elizabeth, Susanna and Catharine.

Feb 1, 1804   Feb 27, 1814
Muhlheim, Nicholas. Executor: Peter Muhlheim. Manheim Township. Brothers and Sisters: Peter, Christian, Jacob, John, Magdalena, Rosana, and Eve.

Feb 8, 1813   Feb 28, 1814
Danner, Henry. Executors: Elizabeth and David Danner. Manheim Township. Wife: Elizabeth Danner. Children: Henry, David, Anna, Rachel, Leah, and Solome.

Aug 19, 1813   Mar 11, 1814
Sholl, Lewis. Executor: George Gabel. Manheim Township. Wife: Catharine Sholl.

--- --, ----   Mar 13, 1814
Hartman, Francis. Executor: George Anstein. Hopewell Township. Children: David, Magdalena wife of Jon Swindel, Frederick, Catharine wife of John Richy, Rebecca wife of Thomas Uinas, Sarah, Nicholas, Henry, and Marian.

Jan 11, 1812   Mar 14, 1814
Bane, James. Executors: William Hooper and Isaac Kirk. Newberry Township. Wife: Margaret Bane. Nephew and Nieces: Nathan, Sarah and Vashti (children of brother John Bane).

Sep 4, 1807   Mar 15, 1814
Beitzel, Jonathan. Executors: Magdalena Beitzel and John Beitzel. Doverzt Township. Wife: Magdalena Beitzel. Children: John, Benjamin, Elizabeth, and Jonathan.

--- --, ----   Mar 16, 1814
Remby, Isreal. Executor: E. Remby. Township: Omitted. (German will.)

Aug 7, 1802   Mar 19, 1814
Frey, Frederick. Executor: John Frey. Windsor Township. Child: John. Grandchildren: John, Frederick, and Henry.

Mar 20, 1814   Mar 25, 1814
Ritz, Anthony. Executors: Margaret and Jacob Ritz. York Boro. Wife: Margaret Ritz. Children: Elizabeth wife of Jacob Frankenberger, Margaret, John, Jacob, Barbara and Catharine.

Jun 13, 1812   Apr 2, 1814
Jones, Daniel. Executors: Benj. Anderson, William Wireman, and John and William Jones. Monaghan Township. Children: John, William, Whirchill, Sarah, Ann, Rebecca, and Peggy. Grandchild: Daniel Smith Jones (parents' names not given).

--- --, ----   Apr 7, 1814
Kelly, Thomas. Executor: Daniel Dubs. Manheim Township. Wife: Mary Kelly. Children: Sarah, Nancy, Patrick, Elizabeth, Thomas, Rachel, John, and Mary.

Apr 14, 1810   Apr 16, 1814
Hershinger, John. Executor: Catharine Hershinger. Hopewell Township.
Wife: Catharine Hershinger. Child: John.

Feb 21, 1814   Apr 16, 1814
Kister, George Jr. Executor: Hannah Kister and Andrew Fortinbaugh.
Newberry Township. Wife: Hannah Kister. Children: (Names and number not given.)

Dec 22, 1812   Apr 18, 1814
Versch, Christopher. Executor: Samuel Kepler. Dover Township.
Children: Catharine Kepler and Catharine Ernst. Grandson: Adam Grish (parents' names not given).

Mar 31, 1814   Apr 25, 1814
Gerverich, Jacob. Executors: John Gerverich and Henry Miller. York County. Wife: Sophia Gerverich. Children: Elizabeth, Henry, Jacob, and John.

Nov 5, 1813   May 10, 1814
Porter, Charles William. Executors: Samuel Nelson and James Smith. Lower Chanceford Township. Wife: Jane Porter. Children: Richard, Martha, Charles, and Jane. N.B. - He wills his son Richard Porter an island in the Susquehannah River.

Apr 27, 1814   May 18, 1814
Neidig, Christiana. Executor: Nicholas Gelwicks. Hanover Township. Children: John, Magdalena wife of Conrad Byerly, Elizabeth wife of Henry Albright, Margaret wife of Michael Frinzer, Christiana wife of Jacob Puderr, Juliana wife of William Chilicoat, and Nancy.

Apr 1, 1812   May 19, 1814
Kline, Henry. Executor: John Kline. New Strasburg Township. Wife: Elizabeth Kline. Children: John, Henry, and Polly.

Jan 7, 1814   May 30, 1814
Ebert, Martin. Executor: Martin, Adam, and Michael Ebert. Manchester Township. Wife: Ann Ebert. Children: Michael, Adam, Martin, Philip, Daniel, Helena, and Ann.

Apr 17, 1814   Jul 27, 1814
Proudfoot, Sarah. Executor: Alexander Tompson. Hopewell Township.
Children: James, Alexander, David, and Robert. Grandchildren: Sarah

Proudfoot (daughter of Alexander), and Sarah Proudfoot (daughter of Robert).

Jun 18, 1814   Aug 2, 1814
Morrison, William. Executors: Samuel Nelson and Matthew Clark. Lower Chanceford Township. Children: John, Samuel, Ann, Jean, Agness, Mary, and Hannah.

Mar 30, 1814   Aug 18, 1814
Hummer, John. Executors: John Hummer and Henry Slagle. Paradise Township. Wife: Susanna Hummer. Children: Daniel, Christiana, Lydia, Susanna wife of Adam Kiener, Eleanor wife of Henry Koche, Elizabeth, Henry, and Catharine wife of John Krister.

Aug 26, 1814   Sep 10, 1814
Urich, Michael. Executors: John Shaffer and George Winebremmer. Washington Township. Wife: Margaret Urich. Children: William, Elizabeth wife of Anthony Erhard. Barbara wife of John Shaffer, Sally wife of John Winebremmer, Susan wife of Jacob Hoak, Molly wife of Timothy Kimmel and Caty wife of Jacob Bradley. Grandchildren: Polly Hoak and Sally Kimmel.

Aug 21, 1813   Sep 27, 1814
Waldasin, Jacob. Executor: Jacob Waldasin. Manheim Township. Wife: Catharine Waldasin. Children: Jacob, Charles, Martin, Juliana and --- Dewald and seven other daughters - names not given. Grandchildren: Sally, Samuel and Charles Dewald.

Apr 9, 1813   Oct 5, 1814
Shelley, John. Executors: Michael Shelley and Peter Baker. Paradise Township. Wife: Maria Barbara Shelley. Children: Michael, Molly wife of Emanuel Houdeshell, Annamaria, John, George, Elizabeth, Sarah, Samuel and Peter.

Aug 4, 1814   Oct 8, 1814
McGraw, Samuel. Executor: Alexander Thompson. Hopewell Township. Children: Mary, William, Jane, Eleanor, Robert, Elizabeth wife of John Johnston, and Agness wife of James Johnston. Grandchild: Agness Johnston (daughter of Elizabeth).

Sep 23, 1814   Oct 14, 1814
Laucks, John. Executor: Peter Laucks. Warrington Township. Brother and Sisters: Michael, Christiana, and Elizabeth.

Sep 23, 1814   Oct 22, 1814
Ziegler, Michael. Executors: Jacob Ruhl and Christian Hetrich. Cordorus Township. Wife: Catharine Ziegler. Children: Peter, Jacob, Elizabeth, John, Philip, Catharine, George, Michael, Nicholas, Susanna and Rachel.

Aug 18, 1814   Oct 31, 1814
Lehr, Philip. Executors: Peter and Casper Lehr. York County. Children: John, Peter, Elizabeth, Catty, Polly, Anny, David, Philip, and Casper.

May 21, 1811   Nov 12, 1814
Newcomer, Christian. Executors: Jacob and Samuel Newcomer. Hellam Township. Wife: Anna Newcomer. Children: Jacob, Abraham, Christian, Barbara, Elizabeth, and Samuel.

Apr 8, 1812   Nov 12, 1814
Boss, Barnet. Executors: Frederick Wiehelm and Frederick Rieman. Shrewsbury Township. Wife: Elizabeth Boss. Children: Catharine, Eve, Barbara, and Christiana.

Jan 9, 1812   Nov 26, 1814
Irwin, Christopher. Executors: Joseph and Samuel Irwin. Fawn Township. Wife: Isabella Irwin. Children: Samuel, Joseph, Elizabeth wife of William Brooks, and Sarah wife of James Willey.

Nov 12, 1814   Dec 3, 1814
Fink, Ferdenand. Executor: John Lehr. York Borough. Wife: Catharine Fink. Children: Ann and Elizabeth.

Jan 6, 1814   Dec 7, 1814
Kleindeinst, Eve. Executor: Andrew Kleindeinst. Cordorus Township. Child: Katharine wife of John Adams. Grandchildren: Anna and Albewer Adams.

Oct 24, 1814   Dec 16, 1814
Ziegler, John. Executors: Henry Wolf and Henry Slagle. West Manchester Township. Children: George, Sarah, Polly, Philip, John, Jacob, Daniel, Caty, Lydia, Elizabeth, Adam, Samuel and Matilda.

Dec 7, 1812   Jan 3, 1815
McFadden, Dennis. Executors: Peter James and Alexander Frazer. Newberry Township. Wife: Catharine McFladden. Children: Dennis, Catharine wife of Hugh McBride, Edward, John, and Hugh.

Grandchildren: Eleanor and Mary McFladden (children of Dennis).

Jul 8, 1814   Jan 4, 1815
Boyard, George Albright. Executors: Philip Fetrow, Jr. and Isaac Kirk. Newberry Township. Wife: Elizabeth Boyard. Children: Mathias, John, Frederick, Mary, Elizabeth wife of Philip Fetrow, Jr., and Catharine.

Dec 24, 1814   Jan 4, 1815
Kister, George. Executors: Christian Kister and Isaac Kirk. Newberry Township. Wife: Anna Kister. Children: George, Mary wife of Nicholas Zimmerman, Ann, Elizabeth, David, Christian, Henry, John, and Jacob.

Aug 18, 1813   Jan 24, 1815
Walck, Detrich. Executors: Jacob Walck and John Geley. Windsor Township. Wife: Magdalena Walck. Children: John, Christianna wife of Leonard Harsh, Christian, Susanna wife of George Fry, Margaret wife of Edward Gibbons, Dietrich, Catharine wife of Martin Fry, Eve, Mary and John Lebernight wife of Barbara wife of John Stauffer.

Nov 18, 1813   Jan 26, 1815
Hoff, Peter. Executor: Isaac Kirk. Newberry Township. Wife: Christiana Hoff. Children: Adam, Peter, Henry, Elizabeth wife of ---- Lutes, Mary, Christian, and Barbara.

Jan 26, 1815   Feb 1, 1815
Pennington, Ehriam. Executor: George Haller. York Borough. Wife: Lydia Pennington. Children: Timothy, Mary wife of John Stoner, Elizabeth wife of Joseph Wampler, Susanna wife of George Haller, and Lydia wife of Robert Hays.

Nov 13, 1814   Feb 7, 1815
Leman, Robert. Executors: Margaret Leman and James Duncan. Fawn Township. Wife: Margaret Leman. Children: William, (and others whose names were not given.)

Jul 7. 1813   Feb 10, 1815
Schenck, Mary. Executor: Henry Strickhouser. Cordorus Township. Daughter of Henry Schenck. (A single woman.) Legatees: (Bro. and Sisters) John, Elizabeth and Margaret.

Aug 14, 1814   Feb 17, 1815
Anderson, John. Executor: Jean Anderson. Fawn Township. Wife: Jean Anderson. Children: Robert, James, David, Mary, Sara and Jean.

Oct 14, 1813   Feb 23, 1815
Sherman, John. Executors: Daniel and John Shelly. Newberry Township. Children: Mary and --- Shelly, Catharine wife of --- Detweiler, Sarah wife of --- Mathias, John, Susanna, Elizabeth, Lydia, Eve and Anna.

Feb 15, 1815   Mar 7, 1815
Low, John. Executors: John and Isaac Low. Shrewsbury Township. Wife: Providen Low. Children: John, Joshua, Ashel, Aquilla, Jeremiah, Hannah, Maria, Rebecca, and Rhode wife of ---- Hendrix. Grandchildren: Jeremiah Low (parents' names not given), and Eli and John Hendrix (children of Rhode).

Feb 10, 1809   Mar 11, 1815
Nace, Mathias. Executors: John Sholl, David Forney, Mathias and George Nace. Hanover Township. Children: George, Mathias, Louisa wife of David Forney, Elizabeth wife of Jacob Eichelberger, and Catharine. Grandchildren: Louisa, Maria, and Eliza Eichelberger.

Feb 2, 1815   Mar 13, 1815
Fisher, Christian. Executors: Catharine Fisher and Jacob Mimermacher. York County. Wife: Catharine Fisher. Children: Catharine, Mary, Margaretta, John, Christian, Jacob, and Elizabeth.

Feb 21, 1814   Mar 17, 1815
Burk, Henry. Executors: Catharine Burk and Abraham Gartner. York Borough. Wife: Catharine Burk. Children: John, Henry, and George.

Mar --, 1814   Mar 22, 1815
Weaver, Ulrich. Executors: Mathias Becker and Jacob Lebernight. Windsor Township. Wife: Julianna Weaver. Children: John, Catharine, Elizabeth, Julianna, Dorothea and Susanna.

Jan 10, 1815   Mar 24, 1815
Robinson, James. Executors: John and George Robinson. Chanceford Township. Wife: Sarah Robinson. Children: Samuel, James, Thomas, John, Betsy wife of Samuel Mitchel, Sarah wife of Thomas Reed, Eleanor, George and Alexander. N.B. This date is wrong on the records - dated 1813, should be 1815.

--- --, ----   Apr 3, 1815
Masemer, Jacob. Executors: Peter Keller and Daniel Hess. Shrewsbury Township. Wife: Barbara Masemer. Children: (Names and number not given.)

Mar 28, 1815   Apr 8, 1815
Morthland, Michael. Executors: Hugh Morthland and Daniel Cookson. Warrington Township. Wife: Rebecca Morthland. Children: Hugh and Susanna.

Mar 18, 1815   Apr 12, 1815
Glatfelder, Felix. Executors: Casper Glatfelder and Philip Glatfelder. Cordorus Township. Wife: Omitted. Children: Frederick, John, Philip, Mary wife of Tobias Hardman, Elizabeth wife of Peter Nes, Casper, Jacob, Margaret, Daniel, and Barbara.

Feb 13, 1806   Apr 17, 1815
Williams, Mary. Executor: Richard Parks. Cumberland Township. Widow of John Williams. Children: Catharine, Margaret wife of Richard Parks, Mary, Betsy, Jenny, James, Abraham, David and Elizabeth.

--- --, ----   Apr 17, 1815
Weshoffer, Abraham. Executor: Omitted. Newberry Township. (German will.)

Apr 14, 1815   Apr 22, 1815
Goodling, Peter. Executors: George Klinefelter and Jacob Falkenstein. Shrewsbury Township. Children: Christian, Adam, Peter, Jacob, and Catharine wife of Maxemilian Marbourg.

Oct 4, 1814   Apr 26, 1815
Mellinger, David. Executors: John Mellinger and Joseph Kaufman. Hellam Township. Children: Francis wife of Martin Slenker, Barbara wife of Christian Lehman, John, Elizabeth, David, Joseph, Christian, and Abraham.

Sep 6, 1814   May 30, 1815
Kraeber, Adam. Executors: John Kraeber and Benjamin Beitzel. York Borough. Wife: Christiana Kraeber. Children: John, Elizabeth wife of Benj. Beitzel, Anna, and Sarah.

May 10, 1815   Jun 7, 1815
Zorger, Frederick. Executor: John Zorger. Newberry Township. Wife: Elizabeth Zorger. Children: Anna wife of Michael Rowe, John, Jacob, Barbara wife of Frederick Shetter, Peter, Lydia, Mathias, Frederick, Michael, George and Elizabeth wife of George Youder. Grandchild: Susanna Youder.

May 18, 1815   Jun 14, 1815
Anderson, James. Executors: Mary Anderson, William Barber and Bushell Carter. York Borough. Wife: Mary Anderson. Children: Mary, James, Joseph, Tate, Margaret, Benjamin, Eliza, David, Ann, Sarah and Jane.

Jan 15, 1814   Jun 27, 1815
Taylor, Philip. Executor: John Wiand. Hopewell Township. Wife: Susanna Taylor. Legatees: (Bros.) John, Michael, Benjamin, Abraham and Jacob.

Jul 5, 1798   June 15, 1815
Weltzhoffer, Jacob. Executors: Jacob Weltzhoffer and George Bard. Hellam Township. Wife: Anna Weltzhoffer. Children: Jacob, Henry, Mary, Catharine, Elizabeth and Susanna.

Apr 18, 1815   Jul 25, 1815
Zanckel, John. Executor: Hannah Zanckel. York County Wife: (name not given) Child: Susanna.

Jun 3, 1815   Aug 17, 1815
Roth, Susanna. Executor: John Zeigler. Cordorus Township. Wife: Christiana Roth. Children: Christiana, Susan, Juliana and John. N.B. The date of probate is wrong on the records - dated 1813, should be 1815.

Aug 31, 1812   Aug 19, 1815
Sharp, John. Executors: John Brillinger and Frederick Kever. Manchester Township. Children: Juliana, Catharine, Erana wife of John Shus, Eva wife of John Ringer, Elizabeth wife of Frederick Kever, George and Rebecca and Peter Huver.

Aug 1, 1804   Aug 19, 1815
Herschy, Elizabeth. Executor: John Martin. Paradise Township. Children: Barbara wife of Martin Huber, Anna wife of ---- Brubaker, Mary wife of Michael Grove, Elizabeth wife of Abraham Kaegy. Grandchildren: Christiana Huber (daughter of Barbara), and Freny Brubaker (daughter of Anna).

Feb 17, 1815   Sep 9, 1815
Ensminger, George. Executor: Sarah Ensminger. Fairview Township. Wife: Sarah Ensminger. Children: (Names and number were not given.)

Sep 6, 1798   Sep 18, 1815
Lan, Anna Mary. Executor: Philip Gentzler. Cordorus Township. (Widow of Michael Lan.) Children: Catharine wife of Christian Mull, Magdalena wife of Henry Wehler, Elizabeth wife of Henry Wunder, Anna wife of Philip Gentzler, Margaret, and Susanna.

Jun 15, 1804   Sep 19, 1815
Miller, Rudolph. Executor: Samuel Moser. Windsor Township. Children: Henry, John, Michael, Jacob, Philip, Kate, Magdalena, Catharine, Margaret, and Rudolph.

Aug 5, 1815   Sep 20, 1815
Shaller, George. Executor: Elizabeth Shaller. York Borough. Wife: Elizabeth Shaller.

Mar 2, 1811   Sep 25, 1815
Overdeer, Ludwig. Executors: Peter Overdeer and Jacob Folk. Manheim Township. Children: John, Jacob, Peter, Catharine, Henry, and Frederick.

Apr 14, 1814   Sep 28, 1815
Johnston, Andrew. Executor: Christian Lanius. York Borough. Wife: Barbara Johnston.

May 1, 1815   Oct 2, 1815
Baer, Michael. Executors: Henry Baer and Philip Kromer. Manheim Township. Wife: Margaret Baer. Children: Magdalena, Michael, John, Samuel, Henry, Jacob, Barbara wife of Jacob Noll, Mary wife of John Baughman, George, Margaret, Susan, Elizabeth, Julian, and Eve.

Sep 25, 1815   Oct 6, 1815
Wickersham, James. Executors: William and Enoch Wickersham. Newberry Township. Children: William, Enoch and Mary wife of Thomas Fugate.

May 7, 1813   Oct 7, 1815
Schlosser, George. Executors: J.F. Williams and Jacob Schlosser. York Borough. Wife: Annamary Schlosser. Children: John, Jacob, Betsy, George and Polly wife of Peter Myers.

Sep 17, 1807   Oct 10, 1815
Small, Killian. Executors: Jacob and John Small. York Borough. Children: Jacob, John, George, Michael, Joseph, Peter and Henry.

Jul 5, 1815   Oct 13, 1815
Hoffman, Nicholas. Executors: Richard Bull and Jacob Hoffman. Dover Township. Wife: Philibina Hoffman. Children: John, Henry, Nicholas, Mary wife of Richard Bull, Catharine, Susanna, Eve, and Elizabeth.

May 25, 1810   Oct 17, 1815
Ruhl, Frederick. Executors: Henry Ruhl and Margaret Erick. Shrewsbury Township. Wife: Catharine Ruhl. Children: Henry, John, Elizabeth wife of John Greenwalt, Juliana wife of Michael Eurich, Margaret wife of John Reber and Michael.

--- --, ----   Oct 20, 1815
Stein, Frederick. Executor: omitted. Omitted Township. (German will.)

Oct 10, 1815   Nov 1, 1815
Buscksler, Conrad. Executors: George Leitner and Henry Goo. Manchester Township. Wife: Anna Buscksler. Children: Christian, John, Magdalena, Elizabeth, and Anna.

Sep 9, 1815   Nov 1, 1815
Miller, Michael. Executors: Jacob March and George Enders. Dover Township. Wife: Elizabeth Miller. Children: Bennet, Samuel, Michael, Elizabeth wife of George Enders, Catharine, and Lydia.

Nov 1, 1814   Nov 15, 1815
Gobrecht, Christopher. Executors: David Gobrecht and Adam Furney. Hanover Township. Children: Salley and David.

Oct 24, 1814   Nov 27, 1815
Lawson, Joseph. Executor: Magdalena Lawson. Cordorus Township. Wife: Magdalena Lawson. Children: Susanna, Catharine, John, Samuel, and William.

Oct 20, 1815   Dec 2, 1815
Edmundson, William. Executors: Thomas Edmundson and Thomas McMillan. Warrington Township. Brother: Thomas Edmundson.

Oct 2, 1815   Dec 22, 1815
Shultz, Peter. Executor: Henry Shultz. Hanover Township. Wife: Catharine Shultz. Children: Catharine wife of --- Miller Peter, Juliana wife of Martin Movofsky, John, Jacob, Margaret wife of Daniel Duden, Eve (a widow - name omitted) and Mary wife of Andrew Goodinlinger. Grandchild: John Miller.

Jun 3, 1814   Dec 28, 1815
Collingwood, Richard. Executor: Frederick Hartman. Windsor Township. Children: William and Martha. Grandchild: Thomas (son of William).

Aug 28, 1794   Jan 11, 1816
Shafer, Catharine. Executor: Henry Shafer. York County. Widow of Abraham Shafer. Children: Charles, Peter, Elizabeth, Anna and Henry.

--- --, ----   Jan 16, 1816
Keyser, Jacob. Executors: Jacob and Samuel Keyser. Shrewsbury Township. Child: Samuel Grandchildren: Jacob, Samuel, John, Catharine, and Elizabeth Keyser.

Dec 7, 1815   Jan 18, 1816
Thompson, Joseph. Executors: Archibald and Joseph Thompson. Chanceford Township. Wife: Mary Thompson. Children: Joseph, Agness wife of Robert Anderson, Alexander James, Margaret, Mary, Samuel, William, Andrew and Archibald.

Jan 6, 1812   Jan 25, 1816
Fishel, Michael. Executors: John Menges and Harry Strickhouser. Paradise Township. Wife: Magdalena Fishel. Children: Michael, (names of others not given.)

May 5, 1814   Feb 1, 1816
Rieb, Nicholas. Executors: Henry Rieb and Peter Brillhart. Shrewsbury Township. Children: Henry, Catharine, Peter, Barbara, Elizabeth, Jacob and Eve wife of Nicholas Etter.

Apr 7, 1814   Feb 6, 1816
Walfahart, Ferdinand. Executors: Jacob, Samuel and George Keller. Manheim Township. Legatees: Jacob Keller and others. N.B. This will is written in Latin.

Jan 27, 1813   Feb 12, 1816
Richey, Elizabeth. Executor: Emanuel Bare. Newberry Township. Legatee: Margaret Nicholas (sister).

Nov 5, 1815   Feb 20, 1816
Banix, Henry. Executor: Catharine Banix. York Borough. Wife: Catharine Banix. Sister: Magdalena Banix.

Jan 28, 1816   Feb 21, 1816
Shaull, Henry. Executors: Jacob and Joseph Shaull. Lower Chanceford Township. Legatees: (Mother) Catherine Shaull, (Bros. and Sisters) John, Jacob, Joseph, Mary Wize and Catharine Ellis.

Aug 14, 1815   Mar 4, 1816
Doll, Conrad. Executors: Conrad Doll and Ludwig Myers. Paradise Township. Wife: Elizabeth Doll. Children: Elizabeth, Conrad, Barbara, Ann, John, and Joseph.

Feb 24, 1816   Mar 8, 1816
Bare, John. Executor: Anna Bare. York Borough. Sister: Anna Bare.

Oct 4, 1807   Mar 9, 1816
Moatz, Catharine. Executor: Peter Kern. Dover Township. Children: George, Jacob, Henry, and John.

Feb 5, 1816   Mar 21, 1816
Ross, Alexander. Executors: William and James Ross. Warrington Township. Wife: Margaret Ross. Children: James, Jane, Martha, William, Thomas, Margaret and Elizabeth.

Dec 28, 1814   Mar 21, 1816
Cramer, David. Executors: Barbara Cramer and William Nes. York Borough. Wife: Barbara Cramer. Children: Polly, Elizabeth, Juliana and Casandra.

Mar 10, 1816   Mar 23, 1816
Heiner, Yost. Executors: Jacob and Joseph Shaeffer. Paradise Township. Wife: Omitted. Children: Michael, George, Elizabeth wife of Michael Fishell, Caroline wife of John Barker, Polly wife of David Ditzell, and Mary wife of George Shaeffer.

Jun 2, 1815   Apr 4, 1816
Cooper, John. Executors: Archibald and Mary Cooper. Fawn Township. Wife: Mary Cooper. Children: Margaret, Nancy, and Archibald.

Jun 7, 1816   Apr 10, 1816
Mitchell, George. Executor: John Livingston. Fawn Township. Wife: Mitchell. Children: Violet, John, Thomas, William, George, James, Robert, Joseph, and Elizabeth wife of John Theaker.

Mar 7, 1808   Apr 10, 1816
Meyer, John. Executors: Abraham Meyer and Adam Ettinger. Warrington Township. Wife: Margaret Meyer. Children: Hannah, Abraham, John, Jacob, Henry, George, Margaret, Elizabeth, Susanna, Anna, Sarah, Lydia, and Catharine.

Mar 4, 1800   Apr 16, 1816
Ohail, Edward. Executor: Hugh Ohail. Monaghan Township. Wife: Jean Ohail. Children: Hugh, Elizabeth, Martha, Thomas, and James.

Mar 11, 1816   Apr 26, 1816
Kauffman, Joseph. Executors: David Witmer, Samuel Stein and Catharine Kauffman. Hellam Township. Wife: Catharine Kauffman. Children: Joseph, Catharine, and Mary.

Feb 16, 1816   Apr 27, 1816
Muhs, Daniel. Executor: David Muhs. Manheim Township. Sister and Brother: Elizabeth and David Muhs.

Mar 13, 1816   Apr 30, 1816
Taylor, Joseph. Executor: David Warren. Newberry Township. Children: Geroge (and others - names not given).

Apr 3, 1816   Apr 30, 1816
Wickersham, Ann. Executor: Jesse Wickersham. Newberry Township. Legatees: (Bro.) Jesse Wickersham, (Mother) Ann Wickersham and (Sisters) Ruth, Mary and Hannah Wickersham.

May 7, 1816   May 8, 1816
Kelly, Eleanor. Executors: Thomas McAlier and Richard Koch. York Borough. (Widow of John Kelly.) Legatee: The Roman Catholic Church of York.

Apr 28, 1816   May 8, 1816
Schriver, John. Executor: William McMullin. Franklin Township. (The names of wife and children not given.)

Aug 1, 1811   May 20, 1816
Moser, Samuel. Executors: Adam and George Moser. York Borough. Wife: Barbara Moser. Children: Adam, George, and Catharine.

Jun 3, 1816   Jun 20, 1816
Gibbs, Boroughs. Executors: Sarah Gibbs and Nicholas Phyles. Hanover

Township. Wife: Sarah Gibbs. Child: Emely.

Jul --, 1815   Jun 24, 1816
Funk, Jacob. Executors: Maria E., Daniel and Joseph Funk. York Borough. Wife: Maria Elizabeth Funk. Children: Jacob, John, Daniel, Joseph, Maria wife of Dutsich Wheler, and Susanna wife of Lewis Wampler.

Mar 11, 1815   Jul 13, 1816
Heisse, Wendle. Executors: Daniel Heisse and Peter Klinefelter. Shrewsbury Township. Wife: Elizabeth Heisse. Children: Henry, Jacob, Eve, Daniel, George, Margaret, and John.

--- --, ----   Jul 18, 1816
Kohler, Joseph. Executor: Omitted. Manchester Township. Legatee: The Roman Catholic Church of York Borough.

Jun 19, 1816   Jul 20, 1816
Drever, John. Executors: Sarah Drever and Philip Zeigler. Dover Township. Wife: Sarah Drever.

Dec 17, 1810   Jul 23, 1816
Lauer, Magdalena. Executor: John Lauer. Dover Township. Brothers: Jacob and John Lauer.

Jul 5, 1816   Aug 5, 1816
Benedict, George. Executors: Henry Stover and Susanna Benedict. Dover Township. Wife: Susanna Benedict. Children: Elizabeth, George, John, Philip, Susanna, Samuel, Catharine, Margaret, Lydia, and David.

Jul 11, 1816   Aug 13, 1816
Kunkle, John. Executor: Jacob Markey. Hopewell Township. Wife: Eve Kunkle. Children: Sally, Samuel, Magdalena, and Alexander.

Jul 2, 1816   Aug 16, 1816
Kuntz, George. Executors: John Kuntz and Godfrey Lenhart. York Borough. Wife: Margaret Kuntz. Children: Francis, William, Elizabeth, and Margaret.

Aug 7, 1816   Aug 20, 1816
Miller, Jesse. Executors: Jacob Hart and Isaac Kirk. Fairview Township. Wife: Abigail Miller. Children: Mary wife of Casper Shup, Jr., Elizabeth, Hannah, and Isabella.

Jun 7, 1816 Aug 20, 1816
Pflieger, Maria Margaret. Executor: Henry Pflieger. York County. Widow of Frederick Pflieger. Child: Henry.

Aug 6, 1816 Aug 25, 1816
Chester, Richard. Executor: Frederick Bentz. Hanover Township. Wife: Elizabeth Chester.

Aug 3, 1816 Sep 9, 1816
Hartman, Frederick. Executors: Elizabeth Hartman, John Mosey, and George Hecker. York County. Wife: Elizabeth Hartman. Child: Charles.

Oct 4, 1815 Sep 13, 1816
Gelwicks, Nicholas. Hanover Township. Wife: Mary Gelwicks. Children: Catharine wife of Philip Youse, and Polly wife of Henry Morningstar.

Apr 4, 1810 Sep 16, 1816
Hemes, Christian. Executors: George Whrley and John Hemes. Paradise Township. Children: Abraham, John, Sally wife of George Whrley, and Christiana wife of Benjamin Hemes. Grandchild: George (son of Benjamin).

Aug 14, 1816 Sep 23, 1816
Alt, Henry. Executors: Peter Fyser and Michael Hess. Shrewsberry Township. Wife: Christiana Alt. Children: Valentine, Philip, John, Isaac, Frederick, Lewis and Henry. *(Note: Henry Alt's will plainly states his children's names (a) by 1st marriage: Valentine, Phillip, John, Jacob, Fred.; (b) by 2nd marriage: Ludwig, Henry, Christina, Elizabeth).*

Sep 25, 1816 Oct 17, 1816
McCann, Henry. Executor: Omitted. Wrightsville. Wife: Dorothea McCann.

Dec 4, 1815 Nov 4, 1816
Wentz, Anna Mary. Executor: John Wentz. Dover Township. Children: John, Adam, Henry, Philip, Michael, Peter, Christian, Anna, Elizabeth and Margaret wife of --- Foltz. Grandchild: Jacob Foltz.

Oct 17, 1816 Nov 4, 1816
Wentz, John. Executors: George and John Wentz. Dover Township. Wife: Catharine Wentz. Children: George, John, Jacob, Elizabeth and Mary.

--- --, ----   Nov 14, 1816
Shultz, Henry. Executors: Alexander Trecker and Catharine Shultz. omitted Township. (German will.)

Sep 19, 1816   Nov 28, 1816
McPherson, Frederick. Executor: William McPherson. Lower Chanceford Township. Wife: Isabella McPherson. Children: Elizabeth, Ann, Latitia, Frederick, John, William, Samuel, Grace, Mary, and Isabella.

--- --, ----   Dec 2, 1816
Kelly, Mary. Executor: James Kelly. Manheim Township.

Oct 29, 1816   Dec 3, 1816
Knoedler, Casper. Executors: John Koch, Jr. and Ignatus Lightner. West Manchester Township. Wife: Magdalena Knoedler. Children: Judith, Joseph, Magdalena, George, and Jacob.

--- --, ----   Dec 6, 1816
Banger, William. Executor: Omitted. German will.

Sep 9, 1816   Dec 9, 1816
Flickinger, Samuel. Executors: Andrew Flickinger and George Throne. Heidelberg Township. Wife: Eve Flickinger. Children: Eve, Andrew, Peter, Rachel, Joseph, Moses, Samuel, and Susanna.

Apr 26, 1815   Dec 17, 1816
Hinkle, John. Executors: John Hinkle and William Albright. Heidelberg Township. Wife: Rachel Hinkle. Children: William, Anthony, Elizabeth, and Margaret. Grandchildren: John Chambers, William and Sarah Albright (parents' names not given).

Feb 1, 1813   Jan 14, 1817
Youse, Frederick. Executors: John Haller and John Stroman. York Borough. Wife: Anna Youse. Children: George, Jacob, John, Elizabeth wife of Daniel Weaver, Catharine wife of Rev. George Kreaner and Polly.

Jan 3, 1814   Jan 28, 1817
Shup, Casper. Executor: Daniel Gilmore. Omitted Township. Wife: Barbara Shup. Children: Jacob, Peter, Jasper, Barbara wife of George Miller and Elizabeth wife of George Wood.

Dec 27, 1816   Jan 28, 1817
Rubel, Christian. Executors: Henry Strickhouser and Conrad Mayer.

Cordorus Township. Wife: Anna Rubel. Child: Esther.

Dec 26, 1816   Feb 4, 1817
Ziegel, Thomas. Executors: John and Elizabeth Ziegel. York Borough. Wife: Elizabeth Ziegel. Children: John, Gotlieb, Elizabeth wife of Conrad Brubacher and Lydia.

Jan 1, 1817   Feb 8, 1817
Felde, John. Executors: Frederick Geiseman and Jacob Falkenstein. Shrewsbury Township. Wife: Mary Felde. Children: (One son and one daughter, names not given.)

Feb 8, 1817   Feb 12, 1817
Gobrecht, David. Executor: Daniel Gobrecht. Hanover Township. Wife: Anna Christiana Gobrecht.

Mar 5, 1816   Feb 21, 1817
Miller, Harman. Executor: Michael Miller. Hopewell Township. Wife: Barbara Miller. Children: (Names and number not given.)

Jan 20, 1817   Feb 22, 1817
Groce, Andrew. Executors: Philip and John Groce. Dover Township. Wife: Barbara Groce. Children: Philip, Margaret, Wendel, Polly wife of Jacob Stover, Henry, and Catharine wife of Kenry Hoover.

Feb 13, 1817   Feb 26, 1817
Stroman, John Jr. Executors: John Stroman and Ignatus Leitner. York Borough. Wife: Mary Stroman. Children: Elton, Susanna, Louisa, Leitner and Mary.

--- --, 1815   Mar 12, 1817
Fitz, Frederick. Executors: Henry Schnell and Jacob Falkenstein. York Borough. Wife: Elizabeth Fitz. Children: Elizabeth wife of Henry Schnell, Peter, Samuel, and John.

Dec 16, 1815   Mar 12, 1817
Goolden, Charles. Executor: John L. Hinkle. Manheim Township. Wife: Elizabeth Goolden.

Oct 29, 1811   Mar 22, 1817
Streher, Peter. Executor: J. Householder. Hopewell Township. Wife: Christiana Streher. Children: John, Peter, Magdalena, Adam, Elizabeth, Catharine, Christian and Jacob.

261

Jun 13, 1817 Mar 29, 1817
Morrison, Martha. Executor: John Smith. Lower Chanceford Township. Children: Margaret wife of John Martin, Jean wife of ---- Snodgrass, and Mary wife of Alfred Beaty. Grandchildren: Martha, John, Mary and William Snodgrass; Henry and Mary Beaty.

Feb 2, 1817 Apr 16, 1817
Melaun, John. Executors: John Asper and Henry Slyder. Washington Township. Wife: Sally Melaun Children: Sarah, Elizabeth, Catharine, Susanna, John, Benjamin, and Alva.

Mar 4, 1817 Apr 25, 1817
Immell, George. Executor: John Stauter. Hanover Township. Mother: Dorothea Meyers.

--- --, ---- Apr 25, 1817
Hoffman, Philip. Executor: Omitted. York County. German will.

Apr 9, 1817 May 2, 1817
Crone, George. Executors: George Neiman and Andrew Weiser. Dover Township. Wife: Catharine Crone. Children: George, Jacob, David, Elizabeth wife of Andrew Weiger, Susanna, Catharine, Benjamin, Leah, and Sally.

Jun 21, 1816 May 7, 1817
Dundore, Henry. Executors: Henry Stover and Susanna Krisley. Dover Township. Wife: Hannah Dundore. Children: Lydia, John, Barbara, Margaret, Catharine, Susanna, and Maria wife of ---- Schlothour.

--- --, ---- May 7, 1817
Ortt, Catharine. Executor: Adam Ortt. Manchester Township. (German will.)

Mar 6, 1817 May 10, 1817
Dewald, Henry. Executors: Jacob Dewald and Samuel Long. Manheim Township. Wife: Mary Dewald. Children: Valentine, Frederick, Jacob, Maria, Mary wife of Samuel Long, Elizabeth wife of John Ketzmieller, Catharine wife of Nicholas Kesfaber, Philip, Juliana, Grabriel, and Donald.

Apr 7, 1817 May 10, 1817
Brubacher, Conrad. Executors: Conrad Brubacher and Christian Rathfon. Windsor Township. Wife: Christiana Brubacher. Children: John, Daniel, Rebecca, Helen, and Catharine wife of Conrad Beverson.

Aug 4, 1808   May 13, 1817
Watts, Thomas. Executors: Mary Watts and Daniel Cookson. Warrington Township. Wife: Mary Watts. The names and number of children not given.

May 2, 1796   May 17, 1817
Miller, Barbara. Executor: David Danner. Cordorus Township. Widow of Andrew Miller. Children: (Names and number not given.)

--- ---, ----   May 22, 1817
Fishell, Frederick. Executor: Omitted. Paradise Township. (German will.)

May 22, 1817   May 29, 1817
Shuler, Andrew. Executors: Jacob Eicholtz and Mosey Bare. Manchester Township. Wife: Margaret Shuler. Children: (the names and number not given).

Jan 9, 1816   Jun 5, 1817
Becker, Philip. Executors: Philip Becker and William Metzar. Newberry Township. Wife: Eve Becker. Children: John, Jacob, Philip, Eve wife of Philip Metzgar, Elizabeth, Catharine wife of Michael Neiman, Margaret wife of John Childer.

--- ---, ----   Jun 13, 1817
Mackaway, Daniel. Executor and Township: Omitted. (German will.)

Apr 1, 1817   Jun 16, 1817
Myers, Michael. Executor: Samuel Jordan. Peach Bottom Township. Wife: Elizabeth Myers. Children: Catharine, Susan, Jacob, Henry, Michael, and John. Grandchildren: Henry and Barbara Kunkle (parents' names not given).

Apr 7, 1816   Jun 28, 1817
Hendrix, Isaac. Executors: Joshua and Joseph Hendrix. Shrewsbury Township. Children: Adam, Isaac, Joshua, Thomas, Joseph, Hannah, Ruth, and John.

Jul 3, 1817   Jul 28, 1817
Miller, Adam. Executors: Peter Good and Michael Livingston. Manchester Township. Wife: Anna Miller. Children: John, Maria wife of ---- Michael, Magdalena wife of John Wealdy, Elizabeth and George Snyder, Henry, Susanna, Samuel, Jacob, Rudolph, Polly, Adam, and Lea.

Jul 15, 1817   Aug 4, 1817
Koutz, Peter. Executor: Catharine Koutz. Manheim Township. Wife: Catharine Koutz. Children: Conrad and Jacob.

Mar 11, 1817   Aug 14, 1817
Spies, Charles. Executor: David Gilmore. York County. Wife: Catharine Spies.

Dec 1, 1810   Aug 16, 1817
Hartman, Tobias. Executors: Frederick and Tobias Hartman. Shrewsbury Township. Wife: Maria Elizabeth Hartman. Children: John, Ludwick, Tobias, Frederick, Philibina wife of Jacob Dipple, and Maria wife of George Boyer.

--- ---, ----   Aug 18, 1817
Diehl, Charles. Executor: Omitted. German will.

Jul 21, 1817   Aug 23, 1817
Bull, John. Executors: Elizabeth and John Bull. Dover Township. Wife: Sarah Bull. Children: Richard, Elizabeth, Eliza, John, and Ross.

Jun 1, 1816   Aug 25, 1817
Diem, Andrew. Executor: Omitted. York County. Children: George, and Elizabeth wife of John Shoemaker.

Oct 19, 1810   Aug 30, 1817
Zeck, Michael. Executor: William Zeck and Jacob Falkinstein. Shrewsbury Township. Wife: Dorothea Zeck. Children: William, Michael, Jacob, Peter, Anamaria wife of Henry Schwartz, Rosana wife of John Schwartz, Catharine wife of Philip Hart, Dorothea wife of Michael Walter, Magdalena wife of --- Clatfelter, Eve, Christiana and Henry.

Sep 18, 1815   Sep 5, 1817
Miller, Anna. Executor: Henry Forry. Hanover Township. Children: Elizabeth wife of John Bolton, Jacob, Abraham, Veronica wife of Jacob Overdeer, Henry, Lancy wife of ---- Blinzinger, and Mary. N.B.: The last name of the these children appears to be Forry. The first one named in the will is Jacob Forry and so continues. There is no mention of children bearing the name of Miller, yet these are spoken of in the will as the children of Ann Miller.

Aug 4, 1817   Sep 8, 1817
Dubinger, Susanna. Executor: Jacob Hope. York Borough. (Bequests to

the German Reform Church.)

Jan 30, 1814   Oct 19, 1817
Long, Isabella. Executor: Hugh Long. Chanceford Township. Children: John, Elizabeth, Hugh, Martha, and George. Grandchild: Isabella Long (child of John).

Aug 27, 1817   Nov 6, 1817
Meiley, Martin. Executors: Jacob Stucher and William Metzger. Manchester Township. Children: Catharine wife of Jacob Stucher, Henry, and Anna wife of --- Bolshor.

Mar 13, 1815   Nov 10, 1817
Hoffman, Henry. Executors: Henry Stoner and Moses Bear. Manchester Township. Wife: Elizabeth Hoffman. Children: Philip and Henry.

Jul 8, 1817   Nov 11, 1817
Wiley, David. Executors: Reobert Gemmil, Ann and David Wiley. Hopewell Township. Wife: Ann Wiley. Children: David, Jannet wife of James Eaday, Margaret wife of David Gemill and Mary wife of Thomas Baird. Grandchildren: Susan, Ann and Nancy Brook (parents' names not given) and Anna, Mary and John Baird.

Feb 22, 1816   Nov 18, 1817
Hake, Frederick. Executors: Frederick and Jacob Hake. Manchester Township. Wife: Anna Maria Hake. Children: Jacob, Frederick, Elizabeth wife of George Smid, Henry, Anna wife of George Grass, John, and Peter.

Dec 1, 1813   Dec 2, 1817
Machlin, Philip. Executors: Solomon and Daniel Machlin. York County. Children: Philip, Catharine wife of John Edgedena, Jonathan, Salome, Daniel, John, and Elizabeth wife of Michael Frank.

Jul 29, 1815   Dec 11, 1817
Leatherman, Conrad. Executors: Dr. John Spangler and Daniel Cassat. York Borough. Child: Margaret wife of Dr. John Spangler. Grandchild: Ferdinand (son of Margaret).

May 5, 1817   Dec 13, 1817
Strickler, John. Executors: Ulrich and John Strickler. York County. Wife: Catharine Strickler. Chlidren: Ulrich, John, Michael, Jacob (four others - names not given).

Dec 3, 1817   Dec 13, 1817
Hurl, Edward. Executors: John Kosh and Ignatus Leetner. York Borough. Wife: Elizabeth Hurl.

Jul 29, 1815   Dec 15, 1817
Ness, Jacob Jr. Executor: Michael Ness. Shrewsbury Township. Children: Margaret wife of Dr. John Spangler. Grandchild: Frederick G. Spangler.

Nov 29, 1817   Dec 15, 1817
Haller, Adam. Executors: Charles A. Barnitz and Abraham Danner, Jr. York County. Wife: Omitted. Children: Elizabeth, Charlotte, Sarah, and Marian.

July 4, 1817   Dec 18, 1817
Akins, William. Executor: Agness Akins. Fawn Township. Wife: Agness Akins.

Apr 12, 1815   Jan 1, 1818
Dritt, Jacob. Executors: William Barber, D. Cassat, and Susan Spangler. Windsor Township. Wife: Elizabeth Dritt. Children: Elizabeth, Magdalena, and Margaret.

Oct 14, 1816   Jan 6, 1818
Etter, Mary. Executors: George and Lawrance Etter. Shrewsbury Township. Children: Michael, George, Lawrance, Catharine wife of Conrad Keesy, and Elizabeth.

--- --, 1811   Jan 10, 1818
Bentz, Michael. Executors: Peter Bentz and Jacob Weygle. West Manchester Township. Wife: Margaret Bentz. Children: Peter, Jacob, Catharine wife of John Eichingers, and Elizabeth wife of John Schroms.

Dec 27, 1815   Jan 13, 1818
Doll, John. Executors: Thomas Jordan and George McMullen. Children: Jacob, Conrad, Catharine wife of Jacob Tressler, Mary wife of Peter Harold, Joseph, Fornica wife of Henry Graeff, Lettia wife of John Lebberl, Elizabeth wife of ---- Marx, Magdalena wife of Nicholas Henry, Christiana wife of Jacob Harr, Susanna wife of George Hoar, Margaret wife of David Wilson, and Barbara wife of Peter Noll. Grandchildren: John, Elizabeth, Polly, Jacob, Joseph, and Catharine (children of Conrad Doll).

Apr 6, 1814   Jan 20, 1818
McMullen, James. Executors: Thomas Jordan and George McMullan.
Fawn Township. Wife: Jean McMullan. Child: George. Grandchild:
Maria Caster (parents' names not given).

May 2, 1813   Jan 26, 1818
Welsh, John. Executor: M. Eichelberger. York Borough. Wife:
Catharine Welsh. Children: John, Jacob, Martin, Esther wife of Joseph
Doll, Catharine wife of Jacob Small, Polly wife of Martin Eichelberger and
Sarah wife of Philip Butler.

Jan 13, 1818   Jan 28, 1818
Schweitzer, Andrew. Executor: Andrew Schweitzer. Fawn Township.
Wife: Elizabeth Schweitzer. Children: Adam, Elizabeth wife of George
Pitts, Mary wife of Adam Pitts, Catharine wife of Henry Woliver, Barbara
and George Shaul and Susanna.

--- --, ----   Feb 3, 1818
Campbell, Elizabeth. Executor: William Whiteford. Chanceford
Township. Children: James and Daniel. Grandchildren: John Denern,
Eleanor Morgan and Elizabeth Prigg (parents' names not given).

Jan 8, 1810   Feb 4, 1818
Doll, Margaret. Executor: Jacob Ernst. Paradise Township. Children:
Catharine wife of George Wallet, Mary wife of John Mouselto and
Elizabeth wife of James Griffith. Grandchildren: Elizabeth, Catharine and
Polly Wallet. (daughters of Catharine Wallet.)

Dec 15, 1817   Feb 16, 1818
Glasgow, Hugh. Executors: John Kirk, Maria and John Glasgow. Peach
Botton Township. Wife: Maria Glasgow. Children: John, Eliza, James,
Hugh, Samuel, William, Walter, and Cunningham.

Jan 22, 1818   Feb 17, 1818
Grass, Andrew. Executors: Peter Grass and John Quickel. Manchester
Township. Wife: Catharine Grass. Children: (Names and number not
given.)

Feb 18, 1817   Feb 20, 1818
Grundy, Jacob. Executors: Henry Etter, and John Prunk. Newberry
Township. Children: John, Daniel, Carray, and Jacaob.

Mar 5, 1818   Mar 21, 1818
Albright, Bernard. Executor: Michael Erhart. Manheim Township. Wife: Anna Mary Albright. Children: Jacob, John, Henry, Daniel, Elizabeth wife of Daniel Bauer, Catharine wife of John Hamm, and Juliana.

Jan 16, 1818   Mar 27, 1818
Sheffer, Rudolph. Executor: Nicholas Sheffer. Cordorus Township. Wife: Christiana Sheffer.

--- --, ----   Apr 6, 1818
Becker, Philip. Executor: Omitted. German will.

Feb 18, 1818   Apr 8, 1818
Ross, William. Executor: Hugh Ross. Lower Chanceford Township. Wife: Margaret Ross. Children: Hugh, Sarah and Elizabeth.

Aug 30, 1814   Apr 28, 1818
Helman, Michael. Executors: Elizabeth Helman and George Mace. Hanover Township. Wife: Elizabeth Helman. Children: (Names and number not given.)

--- --, ----   Apr 29, 1818
Meyer, Philip. Executor: John Koch, Jr. York Borough. Brothers: Henry and Simon Meyer. Sister: Catharine wife of John Becker.

Feb 5, 1817   May 6, 1818
Ohail, Jane. Executors: Hugh and Thomas Ohail. Monaghan Township. Children: Hugh, Thomas, James, Elizabeth, Martha, Mary, Nancy, and Jenny.

Jul 7, 1812   May 7, 1818
Winter, Peter. Executor: Anna Mary Winter. Windsor Township. Wife: Anna Mary Winter. (There were three children and four grandchildren - names not given.)

Apr 1, 1818   May 12, 1818
Smith, Henry. Executor: John Deardorff. Washington Township. Children: Christiana, Ann, Jacob, Abraham and John.

Apr 9, 1817   May 19, 1818
Bleimeyer, Abraham. Executors: Catharine Schram and John Mosey. York Borough. Child: Catharine wife of David Schram.

May 12, 1818   May 26, 1818
Brenise, John. Executors: William and John Brenise. York Borough. Wife: Catharine Brenise. Children: Lydia wife of John Wolf, and Elizabeth.

--- ---, ---   May 28, 1818
Shisler, Henrich. Executor: John Weist. Omitted Township. (German will.)

Mar 17, 1818   Jun 7, 1818
Dibble, Eve. Executor: John Dibble. Hopewell Township. Children: Catharine and John.

Mar 5, 1818   Jun 9, 1818
Brown, James. Executor: John Brown. Fawn Township. Wife: Margaret Brown. Brother: John Brown.

Aug 4, 1818   Aug 14, 1818
Marshall, William. Executors: Adam Hendrix and Elizabeth Marshall. Shrewsbury Township. Wife: Elizabeth Marshall. Child: Elizabeth.

Aug 4, 1818   Aug 18, 1818
Hoffacre, Michael. Executor: Peter Runk. Manheim Township. Wife: Elizabeth Hoffacre. Children: Henry, Michael, John, Barbara, Elizabeth wife of John Shaffer, Jacob, Catharine wife of George Shoeman, and Anna wife of Henry Miller. Grandchildren: Elizabeth Fair and Susanna McClass (daughters of Barbara), and Elizabeth Hoffacre (daughter of Jacob).

Nov 5, 1817   Aug 20, 1818
Rohrback, John. Executors: George Whesley and John Eppley. Manheim Township. Wife: Susanna Rohrback. Children: Christian, Susanna, Magdalena and Elizabeth wife of Peter Fuhrman.

Jul 5, 1815   Aug 22, 1818
Mills, James. Executors: David Warren and Alexander Frazer. Newberry Township. Wife: Joanna Mills. Children: Eli, Amos, James, Edwin, Margery and Lydia. Grandchildren: Eli Mills (son of Eli), Joanna Mills (daughter of Amos), and Franklin Mills (son of James).

Aug 22, 1818   Aug 31, 1818
Himes, William. Executors: Mary Himes. Hanover Township. Wife: Mary Himes. Children: George, Samuel, and Catharine.

Aug 10, 1811   Sep 11, 1818
Windemeyer, Catharine. Executor: George Simon. Dover Township.
Legatees: (Nephews) John Simon and Dewald Hess. N.B. There was a
bequest made to Dover Church - named "Steveyers Church".

Feb 16, 1815   Oct 16, 1818
Cook, Jesse. Executors: Henry, Isaac and Elisha Cook. Franklin
Township. Wife: Mary Cook. Children: Henry, Isaac, John, Samuel, and
Mary wife of Zachariah Reed. Grandchild: Mary (child of Mary).

Aug 11, 1818   Oct 29, 1818
Gruber, Henry. Executors: Margaret Gruber and John Zeigler. Cordorus
Township. Wife: Margaret Gruber.

Oct 9, 1818   Nov 2, 1818
Ziegler, Joseph. Executors: Michael Ziegler and William Coulson. Peach
Bottom Township. Wife: Jane Ziegler. Children: (names not given).

Apr 22, 1818   Nov 3, 1818
Robinson, Sarah. Executors: George and Alexander Robinson. Lower
Chanceford Township. Child: Eleanor.

Oct 30, 1818   Nov 12, 1818
Newcomer, Abraham. Executor: Peter Fried. Hellam Township. Wife:
Margaret Newcomer. Child: Abraham.

Apr 7, 1818   Nov 26, 1818
Yoner, Christian. Executor: Christian Hame. Dover Township. Child:
Mary.

Jul 17, 1801   Nov 27, 1818
Bear, Margaret. Executor: John Lichty. Hempfield Township. Brothers:
Nicholas, John, Philip and Isaac. There was also a bequest left to Benj.
Hershey, a Menonite, for the use of the poor.

Oct 16, 1818   Dec 4, 1818
Manifold, John. Executors: Margaret and William Manifold. Hopewell
Township. Wife: Margaret Manifold. Children: Anabal, Margaret,
Elizabeth, Jean, Mary, Agness, Eleanor, William, Benj, Joseph, and John.

Aug 27, 1818   Dec 11, 1818
McGuire, Peter. Executor: William Smith and William McMullan.
Monaghan Township. Wife: Mary McGuire. Children: William, Peter,

James, John, Ruth, Sarah, and Thomas.

Jun 1, 1805   Dec 14, 1818
Utz, Daniel. Executors: Daniel Dupe and Daniel Utz. Manheim Township. Wife: Mary Utz. Children: Andrew, Daniel, Mary wife of Henry Hoff and Elizabeth.

Dec 16, 1818   Dec 24, 1818
Schneider, Jacob. Executor: George Ebert. Hanover Borough. Wife: Elizabeth Schneider. Children: George, Mary wife of Jacob Wise, Elizabeth wife of Henry Kretzinger, Catharine wife of William Fowler and Susanna wife of Jacob Bower.

Apr 29, 1818   Jan 7, 1819
Leitner, Ignatus. Executors: George Letner and George Kelton. York Borough. Children: Rebecca, Charlotte, Elizabeth, Catharine, Mary wife of Jacob Fahs, Susanna wife of Henry Spangler, Margaret wife of Joseph Russel, Lydia wife of George Skeleton, Jacob, and Joseph. Grandchildren: Henry and Elizabeth Leitner (children of Joseph).

Aug 15, 1818   Jan 19, 1819
Williams, George. Executors: Samuel Bacon and John Beeker. Windsor Township. Wife: Elizabeth Williams. Children: Peter, Sarah wife of Thomas Roberts, Delilah, Ann and Mary wife of John Naeff.

Dec 4, 1818   Feb 3, 1819
Minich, Simon. Executors: Simon Minich and John Bollinger. York County. Wife: Elizabeth Minich. Children: George, Leah, Simon, Catharine, Elizabeth, Margaret, Eve, Sarah, Lydia, John, Jacob, and Matilda.

Sep 2, 1804   Feb 16, 1819
Ziegler, George. Executors: Charles and Jacob Ziegler. Hanover Township. Wife: Anna M. Ziegler. Child: Magdalena.

Feb 1, 1819   Feb 16, 1819
Peter, Elizabeth. Executor: David Peter. Franklin Township. Wife of David Peter. Sole Legatee: Her husband.

Sep 26, 1818   Feb 20, 1819
Kelly, James. Executors: John Quarles, John Hellen, and Charles Barnetz. York Borough. Wife: Mary Kelly. Children: (Five whose names were not given.)

May 2, 1814   Feb 24, 1819
House, Benjamin. Executor: Jacob Hart. Fairview Township. Wife: Elizabeth House. Children: Susanna, Hannah, Joseph, Benjamin, Prudence, and Abigal.

Sep 11, 1814   Feb 24, 1819
Haldeman, Jacob. Executor: Susanna Haldeman. Manheim Township. Sister: Susanna wife of Christian Stoufer.

Feb 2, 1819   Feb 26, 1819
Cross, Randall. Executors: Henry Cross and Tyson. Windsor Township. Brothers: John (of Ohio) and James Cross. Nieces and Nephew: Sarah, Thomas, and Jane Cross (children of James).

Feb 2, 1819   Mar 1, 1819
Meyer, John. Executors: Adam Ettinger. Warrington Township. Wife: Jean Meyer. Children: Mary, Sarah, Elizabeth, and Margaret.

Dec 1, 1817   Mar 12, 1819
Plaff, George. Executors: John Gilbert and Joseph Hamacher. Windsor Township. Children: George, John, Maria wife of Anthony Amend, and Christiana wife of Jacob Reinbine.

Mar 26, 1813   Mar 20, 1819
Schreiber, Philip. Exector: Anna M. Schreiber and Jacob Shaffer. York County. Wife: Anna Maria Schreiber.

Feb 24, 1819   Mar 27, 1819
Updegraff, Joseph. Executors: Joseph and Christian Updegraff. York Borough. Wife: Anna Updegraff. Children: Elizabeth, Jacob, Mary, Joseph, Catharine, Christian, Julian and Benj.

Jan 28, 1817   Mar 30, 1819
McKinly, Stephen. Executors: John Smith, Hugh Long, and Isaac Williams. Chanceford Township. Children: David, Susanna, Esther, Stephen, Elizabeth wife of Robert Alexander, and William. Grandchildren: Elizabeth (daughter of Stephen), Mary, Hannah, and William McKinley (parents' names not given).

Apr 9, 1814   Apr 5, 1819
Wohlfart, Philip. Executors: Catharine Wohlfart and George Yenewins. Manheim Township. Wife: Catharine Wohlfart. Children: Maria wife of George Yenewins, Philip, Elizabeth wife of John Sholl, John, Jacob and

Henry.

Dec 20, 1818   Apr 12, 1819
Welty, George. Executors: Henry and Philip Welty. Manchester Township. Wife: Susanna Welty. Children: Jacob, Philip, Henry and George.

Mar 11, 1819   Apr 15, 1819
Schreiber, Peter. Executors: Emanuel Bare and Casper Lancks. West Manchester Township. Wife: Susanna Schreiber. Children: Daniel, Frederick, Elizabeth, Sarah, Margaret and Susanna.

Dec 4, 1817   Apr 19, 1819
Marks, Sybilla. Executors: John Menges and Henry Meyer. Paradise Township. Children: Barbara, Catharine, Mary, Margaret, and Magdalena.

--- --, ----   Apr 24, 1819
Meyer, George. Executor: Omitted. Conewago Township. (German will.)

Apr 7, 1819   May 12, 1819
Shover, Samuel. Executors: Tempest Wilson and Barbara Shover. Wrightsville. Wife: Barbara Shover. Child: Emanuel.

May 6, 1819   May 17, 1819
Hill, James. Executors: James Bonham and James Hill. Chanceford Township. Wife: Ann Hill. Children: William, Mary wife of ---- Donahay, and James. Grandchild: James (son of Mary).

May 16, 1817   May 20, 1819
Wampler, Jacob. Executor: Christian Wampler. York Borough. Wife: Mary Wampler. Children: Catharine wife of Samuel Gorgas, Barbara wife of John Turner and Mary wife of Abraham Gartman.

Mar 1, 1813   May 31, 1819
Hoff, Daniel. Executor: Henry Hoff. Manheim Township. Wife: Anna Mary Hoff. Children: John, Daniel, Elizabeth, and Magdalena.

Oct 8, 1818   Jun 4, 1819
Riel, Peter. Executor: David Buckler. York County. Wife: Catharine Riel.

Jul 19, 1817   Jun 12, 1819
Segrist, Francis. Executor: John Segrist. Hopewell Township. Wife: Catharine Segrist. Children: Anna, Catharine, Francis, John, Fronica, Michael, Ann, Henry, Barbara, Peter and William.

Apr 22, 1819   Jun 16, 1819
Houston, Joseph. Executors: Robert Cathcart and Jacob Eichelberger. York County. Children: James and Mary.

Mar 8, 1819   Jun 21, 1819
School, Catharine. Executors: Valentine Coleman and Adam Litchenberger. Manchester Township. Legatees: (Bros. and Sister) Anna Coleman, John and George School.

May 18, 1819   Jun 30, 1819
Westhaeffer, Leonard. Executors: Conrad Westhaeffer and George Henisen. Manchester Township. Wife: Catharine Westhaeffer. Children: Conrad, Samuel, Rachel wife of Ludwick Hohr, John, Polly, Peggy, Catharine and George.

May 18, 1818   Jul 1, 1819
Weimert, Andrew. Executors: Jacob Hoke and Catharine Weimert. West Manchester Township. Wife: Catharine Weimert.

Mar 14, 1815   Jul 22, 1819
Becker, Peter. Executors: Christiana Becker and Jacob Schneta. Shrewsbury Township. Wife: Christiana Becker. Children: John, Catharine, Margaret, and Elizabeth.

Jun 21, 1819   Jul 24, 1819
Gutwalt, Felix. Executors: Christian, John and Daniel Gutwalt. York County. Children: Catharine, Jacob, George, John, and Daniel.

Jan 7, 1817   Jul 29, 1819
Welshaus, Jacob. Executor: Abraham Gartman and Jacob Dole. York Borough. Wife: Susanna Welshaus. Children: Jacob, Elizabeth wife of James Griffith and Catharine. Grandson: Jacob Griffith.

Jul 2, 1819   Aug 23, 1819
Lenhart, Godfrey. Executors: William Lenhart, William Barber and John Schmedt. York Borough. Children: William, Henry, Elizabeth wife of John Bayly, Margaret wife of George Kuntz, and Catharine wife of John McPherson.

Aug 11, 1819   Aug 31, 1819
Krantz, Elizabeth. Executors: Jacob Hoke and John Stahle. West
Manchester Township. Children: Ann wife of Jacob Hoke, Christiana
wife of Jacob Small, Catharine, and George.

Aug 9, 1819   Sep 14 1819
Moore, Mordeca. Executor: Michael Hart. Fairview Township. Wife:
Elizabeth Moore. Children: Sarah, Elizabeth, and Isaac.

Apr 30, 1813   Sep 14, 1819
Eipe, Peter. Executors: Frederick Borger and George Small. Manheim
Township. Child: Jacob Eipe.

Sep 4, 1813   Sep 18, 1819
Trostel, Abraham. Executors: Joseph and Abraham Trostel. York
Borough. Wife: Susanna Trostel. Children: Jacob, George, John,
Abraham, Henry, Elizabeth wife of Frederick Rehmer, William, Daniel,
Peter, Catharine and Susanna wife of Jacob Stover.

Apr 27, 1806   Oct 19, 1819
Furst, Barbara. Executor: Frederick Klugh. Dover Township. (Widow of
Adam Furst.) Bequests to nieces and nephews (names not given.)

Sep 14, 1818   Oct 19, 1819
Fulweiler, Michael. Executor: Frederick Klugh. Washington Township.
Children: Mary, Catharine, Joseph, and (five others whose names are not
given.)

Nov 14, 1797   Oct 25, 1819
Emig, Philip. Executors: Charles Emig and Michael Stambach. Wife:
Mary Emig. Children: Jacob, Lorentz, Philip, John, Catharine, Eve,
Elizabeth, and Mary.

Jul 19, 1813   Nov 2, 1819
Lenhart, William. Executors: John and Peter Lenhart. Dover Township.
Wife: Anna Maria Lenhart. Children: Susanna wife of Samuel Close,
Catharine, Elizabeth wife of Henry Miller, George, John, Peter, and
Henry.

Mar 26, 1819   Nov 5, 1819
Beltz, Philip. Executors: Barbara Beltz and John Henke. Hanover
Township. Wife: Barbara Beltz. Children: Eleanor, Catharine, Susan,
Elizabeth, and Jacob.

Oct 6, 1819   Nov 15, 1819
Feiser, Peter. Executors: Peter Feiser and Jacob Falkenstein. Shrewsbury Township. Wife: Maria Feiser. Children: Peter, Jacob, Daniel, and Maria wife of Abraham Yost.

Sep 14, 1819   Dec 8, 1819
Jordan, Thomas. Executors: Archibald and Joseph Jordan. Hopewell Township. Children: John, Archibald, Thomas, Samuel, Benj., and Joseph. Grandchildren: Mary and Hatty Jordan, and Anna and Mary Dickson (daughters of William Dickson of Lancaster, mother's name not given).

Sep 16, 1819   Dec 27, 1819
Anderson, Robert. Executors: James and Andrew Anderson. Hopewell Township. Wife: Sarah Anderson. Robert Anderson (nephew, son of Andrew Anderson) and Jane wife of Archibald Thompson (niece, daughter of Andrew Anderson.

Mar 2, 1819   Dec 27, 1819
Roller, Jacob. Executors: Richard Bull and Daniel Klatfelter. Dover Township. Wife: Catharine Roller. Children: Samuel, John, Ann, Jacob, Sarah and George.

INDEX

ABBOT, Alice, 97
  Catharine, 97
  Edward, 69, 97
  Eleanor, 97
  Elizabeth, 97
  John, 97
  Margaret, 97
  Thomas, 97
ABLENIS, John, 145
  Mary, 145
ABRINETHEY, John, 59
  Mary, 59
ACKERWARE, John, 197
ACTLAND, Elizabeth, 171
  Peter, 171
ADAIR, Hannah, 118
  John, 118
ADAMS, Albewer, 247
  Alexander, 44
  Anna, 247
  David, 101
  Jacob, 166, 179
  John, 98, 247
  Katharine, 247
  Martha, 101
  Mary, 44, 98
  Mathew, 238
  Samuel, 98
  Sara, 238
ADICH, Elizabeth, 100
  George, 100
  Henry, 100
  John, 100
  Maria, 100
  Maria Magdalena, 100
  Peter, 100
ADICK, George, 105
AGNES, Margaret, 75
AGNEW, David, 31, 140, 170
  Elizabeth, 66
  James, 11, 31, 169, 170
  Jane, 170
  Jean, 31
  John, 31, 39, 75, 170
  Margaret, 170
  Martha, 31, 170
  Rebecca, 31
  Samuel, 31, 66
AILKIN, Agness, 236
  Joseph, 236
AINSTIN, Semon, 190
AKINS, Agness, 265
  William, 265
ALBERT, Andrew, 162
  Applonia, 162
  Jacob, 162
  John, 113, 162
  Lawrence, 162
  Margaret, 162
ALBRIGHT, Abigail, 86
  Anna Mary, 267
  Bernard, 267
  Catharine, 164, 267
  Daniel, 267
  Elizabeth, 245, 267
  George, 19, 177
  Henry, 86, 245, 267
  Jacob, 267
  John, 267
  Juliana, 267
  Magdalena, 177
  Peter, 19
  Philip, 19
  William, 259
ALEXANDER, Anne, 3
  Benjamin, 225
  Deborah, 147
  Eleas, 3
  Elizabeth, 271
  Esther, 3
  Francis, 3
  Isaac, 3
  Jane, 27
  Jeddiah, 3
  John, 27
  Lindsey, 27
  Pedons, 27
  Rebecca, 27
  Robert, 271
  Samuel, 27, 110
  Sarah, 110, 147
  Thomas, 3, 147
  William, 3, 147
ALIRESS, Hannah, 235
ALLEN, Elizabeth, 147
  Francis, 123
  James, 147
  Thomas, 72
ALLER, Thomas, 74
ALLEWELT, Bernhart, 84
  Elizabeth, 84
ALLISON, Agnes, 113
  Agness, 77
  Alexander, 77, 113
  Elizabeth, 113, 228, 233
  Francis, 123
  Garvin, 228
  Gavin, 36, 77

James, 77, 228
Jean, 77, 113
John, 77, 228, 233
Joseph, 77, 228
Margaret, 77, 113, 228
William, 77, 228
ALT, Christiana, 258
　Elizabeth, 258
　Frederick, 258
　Henry, 258
　Isaac, 258
　Jacob, 258
　John, 258
　Lewis, 258
　Ludwig, 258
　Philip, 258
　Valentine, 258
AMEN, Anthony, 18
AMEND, Anthony, 271
　Maria, 271
AMENT, Barbara, 31
　Catharine, 31
　Elizabeth, 103
　George, 31
　Jacob, 31
　John, 103
　Marilla, 31
AMERMAN, Anne, 78
　Gerret, 78
　Henry, 78
　James, 78
　Jean, 78
　Mary, 78
　Milly, 78
　Simon, 78
AMMER, Anna, 95
　Barbara, 95
　Catharine, 95
　Daniel, 71, 88, 95, 126
　Veronica, 126

AMMON, Anna, 35
　Conrad, 35
　Elizabeth, 35
　Jacob, 35
　Margaret, 35
　Scharlot, 35
ANDERSON, Agness, 254
　Andrew, 216, 275
　Ann, 251
　Barbara, 93
　Benj., 244
　Benjamin, 251
　David, 248, 251
　Eliza, 251
　Esther, 216
　Hugh, 204
　James, 3, 93, 216, 220, 238, 248, 251, 275
　Jane, 251, 275
　Jean, 52, 248
　Jennet, 216
　John, 216, 248
　Joseph, 251
　Margaret, 236, 251
　Mary, 93, 248, 251
　Rachel, 3, 216
　Rebecca, 106
　Robert, 52, 216, 236, 248, 254, 275
　Sara, 248
　Sarah, 251, 275
　Susanna, 52
　Tate, 251
　Thomas, 106
　William, 3, 93, 157, 185, 212, 229
ANDREW, Elizabeth, 195
　James, 195
　Jannet, 195
　Lennet, 195

　Margaret, 195
　Robert, 195
ANGHINGBOUR-GH, B., 78
ANNE, John, 152
　Sally, 152
ANSTEIN, George, 244
APFEL, Anna, 123
　George, 123
　Wendle, 123
APMEYER, Anna, 143
　Christiana, 143
　Dietrich, 143
　Melcher, 143
　Michael, 143
APPLE, Christian, 69
　Elias, 69
　Eliza, 69
　James, 69
APPLEMAN, Anna Margaret, 97
　Anne, 97
　Christiana, 97
　Conrad, 97
　Elizabeth, 97
　Henry, 97
　Jacob, 97
　John, 97
　Katharine, 97
　Lena, 97
　Margaret, 97
　Philip, 97
ARMAN, Robert L., 165
ARMOR, Anne, 234
　James, 234
　John, 234
　Thomas, 90
ARMSTRONG,
　Elenor, 13
　Isaac, 148, 149
　James, 149

Jennet, 149
John, 13, 149
Margaret, 13
Martin, 195, 216, 233
Quintin, 148, 149
Quinton, 9
Thomas, 13
William, 13
ARNDT, Katharine, 121
Peter, 121
ARNOLD, Catharine, 148
Christiana, 148
Detter, 148
Elizabeth, 148
George, 148
John, 148, 197
Margaret, 148
Nicholas, 148
Peter, 148
Samuel, 81, 85, 95, 133
ARON, Jane, 182
ARTEL, Valentine, 207
ARTHUR, Isaas, 131
Issah, 106
Mary, 106
Thomas, 105, 131
ARTISS, Mary, 3
ASHTON, Margaret Huse, 144
Richard, 144
Thomas, 144
William, 144
ASPER, Abraham, 201
Elizabeth, 19, 201
Frederick, 19, 201
George, 19, 201
Isaas, 201
Jacob, 201
John, 19, 201, 261

Margaret, 201
Mary, 201
Philip, 201
Susanna, 201
Ursella, 19
ASTON, Thomas, 55
William, 55
ATHERTON, Abigail, 77
Elizabeth, 77
Henry, 77
Richard, 77
Thomas, 77
ATKINSON, Caphas, 179
Jane, 179
ATLAND, Andrew, 198
Catharine, 198
Elizabeth, 198
George, 198
Jacob, 198
John, 198
Mally, 133
Peter, 198
Philip, 133, 198
AU, George, 243
Hannah, 243
AUGHINBOUGH, Sally, 153
William, 153
AULENBAUGH, Elizabeth, 202
John, 202
Nicholas, 202
Peter, 202
AUMAN, George, 67
Jacob, 67
John, 67
Margaret, 67
Mary Elizabeth, 67
Michael, 67
Richard, 150

AUSHELMAN, Catharine, 208
Christian, 207
Eve, 207
John, 207
AUSTEIN, Catharine, 175
Sigmond, 175

-B-

BACKLER, John, 238
Mary, 238
BACON, Samuel, 270
BAECHTELL, Samuel, 203
BAEL, Michael, 60
BAER, Anne, 150
Barbara, 213, 252
Catharine, 213
Christian, 150
Elizabeth, 150, 252
Eve, 213, 252
George, 252
Henry, 164, 252
Jacob, 252
Jeremiah, 213
John, 252
Julian, 252
Ludwick, 213
Magdalena, 252
Margaret, 213, 252
Mary, 252
Michael, 150, 213, 252
Peter, 213
Samuel, 252
Susan, 252
William, 213
BAGER, Betey, 141
Catharine, 129
Christina, 129
Elizabeth, 129
George, 129

279

John, 129, 141
Nicholas, 141
Samuel, 129
William, 129
BAHN, Adam, 178
Anna, 27
Catharine, 27
Elizabeth, 27
Eva, 27
Henry, 27
Jacob, 27
Johannes, 27
John, 27
Julianna, 27
BAILE, Caleb, 42
BAILEY, Aaron, 177
Andrew, 128
Daniel, 128, 177
Elizabeth, 128
Hannah, 210
Jane, 128, 210
John, 128, 190
Margaret, 177, 210
Nancy, 128
Rachel, 128
Ruth, 210
Sarah, 128
BAIRD, Mary, 264
Thomas, 264
BAKER, Ann, 76, 234
David, 173
Elizabeth, 85
Henry, 14
James, 234
John, 76, 85, 173
Joseph, 173
Judith, 14
Mary, 76, 173
Mathias, 76
Peter, 173, 246
Philip, 231
BAKERS, Frederick, 155

Margaret, 155
BALDERSTON,
Jacob, 144
John, 136
BALDWIN, Nathaniel, 74
Thomas, 28
BALDY, Freeman, 201
Susanna, 201
BALEY, Eve
Elizabeth, 206
George, 205
Margaret, 205, 206
BALLY, Andrew, 130
BALM, Adam, 190
Elizabeth, 190
Mr., 5
BALTZLY, Anna, 40
Barbara, 40
Elizabeth, 40
Henry, 40
Jacob, 40
Joseph, 40
Mary, 40
BANE, James, 244
John, 244
Margaret, 244
Mary, 229
Nathan, 244
Sarah, 244
Vashti, 244
BANGER, William, 259
BANIX, Catharine, 254
Henry, 254
Magdalena, 254
BANTA, Abraham, 28
Elizabeth, 99
Henry, 37
Peter, 99
BANTERS, Elizabeth, 200

Jacob, 200
BAR, Daniel, 184
BARBER, William, 209, 211, 251, 265
BARD, Barbara, 151
Barne, 12
Catharine, 8
Dorothy, 151
Elizabeth, 155
Fornica, 8
Francis, 8, 12
George, 151, 155, 158, 191, 217, 251
Margaret, 151
Martin, 8, 12
Michael, 14
Paul, 12
Peter, 12
Philip, 8, 12
Savilla, 8, 12
Steom, 8
Susanna, 8
BARDT, Anna, 27
Barbara, 27
Catharine, 27, 73
George, 27
Mandilena, 27
Marlies, 27
Paul, 27
Stephen, 73
Susanna, 27
BARE, Anna, 255
Emanuel, 183, 239, 254, 272
John, 255
Mosey, 262
BARKCLEY, Sarah, 171
William, 171
BARKER, Caroline, 255
Eve, 109
John, 255

Philip, 109
BARMITZ, Jacob, 164
BARMONE, Henry,
  230
  Magdalena, 230
BARNETZ, Charles,
  270
  Charles A., 241
  Jacob, 230
BARNITZ, Ann
  Barbara, 176
  Anna Barbara, 160,
  238
  Barbara, 176
  Catharine, 232
  Charles, 40, 73, 160,
  176
  Charles A., 265
  Daniel, 160, 176
  George, 160, 176,
  184, 232, 240
  Jacob, 98, 160, 176,
  238, 242
  John, 160, 176
  Mary, 98, 242
  Michael, 160, 176,
  238
  Rebecca, 160
  Susan, 160
  Susanna, 176, 238
BARNS, David, 226
  John, 16
  William, 226
BARR, Agnes, 161
  Catharine, 109, 161
  Jacob, 109
  James, 129, 161
  Sarah, 161
BARRINGER,
  Elizabeth, 221
  George, 221
BARTERETT, Daniel,
  70

BASSERMAN,
  Abraham, 144
  Catharine, 144
  Christiana, 144
  Daniel, 144
  Margaret, 144
  Mary, 144
  Peter, 144
  Philip, 144
  Susanna, 144
BATEMAN, Andrew,
  135
  Elizabeth, 135
  Isaac, 135
  Rachel, 135
  Reuben, 135
  William, 135
BAUCHER,
  Catharine, 159
  Frederick, 159
BAUER, Daniel, 267
  Elizabeth, 267
  Martin, 83
  Rosina, 83
BAUGHER, Barbara,
  166
  Catharine, 166
  Christiana, 166
  Elizabeth, 166
  Hannah, 166
  Mary, 166
  Susan, 166
  William, 166
BAUGHMAN, Anna,
  83
  Franey, 83
  Jacob, 83
  John, 83, 252
  Mary, 83, 252
BAUM, Barbara, 189
  Peter, 189
BAUMAN, Anna
  Maria, 174

Barbara, 175
Elizabeth, 174
Eva, 174
Henrich, 175
Jacob, 174, 175
John (Johann), 174
Philip, 174
BAUMGARNER,
  John, 74
  Mary, 74
BAUMGARTNER,
  Henry, 206
  Margaret, 206
BAUP, Evis, 32
  Jacob, 32
BAUSER, Adam, 214
  Andrew, 214
  Benjamin, 214
  Christian, 214
  Daniel, 214
  Elizabeth, 214
  Esther, 214
  Isaac, 214
  Jonas, 214
  Joseph, 214
  Magdalena, 214
  Mary, 214
  Solomon, 214
BAUSMAN, M., 144
BAWCUTT, William,
  81
BAXTER, William, 4,
  136
BAY, Andrew, 11
  Hugh, 11
  John, 124
BAYLY, Elizabeth,
  273
  John, 273
BEACOR, Ann, 96
  Barbara, 96
  Christiana, 96
  Elizabeth, 96

Eve, 96
Frederick, 96
John, 96
Julian, 96
Margaret, 96
Mary, 96
Philip, 96
Rosen, 96
Studebacker, 96
Susanna, 96
BEALER, Jacob, 15
BEALLEY, Joseph, 14
BEALLY, Elizabeth
  Hannah, 14
BEAM, Abraham, 123
  Esther, 123
  Hey, 204
  Magdalena, 204
BEAR, Abee, 229
  Abraham, 32, 80
  Anna, 229
  Barbara, 32, 80, 114
  Benjamin, 229
  Catharine, 238
  Christian, 73
  Daniel, 192, 229
  Elizabeth, 32, 229, 230
  Fornica, 80
  George, 189
  Hannah, 32
  Henry, 32, 80, 229
  Isaac, 269
  Jacob, 49, 55, 80, 229
  John, 32, 80, 238, 269
  Joseph, 102
  Katharine, 229
  Magdalena, 189
  Margaret, 110, 269
  Mary, 32, 80
  Michael, 32, 114, 172
  Moses, 264
  Nancy, 32
  Nicholas, 269
  Philip, 269
  Salome, 32
  Samuel, 32, 80
  Sarah, 32
  Wetzy, 229
  William, 110, 230
BEATTY, Daniel, 129
BEATY, Andrew, 120
  Barbara, 120
  David, 99
  Francis, 6
  Samuel, 19
  Walter, 19
BECHTEL, Barbara, 169
  Samuel, 169
BECHTIL, Samuel, 184
BECK, Ann, 161
  Anna, 157, 158
  Catharine, 161
  Elizabeth, 162
  George, 157, 158
  Jacob, 161, 219
BECKEL, Elizabeth, 211
  Tobias, 211
BECKER, Adam, 74
  Ann, 148, 155
  Anna, 74
  Barbara, 148
  Catharine, 25, 38, 148, 233, 239, 262, 267, 273
  Christiana, 273
  Conrad, 38, 47, 148
  Daniel, 25
  Elizabeth, 25, 148, 217, 233, 239, 262, 273
  Eva, 217
  Eve, 84, 148, 262
  Frederick, 74, 239
  George, 25
  Grabill, 239
  Henry, 84, 217, 239
  Jacob, 148, 217, 243, 262
  John, 25, 74, 84, 148, 262, 267, 273
  John Adam, 74
  Leadia, 217
  Magdalina, 148
  Margaret, 148, 262, 273
  Mary, 84, 148
  Mathias, 148, 217
  Peter, 148, 155, 273
  Philip, 148, 233, 262, 267
  Polly, 217
  Rosana, 217
  Samuel, 148
  Simon, 84
  Susanna, 25
BECKTEL, Christian, 112
BECTHEL, George, 158
  Mary Ann, 158
  Tobias, 158
BEECHER, Adam, 127
  Catharine, 127
BEECHLEY,
  Christian, 51
BEEK, Burk, 61
  Magdelina, 61
BEEKAR, Adolph, 92
  Anna, 92
  Catharine, 92
  Christiana, 92
  Christopher, 92

Coleman, 92
George, 92
Peter, 92
William, 92
BEEKER, John, 84, 270
Michael, 187
BEHLER, Catharine, 146
Jacob, 146
BEIDLE, Ann, 117
Barbara, 117
Freney, 117
BEIGHTELY,
Christian, 10
Martha, 10
Martin, 10
Samuel, 10
BEITLER, Ann, 30
Barbara, 30
Daniel, 30
Jacob, 30
John, 30
BEITZEL, Anna Eliza, 146
Barbara, 146
Benj., 250
Benjamin, 244
Christian, 146
Elizabeth, 146, 244, 250
John, 146, 244
Jonathan, 146, 244
Lorence, 146
Louisa, 146
Magdalena, 146, 244
Margaret, 146
BELK, George, 157
BELLER, Michael, 41
BELTZ, Barbara, 274
Catharine, 274
Eleanor, 274
Elizabeth, 274

Jacob, 118, 128, 274
Philip, 274
Susan, 274
BELY, Eva, 237
George, 237
Jacob, 237
John, 237
Margaret, 237
Rosina, 237
Susanna, 237
BENCE, Caty, 201
David, 201
Elizabeth, 201
George, 201
Henry, 201
Jacob, 201
John, 201
Mary, 201
Philibbina, 201
Susanna, 201
BENDER, Catharine, 99, 121
Conrad, 99, 129
Elizabeth, 99
Henry, 99
Jacob, 99
John, 99, 121
Martin, 160
Mary, 99
Michael, 99
Peter, 160
BENEDICK, John, 238
Juliana, 238
BENEDICT,
Catharine, 86, 257
David, 257
Elizabeth, 228, 257
George, 228, 257
John, 257
Lydia, 257
Margaret, 257
Melchoir, 86

Philip, 257
Samuel, 257
Susanna, 257
BENGHAM, Hugh, 138
John, 138
Thomas, 138
William, 138
Zearr, 138
BENLER, Jacob, 146
BENNER, Adam, 6
Anna, 6
Anna Mary, 6
Barbara, 6
Elizabeth, 6
Eve, 6
Henry, 6
Mary, 6
Philip, 6
BENODT, Catharine, 58
Francis, 58
Henry, 58
Jacob, 58
John, 58
Marials, 58
Mary, 58
BENSEL, Casper, 221
Elizabeth, 221
Jacob, 221
John, 221
Susanna, 221
BENSYL, Casper, 120
Elizabeth, 120
Jacob, 120
Julius, 120
Philip, 120
BENTS, Catharine, 191
BENTZ, Andrew, 226
Anna, 80, 156, 208
Anna Maria, 80, 208
Anna Mary, 156

Barnet, 208
Catharine, 80, 265
Christian, 67, 156
Daniel, 208
Elizabeth, 67, 80,
  156, 208, 226, 265
Frederick, 258
George, 208
Henry, 67
Jacob, 80, 141, 208,
  265
John, 208
Lizzie, 80
Margaret, 67, 265
Mary, 141
Mary Elizabeth, 67
Michael, 265
Peter, 67, 80, 156,
  265
Philip, 67
Polly, 208
Rosina, 67
Salome, 156
Susanna, 80, 156
Ursula, 80, 156
Weerick, 214
Weirick, 206
Whyrich, 80
Whyrick, 156
William, 208
BENTZEL, Barbara,
  56
  Henry, 56
  Johannes, 29
  Sophia, 29
BEON, Mary, 3
BERD, A., 73
  Adam, 166
  George, 166
BEREAU, John, 146
BEREENOUR,
  Anthony, 181
  Barbara, 181

BERGER, Andrew,
  120
  Barbara, 120
  Catharine, 120
  Valentine, 120
BERGHEIMER,
  Caroline, 235
  Henry, 219, 235
  Susanna, 209, 219
  Valentine, 209, 219,
    235
BERKEY, Michael, 33
BERLIN, Ann
  Margaretta, 122
  Catharine, 123
  Christiana, 123
  Frederick, 122
  Jacob, 122
  Nicholas, 122
  Nicolas, 122
BERTH, Michael, 129
  Susanna, 129
BETTINGER,
  Margaret, 20
  Nicholas, 20
BETTY, Samuel, 6
  Walter, 6
  William, 6
BETY, Benjamin, 154
  Elizabeth, 154
  Esther, 154
  Jane, 154
  John, 154
  Lilly, 154
  Margaret, 154
  Mary, 154
  Rachel, 154
  Samuel, 154
  Sarah, 154
  Susanna, 154
  William, 154
BETZ, Elizabeth, 119
  John, 119

BETZEL, John, 198
BEVERSON, Conrad,
  261
BEYER, Catharine,
  214
  John, 135, 214
BICKELER,
  Magdalena, 212
BICKLE, Elizabeth,
  31
  Frederick, 31
  Hannah, 31
  Juliana, 31
  Magdalena, 31
BIEDMYER, Nicholas,
  62
BIEHL, Jacob, 175
BIERER, Barbara, 35
  Conrad, 35
BIGGORS, William, 16
BIGHAM, Abraham,
  169
  Agness, 156
  Byran, 156
  Eleanor, 156
  Eve, 169
  Hugh, 156
  Mary, 156
  Patrick, 156
  Robert, 90, 169
  Samuel, 156, 169
  Thomas, 90
  William, 167, 169
BIGLER, Barbara, 131
  Jacob, 131
  Joseph, 131
  Matalina, 131
  Suvia, 131
BIKEL, Elizabeth, 89
  Francis, 89
  Hannah, 89
  John, 89
  Juliana, 89

Magdalena, 89
BILLET, Eve, 225
Jacob, 225
Magdalena, 225
BILLINGER, Andrew, 69
Jacob, 69
John, 183
Michael, 69
BILLMEYER, Andrew, 99
BILLMYER, Andrew, 204
Ann, 204
Elizabeth, 204
Helena, 204
Michael, 204
Rosina, 204
BILMYER, Jacob, 7
BINDER, Catharine, 213
John, 213
BINGEL, Barbara, 106
Leonard, 106
BINGHAM, Elizabeth, 54
Hugh, 54
Mary, 54
Robert, 54
Samuel, 54
William, 54
BISEL, Abraham, 217
BISHOP, Hannah, 67
Nicholas, 67
BISKING, Casper, 32
Catharine, 32
Henry, 32
Jacob, 32
John, 32
Mary, 32
BITNER, Adam, 213
Catharine, 213

BITTLE, Eve, 60
George, 60
Margaret, 60
Salome, 60
Thomas, 60
BITZEL, Catharine, 145
Lawrence, 145
BIX, Christian, 2
BIXLER, Abraham, 192
Anna, 237
Catharine, 153
Christian, 153
Christley, 124
Conrad, 153
Elizabeth, 19, 153
Eve, 153
Ferena, 145
Jacob, 19, 124, 153, 227
John, 19, 124, 153, 169, 192, 237
Jose, 124
Joseph, 145, 153, 169
Magdalena, 153, 175
Maria, 237
Mary, 19, 192
Michael, 153, 175
Samuel, 19
Susanna, 124, 227
BLACK, Adam, 53
Ann, 174
Anna, 159
David, 54
Elizabeth, 54, 159
Henry, 159, 174, 175
James, 4, 55, 174, 175
Jane, 54
John, 3, 4, 54
Jordon, 54
Mary, 4, 135, 159

Mathew, 4
Michael, 33
Rachel, 174
Robert, 54, 135, 174
Sarah, 54, 159, 174
Spiner, 54
Thomas, 183
William, 3, 4
BLACKBURN, Abigal, 28
Agness, 110
Alexander, 64, 67, 110
Alice, 147
Anthony, 28
Deborah, 139
Eleanor, 28
Hannah, 110
James, 110
John, 54, 63, 110, 147
Joseph, 28, 139
Mary, 110
Sarah, 64, 67, 110
Thomas, 28, 147
William, 110
BLACKFORD, Elizabeth, 136
Joseph, 136
BLAIR, Anna, 93
Barbara, 93
Brice, 180
Brise, 93
Eleanor, 93
James, 93, 180
Jane, 93, 180
John, 52, 93, 180
John Brise, 93
Mary, 93
Susanna, 93
BLASSER, Abraham, 10
Ann, 175

Barbara, 175
Catharine, 175
Harman, 226
John, 219
Magdalena, 175
Mathias, 175
Nicholas, 175
Peter, 175, 226
Philip, 175
Susanna, 175
BLECHHARD,
  Andrew, 38
  Sophia, 38
BLEIMEYER,
  Abraham, 267
  Catharine, 267
BLICK, Henry, 7
BLINZINGER, Lancy, 263
BLYTHE, David, 146
BOB, Catharine, 166
  Elizabeth, 51
  James, 51
  Jannet, 51
  Jenette, 51
  John, 51
  Ludwig, 160
  Peter, 166
  Robert, 51
  Thomas, 51
BOBB, Barbara, 206
  Bernard, 206
  Eve, 206
  Gertrude, 206
  Henry, 206
  John, 206
  Ludwig, 206
  Margaret, 206
  Michael, 206
BODENHIMER,
  Mary, 84
BODINE, Abraham, 100

John, 99, 100
Leine, 99
Lume, 100
BOERSTLER, Anna, 242
Lawrence, 242
BOGLE, Alexander, 178, 179
  Elizabeth, 179
  Joseph, 23
  Malcolm, 178
  William, 149, 178, 179
BOHLY, Daniel, 231
  Rosina, 231
BOHMER, Henry, 109
BOHN, Anna, 200
  Catharine, 200
  Elizabeth, 200
  Jacob, 200
  Ludwig, 200
  Margaret, 201
  Nicholas, 200
BOLEN, Elizabeth, 124
BOLLINGER,
  Abraham, 1
  Anna Mary, 1
  Catharine, 1
  Christian, 1
  Elizabeth, 87
  Eva, 1
  Frederick, 1
  Isaac, 1
  Jacob, 1
  John, 87, 270
  Michael, 1
BOLSHOR, Anna, 264
BOLT, Catharine, 137
  Christiana, 137
  Elizabeth, 137
  Jonas, 137
  Peter, 137

Susan, 137
BOLTON, Elizabeth, 263
  James, 159, 168
  John, 263
BONDABUSH,
  Henry, 25
BONHAM, James, 272
BONINE, Daniel, 83, 94
  Elizabeth, 83
  James, 83
  Mary, 94
  Sarah, 163
  Thomas, 83, 94
BOOSE, Jacob, 222
BOPE, Adam, 142
  Burkhardt, 142
  John, 142
  Ludwick, 142
  Mathias, 142
BOPP, Catharine, 216
  Elizabeth, 216
  Mary, 216
  Peter, 216
BORGER, Frederick, 274
BORHAF, Eva, 151
  Henry, 151
BORHECK, Andrew, 97
  Anna, 97
BOSERMAN,
  Christian, 49
  Michael, 49
BOSERT, Catharine, 191
  Sal, 191
BOSLER, Fornica, 26
  Frederick, 26
  Ulerick, 26
  Veronica, 65
BOSS, Ann, 145

Barbara, 247
Barnet, 247
Catharine, 247
Christiana, 247
Elizabeth, 247
Eve, 135, 247
John, 135
Peter, 145
BOSSERT, Jacob,
 213, 225
BOTE, Ludwig, 161
BOTT, Adelia, 37
 Barbara, 124, 142,
  205
 Cookas, 37
 George, 124, 142
 Herman, 37
 Jacob, 30, 37, 55
 Ludwig, 206
 Mary, 142
 Mary Elizabeth, 124,
  205
 Reinhard, 37
 Reinhart, 109, 124
BOTTENFELD,
 Philip, 207
BOTTENFIELD,
 Adam, 32
BOUMGARTNER,
 Thomas, 208
BOVHAR, Nicholas,
 51
BOWEN, David, 178
 Jane, 178
 John, 178
 Jonathan, 178
 Lydia, 178
 Rachel, 178
 Sarah, 178
 Thomas, 178
 William, 178
BOWER, Abraham,
 148

Barbara, 220
Benjamin, 154
Catharine, 87, 205
Christiana, 215
Christopher, 215
Daniel, 194
Elizabeth, 194
Eve, 215
Frederick, 73
George, 73, 125
George Adam, 215
Henry, 87, 194, 215
Infarth, 220
Isaac, 194
Jacob, 215, 270
John, 194, 215
Joseph, 205
Martin, 215
Mary, 194
Michael, 125, 194
Samuel, 194
Sarah, 194
Susanna, 194, 270
BOWERRAX, John,
 230
 Margaret, 230
BOWMAN, Hy, 174
 John, 174
 Margaret, 79
 William, 79
BOWSER, Mathias, 34
BOYARD, Catharine,
 248
 Elizabeth, 248
 Frederick, 248
 George, 248
 John, 248
 Mary, 248
 Mathias, 248
BOYD, Agness, 194
 Ann, 34, 158
 Archibald, 95
 Benjamin, 95

Catharine, 45, 49,
 55, 95, 158
Elizabeth, 34, 95
George, 34, 158
Isabella, 24
James, 24, 158, 194
Jane, 34, 55, 158
Janet, 27, 95
John, 34, 95
Margaret, 2, 24, 55
Mary, 2, 27, 95
Moses, 24, 55
Rachel, 158
Robert, 24, 95
Samuel, 5, 24, 34
Sarah, 34, 55
William, 2, 24, 34,
 49, 95
BOYER, Barbara, 237
 Benjamin, 221
 Christian, 221, 237
 Daniel, 221, 237
 Elizabeth, 221
 George, 263
 Henry, 221, 237
 John, 221, 224, 237
 Magdalena, 221, 237
 Maria, 263
 Susanna, 221
BRACKBILL,
 Benjamin, 82
BRACKEN, Caleb, 59
 Hannah, 67
 James, 59, 67
 Jean, 67
 John, 67
 Margaret, 67
 Martha, 67
 Mary, 59, 67
 Thomas, 59, 67
 William, 67
BRACKON, Christian,
 74

Elizabeth, 74
John, 74
Margaret, 74
Martha, 74
Mary, 74
Thomas, 74
BRADLEE, Thomas W., 237
BRADLEY, Caty, 246
Jacob, 246
James, 156
Joseph, 176
Katharine, 156
Mary, 176
BRADLY, John, 5
BRAND, Adam, 198, 217
BRANDAGE,
  Catharine, 194
  Joseph, 194
BRANDON,
  Alexander, 44
  Elizabeth, 140
  George, 140
  James, 44, 140
  Jane, 140
  John, 18, 44
  Joseph, 44
  Mary, 18, 44, 139
  Richard, 18, 44
  Thomas, 44, 140
  Walter, 44
  William, 44
BRANDT, Anna, 212
  Mary, 242
BRANEMAN,
  Benjamin, 218
  Joseph, 218
  Mary, 104
  Samuel, 218
  Wilhelm, 218
  William, 104
BRAUIN, Catharine, 152
  Christiana, 152
  Jacob, 152
BREADY, Ann, 34
BREASSEL, Michael, 33
BREDEN, Elizabeth, 125
  James, 125
  Walter, 125
BREEDERLINE,
  Charles, 48
  Elizabeth, 48
BREHM, Breshen, 145
  Catharine, 145
  Esther, 180
  Henry, 145
  Jacob, 145
  Magdalena, 180
  Samuel, 145, 180
BREIGNER, Barbara, 105
BREMMER, Peter Wine, 111
BRENEMIN,
  Catharine, 233
  Jacob, 233
BRENISE, Catharine, 268
  Elizabeth, 268
  John, 268
  Lydia, 268
  William, 268
BRENNEISSY,
  Catharine, 148
  John, 148
BRENNER, Adam, 80
  Anna Maria, 80
  Frederick, 166
BRESSEL, David, 105
  Henry, 25
BREWA, Catharine, 196
  Daniel, 196
BRICKER, Agness, 242
  Ann, 93
  Anna Mary, 193
  Christopher, 93
  Jacob, 93, 193, 242
  John, 242
  Joseph, 242
  Juliana, 93
  Margaret, 93
  Nicholas, 193
BRICKNER,
  Catharine, 203
  Elizabeth, 203
  Emanuel, 203
  John, 203
  Joseph, 203
  Kaleb, 203
  Mary, 203
  Peter, 203
BRILHART, Christian, 219
BRILINGER,
  Catharine, 239
  John, 239
BRILLHARDT, Anna, 104
  Christian, 104
  David, 104
  Johanna, 104
  Joseph, 104
  Richard, 104
  Sarah, 104
  William, 104
BRILLHART, Anna, 78
  Barbara, 78
  Cary, 10
  Christian, 78
  David, 231
  Elizabeth, 78, 231
  Eve, 78

Jacob, 78, 197, 231
John, 78
Margaret, 231
Mary, 78
Peter, 10, 75, 78,
  115, 126, 197, 231,
  254
Samuel, 231
BRILLINGER, John,
  187, 188, 197, 251
BRINGMAN,
  Catharine, 150
  Frederick, 150
  John, 150
BRINKELHOF,
  James, 78
BRISSEL, Elizabeth,
  25
BROADENHEIMER,
  Alse, 114
  Ann, 114
  Christiana, 114
  Eve, 114
  Handiel, 114
  Jacob, 114
  John, 114
  Mary, 114
  William, 114
BROBECK, Catharine,
  165
  Mathias, 165
BROCA, Abraham, 99
  Jane, 99
BROKAW, Abraham,
  146
  Ann, 146
  George, 146
  John, 146
  Lena, 146
  Margaret, 146
  Mary, 146
  Peter, 146
BROOK, Ann, 264

Nancy, 264
Susan, 264
BROOKS, Elizabeth,
  247
  William, 247
BROTHBECK, Ann,
  183
  Barbara, 183
  Catharine, 183
  Christian, 183
  Elizabeth, 183
  John, 183
  Magdalena, 183
  Margaret, 183
  Zacharius, 183
BROUGH, Christiana,
  181
  Herman, 181
BROUSTER, Ann, 44
  John, 44
  Joseph, 32
  Margaret, 44
  Mary, 32, 44
  William, 44
BROWN, Agness, 104,
  113, 154
  Alexander, 25, 81
  Andrew, 182
  Ann, 182
  Anna Mary, 204
  Barbara, 213
  Benj., 104
  Catharine, 182, 204,
   235
  Daniel, 144, 210
  David, 144, 204
  Elizabeth, 118, 140,
   152
  George, 2, 37, 128,
   140
  James, 118, 160, 268
  John, 128, 140, 152,
   158, 160, 182, 268

Joseph, 79
Magdalena, 204
Margaret, 182, 268
Martha, 79, 182
Mary, 79, 118, 128,
  158
Mathias, 204, 213
Phebe, 128, 158
Rebecca, 79
Richard, 11, 160
Robert, 182
Sarah, 79, 158, 182
Sebastian, 204
Stoman, 235
Susanna, 118, 144,
  160, 210
Thomas, 118
Wiliam, 118
William, 72, 160
BRUBACHER, Ann,
  202
  Catharine, 261
  Christiana, 261
  Conrad, 260, 261
  Daniel, 261
  Dietrich, 202
  Elizabeth, 260
  Helen, 261
  John, 202, 261
  Mary, 202
  Rebecca, 261
  Veronica, 202
BRUBAKER, Anna,
  216, 251
  Catharine, 225
  Conrad, 19, 82, 225
  Deitrich, 177
  Deitrick, 207
  Detrick, 112
  Dietrich, 123
  Freny, 251
  Jacob, 88
  John, 216

BRUCKHARD,
  Barbara, 47
  Jacob, 47
  John, 47
  Magdalena, 47
  Michael, 47
  Philip, 47
BRUGH, Jacob, 153
  Sophia, 153
BRUNKHARD, Jacob, 94
BRUNNER, Christian, 139
  Henry, 139
BRUNTER, John, 113
BRUSE, Jane, 34
  William, 34
BRUSKHART,
  Margaret, 205
BRUTHER, Francy, 47
  Henry, 47
BRWEE, Mary, 162
  Paul, 162
BUCHANAN,
  Andrew, 147, 225
  Ann, 111, 114
  Anna, 84, 114
  Barbara, 84
  David, 114
  Ebeneser, 225
  Elizabeth, 111, 147
  Eva, 114
  Eva Mary, 114
  Fornica, 84
  Frederick, 114
  George, 225
  Jacob, 84
  James, 39, 47, 111, 225
  Jane, 225
  Jennet, 111
  John, 39, 84, 225
  Margaret, 23, 47, 111, 225
  Martha, 225
  Mary, 84, 111
  McCarrel, 39
  Nancy, 225
  Robert, 111
  Simpson, 39
  Thomas, 225
  Walter, 111
  William, 45, 111, 197, 225
BUCHANNAN,
  Elizabeth, 18
  James, 18
  Jane, 18
  Margaret, 18
  Thomas, 18
  William, 18
BUCHER, Adam, 169
  Anna, 169
  Elizabeth, 143
  Michael, 143
BUCHNAAN, James, 197
BUCKER, Christian, 211
  Elizabeth, 211
BUCKLER, David, 272
BUDISELL, John, 70
BULL, Eliza, 263
  Elizabeth, 263
  John, 167, 170, 263
  Mary, 253
  Richard, 253, 263, 275
  Ross, 263
  Sarah, 263
BUNTIN, John, 43
  Mary, 43
  Rachel, 43
  Thomas, 43

BURCHART, Julius, 138
BURGER, Elizabeth, 48
  George, 48
  Margaret, 48
  Mathias, 48
BURK, Catharine, 249
  George, 249
  Henry, 249
  John, 249
BURKHOLDER,
  Abraham, 168
  Barbara, 131
  Cabien, 206
  Catharine, 168, 206
  Christian, 217
  Elizabeth, 131, 168
  Frederick, 217
  Hannah, 131
  Henry, 131
  Jacob, 131
  John, 131
  Mary, 131
  Rachel, 131
  Sarah, 131
  William, 217
BURN, Betsy, 217
  Francis, 217
  Joseph, 217
BURNHART,
  Catharine, 103
  Jacob, 103
BURNS, Barbara, 40
  John, 40
BUSCKSLER, Anna, 253
  Christian, 253
  Conrad, 253
  Elizabeth, 253
  John, 253
  Magdalena, 253
BUSEL, Elizabeth,

230
Magdalena, 230
Margaret, 230
Thomas, 230
BUSH, Anna, 72
Barara, 72
Barbara, 183
Catharine, 72, 183
Christiana, 72
Elizabeth, 72, 183, 213
George, 183
Henry, 183, 213
Herman, 183
Jacob, 72
Jieleana, 72
John, 72, 183
Mary, 183
Mathias, 183
Peter, 183
Rosina, 72
Susanna, 183
BUSHANGIN, John, 48
BUSHEY, Henry, 201
Susanna, 201
BUSHONG,
Elizabeth, 36
John, 36, 50
BUSS, Elizabeth, 155, 156, 230
Jacob, 155
John, 155, 230
Mary, 155
Peter, 153, 155
BUTLER, John, 222
Margaret, 28
Mary, 28, 81
Philip, 266
Sarah, 28, 81, 266
Thomas, 27, 28
BUTT, Rienhart, 35
BUVER, Jacob, 225

BWEHER, Anne, 150
Nicholas, 150
BYER, Barara, 123
David, 123
Elizabeth, 53
Esther, 123
George, 53
Henry, 53
Jacob, 53
John, 53, 123
Jonas, 123
Margaret, 53
Mary, 53, 123
Peter, 53
Philip, 53
Samuel, 123
Treat, 53
BYERLY, Conrad, 245
Magdalena, 245
BYERMISTER, Anna, 159
Christiana, 160
Christopher, 159
Elizabeth, 160
Frederick, 159
BYERS, Andrew, 170
Elizabeth, 170
Esther, 170
James, 170
John, 170, 235
Margaret, 170
Martha, 170
Rachel, 170
Samuel, 170
William, 170

-C-
CABELL, Abraham, 65
Barbara, 65
Benjamin, 65
Jacob, 65
Mary, 65

Philip, 65
Salome, 65
CADWALADER,
David, 184
James, 92, 184
Margaret, 184
Mary, 184
CADWALEDER,
David, 219
Elizabeth, 219
CALDWELL,
Catharine, 60
Elizabeth, 60
Hugh, 101
Isabell, 60
James, 11
Jane, 101
Janet, 60
Jean, 60
Martha, 60
Mary, 60
Robert, 60
William, 60
William Hall, 101
CAMBEL, Elizabeth, 6
Janet, 6
John, 6
Marthon, 6
Thomas, 5
CAMPBEL, Archibald, 91
John, 91
Thomas, 91
CAMPBELL, Adam, 48
Agnes, 128
Alexander, 169, 170
Ann, 11, 48, 235
Anna, 48
Armstrong, 170
Charles, 48
Daniel, 222, 266
Donnal, 222

Elizabeth, 11, 222,
266
Esther, 222
George, 54
Hugh, 169
Isabella, 54
James, 48, 222, 266
Jane, 11
Janet, 54
Jennet, 128
John, 11, 48, 128,
222
Joseph, 235
Margaret, 54, 170
Marrion, 54
Martha, 11
Mary, 11, 170, 222
Rebecca, 170, 222
Robert, 148, 170, 171
Sally, 222
Thomas, 11, 132
William, 11, 48
CANDLER, Catharine,
184
David, 184
CANNON, Agness, 30
Elizabeth, 30
Hannah, 30
Jane, 30
John, 30
Mary, 30
Robert, 30
Samuel, 30
Thomas, 30
William, 30
CARETHERS,
Armstrong, 151
Elizabeth, 151
CARITHERS, Agness,
44
James, 44
CARL, Michael, 35,
113

CARLE, Michael, 18,
94
CARSON, Ann, 4
David, 14
Elizabeth, 14
George, 14
Janeat, 14
Janet, 57
John, 14, 57
Mary, 4
Rachel, 4
Robert, 57
Samuel, 14
Sarah, 73
William, 4, 14, 18
CARTER, Bushell, 251
CARUTHERS,
Andrew, 117
James, 117
Jean, 117
John, 117
Thomas, 117
CASPER, Adam, 102
CASSART, D., 265
David, 152
Sarah, 152
CASSAT, Daniel, 264
Francis, 99
CASSET, Jacob, 211
Margaret, 211
CASTER, Maria, 266
CATHCART, Robert,
215, 219, 241, 273
CAVEN, John, 95
Mary, 95
CAVIN, Alexander, 49
Elizabeth, 49
Fergus, 49
James, 49
Jean, 49
John, 49
CAYLER, Daniel, 99
Elizabeth, 98

CEARSON, William,
41
CESSENHOWER,
Elizabeth, 188
Leonard, 188
CESSNA, John, 5
Priscella, 5
CESTER, Robert, 79
CHALMERS, William,
78
CHAMBERLIN, J., 82
James, 49, 133
Jeremiah, 49
John, 49
Margaret, 49
Martha, 49
Nemen, 49
CHAMBERS, Agness,
94
Arthur, 94
Catharine, 178
Henry, 94, 178
Jacob, 178
James, 94
John, 94, 178, 259
Mary, 217
Rachel, 178
Robert, 94
Roland, 94
Rosana, 178
Solomon, 178
CHAPMAN, Mary,
171
William, 171
CHARLES, George,
176
CHESNEY, Elizabeth,
78
William, 78
CHESTER, Elizabeth,
119, 230, 258
James, 119
John, 119

Mary, 119
Richard, 119, 230, 258
Robert Johnson, 111
Robert Johnston, 119
William, 119
CHILDER, John, 262
Margaret, 262
CHILICOAT, Juliana, 245
William, 245
CHRIST, Adam, 102
Elizabeth, 150
John, 102
Leonard, 36
Maria, 36
Maria Magdalena, 36
Philip, 102, 150
CHURCH, Andrew, 138
Elizabeth, 138
CINAGAN, Charles, 51
CLACK, Martin, 217
CLAPSADDLE,
George, 157
Solome, 157
CLAPSADLE,
Barbara, 102
Catharine, 102
Catin, 160
Daniel, 102
Francis, 102
George, 102
Mary, 102
Michael, 27, 102, 160
Paul, 102
CLARK, Daniel, 32
Eleanor, 14
Elizabeth, 14
Hannah, 14
Henry, 5

Keziah, 32
Margaret, 14
Mary, 14, 52
Matthew, 246
Timothy, 14
CLARKSON, Agness, 229
Andrew, 229
Ephraim, 229
James, 132, 229
John, 229
Susanna, 229
Thomas, 229
CLATFELTER,
Magdalena, 263
CLAY, Nicholas, 2
CLEAR, Simon, 89
CLEAVER, Elizabeth, 153
John, 153
Marian, 153
Peter, 153
Sarah, 153
William, 153
CLEMENTZ, Henry, 171
Sophia, 171
CLIMMER, Elemer, 95
Elizabeth, 95
George, 95
John, 95
Margaret, 95
Susanna, 95
Valentine, 95
CLINE, David, 224
Magdalena, 224
CLINGAN, Catharine, 57
David, 57
Elizabeth, 57, 98
George, 57
Hananh, 57

Margaret, 57
Mary, 57
Thomas, 57, 98
CLINGMAN,
Catharine, 142
Jacob, 142
CLOAS, Christian, 49
CLOGSTON,
Elizabeth, 167
Jane, 167
John, 167
Joseph, 167
Margaret, 167
Mary, 167
Robert, 167
William, 167
CLONINGER,
Barbara, 217
Michael, 217
CLOSE, Christian, 32, 118
COAL, Elizazbeth, 84
Jacob, 131
John, 131
Mary, 131
Michael, 84
COBAR, Baltzer, 29
McArillis, 29
COBB, John, 189
COBEAN, Samuel, 140
COCHRAN, Andrew, 34, 71, 85
Isabella, 106
James, 71, 85
John, 71, 85
Margaret, 34, 71
Mary, 71, 85
Oliver, 85
Phebe, 106
Sarah, 85
William, 85, 87, 106
COFFMAN, Barbara,

10
Jacob, 10
COHOON, John, 6
Rachel, 6
Thomas, 6
COIN, John, 228
COLAR, Baltzer, 188, 189
Christiana, 189
Jacob, 122
COLEMAN, Anna, 225, 273
Conrad, 170
Joseph, 170
Margaret, 170
Valentine, 225, 273
COLLINGS, John, 25
Joseph, 25
Mary, 25
Rose, 25
COLLINGWOOD,
Martha, 254
Richard, 254
Thomas, 254
William, 254
COLLINS, Ann, 241
Elizabeth, 241
Grace, 241
Isabell, 241
John, 241
Samuel, 241
William, 241
COLVER, Ephraim, 57
Magdalena, 57
William, 212
COLVIN, Margaret, 222
Robert, 222, 224
COLWELL, Margaret, 66
COMFORT, Andrew, 118

Henry, 118
Jacob, 118
John, 118
Mary, 118
Mary E., 118
CONAWARE, Martin, 242
CONRAD, Agness, 227
Catharine, 148
Jacob, 227
John, 227
Leah, 224
Martin, 166
Philip, 224
COOK, Ann, 85, 86
David, 189
Elisha, 180, 269
Elizabeth, 106, 210
Hannah, 85, 86, 180
Henry, 269
Isaac, 269
Isreal, 180
Jesse, 85, 210, 269
John, 106, 269
Joseph, 85, 106
Mary, 269
Peter, 85, 86
Rebecca, 86, 180
Ruth, 180
Samuel, 85, 86, 180, 210, 269
Sarah, 85, 86, 180
William, 180
COOKSON, Daniel, 250, 262
COONS, Catharine, 10
Fronica, 10
John, 10
Juliana, 10
COOPER, Adam, 20
Alice, 171
Archibald, 255

Armfield, 168
Christiana Elizabeth, 155
Eccy, 168
Elizabeth, 20, 171, 201, 213
Eve, 20
Finwell, 155
Haggie, 201, 213
Hannah, 44, 171
Isabella, 165
James, 154
Jannet, 155
John, 44, 155, 255
Joshua, 171
Margaret, 20, 255
Mary, 155, 168, 171, 255
Nancy, 255
Nelly, 171
Nicholas, 44, 171
Nieely, 155
Peter, 20
Priscilla, 44, 171
Rachel, 155
Robert, 155
Sarah, 44, 171
Stephen, 168, 171
Thomas, 44, 168
William, 155
COPE, John, 232
Mary, 232
COPELAND,
Elizabeth, 13
COPLAND, Thomas, 13
William, 13
COPPENHAFFER,
Barara, 189
Benjamin, 189
Catharine, 189
Elizabeth, 189
John, 189

Martin, 189
Michael, 189
Simon, 189
COPPENHEFFLER,
  Michael, 236
COPPENHOEFFER,
  Catharine, 148
  Elizabeth, 148
  Valentine, 148
COPPINHOFFER,
  Elizabeth, 120
COPWALT, Jacob,
  213
  Sophia, 213
CORD, Agness, 120
  John, 120
CORREL, Christiana,
  88
  Jacob, 88, 107
  Magdalena, 107
COSINE, Anaty, 99
  Ann, 99
  Cornelius, 99
  Elizabeth, 99
  Garard, 99
  Jane, 99
  John, 99
  Leine, 99
  Mary, 99
COSSINE, Cornelius,
  63
  Elizabeth, 63
  Martinus, 63
  Peter, 63
  Williampe, 63
COUDRY, John, 194
  Leah, 194
COUGH, John, 78
  Ursilla, 78
COULSON, Charles,
  47, 130
  David, 130
  Francis, 130, 235

Jane, 130
John, 130
Jospeh, 5
Mary, 130
Niblock, 130
Rebecca, 130
William, 130, 269
COULTER, Jannet, 86
  John, 86
  Martha, 86
  Mary, 86
  Susanna, 86
COWAN, Alexander,
  73
  Gun, 73
  Henry, 73
  Jenny, 73
  Robert, 73
  Samuel, 73
  William, 73
COWEN, James, 135
  Jean, 135
COWGELL, Alice, 28
  Allen, 28
  Henry, 28
  John, 28
  Lydia, 28
  Rachel, 28
  Sarah, 28
COWLEY, Henry, 162
  Mary, 162
  Thomas, 162
COX, Casper, 198
  Catharine, 198
  Conrad, 55
  Elizabeth, 55, 198
  Emmy, 144
  Jesse, 144
  John, 55, 136
  Joshua, 144
  Naomi, 144
  Susanna, 144
  Thomas, 5

William, 144
COXEN, Casper, 146
COYLE, Daniel, 14
  Margaret, 14
COZINE, Cornelius,
  38
CRAFF, Barbara, 73
  George, 73
  Jacob, 73
  Juliana, 73
  Ludwig, 73
  Margaret, 73
  Mary, 73
CRAIG, Anna, 110
  Bobet, 110
  Elizabeth, 56
  Jean, 110
  John, 110
  Margaret, 56
  Robert, 110
CRAMER, Andrew,
  220, 222
  Anna, 162
  Barbara, 255
  Casandra, 255
  Daniel, 64
  David, 255
  elizabeth, 255
  Eve Elizabeth, 162
  Haefer, 64
  Helfrig, 162
  Henry, 162
  John, 162
  Juliana, 255
  Margaret, 162
  Philip, 162
  Polly, 255
CRASSER, Adam, 102
  Barbara, 102
CRATSELDER, Lelia,
  182
  Mary, 182
CRAWFORD, Edward,

2
Eleanor, 92
Hannah, 62
Hugh, 62
James, 35, 62
John, 35
Margaret, 62
Mary, 62
Robert, 92
William, 62
CREARY, John M., 78
CREIGHTON, Agness, 186
Eleanor, 195
Esther, 186
James, 186
Patty, 186
Robert, 195
CREMER, Abraham, 178
Adam, 178
Andrew, 232
Ann Elizabeth, 178
Catharine, 117, 178
David, 117
Elizabeth, 232
Eve, 178
Jacob, 178
Margaret, 234
Peter, 178, 234
CRIGLO, Elizabeth, 20
John, 20
CROLL, Christian, 12
Clara, 82
Daniel, 82
Elizabeth, 12
Henry, 12
Hubly, 82
John, 12, 82
Magdalena, 82
Mary, 12
Michael, 12

Philip, 12
Susanna, 82
CROMBACH,
Barbara, 59
George, 59
CROMBAUCH,
Barbara, 154
CRON, Barbara, 14
Elizabeth, 14
Henrich, 14
Henry, 14
John, 63
CRONBAEK,
Christiana, 160
Elizabeth, 160
George, 160
Henry, 160
Jacob, 160
John, 160
Philip, 160
CRONE, Benjamin, 261
Catharine, 261
Christian, 198
Christiana, 203
Daniel, 198
David, 198, 261
Elizabeth, 261
George, 198, 261
Jacob, 261
John, 200, 203
John Philip, 198
Katharine, 198
Leah, 261
Lorentz, 34
Mary, 198
Mary Elizabeth, 198
Rosanna, 34
Sally, 261
Susanna, 198, 261
CRONEBAUGH,
Elizabeth, 42
Eve, 42

George, 42
Henry, 42
Jacob, 42
Peter, 42
Philip, 42
CRONEMILLER, Ann E., 50
Anna Elizabeth, 32
Dorothea, 32
George, 32
Jacob, 32
John, 32
Martin, 32
Philip, 32
Thomas, 32
CRONESTER,
Barbara, 74
Conrad, 74
Elizabeth, 74
John, 74
Mary, 74
Susanna, 74
CRONMILLER,
Barbara, 118
Martin, 118
CROSBY, David, 191
James, 190
John, 191
Mary, 191
Rachel, 191
Sarah, 191
William, 191
CROSE, Catharine, 238
CROSS, Catharine, 202
George, 202
Henry, 271
James, 225, 226, 232, 271
Jane, 271
John, 193, 271
Randall, 271

Sarah, 271
Thomas, 1
CROUSTER, J., 10
  Metzel, 10
  Y., 10
CROW, Alexander, 91
  Catharine, 92
  Elizabeth, 91
  Leonard, 91
  Michael, 91
  Susanna, 91
CROWELL, Anna, 59
  Anna Maria, 59
  Catharine, 59
  Conrad, 59
  George, 59
  Henry, 59
  Michael, 59
  Peter, 59
  William, 59
CROZLY, Elizabeth, 191
  John, 191
CUIN, Barbara, 155
  Charles, 155
CULLY, John, 39
  Mary, 39
  Thomas, 39
  William, 39
CULP, Madlene, 90
  magdalena, 90
CUMINS, Elen, 91
  Hugh, 91
CUMMINS, Jane, 214
  John, 214
  Rebecca, 214
  Samuel, 214
  William, 214
CUNKERLAND, Adam, 49
  Catharine, 49
CUNNINGHAM, Ambrose, 191, 222

Ann, 191
Benajamin, 191
Elizabeth, 191
Hugh, 191
Jean, 191
Joseph, 191
Lates, 191
Lydia, 222
Mary, 191
Robert, 136
Samuel, 191
Sarah, 191
CURRAN, John, 15
CURRY, Ann, 76
  Elinor, 76
  Francis, 76
  Mary, 76
CUTHBERTSON, Allen, 82
  Lettis, 82
  Nancy, 82
  Rosanna, 82
  William, 82

-D-
DAKIN, Dorothea, 24
  George, 24
  John, 24
  Mary, 24
DALMAN, Ann, 48
  Henry, 48
  John, 48
  Rejena, 48
DALPH, Frederick, 238
  Margaret, 238
DANNER, Abraham, 208, 218, 265
  Anna, 243
  Catharine, 218
  David, 243, 262
  Elizabeth, 218, 243
  Henry, 82, 116, 118,

123, 136, 243
  Jacob, 10
  Leah, 243
  Margaret, 159
  Martin, 218
  Michael, 8, 17, 48, 35
  Philip, 159
  Rachel, 243
  Solome, 243
DAPPER, Andrew, 116
  Christian, 116
  Elizabeth, 116
  John, 116
  Magdalena, 116
  Maria, 116
DARBY, Barbara, 12
  Elizabeth, 12
  George, 41
  James, 12
  John, 12
  Margaret, 12
  Mary, 12
DARON, Adam, 232
  Barbara, 232
  George, 232
  Henry, 232
  Jacob, 232
  John, 232
  Michael, 232
  Philip, 232
DARR, Frederick, 210
  Lydia, 210
DAVIS, Anna, 17
  Anne, 219
  Barbara, 216
  Elizabeth, 219
  Francis, 27
  Hannah, 219
  Jacob, 216
  James, 11
  John, 11, 219
  Mary, 11

Robert, 219
Thomas, 17
Walter, 11
William, 17
DAVISON, Bleam, 110
Eleanor, 33
James, 33, 110
John, 33
Olivia, 33
Peter, 110
Sarah, 33, 110
Thomas, 110
William, 33, 164
DAVON, George, 230
Margaret, 230
DAVY, Ann, 42
George, 42
John, 42
Jonathan, 42
Mary, 42
Rachel, 42
Samuel, 42
DAY, Ann, 191, 204
Anne, 170
Elizabeth, 242
George, 191, 204
Isabella, 170, 191, 204
John, 14, 191, 204
Joseph, 14
Leah, 207
Philip, 242
Rachel, 207
Rebecca, 14, 191, 204
Samuel, 14, 170, 191
Silvina, 14
Solomon, 14
Stephen, 14
Thomas, 14
DEAN, Hans, 6
Jennet, 6
DEARDOFF, Peter, 48, 85

DEARDORF,
Anthony, 113
Caty, 113
John, 113
Mary, 113
Peter, 78, 113
DEARDORFF,
Abraham, 49, 165
Andrew, 181
Ann, 234
Ann Mary, 181
Anna, 192
Anthony, 49, 153, 181, 210
Barbara, 49
Catharine, 49, 181
Christiana, 49, 181
Daniel, 49, 165, 210
David, 210
Elizabeth, 165, 210
Eve, 173
Hannah, 49, 165
Henry, 163, 165, 211, 234
Ira, 234
Isaac, 92, 94, 165, 173
Jacob, 165, 234
John, 49, 165, 176, 210, 211, 267
Jonas, 234
Joseph, 210, 234
Margaret, 49
Mary, 153, 165, 210, 234
Molly, 210
Paul, 181
Peter, 165, 181
Rebecca, 165, 234
Sally, 92
Samuel, 165, 210
Sarah, 165
Susanna, 49, 210

DEATS, George, 34, 139
Magdalena, 34
DEBELLEOWE, Le Brown, 81
DECKART, Elizabeth, 80
Peter, 80
DECKER, Henry, 113
Maria, 113
Mary, 166
Philip, 166, 195
DEEL, Christiana, 144
Jacob, 144
DEELL, Adam, 7
Correll, 7
Daniel, 7
Englis, 7
Evagreda, 7
George, 7
Maria, 7
Mary Catharine, 7
Nicholas, 7
Peter, 7
DEEPSON, James, 108
Margaret, 108
DEERDORF, David, 232
Elizabeth, 232
DEGAN, Elizabeth, 126
John, 126
DEGOMA, Adam, 35
DEGROFF, Abraham, 141
Ann, 141
Catharine, 141
Elizabeth, 141
Esther, 141
Hannah, 141
James, 141
Margaret, 141

Michael, 141
Moses, 141
Nelly, 141
Rachel, 141
Richard, 141
Samuel, 141
William, 141
DEGROSCH, John, 9
  Marilis, 9
DEHOFF, Catharine, 94
  George, 94
  Nicholas, 94
DEHUFF, Barbara, 226
  Catharine, 226
  Christian, 226
  Christiana, 226
  Elizabeth, 226
  George, 226
  Jacob, 226
  John, 226
  Philip, 226
  Susanna, 226
DEITCH, Eve, 116
  Hartman, 116
  Margaret, 116
  Philip, 116
DEITRICH, Jacob, 130
  Margaret, 130
DEITZ, George, 145
  Jacob, 213
DELAP, Catharine, 166
  Robert, 133, 166
  William, 22, 77, 87
DELL, Eizabeth, 208
  Nicholas, 208
DELLINGER,
  Barbara, 86
  Jacob, 86
  John, 86

DELLONE, Michael, 189
DELLOWN, Barbara, 181
  Catharine, 181
  Elizabeth, 181
  Hannah, 181
  Margaretta, 181
  Maria, 181
  Nicholas, 181
DEMERCE, Daniel, 145
  Elizabeth, 145
DEMORE, David, 151
DENBINER,
  Christiana, 86
DENERN, John, 266
DENTZLER,
  Frederick, 40
  Gertrude, 40
DENWODY, David, 52, 82
  Hugh, 52
  James, 52
  Jean, 52
  John, 52
  Robert, 52
  Ronana, 52
DENWOODY, Agness, 77
  Francis, 77
  Joseph, 77
  Sarah, 77
DERR, John, 178
DERRES, Benjamin, 188
  John, 188
DERRINGER, Kilian, 225
  Susanna, 225
DERRIS, Elizabeth, 124
  John, 124

DERSTEEN, Michael, 166
  Susanna, 166
DERSTEIN, Barbara, 82
  Christly, 82
  Elizabeth, 82
  Magdalena, 82
  Mary, 82
  Michael, 82
DESENBERG,
  Anthony, 202
  Margaret, 202
  Peter, 202
DESHNER, Anna, 98
  Barbara, 98
  Elizabeth, 98
  George, 98
  John, 98
  Mary, 98
DETTEMER,
  Dorothea, 71
  John, 71
DETTER, Catharine, 188, 236
  Elizabeth, 188, 236
  Esther, 236
  John, 188, 236
  Lawrence, 236
  Lorentrz, 140
  Magdalena, 188, 236
  Margaret, 236
  Mathias, 140, 236
  Matthias, 188
  Nicholas, 140, 188, 236
  Peter, 236
  Susanna, 188, 236
DETWEILER,
  Catharine, 249
DEVENEY, Aaron, 174
  Sarah, 174

DEVOLT, Margaret, 117
Peter, 117
DEWALD, Catharine, 261
  Charles, 246
  Donald, 261
  Elizabeth, 261
  Frederick, 261
  Grabriel, 261
  Henry, 261
  Jacob, 261
  Juliana, 246, 261
  Maria, 261
  Mary, 261
  Philip, 261
  Sally, 246
  Samuel, 246
  Valentine, 261
DEWALT, Eve, 159
  Philip, 159
DEWES, John, 217
DEWIS, Catharine, 110
  Christiana, 110
  Dorothea, 110
  Elizabeth, 110
  Henry, 110
  John, 110
  Margaret, 110
  Mary, 110
  Mary Barbara, 110
DIBBLE, Catharine, 268
  Eve, 268
  John, 268
DICE, George, 98
  Mary, 98
DICK, Adam, 180
  Catharine, 34
  Christian, 34
DICKE, Daniel, 219
DICKLE, Elizabeth, 221
  Peter, 221
DICKS, Deborah, 147
  Job, 147
  John, 147
  Martha, 147
  Mary, 147
  Peter, 147
  Ruth, 147
  Sarah, 147
DICKSON, Ann, 25
  Anna, 275
  Elizabeth, 23
  Esther, 186
  Hannah, 25
  Isabella, 23
  James, 23, 25, 46, 152
  Jane, 23
  John, 6, 152
  Margaret, 6, 23, 25, 152
  Mary, 23, 275
  Samuel, 23, 152
  Sarah, 6, 152
  Susanna, 152
  Thomas, 186
  William, 6, 275
DIDRICH, William, 31
DIDRICK, Modelena, 31
DIEHL, Adam, 197, 200
  Ann, 200
  Catharine, 200, 239
  Charles, 68, 200, 263
  Christiana, 163, 200
  Daniel, 200, 239
  David, 200
  Elizabeth, 239
  Esther, 200
  Eve, 200
  George, 163, 200
  Jacob, 168, 200, 239
  Nicholas, 239
  Peter, 88, 131, 164, 196, 204, 239
DIEL, Adam, 122
  Catharine, 122
  Daniel, 122
  Nicholas, 122
  Peter, 122
DIEM, Andrew, 263
  Elizabeth, 263
  George, 263
DIERDORF, Peter, 83
DIETZ, George, 195
DIFFENBACH, George, 170
  Magdalena, 170, 229
DIGGS, Ann, 68
  Edward, 68
  Eleanor, 68
  Elizabeth, 68
  John, 68
  Mary, 68
DIHL, Peter, 84
DILL, Agness, 62
  Armstrong, 112
  Eve, 99
  James, 4, 62
  Jean, 67
  John, 4, 112
  Mary, 4
  Mathew, 67
  Matthew, 4
  Nancy, 4
  Nicholas, 99
  Sarah, 4
  Thomas, 4
DINKEL, Daniel, 71
  Margaret, 71
DINKLE, Anna, 8
  Anshilla, 8
  Daniel, 8
  Dorothea, 8

Margaret, 8
Mary, 8
Peter, 8
DINSMORE, Andrew, 224
  George, 224
  Jane, 224
  John, 224
  Martha, 224
  Nancy, 224
  Polly, 224
DIPPLE, Jacob, 263
  Philibina, 263
DISSE, Andrew, 187
  John, 187
  Michael, 187
DITTY, Mary, 78
  Peter, 78
DIXON, James, 24, 106
DOBBIN, Alexander, 125
DOBS, Daniel, 21
  Oswald, 21
  Salome, 21
DODDS, Catharine, 166
  Elizabeth, 166
  Isabella, 166
  Joseph, 166
  William, 166
DODE, Mary, 152
DODS, Agness, 7
  Francis, 7
  James, 7
  Janet, 7, 21
  Jean, 7
  John, 7
  Joseph, 7, 21
  Margaret, 7
  Mary, 7, 21
  Rosena, 7
  Sarah, 7

Susanna, 21
William, 7, 21
DOGOMA, Eve, 35
DOLE, Daniel, 15
  Jacob, 273
DOLL, Ann, 255
  Barbara, 190, 232, 255, 265
  Catharine, 265
  Christiana, 265
  Conrad, 149, 157, 158, 187, 255, 265
  Elizabeth, 157, 158, 255, 265
  Esther, 266
  Fornica, 265
  Jacob, 265
  John, 115, 190, 255, 265
  Joseph, 255, 265, 266
  Lettia, 265
  Magdalena, 265
  Margaret, 265, 266
  Mary, 265
  Polly, 265
  Susanna, 265
DOLLMAN, Anna Mary, 190
  Catharine, 190
  Elizabeth, 190
  John, 190
  Mary, 190
DOMAN, Polly, 217
DOMBAR, James, 30
  Janet, 30
  John, 30, 31
  Margaret, 30
  Mary, 31
DONAHAY, James, 272
  Mary, 272
DONALDSON, Alice, 97

Joseph, 52
Lucia, 124
Patrick, 124
DONDEL, Michael, 73, 124
DONDELL, Michael, 82
DONNALSON, Elizabeth, 126
  John, 126
  William, 126
DORGIS, Barbara, 141
  Dorothea, 140
  Frederick, 141
  Henry, 140, 141
  Michael, 140
  Rosinah, 141
DORLAND, Garret, 105
DORMAN, John, 1
DORROUGH, John, 9
  Joseph, 9
  Margaret, 9
  Mary, 9
  William, 9
DOTTERER, Anny, 99
  Conrad, 99
  Margaret, 99
  Mary, 99
  Michael, 99
  Sophia, 99
DOUDLE, Margaret, 191
  Michael, 141, 191
DOUGHERTY, John, 176
  Salome, 176
DOUGLAS, Archibald, 136
  David, 162
  Elizabeth, 162
  James, 162

John, 162
Margaret, 136
Robert, 136
Thomas, 43, 108, 136
Timothy, 136
William, 136, 162
DOWNING, Alex., 132
DREICHLER,
 Barbara, 192
DRESSLER, Anna,
 205
 Catharine, 205
 Frederick, 205
 George, 205
DREVER, John, 257
 Sarah, 257
DRITT, Elizabeth, 265
 Jacob, 265
 Magdalena, 265
 Margaret, 265
DRORBACH, Adam,
 29
 Nicholas, 29
 Wilhelm, 29
DRUMGOLD,
 Michael, 7
DRUNGOLD,
 Alexander, 24
 James, 24
 John, 24
 Margaret, 24
 Michael, 24
DUBINGER, Susanna,
 263
DUBS, Daniel, 2, 123,
 184, 244
 Salome, 2
DUCKET, Thomas, 1
DUDEN, Daniel, 253
 Margaret, 253
DUFFIELD,
 Elizabeth, 64, 67
 George, 32, 64, 67

DUGLAS, Thomas, 55
 William, 111
DUGLES, Eunics, 151
 Jean, 151
 Margaret, 151
 Mary, 151
 William, 151
DULLINGER,
 Catharine, 163
 George, 163
 John, 163
DUN, John, 204
DUNBAR, William, 11
DUNCAN, Abner, 143
 Christiana, 143
 Elizabeth, 74
 Hannah, 143
 James, 74, 143, 248
 Jean, 74
 John, 74, 143
 Joseph, 143
 Martha, 143
 Matthew, 143
 Rudsand, 74
 Sarah, 74
 Seth, 143
 William, 143
DUNDINGER, Anna,
 58
 Daniel, 58
 Nicholas, 58
DUNDORE, Barbara,
 261
 Catharine, 261
 Hannah, 261
 Henry, 261
 John, 261
 Lydia, 261
 Margaret, 261
 Maria, 261
 Susanna, 261
DUNLAP, William, 18
DUNN, Margaret, 191

 Michael, 191
 Robert, 191
DUNWOODIE, Jane,
 35
 John, 35
DUNWOODY, Daniel,
 112
DUPE, Daniel, 270
DUPES, Oswald, 206
DURNBACH,
 Catharine, 184
 Joseph, 184
DUSTIN, Barbara,
 166
 James, 166

-E-
EABY, Ann, 83
 Barbara, 83
 Christian, 83
 Elizabeth, 83
 Henry, 83
 Jacob, 83
 John, 83
 John J., 83
 Magdalena, 83
EADAY, James, 264
 Jannet, 264
EAGER, Agness, 55
EAGON, Hugh, 28
EAHEN, William, 73
EARLY, Catharine, 5
 Daniel, 5
 Edward, 5
 John, 5
 Patrick, 5
 Sarah, 5
EATTEN, Catharine,
 108
 James, 108
 John, 108
 Samuel, 108
EBBERT, Martin, 117

EBECH, Elizabeth, 101
Michael, 101
EBERHARD,
  Abraham, 121
  Catharine, 121
  Eve, 121
  John, 121
EBERLY, Catharine, 132
  Michael, 132
EBERT, Adam, 93, 245
  Ann, 245
  Anna, 57
  Daniel, 245
  Elizabeth, 93, 228
  Eve, 93
  George, 270
  Helena, 93, 245
  John, 93, 228
  Martin, 57, 93, 111, 126, 203, 214, 245
  Michael, 56, 93, 245
  Philip, 93, 245
EBY, Christian, 134
ECKENROAD, Henry, 210
  Molly, 210
ECKERT, John, 134
EDGAR, Ann, 160
  David, 160
  Ellener, 160
  Jennet, 160
  Joseph, 160, 236
  Libbie, 160
  Thomas, 160
  William, 160
EDGE, James, 47, 57
EDGEDENA,
  Catharine, 264
  John, 264
EDGER, Hugh, 43
  James, 43, 61, 137
  Margaret, 43, 61
  Samuel, 43
  William, 43
EDIE, Daniel, 158
  John, 109, 164
  Samuel, 52, 109
EDINGER, Adam, 223
  Anna Mary, 223
  Benjamin, 223
  Daniel, 223
  Elizabeth, 223
  Jacob, 223
  John, 223
  Jonas, 223
  Joseph, 223
  Leah, 223
  Mary, 223
EDMUNDS, John, 34
EDMUNDSON,
  Abigail, 224
  Caleb, 79
  Esther, 79
  Hannah, 224
  John, 79
  Joseph, 79
  Mary, 224
  Rachel, 79
  Sarah, 79
  Thomas, 79, 224, 253
  William, 224, 253
EDWARDS, Edward, 205
  John, 205
  Unity, 205
EGE, Dorothea, 155
  Michael, 155
EGER, James, 6
EHRESMAN, Jacob, 141
EHRMAN, Appolonia, 167
  Catharine, 167
  Joseph, 167
  Mary, 167
EHRMIG, John, 182
  Margaret, 182
EICHELBERGE,
  Barnett, 70
  Daniel, 70
  George, 70
  Mary, 70
  Susanna, 70
EICHELBERGER,
  Adam, 69, 98, 106
  Anna Maria, 69
  Barbara, 151
  Barnet, 69
  Catharine, 249
  Eliza, 249
  Frederick, 1, 69, 106, 122, 203
  George, 69
  Jabob, 151
  Jacob, 69, 122, 249, 273
  Joseph, 106
  Leonard, 122
  Louisa, 249
  Ludwick, 122
  M., 19, 266
  Magdalena, 106, 122
  Maria, 249
  Martin, 12, 69, 266
  Mary, 69
  Michael, 106
  Polly, 266
  Salome, 106
  Samuel, 106
  Susanna, 69, 106
  Thomas, 220
EICHELERGER,
  Elizabeth, 241
  John, 214
  Lydia, 214
  Martin, 241

EICHINGERS,
  Catharine, 265
  John, 265
EICHLER, George,
  148
EICHOLTZ, Anna,
  161
  Anna B., 161
  Barbara, 70
  Catharine, 161
  Elizabeth, 148
  Frederick, 84, 161
  G. Mathias, 161
  George, 148, 161
  Jacob, 262
  Mathias, 70, 161
  Peter, 233
EICKELBERGER,
  George, 26
  Lydia, 26
EILER, John, 58
EIP, Eve, 211
  Jacob, 211
EIPE, Jacob, 274
  Peter, 274
EISELBERGER,
  Jacob, 134
EISENHARD, Ann, 73
  Catharine, 73
  Conrad, 73
  George, 73
EISENHARDT,
  Elizabeth, 71
  George, 71
EISTER, Anna, 37
  Catharine, 195
  Elias, 37
  Elizabeth, 195
  George, 195
  Peter, 195
ELDER, Andrew, 119
  Benj., 119
  Benjamin, 119

  James, 119
  Joseph, 119
  Mary, 119
  Rosanna, 119
ELEBERGER, Mary,
  145
  Peter, 145
ELECKER, Jacob, 240
ELGAR, John, 232
  Joseph, 232
  Margaret, 232
ELICKER, Henry, 146
ELIEKER, Casper,
  201
  Elizabeth, 201
ELIOT, Anne, 56
  James, 56
  John J., 56
ELLENBERGER,
  Peter, 156
ELLIKER, Casper, 20
  Henry, 20
  Susanna, 20
ELLIOT, Benjamin,
  191
  John, 191
  Lydia, 191
  Mary, 191
ELLIOTT, Agness, 97
  John, 1
ELLIS, Catharine,
  242, 255
  David, 242
ELLISON, Ellen, 17
  John, 17
  Mary, 17
  Matthew, 17
ELLOT, James, 133
  Jennet, 133
  John, 133
  Margaret, 133
  Samuel, 133
  William, 133

ELOCK, Rebecca, 234
ELSROTH, Susanna,
  47
  Valentine, 47
EMERY, Samuel, 81
EMICH, John, 37
EMICK, Christiana,
  215
EMIG, Ann, 182
  Catharine, 274
  Charles, 274
  Elizabeth, 274
  Eve, 274
  Jacob, 274
  James, 192
  John, 164, 182, 209,
    274
  Lorentz, 274
  Mary, 274
  Michael, 182
  Philip, 274
EMLER, Mary, 62
EMMERICK, Barara,
  195
  Catharine, 195
  Elizabeth, 195
  Jacob, 195
  John, 195
  Mary, 195
EMMIT, Joseph, 118
  Mary, 118
  Sarah, 118
  Susanna, 118
EMMITT, Josiah, 64
  Mary, 64
  Sarah, 64
  Susanna, 64
ENDERS, Catharine,
  226
  Elizabeth, 226, 253
  Esther, 226
  Frederick, 226
  George, 226, 253

Jacob, 226
John, 226
Mary, 226
Nicholas, 226
Susanna, 226
ENSIMINGER,
 Catharine, 119
 Christiana, 119
 Conrad, 119
 George, 119
 Henry, 119
 John, 125
 Magdalena, 119
ENSMINGER,
 Conrad, 109
 George, 251
 Henry, 231
 Maria, 109
 Sarah, 251
ENTLER, Magdalena, 38
 Philip, 38
ENTRIKIN, Elizabeth, 46
 James, 46
EPLY, Hanspeter, 153
 John, 153
 Matthias, 153
 Rosina, 153
EPPLE, Anna, 127
 John, 127
EPPLEMAN, Anna Margaret, 97
 Christiana, 97
 Conrad, 97
 Elizabeth, 97
 Henry, 97
 Jacob, 97
 John, 97
 Katharine, 97
 Margaret, 97
 Philip, 97
EPPLEY, Henry, 164

John, 268
EPPLY, John, 178
 Sophia, 178
EREHARD, Anna, 159
 George, 159
ERHARD, Anthony, 246
 Catharine, 234
 Elizabeth, 246
 Margaret, 234
 Michael, 234
 Nicholas, 234
 Peter, 234
 Philip, 234
ERHART, Ann, 46
 Anthony, 46
 Barbara, 46
 Catharine, 46
 David, 30, 46
 Elizabeth, 46
 Esther, 46
 Jacob, 68
 John, 46, 220
 Margaret, 30, 46, 220
 Mary, 148
 Michael, 267
 Philip, 46, 148
 Susanna, 46
 Thomas, 68
 William, 68
ERICK, Margaret, 253
ERION, Catharine, 195
 George, 195
 Jacob, 195
ERISMAN, Jacob, 188
 Susanna, 188
ERMAN, John, 230
 Margaret, 230
ERNST, Adam, 235, 236
 Catharine, 245

Jacob, 266
John, 235, 236
Samuel, 236
Susanna, 236
ERUNST, Adam, 182
 Susanna, 182
ERVIN, Julie, 166
 Patrick, 166
ERWIN, Archibald, 45
 Arthur, 45, 209
 James, 35
 John, 35
 Joseph, 35, 209
 Margaret, 209
 Mary, 35, 45
 Rachel, 45
 Rebecca, 98
 Samuel, 98
 Sarah, 35
 William, 45
ESCCKS, James, 112
ESENHOWER,
 Leonard, 188
ESHLEMAN, Ann, 46
 Elizabeth, 46
 Jacob, 46
 John, 46
 Peter, 46
ESMINGER,
 Catharine, 92
 Nicholas, 92
ESSICK, Simon, 121
 Ule, 121
ESTEL, Catharine, 181
 Valentine, 181
ETTARE, Lawrence, 72
 Margaret, 72
ETTER, Abraham, 52
 Catharine, 206, 265
 Elizabeth, 206, 265
 Eve, 254

George, 206, 265
Henry, 266
Jacob, 206
John, 206
Laurence, 206
Lawrance, 265
Lawrence, 206
Mary, 265
Michael, 206, 265
Nicholas, 254
Susanna, 52
ETTINGER, Adam,
　256, 271
ETZLER, Andrew, 242
　Catharine, 242
　Elizabeth, 202, 242
　Fransina, 242
　George, 242
　Joseph, 202
　Mary, 242
　Michael, 242
EUHILBERGER,
　Elizabeth, 57
　Leonard, 57
EUHILERGER,
　Elizabeth, 234
　Thomas, 234
EURICH, Juliana, 253
　Michael, 253
EURIG, Elizabeth,
　172
　George, 172
　Grace, 172
　James, 172
　John, 172
　Margaret, 172
EVANS, Betsy, 165
　Catharine, 165
　David, 165
　Elizabeth, 33
　Evan, 124
　Eve, 165
　Henry, 33

Joseph, 12
Mary, 33
Peter, 165
Sarah, 165, 184
Thomas, 165, 211
EVERIT, John, 213
EVERSOLT, Jacob, 36
　Magdalena, 36
EVIN, Alexander, 26
　Isaac, 26
　John, 26
　Martha, 26
　Robert, 26
　Samuel, 26
EWING, Ann, 98
　Eleanor, 98
　Elizabeth, 98, 101
　Isaac, 127
　James, 98, 209
　John, 101, 127
　Margaret, 98
　Martha, 98, 127
　Robert, 127
　Samuel, 127
　Thomas, 98
　William, 98
EYECHELBERGER,
　Anna, 124
　Jacob, 124
EYECHILBERGER,
　Anna, 159
　Frederick, 159
EYEN, Catharine, 218
　Charlotte, 218
EYKELBERGER,
　Martin, 12
EYLER, Christiana,
　193
　Jacob, 121
　John, 193
EYSTER, Christian,
　155
　Daniel, 1

Elizabeth, 1
George, 121
Magdalena, 121
Margaret, 145, 155
Peter, 145, 155

-F-
FACKENROTH,
　George, 196
FACKLER, Adam, 33
　Anna Magdalena,
　107
　Catharine, 33
　Elizabeth, 33
　Eva, 33
　George, 33
　Gotleib, 142
　Gottleib, 33
　Jacob, 33, 48
　Magdalena, 33, 48
　Maria F., 33
　Peter, 185
　Susanna, 185
FAERENBACH,
　Catharine, 236
　Joseph, 236
FAGOT, Daniel, 74
FAHENSTOCK,
　Samuel, 146
FAHNESTICK, Benj.,
　104
FAHNESTOCK,
　Bovins, 165
　Samuel, 149, 179
FAHNSTICK,
　Eleanor, 78
FAHNSTOCK, Boris,
　165
FAHS, Abraham, 220,
　239
　Anna Maria, 220
　Catharine, 239
　Elizabeth, 239

Henry, 220, 239
Jacob, 220, 239, 270
John, 220, 239
Joseph, 239
Mary, 270
Philip, 239
Susanna, 220
Tovias, 239
Zachariah, 220
FAINMAN, Philip, 24
FAIR, Elizabeth, 268
FAKE, Ericona, 139
  John, 139
FALKENSTEIN,
  JAcob, 260
  Jacob, 250, 260, 275
FALKINSTEIN,
  Jacob, 263
FALLER, Adam, 89,
    181, 189
  Dorothea, 89
  Elizabeth, 89
  John, 89
  Maria, 89
FANSTICK, Detrich,
    83
  Margaret, 83
FAR, George, 5
  Hannah, 5
FARRA, James, 55
  John, 55, 146
  Katharine, 55
  Martha, 55
  Mary, 55
  Rebecca, 55
  Samuel, 55, 146
  Sarah, 55, 146
  Thomas, 55
  William, 55, 146
FARRE, Rachel, 207
  Thomas, 207
FASS, Christian, 150
  Elizabeth, 150

FAUSTER, Adam, 62
  Christiana, 62
  Mary, 62
FEATORY, Modelena,
    31
FEAVOUR, George,
    18
FEDROE, Andrew,
    127
  John, 127
  Joseph, 127
  Mary, 127
  Michael, 127
  Philip, 127
FEED, Abraham, 202
FEELLY, Mary, 120
  Thomas, 120
FEESER, Anna, 54
  Jacob, 54
  Nicholas, 54
FEGELY, Anna, 157
  Barbara, 157
  Elizabeth, 157
  Paul, 157
FEIGELY, Martin,
    197
FEISER, Anamary,
    211
  Christiana, 211
  Daniel, 275
  Elizabeth, 211
  Jacob, 275
  Maria, 275
  Mary, 275
  Peter, 92, 126, 211,
    275
FEISSER, Barbara,
    227
  Barnet, 227
  Elizabeth, 69
  John, 69
  Mary, 227
  Peter, 69

FELDE, John, 260
  Mary, 260
FELGER, Ann, 111
  Anna Mary, 111
  Barbara, 111
  Eve, 111
  Henry, 111
  Jacob, 111
FELKER, Christiana,
    98
  Dorothea, 98
  Frederick, 98
  John, 176
  Yost, 98
FELTY, Elizabeth, 113
  Henry, 234
  John, 113
  Polly, 234
FELTZ, Henry, 230
FENLEY, William, 72
FENTER, Barbara,
    223
  John, 223
  Martin, 223
  Susanna, 223
FERGUS, Hugh, 152
  Samuel, 152
  Sarah, 86
  Thomas, 86, 152
FERGUSON, James,
    26, 72
FERREE, Andrew,
    175
FESSEL, Adam, 129
  Elizabeth, 129
FETROW, Elizabeth,
    248
  Philip, 248
FETTER, John, 80
  Mary, 80
FETZ, Frederick, 96
  Jacob, 211
  Susanna, 211

FEYERSTON,
    Nicholas, 40
FICHEL, Barbara, 226
    Henry, 227
FICKES, Abraham,
    75, 169
    Elizabeth, 75, 211
    Isaac, 75
    Jacob, 75
    John, 75, 211
    Margaret, 75
    Rebecca, 75
    Valentine, 75
FICKIES, Barbara, 95
    Elizabeth, 88
    John, 88
    Valentine, 95
FIESTER, Catharine,
    212
    Jacob, 212
    Susanna, 212
FILE, Elizabeth, 193
    John, 193
FILEY, Catharine, 196
    Jacob, 196
    John, 196
    Mary, 196
    Sophia, 196
    Susan, 196
FILKERN, Dorothea,
    196
    Elizabeth, 196
    Frederick, 196
    George, 196
    Jacob, 196
    William, 196
FINCH, Catharine,
    123
    Michael, 123
FINDLY, Nicholas,
    107
FINGERY, Christian,
    10

FINK, Ann, 247
    Catharine, 247
    Elizabeth, 109, 247
    Ferdenand, 247
    George, 109, 118
    Henry, 176
    Margaret, 118
FINLEY, Aaron, 146
    Alexander, 126
    Andrew, 112, 215
    Ann, 94
    Ebeneer, 94
    James, 18
    Jean, 18
    John, 217
    Joseph, 94
    Margaret, 18, 146
    Maria, 146
    Martha, 217
    Michael, 94, 146
    William, 146
FINLY, Michael, 52
FIRESTONE,
    Margaret, 236
    William, 236
FISCHEL, Ann, 122
    Barbara, 122, 226
    Catharine, 227
    Charles, 208
    Christiana, 208
    Conrad, 227
    Elizabeth, 226
    Frederick, 227
    Henry, 122
    Jacob, 208
    John, 122, 227
    Kratchan, 227
    Margaret, 122
    Mary, 122
    Michael, 226, 227
    Philip, 122, 227
    Wendel, 122
FISHALL, Adam, 187

FISHEL, Anna Maria,
    236
    Barbara, 56, 188
    Elizabeth, 56, 188,
        236
    Frederick, 236
    George, 236
    Henry, 56, 188, 236
    Jacob, 188, 236
    John, 56, 188
    Magdalena, 254
    Margaret, 56
    Margaretta, 188
    Matalena, 188
    Michael, 188, 236,
        254
    Peter, 56
    Philippp, 56
FISHELL, Adam, 97
    Anna, 97
    Anna Maria, 97
    Elizabeth, 255
    Frederick, 262
    John, 97
    Margaret, 97
    Michael, 97, 255
    Rosina, 97
FISHER, Adolph, 92
    Alice, 179
    Ann, 92, 127
    Barbara, 220
    Casper, 127
    Catharine, 127, 140,
        183, 249
    Charles, 220, 233
    Christian, 183, 249
    Christiana, 92
    Christopher, 92, 127
    Coleman, 92
    Elizabeth, 127, 140,
        179, 249
    Eve, 20, 140
    Frederick, 126

George, 92, 140, 220
Henry, 140
Isaac, 179
Jacob, 249
James, 140, 179
Jane, 179
John, 127, 160, 220, 249
John Casper, 126
John J., 220
Juliana, 57
Magdalena, 232
Margaret, 127
Margaretta, 249
Maria, 92
Marian, 179
Mary, 140, 249
Michael, 57
Nicholas, 92
Peter, 92
Samuel, 185
Suannah, 185
Thomas, 20, 45, 62, 140
Valentine, 67, 92
FISSEI, John M., 118
John Michael, 118
FISSEL, Adam, 119
Barbara, 119
Catharine, 119
Elizabeth, 119
Gillian, 119
Henry, 119
John, 121
Lena, 121
Margaret, 119
FITTLER, Peter, 129
Philip, 129
FITZ, Barbara, 123
Braltzer, 145
Elizabeth, 260
Frederick, 123, 229, 260

John, 260
Peter, 260
Samuel, 260
FLATFELDER, Felix, 115
FLECKINGER, Samuel, 192
FLEISHAMAN, Martin, 211
FLEITZ, Catharine, 161
John, 161
FLEMING, Alice, 82
Dorothea, 87
Robert, 82, 87
Samuel, 87
FLEMMING, Elizabeth, 82
John, 82
FLETCHER, Archibald, 44
Elizabeth, 210
Joseph, 210
Rebecca, 44
FLETZER, Jacob, 12
FLICK, Henry, 15
FLICKINGER, Andrew, 114, 259
Anna, 114
Barbara, 114
Elizabeth, 114
Eve, 78, 259
Hans, 114
Jacob, 114
Joseph, 259
Magdalena, 114
Moses, 259
Peter, 114, 259
Rachel, 259
Samuel, 68, 78, 114, 130, 259
Susanna, 259
FLOCK, David, 125

FLORE, Conrad, 200
Elizabeth, 200
Susanna, 200
Valentine, 200
FLORY, Magdalena, 102
FLOWERS, Alice, 36
Ann, 36
David, 36
Elizabeth, 36
James, 36
John, 36
Mary, 36
Sarah, 36
Thomas, 36
FLUREY, Ann, 117
Daniel, 117
FLURY, Abraham, 211
Caty, 211
Jacob, 240
FOCKLER, Barbara, 142
Jacob, 142
FODERMAN, Elizabeth, 182
Jacob, 182
FOGELSON, Barbara, 164
Catharine, 164
Christiana, 164
Christopher, 164
Nicholas, 164
Philip, 164
FOLK, Elizabeth, 237
Jacob, 252
FOLKE, Catharine, 199
John, 139
Peter, 199
Rosand, 139
FOLKIMMER, George, 243

FOLTZ, Jacob, 258
  Margaret, 258
FORD, Louise, 31
  William, 31
FOREMAN,
  Catharine, 157
  Peter, 157
FORMAN, Jacob, 77
FORNEY, Adam, 79,
  134, 196
  Adams, 196
  Andrew, 197
  Catharine, 196
  Christian, 196
  Daniel, 196
  David, 80, 249
  Elizabeth, 79, 80
  Eve, 196
  Hannah, 80
  Henry, 157
  Jacob, 80
  Louisa, 249
  Louise, 80
  Marks, 196
  Mary, 80
  Peter, 80
  Philip, 79
  Salome, 80
  Samuel, 79
  Susanna, 80, 157
FORRINGER, David,
  232
FORRY, Henry, 263
  M., 73
FORSH, Adam, 198
  Barbara, 198
  John, 198
FORSYTH, John, 69
  Susanna, 69
FORSYTHE, John,
  114, 182
FORTINBAUGH,
  Andrew, 245

FOULK, Jane, 235
  Stephen, 235
FOUR, Ann, 112
  Jacob, 112
FOUST, Barbara, 232
  Elizabeth, 232
  Frederick, 232
  Jacob, 232
  John, 232
  Martin, 232
FOUTS, Catharine, 47
  Jacob, 47
FOUTZ, Jacob, 8, 146
  Mary, 146
FOWLER, Catharine,
  270
  William, 270
FOX, Abraham, 169
  Catharine, 37, 157
  Conrad, 220
  Elizabeth, 169, 220
  Eve, 169, 220
  George, 220
  Henry, 37
  Jacob, 169
  John, 157, 220
  Joseph, 220
  Justina, 37
  Margaret, 46, 157
  Peter, 46, 157
  Salome, 157
  Samuel, 169
FRAIMER, Andrew,
  24
FRANCIS, Peter, 53
FRANCISCUS,
  Margaret, 100
FRANK, Adam, 73
  Anna Mary, 94
  David, 94
  Elizabeth, 264
  Mary, 73
  Michael, 264

FRANKEBERGER,
  John, 108
  Margaret, 108
FRANKELBERGER,
  Barbara, 61
  Caty, 61
  Conrad, 61
  Elizabeth, 61
  George, 61
  Henry, 61
  Jacob, 61
  John, 61
  Margaret, 61
  Molly, 61
  Philip, 61
  William, 61
FRANKENBERGER,
  Elizabeth, 244
  Jacob, 244
FRANKS, Lilly, 154
  Ludwick, 154
FRAZER, Alexander,
  247, 268
FRAZIER, James, 6
  Rebecca, 6
FREDERICK,
  Andrew, 58
  Ann Elizabeth, 58
  Anna Elizabeth, 71
  Catharine, 58
  Elizabeth, 58, 71
  Hannah, 71
  John, 71
  Juliana, 58
  Magdalena, 58
  Michael, 58, 71, 116
  Philip, 214
  Susanna, 58, 71
FREE, Catharine, 243
  Conrad, 243
  Elizabeth, 243
  John, 243
  Magdalena, 243

Maria, 243
Michael, 243
Peter, 243
Susanna, 243
FREED, Peter, 10
FREEMAN, Henry, 37
  Isabella, 37
FREETZ, Adam, 9
  Anna, 9
  Anna Catharine, 9
  Elizabeth, 9
  Julianna, 9
  Philip, 9
FREY, Anna, 65
  Anna Mary, 65
  Barbara, 231
  Barnet, 115
  Conrad, 231
  Elizabeth, 65
  Frederick, 244
  George, 116
  Gottfried, 38, 76
  Henry, 244
  John, 116, 244
  Margaret, 65
  Martin, 65
  Mary, 116
  Philip, 116
FRICHLER, John, 82
FRICKER, Tempest, 147
FRIED, Peter, 269
FRIES, Ann, 139
  Catharine, 139
  Christian, 139
  David, 139
  Elizabeth, 139
  Ericona, 139
  George, 139
  Jacob, 139
  Martin, 139
  Michael, 139
  Simon, 139

FRINZER, Margaret, 245
  Michael, 245
FRISS, Simon, 204
FRITZ, Adam, 217
  Anna, 192
  Baltzer, 192
  Barbara, 192, 217
  Catharine, 217
  Christiana, 192
  Elizabeth, 192
  Fretz, 217
  Henry, 217
  Jacob, 192, 217
  John, 192, 217
  Juleana, 217
  Magdalena, 192
  Mary, 192
  Philip, 217
  Susanna, 192
FRITZLUN, Anna Mary, 179
  George, 179
FROESHER, Barbara, 230
  Catharine, 230
  Charlotte, 230
  Christiana, 230
  Elizabeth, 230
  Eve, 230
  Frederick, 230
  John, 230
  Lutwig, 230
  Magdalena, 230
  Margaret, 230
  Peter, 230
  Rosina, 230
FROSTER, Abraham, 156
FROSTLE, Abraham, 80, 141
  Susanna, 80
FRUT, Ann, 58

  Christian, 58
  Jacob, 58
  John, 58
  Juliana, 58
  Peter, 58
FRY, Adam, 199
  Anna, 188
  Catharine, 248
  Conrad, 188, 195
  Elizabeth, 195
  George, 60, 195, 248
  Hannah, 199
  Magdalena, 60
  Martin, 248
  Susanna, 248
FUCKS, Catharine, 230
  George, 230
  John, 230
  Margaret, 230
  Molly, 230
FUGATE, Mary, 252
  Thomas, 252
FUHRMAN, Elizabeth, 268
  Peter, 268
FULLERTON, Adam, 235
  Ann, 235
  Isabella, 235
  Jean, 107
  John, 107, 235
  Margaret, 235
  Mary, 107, 235
  Robert, 235
  Samuel, 107, 235
  William, 235
FULTON, Alexander, 72
  Andrew, 37, 54
  David, 37, 54
  Ealse, 137
  Elijah, 72

Hugh, 37, 54, 204
James, 37, 54, 72
Jane, 54
Jean, 37
Jennet, 37
Jesse, 137
John, 37, 72
Joseph, 78
Katharine, 229
Margaret, 202, 204
Mary, 72, 204
Richard, 78
Samuel, 229
William, 20, 37, 72
FULWEILER,
  Catharine, 274
  Joseph, 274
  Mary, 274
  Michael, 274
FUNK, Daniel, 257
  Jacob, 69, 257
  John, 257
  Joseph, 257
  Maria, 257
  Maria E., 257
  Maria Elizabeth, 257
  Marilis, 69
  Susanna, 257
FURMAN, Catharine, 68
  Eva, 68
  Michael, 68
  Stephen, 68
  Valentine, 68
FURNEY, Adam, 253
FURRER, Christian, 82
  Daniel, 82
  Elizabeth, 82
  Henry, 82
  Samuel, 82
FURREY, Christian, 43

FURST, Adam, 274
  Barbara, 274
FYSER, Peter, 258

-G-
GABEL, Catharine, 230
  George, 230, 244
GALAHAR, Abraham, 226
  Isabella, 226
  John, 226
  Mary, 226
GALAHER, Isabella, 232
  Jennet, 232
  John, 232
  Martha Isabella, 232
GALBRAITH,
  Isabella, 38
  James, 38
  Nancy, 38
  Robert, 38
  William, 38
GALBREAITH,
  Agness, 28
  Catharine, 28, 58
  Cathren, 28
  Elizabeth, 28
  John, 28
  Rebecca, 28
  Robert, 28, 58
  Thomas, 58
GALT, Martha, 5
GALVIX, Frederick, 89
  Susanna, 89
GALWAX, Andrew, 112
  Christiana, 129
  Daniel, 111, 112, 129
  Katharine, 112
  Magdalena, 129

Tobias, 112
GAMMEL, Agness, 57
  James, 57
  John, 57
  Margaret, 57
  William, 57
GAMMILL, James, 209
  Sarah, 209
GANS, George, 217
GANTZ, George, 190
GANTZER, Andrew, 1
  Catharine, 38
  Elizabeth, 38
  Matthias, 38
GARDNER, Adam, 140
  Catharine, 140
  Elizabeth, 140
  Eve, 140
  George, 140
  Henry, 140
  Jacob, 140
  Lersh, 140
  Margaret, 140
  Martin, 140
  Michael, 140
  Peter, 140
  Philip, 140
GARMAN, Catharine, 216
  Isaac, 216
GARNER, Anna Mary, 172
  Marks, 172
GARRETSON, Aaron, 136
  Ann, 163
  Anna, 136, 231
  Cornelius, 163, 165, 167
  Elizabeth, 136
  James, 231

John, 6, 136, 163
Joseph, 151, 163, 231
Marion, 136
Naomi, 136
Samuel, 163
Sarah, 136, 163
William, 10, 45, 136, 163
GARRISON, Aaron, 104
John, 104
Mary, 103
Tamer, 104
GARRITSON, John, 14
Rebecca, 14
GARTMAN, Abraham, 272, 273
Catharine, 208
Elizabeth, 117, 208
Isaac, 117, 123, 216
Magdalena, 117
Mary, 117, 272
GARTNER, Abraham, 249
Adam, 31, 65
Elizabeth, 65
George, 92
Jacob, 65, 186
Marilla, 31
Martin, 217
Philip, 65
Susanna, 92
GATFELDER,
Barbara, 250
Casper, 250
Daniel, 250
Elizabeth, 250
Felix, 250
Frederick, 250
Jacob, 250
John, 250
Margaret, 250

Mary, 250
Philip, 250
GATTLIP, Samuel, 52
GAUFF, Catharine, 141
George, 141
Philip, 53
GAYER, Andrew, 201
Margaret, 201
GAYLEY, John, 223
GEAR, David, 213
GEARY, Catharine, 70
William, 70
GEBRICK, Barbara, 206
Catharine, 206
GEDDES, Henry, 215
Sarah, 215
GEEDING, Catharine, 145
Ludwig, 145
GEENTIL, Adam, 87
Anna Margaret, 87
GEHLER, Abraham, 16
GEIGER, Catharine, 135
Jacob, 135
GEINLING, Barhard, 21
Barnhard, 21
Christiana, 21
GEIP, Ann, 78
Charlotte, 78
Elizabeth, 78
Eve, 206
Henry, 78
Mary, 78
Michael, 206
Nicholas, 78
Peter, 78
GEIPE, Henry, 117
Peter, 117

GEISEL, Leonard, 18
GEISELMAN,
Catharine, 88
Christiana, 88
Elizabeth, 88
Eve, 88
F., 238
Frederick, 88
George, 87
Jacob, 88
John, 88, 222
Magdalena, 88
Margaret, 87
Michael, 87, 88
Rosina, 222
GEISEMAN,
Frederick, 260
GELEY, Christiana, 248
GELLAND, William, 120
GELWEKS, Nicholas, 206
GELWICKS,
Catharine, 258
Charles, 80
Daniel, 80
Eve, 80
Frederick, 80
George, 80
Mary, 258
Mary Dorothea, 80
Nicholas, 80, 245, 258
Peter, 80
Polly, 258
GEMILL, David, 264
Margaret, 264
Robert, 264
GEMMEL, Ann, 148
David, 147
James, 147
Jannet, 147

Jean, 147
John, 148
Margaret, 148
Mary, 148
Robert, 147, 215
Thomas, 148
William, 147
GEMMELL, William, 67
GEMMILL, Agness, 165
Ann, 112, 165
David, 112, 165
Elizabeth, 164, 165, 242
J. Jannet, 112
James, 112, 165
Jane, 242
Jannet, 165
Jean, 165
John, 112, 164, 165
Margaret, 112, 165
Mary, 165, 242
Robert, 112, 165, 186, 229, 242
Sarah, 165, 229, 242
William, 36, 58, 112, 165
GENGRICH,
Christian, 237
Eve, 237
GENTER, Christiana, 178
Conrad, 178
John, 178
Nicholas, 178
GENTLZER, George, 55
Gertrude, 55
Magdalena, 55
Philip, 55
GENTZER, George, 209

Magdalena, 209
GENTZLER, Anna, 252
Conrad, 55
Julianna, 45
Philip, 45, 252
GEORGE, David, 235
Frederick, 196
Mary, 235
GEORING, Barbara, 218
Elizabeth, 218
Jacob, 218
John, 218
Lydia, 218
Margaret, 218
Maria, 218
Sarah, 218
GERBER, Andrew, 192
Catharine, 203
Christian, 203
Elizabeth, 203
John, 203, 205
Nicholas, 203
GERBRICK,
Elizabeth, 205
Eve, 205
Frederick, 205
George, 205
Jacob, 205
John, 205
Joseph, 205
Margaret, 205
Maria, 205
Michael, 205
Peter, 205
Susan, 205
GERLACK, Henry, 17
GERLIN, Catharine, 226
Valentine, 226
GERNER, George,

175
John Geo., 175
GERVERICH,
Elizabeth, 245
Henry, 245
Jacob, 245
John, 245
Sophia, 245
GESLER, Daniel, 242
Henry, 242
John, 242
Margaret, 242
Michael, 242
Peggy, 242
GETTING, John, 8
GETTY, James, 82
GEWICKS, Nicholas, 218
GEYER, Adam, 62
Anna, 62
Catharine, 62
Conrad, 62
George, 62, 97
Maria, 62
Paul, 62
Peter, 62
Rosina, 97
Sabina M., 62
Sabina Margaret, 62
GIBBONS, Catharine, 190
Edward, 248
Margaret, 248
Matthew, 190
GIBBS, Boroughs, 256
Emely, 257
Sarah, 256, 257
GIBSON, Andrew, 222
Ann, 222
Anna, 222
George, 222
Hugh, 191, 222
Jacob, 57, 118, 222

James, 79
Jane, 222
Jennet, 79
John, 54, 79, 222
Joseph, 222
Lates, 191
Lydia, 222
Margaret, 222
Martha, 54
Mary, 222
Robert, 240
Thomas, 222
GICH, Catharine, 188
Ludwig, 188
GIERR, Peter, 226
Susanna, 226
GILBERT, John, 271
GILKEY, John, 5
Mary, 5
Walter, 5
GILL, Gabriel, 124
Rebecca, 124
GILLAND, William, 140
GILLELAND, James, 116
Jane, 116
John, 116
Samuel, 116
William, 116
GILLEREES, Agness, 74
James, 74
John, 74
Margaret, 74
Robert, 74
William, 74
GILLILAND, William, 106, 120, 151
GILLILANS, William, 126
GILLISPIE, Barbara, 198

Daniel, 198
Francis, 198
John, 198
GILMORE, Daniel, 259
David, 263
GIMMILL, Catharine, 199
Robert, 199
GINGLES, Margaret, 45
Samuel, 45
GINKIN, Moses, 24
GINTER, Anna, 44
Christiana, 44
Dewalt, 44
GINTON, Elizabeth, 200
Sarah, 200
GIPE, Catharine, 189
Henry, 188, 189
GIRBIN, Elizabeth, 125
Mary, 125
GISE, George, 200
Jacob, 200
Peter, 200
Susanna, 200
GISLER, Adam, 118
Anna, 118
John, 118
Magdalena, 118
GISON, John, 4
Mary, 4
GLABSATLE, Daniel, 118
Justina, 118
GLADUS, Anna, 199
Peter, 199
GLANCY, Joseph, 113
GLARRICK,
Catherine, 226
Samuel, 226

GLASGO, Eliza, 219
James, 219
John, 219
GLASGOW,
Cunningham, 266
Eliza, 266
Hugh, 266
James, 266
John, 266
Maria, 266
Samuel, 266
Walter, 266
William, 266
GLASHFATTER,
Falicks, 202
GLASICK, John, 49
Mary, 49
Rachel, 49
Samuel, 49
GOBRECHT, Anna
Christiana, 260
Christopher, 253
Daniel, 260
David, 253, 260
Salley, 253
GOCHENOUER,
Abraham, 228
Anna, 228
Barbara, 228
Christian, 228
Jacob, 228
John, 228
Joseph, 228
Martin, 228
Mary, 228
Michael, 228
Samuel, 228
GODFREY, Charles, 235
Hannah, 235
Jane, 235
Mary, 235
Thomas, 235

William, 235
GODWALD, Andrew, 212
Catharine, 212
Daniel, 212
Elizabeth, 212
George, 212
Henry, 212
Jacob, 212
John, 212
Magdalena, 212
GOERING, Elizabeth, 229
Jacob, 144
GOGHENAUR, John, 150
GOHN, Adam, 41
Anna, 164
Catharine, 41, 99, 196
Elizabeth, 41, 231
George, 196, 231
Henry, 41, 231
Jacob, 231
John, 41, 99, 196, 231
Magdalena, 41
Margaret, 41, 164
Mary, 41
Peter, 41
Philip, 41, 231
Rebecca, 196
Sophia, 41, 231
GOLDING, Eve, 145
Nancy, 145
GOO, Henry, 253
GOOD, Anna, 102
Anna Mary, 102
David, 102
Peter, 262
GOODBRED, Ludwick, 49
Philip, 50

Turless, 49, 50
GOODINLINGER, Andrew, 253
Mary, 253
GOODLING, Adam, 250
Catharine, 250
Christian, 250
Jacob, 250
Peter, 250
GOODWIN, Margaret, 116
Matthew, 116
GOODY, Anne
Elizabeth, 133
George, 133
GOODYEAR, George, 134
GOOLDEN, Charles, 260
Elizabeth, 260
GORDAN, James, 223
Janet, 223
Robert, 214
GORDEN, Robert, 239
GORDMAN, Isaac, 111
GORDON, Catharine, 193
Elizabeth, 193
Isabella, 193
James, 193
Martha, 193
Mary, 193
Matthew, 193
Robert, 193, 229
GORGAAS, Catharine, 272
Samuel, 272
GOSSLER, John, 170
Philip, 178
GOSSWEILER, John, 156

GOTTWALT, Andrew, 120, 146
Catharine, 120, 146, 147
Elizabeth, 120
George, 120, 146
Jacob, 120
Maria Catharine, 120
Mary C., 120
GOUFF, Philip, 49
GOULD, Catharine, 201
Elizabeth, 201
Jane, 201
Mary, 201
Susanna, 201
Thomas, 201
GOUTZ, George, 232
GRABELL, Joseph, 78
Mary, 78
GRABILL, Samuel, 202
Veronica, 202
GRAEFF, Fronica, 265
Henry, 265
GRAFF, Anna, 141
Catharine, 141
Christian, 141
Gertrude, 141
Henry, 141
Mathias, 141
GRAFFIN, Abraham, 206
GRAFINS, Rebecca, 178
GRAFIUS, Abraham, 191
GRAFUS, Abraham, 224
GRAHAM, James, 236
Michael, 215
Rebecca, 157, 185
GRAIF, Elizabeth, 187

GRAME, Agness, 214
  Conrad, 214
  Frederick, 214
  Gertrude, 214
  Peter, 214
  Susanna, 214
  T., 214
GRASEAS, Christiana, 89
GRASS, Andrew, 28, 266
  Anna, 264
  Catharine, 266
  George, 264
  Peter, 266
GRASSER, Adam, 169
  Anna, 169
  Catharine, 169
  Henry, 169
  Jacob, 169
  Leonhart, 169
GRAUL, Jacob, 188
  Magdalena, 188
GRAW, John, 182
GRAY, Anna, 187
  Charles, 187
  Sarah, 187
  Thomas, 9
  William, 187
GRAYBELL, Hannah, 184
  Jacob, 184
  Polly, 184
GRAYBILL, Anna, 46
  Barbara, 46
  Christian, 46
  Eve, 46
  Johannes, 46
  John, 46
GREEN, John, 97
  Margaret, 97
GREENWALD,
  Christopher, 74

Mary, 74
GREENWALT,
  Christian, 33
  Elizabeth, 253
  John, 253
GREESEMER, Adam, 98
  Catharine, 98
  Elizabeth, 98
  Henry, 98
GREFF, Catharine, 39
  Gerhard, 39
GRENBLAD, Barara, 216
  Philip, 216
GRENN, Philip, 86
GRET, Ann Elizabeth, 161
  Apolonia, 161
  Christiana, 161
  Eve, 161
  Jacob, 161
  John, 161
  Joseph, 161
  Michael, 161
  Nicholas, 161
GREVER, Adam, 32
  Anna Maria, 33
  Anthony, 32
  Elizabeth, 33
  Margaret, 32, 33
  Mary, 32
GREY, Christiana, 177
  Elizabeth, 101
  Isabella, 101
  John, 101
  Joseph, 101
  Thomas, 101
  William, 101
GRIBBLE, Archibald, 102
  Elizabeth, 102
  Jane, 102

John, 102
Mary, 102
Vevi, 102
Vincent, 102
GRIENEWALT,
  Abraham, 207
  Anna, 207
  Catharine, 207
  Christopher, 207
  Frederick, 207
  Jacob, 207
  John, 207
  Maria, 207
GRIER, Agness, 123
  Anna, 241
  David, 123
  Jane, 241
  Jennet, 123, 241
  John, 184
  Margaret, 123, 241
  Mary, 123
GRIEST, John, 144
  Joseph, 194, 218
  Rebecca, 218
  Sarah, 144
  William, 194
GRIFF, John, 95
  Lydia, 95
GRIFFE, Eve, 20
  Magdalena, 20
  Sarah, 20
  Stephen, 20
GRIFFETH, William, 10
GRIFFIN, William, 41
GRIFFITH, Abraham, 144
  Ann, 147
  Anna, 180
  Benj., 144
  Caleb, 180
  Daniel, 31
  David, 69, 144, 147,

180
Debora, 144
Elizabeth, 147, 241,
  266, 273
Esther, 69
Even, 69
Hannah, 69
Jacob, 144, 218, 273
James, 147, 241, 266,
  273
Jane, 241
Jenny, 241
John, 108, 147, 241
Joseph, 144, 180, 241
Lydia, 218
Martha, 108, 147,
  241
Mary, 144
Rachel, 147
Rebecca, 147, 180
Robert, 241
Sarah, 69, 103, 147,
  180
Susanna, 69
William, 103, 144,
  180, 241
GRIHAMS, Ann, 149
  Margaret, 149
  Martha, 149
  Robert, 149
  Thomas, 149
  William, 149
GRIMES, Conrad, 137
  David, 137
  Henry, 137
  John, 137
  Margaret, 137
  Mary, 80
  Nathan, 80
GRIMM, Barbara, 142
  Christiana, 142
  Daniel, 142
  Dorothea, 142

John, 142
Michael, 142
Peter, 142
Philip, 142
GRISH, Adam, 245
GRITT, John, 74
GRIVER, Ludwick,
  154
GROCE, Andrew, 260
  Barbara, 260
  Catharine, 260
  Henry, 260
  John, 260
  Margaret, 260
  Philip, 260
  Polly, 260
  Wendel, 260
GRODDEN, Moses, 5
GROFE, John, 117
  Magdalena, 117
  Margaret, 117
  Michael, 117
  Valentine, 117
GROFF, Francis, 121
GROSGRAS, Jacob,
  112
  Martha, 112
GROSS, Esther, 135
  Jacob, 135
  Samuel, 125, 135,
  138, 205
GROUL, Catharine,
  227
  Henry, 227
GROVE, Allner, 187
  Anna Mary, 66
  Cambel, 187
  Catharine, 66, 119,
  223, 234
  Caty, 85
  Christian, 85
  Elizabeth, 66, 187,
  223

Francis, 187, 223,
  234
Frederick, 223, 234
George, 66
Henry, 66
Jacob, 66, 187
John, 223, 234
Margaret, 187, 223,
  234
Mary, 251
Michael, 169, 234,
  251
Nicholas, 164
Salley, 223
Samuel, 119
Susanna, 223
Thomas, 67, 187
GROVER, Francis,
  227
GRUBB, John, 214
GRUBER, Henry, 269
  Margaret, 269
GRUNBLAD,
  Barbara, 216
  Philip, 216
GRUNDY, Carray, 266
  Daniel, 266
  Jacaob, 266
  Jacob, 266
  John, 266
  Peter, 111
GRUNWALD,
  Frederick, 163
GUCKES, Adam, 211
  Catharine, 211
  Dorothea, 211
  John, 211
  Julianna, 211
GUILLILAND,
  Matthew, 57
  William, 57
GUMP, Barbara, 134
  Catharine, 134

Dorothea, 134
Elizabeth, 134
George, 58, 134
Hannah, 134
John, 134
Margaret, 134
Rosana, 134
Salome, 134
GUNACKER,
  Barbara, 132
  Michael, 132
GUNKLE, Anna, 237
  Anna Maria, 237
  Balzer, 237
  Catharine, 237
  Charles, 237
  Eve, 237
  Maria, 237
GUSE, John, 135
GUTH, Charles, 102
  Jacob, 143
  Mary, 143
  Peter, 169
GUTTORY, James, 67
  Mary, 67
GUTWALT,
  Catharine, 273
  Christian, 273
  Daniel, 273
  Felix, 273
  George, 273
  Jacob, 273
  John, 273
GYER, Anna
  Catharine, 33
  Paul, 33

-H-

HAAR, Eizabeth, 241
  George, 241
  Jacob, 241
HAAS, Maria
  Magdalena, 100

HAASE, Adam, 243
  John, 243
  Kreta, 243
HABERSOCK,
  Andrew, 117
  Magdalena, 117
HACK, Andrew, 208
  Mary, 208
HACKEN, Elizabeth,
  232
  Jacob, 232
HAEFFNER,
  Matheisz, 94
HAGEN, Andrew, 62
  David, 62
  Edward, 62
  Elizabeth, 62
  Henry, 62
  James, 62
  John, 62
  Patrick, 62
HAGENBERGER,
  John, 28
  Mary, 28
  Reinhart, 28
  Rosina, 28
HAGENER, Adelia, 37
  John, 37
HAGY, Jacob, 1
  John, 134
HAHN, Barbara, 210
  Catharine, 166
  David, 210
  Elizabeth, 67
  John, 67
  Michael, 67
  Philipina, 210
  Rosina, 67
  Soloman, 166
HAINDLY, Adam, 18
HAINES, Sophia, 135
  William, 135
HAKE, Anna, 264

Anna Maria, 264
Benjamin, 233
Catharine, 233
Conrad, 233
Elizabeth, 233, 264
Frederick, 233, 264
Henry, 264
Jacob, 233, 264
John, 233, 264
Peter, 264
Samuel, 233
William, 233
HALDEMAN, Jacob,
  271
  Jacob M., 241
  Susanna, 271
HALE, Hannah, 15
  John, 15
  Joseph, 15
  Sarah, 15
  Thomas, 15
HALL, Christiana, 123
  Edward, 46, 170
  Elizabeth, 46
  Else, 46
  Esther, 46
  Isaac, 123
  James, 182
  Jean, 46
  John, 46
  Martha, 170
  Mary, 46
  Michael, 123
  William, 46
HALLER, Adam, 265
  Anne Maria, 52
  Charlotte, 265
  Christopher, 52
  Elizabeth, 265
  George, 248
  John, 139, 141, 173,
    195, 205, 216, 259
  Marian, 265

Sarah, 265
Susanna, 52, 248
HALLERPETER,
  Mathias, 119
HAM, Baltzer, 21
  Christian, 21
  Daniel, 149
  Jacob, 149
  John, 149
  Louisa, 21
  Mary, 21
  Peter, 149
  Valleendin, 21
HAMACHER,
  Christian, 200
  Joseph, 271
HAMBRECHT,
  Christiana, 56
  Martin, 56
HAME, Christian, 269
HAMEISSE, John, 84
HAMEL, James, 18
  Mary, 18
  Rachel, 18
HAMERSBY, Mary, 157
  Robert, 157
HAMERSLEY,
  Robert, 210
HAMERSLY, Robert, 158
  William, 158
HAMILTON, Ann, 76
  Catharine, 140
  Francis, 76
  George, 36
  Guain, 36
  Hance, 36
  James, 36, 76
  John, 36
  Mary, 36, 76
  Sarah, 36
  Thomas, 36

  William, 36, 76, 140, 149
HAMLETON,
  Margaret, 215
HAMM, Balthasser, 207
  Catharine, 207
HAMMER, Catharine, 159
  Conrad, 159
HAMMOND, Daniel, 87
  Deborah, 103
  Elizabeth, 87, 103
  George, 95, 140
  James, 95, 140
  John, 103, 140
  Margaret, 140
  Mary, 103, 140
  Nathan, 103
  Sarah, 103
  Thomas, 140
HANCE, Christiana, 99
  Jacob, 99
HANCOCK, Benjamin, 154
  Elizabeth, 154
  James, 154
  Joel, 154
  John, 154
  Sarah, 154
HANIMAN, Philip, 32
HANS, John, 122
  Margaret, 122
HANTZ, Andrew, 102
  Barbara, 102
  Catharine, 102
  Jacob, 102, 183
  John, 102
  Mary, 183
HARA, Charles, 30
  Daniel, 30

  Mary, 30
  Patraick, 30
HARBAUGH,
  Barbara, 34
  Jacob, 34
HARBISON, Francis, 75
HARBOLD,
  Catharine, 110, 120
  Elizabeth, 120
  George, 110, 120
  Henry, 120
  Leonard, 120
  Michael, 120
  William, 120
HARBOLT, Dorothea, 110
  William, 110
HARDMAN, Mary, 250
  Tobias, 250
HARING, Christiana, 184
  George, 184
  Henry, 184
  Jacob, 184
  John, 184
  Juliana, 184
  Lewis, 184
  Mary, 184
  Philipena, 184
HARKINS, Samuel, 51
HARMAN, Adam, 79
  Elizabeth, 79
  Esther, 18
  Frederick, 79
  George, 79, 148
  Honickle, 18
  John, 79
HARMON, John, 177
HARNISCH, Samuel, 203
HARNISH, Elizabeth,

186
Machael, 186
HARNIST, Barbara,
  122
John, 122
HAROLD, Mary, 265
Peter, 265
HARPER, Agness, 69
James, 57, 69
Jane, 198
Jean, 69
Jennet, 69
Margaret, 57
Samuel, 69, 198
HARR, Christiana, 265
Jacob, 265
HARRIS, Bulah, 210
Elisha, 210
Elizabeth, 205, 210
George, 128, 210
Hannah, 210
James, 210
John, 205, 210
Lydia, 210
Mary, 210
Richard, 210
HARRISON, Ann,
  125, 182
Hannah, 125, 182
John, 125
Thomas, 125, 182
HARRY, Stephen, 233
HARSH, Christiana,
  248
Leonard, 248
HART, Andrew, 79
Catharine, 263
David, 79
Elijah, 79
Isabella, 79
Jacob, 100, 236, 257,
  271
Jean, 79

John, 79, 177
Margaret, 34, 79
Mary, 79, 155
Michael, 238, 274
Philip, 263
Sarah, 177
Tracy, 177
William, 34, 155
HARTLEY, Charles,
  182
Thomas, 2, 51, 182
HARTMAN, Andrew,
  186
Anna, 113
Catharine, 244
Charles, 258
David, 244
Elizabeth, 236, 258
Eve, 186
Francis, 244
Frederick, 190, 244,
  254, 258, 263
Henry, 157, 244
Jacob, 113, 236
John, 263
Ludwick, 263
Magdalena, 244
Margaret, 157
Maria, 263
Maria Elizabeth, 263
Marian, 244
Nicholas, 244
Philibina, 263
Rebecca, 244
Sarah, 244
Tobias, 263
HARTZOUGH,
  Andrew, 32
Ann Maria, 32
Anna, 32
Catharine, 32
Dorothea, 32
George, 32

Magdalena, 32
Maria, 32
HASSLER, Abraham,
  42
Christian, 42
George, 42
Joseph, 42
Magdalena, 42
Margaret, 42
Michael, 42
HASTY, Able, 120
Elizabeth, 120
HATTAN, Leonard, 31
HATTON, Ann, 64
Edward, 64, 83
Elizabeth, 83
James, 64, 83
Jane, 64, 83
John, 64, 139
Leonard, 64, 83
Mary, 64
Rachel, 64, 83
Rebecca, 139
Robert, 64, 83
William, 61
HAUSMAN,
  Christian, 178
Conrad, 178
HAWMMEL, Anna, 96
Anna Mary, 96
Conrad, 96
Daniel, 96
Elizabeth, 96
Eve, 96
Jacob, 96
Philip, 96
HAY, Allen, 55
Catharine, 243
Christiana, 221
Elizabeth, 243
George, 243
Jacob, 218, 220, 243
James, 221

John, 33, 48, 76, 80,
  86, 116, 228
Susanna, 228, 243
William, 243
HAYD, Anna Mary,
  171
HAYNEY, Ann, 95
  Catharine, 95
  Edward, 95
  Mary, 95
  Patrick, 95
  Sarah, 95
HAYNS, Barbara, 55
  Catharine, 55
  Christiana, 55
  Elizabeth, 55
  Eve, 55
  Jacob, 55
  Philip, 55
  Susanna, 55
HAYS, Adam, 163
  Alexander, 163
  Charity, 163
  George, 163
  John, 163
  Lessy, 163
  Lydia, 248
  Nancy, 152
  Patrick, 152
  Robert, 248
  Sarah, 163
  William, 163
HEADRICH,
  Abraham, 71
  Appolonia, 71
  Catharine, 71
  Christely, 71
  Christian, 71
  Elizabeth, 71
  Jacob, 71
  John, 71
HEAGY, George, 157
HEALMAN, Dorothea,
    141
  Philip, 141
HEAR, Elizabeth, 58
  Michael, 58
HECKENDORN, Ann,
    95
  Barbara, 95
  Catharine, 95
  Christian, 95
  Elizabeth, 95
  John, 95
  Maria, 95
HECKENTHON,
  John, 32
HECKER, George,
    258
HECKERT, Catharine,
    230
  Charles, 238
  Daniel, 238
  Dorothea, 238
  George, 187, 230,
    238
  Jacob, 230
  Joseph, 230
  Magdalena, 230
  Mary, 238
  Philip, 230, 238
  Sarah, 238
  Susanna, 187
HECKMAN, John, 92
HEGAS, Magdalena,
    180
  Valentine, 180
HEHL, Leonard, 134
  Margaret, 134
HEIBLE, Christopher,
    166
  George, 166
  Jacob, 166
  Louisa Catharine,
    166
  Michael, 166
HEIBLEY, Anna, 98
  Christian, 98
  Christopher, 98
  Jacob, 98
  John, 98
  Juliano, 98
  Magdalena, 98
  Michael, 98
  Paul, 98
  Sophia, 98
HEIBLY, Anna, 223
  Jacob, 223
  John, 223
  Juliana, 223
  Michael, 223
  Sophia, 223
HEIDLER, Catharine,
    212
  Elizabeth, 212
  John, 34, 68, 212
  Judith, 212
  Magdalena, 212
  Margaret, 212
  Mary, 212
HEIGES, Christian,
    222
  Elizabeth, 222
  George, 222
  Jacob, 222
  John, 222
  Mary, 222
HEILMAN, Catharine,
    141
  Peter, 141
HEINDAL, Barbara,
    169
  Jacob, 169
HEINE, Joseph, 114
HEINEN, Elizabeth,
    242
  Henry, 242
HEINER, Caroline,
    255

Elizabeth, 255
George, 255
Mary, 255
Michael, 255
Polly, 255
Yost, 255
HEISLAND,
  Abraham, 231
HEISMAN, Catharine,
  130
Henry, 130
HEISSE, Daniel, 257
  Elizabth, 257
  Eve, 257
  George, 257
  Henry, 257
  Jacob, 257
  John, 257
  Margaret, 257
  Wendle, 257
HEISTAND,
  Abraham, 192
  Catharine, 207
  John, 207
HEITZEL, Catharine,
  96
  Jacob, 96
HELFRICH,
  Christian, 140
  Christiana, 140
  George, 139
  Mary, 140
HELLEN, John, 270
HELLER, Catharine,
  80
  Jacob, 80
  John, 142
  Samuel, 189
HELLJET, Anna, 35
  Tobias, 35
HELLMAN, George,
  94
  Herman, 182

Jacob, 99
Magdalena, 99, 182
HELMAN, Anamary,
  101
Barbara, 114
Catharine, 101
Christian, 114
Elizabeth, 267
Eve, 114
Jacob, 114
John, 101
Margaret, 114
Martin, 114
Michael, 101, 114,
  206, 221, 229, 237,
  267
Philip, 101
William, 114
HELMER, Ann, 76
  Christian, 76
HELTZEL, Anna, 135
  Anna Maria, 166
  Bernard, 166
  Catharine, 135, 166
  Christiana, 166
  Eve, 135
  Frederick, 166
  Henry, 135
  Jacob, 166
  John, 135, 166
  Margaret, 135
  Philip, 135
  Scharlot, 135
  Sophia, 135
  Tobias, 135, 166
HEMES, Abraham,
  258
  Benjamin, 258
  Christian, 258
  Christiana, 258
  John, 258
  Sally, 258
HENDERSON,

Francis, 2
James, 2
Jane, 140
John, 2
Letiss, 42
William, 2
HENDRICKS, Alice,
  80
  Ann, 80
  Elizabeth, 80
  Hannah, 80
  Lydia, 80
  Margaret, 36
  Martha, 80
  Nathan, 80
  Patience, 80
  Samuel, 80
  Stephen, 80
  Tobias, 36
HENDRIX, Adam,
  262, 268
  Eli, 249
  Hannah, 262
  Isaac, 262
  James, 27
  John, 249, 262
  Joseph, 262
  Joshua, 262
  Rhode, 249
  Ruth, 262
  Thomas, 262
  William, 27
HENEISE, Catharine,
  227
  Elizabeth, 227
  George, 227
  John, 227
  Margaret, 227
  Mary, 227
  Philip, 227
HENEISSEN, Philip,
  201
HENEMAN,

Catharine, 46
John, 46
Margaret, 46
Mary, 46
Philip, 30, 46
HENGST, Catharine,
  187
  Elizabeth, 187
  Eve, 187
  Jacob, 187
  Juliana, 190
  Margaret, 187
  Michael, 187, 190
HENICK, Catharine,
  129
  John, 129
HENISEN, George,
  273
  John, 161
HENKE, John, 274
HENKELL, Anthony,
  184
HENKLE, Anthony,
  199
HENLY, John, 111
HENNINGER,
  Dorothea, 115
HENRY, Anna, 156,
  188
  Cathrine, 188
  Christian, 188
  Daniel, 156
  Elizabeth, 78, 188
  George, 78, 215
  Jacob, 209
  Jane, 215
  Joel, 156
  John, 156, 188
  Joseph, 156
  Magdalena, 188, 265
  Margery, 215
  Michael, 188
  Nicholas, 265

Peter, 156
Samuel, 156
William, 78, 215
HENTIL, Catharine,
  237
  Larentz, 237
  Laurentz, 236
HENTZ, Anna, 71
  Barbara, 71
  Catharine, 71
  Christiana, 142
  Elizabeth, 71
  Henry, 71
  John, 71
  Maria, 71
  Mark, 71
  Martin, 71
  Mary, 71
  Nicholas, 71
  Peter, 71
  Philip, 71
HENTZEL, Casper,
  203
  Catharine, 203
  George, 203
  Mary, 203
HERBACH, Elizabeth,
  190, 240
  George, 190
  John, 43, 62, 157,
  190, 240
  Juliana, 190
  Magdalena, 190
  Margaret, 190
  Polly, 190
  Salome, 240
  Yost, 221
HERBACK,
  Catharine, 16
  George, 16
  Jacob, 16
  John, 16, 87
  Jost, 169

Leonard, 16
Margaret, 16
Mary, 16
Mary Eliza, 16
Yost, 16
HEREH, Catharine,
  172
  John, 172
HERING, Catharine,
  62
  Christiana, 62, 151
  Dorothea, 62
  Elizabeth, 62
  Eve, 213
  Henry, 62, 199
  John, 151
  Margaret, 199
  Mary, 62
  Michael, 62
  Philip, 62, 213
HERLEMAN, Conrad,
  142
  Sebastian, 142
HERMAN, Abraham,
  240
  Ann, 240
  Anna, 113
  Applonia, 162
  Christian, 194
  David, 240
  Elizabeth, 194
  Emanuel, 73, 143
  Eve, 143
  George, 113, 162,
  209
  Henry, 113
  Jane, 201
  John, 97, 201
  Joseph, 240
  Lydia, 240
  Maria, 113
  Mary, 143, 240
  Philip, 214

Samuel, 240
Suanna, 240
HEROLD, Mary, 136
Peter, 136
Rebecca, 136
HERR, Anna, 210
Caty, 211
Elizabeth, 211, 216
John, 110, 210, 216
Mary, 210
Rudy, 210
Susanna, 211
HERRINGTON,
Jacob, 30
Mary, 30
HERSCHY, Andrew,
164, 177
Anna, 169, 177, 251
Barbara, 164, 169,
251
Christian, 164, 169,
177
Elizabeth, 164, 169,
177, 251
Jacob, 177
John, 169
Joseph, 164, 177
Magdalena, 164
Mary, 251
Peter, 177
HERSH, Benjamin,
231
John, 231
Mary, 231
HERSHAW, Christian,
73
Mary, 73
HERSHEY, Barbara,
207
Benj., 269
Christian, 147, 150,
169, 230
Elizabeth, 169

John, 207
Joseph, 230
Katharine, 230
Peter, 229
Reed, 29
HERSHINGER,
Catharine, 245
John, 245
HERSHNER, Andrew,
235
Anna, 235
Barbara, 235
Henry, 235
Jacob, 169
Lawrence, 63
HERTH, Henry, 182
Susanna, 182
HERTSEL, George,
112
HERTZOG, Andrew,
53
HESHNER, Eve, 169
HESLET, James, 14
John, 14
Mary, 14
Robert, 14
Sarah, 14
William, 14
HESS, Christiana, 126
Daniel, 249
Dewald, 269
Elizabeth, 93, 174
Henrich, 175
Henry, 93, 124, 174
Isaac, 93
Michael, 126, 258
Rachel, 93
Ulrich, 124
Ursula, 124
Valentine, 93
HESSEY, John, 29
HESSLET, Agness, 23
Esther, 23

Joseph, 23
Mary, 23
HETERICK, Barbara,
206
Christian, 206
HETIG, Ludwig, 37
Sabina, 37
HETRICH, Christian,
247
HETRICK, Ann, 229
Christian, 229
Elizabeth, 229
John, 229
HEUISEN, John, 69
HEUREMAN,
Barbara, 235
Christian, 235
HEYER, Barbara, 166
John, 166
HICKER, George, 42
HICKES, Barbara,
178
Catharine, 178
Christiana, 178
Frederick, 178
George, 178
Henry, 178
Jacob, 178
John, 178
Laurence, 178
Mary, 178
HICKS, Catharine,
209
Jacob, 209
Laurence, 209
Lawrence, 209
Mary, 209
Rebecca, 209
Susanna, 209
HIDEY, Philip, 203
HIEPERT, Baltzer,
203
HIESTAND, Anna,

192
Jacob, 23
HIGAS, John, 235
HIGHGAS, Abraham,
  199
  Catharine, 199
  Elizabeth, 199
  George, 199
  Hannah, 199
  Henry, 199
  Jacob, 199
  John, 199
  Magdalena, 180, 199
  Margaret, 199
  Mary, 199
  Sareina, 199
  Valentine, 180
  William, 199
HIKE, Frederick, 186
HILDEBRAND, Felix,
  80
  John, 80
HILL, Alexander, 8
  Ann, 272
  Edward, 7
  Eleanor, 8
  Elizabeth, 8, 7
  James, 7, 272
  Jane, 7
  John, 8, 7
  Margaret, 7
  Mary, 7, 272
  Rachel, 7
  Robert, 7
  Samuel, 8, 7
  William, 272
HILLER, Martin, 170
HILT, Elizabeth, 181
  Joseph, 181
HIMAN, Gottleib, 224
  Hannah, 224
  Jacob, 224
  John, 224

Magdalena, 224
HIMES, Catharine,
  230, 268
  Charles, 113
  Elizabeth, 230
  Francis, 153, 230
  George, 230, 268
  John, 230
  Mary, 113, 268
  Samuel, 230, 268
  Solome, 230
  William, 230, 268
HIND, Christiana, 121
  Peter, 121
HINEGO, Elizabeth,
  229
  Michael, 229
HINER, Barbara, 157
  Ludwig, 157
HINES, Anthony, 215
  James, 215
  Mary, 215
  Rosanna, 215
  Ruth, 215
  Sarah, 215
  Susanna, 215
HINKLE, Adam, 139
  Ann, 139
  Anthony, 121, 259
  Elizabeth, 259
  John, 259
  John L., 260
  Margaret, 259
  Rachel, 259
  Salome, 121
  Sarah, 259
HIRDT, Barbara, 169
  Christiana, 169
  Daniel, 169
  David, 169
  Eve, 169
  Martin, 169
HITTABRAND,

Casper, 202
HOAK, Catharine, 31
  Conrad, 31
  Jacob, 246
  Polly, 246
  Susan, 246
HOAR, George, 265
  Susanna, 265
HOBBACH,
  Catharine, 172
  Christiana, 172
  Conrad, 172
  Elizabeth, 172
  George, 172
  John, 172
  Margaret, 172
  Mary, 172
  Peter, 172
  Philip, 172
HOBIAS, Frederick,
  69
  Margaret, 69
HOBSON, Francis, 61
  Joseph, 61
HOCKDELIN, Ann,
  146
  William, 146
HOCKINBOUGH, B.,
  30
HODGE, John, 24
  Margaret, 24
  Mary, 24
  Samuel, 24
  Sarah, 24
  William, 5, 24
HOFERMAN, Adam,
  233
HOFF, Adam, 96, 231,
  248
  Barbara, 248
  Christian, 248
  Christiana, 248
  Daniel, 272

Elizabeth, 248, 272
Eve, 231
Francis, 96, 231
Henry, 248, 270, 272
John, 272
Juleana, 96
Magdalena, 272
Mary, 248, 270, 272
Peter, 248
HOFFACRE, Anna, 268
Barbara, 268
Catharine, 268
Elizabeth, 268
Henry, 268
Jacob, 268
John, 268
Michael, 268
HOFFMAN, Adam, 154
Anna Elizabeth, 122
Barbara, 154
Catharine, 156, 173, 208, 237, 253
Charles, 154, 201
Christian, 160
Christiana, 154
Daniel, 154, 208
Elizabeth, 154, 253, 264
Eve, 148, 208, 215, 253
Frederick, 154
Hannah, 154
Henry, 154, 253, 264
Jacob, 148, 188, 253
John, 208, 253
Leach, 237
Magdalena, 208
Martin, 156
Mary, 154, 201, 237, 253
Mathias, 122

Michael, 122
Nicholas, 253
Philibina, 253
Philip, 173, 188, 261, 264
Sarah, 188
Susanna, 208, 253
HOGHAN, Ann, 11
Catharine, 11
Chatronary, 11
Nicholas, 11
HOH, Martin, 1
HOHF, Anna, 82
Barbara, 82
Henry, 82
Mary, 82
Michael, 213
Nicholas, 82
HOHFF, Henry, 68
HOHR, Ludwick, 273
Rachel, 273
HOKE, Andrew, 33, 72, 122
Ann, 274
Barbara, 122
Casper, 33, 172
Catharine, 203
Conrad, 33
Daniel, 72
Dorothea, 57, 203
Elizabeth, 122
Frederick, 33, 72
George, 72, 203
Gloria, 122, 203
Henry, 33, 118
Jacob, 203, 273, 274
John, 33, 72
Margaret, 172
Mary, 203
Michael, 203
Peter, 57, 203
Sabina, 72, 203
HOLDER, Barbara, 187
John, 187
HOLDSWORTH, Catharine, 108
Jane, 108
John, 108
Joseph, 108
Margaret, 108
Samuel, 108
HOLK, John, 90
HOLL, Abraham, 111
Andrew, 111
Anna, 36, 184
Barbara, 91
Catharine, 111
George, 91, 111
Henry, 111, 114, 184
Jacob, 36, 111
John, 111, 184
Martin, 184
Mary, 91, 111
Nicholas, 111
Peter, 111
Philip, 111
HOLLAND, Mary, 106
Thomas, 106
HOLLER, Catharine, 188
Francis, 188
Sarah, 188
HOLLIDAY, Charles, 45
James, 45
Mary, 45
HOLLINGER, Christopher, 123
HOLLOPETER, Abraham, 173
Andrew, 173
Barbara, 173
Christiana, 173
Frederick, 173
John, 173

Mary, 173
Matthias, 173
Susanna, 173
HOLSABLE, Adam,
 142
Barbara, 142
Catharine, 142
Christiana, 142
Elizabeth, 142
Erasmus, 142
Henry, 142
Jacob, 142
Margaret, 142
HOLTZAFFEL, Adam,
 207
HOLTZENGER,
Barnet, 52
Catharine, 52
Elizabeth, 51, 52
Jacob, 52
Joseph, 52
HOLTZINGER, Jacob,
 2
HOLTZRAPPLE,
Barnet, 149
HOMAN, Elizabeth,
 27
Godleap, 27
Michael, 27
HOMER, Joseph, 137
HONING, Elizabeth, 5
John, 5
Nicholas, 5
HONSICKER,
Catherine, 17
Jacob, 17
HOOBER, Barbara, 45
Frederick, 142
George, 45, 240
Henry, 130
John, 45
Margaret, 142
HOOD, Elizabeth, 11

HOOKAS, Catharine,
 71
Harman, 71
HOOPARD,
Catharine, 120
Christiana, 120
Daniel, 120
Elizabeth, 120
Eve, 120
George, 120
John, 120
Mary, 120
HOOPER, Elizabeth,
 202
Hannah, 124
Jannet, 202
John, 124, 202
Mary, 202
William, 244
HOOPERT,
Catharine, 132
George, 132
HOOPPERT, Polly,
 234
HOOVER, Adam, 100
Anna, 158
Catharine, 110, 260
Christian, 32, 110
David, 110
Elizabeth, 153
George, 100
Henry, 260
Isaac, 110
Jacob, 158
John, 153, 158
John George, 100
Joseph, 110
Martin, 110
Mary, 32, 100, 110
Susanna, 158
HOPE, Adam, 126
Andrew, 126
Jacob, 264

Jannet, 198
HOPPERT, Catharine,
 234
HORN, Jacob, 57
HORNEY, Benedict,
 134
Elizabeth, 134
Henry, 134
HORST, Amanuel, 43
Ann, 43
Barbara, 43
Daniel, 43
Jacob, 43
John, 43
HOSE, Dietrich, 109
Elizabeth, 109
Eve, 109
Jacob, 109
Magdalena, 109
Peter, 109
Philip, 109
HOSSACK, David, 135
Henry, 135
Jean, 135
John, 135
Mary, 135
Thomas, 135
HOSSELBERGER,
Catharine, 22
George, 22
Maria, 22
Michael, 22
Philip, 22
HOSTETTER,
Elizabeth, 243
Jacob, 210
Samuel, 243
HOTLZAFFEL,
Catharine, 207
Margaret, 207
HOUCK, Anna Mary,
 119
Barbara, 16

Catharine, 120
Christiana, 120
David, 209
Elizabeth, 16, 120
Eva, 16
Eve, 16
George, 16
Hannah, 120
Jacob, 16, 119, 120
Lorentz, 119
Maria, 209
Peter, 119
Philip, 16
Susanna, 120
HOUDESHELL,
  Emanuel, 246
  Molly, 246
HOUK, Christopher,
  50
HOULTON, Ann, 60
  Benjamin, 60
  Elizabeth, 60
  Francis, 15, 60
  John, 60
  Joseph, 60
  Margery, 60
  Mary, 60
  Samuel, 60
  William, 60
HOUSE, Abigal, 271
  Benjamin, 271
  Elizabeth, 271
  Hannah, 271
  Joseph, 271
  Prudence, 271
  Susanna, 271
HOUSEHOLDER,
  Abraham, 221
  Elizabeth, 221
  Henry, 221
  J., 260
  Jacob, 221
  John, 221

Mary, 221
Nancy, 221
HOUSEMAN, Philip,
  10
HOUSER, Elizabeth,
  17, 115
  George, 17, 142
  Henry, 17
  Jacob, 17
  John, 17, 142
  Mary, 17
  Peter, 17
  Yuleyane, 17
HOUSMAN, Barbara,
  99
  Catharine, 99
  Charles, 99
  Christian, 99
  Christiana, 99
  Jacob, 99
  Michael, 99
HOUSTON, James,
  273
  Joseph, 273
  Mary, 273
HOUTS, Catharine,
  70
  Christiana, 70
  Christopher, 70
  Elizabeth, 70
  Ida, 70
  Jacob, 70
  John, 70
  Margaret, 70
HOW, Abraham, 21,
  30
  Elizabeth, 21, 30
  Mary, 21
  Samuel, 21
  William, 119
HOWER, Anthony,
  197
  Barbara, 197

  Elizabeth, 215
  Eve, 215
  George, 215
  Henry, 215
  Michael, 215
  Peter, 197
HUBER, Adam, 145
  Andrew, 177
  Barbara, 251
  Catharine, 177
  Christiana, 251
  David, 177
  George, 177
  Henry, 177
  John, 177
  Martin, 210, 251
  Michael, 177
  Ulerick, 165
HUBLEY, Frederick,
  181
  Magdalena, 181
HUGGINS, Ann, 81
  George, 81
  Isabella, 81
  Jacob, 81
  Margaret, 81
HUGHES, Eleanor, 28
  John, 28
  Jonathan, 28
HUGHS, Ann, 58
  Catharine, 58
  Charles, 58
  Christian, 58
  Daniel, 58
  Elizabeth, 60
  Francis, 58
  Hannah, 58
  Henry, 58
  Isabella, 60
  James, 58, 60
  John, 58, 60
  Joseph, 58
  Mary, 58

Patrick, 58
Robert, 60
Rowland, 60
Samuel, 60
Symly, 60
Tamer, 58
Valentine, 180
William, 60
HULE, Abraham, 27
HULL, Ann, 89, 113
Elizabeth, 89
Henry, 105
Isaac, 89
Magdalena, 89
Mary, 89
Nicholas, 113
Samuel, 89
HUMMEL, Barbara, 136
Catharine, 136
Frederick, 136
George, 136
Jacob, 136
HUMMER, Catharine, 246
Christiana, 246
Daniel, 246
Eleanor, 246
Elizabeth, 246
Henry, 246
John, 246
Lydia, 246
Susanna, 246
HUNSECHER, Johannes, 18
HUNT, Edward, 79, 101, 107
Elisha, 218
Elizabeth, 79, 101
Jane, 79, 101
John, 79
Margaret, 79
Mary, 79, 218

Rodger, 79
Roger, 101
Samuel, 79
William, 79
HUNTER, Agness, 77
Alexander, 77
Alice, 55
Allen, 184
Betty, 176
Elias, 184
Elizabeth, 58
Ephraim, 55, 184
Francis, 77
Isabella, 58
Jacob, 184
James, 55, 58, 170
Jane, 55
Jean, 184
Joseph, 55, 58, 77, 184
Margaret, 55, 184
Mary, 55, 58, 184
Nancy, 55
Samuel, 58, 134, 145
Sarah, 77
Thomas, 55
William, 55, 66, 176, 184
HUNTZ, Elizabeth, 89
Francis, 89
HUPARD, Adam, 70, 71
Anamary, 71
Catharine, 70, 71
Eve, 71
HURL, Edward, 265
Elizabeth, 265
HURST, Ann, 198
Henry, 189
Jacob, 150
John, 150, 198
HUSSEY, Amos, 85, 218

Edith, 218
Hannah, 47, 218
Lydia, 218
Marian, 85
Mary, 218
Miriam, 218
Nathan, 47
Rebecca, 218
Riccord, 85
Ruth, 218
HUTCHINSON, Ann, 147
Esther, 147
James, 147
Jennet, 147
John, 147
Leech, 147
Martha, 147
Robert, 147
Samuel, 147
HUTTON, Betty, 34
Joseph, 34
Joshua, 34, 115
Rachel, 34, 115
Simeon, 34
HUVER, Peter, 251
Rebecca, 251
HUZZY, Hannah, 218
Judia, 218
Nathan, 218
HYAS, Lawrance, 162
Margaret, 162
HYRE, Charles, 155, 182
Elizabeth, 155
Frederick, 155
Jacob, 155, 182
Magdalena, 155

-I-
ICKIS, Dorothea, 119
Peter, 119
ILGENFRETZ, Anna,

238
Catharine, 238
Daniel, 238
Elizabeth, 238
Hannah, 238
Jacob, 238
Joseph, 238
Juliana, 238
Margaret, 238
Martin, 238
Sarah, 238
ILGENFRITZ,
 Elizabeth, 190
 Jacob, 190
 Samuel, 198
IMMEL, Abraham, 37
 Barbara, 56
 Christiana, 56
 Daniel, 109
 Dorothea, 109
 Eva, 56
 Eve, 37
 George, 109
 John, 56, 109
 Leonard, 56
 Magdalena, 56
 Margaret, 56
 Maria, 56
 Michael, 56
 Sevilla, 56
IMMELL, George, 261
IMSRVILLER,
 Catharine, 86
IMSWILLER, Mary
 Eva, 38
 Peter, 38
INGLEFRITZ,
 George, 35
 Margaret, 35
IRWIN, Christopher,
 247
 Elizabeth, 247
 George, 218, 235

Gerrerd, 218
Henry, 235
Isabella, 34, 247
John, 218, 235
Joseph, 247
Martha, 235
Robert, 34
Samuel, 247
Sarah, 247
William, 218

-J-
JACK, Agness, 66
 Andrew, 66
 Elizabeth, 66
 Esther, 66
 James, 66
 Jean, 66
 John, 66, 171
 Lidia, 66
 Margaret, 171
 Sarah, 66
JACOB, Anna, 203
 Catharine, 203
 Daniel, 203
 David, 203
 Elias, 203
 Elizabeth, 189, 203,
  208
 George, 189, 208
 Henry, 208
 John, 203
 Mary, 203, 208
JACOBS, Abraham,
 133
 Barbara, 133
 Catharine, 133
 Daniel, 48, 133
 Elizabeth, 133
 Henry, 133
 James, 222
 John, 133
 Lydia, 222

Magdalena, 48
Mally, 133
Nancy, 133
Peter, 133
Philip, 30, 48, 133
Salome, 133
Samuel, 48, 133
Susanna, 30, 133
William, 133
JACOBY, Catharine,
 228
 John, 138, 228
JAIMESON, Enis, 132
 Mary, 132
JAMES, Hannah, 180
 Jacob, 239
 Peter, 247
 Thomas, 180
JAMESON, David,
 223
 Juliana, 223
 Mary, 204
 William, 204
JAMISON, Robert, 48
 Samuel, 48
 Sarah, 48
 Susanna, 48
JANS, Frederick, 48
JARDIN, David, 54
JEFFERIES, Joseph,
 51
JEIGLER, Ann, 95
 Anna, 95
 John, 95
JELLERS, Catharine,
 198
 Christian, 198
JENEWEIN, Leonard,
 49
JENEWIN, Leonard,
 133
JENKINS, Francis,
 112

Moses, 112
Walter, 112
JENNINGS, Esther,
  183
  Thomas, 183
JESSOP, Jonathan,
  231
JESSUP, Jonathan,
  232
JOHN, Ann, 165
  Anna, 167
  Elizabeth, 165
  Griffith, 165, 167
  Hannah, 165, 167
  Isaah, 165, 167
  Isabella, 165
  Joshua, 165, 167
  Rachel, 165, 167
  Sarah, 165, 167
JOHNSON, Agness,
  66
  Elizabeth, 38, 66
  Ephraim, 28, 66
  James, 66, 83, 211
  John, 66
  Robert, 79
  Susanna, 38
  Thomas, 85
JOHNSTON, Able, 30
  Agness, 41, 76, 152,
  246
  Alexander, 52
  Andrew, 252
  Ann, 30
  Barbara, 252
  Benjamin, 30
  Caleb, 30
  Catharine, 2
  Daniel, 2
  Eleanor, 41
  Elizabeth, 41, 76,
  152, 246
  Ephraim, 30, 76, 152

Jacob, 30, 52
James, 41, 76, 128,
  152, 165, 246
Jean, 41, 152
Jennet, 133
John, 52, 82, 117,
  246
Margaret, 41, 76
Mary, 2, 30, 41, 82,
  133
Nathan, 76
Polly, 190
Robert, 2, 30
Samuel, 165
Sarah, 41, 76
Thomas, 2, 52
William, 133, 152,
  190
JOHNTZ, Elizabeth,
  149
  Henry, 149
  Jacob, 149
  Peter, 149
  Susanna, 149
JOLLY, John, 50
JONCE, Barbara, 96
  Catharine, 96
  Elizabeth, 96
  John, 96
  Magdalena, 96
JONES, Alice, 171
  Ann, 244
  Charles, 13
  Daniel, 244
  Daniel Smith, 244
  Edward, 163
  Elizabeth, 13, 15,
  125
  Engel, 15
  Ezekiel, 171
  Hannah, 125, 163
  Henry, 125
  Jacob, 141

Jane, 163
John, 184, 244
Margery, 125
Maria, 185
Mary, 15, 78, 125
Mary E., 15
Michael, 15, 67
Peggy, 244
Phebe, 163
Rachel, 125
Rebecca, 244
Robert, 13
Roert, 125
Sarah, 184, 244
Whirchill, 244
William, 185, 244
JONEST, J., 100
JORDAN, Archibald,
  275
  Benj., 275
  Elisha, 127
  Hatty, 275
  John, 63, 275
  Joseph, 275
  Joshia, 127
  Lydia, 127
  Mary, 275
  Samuel, 262, 275
  Thomas, 265, 266,
  275
JOSEPH, John, 135
JOST, Christiana, 25
  Conrad, 25
  Herman, 25
JULIUS, George, 160,
  180
  James, 221
JUNG, Baker, 155
  Baltzer, 156
  Mary, 155

-K-
KACKLER, Mary, 121

Peter, 121
KAEFFNER, Ann, 93
  Apolon, 93
  Margaret, 93
  Mary, 93
  Mattheis, 93
KAEGY, Abraham, 251
  Elizabeth, 251
KAETRICTER,
  Elizabeth, 190
  George, 190
KAGEY, Abraham, 112
  Ann, 112
  Barbara, 112
  Jacob, 112
  John, 112
KALLER, Abraham, 165
  Barbara, 165
  Catharine, 165
  Christiana, 165, 166
  Elizabeth, 165
  George, 165
  Jacob, 165
KAMSEY, James R., 194
KANN, George, 53
KANTZ, Elizabeth, 51
  Valentine, 51
KAP, Dorothea, 62
  Margaret, 62
KAPP, Eve Maria, 170
  Martin, 170
KARL, Anna, 65
  Anna Maria, 65
  George, 65
  Martin, 65
  Michael, 65
KARWER, Henry, 41
  Mary Elizabeth, 41
KATZ, Anna, 193

John, 193
KAUB, Peter, 62
KAUFFELT, John, 239
  Mary, 239
KAUFFMAN, Anna, 200
  Barbara, 200
  Catharine, 256
  Christian, 200
  Christiana, 200
  Elizabeth, 200
  John, 166
  Joseph, 256
  Magdalena, 166
  Mary, 256
KAUFMAN, Barbara, 187
  Catharine, 187
  Christian, 233
  Elizabeth, 187
  Feronica, 187
  Henry, 187
  John, 187, 230
  Joseph, 250
  Maria, 230
  Michael, 233
  Peter, 187
  Soloman, 187
  Susanna, 187
KAUN, Barbara, 166
  Catharine, 166
  Daniel, 166
  Henry, 166
  John, 166
  Magdalena, 166
  Mary, 166
  Michael, 166
  Philip, 166
  Susanna, 166
KAUTER, Bernhard, 161
  Catharine, 161

Philip, 161
KAUTZ, George, 20
KAWFELT, Michael, 164
KEARNS, Rebecca, 132
  William, 132
KEAS, Catharine, 140
  Elizabeth, 140
  Jane, 140
  John, 140
  Margaret, 140
  Mary, 140
KEAWEY, Catherine, 56
  John, 56
KEEB, Stephen, 161
KEEFER, Eve, 185
  Henry, 185
KEENTZ, Catharine, 54
  George, 17, 23, 31, 37, 45, 54
  Maria Elizabeth, 45
  Marie E., 45
  Mary Elizabeth, 53
KEENY, Anna, 114
  John, 114
KEESY, Catharine, 265
  Conrad, 265
KEFFER, Barbara, 153
  Catharine, 153
  Elizabeth, 153
  Eve, 153
  Frederick, 99
  Jacob, 153
  John, 153
  Joseph, 153
  Ludwig, 153
  Mary, 153
  Mary Elizabeth, 153

Mathias, 153
KEGY, John, 77
  Sarah, 77
KEHLER, Martin, 84
KEHR, Christian, 143
  Elizabeth, 143
  John, 114, 143
  Mary, 143
  Samuel, 143
KEIFER, Dorothea, 45
  Peter, 45
KEIFFER, Ann, 33, 233
  Catharine, 33, 233
  Dorothea, 33, 233
  John, 33, 68, 233
  Margaret, 33
  Maria, 233
  Peter, 33, 233
KEILER, Barbara, 236
  Henry, 236
  John, 236
KEINTZ, George, 15
KEIPER, James, 219
  John, 219
  Samuel, 219
KEIZER, Henry, 192
KELLER, Catharine, 225
  Christian, 129, 132, 186
  Christiana, 132
  Elizabeth, 132, 203, 225
  Esther, 225
  George, 132, 254
  Henry, 132
  Jacob, 129, 135, 203, 213, 225, 254
  John, 186, 213, 225
  Margaret, 186
  Maria, 225
  Mary, 186
  Peter, 249
  Samuel, 185, 186, 254
  Veronica, 132
KELLY, Ann, 229
  Catharine, 229
  Egemyah, 96
  Eleanor, 256
  Elizabeth, 244
  Henry, 222
  James, 96, 259, 270
  John, 96, 111, 116, 164, 210, 229, 244, 256
  Mary, 96, 244, 259, 270
  Nancy, 244
  Patrick, 244
  Rachel, 244
  Rebecca, 96
  Sarah, 244
  Thomas, 96, 244
KELSO, Joseph, 241
  Rebecca, 241
KELTON, George, 270
KEMBERLY,
  Elizabeth, 91
  Paul, 92
KEMERLY, Jacob, 133
  Margaret, 133
KEND, Abraham, 193
  Anna, 193
  Anna Mary, 193
  Christian, 193
  Malin, 193
  Nicholas, 193
  Susanna, 193
KENDRICH, Henry, 123
KENDWORTH,
  Rebecca, 47
KENDWORTHY,
  David, 47
  Rebecca, 47
KENLY, Daniel, 3
KENNARD, Anthony, 136
  Eby, 136
  Elizabeth, 136
  Hannah, 136, 144
  Jesse, 144
  Joseph, 136
  Levi, 136
  Mary, 136
  Phebe, 136
  Tacy, 136
KENNEDY,
  Alexander, 126
  David, 108
  George, 126
  Mary, 108
  William, 126
KENNERLY,
  Catharine, 193
  Jacob, 193
KEPLER, Abijah, 207
  Catharine, 207
  Elizabeth, 207
  George, 207
  Jacob, 207
  Leah, 207
  Martha, 194
  Mary, 207
  Nancy, 207
  Rachel, 207
KEPLINGER,
  Anamary, 152
  Catharine, 152
  Daniel, 152
  Elizabeth, 152
  Hannah, 152
  Peter, 152
  Samuel, 152
KEPNER, Andrew, 119

335

Catharine, 119
Dorothea, 119
Elizabeth, 119
Henry, 119
Mary, 119, 122
Tobias, 119, 121,
  122, 200, 212
William, 119
KEPP, Barbara, 175
George, 175
KEPPLER, Samuel,
  245
KERBACH, Jost, 163
KERBER, Casper, 37
Maria, 37
KERCKHART,
  Anthony, 43
  John, 43
  Veronica, 43
KERMAN, Mathias,
  219
KERN, Barbara, 192
Catharine, 173, 192
Elizabeth, 173
Eve, 192
Frederick, 183
Jacob, 173
John, 173
Joseph, 173
Judith, 192
Margaret, 192
Mary, 192
Michael, 192
Peter, 199, 200, 255
Susanna, 192
KERNAHAN, Agness,
  66
James, 66
KERR, Agness, 108
Alexander, 86
Andrew, 13
David, 153
Eleanor, 153

Eliza, 108
George, 13
Hans, 39
James, 13, 108, 153
Jane, 153
John, 13, 86, 98, 101,
  108, 153
Joseph, 108
Josiah, 86
Margaret, 108
Martha, 13
Mary, 86, 108
Nancy, 108
Robert, 108
Samuel, 13
Sarah, 101
Susanna, 86
Thomas, 13
William, 13, 86, 108,
  153
KESFABER,
  Catharine, 261
  Nicholas, 261
KESSLER, Christiana,
  196
Henry, 64
Magdalena, 196
Michael, 196
KETSMILLER, G., 85
KETZMILLER,
  Elizabeth, 261
  Hannah, 40
  John, 261
  Leonard, 40
KEVER, Elizabeth,
  251
  Frederick, 251
KEYSER, Catharine,
  254
Elizabeth, 254
Jacob, 254
John, 254
Samuel, 254

KIEFBRALER,
  Catherine, 196
  Nicholas, 196
KIENER, Adam, 246
  Susanna, 246
KILGORE, John, 223
  Matthew, 52
  Soloman, 219
  Thomas, 219
KILMORE, Elizabeth,
  165
KIMMEL, Michael, 78
  Molly, 246
  Sally, 246
  Timothy, 246
KINACRE, Anna, 65
  Caspar, 65
KINCAID, Joseph, 229
  Joshua, 229
  Michael, 91
  Nancy, 229
  Samuel, 229
  Thomas, 229
KINEFELTER,
  Michael, 27
KING, Abraham, 20
  Adam, 131
  Ann, 50, 78
  Anna, 97, 131
  Barbara, 50, 101,
    131, 208
  Catharine, 53, 131,
    208
  Charles, 101
  Christiana, 208
  Elizabeth, 131, 139,
    208, 239
  George, 20, 131, 208
  Godfrey, 50, 208
  Henry, 53, 80, 131,
    236
  Hey, 239
  Hugh, 46, 147

Jacob, 101, 131
Jeasus, 37
John, 139, 147
Maria, 53
Michael, 78
Nicholas, 50
Peter, 131
Philip, 32, 50, 131
Philip Jacob, 208
Salome, 139
Susanna, 50
Thomas, 139
Ursula, 80
Victor, 46, 147
William, 46, 97, 106, 147
KINHEAD, Michael, 39
KINKAID, Mary, 112
KINKCAID, John, 61
  Mary, 61
  Michael, 61
  Samuel, 61
KINLY(KING), H., 46
KINSELY, John, 195
KINSER, Jacob, 93
KINSLER, Michael, 221
  Rebecca, 221
KINSTLER, Rebecca, 219
KINTIG, Anna, 169
KINTZLEIN,
  Catharine, 220
  Christian, 220
  Elizabeth, 220
  Jacob, 220
  John, 220
  Magdalena, 220
  Susanna, 220
KINZER, Jacob, 107
KIRK, Aquila, 121
  Caleb, 167

Edith, 186
Eli, 186
Elisha, 83, 121
Elizabeth, 163
Ezekiel, 115
Isaac, 231, 244, 248, 257
John, 266
Jonathon, 115
Lydia, 167
Mathias, 163
Priscilla, 121
Rachel, 115
Ruth, 121
Sarah, 115
Thomas, 115
Timothy, 115
William, 115
KIRKHAN, Anthony, 10
KIRKPATRICK,
  David, 27
  Elizabeth, 27
  Hannah, 27
  Hugh, 27
  James, 27
  Mary, 27
  Susanna, 27
KISER, Catharine, 33
  David, 33
KISSINGER, Anna, 200
  Conrad, 88
  Elizabeth, 88
  Philip, 200
KISTER, Ann, 248
  Anna, 248
  Christian, 248
  David, 248
  Elizabeth, 171, 248
  George, 171, 245, 248
  Hannah, 245

Henry, 248
Jacob, 248
John, 248
Ludwig, 171
Mary, 248
KITZMILLER,
  Catharine, 108
  George, 108
  Jacob, 108
  John, 108
  Juliana, 108
  Martin, 108
  Mary, 108
KLATFELTER,
  Daniel, 275
KLEBER, Elizabeth, 199
  John, 199
KLEIN, Ann, 96
  Catharine, 96
  Christian, 96
  Elizabeth, 168
  Eve, 96
  George, 96
  Henry, 168
  Jacob, 168
  John, 96, 142, 168
  John Ludwig, 100
  Sally, 168
KLEINDEINST,
  Andrew, 247
  Eve, 247
  Katharine, 247
KLEINDINZT,
  Andrew, 168
  David, 168
  Elizabeth, 168
  John, 168
  Polly, 168
  Sabina, 168
KLEINDRENST,
  Godfrey, 187
  Margaret, 187

KLEINFELTER,
   Jacob, 205
KLEPFER, Frederick,
   164
KLINDIENS, Godfrey,
   101
KLINE, Adam, 89
   Anna, 72, 160
   Christiana, 121
   Christopher, 72
   Elizabeth, 78, 207,
      245
   Henry, 108, 245
   John, 121, 245
   Mary, 108
   Mathias, 207
   Michael, 160
   Peter, 78
   Polly, 245
KLINE (OR LITTLE),
   Frederick, 100
   Margaret, 100
   Mary Eva, 100
   Peter, 100
KLINEDIENZT,
   Andrew, 167
   Barbara, 167
   Christian, 167
   Daniel, 167
   David, 167
   Eve, 167
   Godfrey, 167
   Magdalena, 167
   Michael, 167
KLINEFELTER,
   George, 250
   Jacob, 196
   Michael, 208
   Peter, 257
KLINEPETER, Adam,
   150, 222
   Anna, 150
   Casper, 222

Catharine, 222
Elizabeth, 222
Frederick, 222
Henry, 222
John, 222
Margaret, 222
Mary, 222
Rudolph, 222
KLUGH, Frederick,
   274
KLUNK, Ann, 67
   Elizabeth, 67
   Magdalena, 67
   Margaret, 67
   Martin, 67
   Mary, 67
   Peter, 67
KNAB, Catharine, 200
   Jacob, 200
KNASH, Elizabeth,
   157
   William, 157
KNAUB, Elizabeth,
   181
   Peter, 181
KNAUR, Christiana,
   173
   David, 173
KNERTZER, Andrew,
   22, 28
   Anna, 22
   Baltzer, 22, 28
   Catharine, 22, 28
   Christopher, 22
   Dorothea, 28
   George, 28
   Margaret, 22, 28
   Nicholas, 22, 28
KNETZINGER,
   Elizabeth, 222
   Frederick, 222
KNIPPLE, Anna
   Maria, 47

Baltzer, 47
Christopher, 47
KNISEL, Mary, 119
   Samuel, 119
KNISELLEY,
   Abraham, 122
   John, 121, 122
   Mary, 121, 122
   Samuel, 121
KNISELY, Abraham,
   183
   Anna, 183
   Anthony, 183
   Eve, 183
   George, 183
   Jacob, 183
   John, 183
   Mary, 183
   Michael, 183
   Samuel, 183
   Soloman, 183
KNOB, Casper, 201
   Margaret, 201
KNOEDLER, Casper,
   259
   George, 259
   Jacob, 259
   Joseph, 259
   Judith, 259
   Magdalena, 259
KNOUSE, Francis,
   121
KNUES, Daniel, 59
   Elizabeth, 59
   Eve, 59
   Francis, 59
   Henry, 59
   Mary, 59
KOBELL, Jost, 179
KOCH, Barbara, 199
   Catharine, 118
   Elizabeth, 176
   Feronica, 187

George, 134, 176
Jacob, 176
Johannes, 81
John, 118, 134, 176, 259, 267
Margaret, 199
Mary, 81, 176, 199
Nicholas, 187
Peter, 176
Richard, 199, 256
Salome, 176
KOCHE, Eleanor, 246
Henry, 246
KOCHENOUR, John, 109
KOCK, Margaret, 144
Peter, 144
KOELLER, Henry, 138
KOHL, John, 130
Mary, 130
KOHL(COHL), Jacob, 130
KOHLER, Andrew, 101
Joseph, 101, 257
Magdalina, 148
Maria, 101
Valentine, 148
KOHLMAN, Catharine, 237
Jacob, 237
Valentine, 163
KOLP, Magdalena, 199
Philip, 199
KOMFORT, Andreas, 29
Andrew, 29
Ann, 29
John, 29
Leonard, 29
Mary Vernoica, 29

KOOMBS, Elizabeth, 31
Francis, 31
KOPPENHEFFER, Conrad, 214
Elizabeth, 214
KORBMAN, Catharine, 222
Christiana, 222
Eve, 222
George, 222
Henry, 222
John, 222
Michael, 222
Rosina, 222
KOSH, John, 265
KOUR, John, 114
KOUTZ, Catharine, 263
Conrad, 263
Jacob, 263
Peter, 263
KRAEBER, Adam, 250
Anna, 250
Christiana, 250
Elizabeth, 250
John, 250
Sarah, 250
KRAHMER, Barbara, 181
David, 181
KRAMER, Daniel, 64
Jacob, 169
KRANTZ, Ann, 274
Catharine, 274
Christiana, 274
Elizabeth, 274
George, 274
KREANER, Catharine, 259
George, 259
KREBER, Adam, 21, 93, 116, 124

Catharine, 207
Christiana, 93
Elizabeth, 207
Jacob, 207
John, 207
Margaret, 207
Martin, 93
Phileip, 93
Philip, 207
Susanna, 207
KREBS, Anna, 133
Christian, 133
Elizabeth, 85
George, 85, 133
Henry, 133
Jeremiah, 85
John, 133
Katharina, 85
Ludwig, 85
Margaret, 85
Mary, 133
Peter, 85, 133
KREBS (CREBS), Christiana, 133
KREEBER, Henry, 6
Philip, 6
KREIDER, Elizabeth, 109
Michael, 109
KREITLER, Anna, 215
Christian, 215
KRETZINGER, Elizabeth, 270
Henry, 270
KRIDER, Barbara, 109
KRIEGER, Catharine, 38
Peter, 38
KRISLEY, Susanna, 261
KRISTER, Catharine,

246
John, 246
KROAN, Samuel, 94
KROBER, Adam, 184
  Catharine, 184
  Elizabeth, 184
  Gertrude, 184
  Henry, 26
  John, 184
KROH, John, 111
KROLL, John, 101
KROMEIN, Dorothea, 37
  Sabina, 37
  Thomas, 37
KROMER, Philip, 252
KROMLICK, Anna, 47
  Henry, 47
  Mary, 47
KROUSE, Elizabeth, 233
  Hannah, 233
  Jacob, 1
  Mary, 233
  Susanna, 233
KUENY, Anna, 68
  Henry, 68
  John, 68
KUHL, John, 190
  Margaret, 190
  Peter, 190
  Yost, 190
KUHN, Barbara, 56
  Catharine, 56, 124
  Frederick, 56
  George, 56, 124
  Henry, 56
  Jacob, 56, 167
  John, 153, 159, 176
  Mary, 56
  Susanna, 56
KULP, Henry, 196
  Sarah, 196

KUNCKEL, Anna Maria, 237
  Baltzer, 237
  Catharine, 237
  Christian, 237
  Elizabeth, 237
  Eve, 237
  Jacob, 237
  Maria, 237
KUNKEL, Catharine, 125
  Eve, 125
  Jacob, 125
  John, 125
KUNKLE, Alexander, 257
  Barbara, 262
  Eve, 257
  Henry, 262
  John, 88, 257
  Magdalena, 88, 257
  Sally, 257
  Samuel, 257
KUNTZ, Abraham, 127
  Anna, 127
  Catharine, 68, 101, 127
  Elizabeth, 68, 199, 257
  Francis, 199, 257
  George, 6, 27, 28, 91, 99, 257, 273
  John, 127, 167, 257
  Margaret, 257, 273
  Michael, 127
  Peter, 101, 127
  William, 68, 257
KUNY, Anna, 118
  John, 118
KURK, Furgerson, 167
  Mary, 167

Peter, 167
KURTZ, Anna, 185
  Anna Mary, 185, 209
  Benjamin, 144
  Catharine, 54
  Christian, 140, 144
  Christiana, 54, 185, 209
  Christopher, 54
  Daniel, 144
  Elizabeth, 54, 140, 144, 185
  Eve, 185
  Frederick, 144
  George, 144
  Jacob, 144
  John, 54, 144
  Margaret, 185
  Maria, 185
  Martin, 54
  Mary, 144
  Michael, 54, 185, 202, 209
  Nicholas, 144, 185
  Peter, 54, 144
  Philipina, 54
  Susanna, 185
  Thomas, 54
KUTTER, Peter, 184

-L-

LABO, Adam, 193
LACKEY, Alexander, 88
  Catharine, 88
  George, 88
  Margaret, 88
  Mary, 88
  Sarah, 88
LAFERTY, John, 233
LAGER, Thomas, 54
LAIRD, Andrew, 215
  Anna, 17

Baxter, 215
Ellener, 215
Hugh, 216, 240
James, 17, 216, 240
Jane, 216
Janet, 240
Jennet, 17
John, 240
Margaret, 17
Martha, 17
Mary, 17, 215, 216
Polly, 217
Rebecca, 240
Robert, 240
Samuel, 17
Sarah, 17
William, 216
LALTA, Thomas, 110
LAMB, Abraham, 103
  Ann, 103
  Catharine, 103
  Conrad, 103, 136
  Hannah, 162
  John, 162
  Mary, 103
LAMBARD, Ann, 9
  Caspar, 9
  Catharine, 9
  George, 9
  Jacob, 9
  Mathias, 9
LAMBERGER, Mary, 60
LAMBERT, Ann, 107
  Casper, 38, 63
  Catharine, 107
  Elizabeth, 107
  George, 107
  Jacob, 107
  John, 107
  Mary, 107
  Matalina, 107
LAN, Andrew, 150, 209
  Anna, 37, 209, 252
  Anna Mary, 150, 252
  Anna Oleva, 37
  Catharine, 209, 252
  Christian, 37
  Elizabeth, 252
  Eve, 209
  George, 209
  Magdalena, 209, 252
  Margaret, 252
  Maria, 37
  Michael, 37, 150, 252
  Peter, 37, 150, 209
  Philip, 37
  Susanna, 209, 252
LANAUS, William, 55
LANCKS, Casper, 272
LANDES, Abraham, 73
  Barbara, 73
  Benjamin, 73
  Christian, 73
  Daniel, 73
  David, 73
  Elizabeth, 73
  Henry, 73
  Jacob, 73
  John, 73
  Magdalena, 73
  Maria, 73
  Samuel, 73
  Stephen, 73
LANDIS, Anna, 123
  Barbara, 123
  Elizabeth, 123
  John, 185, 189, 208
  Magdalena, 123
  Samuel, 51, 96, 123
LANDRS, Stephen, 83
LANE, Abraham, 146
  Catharine, 146
  John, 146
  Mary, 146
  Peter, 146
  Samuel, 146
  Thomas, 146
LANER, Philip, 215
LANG, Elizabeth, 116
  Frederick, 116
  John, 116
  Mary, 116
LANGEL, Nicholas, 88
LANGWORTHY, E., 82
LANIUS, Barbara, 108
  Catharine, 57, 108
  Christian, 219, 252
  Elizabeth, 220
  Harvey, 57
  Henry, 57, 64, 108, 219
  Jacob, 57, 86, 108
  John, 57, 108
  Juliana, 57
  Magdalena, 57
  Mary, 57
  William, 57, 64, 95, 108
LANTZ, Catharine, 189
  Christiana, 189
  Elizabeth, 188
  Henry, 189
  Marelise, 189
  Philip, 188
LANTZEL, Anna, 199
  Catharine, 199
  George, 199
LARCH, Elizabeth, 159
  Jacob, 159
LARIMER, Esther, 134
  James, 41

Jane, 41
John, 134
Mary, 41
Robert, 134
Thomas, 134
Victor, 41
William, 41, 134
LATSHAW,
  Catharine, 181
  Isaac, 181
LATTA, Debora, 52
  Thomas, 52
LAUB, Conrad, 164
LAUCKS, Christiana, 246
  Elizabeth, 246
  John, 209, 246
  Michael, 246
  Peter, 246
LAUER, Abraham, 121
  Anamary, 121
  Anna, 225
  Barbara, 225
  Catharine, 121, 225
  Christiana, 121, 225
  Conrad, 121
  Elizabeth, 121, 225
  Henry, 121
  Jacob, 121, 225, 257
  John, 121, 225, 257
  Ludwick, 121
  Magdalena, 225, 257
  Margaret, 121
  Mary, 225
  Mathias, 121
  Philip, 225
LAUGHLIN, Jean, 19
  Robert, 19
  Samuel, 19
  Sarah, 154
  William, 154
LAUMAN, Anna

Maria, 55
Catharine, 55, 134
Christian, 116
Christopher, 55
Gottleib, 55
Mary, 55, 134
Susanna, 134
LAUMASTER,
  Elizabeth, 163
  Frederick, 163
  Wendle, 163
LAURER, Abraham, 225
  Anna, 225
  Elizabeth, 225
  John, 225
  Molly, 225
  Nancy, 225
  Philip, 225
  Susanna, 225
LAUSON, Benj., 50
  Edward, 50
  Francis, 50
  Joseph, 50
  Mary, 50
  Moses, 50
  Richard, 50
LAUTSHAW,
  Elizabeth, 15
  Isaac, 15
  Jacob, 15
  John, 15
  Joseph, 15
  Mary, 15
  Peter, 15
LAW, Mary, 182
  Peter, 182
LAWMAN, Catharine, 100
  Christian, 67, 100
  Christopher, 100
  Mary, 100
  Susanna, 100

LAWRENCE,
  Elizabeth, 133
LAWSON, Benj., 224
  Catharine, 253
  Edward, 224
  Fanny, 224
  John, 253
  Joseph, 224, 253
  Magdalena, 253
  Mary, 224
  Moses, 224
  Richard, 224
  Samuel, 253
  Susanna, 253
  William, 253
LAY, John, 202
LEAMER, Conrad, 119
  Elizabeth, 119
LEANY, Catharine, 120
  Isaac, 120
LEARD, John, 20
  Joseph, 52
  Martha, 20
  Mary, 20
  Robert, 52
  William, 20, 52
LEAS, Abraham, 78
  Asper, 172
  Barbara, 212
  Benjamin, 78
  Catharine, 78
  Daniel, 78, 212
  Eleanor, 78
  Elizabeth, 212
  Hannah, 172
  Jacob, 78, 212
  John, 78, 160, 172
  Leonard, 78, 172
  Margaret, 212
  Mary, 78, 172
  Philip, 172

Samuel, 172
Sarah, 78, 212
Stephen, 172
Susanna, 172, 212
Ursilla, 78
Valentine, 212
William, 78, 212
LEASE, Leonard, 80
Louise, 80
LEAST, John, 190
Philip, 190
LEATHERMAN,
  Conrad, 56, 264
  Margaret, 56, 264
  Michael, 56
LEBBERL, John, 265
Lettia, 265
LEBERNIGHT, Jacob, 249
  John, 248
  Mary, 248
LECHNER,
  Catharine, 121
  Christiana, 121
  Elizabeth, 121
  George, 121
  John, 121
  Juliana, 121
  Lena, 121
  Mary, 121
  Micheal, 121
  Salome, 121
LECKRONE, George, 226
  Gerard, 226
  Leonard, 226
  Peter, 226
LEDDER, Jacob, 19
  Margaret, 19
LEE, John, 206
LEECH, Ann, 98, 139
  Barbara, 139
  Henry, 139

James, 139
Jane, 105
Jean, 139
Jenet, 139
Jennet, 147
Mary, 139
Rachel, 105
Robert, 139
Samuel, 98, 139
Sarah, 34, 105
Thomas, 105, 158
LEETENBERGER,
  Casper, 201
LEETNER, Ignatus, 265
LEFER, James, 27
LEFEVER, Catharine, 87
  George, 30
  Jacob, 87
LEFFER, George Lewis, 80
LEFLER, Elizabeth, 240
  George, 56
  George Lewis, 82, 160, 240
  Margaret, 56
  Mary, 240
LEGGET, Ellener, 160
  William, 160
LEH, Barbara, 187
  John, 187
LEHMAN, Abraham, 161, 184, 206
  Ann, 40, 202
  Anna, 239
  Barbara, 10, 250
  Christian, 89, 161, 202, 250
  Elizabeth, 239
  Frederick, 239
  Henry, 161

Jacob, 40, 239
John, 161
Maria, 40
Mary, 40, 206, 239
Peter, 10, 40
Susanna, 161
LEHMER, Abraham, 148
  Catharine, 148, 180
  David, 148
  Elizabeth, 148, 180
  Eve, 148
  Henry, 148, 152, 180
  Jacob, 148, 180
  John, 148, 180
  Mary, 148
  Philip, 148
  Sarah, 148
  Susanna, 148, 180
  William, 148, 180
LEHN, Abraham, 149
  Catharine, 81
  Elizabeth, 81
  Hannah, 81, 149
  John, 81
  Jonathan, 81
  Margaret, 81
  Mary, 81
  Peter, 81, 149
  Thomas, 149
LEHR, Anny, 247
  Casper, 247
  Catty, 247
  David, 247
  Elizabeth, 247
  John, 247
  Peter, 247
  Philip, 247
  Polly, 247
LEIB, Abraham, 155, 156
  Ann, 155
  Barbara, 101

Catharine, 155
Christian, 73, 155
Godrey, 101
Henry, 215
John, 215, 235
Magdalena, 155, 215
Nancy, 215
Tobias, 107
LEIBBHART, Henry, 140
LEIBENSTEIN,
  Adam, 35
  Ann, 35
  Catharine, 35
  Christian, 35
  Elizabeth, 35
  Eve, 35
  George, 35
  Jacob, 35
  John, 35
  Maria, 35
  Michael, 35
LEIBHART,
  Elizabeth, 231
  Henry, 231
LEIDIG, Michael, 186
  Sarah, 186
LEIDY, Catharine, 204
  Jacob, 204
LEIL, Barbara, 166
  Christian, 166
LEINBACHER, Anna, 39
  Catharine, 39
  Conrad, 39
  Felix, 39
  Henry, 39
LEININGER,
  Catharine, 76
  Elizabeth, 217
  George, 76, 128, 217
  Magdalena, 128

LEIPHARD, Henry, 99
LEISS, Elizabeth, 238
  Peter, 238
LEITNER, Adam, 55
  Catharine, 270
  Charlotte, 270
  ELizabeth, 270
  George, 253, 270
  Henry, 270
  Ignatus, 65, 233, 260, 270
  Jacob, 270
  Joseph, 270
  Lydia, 270
  Margaret, 270
  Mary, 270
  Rebecca, 270
  Suanna, 270
LELLEY, Thomas, 12
LEMAN, Barbara, 30
  Christian, 30
  David, 30
  Frena, 30
  John, 30
  Maney, 30
  Margaret, 248
  Robert, 248
  Rude, 30
  William, 248
LENHART, Anna
  Maria, 274
  Cataharine, 232
  Catharine, 273, 274
  Elizabeth, 148, 232, 273, 274
  George, 274
  Godfrey, 148, 257, 273
  Henry, 273, 274
  John, 274
  Margaret, 273
  Peter, 274

Susanna, 274
William, 273, 274
LENIUS, Hey, 97
  Margaret, 97
LENN, Adam, 3
LENUS, Henry, 72
  Jacob, 72
LEONHART,
  Christopher, 43
  Frederick, 43
  George, 43
  Godrey, 43
  Henry, 43
  Jacob, 43
  Margaret, 43
  Peter, 43
  Philip, 43
  William, 43
LEPE, Christian, 44, 89
LEPHARD, Appolonia, 117
  Henry, 50
  Valentine, 117
LEPHART, Anna, 117
  Catharine, 39
  George, 39
  Henry, 39
  Jacob, 39
  John, 39
  Mary, 39
  Valentine, 39
LEREW, Jacob, 163
LERSH, Abraham, 140
  Margaret, 140
LERUE, Abraham, 10
  Francis, 10
  Jacob, 94
  Mary, 10
LERY, Elizabeth, 26
LESHY, Susanna, 146
LESSEL, John, 185

Margaret, 185
LETH, William, 81
LETSHAW, Jacob, 77
　Marlina, 77
LEVERKNIGHT,
　Catharine, 243
　Frederick, 243
　John, 243
LEVESTON, Barbara, 87
　John, 87
LEVISTON, Andrew, 3
　George, 16
LEWIG, Anna, 212
　Philip, 212
LEWIS, Eli, 148
　Ellis, 29, 148
　Jacob, 148
　Lewis, 59
　Mary, 148
　Ruth, 148
　Susanna, 233
LEYTY, Catharine, 9
　Christian, 9
　John, 9
　Jonas, 9
LIBHART, Henry, 63
LICHDEBERGER, A., 192
　C., 192
LICHENKNECHT, F., 98
LICHTENBERGER,
　Adam, 200, 202, 207, 218, 225
　Casper, 50
　Elizabeth, 200
　George, 200
　Killean, 74
LICHTENWALTER,
　Abraham, 168
LICHTINBERGER,
　Adam, 196
　Conrad, 196
LICHTY, Barbara, 213
　John, 269
　Nicholas, 213
LIEBHART,
　Appolonia, 213
　Barbara, 213
　Catharine, 213
　Elizabeth, 213
　Henry, 213
　Jacob, 213
　John, 213
　Philip, 213
　Susanna, 213
　Valentine, 213
LIFLER, Grace Lewis, 86
LIGGIT, Alexander, 17, 195
　Eleanor, 195
　Elizabeth, 17
　Francis, 17
　George, 17
　John, 17
　Margaret, 17, 195
　William, 195
LIGHTNER, Adam, 17, 45
LIGHTY, Abraham, 214
　John, 36, 214
　Jonas, 51
　Mary, 36
LIKE, Chrisle, 46
LILLEY, Samuel, 12
　Thomas, 12
LILLY, Anna, 104
　Thomas, 27, 58, 104
LIND, Peter, 47
LINDSEY, Mary, 6
　William, 6
LINDY, Catharine, 139
　Christiana, 139
　Dorothea, 139
　Elizabeth, 139
　Eve, 139
　Jacob, 139
　John, 139
　Rosand, 139
LINE, William, 242
LINN, Andrew, 141
　David, 141
　Hugh, 141
　Jennet, 141
　John, 22, 44, 51, 141
　Margaret, 141
　Rachel, 174
　Samuel, 141, 174
　William, 141
LINTON, Elizabeth, 192
　Sarah, 192
LIPE, Christian, 33
　Mary, 32
LITCH, Elizabeth, 59
　James, 59
　Jean, 59
　Joseph, 59
LITCHENBERGER,
　Adam, 273
LITTLE, Adam, 83
　Andrew, 83
　Casper, 83
　Catharine, 83
　David, 83
　Frederick, 100
　George, 83
　Hannah, 83
　Henry, 83
　Jacob, 83
　John, 83
　John Ludwig, 100
　Joseph, 83
　Margaret, 100

Mary Eva, 100
Peter, 83, 100
Samuel, 83
Susanna, 83
Trony, 83
LIVE, Elizabeth, 59
Michael, 59
LIVINGSTON, Adam, 44
Agness, 133
Andrew, 44
Eals, 133
George, 44
James, 133
Jean, 133
John, 55, 133, 229, 255
Margaret, 55
Mary, 133
Michael, 262
Sarah, 133
William, 55, 133
LOBACH, Andrew, 183
Eve, 183
LOBOOB, Christiana, 68
Dorothea, 68
Elizabeth, 68
Maria, 68
Michael, 68
LOCHNER, Anna, 130
Henry, 130
LOEB, Ann, 199
Daniel, 199
LOGAN, Agness, 156
Esther, 173
Henry, 156
Jenny, 156
John, 156
Nancy, 156
LOGUE, James, 72, 127, 197, 235, 238

LOHRA, Michael, 26
Regena, 26
LOMER, Adam, 121
Catharine, 121
LONG, Andrew, 56
Ann, 150
Anna, 159
Anna Maria, 159
Barbara, 223
Catharine, 150
Christiana, 159, 192, 214
Conrad, 150, 159
Elizabeth, 22, 23, 150, 159, 264
Enis, 150
Frederick, 90, 214, 223
George, 22, 36, 264
Hannah, 172
Henry, 23, 39, 150
Herman, 192
Hugh, 264, 271
Isabella, 172, 264
Jacob, 150
James, 39, 78
Jane, 172
Jennet, 23
John, 159, 172, 223, 264
Joseph, 172
Juliana, 159
Margaret, 23, 172
Martha, 264
Mary, 23, 39, 172, 192, 261
Mary C., 223
Matthew, 23
Michael, 56, 223
Peter, 56
Philip, 76
Polly, 208
Rachel, 172

Rebecca, 106
Regina Magdalena, 56
Samuel, 208, 261
Sarah, 171
Susanna, 150
Thomas, 172
William, 106, 150
LOOP, Christian, 90
Christiana, 90
LORA, Henrich, 18
LORICH, Barbara, 216
Effa, 216
Jacob, 216
Michael, 216
LORY, Philip, 158
LOSH, Catharine, 217
Elizabeth, 217
Henry, 217
Zacharius, 217
LOTT, Cornelius, 146
Cyrus, 240
David, 240
Elizabeth, 240
Hannah, 240
James, 240
John, 240
Lena, 146
Mary, 240
Ruth, 240
Susanna, 240
LOTTMAN, Barbara, 234
Catharine, 234
Elizabeth, 234
George, 233, 234
Jacob, 234
John, 233, 234
Mary, 234
Sarah, 234
LOUDWICK, Abraham, 94

Anna Mary, 93
Christopher, 94
Conrad, 93
Jacob, 93, 94
Michael George, 94
LOVE, Anna, 232
Eleanor, 7
Elizabeth, 7
James, 83
Jane, 7
John, 7, 83, 137, 185, 232
Margaret, 7
Mary, 83
Thomas, 83
William, 7, 24, 83
LOVINE, Abraham, 35
LOW, Andrew, 70
Ann, 220
Aquilla, 249
Ashel, 249
Caleb, 16, 220
Conrad, 5
Elizabeth, 70
Gertrude, 70
Hannah, 249
Henry, 70
Isaac, 249
Jeremiah, 249
Jesse, 220
John, 249
Joshua, 16, 220, 249
Magdalena, 70
Maria, 249
Mary, 16, 220
Michael, 70
Peter, 24
Philip, 70
Providen, 249
Rebecca, 249
Rhode, 249
LOWMAN, Ann, 30

Anna Margaret, 30
Barnet, 30
Bernhart, 6
Christopher, 30, 132
Gotleep, 30
Magdalena, 30
Stophel, 50
LOYD, Walter, 3
William, 3
LUCHENBACH,
Elizabeth, 35
Henry, 35
LUCK, Thomas, 177
LUDER, Frederick, 196
LUDWICK, Elizabeth, 185
George, 185
John, 185
Laurence, 185
Lawrence, 185
Mary, 185
Philip, 185
LUDWIG, Abraham, 93
Ann, 93
Anna Mary, 93
Barbara, 158
Conrad, 93
Geroge, 93
Jacob, 93
Markret, 93
Milzer, 109
LUENEY, Mary, 154
LUSK, David, 106
Elizabeth, 106
LUTES, Adam, 224
Elizabeth, 224, 248
Henry, 224
John, 224
Leah, 224
Magdalena, 224
Margaret, 224

Sarah, 224

-M-
M., Catharine, 59
Vernor, 59
MCADAMS, John, 15, 179
Marian, 179
Samuel, 15
Sarah, 15
MCALESTER, Elen, 91
Gabriel, 91
James, 91
John, 91
MCALIER, Thomas, 256
MCALISTER, Abigail, 136
Alexander, 45
Charles, 45, 77
Hugh, 77
James, 45, 77
John, 45
Margaret, 45
Mary, 45, 77
Richard, 136
Rosanna, 45
Sarah, 77
MCALLISTER,
Elizabeth, 159
Jesse, 159
MCANULTY, James, 43
Jeseph, 43
John, 43, 55
Mary, 43, 55
Michael, 43, 54
Richard, 111
Robert, 55
William, 43
MCBRIDE, Andrew, 101

Catharine, 247
Daniel, 41
Elinor, 76
Hugh, 41, 247
James, 101
Jean, 101
Margaret, 41, 101
Neal, 41
Susanna, 101
William, 76
MCCAIN, Catharine, 107
Joseph, 107
MCCALISTER,
  Archibald, 152
  Elizabeth, 152
  Jean, 152
  Jessee, 152
  John, 152
  Matthew, 152
  Nancy, 152
  Richard, 152
  Sally, 152
MCCALL, Alexander, 7
  Elizabeth, 7
  James, 7
  Jennet, 7
  John, 7, 156
  Margaret, 7
  Martha, 7
  Matthew, 68, 156
  Robert, 68, 156
  Samuel, 7
  Susanna, 68
  Thomas, 7
MCCALLY, John, 222
  William, 222
MCCAN, Ann, 13
  Daniel, 13
  Patrick, 13
  Timothy, 13
MCCANDLES,
  Alexander, 21
  James, 21
  Jean, 21
  Margaret, 21
  Martha, 21
  Sarah, 21
  William, 21
MCCANDLESS,
  Agness, 239
  Alexander, 65, 110, 116, 239
  Elizabeth, 65
  Esther, 110, 116
  George, 156
  Hannah, 239
  James, 110, 116, 156, 239
  John, 156, 239
  Katharine, 156
  Mary, 156
  R., 110
  Ruthia, 110, 116, 239
  Sarah, 110, 116
  William, 110, 116
MCCANLEY, Eve, 220
  Robert, 220
MCCANN, Dorothea, 258
  George, 147
  Henry, 258
  Martha, 147
MCCARRA, James, 39
MCCARRLL, Ann, 22
  Elizabeth, 22
  Esther, 22
  James, 22
  John, 22
  Mary, 22
MCCARRY, Yeancy, 3
MCCARTER,
  Alexander, 14, 22
  Elizabeth, 14
MCCASKEY, Neall, 27

William, 27
MCCAULEY, Jennet, 242
  Susanna, 242
  William, 242
MCCAY, John, 229
MCCHANCE,
  Andrew, 75
  David, 74, 75
  George, 74, 75
  John, 74
  Margaret, 75
MCCLAIN, Elizabeth, 220
  Jacob, 220
  Moses, 98
  Peter, 62
  William, 35
MCCLARIE, Andrew, 196
  John, 196
  Margaret, 196
MCCLASS, Barbara, 268
  Susanna, 268
MCCLEAN,
  Alexander, 98
  Ann, 98
  Anna Maria, 167
  Archibald, 98
  Catharine, 7
  Elizabeth, 98
  Esther, 98
  James, 7
  John, 7
  Mary, 98
  Moses, 98, 159
  Rebecca, 98
  William, 7, 55, 167
MCCLEARY, Agness, 212
  Andrew, 233
  Elizabeth, 233

Isabella, 212
Jane, 233, 236
Jean, 212
John, 212, 233, 236
Margaret, 212
Martha, 233
Nathan, 212
Sarah, 233
William, 233
MCCLELLAN, Ann, 210
David, 7, 91, 158, 210
Elizabeth, 7, 76
Jacob, 7
James, 158
Jane, 76
John, 7, 76
Margaret, 76, 158, 210
Martha, 158
Mary, 7, 76
Samuel, 158
Thomas, 136
William, 7, 76, 158
MCCLELLAND,
Agness, 152
David, 122
Elizabeth, 122
Jacob, 122
Jannet, 122
John, 122
Mary, 122
Robert, 122
Walter, 122
William, 122
MCCLELLEAN,
David, 111
MCCLENTOR, James, 20
Jean, 20
Jenny, 20
MCCLERY, Andrew, 31
John, 31
Martha, 31
Mary, 31
Sarah, 31
MCCLURE, Agness, 109
Ann, 109
Elizabeth, 75, 109
Jane, 109
John, 75, 97
Margaret, 75, 109
Mary, 75, 109
Sarah, 109
Thomas, 75
Violet, 97
MCCLURE(MCLURE), James, 109
MCCONNELL,
Ebenezer, 42
Margaret, 42
MCCONOUGHY,
Samuel, 39
MCCORMICK, James, 66
Mary, 66
MCCORRISON, Cary, 11
John, 11
Margery, 11
William, 11
MCCORTEL,
Margaret, 66
Robert, 66
MCCOSH, James, 54
John, 54
Mary, 54
Nathaniel, 54
Samuel, 54
Sarah, 54
MCCOULLATH,
Anna, 34
Elizabeth, 34
Esther, 34
Isabella, 34
Jane, 34
Margaret, 34
Samuel, 34
William, 34
MCCOY, Agness, 205
Elizabeth, 205
Esther, 6
James, 205
Jenny, 205
John, 205
Lydia, 205
William, 205
MCCRACKEN,
Anthony, 44
Elizabeth, 44
James, 44
Margaret, 158
Mary, 44
Rebecca, 44
Robert, 158
MCCREARY, Andrew
Agnew, 170
George, 120
Hannah, 130
James, 148, 170
James Agnew, 170
Jannet, 148
John, 148, 154
John Agnew, 170
Margaret, 30, 148
Mary, 120
Sarah, 130
Thomas, 119, 180
William, 30, 55, 148
MCCREERY, Jane, 171
Margaret, 171
MCCRERY, Marion, 136
Thomas, 136
MCCUER, James, 190

Susanna, 190
MCCULLEN, Agness,
  113
  Jennet, 113
  Mary, 113
MCCULLOCH,
  Margaret, 39
  Mary, 39
  Samuel, 39
MCCULLOUGH,
  Hugh, 54
  Jacob, 108
  James, 108
  John, 108
  Margaret, 108
  Mary, 54, 108
  Rebecca, 108
  Samuel, 150
  Sarah, 108
  William, 108
MCCUNE, Martha,
  110
  Samuel, 110
  Sarah, 110
  Thomas, 110
MCCURDY, Agness,
  70
  Alexander, 44, 198
  Grace, 106
  Hugh, 106
  James, 63
  Jeseph, 70
  John, 70
  Margaret, 70, 198
  Mary, 70, 106
  Robert, 70
  Sarah, 44, 70
MCCURRY, George,
  52
  James, 52
  John, 52
  Joseph, 52
  William, 52

MCDANIEL, James,
  186
  Jane, 186
  John, 186
MCDAVIT, Barbara,
  189
  George, 189
MCDERMOND, John,
  123
  Mary, 123
  Sarah, 123
MCDONALD, Agness,
  116
  Anna, 168
  Aquilla, 116, 168
  Daniel, 158
  Duncan, 41
  Elizabeth, 116, 168,
    239
  Grazel, 168
  Jane, 116, 168, 189
  John, 158, 239
  Margaret, 116, 168
  Martha, 76
  Mary, 76, 116, 168
  Persilla, 116, 168
  Richard, 116, 168
  Robert, 116, 168
  Samuel, 76
  Susanna, 239
MCDONAUGH, Ann,
  11
  Elizabeth, 11
  Henry, 11
  Jean, 11
  John, 11
  Joseph, 11
  Margaret, 11
  Mary, 11
MCDONNALD, Mary,
  219
MCDOWEL, Agness,
  61

  Elizabeth, 61
  John, 61
  Margaret, 61
  William, 61
MCDOWELL, Agness,
  81
  Andrew, 38
  James, 81
  Joseph, 91
  Manuell, 210
  Sarah, 91
MACE, George, 267
MCELHENNY,
  Elizabeth, 50
  Robert, 151
MCELWAIN,
  Elizabeth, 44
  William, 44
MCFADDEN,
  Catharine, 247
  Dennis, 247
  Edward, 247
  Hugh, 247
  John, 247
MCFARLAN, Alice, 82
  James, 82
  John, 149
  Mary, 82
  Sarah, 82
  Thomas, 82
  William, 82
MCFARLAND, James,
  70
  Margaret, 154
  Thomas, 66, 154
MCFARRAN, Samuel,
  6, 12
MCFERRAN, Agness,
  79
  Andrew, 79
  Anne, 79
  Elizabeth, 79
  Jane, 79

John, 79
Martha, 79
Mary, 79
Samuel, 79
Susanna, 79
William, 79
MCFERSON, Hugh, 2
Jane, 2
John, 2
Robert, 2
MCFLADDEN,
Dennis, 248
Eleanor, 248
Mary, 248
MCFLADDIN,
Catherine, 248
MCGAHEY,
Alexander, 53
Jann, 53
John, 53
Martha, 53
Mary, 53
Thomas, 53
MCGANGHY, James, 79
William, 2
MCGAUGHEY,
Agness, 77
William, 77
MCGAUGHY, Agness, 169
Alexander, 3, 169
Ann, 169
Hugh, 169
James, 3, 169
John, 3
Margaret, 3
William, 3, 169
MCGEE, James, 111
Jean, 20
Patrick, 111
MCGENNIS, Dennis, 4

James, 4
John, 4
William, 4
MCGILL, Agness, 156
John, 156
MCGIMSEY, Anna, 172
Joseph, 172
Mary, 172
Robert, 172
William, 172
MCGINLEY, Abigail, 159
Alexander, 159
Ebenezer, 159
Edward, 159
Jane, 159
John, 159
Joseph, 159
Margaret, 159
Mary, 159
MCGLAUGEN,
Margaret, 196
MCGLAUGLEN,
James, 196
MCGOWN, Andrew, 53
James, 53
John, 53
Mary, 53
Robert, 53
Samuel, 53
William, 53
MCGRAW, Agness, 246
Eleanor, 246
Elizabeth, 246
Jane, 246
Mary, 246
Robert, 246
Samuel, 246
William, 246
MCGREW, A., 46

Alexander, 134
Alexnader, 139
Ann, 139
Archibald, 19, 22, 30, 37, 46, 49, 64, 67, 87, 97
Catharine, 49
David, 11
Deborah, 139
Elizabeth, 22, 49
Finley, 22, 26, 117, 139, 152
James, 22, 139
Jean, 139
John, 49, 97, 132, 139, 166
Margaret, 67
Mary, 110, 139
Nathan, 22, 26
Peter, 22
Rachel, 26
Rebecca, 26
Robert, 114
Simeon, 139
William, 22, 49, 110, 114
MCGRUE, John, 59
MCGUIRE, James, 270
John, 270
Mary, 269
Peter, 269
Ruth, 270
Sarah, 270
Thomas, 270
William, 269
MACHLAN,
Elizabeth, 65
George, 65
James, 65
John, 65
Lydia, 65
Margaret, 65

Mary, 65
Rebecca, 65
Sarah, 65
William, 65
MACHLIN, Catharine, 264
Daniel, 264
Elizabeth, 264
John, 264
Jonathan, 264
Philip, 264
Salome, 264
Solomon, 264
MCILHENNEY, James, 60
Robert, 140
MCILHENNY, Esther, 173
Ezekiel, 173
James, 86, 173
Robert, 89, 173
Samuel, 173
Sophia, 173
MCILHENY, Agness, 97
Anna, 97
Margaret, 97
Robert, 97
Violet, 97
William, 97
MCILHERSON, Eleanor, 80
MCILVAIN, Alexer., 138
Andrew, 101, 138
John, 138
Moses, 138
Rebecca, 138
William, 138
MCINTYRE, Alexander, 101
Jane, 101
John, 101

Martha, 101
Sarah, 101
MCIUOWN, Thomas, 120
MACKAWAY, Daniel, 262
MCKEAN, Alexander, 130
Hugh, 130
James, 130
John, 130
Martin, 130
Mary, 130
Robert, 130
Thomas, 130
MCKEE, Andrew, 52
Betsy, 127
James, 11
Jean, 111
John, 111, 127
Joseph, 115, 127
Polly, 111
Robert, 111
Sally, 127
Thomas, 127
William, 127
MCKEEN, Alexander, 36
Hugh, 36
Mary, 36
Sarah, 36
MCKESSON,
  Alexander, 34
  Ebenezer, 34
  James, 34, 42, 71
  John, 34
  Margaret, 34
  Mary, 34
  William, 34, 42, 71
MACKEY, Eleanor, 97
James, 97
MCKINLEY, Andrew, 157

Ann, 106
Benjamin, 157
Catharine, 157
David, 59, 271
Elizabeth, 106, 271
Esther, 271
Hannah, 271
Hugh, 54
Isaac, 106
James, 106
John, 27, 54, 59, 157
Margaret, 59, 106
Martha, 106
Mary, 54, 271
Phebe, 106
Rebecca, 106
Sarah, 106
Stephen, 142, 271
Susanna, 271
Thomas, 216
William, 106, 271
MCKINLY, Isaac, 11
MCKINNEY, Anna, 230
MCKNIGHT, James, 32
MCKUITT, James, 191
Jean, 191
MCLAUGHLIN, John, 143
Mary, 143
MCLEAN, Ann, 83
James, 83
Jean, 75
Moses, 83
William, 75, 152
MCMIHLHEIM, George, 159
MCMILLAN, Abigail, 130
Ann, 151
Deborah, 151

Esther, 144
George, 151
Jacob, 151
James, 130, 144
Joanna, 144
John, 130, 144, 158
Joseph, 151
Mary, 144, 151
Rebecca, 151
Ruth, 144
Thomas, 130, 151, 253
William, 38
MCMILLEN, Thomas, 218
William, 34
MCMILLIN, Samuel, 38
MACMON, William, 241
MCMORDIE, James, 84
MCMULLAN, George, 266
William, 269
MCMULLEN,
　Charles, 9
　George, 265, 266
　James, 15, 207, 266
　Jean, 15, 266
　Mary, 15
　Matthew, 117
　Robert, 15, 117
　Samuel, 117, 207
　William, 207
MCMULLIN, Ealse, 137
　Elizabeth, 137
　George, 137
　Hugh, 137
　Jane, 137
　Mary, 137
　William, 256

MCNAGTEN,
　Elizabeth, 64, 67
　John, 64, 67
　Margaret, 64, 67
　Margerey, 64
　Margery, 67
　Neal, 64
　Sarah, 64, 67
　Thomas, 64, 67
MCNAIR, Alexander, 153
MCNARY, Agness, 187
　Alexander, 187
　Elizabeth, 187
　Esther, 187
　James, 187, 202
　Jannet, 187
　Jean, 187
　John, 187
　Margaret, 187, 202
　Mary, 187
MCNEIL, Ephriam, 13
　John, 13
　Robert, 13
MCNUTT, Francis, 43
　John, 43
　Samuel, 43
　Susanna, 43
MCPERSON, William, 112
MCPHERSON,
　Agness, 27
　Ann, 259
　Catharine, 273
　Elizabeth, 259
　Frederick, 259
　Grace, 241, 259
　Hugh, 27
　Isabella, 241, 259
　James, 26
　Janet, 27
　Jannet, 27

John, 227, 259, 273
Latitia, 259
Mary, 259
Polly, 241
Robert, 26, 27, 36, 76
Samuel, 259
William, 82, 227, 241, 259
MCPHESON, Agness, 139
　John, 139
　Robert, 139
　William, 139
MCPIKE, Anna, 105
　Daniel, 105
　James, 105
　John, 105
　Margaret, 105
　William, 105
MCQUEEN,
　Elizabeth, 151
　Isabella, 151
　Josiah, 151
　Susanna, 151
MCQUOWN,
　Catharine, 120
　David, 120
　Eleanor, 120
　Elizabeth, 120
　James, 120
　Jean, 120
　John, 120
　Laurence, 120
　Margaret, 120
　Mary, 120
　Rebecca, 120
　Thomas, 120
　William, 120
MCRAIL, Owen, 117
MCRANDLES, Ann, 64
　Joseph, 64

Roland, 64
MCSHERRY, Barbara, 169
  Barnabus, 151
  Catherine, 151
  Hugh, 151
  James, 151
  John, 151
  Mary, 151
  Patrick, 62, 151
  Sarah, 151
MCTEETH, Jean, 143
  John, 143
MCWILLIAM, James, 13
MCWILLIAMS,
  James, 81
  John, 81
MADOK, Dorothea, 62
  George, 62
MAFFIT, James, 77
MAGOLD, Barara, 137
  Catharine, 137
  Elizabeth, 137
  George, 137
MAICH, David, 224
MAIER, Andrew, 62
  Christian, 62
  Elizabeth, 62
  Francis, 62
  Hannah, 62
  John, 62
MAINS, Culbert, 28
  Elizabeth, 28
  Isaac, 28
  Robert, 28
MAIR, Daniel, 152
MAISH, John George, 204
  Joseph, 193, 204
MAISK, George, 145
MAJOR, Agness, 197

Alexander, 197
Andrew, 197
Anne, 197
Archibald, 197
John, 197
Thomas, 197
MALAWN, Anna, 36
  Catharine, 36
  Hannah, 36
  John, 36
  Mary, 36
  Mathias, 36
  Rebecca, 36
MALE, George, 73
MALERIS, Catharine, 233
  Jacob, 233
MALES, Elizabeth, 99
  Jacob, 99
MALOAN, Mathias, 78
MALTER, Henry, 215
MAMAUGH, John, 210
MAMBER, Christiana, 214
  Michael, 213, 214
MANGES, Catharine, 211
  Elizabeth, 211
  Eve, 211
  Jacob, 211
  John, 211
  Margaret, 211
  Peter, 205, 211
MANIFOLD, Agness, 269
  Anabel, 269
  Anibale, 185
  Benj., 185, 269
  Eleanor, 185, 269
  Elizabeth, 269
  Henry, 185

Jean, 269
John, 168, 185, 269
Joseph, 185, 269
Lydia, 185
Margaret, 269
Mary, 185, 269
William, 185, 269
MANIFORD, Joseph, 116
MANSBERGER,
  George, 194
MANSPERGER,
  George, 46, 74
  John, 46
  Margaret, 46
  Martin, 46
MAPPEN, Mary, 5
  Moses, 5
MARBOURG,
  Catharine, 250
  Maxemilian, 250
MARCH, Andony, 131
  Catharine, 131
  George, 131
  Gertrude, 131
  Jacob, 131, 168
  John, 131
  Joseph, 192
  Mary Catharine, 131
  Nancy, 131
  Polly, 131
  Susanna, 131
MARCKS, John, 109
  Sybilla, 109
MARKER, Catharine, 8
  Mathias, 8
MARKEY, Jacob, 257
MARKLE, Henry, 81
MARKS, Barbara, 272
  Catharine, 272
  Magdalena, 272
  Margaret, 272

Mary, 272
Sybilla, 272
MARLEN, Jean, 38
John, 38
Mary, 38
Rachel, 38
William, 38
MARLIN, Agness, 72
Alexander, 107
David, 126
Elizabeth, 72
James, 107, 127
Jean, 72
John, 127
Mary, 72
Rachel, 72, 127
Sarah, 107, 126
Susanna, 72
William, 72, 127
MARSDEN, Edward, 144
Elizabeth, 144
James, 144
Jean, 144
Matthew, 144
MARSH, Catharine, 213
Deborah, 113
Edith, 218
Elizabeth, 197
Esther, 113
Hannah, 197, 218
Hugh, 197, 213
James, 218
Jane, 34, 113
John, 113, 197, 213, 218
Jonathan, 113, 197
Lidia, 197
Lydia, 113
Margaret, 197
Mary, 113, 197
Peter, 113

Rachel, 113
Rebecca, 113, 197
Susanna, 197
William, 197
MARSHALL,
Catharine, 95
Elizabeth, 268
James, 77
Nicholas, 95
William, 268
MARSHEL, Elizabeth, 189
James, 189
Susanna, 189
William, 189
MARTER, Anna, 159
Catharine, 159
George, 159
Henry, 159
Jacob, 159
Ludwig, 159
Valentine, 159
MARTIN, Andrew, 182, 195
Charles, 81
Christian, 224
Edward, 16
Elizabeth, 182, 195
Henry, 49
Isabel, 195
Jacob, 110
James, 79, 195
Jean, 182, 195
Jennet, 79
John, 127, 182
Margaret, 182
Mary, 16, 196
Peter, 195
Samuel, 195
Sarah, 79
Thomas, 79, 182
William, 72, 196
MARTZEN,

Catharina, 168
MARWELL, James, 95
MARX, Elizabeth, 265
Mary, 122
Peter, 122
MASEMER, Barbara, 249
Jacob, 249
MASON, Janet, 57
Joseph, 16
MASTER, George, 162
Susanna, 162
MATE, Anna, 117
Appolonia, 117
Casper, 117
Elizabeth, 190
John, 96, 117
Magdalena, 117
Philip, 117, 190
MATEER, Mary, 238
Warren, 238
MATEERS, Samuel, 204
MATHER, George, 25, 121
Henry, 188
Jean, 9
Lydia, 178
Richard, 9
Sarah, 9
Thomas, 178
MATHERS, Mary, 107
MATHIAS, Henry, 109
Sarah, 249
MATTER, Henry, 204
MATTHEW, Hannah, 133
William, 29, 133
MATTHEWS,
Hannah, 147
Mordica, 218
Ruth, 218

William, 34
MATTHIAS,
  Catharine, 213
  Elizabeth, 213
  Henry, 213
  John, 213
  Mary, 213
  Peter, 213
  Sophia, 213
MAUL, Bartholomew, 8
  Catharine, 8
  George, 8, 65
  Mary, 8
  Mary Elizabeth, 8
  Peter, 8
  Tullinar, 8
MAURER, Adam, 81
  Andrew, 84
  Anna Maria, 81
  Catharine, 81, 84
  Elizabeth, 81
  George, 81
  Herman, 81
  John, 81
  Juliana, 81
MAXWELL, Isabel, 152
  Isabella, 134
  James, 49, 83, 133, 134
  John, 49, 134
  Robert, 49, 134
MAY, Barbara, 156
  Daniel, 108, 110, 131, 156
  Jacob, 21, 131
  John, 238
  Jones, 156
  Joseph, 156
  Lewis, 21
  Samuel, 156
  Sarah, 156

MAYER, Andrew, 134
  Anna, 240
  Catharine, 172
  Conrad, 259
  Elizabeth, 240
  Frederick, 240
  Hansly, 17
  Margaret, 240
  Mary, 240
  Peter, 240
MAYES, Charles, 70
  Dorcas, 70
  John, 70
  William, 70
MAYR, Catharine, 99
  Henry, 99
MAYRS, Barbara, 89
  Catharine, 89
  George, 89
  Henry, 89
  Jacob, 89
  John, 89
MAYS, Andrew, 24
  Charles, 92
  Dorcas, 92
  Elizabeth, 92
  John, 92
  Samuel, 92
  William, 92
MEALHOOF,
  Annamary, 87
  John, 87
MEARNS, Agness, 16
  Elizabeth, 16
  Martha, 16
  William, 16
MEAS, Henry, 149
  Magdalena, 149
MECKLE, Anna, 213
  Barbara, 213
  Catharine, 213
  Christian, 213
  Elizabeth, 213

  George, 213
  Henry, 213
  Jacob, 213
  John, 213
  Michael, 213
MEELY, Esther, 162
  Isabella, 166
  John, 166
  William, 162
MEEM, John, 51
MEILEY, Anna, 264
  Catharine, 264
  Henry, 264
  Martin, 264
MEISSENKOP, Anna, 191
MELANN, Anna, 165
  Catharine, 165
  Elizabeth, 165
  John, 165
  Mathias, 165
  Rachel, 165
  Rebecca, 165
  Sarah, 165
MELAUN, Ava, 261
  Benj., 141
  Benjamin, 261
  Catharine, 261
  Elizabeth, 261
  Hannah, 141
  John, 141, 194, 261
  Mary, 141
  Mathias, 141
  Rebecca, 141
  Sally, 261
  Sarah, 141, 194, 261
  Susanna, 141, 261
MELHORN, Andrew, 47, 113
  Anna Barbara, 113
  Barbara, 47, 113
  Casper, 113
  David, 113

Elizabeth, 113
Frederick, 113
George, 47
John, 47, 113
Magdalena, 47
Mary, 47, 113
Michael, 47
Simon, 47, 113
MELLER, George,
  102, 215
MELLINGER,
  Abraham, 250
  Barbara, 250
  Christian, 250
  David, 250
  Elizabeth, 250
  Francis, 250
  John, 250
  Joseph, 250
MELOAN, Hannah, 88
  John, 88
  Mathias, 88
MENGES, John, 226,
  254, 272
  Maria, 170
  Michael, 187
  Peter, 170
MENTEITH, Daniel,
  88, 115
  Janet, 115
  John, 115
MENTEL, George,
  117
  Magdalena, 117
MEOW, Michael, 138
MEREDITH, Thomas,
  152
MERMER, Jacob, 227
MERTZ, Jacob, 191
MESEMER, Anna
  Mary, 157
  Elizabeth, 157
  Henry, 157

Jacob, 157
John, 157
Mary, 157
Yodorus, 157
MESS, Elizabeth, 232
  William, 232
MESSERLY,
  Abraham, 158
  Anna, 158
  Daniel, 49, 57, 81,
  158
  Peter, 158
  Susanna, 158
MESSING, Anne, 210
  Frederick, 210
  John, 210
  Sophia C., 210
MESSONCOPP,
  Jacob, 188
METIER, Hannah,
  186
  Samuel, 186
METZAR, William,
  262
METZEL, U., 10
METZGAR, Adam, 38
  Dorothea, 38
  Eve, 222, 262
  George, 222, 231
  Jacob, 197
  Magdalena, 197
  Margaret, 231
  Philip, 262
  William, 197, 231
METZGER, William,
  217, 231, 264
METZLER, Elizabeth,
  115
  George, 115
  Margaretta, 115
MEYER, Abraham,
  256
  Adam, 151

Adolph, 143
Albert, 103
Andrew, 129
Ann, 143
Anna, 131, 256
Catharine, 131, 199,
  256, 267
Christiana, 151, 208
Conrad, 151
David, 103, 131, 151
Dorothea, 101
ELizabeth, 256
Elizabeth, 103, 143,
  151, 200, 271
Frederick, 151
Freney, 207
George, 101, 136,
  200, 256, 272
Hannah, 256
Henry, 81, 131, 151,
  256, 267, 272
Jacob, 103, 136, 256
Jean, 271
John, 65, 81, 96, 103,
  131, 143, 199, 207,
  208, 256, 271
Joseph, 143
Ludwig, 103
Lydia, 256
Magdalena, 65, 81
Margaret, 103, 131,
  256, 271
Mary, 103, 143, 271
Mary Ann, 143
Mathias, 151
Michael, 75, 131, 143
Nicholas, 103, 143
Peter, 91, 103, 134,
  143, 151, 192
Philip, 103, 267
Regina, 151
Sarah, 256, 271
Simon, 267

Susanna, 103, 256
William, 103
MEYERS, Dorothea,
  261
  Hannah, 235
  Jacob, 235
MICAWEE, Benjamin,
  52
MICHAEL, Adam,
  127, 237
  Ann, 39
  Anna, 39, 127, 243
  Anna Maria, 237
  Catharine, 243
  Catherine, 62
  Charles, 243
  Christiana, 25, 234
  Elizabeth, 243
  Henrietta, 243
  Henry, 25, 234
  Jacob, 243
  Jean, 39
  John, 234, 243
  Lewis, 234
  Margaret, 25, 234,
    243
  Maria, 262
  Mary, 234
  Nicholas, 62, 237
  Paul, 25
  Wendle, 234
  William, 25, 39, 243
MICHENFEL,
  Barbara, 166
  Casper, 166
MICKEL, Anna, 181
  Barbara, 181
  Catharine, 181
  Christian, 181
  Elizabeth, 181
  George, 181
  Henry, 181
  Jacob, 181

John, 181
Margaret, 181
Michael, 181
MICKEY, David, 102
  Egemyah, 96
  Robert, 96
MICKLE, Elijah, 117
  Griziel, 136
  Hannah, 117
  Jane, 117
  John, 4, 117
  Mary, 117
  Sarah, 117
  Thomas, 136
MICLHEIM,
  Catharine, 159
  Christian, 159
  Eve, 159
  George, 159
  Margaret, 159
MIEHEIMER,
  Christian, 120
MIER, Daniel, 44
  Emanuel, 44
  Jacob, 44
  Katharine, 44
  Martin, 44
MIERS, Peter, 153
MIESENHELTER,
  David, 207
MIFFLIN, James
  Ewing, 210
MILEN, Anna, 72
  Frantz J., 72
MILHEIM, Christian,
  193
  Christiana, 193
  Elizabeth, 193
  George, 193
MILLER, Abigail, 257
  Abraham, 96, 166,
    168, 263
  Adam, 96, 206, 262

Agness, 144
Alice, 69
Andrew, 28, 31, 39,
  168, 262
Ann, 110, 127
Ann Elizabeth, 68
Anna, 9, 110, 158,
  164, 166, 191, 206,
  262, 263, 268
Anna Barbara, 110
Anna M., 238
Anna Margaret, 238
Anna Mary, 127
Barbara, 39, 68, 96,
  110, 122, 158, 188,
  238, 259, 260, 262
Bennet, 253
Bernard, 182
Casper, 84
Catharine, 84, 85,
  88, 122, 155, 182,
  191, 196, 238, 243,
  252, 253
Christian, 82, 149,
  155, 164, 170, 191,
  230
Christiana, 211
Conrad, 82, 142
Deborah, 69
Dolly, 206
Dorothea, 28, 142
Ebenezer, 69
Eli, 29
Elizabeth, 13, 62, 88,
  89, 122, 154, 155,
  156, 158, 182, 191,
  196, 201, 206, 213,
  238, 253, 257, 262,
  263
Esther, 206
Eve, 122, 149, 166
Fanny, 96
Francis, 58

Frederick, 70, 82, 191
George, 39, 62, 154, 155, 182, 191, 203, 206, 211, 238, 259
Gertrude, 70
Hannah, 163, 243, 257
Harman, 82, 260
Henry, 62, 82, 88, 96, 116, 122, 123, 201, 206, 223, 240, 243, 245, 252, 262, 263
Herman, 82
Isabella, 144, 257
Jacob, 39, 68, 85, 107, 192, 206, 238, 252, 262, 263
James, 9, 144, 166
Jean, 220
Jesse, 257
Johannes, 68
John, 8, 19, 69, 88, 89, 96, 106, 144, 168, 170, 183, 196, 201, 206, 211, 227, 252, 253, 262
John L., 226
Jonathan, 206
Joseph, 29, 163, 206
Joshua, 69
Juliana, 155
Kate, 252
Lancy, 263
Lea, 262
Levi, 29
Lovice, 82
Ludwig, 110, 168
Lydia, 253
Magdalena, 89, 182, 191, 214, 238, 252, 262

Margaret, 29, 88, 96, 122, 127, 163, 168, 201, 213, 252
Maria, 238, 262
Martin, 122, 159, 238
Mary, 19, 28, 31, 109, 122, 127, 155, 163, 206, 220, 227, 238, 257, 263
Mary Eve, 170
Matthew, 9
Michael, 7, 65, 82, 88, 98, 133, 155, 158, 165, 166, 191, 252, 253, 260
Milley, 196
Nathaniel, 8
Nicholas, 20, 85, 110, 125, 127, 214
Paul, 156, 159, 180
Peter, 68, 127, 238
Phebe, 29
Philip, 68, 109, 155, 188, 252
Polly, 262
Rebecca, 106, 186
Richard, 220
Robert, 13, 128, 163, 201, 213
Rudolph, 252, 262
Salome, 182
Samuel, 44, 163, 177, 186, 220, 253, 262
Sarah, 8, 163, 196
Sebilla Catharine, 107
Simeon, 82
Simon, 168
Solome, 206
Sophia, 223, 238
Susanna, 9, 68, 88, 192, 262
Suvley, 196

Thomas, 13, 163, 201, 213
Tobias, 155
Ursula, 182
Valentine, 182, 191
Veronica, 263
William, 144, 170, 201, 213
MILLIKEN, Elizabeth, 212
James, 212
Jean, 212
Martha, 212
Thomas, 212
MILLIKIN, Jennet, 128
Mark, 128
MILLIRON, Jacob, 102
John, 102
Regena, 102
MILLS, Amos, 268
Edwin, 268
Eli, 268
Elizabeth, 59
Esther, 221
Franklin, 268
James, 59, 268
Joanna, 268
John, 59
Lydia, 268
Margery, 268
Mary, 59, 221
Rachel, 221
Robert, 59, 220
Susanna, 59
Thomas, 220, 221
MIMERMACHER, Jacob, 249
MINCH, Michael, 164
Simon, 164
MINER, Mary, 4
Samuel, 4

Thomas, 4
MINGER, Peter, 70
MINICH, Catharine, 270
  Elizabeth, 270
  Eve, 270
  George, 270
  Jacob, 270
  John, 270
  Leah, 270
  Lydia, 270
  Margaret, 270
  Matilda, 270
  Sarah, 270
MINSHALL, Thomas, 11
MINTER, Martin, 76
MIRS, Elizabeth, 17
  John Jr., 17
MITCHEL, Amelia, 92
  Andrew, 92
  Betsy, 249
  Catharine, 29
  Ebenezer, 104
  Jean, 104
  John, 29, 59
  John George, 29
  Margaret, 152
  Mary, 104
  Matthew, 104
  Samuel, 249
  William, 59, 128
MITCHELL,
  Elizabeth, 255
  George, 255
  James, 255
  John, 255
  Joseph, 255
  Robert, 255
  Samuel, 4
  Thomas, 255
  Violet, 255
  William, 76, 255

MITTMAR, Barbara, 148
  Charles, 148
MIXELL, Adam, 70
  Barbara, 70
  Catharine, 70
  Conrad, 70
  Elizabeth, 70
  George, 70
  Jacob, 70
  John, 70
  Margaret, 70
  Mary, 70
MOATZ, Catharine, 255
  George, 255
  Henry, 255
  Jacob, 255
  John, 255
MOHLER, Ezra, 227
  Jacob, 227
  Maria, 227
  Ruth, 227
MOHR, Barbara, 161
  Catharine, 63, 148, 161
  Christian, 148
  Christiana, 139
  Elizabeth, 161
  Eve, 161
  George, 63
  Gertrude, 161
  Jacob, 161
  John, 161
  Magdalena, 161
  Margaret, 161
  Mary, 63
  Nicholas, 158
  Peter, 158, 161, 187, 200, 207
  Philip, 63, 158
  Sophia, 63
  Yost, 139

MOKLIN, Hugh, 113
MOLL, Catharine, 129
  Henry, 129
  John, 129
  Ludwig, 129
  Margaret, 129
  Mary, 129
MONFORT, Charity, 84
  John, 53
  Lawrence, 84
  Peter, 84
MONGES, Adam, 98
  Ann, 98
  Charles, 98
  Elizabeth, 98
  Jacob, 98
  John, 98
  Mary, 98
  Mary Elizabeth, 98
  Michael, 98
  Peter, 98, 200
MONTFORT,
  Abraham, 28
  Anamary, 28
  Catharine, 28
  Cneartie, 53
  Johannah, 28
  John, 28, 53, 125
  Larence, 53
  Margaret, 28
  Mary, 53
  Peter, 28, 53
  Sarah, 28
MONTGOMERY,
  James, 103, 186
  John, 103
  Mary, 186
  Patrick, 103
MONTGUMERY,
  Elizabeth, 21
  Hugh, 21
  James, 21

Jean, 21
John, 21
Margaret, 21
Martha, 21
William, 21
MONTORFF, John, 88
MOODY, Margaret, 97
Samuel, 97
MOORE, Alexander, 136
Anna, 161
Annamaria, 161
Anthony, 161
David, 9, 105, 158
Elizabeth, 82, 274
Isaac, 159, 274
James, 12, 165
Jean, 9, 12
Job, 161
John, 161, 222
Joseph, 33
Margaret, 159
Matley, 165
Mordeca, 274
Mordica, 161
Peggy, 165
Robert, 12
Samuel, 9, 84
Sarah, 222, 274
Thomas, 9
William, 12
MORE, Catharine, 207
Jacob, 208
Mary, 208
MORGAN, Catharine, 103
David, 103
Eleanor, 266
Elizabeth, 24, 103
John, 24, 103
Margaret, 103
Mary, 24, 103

Nathaniel, 24, 103
Thomas, 24
William, 24, 103
MORGENSTERN, John, 67
MORNINGSTAR, Adam, 113
Ann, 113
C., 67
Catharine, 113, 199
Elizabeth, 113, 199
George, 113, 199
Henry, 113, 199, 258
John, 113, 199
Juliana, 113
Philip, 113
Polly, 258
Salome, 113
MORRIS, Barbara, 220, 226, 236
Charles, 200, 220
John, 181, 220, 226, 236
Martha, 207
Nathan, 207
MORRISON, Agness, 246
Ann, 15, 111, 246
Anna, 57
Ebenezer, 111
Elizabeth, 15, 111
Hannah, 46, 246
Hans, 111
Hugh, 111
James, 111
Jane, 53
Janet, 45
Jean, 246
John, 25, 46, 111, 246
Joseph, 45, 46, 53, 161
Margery, 15

Martha, 261
Mary, 15, 46, 53, 209, 246
Richard, 111
Samuel, 46, 127, 209, 246
William, 46, 57, 191, 246
MORRON, John, 108
MORROW, Jane, 54
William, 54
MORTAR, George, 39
MORTER, Henry, 199
MORTHLAND,
Agness, 14
Catharine, 234
Charles, 14
Hugh, 14, 88, 234, 250
Margaret, 14
Michael, 234, 250
Rebecca, 14, 234, 250
Samuel, 14, 45
Susanna, 250
William, 14
MORTON, Emmy, 144
John, 144
Thomas, 21
MOSER, Abraham, 60
Adam, 256
Barbara, 256
Catharine, 256
Elizabeth, 239
Eve, 88
George, 256
Samuel, 18, 88, 157, 252, 256
Solome, 157
MOSEY, Ann, 102
John, 102, 258, 267
Mary, 102
MOSSER, Catharine, 139

Jacob, 239
John, 139
Samuel, 139
MOTZ, Barbara, 194
  Catharine, 194
  Jacob, 194
MOUCH, John, 102
MOUL, George, 57
  Rosanna, 57
MOURER, Charlotte, 218
  Henry, 218
MOUSELTO, John, 266
  Mary, 266
MOUTEETH, Daniel, 151
MOVOFSKY, Juliana, 253
  Martin, 253
MOYER, Barbara, 110
  Henry, 110
MUHLHEIM,
  Christian, 243
  Eve, 243
  Jacob, 243
  John, 243
  Magdalena, 243
  Nicholas, 243
  Peter, 243
  Rosana, 243
MUHS, Daniel, 256
  David, 256
  Elizabeth, 256
MULL, Catharine, 252
  Christian, 252
MULLER, John S., 21
MULLIN, Agness, 128
  Henry, 128
  John, 128
MUMMARD, Richad, 154
MUMMER, Frederick, 123
  William, 34, 88
MUMMERT, Anna, 179
  Catharine, 30, 36, 179
  Dietrich, 30
  Elizabeth, 30
  Jacob, 179
  John, 179
  Margaret, 30
  Mary, 30
  Mathias, 179
  Peggy, 179
  Richard, 179
  Susanna, 30, 179
  William, 30, 36, 117, 179
MUNDERFF, Peter, 181
MUNDORF, Peter, 125
MUNDORFF, Mary, 20
  Mary Magdalena, 241
  Peter, 20, 241
MUNICH, Simon, 115
MUNNAMACHER,
  Anna, 191
  Jacob, 191
MUNTFORT, John, 78
MURDOCK, Jennet, 80
  John, 80
MURDOUGH, Anne, 118
  Robert, 118
MURPHY, Alexander, 13
  Archibald, 13
  Daniel, 167
  Hugh, 167
  James, 13, 51, 238
  John, 167
  Martha, 167
  Samuel, 167
MURRAY, Duncan, 91
  Eleanor, 91
  Elizabeth, 85
  John, 85, 91
  Mary, 85
MURRY, Samuel, 3
MUSSER, Daniel, 84
MUTCHLER, Jacob, 141
  Susanna, 141
MYER, Abraham, 145
  Anamary, 152
  Ann, 145
  Anna Barbara, 118
  Barbara, 118
  Catharine, 10, 94, 118, 179, 197
  Christian, 10
  Elizabeth, 172, 197
  Frances, 172
  Frederick, 41, 118
  George, 19, 53, 118
  Henry, 10, 118, 197
  Hy., 10
  Jacob, 94, 118
  Johannes, 61
  John, 10, 118, 152
  Joseph, 172
  Margaret, 41, 118
  Maria, 197
  Maria Catharine, 61
  Martin, 94
  Mary, 172
  Mathias, 179
  Michael, 172
  Peter, 118, 197
  Sarah, 197
  Simon, 197

Tobias, 239
MYERS, Catharine, 262
Conrad, 182
Elizabeth, 262
Eve, 80, 84, 239
George, 239
Hannah, 49
Henry, 225, 262
Jacob, 262
John, 262
Ludwig, 255
Margaret, 182
Mary, 178, 239, 241
Michael, 262
Mirecles, 239
Nicholas, 49
Peter, 252
Philip, 80, 111, 178
Polly, 252
Susan, 262
Thurley, 239
MYRISE, Adam, 177
George, 177
John, 177
Margaret, 177

-N-
NACE, Adam, 237
Catharine, 249
Elizabeth, 237, 249
George, 249
John, 237
Louisa, 249
Mathias, 249
NAEFF, John, 270
Mary, 270
NAFE, Ann, 236
Christian, 236
Susanna, 236
NAGEL, Jacob, 179
Susanna, 179
NAGLE, Catharine, 34

Jacob, 34
John, 34
Margaret, 34
Sophia, 210
NAIL, James O., 137
Mary, 137
NAILER, Elizabeth, 63
Ewing, 63
James, 63
John, 63
Mary, 63
Ralph, 63
Thomas, 63
William, 63
NEAL, Agness, 71
David, 42
Hugh, 42
John, 42, 71
Letiss, 42
Margaret, 71
Mary, 42
Matthew, 42
Susanna, 42
Thomas, 71
NEAS, George, 78
Mary, 78
Mathias, 168
NEBINGER, Andress, 63
Anna Maria, 63
Catharine, 63
George, 63
NEEL, William, 217
NEELY, Agness, 44
Anna, 159
Catharine, 97
Elizabeth, 44, 176
Henry, 97
Jackson, 44, 169
James, 44, 176
Jean, 44
Jennet, 159

John, 44, 176
Jonathan, 44, 159
Joseph, 97
Margaret, 44
Mary, 44, 97, 159
Peter, 97
Samuel, 44, 169
Sarah, 44
Susanna, 169
Thomas, 44, 169
William, 44, 97
NEFF, Anna, 25, 134
Catharine, 134
Elizabeth, 25, 134
Henry, 134
John, 25
Magdalena, 134
Mary, 134
Peter, 25, 175
Susanna, 175
NEHRBAS, Catharine, 119
Frances, 119
NEIDIG, Christiana, 245
Elizabeth, 245
John, 245
Juliana, 245
Magdalena, 245
Margaret, 245
Nancy, 245
NEIGHCOMER, Anna, 123
NEIL, Hugh, 189
James, 189
Jennet, 189
John, 189
William, 189
NEILL, Alexander, 219
Lewis, 219
Thomas, 219
NEILSON, Agness, 58

Elizabeth, 190
Hugh, 58
Jenny, 190
John, 58
Margaret, 190
Mary, 190
Rebecca, 190
Robert, 58
Roberts, 190
Samuel, 190
Susanna, 190
William, 190
NEIMAN, Catharine, 262
George, 261
Michael, 262
NEISCHWANGER, Joseph, 47
Peter, 47
NELSON, Elizabeth, 223
Harriet, 241
John, 223
Mary, 186
Nancy, 186
Rebecca, 223
Robert, 223
Samuel, 40, 68, 117, 223, 245, 246
Thomas, 186
Wiliam, 21
NELY, Jonathan, 159
Sarah, 159
NENKOMENT, Magdalena, 104
Ulrich, 104
NES, Elizabeth, 250
Peter, 250
William, 255
NESBIT, Hannah, 186
Jane, 186
Jean, 204
Jenny, 186

John, 15, 52, 186
Martha, 186
Mary, 186
Nancy, 186
Rebecca, 186
William, 186
NESS, Catharine, 24
Henry, 24
Jacob, 24, 265
Margaret, 265
Mary, 24
Mathias, 24
Michael, 265
Peter, 24
Susan, 24
NESSERLY, Daniel, 43
NEVIS, Christopher, 125
Ida, 125
John, 125
Martin, 125
NEVITT, Hannah, 210
NEWCOMER,
Abraham, 247, 269
Anna, 92, 247
Barbara, 247
C., 42
Christian, 92, 247
David, 192
Elizabeth, 247
George, 92
Jacob, 247
Magdalena, 192
Margaret, 269
Sally, 92
Samuel, 247
NEWLAND, Anna, 30
Benjamin, 30
David, 30
Deborah, 30
Elijah, 30
Hannah, 29, 30

James, 30
John, 30
William, 29, 30
NEWMAN, Andrew, 228
Anna, 228
Catharine, 152, 228
David, 48, 197, 229
Elizabeth, 228
George, 152, 228
Jacob, 48
Magdalena, 197
Margaret, 228
Mariles, 48
Mary Elizabeth, 228
Michael, 31, 197, 229
Susanna, 228
William, 197
NEWSCHWANGE,
Emanuel, 164
Magdalena, 164
NEWTIN, Ebenezer, 18
NICHOL, Anthony, 195
NICHOLAS, Jane, 128
John, 128, 158
Margaret, 254
NICKEY, David, 96, 103
NICKLESON,
Hannah, 143
John, 143
NICKY, David, 141
NICOL, James, 40
Mary, 40
Samuel, 40
Sarah, 40
William, 40
NICOLAS, Jane, 112
NOBLIT, Abraham, 19, 157
Ann, 157

Anna, 19
James, 157
John, 19, 157
Mary, 157
Rebecca, 157
Rhodes, 157
Thomas, 19
William, 19, 157
NOEL, Andrew, 20
Casper, 20
Jacob, 20, 105
Joel, 189
John, 20
Margaret, 20
Nicholas, 20
Peter, 20
Philip, 20
Philpina, 189
NOELL, Barbara, 34
Daniel, 34
John, 34
Magdelena, 34
Margaret, 34
Mary, 34
Peter, 34
NOLL, Anna
Margaret, 36
Anthony, 36
Barbara, 252, 265
Christiana, 89
Daniel, 39
Elizabeth, 36, 89, 218
Francis, 35, 218
George, 89, 218
Henry, 36
Jacob, 218, 252
John, 89, 218
Margaret, 36
Mary, 89, 218
Peter, 265
Philip, 89
Sarah, 218

Susanna, 89, 218
NORTON, Isaac, 55
Joseph, 55
Rebecca, 55
NUNEMACHER, Ann, 228
Anna Mary, 228
Barbara, 189, 228
Catharine, 189, 228
Christiana, 189
Daniel, 228
Eve, 189
George, 189, 228
Gotleib, 189
Jacob, 189, 228
John, 228
Magdalena, 189
Margaretta, 189
Mary, 228
Philip, 189
Soloman, 228
Solomon, 228
NUNNAMACHER,
Abraham, 130
Anna, 130
Christiana, 130
Nicholas, 130

-O-

OB, Jacob, 142
Philip, 142
OBALT, Boston, 81
OBEDIER, Jacob, 172
OBERDORFF,
George, 188
OBERDORPH,
George, 220
OBERLIN, Catharine, 232
Christiana, 232
Christopher, 232
Elizabeth, 232
George, 232

Hannah, 232
Jacob, 232
Polly, 232
Susanna, 232
OBERTWIFF, George, 116
OBOLT, Sabastian, 113
Sebastian, 68, 102
OCHER, Christiana, 15
Hannickel, 15
John, 15
Margaret, 15
Susanna, 15
ODEMAN, J. G., 150
ODERMAN, John G., 171, 205
OHAALL, Edward, 137
OHAIL, Edward, 256
Elizabeth, 256, 267
Hugh, 256, 267
James, 256, 267
Jane, 267
Jean, 256
Jenny, 267
Martha, 256, 267
Mary, 267
Nancy, 267
Thomas, 256, 267
OHARD, Patrick, 1
OHMET, Anna, 188
John, 188
OILER, Christiana, 121
Frederick, 121
Jacob, 121
John, 121
Katharine, 121
Magdalena, 121
Mary, 121
Susanna, 121

Valentine, 121
OLDHAM, Hananh, 125
Thomas, 125
OLER, Anthony, 34
Catharine, 34
OLLIGNER, Adam, 182
Barbara, 182
Catharine, 183
Elizabeth, 183
Jacob, 183
John, 182, 183
Peter, 182
OLP, Catharine, 237
Dorothea, 237
Jacob, 237
John, 236, 237
Peter, 237
OPP, Andrew, 38
Barbara, 38
Catharine, 38
Dorothea, 38
Elizabeth, 38
Jacob, 38
Magdalena, 38
Margaret, 38
Maria, 38
Peter, 38, 233
Sophia, 38
ORIN, Benjamin, 132
Elizabeth, 132
John, 132
Mary, 132
Rachel, 132
Rebecca, 132
William, 132
ORMAN, Margaret, 126
ORMOND, Alexander Poe, 107
Margaret, 107
Thomas, 107

ORR, Arthur, 138
James, 13
John, 23
Robert, 101
William, 79
ORSON, Anna, 187
George, 187
John, 187
Joseph, 187
Mary, 187
Rebecca, 187
Sarah, 187
William, 187
ORT, Milzer, 109
ORTT, Adam, 261
Catharine, 261
Henry, 242
OSBURN, Francis, 4
Margaret, 4
Martha, 127
Noble, 4, 127
Thomas, 4
OTTILIA, Anna, 134
OTTINGER, Clara, 71
Dorothea, 71
Elizabeth, 71
Hannah, 71
Henry, 71
Jacob, 71
Peter, 71
OTTMAN, Catharine, 72
John, 64, 72
OVERDEER, Benj., 240
Catharine, 240, 252
Christian, 240
David, 240
Frederick, 252
Freney, 240
Henry, 252
Hyster, 240
Jacob, 240, 252, 263

John, 240, 252
Ludwig, 252
Peter, 240, 252
Veronica, 263
OVERDORPH,
Elizabeth, 109
George, 109
OVERDURFF,
George, 135
OVERLANDER,
Jacob, 166
Susan, 166
OWENS, Jane, 189
Susanna, 189
OWINGS, Charles, 13
Hannah, 13, 77, 86
John, 13, 65
Joseph, 65
Joshua, 13, 77
Mary, 13, 151
Mary Ann, 65
Rachael, 13
Robert, 13
Susanna, 13, 77, 86
Thomas, 13
William, 13, 151

-P-
PACKER, Aaron, 164
George, 164
Hannah, 164
James, 164
John, 164
Lydia, 164
Moses, 164
Philip, 164
PADEN, David, 126
Mary, 126
PAIN, Jonathan, 95
PAINDER, Abraham, 226
Elizabeth, 226
PAINTER, Andrew,

89
  Christiana, 89
  George, 89
  Jacob, 89
  John, 89
  Magdalena, 89
  Valentine, 89
PALM, Ann, 69
  Jacob, 68
PANTAN, David, 120
  Jean, 120
PARK, Andrew, 34
  Elihu, 211
  Elizabeth, 211
  Francis, 211
  Joseph, 211
  Mary, 6, 34, 211
  William, 6, 211
PARKER, Ann, 191
  Anna, 57
  Catharine, 234
  George, 24
  James, 24, 57
  John, 57, 234
  Margaret, 24
  Mary, 24
  Rebecca, 24
  Samuel, 57, 191
  Sarah, 191
PARKS, Andrew, 54
  Hoge, 54
  James, 39, 54, 127
  Jane, 54
  John, 54, 75
  Joseph, 127
  Margaret, 54, 250
  Martha, 54
  Mary, 39, 54
  Richard, 250
  Robert, 54, 127
  Sarah, 77
  William, 77
PATHER, Anna

  Barbara, 84
  Catharine, 84
  Elizabeth, 84
  Margaret, 84
  Philip, 84
  Susanna, 84
PATTERSON, Anna, 176
  Betty, 176
  Hugh, 176, 207
  James, 111, 112, 129, 205, 207, 242
  Jenny, 176
  John, 176
  Martha, 207
  Mary, 176, 207
  Samuel, 112
  Susanna, 112, 129
  Thomas, 176
PATTON, James, 238
  Mary, 98
  Robert, 98
  Sophia, 238
PAULOS, Adam, 135
PAXTON, Andrew, 132
  Ann, 132
  Benj., 137
  David, 137
  Elizabeth, 86
  George, 137
  Grisle, 137
  Hannah, 15
  Hugh, 137
  Isaac, 86
  Isabella, 137
  James, 60, 132
  Jane, 137
  Jean, 132
  Jennet, 132
  John, 15, 86, 137
  Jonathan, 137
  Joseph, 15, 137

  Margaret, 132
  Margery, 137
  Mary, 86, 137
  Moses, 137
  Nathaniel, 15, 106, 137, 138
  Rachel, 137
  Robert, 137
  Samuel, 137
  Sarah, 86, 137
  Thomas, 137
PAYNE, George, 28
PEACHER, Catharine, 153
  Christiana, 153
  Elizabeth, 153
  Henry, 153
  John, 153
  Simon, 153
PEADOL, Thomas, 241
PEAR, Anna, 213
  David, 213
PECHER, Elizabeth, 84
  Eve, 84
  Henry, 84
  John, 84
  Mary, 84
  Simeon, 84
  Simon, 84
PECK, Elizabeth, 198
  John, 198
PEDAN, Benjamin, 242
  David, 242
  Eleanor, 242
  Isabella, 242
  James, 242
  Jannet, 242
  John, 242
  Martha, 242
  Mary, 107

Susanna, 242
PENCE, Catharine, 91
Elizabeth, 22, 91
Henry, 91
John, 91
Joseph, 91
Mary, 91
Michael, 91
Philip, 91
PENNINGTON,
  Ehraim, 248
  Elizabeth, 248
  Lydia, 248
  Mary, 248
  Susanna, 248
  Timothy, 248
PENROSE, Ann, 94
  Jane, 94
  John, 94
  Mary, 94
  Phebe, 94
  Susanna, 94
  Thomas, 94
  William, 34, 94
PENRY, Alle, 100
  Eleanor, 100
  Elizabeth, 100
  James, 100
  Robert, 100
PENTZ, Caty, 201
  David, 201
  Elizabeth, 201
  George, 201
  Henry, 201
  Jacob, 201
  John, 201, 203
  Mary, 201
  Philibina, 201
  Sabina, 203
  Susan, 201
PERCEL, Catharine, 76
  Elizabeth, 76

Hannah, 76
Hilgath, 76
Isaac, 76
John, 76
Mary, 76
Peter, 76
Richard, 76
Rulit, 76
Sarah, 76
PERRY, Samuel, 10
PERSON, Benjamin, 3
  Jenn, 3
  John, 3
  Joseph, 209
  William, 3
PETER, Anna, 125
  Barbara, 38
  Catharine, 38
  David, 270
  Elizabeth, 270
  Henry, 125
  Magdalena, 38, 125
  Mary Margaret, 125
  Peter, 125
  Philip, 38
PETERMAN, Andrew, 87
  Anna Mary, 87
  Annamary, 87
  Barbara, 123
  Catharine, 87
  Daniel, 56
  Dorothea, 123
  Elizabeth, 87
  George, 87
  Jacob, 87
  John, 87
  Margaret, 87
  Michael, 87
  Richard, 87
PETERS, Abijah, 194
  Garred, 194
PETERY, Anna, 136

George, 136, 155
Henry, 136
Jacob, 136
Magdalena, 136
Michael, 136
Stephen, 82, 136
PETIT, Abigail, 32
  Eve, 32
  Hannah, 32
  James, 32
  Keziah, 32
  Priscilla, 32
  Stephen, 32
  Thomas, 32, 180
PETRE, George, 186
  Martha, 186
PETRY, George, 123
PETTERSON,
  Andrew, 34, 35
  Eleanor, 35
  Iabella, 35
  James, 35
  John, 35
  Mary, 35
  Nathan, 34, 35
  Sarah, 34, 35
PETTIT, Hannah, 124
  Lucia, 124
  Priscilla, 124
  Rebecca, 124
  Thomas, 124, 182
PFLIEGED,
  Catharine, 181
  John, 181
PFLIEGER, Abraham, 126
  Christiana, 126
  Frederick, 126, 258
  George, 126
  Henry, 126, 258
  Jacob, 126
  John, 126
  Maria Margaret, 126,

258
Michael, 126
PHILEGER, Barnet, 242
  Charles, 242
  Daniel, 242
  Polly, 242
  Sarah, 242
PHILIPS, Edmond, 48
  Elizabeth, 48
  Eve, 187
  George, 187
  Jane, 48
  John, 48, 237
  Mary, 48
  Nathan, 48
  Patience, 48
  Phebe, 48
PHILLIPS, Priscilla, 147
PHILLIPSE, George, 34
  Margaret, 34
PHYLES, Nicholas, 256
PICKART, Henry, 9
PICKING, Christiana, 153
  Jacob, 153
PIEPER, Adam, 126
  Catharine, 126
PIERSON, Elias, 102
PIKE, Daniel, 223
  David, 223
  Elizabeth, 128, 223
  John, 128, 223
  Mary, 201
  Moses, 201, 223
  Mosey, 128
  Phebe, 223
  Pheby, 128
  Rebecca, 128, 223
  Ruth, 128, 223
  Sarah, 223
PILER, Conrad, 177
  Elizabeth, 177
PILES, Ann, 134
  Christian, 134
PITTS, Adam, 266
  Elizabeth, 266
  George, 266
  Mary, 266
PIXLER, Elizabeth, 78
  Samuel, 78
PLAFF, Christiana, 271
  George, 271
  John, 271
  Maria, 271
PLOW, John, 27
PLUNKET, Eleanor, 132
  Francis, 132
  Thomas, 132
POAKE, Anne, 176
  David, 176
  Elizabeth, 176
  James, 176
  John, 176
  Martha, 176
  Mary, 176
  Rachel, 176
  Robert, 176
POARDS, Philip, 32
POE, Alexander, 107
  John, 107, 126
  Margaret, 107, 126
  Mary, 126
  Sarah, 107, 126
POFELBERGER, Barbara, 88
  George, 88
  John, 88
  Katharine, 88
  Margaret, 88
  Peter, 88
POLASAEI, Catharine, 25
POLASEI, Adam, 25
  Catharine, 25
  Lorance, 25
POLK, David, 154
  Esther, 154
  John, 154
  Rachel, 154
POPE, John, 34, 87
  Samuel, 87
PORTER, Agness, 49
  Alexander, 49, 80, 98
  Andrew, 49, 77
  Charles William, 245
  David, 49
  Jane, 245
  Martha, 245
  Mary, 49, 77
  Matthew, 49
  Rebecca, 27
  Richard, 245
  Samuel, 49
  Sarah, 64, 106
  Thomas, 106
  William, 52, 64, 85, 87, 119
POSSILER, Gertrude, 214
  Jacob, 214
POTT, Benjamin, 42
  Catharine, 42
  Degenbart, 42
  Jacob, 42
  John, 42
  Margaret, 42
  William, 42
POULLY, Andrew, 96
POWELL, David, 114
  Elizabeth, 114
  Emas, 114
  George, 114
  Hannah, 114

Mary, 114
PRAXTON, John, 21
Thomas, 21
PREME, Esther, 180
Samuel, 180
PRENEMAN, John, 213
Mary, 213
PRESSEL, Catharine, 105, 217
Daniel, 105
David, 105, 143
Elizabeth, 105, 217
Henry, 143
Margaret, 217
Mary, 105
Michael, 143
Sarah, 143
Valentine, 105, 143, 217
PRICE, Joseph, 28
Phebe, 28
PRIER, Elizabeth, 83
Thomas, 83
PRIGG, Elizabeth, 266
PRINIMEN, Frainy, 90
PRITT, Jacob, 106
PROBST, Anna, 69
Anna Elizabeth, 69
Jacob, 69
John, 69
Marilis, 69
PROSE, Elizabeth, 79
PROUDFITS,
Alexander, 233
Martha, 233
PROUDFOOT,
Alexander, 214, 245, 246
Andrew, 57, 214
Daniel, 188
David, 214, 245

James, 214, 245
Mary, 188
Robert, 188, 214, 245
Rudolph, 188
Sarah, 214, 245, 246
PRUNK, John, 266
PUDERR, Christiana, 245
Jacob, 245
PUGH, David, 222
Joseph, 222
Lydia, 222
Mordica, 222
Sarah, 222
PURDY, Archibald, 198
B. L., 186
Esther, 186
Jane, 198
Jennet, 186
Mary, 198
Patty, 186
PUTT, Mary, 235
William, 235

-Q-
QUARLES, John, 270
QUICKEL, Ann, 188
Anna, 109, 188
Balthasser, 188
Baltzer, 109
Barbara, 109, 188
Catharine, 109
Elizabeth, 109
George, 84
John, 109, 188, 212, 217, 266
Maria, 109
Michael, 109
Peter, 2

-R-
RAAB, Peter, 122

RACHSER, Effa, 216
Elizabeth, 216
William, 216
RAEBER, Catharine, 179
Christiana, 179
Elizabeth, 179
Henry, 179
John, 179
Jonas, 179
RAFFENSBERGER,
Martin, 165
RAFINSBERGER,
Catharina, 105
Christian, 105
RAHAUSER, Jacob, 156
RAHL, Henry, 217
RALSON, John, 13
RALSTON, James, 157, 185
John, 157
Mary, 157, 185
RAMGIER, Ann, 114
John, 114
RAMSAY, Alexander, 65
Catharine, 219
James, 219
Martha, 52
Mary, 65
Oliver, 65
Raymond, 52
Reynold, 52
Sarah, 65, 219
Thomas, 65
William, 52, 65, 219
RAMSEY, James, 9
Mary, 9
Robert, 217
RANCK, Yost, 231
RANDEL, Elizabeth, 180

Hannah, 179
Mary, 179
William, 179
RANDELS, Hannah, 132
Hugh, 132
Jannett, 132
Martha, 132
William, 132
RANGE, Elizabeth, 129
John, 111, 112, 129
Magdalena, 112, 129
Sholas, 112
Theobald, 129
RANKIN, Abraham, 189
Catharine, 189
Elizabeth, 95
Hanna, 95
James, 44, 159
John, 95
Mary, 159
Moses, 95
Rebecca, 95
William, 159
RAPE, Emanuel, 177
Margaret, 177
Martin, 177
RASER, Adam, 146
Catharine, 146
John, 146
Laurence, 146
Lawrence, 146
Philip, 146
RATCAKIN, Jane, 92
Sarah, 92
RATHFON, Christian, 261
RATHFOU,
Catharine, 138
Christian, 138
Elizabeth, 138

Frederick, 138
George, 138
Jacob, 138
Leonard, 138
Margaret, 138
RATZ, Godfried, 171
Margaret, 171
RAUHAUSER, Daniel, 146
RAUKAUSER, Daniel, 201
John, 201
RAUS, Anna, 87
Catharine, 87
George, 87
RAUTENBUSH,
Anna, 85
Caty, 85
Daniel, 85
Elizabeth, 85
Esther, 85
Henry, 85
Jacob, 85
John, 85
Michael, 85
Soloman, 85
RAYMER, Adam, 86
Catharine, 86
Frantz J., 56
Frederick, 86
John, 86
READ, Agness, 59
Ann, 202
David, 112
Elizabeth, 59
Esther, 116, 202
Hugh, 59
James, 13, 59, 202
Janet, 202
Jean, 59
John, 13, 59
Joseph, 202
Margaret, 13, 59,

202
Mary, 59, 112
Minor, 112
Nicholas, 202
Robert, 13
William, 13, 112, 116, 202
REAGAN, Frederick, 219
REAPLOGE,
Reinhart, 20
REDETT, Andrew, 50
REDITT, John, 50
REEAD, James, 30
Janet, 30
REED, Agness, 144
Arthur, 138
Daniel, 66
Fanny, 24
Hannah, 24, 210
Hugh, 65, 138, 210
James, 115, 127, 148
Jane, 24, 115, 127, 138
Jean, 115
John, 4, 24, 54, 66, 127, 138
Joseph, 65, 187, 235
Margaret, 128, 138
Mary, 65, 115, 127, 269
Matthew, 24
Rebecca, 24
Samuel, 24, 128
Sarah, 249
Thomas, 24, 127, 249
William, 24, 66, 115, 127, 144
Zachariah, 269
REEP, Stephen, 104
REGAL, Elizabeth, 166
Jacob, 166

REGAN, Daniel, 243
Ruth, 243
REHMER, Elizabeth, 274
Frederick, 274
REIBER, Kratchan, 227
Lenhart, 227
REIBOLT, Andrew, 190
Barbara, 190
Henry, 190
Martha, 190
REID, Elizabeth, 78
George, 78
James, 75, 78
James R., 75
Jean, 78
Jennet, 78
John, 78
Joseph, 75, 78
Samuel, 75
Thomas, 75
William, 75, 78
REIDER, Gertraut, 118
REIFF, Catharine, 210
Joseph, 210
REIGER, Anna Lees, 91
Elizabeth, 221
Gertrude, 221
John, 91
Ludwick, 221
Margaret, 221
Peter, 221
REIGLE, Ludwig, 135
REIGNBERGER, Philip, 189
REINBINE, Christiana, 271
Jacob, 271
REINBOLT, Henry, 232
REINECKER, Anna, 124
Casper, 124
Catharine, 124
Conrad, 124
Elizabeth, 124
George, 124
Gloria, 124
Maney, 124
Nancy, 124
REINHARD, Anna, 114
George, 114
REINHART,
Abraham, 183
Anna, 183
Barbara, 226
Catharine, 183
Charles, 183
David, 183
Elias, 183, 226
George, 183
Henry, 183
Jacob, 183
John, 183
Magdalena, 183
Mary, 183
Peter, 183
Simon, 183
Susanna, 183
REISINGER,
Catharine, 230
Eve, 185
John, 89, 185
Martin, 74
Peter, 163, 185, 230
REITER, Catharine, 96
Christopher, 96
Gertrude, 96
John, 96
Lawrence, 96
REITINGER, Anna, 224
Michael, 224
REMACK, Jacob, 233
REMBY, E., 244
Isreal, 244
RENBARGER,
Barbara, 98
Henry, 98
RENECKER, Eve, 199
Michael, 199
RENILL, Barbara, 182
Christian, 182
Daniel, 182
Darrell, 182
Jacob, 182
Margaret, 182
Mary, 182
Peter, 182
Susanna, 182
RESSLER, Catharine, 102
Dena, 102
Elizabeth, 102
Henry, 102
Mathias, 102
Michael, 102
RESTER, Eve, 140
Philip, 140
RETOW, Francis, 10
Mary, 10
RETOW (LERUE),
Abraham, 10
RETROF, John, 81
RETTER, Jacob, 209
REVER, Catharine, 101
John, 101
REYNOLD, Anna, 209
Daniel, 209
Eve, 209
Peter, 209
REYNOLDS, Martha,

10, 11
Mary, 11
Samuel, 10
RHEIL, Peter, 63
RHODE, Anthony, 89, 90
    Christian, 90
    Elizabeth, 90
    Frainey, 89
    Frederick, 90
    Henry, 89
    John, 89
    Magdalena, 89, 90
RHODES, Ann, 90
    Frainy, 90
    Henry, 90
    John, 90
RHORBACK,
    Christian, 118
    Henry, 118
    John, 118
    Lawrence, 118
    Susanna, 118
RICHARD, John, 160
RICHARDS, John, 128
    Sarah, 128
    Stewart, 128
RICHEY, Elizabeth, 254
RICHMAN, Agness, 198
    Archibald, 198
    John, 128, 198
    Pheby, 128
    Samuel, 198
RICHMOND, John, 223
    Phebe, 223
RICHTER, Barbara, 74
    George, 74
RICHWINE, John, 152

Susanna, 152
RICHY, Catharine, 244
    John, 244
RICKEL, Isabella, 104
    James, 104
RICKEY, Andrew, 162
    David, 162
    Esther, 162
    Hannah, 162
    John, 162
    Sarah, 162
    Thomas, 162
RIDAR, Barbara, 225
    Catharine, 225
    Epfriam, 225
    Frederick, 225
    Hannah, 225
    John, 225
    Rosanna, 225
    Sophia, 225
RIDDLE, David, 115
    George, 115
    James, 115, 123
    John, 115, 127
    Joseph, 115
    Joshua, 115
    Robert, 115
    Samuel, 115
    William, 115
RIDER, Christiana, 110
    Frederick, 81
    Jacob, 69
    Paul, 110
RIEB, Barbara, 254
    Catharine, 254
    Elizabeth, 254
    Eve, 254
    Henry, 254
    Jacob, 254
    Nicholas, 254
    Peter, 254

RIEHL, Catharine, 71
    Gertrude, 71
    Margaret, 71
    William, 71
RIEL, Catharine, 272
    Peter, 272
RIEMAN, Frederick, 247
    Jacob, 43
RIGEL, Peter, 206
RIKE, Abraham, 210
RINGER, Barbara, 201
    Catharine, 125
    Christiana, 125
    Elizabeth, 183
    Eva, 183, 251
    George, 125, 183, 201
    John, 125, 183, 251
    Michael, 125
RITCHEY, Adam, 104
    Agness, 104
    Anna, 104
    David, 104
    George, 104
    Isabella, 104
    James, 104
    Jean, 104
    John, 104
    Margaret, 104
    Mary, 104
    Matthew, 104
    Rachel, 104
    Rebecca, 104
    Robert, 104
    William, 104
RITTER, Andrew, 101
    Mary, 101
RITZ, Anthony, 244
    Barbara, 244
    Catharine, 244
    Elizabeth, 244

Jacob, 244
John, 244
Margaret, 244
ROAD, Abraham, 88
　Anna, 88
　Anna Maria, 88
　Catharine, 88
　Christian, 88
　Elizabeth, 88
　Ferona, 88
　Jacob, 88
　Joseph, 88
　Magdalena, 88
　Maria, 88
ROAT, Herman, 84
　Margaret, 84
ROBENSTEIN,
　Albrak, 120
　Christiana, 120
　David, 120
　Leonard, 120
ROBERTS, Ann, 59
　Benjamin, 59
　Jacob, 59
　John, 59
　Mary, 59
　Moses, 59
　Patrick, 59
　Peter, 59
　Rachel, 59
　Sarah, 270
　Thomas, 270
　Zachariah, 59
ROBINET, George,
　131, 165
ROBINETT, George,
　162
ROBINETTE, James,
　235
ROBINSON,
　Abraham, 4
　Alexander, 249, 269
　Betsy, 249

Catharine, 155
Eleanor, 249, 269
Elizabeth, 5
George, 249, 269
Henry, 36
Isaac, 155
Jacob, 155
James, 4, 36, 100,
　154, 249
Jane, 155
John, 5, 36, 155, 249
Margaret, 5
Margerey, 67
Margery, 64
Mary, 4, 5, 36, 155
Robert, 36
Samuel, 154, 155,
　249
Sarah, 36, 155, 249,
　269
Thomas, 5, 249
William, 36, 64, 67
ROCKENBAUGH,
　Catharine, 41
　Jacob, 41
　Mathias, 41
ROCKEY, Barbara, 91
　Christopher, 91
　Elizabeth, 208
　Frederick, 208
　Hans, 91
　Henry, 91
　Margaret, 91
　Susanna, 84
　Wendle, 84
ROGERS, Adam, 16
　Eleanor, 16
　John, 16
　William, 16
ROHBACK, John, 268
ROHMER, Catharine,
　57
　Frederick, 57

ROHRACK, Christian,
　268
　Elizabeth, 268
　Magdalena, 268
　Susanna, 268
ROHRAUGH,
　Christian, 69
ROHRBAUGH, Adam,
　145
　Barbara, 145
　Christiana, 145
　John, 145
　Rachel, 145
　Zacarias, 145
ROHREBACH,
　Christiana, 132
ROLAND, Agness, 61
　Ann, 61
　Isabella, 61
　James, 61
　John, 61
　Margaret, 61
　Mary, 61
　Matthew, 61
　Robert, 61
ROLLER, Ann, 275
　Catharine, 275
　George, 275
　Jacob, 275
　John, 275
　Samuel, 275
　Sarah, 275
ROOSE, Andrew, 91
　Barbara, 91
　Christiana, 91
　Frederick, 91
　Rosanna, 91
RORAHBAH,
　Barbara, 25
　Jacob, 25
　John, 25
　Lairriah, 25
　Margaret, 25

373

RORRSICH,
  Catharine, 141
  Christiana, 141
  Dorothea, 141
  Eve, 141
  George, 141
  Mary, 141
  Michael, 141
  Susanna, 141
ROSE, Frederick, 146
  Jacob, 131
ROSEBOROUGH,
  Eleanor, 45
  John, 45
  Mary, 45
  Robert, 45
ROSEMILLER,
  Ludwig, 73
ROSS, Agness, 162
  Alexander, 52, 186,
    190, 204, 207, 208,
    255
  Ann, 10, 52
  David, 162
  Dorcas, 198
  Eleanor, 10, 162
  Elizabeth, 10, 52, 65,
    192, 200, 255, 267
  George, 10, 200
  Hugh, 64, 267
  Isabella, 162
  James, 9, 10, 52,
    162, 198, 255
  Jane, 255
  Jean, 52, 162
  John, 10, 162, 200
  Joseph, 15, 65
  Margaret, 255, 267
  Martha, 52, 255
  Mary, 10, 52, 65
  Rebecca, 10
  Richard, 10, 200
  Sarah, 10, 200, 267

  Suisanna, 162
  Susanna, 10
  Thomas, 255
  William, 8, 9, 46, 52,
    64, 65, 78, 162, 255,
    267
ROSSAR, Adam, 216
ROTH, Abraham, 215,
  227
  Catharine, 155, 227
  Christiana, 251
  Elizabeth, 215, 227
  Henry, 227
  Jacob, 89
  John, 155, 251
  Juliana, 251
  Mary, 89
  Salome, 227
  Susan, 251
  Susanna, 251
ROTHBAUST, Anna,
  216
  John, 216
ROTHRACK, John,
  134
ROTHROCK, Anna,
  191
  Benj., 191
  Catharine, 191
  Eleanor, 191
  Frederick, 191
  George, 191
  Jacob, 191
  John, 52, 140, 191
  Joseph, 191
  Peter, 191
  Philip, 55, 191
  Valentine, 191
ROWAN, Agnes, 29
  Andrew, 29
  Jean, 29
  Margaret, 29
  Mary, 29

  Susanna, 29
  William, 29
ROWE, Anna, 250
  Michael, 250
ROWES, Becky, 109
  Johanna, 109
  John, 109
  Lucas, 109
  Sophia, 109
ROYL, Hannah, 117
  William, 117
RUBEL, Anna, 260
  Barbara, 145
  Christian, 145, 259
  Esther, 260
RUBEY, John, 186
RUBLE, Abraham, 39
  Anna, 39
  Christian, 39
  Matthew, 39
  Peter, 39
RUBY, Casper, 50
RUDESILTZ, James,
  8
RUDISEL, Elizabeth,
  213
  John, 213
RUDISELL, Baltzer,
  129
  Charlotte, 230
  Jacob, 120, 121, 124,
    230
RUDISELLY, Balthus,
  53
  John, 179
  Ludwig, 179
RUDISERE, Baltzer,
  101
  Barbara, 101
  Catharine, 101
  Dorothea, 101
  Elizabeth, 101
  Henry, 101

Jacob, 101
John, 101
Jonas, 101
Mary, 101
Philip, 101
Susanna, 101
RUDISILL, Catharine, 192
  Jacob, 152
RUDISILLY,
  Elizabeth, 215
  Jacob, 215
  John, 215
  Jonas, 97
  Ludwig, 215
RUDISILY, Andrew, 199
  Mary, 199
RUDSILL, Ann, 182
  Barbara, 182
  Catharine, 182
  Elizabeth, 182
  John, 182
  Margaret, 182
  Susanna, 182
  Werrick, 182
RUDSILLY, Ludwick, 77
RUDY, Anna, 80
  Barbara, 201
  George, 72, 80, 201
  Henry, 151, 201
  Jacob, 117
  Maria, 151
  Mary, 117
  Michael, 185
RUHL, Catharine, 166, 253
  Elizabeth, 253
  Frederick, 166, 253
  Henry, 231, 237, 243, 253
  Jacob, 247

John, 71, 126, 190, 253
Juliana, 253
Margaret, 253
Michael, 253
Yost, 190
RUMAN, Henry, 228
RUMEL, Elizabeth, 88
  Frederick, 88
  Jacob, 116
  Margaret, 116
RUNK, Jost, 119
  Peter, 268
  Yost, 72
RUNKLE, Anna Mary, 146
  Catharine, 146
  Christian, 182
  Henry, 182
  Jacob, 146
  John, 146
  Ludwick, 146
RUPARD, Adam, 149
  Christiana, 149
RUPP, Baltzer, 159
  Catharine, 217
  Christian, 159
  Elizabeth, 159, 187
  Gotlieb, 159, 187
  Jacob, 159
  Philip, 217
RUSE, Andrew, 148
  John, 190
RUSK, Sarah, 95
  William, 95
RUSSEL, Catharine, 105
  Joseph, 270
  Margaret, 270
  Patrick, 178
  Rachel, 178
  Valentine, 105
RUSSELL, Alexander, 153
  James, 43
RUTTER, Adam, 208
  Barbara, 208
  Samuel, 208
RYAN, Ann, 29
  Cornelius, 29
RYDER, Peter, 235

-S-
SADDLER, Mary, 158
SADLER, Isaac, 34
SAHLER, Eleanor, 124
  Isaac, 124
SAILOR, Caspar, 197
  John, 197
  Peter, 197
  Susanna, 197
SALEGEVER, Casper, 198
  Catharine, 198
SALTZGEBER,
  Casper, 16
  Detrick, 16
  Elizabeth, 16
  Jacob, 16
  Margaret, 16
  Mary, 16
SAMPLE, Agness, 194
  Ann, 194
  Catharine, 194
  Cunningham, 194
  Elizabeth, 194
  John, 194
  Mildridge, 194
  Nathaniel, 194
  Sarah, 194
SANDERS, Jenny, 186
  John, 186
SANDERSON,
  Alexander, 102

James, 190
Jean, 190
John, 190
SANDS, Elizabeth,
　189
John, 189
SANGRY, Cabien, 206
Catharine, 206, 221
Charlotte, 221
Chrisly, 206
Christian, 221
Christiana, 221
Elizabeth, 221
Jacob, 221
John, 221
Michael, 189, 221
Peter, 221
SANSANY, Peter, 99
SARBACK, Catharine,
　105, 152
Christian, 105
Christiana, 105, 152
David, 105, 152
Elizabeth, 105, 152
Jacob, 105, 152
Michael, 105, 152
Susanna, 105
SAUNDERSON,
　Barbara, 131
　James, 131
SAUNNOT, Daniel, 80
Elizabeth, 80
SAWER, Philip, 10
SAWMILLER,
　Frederick, 195
SAY, Mary, 24
Richard, 24
SAYLOR, Benjamin, 7
Catharine, 7
SCANNAL, Catharine,
　95
Lorentz, 95
SCHAEDEL, George,

　128
SCHAFFER, Jacob,
　188
Magdalena, 188
SCHALL, Fent, 9
John, 9
Susanna, 9
SCHANTZ, Elizabeth,
　149
Henry, 149
Jacob, 149
Juliana, 149
Peter, 149
Susanna, 149
SCHARTZ, Andrew,
　33
George, 33
Margelton, 33
Mary, 33
Michael, 33
Philip, 33
SCHARWARTZWELD
　ER, Elizabeth, 139
Philip, 139
SCHATTEL,
　Catharine, 228
George, 228
John, 228
Margaret, 228
Michael, 228
Susanna, 228
SCHAUM, Elizabeth,
　22
Isaac, 22
John, 22
Leonard, 22
Mary Ann, 22
Nicholas, 22
SCHEAFFER, George,
　194
SCHEIBLEY,
　Barbara, 42
Christian, 42

Elizabeth, 42
Esther, 42
John, 42
Susanna, 42
SCHENCK, Ann, 207
Barbara, 207
Elizabeth, 207, 248
Freney, 207
Henry, 207, 248
John, 207, 233, 248
Magdalena, 233
Margaret, 207, 233,
　248
Maria, 233
Mary, 248
Mary Magdalena,
　207
Michael, 207
SCHEYERMAN, Ann,
　122
Theobald, 122
SCHICKLEY, Jacob,
　27
SCHITZ, Margaret, 89
SCHLAR, Catharine,
　145
Henry, 145
SCHLOSSER,
　Annamary, 252
Betsy, 252
George, 252
Jacob, 252
John, 252
Peter, 173
Polly, 252
SCHLOTHAUER, A.
　E., 64
Anna, 64
Anthony, 64
Nicholas, 64
SCHLOTHOUR,
　Maria, 261
SCHLOTT, Adam, 203

Catharine, 204
Elizabeth, 204
John, 203
Magdalena, 204
Margaret, 204
Mary C., 203
Mary Catharine, 203
Michael, 203, 204
Philip, 204
Sophia, 204
Susan, 203
SCHMEDT, John, 273
SCHMEISER, Anna,
  39, 57
Barbara, 155
Dorothea, 57
Elizabeth, 57
Jacob, 57, 70, 109
Mathias, 39, 57
Michael, 57
Peter, 155
Rosanna, 57
Sabina, 57
Susanna, 57
SCHMITH, Barbara,
  164
Daniel, 194
David, 194
John, 194
William, 194
SCHMOK, Catharine,
  115
Jacob, 115
John, 115
SCHMUCK, Anna,
  193
Catharine, 181, 193
Elizabeth, 181
George, 181, 193
John, 181, 193
Mary, 190
Michael, 190, 193
Peter, 179

Susanna, 179
SCHMUTZER, Jacob,
  70
SCHMYSER, Anna,
  228
Anna Maria, 228
Elizabeth, 228
Jacob, 228
John, 228
Michael, 228
Peter, 228
Polly, 228
Sarah, 228
Susanna, 228
SCHNEBZ, Jacob, 221
Susanna, 221
SCHNECK, Henry, 26
SCHNEIDER,
  Abraham, 77
  Adam, 77
  Ann, 203
  Anthony, 194
  Casper, 194
  Catharine, 197, 270
  Christiana, 197
  Daniel, 203
  Elizabeth, 197, 203,
    270
  Eve, 77
  George, 203, 270
  Henry, 89
  Jacob, 194, 197, 270
  John, 77
  Magdalena, 197
  Margaret, 89, 203
  Marlina, 77
  Mary, 89, 197, 270
  Nicholas, 197
  Peter, 197
  Philip, 197
  Rebecca, 197
  Salome, 203
  Sarah, 77

Susanna, 89, 270
Theobald, 89
Theobold, 177
SCHNELL, Elizabeth,
  260
Henry, 260
SCHNERR, Casper,
  121
Catharine, 121
Elizabeth, 121
Madlen, 121
Mary, 121
Ule, 121
SCHNETA, Jacob, 273
SCHNYDER,
  Elizabeth, 125
  George, 125
  Susanna, 125
SCHOLL, Catharine,
  64
  Dorothea, 64
  John, 64
  John Jacob, 64
  Mary, 64
SCHONK, Joseph, 117
SCHOOL, Catharine,
  273
  George, 273
  John, 273
SCHOOLER, John, 61
SCHOOOL, John, 202
SCHOSP, Adam, 168
  Andrew, 168
  Elizabeth, 168
  Jacob, 168
  John, 168
  Peter, 168
  Stephen, 168
SCHOUK, Barbara,
  117
  Elizabeth, 117
  George, 117
  John, 117

SCHRAM, Catharine, 267
David, 267
SCHREIBER,
  Andrew, 199, 203
  Anna M., 271
  Anna Maria, 271
  Daniel, 272
  Eliza, 164
  Elizabeth, 164, 182, 199, 272
  Frederick, 272
  George, 199
  Henry, 199
  Isabella, 199
  Jacob, 182, 199
  John, 199
  Margaret, 164, 272
  Maria, 164
  Mary, 203
  Michael, 164, 199
  Peter, 199, 272
  Philip, 271
  Sarah, 272
  Susanna, 164, 272
SCHREINER, Philip, 185
SCHRIBER, Andrew, 40
SCHRIEBER, Michael, 151
  John, 56, 151
SCHRIVER, John, 256
  Michael, 56
  Sevilla, 56
SCHROMS, Elizabeth, 265
  John, 265
SCHROTH,
  Christopher, 94
SCHRYOCK, Anna M., 107
  Christian, 107
  Helena, 107
  Jacob, 107
  John, 107
  Leonard, 107
  Michael, 107
SCHUH, Elizabeth, 215
  Isaac, 215
SCHULER, Andrew, 61
  Christian, 61
  Christly, 61
  George, 61
  John, 61
  Mary, 61
SCHULLER, Anna, 145
  John Adam, 145
SCHULTZ, Henry, 9
  Martin, 135
  Scharlot, 135
SCHUYOCK, John, 107
SCHWARTZ,
  Abraham, 174, 209
  Adam, 148
  Anamaria, 263
  Andreas, 51
  Andrew, 115
  Anna M., 198
  Anna Maria, 174, 209
  Catharine, 148, 149, 226
  Charles, 198
  Christian, 149
  Christopher, 198
  Conrad, 53, 115
  Elizabeth, 51
  George, 149
  Henry, 177, 263
  John, 226, 263
  Magdalena, 149
  Rosana, 263
  Sally, 149
SCHWEISGUTE,
  Adam, 171
  Anna, 171
  Catharine, 171
  Elizabeth, 171
  John, 171
  Laurence, 171
  Margaret, 171
  Philip, 171
  Sophia, 171
SCHWEITZER, Adam, 266
  Andrew, 266
  Barbara, 266
  Catharine, 266
  Elizabeth, 266
  Mary, 266
  Susanna, 266
SCHWRTZMAN,
  Andrew, 156
  Joseph, 156
SCHYROCK, John, 107
SCOTT, Abraham, 56, 61
  Anne, 87
  Christian, 61
  David, 11
  Hugh, 27
  Janet, 11
  Jean, 87
  John, 11, 52
  Leivinia, 87
  Margaret, 87
  Martha, 87
  Mary, 56, 87
  Patrick, 43, 194
  Richard, 11
  William, 87, 126, 143
SCREIBER, Jacob, 164

SCRINER, Catharine, 60
Elizabeth, 60
George, 60
Margaret, 60
Mary E., 60
SEBASTIAN,
  Elizabeth, 188
George, 188
Marelise, 189
Michael, 189
SEEGRIST, Hans
  Urick, 50
SEFFERENCE,
  Martha, 215
Nancy, 215
SEFFRENTZ,
  Catharine, 202
George, 202
SEGRIST, Ann, 273
Anna, 273
Barbara, 273
Catharine, 273
Francis, 273
Fronica, 273
Henry, 273
John, 273
Michael, 212, 273
Peter, 273
William, 273
SEIFERT, Adam, 107
Anna Maria, 107
Michael, 107
SEIP, Christiana, 155
Joseph, 155
SEITZ, Aaron, 134
Adam, 228
Anna, 134
Anna Elizabeth, 228
Benjamin, 134
Catharine, 138
Christiana, 228
Jacob, 134

John, 138, 228
Joseph, 138, 228
SELL, Abraham, 99
Adam, 99
Anthony, 34
Catharine, 99
Caty, 113
Eve, 99
Hannah, 99
Isaac, 177
Jacob, 99, 177
James, 99
Ludwick, 113
Margaret, 177
Mary, 34
SELLIX, Agness, 120
Hamilton, 120
Margaret, 120
Mary, 120
Thomas, 120
Tobias, 120
SELLY, John, 210
SELY, Henry, 165
Mary, 165
SEMONDS, Adam, 64
SEMPLE, John, 54, 108, 111
SENFERT, Adam, 205
Anna Maria, 205
Barbara, 205
Catharine, 205
Elizabeth, 205
George, 205
John, 205
Mary, 205
Michael, 205
Philip, 205
Susanna, 205
SENFF, Andrew, 121, 142
Juliana, 121
SENFT, Andrew, 167
Anna Mary, 167

John Philip, 167
Peter, 167
Philip, 72
SENNARD, Abraham, 67
Eleanor, 67
Elizabeth, 67
John, 67
Jonathan, 67
Margaret, 67
Mary, 67
Sarah, 67
Susanna, 67
Thomas, 67
SEYMONDS, Adam, 64
Mary, 64
SHAEFER, Anna, 109
Catharine, 180
Christiana, 109
Christofel, 109
Elizabeth, 109
Frederick, 180
George, 180
Jacob, 180
John, 180
Margaret, 180
Molly, 180
Sally, 180
Samuel, 180
Susanna, 180
SHAEFFER,
  Christiana, 232
George, 255
Jacob, 255
John, 232
Joseph, 255
Mary, 255
SHAFER, Abraham, 254
Anna, 254
Catharine, 254
Charles, 254

Elizabeth, 254
Henry, 254
Peter, 254
SHAFFER, Abigal, 86
  Adam, 206
  Ann, 204
  Anna E., 86
  Anna Margaret, 92
  Barbara, 86, 228, 246
  Catharine, 86
  Christiana, 86
  David, 228
  Elizabeth, 40, 268
  Hannah, 228
  Henry, 204
  Jacob, 50, 271
  John, 211, 246, 268
  Margaret, 211
  Michael, 50
  Nicholas, 40, 50
  Paul, 86
SHAHR, Frederick, 53
SHAILEY, Andrews, 103
  Jacob, 103
  John, 103
SHALL, Barbara, 23
  Catharine, 23
  George, 23
  Mary, 23
  Vliana, 23
SHALLER, Elizabeth, 252
  Eve, 192
  George, 192, 252
SHAM, Frederick, 49
SHAMBERGER,
  Baltzer, 3
  Margaret, 3
SHANCK, Elizabeth, 165
  George, 165
  Joseph, 165

SHANEY, George, 234
  Margaret, 234
SHANK, Adam, 130
  Christian, 130
  Elizabeth, 130
  Franey, 130
  Jacob, 130
  John, 130
  Mary, 130
  Michael, 130
  Myri, 130
SHANKES, Christian, 17
SHANKS, David, 208
  Elizabeth, 208
  James, 208
  Mary, 208
  Sarah, 208
  Thomas, 208
  William, 208
SHANNON, Andrew, 16
  Joseph, 162
  Margaret, 16
  Mary, 16, 162
  Rebecca, 16
  Richard, 16
  Samuel, 16, 43
  Sarah, 16
  Thomas, 162
  William, 16
SHARER, Jacob, 86
  John D., 86
SHARES, Jacob, 64
SHARP, Andrew, 62
  Ann, 66
  Catharine, 251
  Dorcas, 66
  Elizabeth, 59, 251
  Erana, 251
  Eva, 251
  George, 251
  Hannah, 66

James, 62, 66
Jannet, 62, 66
Jean, 66
John, 59, 154, 200, 203, 205, 240, 251
Juliana, 251
Kezia, 3
Rebecca, 251
Robert, 66
Susanna, 203
Thomas, 3
SHARRON, Eva, 48
  Margaret, 48
  Philibina, 48
SHAUL, Barbara, 266
  Catharine, 242
  George, 242, 266
  Henry, 242
  Jacob, 242
  John, 242
  Joseph, 242
  Mary, 242
SHAULL, Catherine, 255
  Henry, 255
  Jacob, 255
  John, 255
  Joseph, 255
SHAW, Isabella, 223
  Jean, 16
  John, 16
  Margaret, 16
  Nancy, 223
  Robert, 16
  William, 6, 16, 223
SHAWER, Christiana, 226
  Jacob, 226
SHEARER, Daniel, 126
  George, 126
  Henry, 126
  Jacob, 126

John, 126
Maria, 126
SHEARLY, Elizabeth, 157
Nicholas, 157
SHEELY, Abraham, 60
Catharine, 60, 179
Christopher, 179
Elizabeth, 60
George, 60, 179
Godfrey, 60
Henry, 60
John, 60
Mary, 179
Stophel, 60
SHEFER, Christiana, 124
John, 124
SHEFFER, Ann, 145
Anna, 29
Barbara, 155
Catharine, 29, 155
Charles, 29
Christiana, 109, 155, 267
David, 29
Elizabeth, 29, 109, 145, 155
Henry, 109
Jacob, 145
John, 109, 145, 219
Katherine, 29
Malcher, 155
Margaret, 29, 145, 155
Maria, 29
Mary Catharine, 145
McArillis, 29
Natalina, 29
Nicholas, 267
Peter, 145
Philip, 29, 155

Rudol[h, 267
Sheffer, 267
SHEKLEY, William, 23
SHELLBECKER, Catharine, 161
SHELLEY,
Annamaria, 246
Elizabeth, 246
George, 246
John, 246
Maria Barbara, 246
Michael, 246
Molly, 246
Samuel, 246
Sarah, 246
SHELLY, Andrew, 139
Ann, 27
Catharine, 27
Daniel, 27, 249
Eve, 139
John, 249
Mary, 27, 249
Peter, 27
SHELTER, Andrew, 56
Christian, 56
Frederick, 56
Henry, 56
Jacob, 56
John, 56
Mary, 56
Michael, 56
SHENBERGER,
Adam, 177
Elizabeth, 177
John, 177
Joseph, 177
Magdalena, 177
Margaret, 177
Mary Susanna, 177
Michael, 177

Rachel, 177
SHEPERD, John, 117
Mary, 117
SHEPHERD, Isaac, 223
Sarah, 223
SHERER, Adaman, 237
Dorothea, 237
SHERFIG, Catharine, 144
Jacob, 144
SHERITZ, Arnold, 96
Catharine, 96
Conrad, 96
Jacob, 96
Ludwick, 96
SHERMAN, Anna, 249
Catharine, 249
Conrad, 121
Eizabeth, 124
Elizabeth, 249
Eve, 249
Helena, 121
John, 249
Lydia, 249
Mary, 249
Sarah, 249
Susanna, 249
SHERRITZ,
Catharine, 131
Conrad, 131
Elizabeth, 131
Frederick, 131
Ludwig, 131
Margaret, 131
Mary, 131
SHETERON, Anna, 35
Anna Maria, 35
Caspar, 35
Catharine, 35

Henry, 35
Jacob, 35
Leonard, 35
Margaret, 35
Trowne, 35
SHETLEY, Elizabeth, 113
Frederick, 113
SHETTER, Andrew, 97
Barbara, 97, 250
David, 97
Dorothea, 97
Elizabeth, 97
Eve, 97
Frederick, 250
John, 97
Mady, 97
Margaret, 97
Martin, 97
Merea, 97
Samuel, 97
Susanna, 97
SHETTERS, Hyster, 240
John, 240
SHETTLE, George, 194
SHETTLER, Andrew, 31, 214
Barbara, 214
Eve, 31, 214
George, 182
Jacob, 214
Lydia, 214
SHETTRON, David, 143
SHICK, Joseph, 110
SHICKARD, Philip, 84
SHIELD, James, 151
Margaret, 151
SHIELDS, Anna, 176
Anne, 176

Betty, 176
Jennet, 80
John, 80
Margaret, 80
Robert, 80
William, 176
SHILTZBERGER,
  Andrew, 87
  Anna B., 87
  Jacob, 87
  Maria, 87
SHINDEL, Frederick, 200
SHINDLER, Conrad, 94
SHIRTS, Mary, 199
  Samuel, 199
SHISLER, Henrich, 268
SHIVE, Ludwick, 180
SHNYDER, Jacob, 125
  Walter, 191
SHOCK, Elizabeth, 142
  Henry, 142
SHOE, Elizabeth, 90
  Frederick, 90
  Henry, 90
  John, 90
  Susanna, 90
SHOEMAKER, Anna, 74
  Jacob, 74
  John, 263
SHOEMAN,
  Catharine, 268
  George, 268
SHOENBERGER,
  Margaret, 133
  Peter, 133
SHOL, Anna, 235
  Anna Elizabeth, 235
  Gacharius, 235

Henry, 235
Isaac, 235
Jacob, 235
John, 235
Peter, 235
SHOLL, Catharine, 244
  Elizabeth, 271
  John, 249, 271
  Lewis, 244
SHOLLAS, Christiana, 129
  Katharine, 112
  Magdalena, 111, 112, 129
  Martha, 112
  Susanna, 112, 129
  Theobald, 111
SHONARD, Abraham, 20
  Eleanor, 20
  Elizabeth, 20
  John, 20
  Jonathan, 20
  Margaret, 20
  Mary, 20
  Susan, 20
  Thomas, 20
  William, 20
SHOOLSBANK,
  Joseph, 4
  Mary, 4
  Michael, 4
  Philip, 4
  William, 4
SHORT, Anthony, 180
  Christiana, 160
  Francis, 180
  Jacob, 180
  James, 126, 164
  Jane, 164
  John, 180
  Joseph, 180

Mary, 180
Peter, 160
SHOTTER, Anna, 163
  Catharine, 163
  Dorothea, 163
  Elizabeth, 163
  Frederick, 163
  Henry, 163
  Margaret, 163
SHOUP, Andrew, 119
  Christian, 119
  Dorothea, 119
  Mathias, 119
  Peter, 119
SHOVER, Barbara, 272
  Samuel, 272
SHRAM, Elizabeth, 38
  George, 38
  Jacob, 38
SHREIBER, Ann, 151
  Catharine, 151
  Eva, 151
  Jacob, 151
  John, 151
  Margaret, 151
  Maria, 151
  Michel, 151
  Peter, 151
SHRETTRONE, Jacob, 38
SHRIBERS, Anna, 238
  Daniel, 238
SHRIEBER, Jacob, 151
  Peter, 151
SHRIENER, Philip, 173
SHRINE, Andrew, 79
SHRINER, Margaret, 194
  Martin, 194

Peter, 196
Philip, 194
Sarah, 196
SHRIVER, Catharine, 157
  Elizabeth, 157
  John, 157, 220
  Ludwick, 80, 157
  Margaret, 157
  Mary, 80
  Peter, 157
  Solome, 157
  Susanna, 157
SHRODER, Martin, 37
  Mary, 37
SHROLL, Anna, 225
  Catharine, 225
  Christian, 225
  Eve, 225
  John, 225
SHROM, Anna Maria, 6
  David, 6
  George, 6
  John, 6
  Nicholas, 6
SHUCK, George, 40, 117
  Margaret, 40
SHUGART, Catharine, 116
  Mary, 26, 116
  Peter, 26
SHULER, Andrew, 262
  Margaret, 262
SHULL, Anna, 183
  Barbara, 42
  Frederick, 42
  Jacob, 42, 183
  John, 42
  Joseph, 42

Mary, 42
Peter, 42
Sally, 42
Samuel, 42
Solomena, 42
SHULTZ, Adam, 145
  Andrew, 141
  Catharine, 31, 113, 145, 253, 259
  Elizabeth, 145
  Eve, 145, 253
  George, 145
  Gertrude, 145
  Henry, 9, 145, 193, 199, 230, 253, 259
  Jacob, 31, 145, 253
  John, 9, 145, 253
  Juliana, 253
  Margaret, 31, 253
  Mary, 253
  Peter, 82, 113, 138, 141, 205, 253
  Samuel, 31
  Susanna, 145
  Valentine, 53
SHUP, Barbara, 259
  Casper, 257, 259
  Elizabeth, 259
  Jacob, 259
  Jasper, 259
  Mary, 257
  Peter, 259
SHUPP, Barbara, 87
  Jacob, 87
  Louis, 87
  Martin, 87
  Peter, 87
SHUS, Erana, 251
  John, 251
SIDLE, Godfrey, 150
SIDLER, Jacob, 80
  Lizzie, 80
SIECHRIST, Ann, 230

Elizabeth, 230
Jacob, 230
Maria, 230
SIEGLE, Anna, 179
  Christiana, 179
  Elizabeth, 179
  George, 179
  Jacob, 179
  Rosanna, 179
SIESS, George, 220
SIMENTON, Ann, 2
SIMON, Casper, 142
  George, 269
  John, 142, 269
  Margaret, 142
SIMPSON, Agness, 84
  Alexander, 84
  Elizabeth, 161
  James, 84, 161
  John, 161
  Jonathan, 84
  Michael, 241
  Robert, 161
  Susanna, 241
SINCKEL, William, 36
SINCLAIRE, Hannah, 127
SINN, Anna, 198
  Barbara, 100
  Catharine, 100
  Christian, 100, 134, 198
  George Christian, 100
  Jacob, 198
  John, 198
  Margaret, 198
  Mary, 100
  Rebecca, 198
SIPE, Charles, 66
  Elizabeth, 66
  George, 66
  Henry, 66
  Jean, 66
  Mary, 66
  Sarah, 66
SIPPIX, Betsy, 112
  Cuff, 112
  Grease, 112
  Jacob, 112
  James, 112
  John, 112
  Sarah, 112
SITTLER, Barbara, 80
  Isaac, 80
SKELETON, George, 270
  Lydia, 270
SLAGEL, Catharine, 63
  Christopher, 63
  Daniel, 63
  Henry, 63
  Jacob, 63
  Magdalena, 63
  Mary, 63
  Susanna, 63
SLAGLE, Barbara, 121
  Catharine, 121, 145
  Christiana, 121
  Christopher, 121
  Daniel, 145
  David, 121, 145
  Elizabeth, 121, 145
  Eve, 121
  George, 121
  Gloria, 121
  Helenea, 121
  Henry, 45, 76, 121, 177, 242, 246, 247
  Jacob, 121, 170
  John, 121
  Joseph, 232
  Joshua, 121
  Louise, 121
  Magdalena, 121
  Margaret, 145, 232
  Mary, 121, 145
  Salomy, 121
  Susanna, 121
SLATER, George, 211
SLAUP, Catharine, 129
  Martin, 129
SLEGERS, Elizabeth, 166
  George, 166
SLEMOUS, James, 171
  John, 171
  Robert, 171
  Sarah, 171
  William, 171
SLENKER, Andrew, 137
  Elizabeth, 137
  Francis, 250
  Jacob, 137
  John, 137
  Martin, 137, 250
SLENTZ, Catharine, 157
  Jacob, 154, 157
  John, 157
  Marilis, 154
  Nicholas, 154
  Philip, 88, 113, 154
SLOTHOUR, Anthony, 155
  Catharine, 155
SLOUGH, Catharine, 112
  Elizabeth, 112
  Jacob, 112
  Mary, 112
  Rosanna, 112
  Susanna, 112
SLYDER, Henry, 261

SMALL, Anna, 233
  Barbara, 56
  Catharine, 233, 266
  Elizabeth, 233
  Enos, 233
  George, 252, 274
  Henry, 252
  Jacob, 56, 233, 252, 266, 274
  John, 177, 233, 252
  John Engle, 177
  Joseph, 233, 252
  Killean, 65
  Killian, 65, 72, 252
  Mary, 177, 232
  Michael, 252
  Peter, 232, 252
  Philibina, 233
  William, 233
SMART, William, 6
SMELSER, Michael, 132
  Philip, 132
SMID, Elizabeth, 264
  George, 264
SMISSER, Louise, 121
  Mathias, 121
SMITH, Abraham, 235, 267
  Adam, 41, 143, 220
  Agness, 77
  Alexander, 199
  Andrew, 101, 122, 212, 215, 236
  Ann, 6, 108, 115, 162, 229, 267
  Anna, 215
  Anthony, 209
  Baltzer, 186
  Barbara, 34, 42, 86, 143, 220, 236
  Barnet, 164, 232
  Catharine, 34, 121, 143, 155, 209, 229, 235, 236
  Christian, 220
  Christiana, 211, 220, 267
  Christopher, 73
  Daniel, 211
  David, 42, 77, 108
  Eleanor, 92, 211
  Elizabeth, 34, 77, 92, 143, 154, 160, 162, 186, 209, 218, 235
  Eve, 186, 236
  Francis, 108
  Frederick, 160
  Gabriel, 160
  George, 34, 92, 154, 209, 236
  Godlip, 121
  Hannah, 92, 235
  Henry, 34, 94, 235, 236, 267
  Hugh, 92
  Jacob, 41, 115, 143, 235, 267
  James, 11, 92, 108, 147, 186, 211, 234, 245
  John, 41, 68, 77, 92, 108, 167, 183, 186, 209, 222, 236, 267, 271
  Joseph, 86, 108
  Juliana, 209
  Katharine, 229
  Magdalena, 34, 186, 209, 236
  Maggie, 34
  Margaret, 34, 41, 92, 143, 164, 195, 209, 220, 229
  Maria Dorothea, 215
  Martha, 108
  Mary, 77, 108, 183, 186, 220, 235
  Mary Anna, 220
  Michael, 218
  Peter, 41, 162, 215, 218, 235
  Polly, 220
  Rebecca, 108, 147
  Robert, 77
  Rosanna, 34
  Salome, 186
  Samuel, 108, 229, 235
  Sarah, 77, 167, 186, 229
  Sophia, 209
  Susanna, 101, 209
  Thomas, 147, 167
  Valentine, 167
  William, 69, 77, 108, 155, 167, 186, 195, 229, 269
SMOCK, Ann, 96, 99
  Barnet, 99
  Mathias, 96
SMYSER, Barbara, 216
  Catharine, 122
  Elizabeth, 142, 143
  Henry, 142, 143
  Jacob, 122, 141, 142, 143, 216, 242
  Martin, 216
  Peggy, 242
  Sarah, 216
SNAR, Casper, 96
SNEARINGER, L., 85
SNEERSY, Joseph, 207
SNEIDER, Christiana, 54
  David, 202
  Elizabeth, 202

Philip, 54
SNEIDMAN, Bastian,
    104
    Daniel, 104
    Loreena, 104
SNELLBECKER,
    Ann, 151
    Barbara, 70
    Catharine, 70
    George, 70, 151
    Jacob, 70
SNIDER, Hy, 99
    Mary, 99
SNODGRASS,
    Agness, 138
    James, 138
    John, 138
    Joseph, 138
    Mary, 138
    Robert, 138
    William, 138
SNYDER, Anthony, 58
    Catharine, 58
    Davolt, 135
    Theobold, 192
SNYUDER, John, 135
SOHN, Elizabeth, 15
    George, 15
    Jacob, 15
    John, 15
    Margaret, 15
SONDAY, Christiana,
    116
    Jacob, 116
    John, 116
    Joseph, 116
    Margaret, 116
    Mathias, 116
SOPHIA, Esther, 173
SOWER, Adam, 73
    Catharine, 73
    Daniel, 73
    David, 73
    Elizabeth, 73
    Eve, 73
    Frederick, 113
    George, 73
    Jacob, 73
    John, 73
    Juliana, 73, 113
    Martin, 73
    Mary, 73
    Susan, 73
SOX, Nicholas, 154
    Sarah, 154
SPAHR, Barbara, 57
    Catharine, 57
    Elizaeth, 57
    Eve, 57
    Frederick, 57
    Hans, 201
    John, 201
    Michael, 57
    Peter, 57
SPANGLER, Andrew,
    160
    Anna, 69, 229
    Anna Maria, 228
    Balser, 89
    Baltzer, 31, 139
    Barnard, 131
    Barned, 122
    Barnet, 14, 196
    Barnhart, 190
    Bernard, 126
    Casper, 14, 240
    Catharine, 171, 232
    Catherine, 17
    Christiana, 234
    Daniel, 31, 89, 181,
        186, 190, 232
    Dorothea, 232
    Elizabeth, 17, 31, 89,
        126, 186, 190, 224,
        232, 240
    Eve, 190
    Ferdinand, 264
    Frederick G., 265
    George, 6, 31, 69, 89,
        139, 167, 228, 229
    Henry, 17, 50, 67,
        224, 270
    Jacob, 158, 186, 190,
        208, 232
    Jesse, 232
    John, 31, 89, 111,
        151, 158, 186, 190,
        229, 264, 265
    John G., 50
    Jonas, 186, 190
    Joseph, 186, 238
    Judith, 14
    Juliana, 31, 89, 158
    Magdalena, 31, 229,
        232
    Margaret, 151, 158,
        196, 232, 240, 264,
        265
    Mary, 89, 158, 186,
        232, 238
    Michael, 31, 89, 139,
        171
    Peter, 135, 186, 232
    Philip, 14
    Rebecca, 158
    Robert, 224
    Rosanna, 6
    Rudolph, 17, 31, 70,
        139, 160, 232, 234
    Rudy, 89
    Sarah, 158
    Susan, 265
    Susanna, 67, 224,
        270
    William, 158
    Zacharia, 158
SPANSELLER,
    Catharine, 177
    Elizabeth, 177

George, 177
Margaret, 177
Rachel, 177
SPEAKMAN, Samuel, 185
SPEER, Christiana, 114
James, 84, 215
Jane, 215
John, 114
William, 72
SPENCE, George, 162
John, 162, 210
SPENCER, Isaac, 63
Jean, 63
John, 63
Mary, 63
Robert, 63
Thomas, 63
William, 63
SPENGLER, Adam, 126
Christiana, 163
Clara, 126
George, 23
Henry, 23, 126
John, 126
John George, 163
Lydia, 126
Rosina, 23
Rudolph, 163
Susanna, 163
SPIES, Catharine, 263
Charles, 263
George, 91
Jacob, 91
Katharine, 91
Peter, 91
Susanna, 91
SPIHR, Barbara, 182
George, 182
SPINCKEL, Anna, 37
Catharine, 36

Charlotte, 36
Daniel, 36
Elizabeth, 36
Eve, 37
Henry, 36
Jacob, 36
Margaret, 36
Mary, 37
Peter, 36
SPITTER, Matthias, 139
SPITTLE, Catharine, 183
Mary, 183
SPITTLES, John, 183
SPITZER, Ann, 236
Barbara, 236
Conrad, 236
John, 236
Susanna, 236
SPONSELLER, Ann, 40
George, 40
Jacob, 89
Margaretta, 40
SPRENCKEL, Anna, 205
Barbara, 205
Daniel, 205
Elizabeth, 205
Frederick, 205
George, 205
John, 205
Magdalena, 205
Michael, 205
SPRENKLE, Anna, 242
Anna Maria, 242
Daniel, 242
Elizabeth, 223, 242
Frederick, 242
John, 223, 242
Peter, 242

Sarah, 242
Wiliam, 242
SPRINCKEL,
Margaret, 127
Peter, 126
SPRINGER, Ann, 112
Isaac, 128
Margaret, 128
SPRINKLE,
Catharine, 217
Henry, 217
SPROCHELL,
Elizabeth, 129
Joanna, 129
Susanna, 129
STAAB, Adam, 40
Anna, 40
Catharine, 40, 102
George, 40
Henry, 40
Jacob, 40
John, 40
Philip, 40
STABLER, George, 191
STAGNER, Catharine, 128
Catherine, 18
Charlotte, 128
Isaac, 18
Mary, 128
Nicholas, 18
Peter, 128
STAHL, Henry, 77
Matalena, 77
STAHLE, John, 274
STAHN, Michael, 67
STAKE, Catharine, 116
Christian, 116
Elizabth, 116
George, 22, 116
Jacob, 116

Lehna, 116
Mary, 116
Michael, 116
Peggy, 116
STALEY, Barbara, 45
STALL, Anna Maria, 5
Jacob, 5
Mary, 5
STAM, Adam, 108
Ann, 109
Catharine, 108
Elizabeth, 109
John, 108
Juliana, 109
Leonard, 109
STAMBACH, Anna, 213
Anna Maria, 233
Barbara, 179
Elizabeth, 233
Henry, 179, 233
Jacob, 179, 204, 213
John, 179, 204
Michael, 233, 274
Peter, 204
Philip, 179, 204, 233
STARBOCK, Martin, 32
STARK, John, 229
STARR, John, 193
Moses, 193
STAUFFER,
Abraham, 94
Anna, 94, 216
Barbara, 216, 248
Christian, 150
Christiana, 94
Elizabeth, 216
Henry, 94, 216
Jacob, 150, 216
John, 94, 199, 216, 248
Margaret, 150

Peter, 150
Polly, 216
Rebecca, 94
STAUSEBERG,
Andrew, 160
Catharine, 160
Conrad, 160
Daniel, 160
Elizabeth, 160
George, 160
Henry, 160
John, 160
Joseph, 160
STAUTER, John, 261
STECKENDOM,
John, 52
STEEDT, James, 151
Mary, 151
STEEL, David, 43
Elizabeth, 72
John, 43, 72
Margaret, 43
Martha, 43
Rachel, 43
Thomas, 43
William, 43
STEELE, George, 57
Mary, 57
STEFFE, Christiana, 189
Michael, 189
STEGMER, Jacob, 193
STEHER, Adam, 260
Catharine, 260
Christian, 260
Christiana, 260
Elizabeth, 260
Jacob, 260
John, 260
Magdalena, 260
STEIGHLETTER,
Elizabeth, 72

George, 72
STEIMAN, Conrad, 172
STEIN, Andrew, 183, 192
Anna, 192
Anna Maria, 192
Catherine, 192
Christiana, 142
David, 142
Elizabeth, 134, 183, 192
Frederick, 134, 192, 253
Jacob, 192
Julianna, 192
Magdalena, 192
Mathias, 192
Samuel, 256
STEINER, Christian, 135
STELEVISH, Anna, 185
George, 185
STEMMERS,
Alexander, 150
John, 150
Margaret, 150
STENTZ, Anna, 12
Catharine, 12
Dorothea, 12
Henry, 12
Jacob, 12
John, 12
Leonard, 12
Maria, 12
Maria Dorothea, 12
STEPHANS, Peter, 49
STEPHENSON,
William, 32
STERBICK, Jacob, 223

STERMER, Barbara, 194
John, 194
STERRET, Benjamin, 80
Margaret, 80
STEVENS, Adam, 237
Anna Mary, 237
Henry, 237
Mary, 237
Philip, 237
STEVINSON,
Elizabeth, 2
George, 2
James, 2
Margaret, 2
William, 2
STEWART, Abraham, 72, 236
Agnes, 94
Andrew, 108, 128, 129
Anna, 210
Barbara, 72, 236
Benj., 120
David, 72
Elizabeth, 72, 128, 129
Elizabth, 236
Eve, 227
Freny, 72
Hugh, 128, 129
Jacob, 72
James, 128
John, 72, 142, 191, 210, 236
Martha, 142
Mary, 72, 128
Mathias, 72, 227
Rachel, 142
Rebecca, 120
Robert, 142
Ruth, 184

Sarah, 129
Thomas, 94
William, 128, 129
STICKLER, Ann, 60
Christopher, 60
George, 60
Jacob, 60
John, 60
Magdalena, 60
Peter, 60
STINE, Abraham, 181
Catharine, 181
Christiana, 181
Frederick, 181
John, 181
Mary, 181
STITT, Rachel, 132
Samuel, 132
STOBLE, Jacob, 212
STOCKSLAGE,
Barbara, 123
John, 123
STOCKTON, Thomas, 12
STOHLY, Barbara, 166
Jacob, 166
STOMINGER,
Michael, 189
STONE, Mary, 202
Samuel, 202
STONER, Adam, 153
Catharine, 228
Christian, 17, 50, 210, 211
Christiana, 153
Frederick, 153, 228
George, 153
Henry, 264
Jacob, 153
John, 248
Mary, 211, 248
Michael, 153

STOP, Barbara, 123
John, 123
STOPHEL, Michael, 39
STORM, Peter, 161
STOSACH, John, 45
STOUCHENBERGER, Conrad, 155
Elizabth, 155
STOUCK, Charlotte, 137
Elizabeth, 137
George, 137
Godfrey, 137
John, 137
Mary, 137
STOUFER, Christian, 271
Susanna, 271
STOUFFER,
Abraham, 49
STOUGH, Andrew, 193
Barbara, 193
Catharine, 193
Frederick, 193
George, 193
Henry, 193
Jaccobin, 193
Jacob, 193
John, 193
Lanhart, 193
Peter, 193
STOUT, Peter, 5
STOVE, George, 212
Jacob, 212
Michael, 212
STOVER, Anna Maria, 99
Catharine, 99
Christian, 99
Elizabeth, 99
Henry, 99, 135, 228,

257, 261
Jacob, 222, 227, 260, 274
Nicholas, 227
Polly, 260
Susanna, 274
STRACK, John Philip, 211
STRADDLER, Jacob, 200
STRAEHER, Andrew, 145
Catharine, 145
Elizabeth, 145
Eve, 145
Jacob, 145
John, 145
Juliana, 145
Magdalena, 145
Mary, 145
Peter, 145
Susanna, 145
STRAKE, George, 103
STRALEY, Andrew, 24
STRASPACH,
Barbara, 34
Peter, 34
STRAWBRADGE,
John, 126
STRAYER, Nicholas, 234
STREBER, Elizabeth, 243
Peter, 224, 243
STRECHER, Peter, 29
STREHER, Peter, 260
STREIPLER,
Elizabeth, 192
John, 192
STREITHOFF, Ann, 103

Francis, 103
STRICKHOUSER,
Elizabeth, 164
Harry, 254
Henry, 164, 233, 243, 248, 259
STRICKLER, Ann, 90, 135
Anna, 135
Barbara, 169
Catharine, 264
Christian, 142
Christiana, 142, 169
Conrad, 142, 169
Elizabeth, 189, 227
Frainey, 89
Henrich, 135
Henry, 17, 73, 82, 99, 102, 117, 123, 135, 156
Jacob, 51, 135, 158, 175, 189, 264
John, 51, 169, 189, 227, 264
Joseph, 227
Magdalena, 73
Michael, 264
Salome, 227
Samuel, 227
Ulrich, 264
William, 227
STRICKOUSER,
Henry, 230
STRIOR, Jacob, 8
John, 8
STROBICH, Anamary, 211
Jacob, 211
STROHMENGER,
Jacob, 100
STROMAN, Elton, 260
John, 241, 259, 260

Leitner, 260
Louisa, 260
Mary, 260
Susanna, 260
STRONAN, John, 234
STRONG, Jacob, 196
James, 196
Mary, 196
STROW, Anna, 92
George, 92
STRUP, Ann, 154
Barbara, 154
Catharine M., 154
Catharine Margaret, 154
Daniel, 154
Elizabeth, 154
John, 154
Martin, 154
Mary, 154
Rachel, 154
Rebecca, 154
Susanna, 154
STUCHER, Catharine, 264
Jacob, 264
STUCK, Conrad, 31
Eve, 31
Hannah, 31
Jacob, 31, 214
Margaret, 31
Martin, 31
Mary, 67
Peter, 31
Susanna, 31
William, 67
STUCKSLAGER,
Albertus, 51
STUM, Mary, 131
STUMP, Baltzer, 172
Barbara, 88
Catharine, 88
Elizabeth, 88

George, 172
Henry, 172
John, 88, 222
Joseph, 172
Margaret, 88, 172, 222
Mathias, 88
STURT, Elizabeth, 110
John, 110
STYER, Magdalena, 36
Tobias, 36
STYVENSON,
  Elizabeth, 182
  George, 182
SUER, Margaret, 33
Tobias, 33
SUGAR, Catharine, 232
Jacob, 232
SULLIVAN, Patrick, 117
Timothy, 84
SULTZBERGER,
  Andrew, 115
  Anna, 115
  Dorothea, 115
SUMBERLAND,
  Elizabeth, 45
  James, 45
  Jean, 45
  John, 45
  William, 45
SUMMER, John, 203
SUMMERS, Agness, 23
Elizabeth, 23
John, 23
Robert, 23
SUMOFON,
  Catharine, 137
  Henry, 137

SUMWALD, Godfrey, 185
SUNDAY, Andrew, 198
Catharine, 198
Charles, 198
Elizabeth, 198
John, 198
SUTOR, John, 32, 107
Sarah, 32
William, 32
SWAGER, Catharine, 196
Jacob, 196
SWARTZ, Andrew, 203
Barbara, 116
Conrad, 192
Dorothea, 203
Felix, 203
George, 115
Jacob, 80, 135, 202, 203
John, 203
Tobias, 203
SWARTZBACK,
  Adam, 134
  Anna, 134
  John, 134
  Magdalena, 134
SWEENEY, Ann, 66
Isaac, 66
James, 66, 105, 173
John, 66, 173
Mary, 66
Miles, 66, 173
Polly, 173
Thomas, 66, 173
SWENEY, Esther, 206
Polly, 206
SWEVANS, Ann, 23
George, 23
SWINDEL, Jon, 244

Magdalena, 244
SWING, George, 72
Margaret, 72
Michael, 72
SWOBENLAND,
  Anna, 179
  Christian, 179
  Ludwig, 179
  Peggy, 179
SWOOPE, Adam, 176
Conrad, 176
George, 176
Gloria, 176
Henry, 176
John, 176
SWOPE, Anna Maria, 75
Catharine, 140
Conrad, 87
Elizabeth, 140
George, 23, 75
Jacob, 57
Michael, 14, 31
Sabina, 57

-T-

TAGGERT, James, 69
TALLER, Adam, 181
Maria, 181
TARNOCK, Jacob, 195
Nancy, 195
TARQUHAR, Lydia, 185
William, 185
TATE, Abigail, 176
Archibald, 143
Elizabeth, 177
George, 176
Hannah, 176
Isaac, 177
Izreal, 177
James, 143

Jean, 143
Jeremiah, 176
Martha, 176
Mary, 143, 176
Sarah, 143
Solomon, 177
William, 143
TAYLOR, Abraham,
  251
Adam, 19
Ann, 5
Benjamin, 5, 251
Eleanor, 17
George, 3, 256
Grace, 5
Hugh, 17
Jacob, 251
James, 212
Jean, 17, 151
John, 3, 5, 17, 251
Joseph, 151, 256
Margaret, 235
Michael, 251
Philip, 251
Rebecca, 5
Robert, 3, 17
Susanna, 251
Thomas, 3
TEETERICH,
  Catharine, 107
  Joseph, 107
  Mary, 107
TEST, Anna, 151
  Anne, 170
  George, 151
  Isabella, 151
  Jacob, 151
  John, 151
  Margaret, 151, 170
THAKER, Jean, 228
  John, 228
  Samuel, 228
  Sarah, 228

William C., 228
THEAKER, Elizabeth,
  255
John, 255
THOMAN, Abraham,
  206
Elizabeth, 206
Henry, 206
Jacob, 206
John, 206
Magdalena, 206
Rudolph, 206
Susanna, 206
THOMAS, Adam, 196
Barbara, 40, 49
Deborah, 241
Dinah, 33
Eleanor, 33
James, 136, 241
John, 33, 119, 210
Jonah, 33
Milley, 196
Naomi, 136
Rebecca, 33
Sarah, 33
William, 49
THOMBURG,
  Thomas, 178
THOMEY, Margaret,
  49
THOMPSON, Agness,
  85, 254
Alexander, 21, 85,
  113, 246
Alexander James,
  254
Allen, 85
Andrew, 4, 15, 104,
  140, 166, 254, 162
Anne, 140
Archibald, 254, 275
Eleanor, 15, 123
Elizabeth, 123, 140

Ephriam, 15
Esther, 21, 140
George, 15
Isaac, 15
James, 85, 150
Jane, 275
John, 15, 26, 52, 63,
  123, 137, 140
Joseph, 85, 254
Margaret, 15, 254
Martha, 123
Mary, 123, 140, 254
Phebe, 123
Robert, 123
Ruth, 123
Samuel, 254
Sarah, 123
Susanna, 123
William, 15, 123, 163,
  254
THORN, Magdalena,
  58
Peter, 58
THOMBURG,
  Thomas, 178
THRON, Barbara, 114
Elizabeth, 114
George, 114
John, 114
Magdalena, 114
Mary, 114
Michael, 114
Samuel, 114
THRONE, Abraham,
  183
Anna, 183
George, 259
John, 183
Magdalena, 183
Mary, 143, 183
Samuel, 143, 183
TIN, Charlotte, 36
Nicholas, 37

TISSELL, John Adam,
  170
TODD, Hannah, 137
  James, 137
  Joseph, 137
  Owen, 137
TOLAND, Anne, 118
  Elizabeth, 118
  James, 118
  Margaret, 118
  Mary, 118
  Susanna, 118
  Thomas, 118
  William, 118
TOMKINS, Benjamin,
  240
  Deborah, 240
  Jacob, 240
  John, 240
  Joseph, 240
  Sarah, 240
TOMPKINS, Benj.,
  124
TOMPSON, Agness,
  23
  Alexander, 23, 214,
    245
  Andrew, 166
  James, 23
  Joseph, 23, 198
  Mary, 198
  Sarah, 77
TONNERAS,
  Elizabeth, 217
  Samuel, 217
TORANCE, Archibald,
  4
  David, 4
  John, 4
  Sarah, 4
TORBET, Agness, 223
  Andrew, 223
  Isabella, 223

Janet, 223
Jean, 223
Robert, 223
TORMIN, Anna Mary,
  33
  Benedict, 33
  John, 33
  Samuel, 33
TORRENS, Aaron, 4
TOUAMPF, Peter,
  234
  Rebecca, 234
TOWBENBERGER,
  Margaret, 133
TOWLE, Ambrose, 6
  Henry, 6
  Jean, 6
  Lettis, 6
  Sarah, 6
TOWNSLEY, George,
  129
  James, 129
  Jean, 129
  John, 129
  Margaret, 129
  Robert, 129
  William, 129
TRAMB, Henry, 104
TREASE, Michael, 34
TRECKER, Alexander,
  259
TREIGHLER, Anna,
  176
  Barbara, 176
  Catharine, 176
  Daniel, 176
  Dorothea, 176
  Elizabeth, 176
  John, 175
  Magdalena, 176
  Maria, 176
  Martin, 176
  Salome, 176

TRENHLER,
  Catharine, 227
  Dorothea, 227
  Elizabeth, 227
  Eve, 227
  Mary, 227
  Salome, 227
  Susanna, 227
TRESSLER,
  Catharine, 265
  Jacob, 265
TREXEL, Anthony,
  167
  Catharine, 167
  John, 167
  Joseph, 167
TRIFAGEL, John, 230
  Molly, 230
TRIMBLE, Agness,
  130
  John, 130
  Mary, 130
TRIMMER, Andrew,
  125, 153
  Ann, 125
  Anna, 153
  Catharine, 173
  Christiana, 125, 153
  David, 125, 153
  Eleanor, 153
  George, 173
  Henry, 172
  John, 125, 153
  Mary, 125, 153
  Mathias, 125
  Matthew, 153
  Nelly, 125
  Peter, 125
  Sally, 153
  Salome, 125
  Sophia, 125, 153
  William, 125, 153
TRINDLE, Alexander,

162
Sarah, 162
TRINE, Christian, 75
Elizabeth, 75
Jacob, 75
Margaret, 75
Peter, 75
Rose, 75
TRONE, George, 25
John, 114, 209
Magdalena, 114
TROSTEL, Abraham, 274
Catharine, 274
Daniel, 274
Elizabeth, 274
George, 274
Henry, 274
John, 274
Joseph, 274
Peter, 274
Susanna, 274
Wiliam, 274
TROUP, Henry, 104
John, 104
Margaret, 104
Mary, 104
Paul, 104
Peter, 104
Philip, 104
Robert, 104
TROUSHELD, Eve, 141
William, 141
TRUMP, Barbara, 199
Elizabeth, 208
Herman, 199
John, 154, 199, 208
Margaret, 199
Mary, 154
Michael, 199
Peter, 199
TSCHUDY, Barbara,

227
Nicholas, 227
TUCKER, Mary, 131
Tempest, 131
TUITZ, Elizabeth, 185
John, 185
Philip, 185
Susanna, 185
TULL, Elizabeth, 21
Ulrich, 21
TURNER, Ann, 8
Barbara, 272
David, 8
John, 8, 272
Lydia, 8
Rebecca, 22
Robert, 8
Sarah, 8
William, 22
TYSON, Benjamin, 103
Elizabeth, 239
Henry, 83, 86, 87, 102, 115, 157, 208
Jacob, 239

-U-
UHLER, Adam, 19
Andrew, 19
Barbara, 19
Catherine, 19
Dietrich, 19
Elizabeth, 19
Erasmus, 19
Eve, 19
Margaret, 19
Rosanna, 19
Savenah, 19
Valentine, 19
UINAS, Rebecca, 244
Thomas, 244
ULHER, Deiter, 12
UMKATONE, George,

10
UNDERWOOD, Abraham, 164
Alexander, 25, 186, 232
Anna, 93, 136
Benj., 93, 194
Benjamin, 25, 194
Elicher, 25
Eliher, 93
Elihn, 91
Elihu, 93, 186
Elinure, 91
Elisha, 136
Frazier, 25
Hannah, 93, 164
Isaac, 195
Jane, 25, 93
Jesse, 93
John, 25
Joseph, 25
Lydia, 93
Margaret, 186
Martha, 195
Mary, 25, 194, 195
Michael, 194
Nehemiah, 194
Obed, 93
Rachel, 93
Rhoda, 232
Ruth, 25, 93
Samuel, 25
Sarah, 195
Susanna, 194
Thomas, 25
William, 25, 93, 194, 195
Zephina, 93
UNKAFARE, George, 18
UNWE, Elizabeth, 184
UPDEGRAEF, Anna
Ursula, 12

Derick, 12
Harman, 12
Herman, 12
John, 12
Joseph, 12
William, 12
UPDEGRAF, Ann, 155
Joseph, 155
UPDEGRAFF,
 Ambrose, 186
 Anna, 232, 271
 Barbara, 103
 Benj., 271
 Catharine, 271
 Christian, 271
 Edith, 186
 Elizabeth, 176, 211, 271
 Hannah, 186, 211
 Henry, 211
 Herman, 211, 232
 Israel, 186
 Jacob, 103, 211, 271
 Jesse, 241
 John, 26
 Joseph, 47, 103, 186, 271
 Josiah, 186
 Julian, 271
 Lydia, 167
 Mary, 167, 186, 232, 271
 Mary Webb, 47
 Nancy, 211
 Nathan, 47, 186
 Peter, 103, 176, 211
 Rhoda, 232
 Samuel, 167, 211
 Sarah, 186
 Susanna, 186, 232, 241
UPDEGROFF, Jacob, 169
UPDERGRAFF,
 Ambrose, 47
 Edith, 47
 Jacob, 23
 Susanna, 47
UPLAND, Dorothea, 237
 Michael, 237
UPP, Catharine, 22
 Elizabeth, 22
 Jacob, 22
 Louisa, 22
 Nicholas, 22
UPPACH, Catharine, 182
 Philip, 182
UREY, Antone, 63
 Barbara, 63
 Elizabeth, 63
 John, 63
 Michael, 63
URICH, Barbara, 246
 Caty, 246
 Elizabeth, 246
 Margaret, 246
 Michael, 246
 Molly, 246
 Sally, 246
 Susan, 246
 William, 246
UTTZ, Daniel, 82
UTZ, Adam, 150
 Andrew, 270
 Catharine, 150
 Daniel, 114, 270
 Elizabeth, 114, 270
 Mary, 270

-V-

VALE, Ann, 176, 241
 Bulah, 241
 Deborah, 241
 Eli, 241
 James, 241
 John, 176
 Joshua, 176
 Lydia, 241
 Phebe, 241
 Robert, 176, 241
 Sarah, 176
 William, 176, 218
VALENTINE, Daniel, 63
 Philip, 63
 Sophia, 63
VANAERSDALEN,
 Antie, 37
 Cornelius, 37
 David, 37
 Elam, 37
 Isaac, 37
 Jannek, 37
 Joannes, 37
 Johanna, 37
 Nettie, 37
VANARSDAEL, G., 84
VANARSDALEN,
 Alleda, 104
 Anna, 104
 Charity, 104
 Cornelius, 78, 104
 Creasy, 104
 Garret, 104
 Ida, 104
 Jack, 104
 Janetec, 104
 Jenne, 104
 John, 104
 Joseph, 104
 Lemon, 63
 Luck, 104
 Margaret, 104
 Sarah, 104
 Simon, 104
 Tracey, 104

William, 104
VANASDALE, Anaty, 99
Simon, 99
VANCE, Agness, 41
Catharine, 133
Charles, 40
Eleanor, 25
Elizabeth, 41
Ezekiel, 25
Hannah, 41
Henry, 133
Hugh, 40
Jean, 41
John, 41
Mary, 41
Robert, 40
Samuel, 41
Sarah, 41
Thomas, 40
William, 25
VANDERBILT,
Catharine, 38
David, 38
Ida, 38
Jacob, 38
Lea, 38
Maria, 38
Nelly, 38
William, 38
VANDERMULLEN,
Catharine, 187
VANDEYNE, Cassar, 152
David, 152
Ida, 152
Sarah, 152
VANDUYN, David, 152
Maria, 152
Mary, 152
Nelly, 152
VANSCOYOE, Enoch,
191
VELTI, Catharine, 181
Dietrich, 181
VENUS, Elizabeth, 53
Philip, 53
VERNON, Aaron, 177
Abraham, 128, 223
Margaret, 177
Mary, 177
Rebecca, 128, 223
Sarah, 177
VERSCH, Catharine, 245
Christopher, 245
VICHELY, Peter, 59
Sarah, 59
VOGAN, Rachel, 185
VOGT, Peter, 125
Susanna, 125
VONCE, Frederick, 69
VONDERAU, Adam, 54
VONGEND, Peter, 1
VONSEYOC, Aaron, 37
Cornelius, 37
Enoch, 37
Isabella, 37
Moses, 37
Rebecca, 37
Tobitha, 37
VORE, Jacob, 65

-W-
WAEF, Michael, 232
Susanna, 232
WAFE, Elizabeth, 93
Martin, 93
WAGNER, Anna, 171
Barbara, 181
Catharine, 181
Elizabeth, 181

Jacob, 171
John, 181
Mary, 181
Rebecca, 181
WAGONER, Ann, 103
Anna, 231
Anna M., 231
Anna Maria, 231
Catharine, 103, 231
Daniel, 231
Elizabeth, 231
George, 231
Joseph, 5, 103
Margaret, 103
Margaretta, 103
Maria, 231
Samuel, 231
William, 231
Yost, 98
WAILER, Elizabeth, 150
Frederick, 150
WALCK, Barbara, 248
Catharine, 248
Christian, 248
Christiana, 248
Detrich, 248
Eve, 248
Jacob, 248
John, 248
Magdalena, 248
Margaret, 248
Mary, 248
Susanna, 248
WALDASIN,
Catharine, 246
Charles, 246
Jacob, 246
Juliana, 246
Martin, 246
WALDENBERGER,
Daniel, 171
Elizabeth, 171

WALFAHART,
  Ferdinand, 254
WALKER, Benjamin,
  86, 172, 219, 231,
  241
  Grace, 106
  James, 106
  Joseph, 106, 165
  Letitia, 106
  Margaret, 106
  Mary, 106, 128, 129
  Samuel, 106
  Sarah, 106
  William, 32, 44, 104,
  108
WALL, John, 221
  Mary, 221
WALLACE, Agness,
  23, 36, 57
  Alexander, 23, 236
  Andrew, 241
  Ann, 241
  Anna, 8
  Christiana, 23
  Christianna, 36
  Daniel, 8
  Eleanor, 230
  Elizabeth, 23
  Geen, 36
  James, 23, 36, 57
  Jane, 78
  Jean, 8, 23
  Jenny, 230
  John, 8, 230
  Joseph, 8
  Ludwick, 8
  Margaret, 23, 36, 43,
  57, 230
  Mary, 8, 230
  Moses, 8, 78
  Nancy, 230
  Peter, 36
  Samuel, 66
  Sarah, 23, 36
  Thomas, 230
  William, 8, 23, 230,
  241
  William Ebram, 36
WALLER, George,
  175
WALLET, Catharine,
  266
  Elizabeth, 266
  George, 266
  Polly, 266
WALLICK,
  Magdalena, 119
  Philip, 119
WALSCH, Elizabeth,
  172
  Michael, 172
WALSHANTZ, Jacob,
  72
WALTER, Anna, 48,
  87
  Anna Maria, 48
  Barbara, 87, 132
  Catharine, 87, 88,
  132
  Dorothea, 263
  Elizabeth, 132, 146
  George, 87, 88
  Henry, 68, 132, 146
  Jacob, 87
  James, 240
  John, 88, 223
  Joseph, 48
  Margaret, 87
  Marilis, 48
  Mary E., 88
  Michael, 263
WALTZ, Magdalena,
  153
  Peter, 153
WAMBACH, Anna,
  213
  Peter, 213
WAMBACK, Anna
  Mary, 223
  Catharine, 223, 226
  Elizabeth, 223
  George, 223, 226
  John, 223, 226
  Magdalena, 223
  Mary, 226
  Michael, 223, 226
WAMPFLER,
  Christian, 18
WAMPLER, Barbara,
  272
  Catharine, 37, 272
  Christian, 272
  Elizabeth, 170, 248
  Jacob, 272
  John, 170
  Joseph, 37, 248
  Lewis, 257
  Ludwick, 37
  Mary, 170, 272
  Susanna, 257
WANBAUGH,
  Barbara, 189
  Catharine, 189
  Jacob, 189
  John, 189
  Mary, 189
  Michael, 189
WANSHOUNG, Ann,
  115
  Conrad, 115
  Margaretta, 115
  Mary Elizabeth, 115
WARNER, Adam, 47
  Catharine, 47, 205
  Christopher, 47
  Francy, 47
  George, 47, 150
  Jacob, 47
  John, 47

WARREN, David, 256, 268
  Margaret, 201, 213
  Thomas, 201, 213, 238
WART, Christian, 97
WARWICK, Andrew, 182, 215
WATSON, Daniel, 26
  Elizabeth, 26
  George, 26
  Hugh, 26
  James, 173
  John, 26
  Joseph, 23
  Katharine, 26
  Patrick, 26
  Sarah, 26
  William, 26
WATT, George, 80
  Jennet, 80
  John, 80
  Martha, 80
  Mary, 80
WATTS, Mary, 262
  Thomas, 262
WATTSON, Patricia, 5
WEAKLEY, James, 106
  Rebecca, 106
  William, 133
WEALDY, John, 262
  Magdalena, 262
WEALER, Frederick, 180
WEAVER, Barbar, 78
  Catharine, 249
  Daniel, 259
  David, 78
  Dorothea, 249
  Elizabeth, 78, 249, 259

John, 78, 249
Julianna, 249
Melcher, 78
Susanna, 249
Ulrich, 249
WEBB, Eleanor, 124
  Joseph, 210
  Mary, 210
WEBER, Abraham, 216
  Anna, 216
  Catharine, 216
  Daniel, 216
  Philip, 216
WEBSTER, Mary, 30
  Samuel, 30
WEEMS, Elizabeth, 159
  John, 159
  Mary, 159
  Sarah, 159
  Thomas, 159
WEHLER, Catharine, 172
  Daniel, 172
  Frederick, 172
  Henry, 172, 252
  John, 172
  Magdalena, 252
WEHN, Elizabeth, 188
  Frederick, 188
WEHR, Elizabeth, 180
  Eve, 180
  George, 69, 180
WEHRLY, George, 206
WEIDER, Christopher, 57
  Mary, 57
WEIGEL, Anna, 216
  Catharine, 216
  Christiana, 123
  Elizabeth, 216

Henry, 216
Jacob, 119, 145
Julianna, 216
Margaret, 216
Martin, 123
Peter, 216
Sebastian, 216
Sebina, 216
Susanna, 216
WEIGER, Andrew, 261
  Elizabeth, 261
WEIGLE, Leonard, 204
  Peter, 208
  Rosina, 204
WEILLEY, Isabella, 101
  John, 101
WEIMERT, Andrew, 273
  Catharine, 273
WEIN, Adam, 105
  Elizabeth, 105
  Henry, 105
  Jacob, 105
WEINAND, Jacob, 130
  John, 130
  Margaret, 130
  Philip, 130
WEINHOLD, George, 100
WEISER, Andrew, 261
  John, 190
WEIST, Christian, 97
  John, 268
WEISZ, Casper, 76
WEIZE, Henry, 242
  Mary, 242
WELCH, Brown, 128
  Catharine, 71

George, 128
Jane, 128
John, 112
Margaret, 128
Mary, 112, 128
Peter, 71
Sarah, 112, 128
William, 112, 128, 151
WELCHANS, Joseph, 38
WELDIE, Abraham, 18
WELLER, Anna Eve, 64
Catharine, 111
Elizabeth, 64
Eve, 111
George, 63, 64
Martin, 64, 111
Philip Rathrock, 64
Savena, 64
WELLS, James, 217
WELSCH, William, 121
WELSH, Anna Maria, 241
Barbara, 91, 117
Catharine, 117, 218, 234, 241, 266
Charles, 241
Christiana, 234
Elizabeth, 41, 117, 206, 241
Esther, 266
Henry, 117, 230, 234, 241
Jacob, 41, 117, 206, 241, 266
James, 44
John, 41, 44, 76, 117, 206, 218, 266
Margaret, 206

Martin, 266
Mary, 241
Michael, 83, 117, 206
Nicholas, 91
Peter, 234
Polly, 266
Sarah, 266
Susanna, 241
William, 158
WELSHANCE,
 Conrad, 17
David, 17
Elizabeth, 17
Eve, 17
Jacob, 17
Magdalena, 17
WELSHANS, Conrad, 149
David, 149
Elizabeth, 149
Eve, 149
Jacob, 149, 200
Magdalena, 149
WELSHANTZ, Jacob, 99
WELSHAUS,
 Catharine, 273
Elizabeth, 273
Jacob, 273
Susanna, 273
WELSHOVER, Jacob, 16
WELT, Catharine, 222
Nicholas, 222
WELTY, Abraham, 8
Catharine, 8
George, 272
Henry, 272
Jacob, 272
John, 8
Peter, 8
Philip, 272
Susanna, 272

WELTZ, Abraham, 145
Ann, 145
Barbara, 145
Catharine, 145
Elizabeth, 145
Eve, 145
Ferena, 145
Jacob, 145
Joh, 145
John, 73, 145
Joseph, 145
Magdalena, 145
Mary, 145
Peter, 145
WELTZHOFFER,
 Anna, 251
Catharine, 251
Elizabeth, 251
Henry, 251
Jacob, 251
Mary, 251
Susannah, 251
WENDLER,
 Catharine, 124
WENKEL, Margaret, 38
Martin, 38
WENNEY, Francis, 225
WENTEROTH, Adam, 89
WENTZ, Adam, 258
Ann, 149
Anna, 258
Anna Mary, 149, 258
Catharine, 258
Christiana, 149
Chrsitian, 258
Elizabeth, 149, 258
George, 258
Harry, 213
Henry, 149

Jacob, 149
John, 149, 258
Margaret, 149, 258
Mary, 258
Michael, 149, 258
Peter, 258
Philip, 149, 258
WERE, Ludwick, 203
WEREMAN, Nicholas, 33
WERKING, Dorothea, 171
  Henry, 171
  Margaret, 171
  Philip, 171
  Philip W., 131, 171
  Philipina, 171
WERLEY, James, 70
WERLY, George, 17
WERMAN, Henry, 42
WERNER, Anna, 206
  Daniel, 206
  Elizabeth, 206
  Francis, 225
  George, 183
  Jacob, 206
  John, 206
  Judith, 206
WERT, Jacob, 214
WERTS, Christian, 196
  Eve, 196
WERTZ, Catharine, 72
  Daniel, 72
  Elizabeth, 72
  Jacob, 72
  John, 72
  Margaret, 83
  Peter, 24, 72, 83
  Rosinna, 72
  Wilhelmus, 83
WESHOFFER, Abraham, 250

WESSELER, Henry, 74
WEST, Charles, 113
  Christian, 42, 205
  G., 100
  George, 100
  Hannah, 113
  John, 113
  Jonathan, 100
  Phebe, 100
  Priscilla, 100
  Rachel, 100
  Samuel, 100
WESTHAEFFER, Catharine, 273
  Conrad, 273
  George, 273
  John, 273
  Leonard, 273
  Peggy, 273
  Polly, 273
  Rachel, 273
  Samuel, 273
WESTHEFFER, Catharine, 227
  Leonard, 227
WETTERRECHT, George, 207
  Susanna, 207
WETZEL, Jacob, 60
  Mary, 60
WEYANT, Anna M.
  Nicholas, 94
  Nicholas, 94
WEYER, Andrew, 202
  Anthony, 202
  Benard, 202
  Daniel, 202
  Elizabeth, 202
  Jacob, 202
  John, 202
  Lydia, 202
  Margaret, 202

  Mary, 202
  Michael, 202
  Susanna, 202
WEYERMAN, Gertrude, 19
  Hannah, 19
  Henry, 19
  John, 19
  Nicholas, 19
  William, 19
WEYGLE, Jacob, 265
WEYLIE, Ann, 112
  David, 112
  Jane, 112
WHEELER, Thomas, 44
WHELER, Dutsich, 257
  Maria, 257
WHERRY, Thomas, 105
WHESLEY, George, 268
WHINERY, Catharine, 130
  Hannah, 130
  Robert, 130
  Thomas, 130
  William, 130
WHINRIY, Thomas, 131
WHITE, Agness, 186
  Andrew, 56, 75
  Ann, 83, 114
  Archibald, 18
  Casper, 76
  Catharine, 218
  Charity, 75
  Dorcas, 83
  Edward, 144
  Elizabeth, 56, 75, 144
  George, 114, 155

Hannah, 114
Henry, 75, 83
Isaah, 83
James, 18, 56, 75
John, 83, 144, 218
Joseph, 56, 114
Joseph Jackson, 56
Mary, 56, 76
Peter, 75
Robert, 83
Sarah, 56, 114, 155
Stephen, 83
Tempest, 114
Thomas, 76, 114
William, 83, 114, 186
WHITEFORD, Ann,
  103, 194
Anna, 103
Cunning, 194
Hugh, 6, 17, 103, 194
John, 103
Mary, 103
William, 73, 266
WHITTLESAY, Eli, 5
WHITTON, Ann, 108
Robert, 108
WHRLEY, George,
  258
WIAND, John, 251
WIBLE, Stephen, 20
WICHERSHAM,
  Enoch, 252
James, 252
Mary, 252
William, 252
WICKER, Baltzer, 40
Margaret, 40
Maria, 40
WICKERSHAM, Ann,
  220, 256
Anna, 183, 193
Hannah, 193, 256
James, 136

Jesse, 193, 256
John, 193
Lydia, 193
Mary, 193, 256
Rachel, 221
Ruth, 193, 256
Sarah, 136
William, 221
WIDEBACH, Henry, 7
WIDEBACK,
  Abraham, 7
Anna, 7
Anna Marcant, 7
John, 7
WIDEMAN,
  Sebastina, 123
WIDT, Adam, 97
Ann, 97
Elizabeth, 97
George, 97
John, 97
Mary, 97
Nicholas, 97
Samuel, 97
Valentine, 97
WIEHELM, Frederick,
  247
WIERMAN, Benj., 178
Nicholas, 178
Phebe, 178
Sarah, 178
William, 178
WIEST, Jacob, 126
WIGLE, Bastian, 12
Dorothea, 12
Elizabeth, 12
Henry, 12
Jacob, 12, 145
Julianna, 12
Leonard, 12
Magdalena, 145
Martin, 12
Peter, 12

WILDASIN, Ann, 199
Anna Mary, 204
Catharine, 199
Eve, 199
George, 199
Jacob, 199, 204
John, 199
Margaret, 199
Mary, 199
Peter, 199
Philip, 199
Samuel, 199, 204
WILDISIN, Margaret,
  123
Samuel, 123
WILEY, Ann, 264
Anna, 264
David, 264
Elizabeth, 148
James, 209, 247
Jannet, 264
Jenny, 209
John, 264
Joseph, 148, 209
Margaret, 264
Mary, 148, 209, 264
Sarah, 209, 247
WILHELM,
  Christiana, 141
John, 141
WILIAMS, Abraham,
  250
Betsy, 250
David, 250
Elizabeth, 250
James, 250
Jenny, 250
Mary, 250
WILKEY, James, 66
Jean, 66
WILKINSON, Ann, 29
Diriah, 29
John, 29

Robert, 29
William, 29
WILL, Catharine, 176
　Henry, 176
　Nicholas, 176
　Peter, 176
WILLED, Anthony,
　234
WILLER, Henry, 209
WILLET, Anthony,
　221
　Elizabeth, 221
WILLEY, Robert, 56
WILLHELM, Adam,
　50
　Barbara, 50
WILLIAM, Elizabeth,
　81
　Frederick, 81
　Peter, 81
WILLIAMS, Ann, 270
　Benjamin, 92
　Catharine, 250
　Delilah, 270
　Edward, 37
　Elizabeth, 270
　George, 21, 99, 270
　Hannah, 231
　Isaac, 61, 195, 271
　J. F., 252
　Jane, 22
　John, 46, 250
　Lewis, 57
　Margaret, 61, 250
　Martha, 92
　Mary, 46, 61, 62, 270
　Mordica, 231
　Peter, 270
　Sara, 92
　Sarah, 231, 270
　Tobitha, 37
WILLIAMSON,
　Cassar, 152
　George, 125, 152
WILLIS, Betty, 185
　Catharine, 19
　Hannah, 185
　Henry, 19
　John, 185
　Joshua, 19
　Lydia, 185
　Mary, 19, 185
　Rachel, 19
　Richrd, 19
　Samuel, 185, 232
　Suannah, 185
　William, 19, 185
WILLISO, David, 187
WILLSON, Catharine,
　115
　Elizabeth, 115
　John, 115
　Joseph, 115
　Margaret, 115
　Martha, 115
　Mary, 115
　Robert, 115
　Thomas, 115
　William, 115
WILOT, Catharine,
　151
　John, 151
WILSHAM, Joseph,
　65
WILSON, Agness,
　171, 236
　Alexander, 78, 163,
　　184, 198
　Andrew, 62, 137,
　　198, 235
　Ann, 133
　Anna, 34, 238
　Anne, 66
　Benj., 95
　Benjamin, 178
　Catharine, 132, 141,
　　173
　Charles, 66
　Daniel, 137
　David, 141, 170, 184,
　　224, 236, 265
　Dorcas, 198
　Elizabeth, 19, 66,
　　171, 235
　Esther, 63
　Francis, 137, 198
　Garret, 3
　George, 95, 173, 235
　Grizal, 78
　Hannah, 185
　Henry, 62
　Hugh, 59, 78, 170
　Isabella, 59, 78
　James, 50, 59, 63,
　　66, 163, 170, 171,
　　184, 189, 224
　Jane, 170, 198, 216,
　　236
　Janet, 3, 137
　Jannet, 62
　Jannett, 224
　Jasper, 31
　Jean, 19, 63
　John, 31, 59, 66, 132,
　　137, 141, 184, 224
　Joseph, 9, 75, 141
　Josiah, 238
　Lydia, 95
　Margaret, 137, 141,
　　184, 235, 236, 265
　Marmaduke, 3, 161
　Marmyduke, 154
　Martha, 170
　Mary, 57, 62, 66,
　　132, 133, 141, 197,
　　235
　McCartha, 3
　Nelly, 173
　Patrick, 3

Rachael, 216
Rachel, 224
Rebecca, 137
Richard, 163
Robert, 66, 171, 224, 235
Robet, 34
Samuel, 3, 57, 59, 185
Sarah, 59, 95, 178
Susanna, 19, 154
Tempest, 272
Thomas, 51, 59, 66, 171, 216
Wiliam, 131
William, 3, 19, 141, 184, 216, 224, 236
WILT, Anne, 181
Barbara, 181
Catharine, 181
Elizabeth, 181, 218
John, 194
Magdalena, 181
Margaret, 213
Nicholas, 181
Paul, 194
Peter, 181
Samuel, 213
Susanna, 181
Valentine, 68, 181
Velantine, 181
WINDEMERE, Philip, 138
WINDEMEYER, Catharine, 269
WINDERWOOD, Elihue, 148
WINEBREMMER, ?, 118
Barbara, 118
Catharine, 128
George, 246
John, 246

Justina, 118
Sally, 246
WINEBRIGHT, Catharine, 95
Michael, 95
WINROTE, Catharine, 177
John, 177
WINTER, Anna Mary, 267
George, 243
Katharine, 243
Kreta, 243
Margaret, 243
Peter, 267
WINTERMEYER, Anna, 166
Anna Gertrude, 45
Anthony, 45, 166
Catharine, 166
Dorothea, 45
Elizabeth, 166
George, 166
Julianna, 45
Julie, 166
Philip, 45, 166
Susanna, 166
Valentine, 166
WINTERODE, Adam, 31
WINTEROTE, Adam, 83
WINTEROTH, Adam, 95
WINTERSMITH, Charles, 74
WEIREMAN, Henry, 59, 77
Herman, 42
Nicholas, 29
William, 244
WIRT, Henry, 18
WISE, Catharine, 189

Christiana, 195
Christianna, 189
George, 195
Jacob, 270
Joseph, 189
Mary, 255, 270
Nancy, 195
Philipina, 189
Sebastian, 189
Sebastine, 189
WISER, Jacob, 196
Sophia, 196
WIST, Christian, 122
Jacob, 221
Susanna, 221
WITHROW, Jean, 75
JOhn, 75
John, 18
Margaret, 75
William, 75
WITMAN, Catharine, 239
Christian, 239
Daniel, 239
Elizabeth, 239
Jacob, 239
Mary, 239
Michael, 239
Rebecca, 239
William, 239
WITMER, David, 256
WITTERCHD, Annamary, 185
Catharine, 185
Christiana, 185
Elizabeth, 185
Filbina, 185
George, 185
Jacob, 185
Peter, 185
Sarah, 185
Susanna, 185
WITTERECHT,

George, 138
Jacob, 138
Michael, 138
Peter, 138
Philip, 138
WITTMEYER,
  Magdalena, 208
  Mary, 208
  Simon, 208
WOEFF, Frederick, 90
WOFGANG, Nicholas,
  94
WOGAN, Anne, 170
  Georgan, 204
  George, 151, 170
  Isabella, 170
  Margaret, 170
WOHLFART, Henry,
  272
WOHLFAURT,
  Catharine, 128
  Christopher, 128
  Mary, 128
  Stofel, 128
WOHLFORT, Philip,
  223
WOLF, Adam, 105
  Alse, 114
  Andrew, 105, 114
  Anna, 40
  Appolonia, 105
  Catharine, 105
  Catharine, 40, 221
  Christian, 116
  Christiana, 105
  Dorothea, 111
  Elizabeth, 40, 105,
    187, 221
  Frederick, 105
  George, 40, 111, 187,
    221
  Henry, 40, 80, 83,
    135, 195, 212, 216,
    221, 247
  Jacob, 40, 105
  Johannes, 40
  John, 35, 40, 105,
    161, 163, 268
  Jonas, 105
  Lydia, 268
  Margaret, 40
  Mary, 135
  Peter, 40, 102, 221
  Sabina, 40
  Scharlot, 35
  Tobias, 40
WOLFART,
  Catharine, 271
  Elizabeth, 271
  Jacob, 271
  John, 271
  Maria, 271
  Philip, 271
WOLFERT, Philip,
  189
WOLFF, Adam, 155
  Andrew, 155
  Ann, 155
  Anne E., 70
  Babara, 155
  Catharine, 155
  Dorothea, 155
  Elizabeth, 155
  Frederick, 113
  George, 70
  Henry, 155
  Margaret, 155
  Peter, 71, 155
WOLFGANG,
  Elizabeth, 71
  Nicholas, 71
WOLIVER, Catharine,
  266
  Henry, 266
WONDER,
  Elizabeth, 150
  Henry, 150
  Margaret, 150
  Sebastian, 150
  Stephen, 150
WOOD, Elias, 121
  Elizabeth, 121, 259
  George, 259
WORLEY, Abigail, 214
  Charity, 26
  Daniel, 26
  Elizabeth, 27, 206
  Francis, 26, 125, 243
  George, 206
  Henry, 26
  Jacob, 26
  James, 26, 214
  Joseph, 243
  Lydia, 214
  Martha, 26
  Mary, 26
  Nathan, 26, 214, 240
  Rachel, 125
  Samuel, 26
  Thomas, 26
WRESTLER,
  Catharine, 138
  Mathias, 138
WRIGHT, Eleanor, 14
  Elizabeth, 103
  James, 14
  John, 14, 103
  Jonathan, 95
  Robert, 14
WUMMARD, Richard,
  198
WUNDER, Elizabeth,
  252
  Henry, 252
WYSON, Ludwig, 88
  Mary, 88

-Y-

YAGER, Henry, 214

405

YAGY, John Adam, 91
YEARMAN, George, 29
  Katerine, 29
YEGER, Adam, 200
  Anna, 200
  Peter, 200
  Susanna, 200
YENCE, Frederick, 33
YENEWINS, George, 271
  Maria, 271
YESSLER, Henry, 67
YIENGER, Jacob, 239
YODER, John, 168
  Martin, 168
  Susanna, 168
YOE, Elizabeth, 126
YONCE, Frederick, 53
YONER, Catharine, 107
  Christian, 269
  Elizabeth, 108
  John, 107
  Mary, 269
  Nicholas, 108
YOST, Abraham, 136, 275
  Catharine, 136
  Elizabeth, 136
  Maria, 275
  Nicholas, 93, 103, 136
  Rachel, 93
  Robert, 93
YOTHER, Elizabeth, 107
  Esther, 107
  Jacob, 107
  John, 107
YOUDER, Elizabeth, 250
  George, 250
  Susanna, 250
YOUKER, Anna, 166
  Casper, 166
YOUND, Catharine, 242
  William, 242
YOUNG, Agness, 22, 42, 92
  Amelia, 92
  Andrew, 40, 42, 61, 105
  Ann, 40, 92
  Anna Maria, 138
  Baltzer, 138, 139
  Barara, 40, 211
  Catharine, 105
  Christian, 105
  David, 16, 22
  Dewalt, 40
  Eleanor, 16
  Elizabeth, 61, 219, 221, 229
  Frederick, 138
  Griziel, 42
  Hannah, 40
  Henry, 221
  Isabel, 42
  Jacob, 113, 221
  James, 16, 22, 61, 165
  Jean, 42
  John, 61, 211
  John Davison, 22
  John Nicholas, 105
  Margaret, 22, 42, 61
  Margaretta, 40
  Mary, 61, 92, 165
  Nancy, 16
  Peggy, 165
  Peter, 40
  Robert, 42
  Samuel, 92
  Tobias, 219, 229
  William, 42, 61, 92, 221
YOUSE, Anna, 259
  Catharine, 258, 259
  Elizabeth, 259
  Frederick, 179, 215, 259
  George, 259
  Jacob, 259
  John, 259
  Philip, 258
  Polly, 259
YUCE, Frederick, 164

-Z-

ZACHARIAS, George, 211
ZANCKEL, Hannah, 251
  John, 251
  Susanna, 251
ZECK, Annamaria, 263
  Catharine, 263
  Christiana, 263
  Dorothea, 263
  Eve, 263
  Henry, 263
  Jacob, 263
  Magdalena, 263
  Michael, 263
  Peter, 263
  Rosana, 263
  William, 263
ZEIGAL, Godleib, 238
ZEIGEL, Maria M., 62
ZEIGER, George P., 91
  Killian, 91
ZEIGLER, Anna, 162
  Barbara, 162
  Barnet, 49, 68, 69, 87, 101, 126, 127,

142, 162
Barney, 118
Catharine, 211
Christiana, 162
George, 42, 137
George P., 209
George Philip, 160
Gotleib, 48
Gotlieb, 23
Gottlieb, 33
Jane, 269
John, 162, 218, 243,
　251, 269
Joseph, 269
Margaret, 190
Martin, 211
Michael, 269
Peter, 190
Philip, 42, 73, 137,
　142, 162, 257
Rosina, 162
Sabina, 162
ZELL, B., 62
　Bartholomew, 62
ZELLER, Catharine,
　213
　Mary, 239
　Peter, 213, 239
ZEMMERMAN,
　Elizabeth, 156
　Lydia, 229
　Michael, 156
ZENK, Hannah, 154
　Jacob, 154
ZERM, Jacob, 219
　Margaret, 219
　Mary, 219
ZIEGEL, Ann, 62
　Barbara, 62
　Christianna, 62
　Elizabeth, 62, 260
　Frederick, 60, 62
　Gotlieb, 260

Gottleib, 60
Jacob, 62
John, 260
Lydia, 260
Magdalena, 60
Maria, 62
Mary Barbara, 60
Thomas, 60, 260
ZIEGLER, Adam, 247
　Anna M., 270
　Anna Mary, 90
　Catharine, 129, 173,
　　227, 247
　Caty, 247
　Charles, 270
　Christiana, 227
　Daniel, 173, 200, 247
　Elizabeth, 129, 173,
　　247
　Eve, 173, 200
　George, 90, 173, 200,
　　247, 270
　Henry, 173
　Jacob, 90, 129, 200,
　　227, 247, 270
　John, 173, 247
　Lydia, 247
　Magdalena, 270
　Margaret, 90
　Martin, 200
　Mary, 173
　Matilda, 247
　Michael, 129, 227,
　　247
　Nicholas, 129, 227,
　　247
　Peter, 200, 247
　Philip, 173, 175, 247
　Polly, 247
　Rachel, 247
　Samuel, 247
　Sarah, 173, 247
　Susanna, 173, 247

Volly, 173
ZIMMERMAN, L., 42
　Mary, 248
　Nicholas, 248
ZINLAUB, Ann, 130
　Catharine, 130
　Christiana, 130
　George, 130
　Henry Heisman, 130
　Margaret, 130
ZINN, Adam, 222
　Ann Kunta, 222
　Barbara, 222
　Catharine, 222
　Christiana, 222
　Elizabeth, 222
　Jacob, 222
　John, 222
　Magdalena, 222
　Margaret, 222
　Mary, 222
　Nicholas, 222
　Philip Jacob, 222
ZOLLINGER,
　Barbara, 137
　Catharine, 126
　Elizabeth, 126
　Henry, 126
　John, 126
　Peter, 126, 137
　Ulrich, 126
　Veronica, 126
ZONCE, Frederick, 60
ZONG, Eva, 48
　Henry, 48
　John, 48
　Margaret, 48
　Philibina, 48
ZORGER, Anna, 250
　Barbara, 250
　Elizabeth, 250
　Eve, 239
　Frederick, 138, 182,

250
George, 239, 250
Jacob, 250
John, 239, 250
Lydia, 250
Margaret, 138
Mathias, 250
Michael, 250
Peter, 250
ZOUCK, Ann, 114
Henry, 114
ZUMWALT, Baltzer, 50

Other Heritage Books by F. Edward Wright:

Abstracts of Bucks County, Pennsylvania Wills, 1685-1785

Abstracts of Cumberland County, Pennsylvania Wills, 1750-1785

Abstracts of Cumberland County, Pennsylvania Wills, 1785-1825

Abstracts of Philadelphia County Wills, 1726-1747

Abstracts of Philadelphia County Wills, 1748-1763

Abstracts of Philadelphia County Wills, 1763-1784

Abstracts of Philadelphia County Wills, 1777-1790

Abstracts of Philadelphia County Wills, 1790-1802

Abstracts of Philadelphia County Wills, 1802-1809

Abstracts of Philadelphia County Wills, 1810-1815

Abstracts of Philadelphia County Wills, 1815-1819

Abstracts of Philadelphia County Wills, 1820-1825

Abstracts of Philadelphia County, Pennsylvania Wills, 1682-1726

Abstracts of South Central Pennsylvania Newspapers, Volume 1, 1785-1790

Abstracts of South Central Pennsylvania Newspapers, Volume 3, 1796-1800

Abstracts of the Newspapers of Georgetown and the Federal City, 1789-99

Abstracts of York County, Pennsylvania Wills, 1749-1819

Bucks County, Pennsylvania Church Records of the 17th and 18th Centuries Volume 2: Quaker Records: Falls and Middletown Monthly Meetings
Anna Miller Watring and F. Edward Wright

Caroline County, Maryland Marriages, Births and Deaths, 1850-1880

Citizens of the Eastern Shore of Maryland, 1659-1750

Cumberland County, Pennsylvania Church Records of the 18th Century

Delaware Newspaper Abstracts, Volume 1: 1786-1795

Early Charles County, Maryland Settlers, 1658-1745
Marlene Strawser Bates and F. Edward Wright

Early Church Records of Alexandria City and Fairfax County, Virginia
F. Edward Wright and Wesley E. Pippenger

Early Church Records of New Castle County, Delaware, Volume 1, 1701-1800

Frederick County Militia in the War of 1812
Sallie A. Mallick and F. Edward Wright

Inhabitants of Baltimore County, 1692-1763

Land Records of Sussex County, Delaware, 1769-1782

Land Records of Sussex County, Delaware, 1782-1789
Elaine Hastings Mason and F. Edward Wright

Marriage Licenses of Washington, District of Columbia, 1811-1830

Marriages and Deaths from the Newspapers of Allegany and Washington Counties, Maryland, 1820-1830

Marriages and Deaths from The York Recorder, 1821-1830

Marriages and Deaths in the Newspapers of Frederick and Montgomery Counties, Maryland, 1820-1830

Marriages and Deaths in the Newspapers of Lancaster County, Pennsylvania, 1821-1830
Marriages and Deaths in the Newspapers of Lancaster County, Pennsylvania, 1831-1840
Marriages and Deaths of Cumberland County, [Pennsylvania], 1821-1830
Maryland Calendar of Wills Volume 9: 1744-1749
Maryland Calendar of Wills Volume 10: 1748-1753
Maryland Calendar of Wills Volume 11: 1753-1760
Maryland Calendar of Wills Volume 12: 1759-1764
Maryland Calendar of Wills Volume 13: 1764-1767
Maryland Calendar of Wills Volume 14: 1767-1772
Maryland Calendar of Wills Volume 15: 1772-1774
Maryland Calendar of Wills Volume 16: 1774-1777
Maryland Eastern Shore Newspaper Abstracts, Volume 1: 1790-1805
Maryland Eastern Shore Newspaper Abstracts, Volume 2: 1806-1812
Maryland Eastern Shore Newspaper Abstracts, Volume 3: 1813-1818
Maryland Eastern Shore Newspaper Abstracts, Volume 4: 1819-1824
Maryland Eastern Shore Newspaper Abstracts, Volume 5: Northern Counties, 1825-1829
F. Edward Wright and Irma Harper
Maryland Eastern Shore Newspaper Abstracts, Volume 6: Southern Counties, 1825-1829
Maryland Eastern Shore Newspaper Abstracts, Volume 7: Northern Counties, 1830-1834
Irma Harper and F. Edward Wright
Maryland Eastern Shore Newspaper Abstracts, Volume 8: Southern Counties, 1830-1834
Maryland Militia in the Revolutionary War
S. Eugene Clements and F. Edward Wright
Newspaper Abstracts of Allegany and Washington Counties, Maryland, 1811-1815
Newspaper Abstracts of Cecil and Harford Counties, Maryland, 1822-1830
Newspaper Abstracts of Frederick County, Maryland, 1816-1819
Newspaper Abstracts of Frederick County, Maryland, 1811-1815
Sketches of Maryland Eastern Shoremen
Tax List of Chester County, Pennsylvania 1768
Tax List of York County, Pennsylvania 1779
Washington County Church Records of the 18th Century, 1768-1800
Western Maryland Newspaper Abstracts, Volume 1: 1786-1798
Western Maryland Newspaper Abstracts, Volume 2: 1799-1805
Western Maryland Newspaper Abstracts, Volume 3: 1806-1810
Wills of Chester County, Pennsylvania, 1766-1778

www.ingramcontent.com/pod-product-compliance
Lightning Source LLC
Chambersburg PA
CBHW071944220426
43662CB00009B/987